AGING
IN WESTERN
SOCIETIES

AGING
IN WESTERN
SOCIETIES

EDITED BY

Ernest W. Burgess

THE UNIVERSITY OF CHICAGO PRESS

Library of Congress Catalog Number: 60-5465

THE UNIVERSITY OF CHICAGO PRESS, CHICAGO 37
Cambridge University Press, London, N.W. 1, England
The University of Toronto Press, Toronto 5, Canada

Foreword

The Gerontological Society, Inc., like other scientific organizations, brings together research investigators who have knowledge of the growing edges of their sciences and an awareness of the emerging needs of their fields. It was just such a circumstance that led the Society in 1955 to establish a committee to consider the pressing question of how to increase the number of university and college teachers equipped to train others in the psychological and social aspects of aging. Initial consideration of the problem by the committee made it evident that far more would be required to accomplish this end than merely convening a representative group of educators to propagandize the need and affirm their intentions to give more instructional emphasis to individual and societal components of aging. The newness and unorganized state of knowledge about psychosocial aging, the breadth of the subject matter to be covered, and the difficulties of introducing a new field of study and inquiry into the established academic structure were problems clearly requiring a comprehensive and creative approach and the investment of the thinking of scholars from a number of disciplines. Accordingly, with the assistance of a grant from the National Institute of Mental Health,[1] the committee convened a working conference of distinguished students of aging in Palm Beach, Florida, in July, 1956, to explore methods and make plans for meeting the need for training of scientific and professional personnel in social gerontology.

At this conference a multiuniversity training project in social gerontology was designed, an executive committee was selected, the director of the project was named, and plans for an Inter-University Council in Social Gerontology representing the sixteen participating universities were drawn up. Subsequently, grants in support of the project were made by the National Institutes of Health[2] to the University of Michigan, Institute for Human Adjustment, Division of Gerontology, which established the Inter-University Training Institute in Social Gerontology in January, 1957, to administer the program.

Thus began what was destined to be the arduous twin tasks of developing and shaping a new scientific field of social gerontology, the subject matter for which was almost momentarily unfolding, and then of introducing the newcomer to the scientific and academic communities. To accomplish these ends, two major lines of action were undertaken. The first, and basic to the field of social gerontology as a proper area of education and research, was the collection, organization, and publication of existing scientific knowledge in the psychological and social aspects of aging to provide comprehensive reference works for use by educators in the training of students for teaching, service, and research in aging. The second was to provide through summer institutes intensive postgraduate training for established university and college faculty members in the psychological and social sciences and al-

[1] Grant No. 3M-9114.

[2] National Institute of Mental Health Grant No. 3M-9118, and National Heart Institute Grant No. HTS-5205.

lied fields. By these means, the Inter-University Council mobilized the most distinguished and sophisticated scholars in aging to delineate the field of social gerontology, to develop teaching tools, and to offer instruction to a total of seventy-five faculty members selected for their interest in and potential for advancing in the field.

It was originally intended that a single handbook of psychosocial gerontology would be prepared. In structuring the field of aging, however, it became evident that somewhat different foci were required to provide the emphasis and perspectives which would make the technical summaries equally useful to those concerned with individual aging and those involved with the nature of social aging and its impacts on the individual and society. Thus two comprehensive reference works have been produced to enable maximum use of the materials.

One of the two, *Handbook of Aging and the Individual: Psychological and Biological Aspects,* was done under the able editorship of James E. Birren, whose position as chief of the Section on Aging of the National Institute of Mental Health made him the natural choice of the Inter-University Council to undertake the creative task of bringing about an orderly conceptualization of the field of human aging and of giving oversight to the preparation of the technical summaries of pertinent research. In these tasks he has given a brilliant account of himself.

The second of the two companion books was the volume *Handbook of Social Gerontology: Societal Aspects of Aging.* The Council considered none other than Clark Tibbitts for its editor because of his long apprenticeship on the national scene as pioneer in social gerontology and because it was he who first glimpsed its potentials for providing a rational approach to aging as a positive force in American life. In 1954 he introduced the term "social gerontology" into the literature when he used

it in a review of the newly published *Older People* by Ruth Albrecht and Robert J. Havighurst. The *Handbook* is testimony of the depth and definitiveness of his encyclopedic knowledge of aging and of his skill in organizing it into a meaningful whole. Under his effective direction the outstanding authorities who contributed to the book offer a dynamic view of the emerging field of social gerontology.

Believing that social gerontology in the United States could be better understood if seen against a background of other cultural groups that had experienced the phenomenon of aging at an earlier date, the Council planned for a third book which would offer a review of major trends and developments in aging in several countries of western Europe and Great Britain. This volume, *Aging in Western Societies: A Survey of Social Gerontology,* was prepared under the editorship of Professor Ernest W. Burgess. There could have been no more fortuitous circumstance than to have had Dr. Burgess available to undertake this assignment. Having achieved one of the most distinguished scientific careers in the United States prior to his retirement as professor and chairman of the Department of Sociology at the University of Chicago, he brought to the project a perspective and sensitivity refined by years of study, research, and experience. Thus he was able to give meaning to the social scene as observed in the various countries and to offer guidance to the contributors in relating these data to current trends in the United States.

As director of the Inter-University Training Project in Social Gerontology, I want to express my thanks not only to the editors of the three books but also to the sixty or more contributors to the volumes. To the members of the Executive Committee and the Inter-University Council, I am indebted for their continued support, dedication, and long hours of work which made possible the achievement of the objectives of the project. The sixteen universities sponsoring the project have been well represented and can take pride in the contribution which their co-operative effort has made to scientific thinking and to the advancement of the understanding and welfare of the older people of our country.

ANN ARBOR, MICHIGAN   WILMA DONAHUE
July 29, 1960

INTER-UNIVERSITY TRAINING INSTITUTE IN SOCIAL GERONTOLOGY

Director: WILMA DONAHUE
University of Michigan

Assistant Project Director: HAROLD L. ORBACH
University of Michigan

EXECUTIVE COMMITTEE

JOHN E. ANDERSON
University of Minnesota
JAMES E. BIRREN
National Institute of Mental Health
ERNEST W. BURGESS
University of Chicago
EWALD W. BUSSE, M.D.
Duke University
ROBERT J. HAVIGHURST
University of Chicago

WOODROW W. MORRIS
State University of Iowa
CLARK TIBBITTS
United States Department of Health, Education, and Welfare
IRVING L. WEBBER
University of Florida
RICHARD C. WILCOCK
University of Illinois

INTER-UNIVERSITY COUNCIL

JOHN S. ALLEN
University of Florida
JOHN E. ANDERSON
University of Minnesota
HARRY W. BRAUN
University of Pittsburgh
JOSEPH H. BRITTON
Pennsylvania State University
MARION E. BUNCH
Washington University (St. Louis)
FEDELE F. FAURI
University of Michigan
ROBBEN W. FLEMING
University of Illinois
EUGENE A. FRIEDMANN
University of Wisconsin

HERBERT C. HUNSAKER
Purdue University
HAROLD E. JONES
University of California
DONALD P. KENT
University of Connecticut
RAYMOND G. KUHLEN
Syracuse University
WOODROW W. MORRIS
State University of Iowa
BERNICE L. NEUGARTEN
University of Chicago
LLOYD SAVILLE
Duke University
GORDON F. STREIB
Cornell University

Preface

This volume is a survey of the problems of older persons and of the solutions for their welfare adopted by societies of Western culture. It attempts to picture the economic and social trends which created the modern problems of aging in industrial societies. It also presents the policies and the programs which have been developed by several European nations to promote the welfare of aging people.

The problems facing older people in all societies of Western culture are similar. They differ mainly in degree and in the extent and in the ways in which they are being met. These problems are inequality of opportunity for employment, inadequate income for livelihood and social living, unsuitable housing, unmet needs for special services, insufficient provision for physical and mental health, stresses and strains in changing family relations, general lack of meaningful activities for retirement, and paucity of significant research on the social and psychological aspects of aging.

The White House Conference on Aging (January, 1961) is having a tremendous impact upon the movement for the welfare of the aging in the United States. There is a great humanitarian motivation behind it. But sentiment, no matter how noble, is not enough. There needs to be rational guidance to prevent costly mistakes in recommendations and in action.

This volume aims to provide the perspective of European experience to help in guiding the welfare movement for the aging in the United States. This perspective is essential for understanding and coping with the situations now facing older people in Western societies. The nature of aging, the problems of older people, and the social action for their welfare will be presented in the context of the three main dimensions of social change: (1) the *economic trends* of the nineteenth and twentieth centuries; (2) the resulting changes in the *socioeconomic structure* of society; and (3) the *cultural differences* which have developed among different countries.

These three dimensions of social change will be analyzed as they affect the problems of the aging population and social action for the welfare of older people.

1. *The economic dimension.*—The basic economic trend of the past fifteen decades in Europe has been the industrialization of the economy and the urbanization of society. Industrialization and urbanization have proceeded at an ever increasing tempo. At first the United States lagged behind European countries in industrial and urban growth. Recently, this country has forged ahead of the other nations of the Old World in its economic and technological development.

This early initial lag and later rapid forward thrust in economic and industrial growth resulted in the backwardness of the United States in meeting the needs of older persons who were trapped in the vortex of the acceleration of economic change.

2. *The societal dimension.*—Industrialization and urbanization effected unplanned and unforeseen changes in the structure of society. The cohesive extended family and its component nuclear family before the industrial revolution had been in practically all societies the unit of the production of

goods and services. Both this large kinship grouping dominated by a patriarch and the small semipatriarchal family lost the age-long function of economic production. Fathers, mothers, and older and even younger children no longer had their work in the home or in the family shop. They went to labor for an employer in the factories which displaced the home in the production of goods.

Older persons were more and more left stranded in this period of economic transition. In the cities their children were less and less able to accommodate aging parents in their homes or to give them other financial assistance. From 1900 to 1950 in the United States and some other countries the proportion of grandparents doubled, while the average number of adult children decreased.

3. *The cultural dimension.*—These economic and societal changes have occurred and are continuing in all countries of Western culture. They have, however, proceeded at a different pace and often in somewhat different forms in the various nations. Nearly every country has pioneered in some outstanding development. This fact makes possible and desirable the drawing of cross-cultural comparisons between the different countries. Thus western Europe provides an unintended laboratory in social gerontology.

Finally, new organizational structures developed for the economic support of older persons. Old age insurance pensions and public assistance were instituted to rescue them from destitution, from growing insecurity in an industrial society, and from the hazards of independence upon the care and aid of their children and other relatives.

This volume, accordingly, will consider all three dimensions of the factors affecting the welfare of the aging as it describes and analyzes the economic and social trends and the present status and problems of the aging in selected western European societies.

The book is divided into three parts. Part I is composed of chapters by different authorities in the field of social gerontology. Background data on representative western European countries are presented in chapter i. Chapters ii–ix describe the various policies, programs, and activities that have been developed for the welfare of older people. Chapter x surveys the basic and applied research on the psychological and social aspects of aging in progress in various countries of western Europe. Chapter xi analyzes the policies and programs from the standpoint of their applicability as guideposts to American planning for the welfare of the aging.

Part II is devoted to "Case Studies." These cases, over half of which were prepared by Europeans, were selected for their current interest in describing certain pioneering projects significant for American consideration for providing insight into human relations in cultures different from our own or for documenting in detail material presented in Part I.

Part III contains fifteen statistical tables of data on the economic and social trends affecting older people and on the characteristics of the aging population. They make possible significant and interesting comparisons between the more and the less industrially developed countries of western Europe (including both Communist and non-Communist countries) and with four non-European industrial countries and with four underdeveloped countries.

In the preparation of the various chapters of this volume the authors have been fortunate in having the generous and valuable co-operation of European gerontologists. Our indebtedness to them is only partially indicated by the acknowledgment at the beginning of each chapter.

All the authors of chapters except Dr. Hauser and Drs. Vera and Jerome Peterson attended the fourth International Congress of Gerontology held in Merano and Venice, Italy, in July, 1957. During the week before the Congress they took part in the Seminar on the Social Health of the Aging in the United States and Europe which enabled them to make contacts with the leading European gerontologists. In addition, they spent some weeks visiting different European countries and gathering information and materials for their respective chapters. The editor wishes to express the gratitude of the authors to our European colleagues for the time they gave in conferences, in arranging appointments, and in reading and criticizing the different chapters and for contributing statements and case studies incorporated in this volume.

The editor gratefully acknowledges the help he received by way of advice, constructive suggestions, and approval of the selection of countries for the survey of Western societies and the outline of the volume from the Inter-University Council of the Institute and especially from his colleagues on the Executive Committee—Wilma Donahue, chairman, John E. Anderson, James E. Birren, Ewald W. Busse, M.D., Woodrow W. Morris, Bernice L. Neugarten, Clark Tibbitts, Irving L. Webber, and Richard C. Wilcock.

Grateful acknowledgments are also made to the Division of Gerontology, the University of Michigan, and to its director, Wilma Donahue, and her staff, especially Dorothy Coons and Harold Orbach, for assuming the task of the major responsibility for checking the data, for proofreading, and for the preparation of the Index.

E. W. B.

Contents

PART ONE

PART TWO

Selected Case Studies

PART THREE

Selected Statistical Tables

PART ONE

I

Aging in Western Culture

ERNEST W. BURGESS

I. Introduction

The purpose of this volume is to present a picture of aging in selected countries of Western culture. Its aim is threefold. First, it seeks to describe the status and problems of the aging in these countries. Second, it attempts to portray the course of social action for the welfare of the aging. Third, it endeavors to compare the developments in European countries with those in the United States and, so far as feasible, to assess the value of their experience for American adoption, adaptation, or rejection.

A. Criteria of Western Cultures

What are the criteria by which Western cultures may be differentiated from those of other peoples?

1. *Industrialization and the growth of cities* is the first and most obvious characteristic. Industrialized countries like France, Italy, the Netherlands, Sweden, the United Kingdom, West Germany, and the United States, whatever the differences among them, are easily distinguished from such economically underdeveloped countries as Mexico, Brazil, Egypt, and India, which have a predominantly rural population. With the growth of cities there has also developed the urban way of life.

2. *The rise of science and technology,* although less apparent, is the basic characteristic of Western culture upon which industrialization and urban life depends.

We are now living in the atomic era, with unlimited possibilities of future developments that will affect the health, activities, and welfare of all age groups.

3. *Medical science and the prolongation of life* are farthest advanced in countries of Western culture. The conquest of diseases and the reduction in morbidity and mortality have been greatest in infancy, childhood, and early and middle adult life. Prospects, however, are bright for the victory of medical science in combating the diseases accompanying the later years of life.

4. *The growth of democracy* is a common characteristic of Western cultures. This includes not only universal suffrage and the guaranties of free speech, free press, and freedom of movement and of association but also industrial democracy.

5. *The development of social gerontology,* or the science of aging in its psychological and social aspects, is a phenomenon of Western culture. It is a recognition of the concern of industrialized countries with the welfare of their aging population. Even more it is a realization that social action on behalf of the aging should be based on research not only of the biological but also of the psychological and social aspects of aging.

B. Selection of Countries

It is not feasible to include in this survey of social gerontology all the countries

3

of Western culture. It was decided instead
to concentrate upon six European nations
which met the criteria outlined above and
at the same time were representative of the
remaining countries of Western culture.
Those selected were France, Italy, the
Netherlands, Sweden, the United Kingdom, and West Germany. Three other
countries are considered in one or more of
the chapters which follow: Belgium, Denmark, and Switzerland. These countries, together with Finland and Norway, were
considered for inclusion in the survey. It
was decided to select Sweden as representative of Scandinavian countries, thereby
excluding Denmark, Finland, and Norway
for systematic treatment. Similarly, the
Netherlands was chosen over Belgium and
Switzerland for inclusion from the smaller
countries.

All these countries meet the criteria of
membership in Western culture. They have
all participated in a common economic,
cultural, social, and political development.
They have all been affected, some to a
greater degree than others, by the industrial revolution. They enjoy in large measure a common cultural and religious heritage. They have taken part in the development of political democracy, with occasional lapses into authoritarian rule in the
cases of France, Italy, and Germany.

Four other countries of Western culture
deserve attention at this point. They are
Australia, Canada, New Zealand, and the
United States. These are all non-European
countries but peopled by Europeans. They
are pioneer areas in the sense that they all
passed from colonial to independent status
and that the transition from agriculture to
industrialization took place later than in
Europe. At present, however, they all fully
measure up to the criteria of membership
in Western culture. Therefore, references
where pertinent will be made to these
countries.

Excluded for purposes of this survey are
Communist-dominated countries. They do
not meet our criteria for membership in
Western culture. The Soviet Union, its sat-

ellites, and Yugoslavia differ widely in
their economic and political values and institutions from those of the countries selected for inclusion. All these countries
have programs of old age pensions which
follow, in general, the same pattern. Statistical data on aging are often lacking for
systematic comparisons, and there is little
or no research in progress in the field of social gerontology. There is, therefore, little
to be learned from their experience which
would be of value to workers in gerontology in the United States and other Western countries.

Also omitted for systematic treatment
are the many comparisons that might be
made to the economically underdeveloped
countries like those of Latin America, Africa, and Asia.

C. The Criterion of Aging

"Aging," as the term implies, is a process. It begins even before birth and continues until death. As such, aging is sy-
nonymous with human development. Cus-
tomarily, however, the term "aging" is
taken to mean the later stage or stages of
the process. For purposes of this survey it
is necessary to define aging, or, more precisely, the later stage of aging, arbitrarily
at a fixed age. But what should this arbitrary age be?

One criterion of the lower limit of old
age would be legal. At what age under the
law is a man or a woman eligible for an
old age pension or for insurance benefits
administered by the government? In eighteen European countries, outside those that
are Communist-dominated, the pensionable ages for old age programs for men are
three at 60, twelve at 65, one at 67, and
two at 70. For women the corresponding
pensionable ages are one at 55, eight at 60,
one at 63, five at 65, two at 67, and two at
70. These figures indicate 65 as the most
frequent age and give support for its selection as the arbitrary age at which aging
may be said to begin.

The age 65 gets unexpected support according to a biological criterion of aging. For all males at birth the average life-expectancy for thirteen European countries of Western culture is 65 years. For females it is somewhat higher. In other words, half of all males live beyond their sixty-fifth birthday. The other half die before reaching this age. All living to be 65 and over have surpassed their life-expectancy at birth. They are living, as the popular expression phrases it, "on borrowed time."

In the future we undoubtedly will have a better criterion than that of chronological age. Havighurst (1959) has proposed a sociological definition of aging in terms of reduction in social competence. Even if we use chronological age, it is evident that it may be desirable for some purposes to shift it earlier, as in the case of eligibility for pensions or insurance for women, or to advance it, as in the case of compulsory retirement for non-manual employment. For purposes of our survey of European cultures the age of 65 as marking the beginning of the later stage of aging will generally be used.

In this introductory chapter answers to four main questions will be sought to provide background for the chapters that follow:

1. What are the trends of social change which underlie the emergence of the problems of aging in countries of Western culture?

2. What have been the effects of these trends on aging and its problems in these European countries?

3. How do these countries differ from one another in the problems of aging?

4. What are the chief areas of societal concern which find expression in social action?

II. Social Trends in Aging

All the countries of Western culture have experienced the economic and social effects of the industrial revolution. The change from agriculture to manufacture as the basic mode of production set in motion a series of economic and social trends. We will now review those which have special significance for an understanding of the problems of aging in modern cultures.

A. The Change from Home to Factory Production

The immediate and most visible effect of the industrial revolution was that the production of goods was taken out of the home and placed in the factory. This meant the separation of work from the home. Earlier the family had been the unit of production as on the farm or in the shop in town.

Another aspect of this change was the great decrease in owners and entrepreneurs.

TABLE 1

Percentage of Self-employed in Five Western European Countries

Country	Early Year	Per Cent	Later Year	Per Cent
France	1936	29.1	1954	28.6
Italy	1936	42.6	1951	37.2
Sweden	1940	28.5	1950	22.2
United Kingdom	1931	13.2	1951	10.5
West Germany	1936	28.0	1950	23.0

The shift was from employer to employee. Instead of operating his own business the average person worked under the direction of his employer.

The proportion of self-employed to all occupied persons not only is small in countries of Western culture but is decreasing, as Table 1 shows. Italy and France have the highest proportion of self-employed because of the large number engaged in agriculture and small business in these countries. The United Kingdom has the lowest proportion of persons working for themselves, which corresponds with its position as a highly industrialized country with a minimum of agriculture. Even in a rural country like Ireland, with a high proportion of self-employed to all employees, the percentage fell from 47.6 in 1936 to 39.8 in 1951. The presumption is that this trend will continue for all countries of Western culture.

Women as well as men left the home to work in the factory. At present the percentage of women and of married women gainfully employed in countries of Western culture is large (Table 2). As they reach working age, children of wage-earning parents enter industry. The members of the family who are gainfully employed are more likely to work for different concerns rather than for the same company or organization.

At any rate, it is clear that the industrial revolution has largely destroyed the family as a unit of economic production. The

TABLE 2

PERCENTAGE OF FEMALES ECONOMICALLY
ACTIVE IN SIX WESTERN EUROPEAN
COUNTRIES

Country	Year	Ages 15–19	Ages 20–64
France.............	1954	43.3	44.0
Italy..............	1955	38.2	26.8
Netherlands........	1947	48.7	25.4
Sweden............	1950	54.3	31.6
United Kingdom.....	1951	78.2	36.0
West Germany......	1950	77.5	40.1

last remaining stronghold of this type of family is on the farm and in the few other kinds of family businesses.

B. From the Rural to the Urban Way of Life

The shift from rural to urban living naturally accompanied industrialization. The countries of Western culture are with few exceptions highly industrialized. This is evident by the small proportion of agricultural production to the total commodity output of a country, as shown in Table 3.

Of these countries, the United Kingdom and West Germany are the most highly industrialized; Sweden and the Netherlands are less industrialized; and France and Italy are semi-agricultural. None of these countries would be classified as mainly ag-

ricultural. Certain European countries, by contrast, are still predominantly agricultural, as shown by the nations for which data are available (Table 4).

In eleven European countries data are available for a year or more of the period 1936–38. For nine of these the percentage of agriculture to total commodity output has declined since then. For the others it has remained stationary. The trend is still

TABLE 3

PERCENTAGE OF AGRICULTURE TO
TOTAL COMMODITY OUTPUT IN
SIX WESTERN EUROPEAN COUN-
TRIES

Country	Year	Per Cent
France..........	1950	31.0
Italy............	1950	43.5
Netherlands.....	1950	24.6
Sweden..........	1950	21.0
United Kingdom.	1949	11.2
West Germany...	1950	14.6

TABLE 4

PERCENTAGE OF AGRICULTURE TO
TOTAL COMMODITY OUTPUT IN
FOUR COUNTRIES

Country	Year	Per Cent
Ireland......	1950	55.5
Greece......	1949	61.4
Spain.......	1951	59.1
Turkey......	1950	75.5

continuing toward a contraction of agriculture in the national economy of Western culture and to the further growth of urban population and the urban way of life.

Urbanization, as well as industrialization, is an outstanding characteristic of Western cultures. The comparison with the predominance of rural settlement in economically underdeveloped countries is striking.

The shift from rural to urban living naturally accompanied industrialization. The countries of Western culture are predomi-

nantly urban, as Table 5 shows. It is interesting that the New World countries of
like industrial development also have correspondingly high proportions of urban
population (Table 6).

The countries of Asia and Latin America, with the exception of Argentina, are
predominantly rural, as seen by the data in
Table 7. Communist countries also have a
small proportion of urban population (Table 8).

The urban way of life develops only in
part because of population density. It
arises even more with the division of labor,

TABLE 5*

PERCENTAGE OF URBAN POPULA-
TION IN SELECTED WESTERN
EUROPEAN COUNTRIES

Country	Year	Per Cent Urban
United Kingdom.	1951	81
West Germany...	1946	69
Netherlands.....	1947	55
France..........	1954	56
Sweden..........	1950	50
Italy............	1936	45

* Source: United Nations, *Demographic
Yearbook, 1957*, Table 7.

TABLE 6*

PERCENTAGE OF URBAN POPULA-
TION IN NEW WORLD INDUS-
TRIAL COUNTRIES

Country	Year	Per Cent Urban
Australia........	1947	69
United States....	1950	64
Canada.........	1951	62
New Zealand.....	1951	60

* Source: United Nations, *Demographic
Yearbook, 1957*.

with the differentiation of economic and
social classes, with the multiplicity of social groupings, and with the specialization
of personal interests, goals, and roles. The
contrasting natures of the rural and urban
ways of life are expressed in the shift from

personal to impersonal social contacts and
relationships, the change in social control
of the conduct of the person from the primary to the secondary group, the decrease
in sentimental and the increase in rational
attitudes, and the decline in concrete and

TABLE 7*

PERCENTAGE OF URBAN POPULA-
TION IN SELECTED UNDER-
DEVELOPED COUNTRIES

Country	Year	Per Cent Urban
Argentina...	1947	62.5
Brazil.......	1950	36.2
Egypt.......	1947	30.1
India.......	1951	17.3
Japan.......	1945	27.8
Mexico......	1950	42.6

* Source: United Nations, *Demographic
Yearbook, 1957*.

TABLE 8*

PERCENTAGE OF URBAN POPULA-
TION IN SIX COMMUNIST
COUNTRIES

Country	Year	Per Cent Urban
Bulgaria.........	1946	24.6
Czechoslovakia...	1947	48.8
Hungary........	1949	34.5
Yugoslavia......	1948	16.2
Poland..........	1946	31.4
Rumania........	1948	23.4

* Source: United Nations, *Demographic
Yearbook, 1957*.

the growth of abstract reactions to experience. The urban way of life increases the
movement of population. All types of mobility are stepped up: residential, social or
vertical, and ideational. There is the
growth of the mass media of communication: newspapers, magazines, motion pictures, radio, and television. Comparative
data are available which show the differences among countries in the numbers of
the audience or public for the various media of mass communication.

The circulation of daily newspapers and

newsprint consumption are closely related to the degree of industrialization and urbanization. The United Kingdom and Sweden are the highest, and Italy the lowest, in newspaper circulation and per capita newsprint consumption (Table 9).

TABLE 9*

NEWSPAPER CIRCULATION AND PER CAPITA NEWSPRINT CONSUMPTION IN SIX WESTERN EUROPEAN COUNTRIES

Country	Year	Daily Newspaper Circulation per 1000 Population	Newsprint Consumption Per Capita
France..........	1956	244	10.2
Italy..........	1956	107	3.6
Netherlands.....	1956	264	11.1
Sweden.........	1956	462	23.3
United Kingdom.	1954	573	19.0†
West Germany..	1956	277	7.2‡

* Source: United Nations, *Statistical Yearbook, 1957*, Tables 184–85; *1958*, Tables 180–81.
† 1956.
‡ West Germany and West Berlin.

TABLE 10*

NEWSPAPER CIRCULATION AND PER CAPITA NEWSPRINT CONSUMPTION IN FOUR NON-EUROPEAN COUNTRIES

Country	Year	Daily Newspaper Circulation per 1000 Population	Newsprint Consumption Per Capita
Canada.........	1956	244	26.0
Australia........	1957	381	28.2
New Zealand....	1956	390	28.7
United States....	1956	337	38.0

* Source: United Nations, *Statistical Yearbook, 1957*, Tables 184–85; *1958*, Tables 180–81.

The non-European countries of Western culture are all relatively high in daily newspaper circulation and per capita newsprint consumption. They are all lower than the United Kingdom in daily newspaper circulation per 1000 population, but their newspapers are larger, as shown by the newsprint consumption, than in the European countries (Table 10).

The underdeveloped countries have low daily newspaper circulation and small use of newsprint per capita, as shown by Table 11.

TABLE 11*

NEWSPAPER CIRCULATION AND PER CAPITA NEWSPRINT CONSUMPTION IN FIVE UNDERDEVELOPED COUNTRIES

Country	Year	Daily Newspaper Circulation per 1000 Population	Newsprint Consumption Per Capita
Argentina.........	1956	159	5.8
Brazil............	1955	50	2.9
Egypt............	1952	25	1.1
India............	1953	7	0.2
Mexico...........	1952	48	2.8

* Source: United Nations, *Statistical Yearbook, 1957*, Tables 184–85; *1958*, Tables 180–81.

TABLE 12*

NEWSPAPER CIRCULATION AND PER CAPITA NEWSPRINT CONSUMPTION IN EIGHT COMMUNIST COUNTRIES

Country	Year	Daily Newspaper Circulation per 1000 Population	Newsprint Consumption Per Capita
Bulgaria........	1956	170	2.0
Czechoslovakia..	1956	170	....
East Germany...	1954	118†	....
Hungary........	1956	122†	....
Poland..........	1956	150	1.8
Rumania.......	1957	149	1.8‡
Yugoslavia......	1956	48	1.2
U.S.S.R........	1956	107	1.6

* Source: United Nations, *Statistical Yearbook, 1957*, Tables 184–85; *1958*, Tables 180–81.
† Estimated.
‡ 1956.

In Communist countries daily newspaper circulation and newsprint consumption are, in general, intermediate between those of countries of Western culture and underdeveloped countries (Table 12).

The United Kingdom has the highest annual per capita motion-picture theater attendance—23.2—in the world. The lowest per capita attendance of our six European countries is in the Netherlands, Sweden, and France (Table 13).

The four non-European countries of Western culture all have relatively high motion-picture theater attendance, as shown in Table 14.

Underdeveloped countries are much lower in per capita attendance at motion-picture theaters (Table 15).

TABLE 13*

PER CAPITA ATTENDANCE AT MO-
TION-PICTURE THEATERS IN SIX
WESTERN EUROPEAN COUN-
TRIES, 1954–58

Country	Year	Per Capita Attend- ance
France..........	1955	9.7
Italy............	1954	16.8
Netherlands.....	1955	6.1
Sweden..........	1958	9.4
United Kingdom.	1955	23.2
West Germany...	1955	15.3

* Source: United Nations: *Statistical Year-book, 1956*, Table 183B; *1957*, Table 187B; and *1958*, Table 183B.

TABLE 14*

PER CAPITA ATTENDANCE AT MO-
TION-PICTURE THEATERS, IN
FOUR NON-EUROPEAN COUN-
TRIES, 1954–57

Country	Year	Per Capita Attend- ance
Australia........	1955	15.0
Canada..........	1954	15.6
New Zealand.....	1957	18.9
United States....	1955	14.5†

* Source: United Nations, *Statistical Year-book, 1956*, Table 183B; *1957*, Table 187B; and *1958*, Table 183B.
† Estimated.

Communist countries, except for Rumania and Yugoslavia, compare quite favorably in attendance at motion-picture theaters with the nations of Western culture, as shown in Table 16.

The relative distribution of radio receivers in use follows the pattern observed in the other media of mass communication. Countries of Western culture are highest in use of radio receivers, underdeveloped countries are lowest, and the

TABLE 15*

PER CAPITA ATTENDANCE AT MO-
TION-PICTURE THEATERS IN
FIVE UNDERDEVELOPED COUN-
TRIES, 1953–57

Country	Year	Per Capita Attend- ance
Argentina.......	1957	3.9
Brazil..........	1955	5.3
Egypt...........	1955	2.8
India...........	1953	2.0†
Mexico..........	1957	8.5

* Source: United Nations, *Statistical Year-book, 1956*, Table 183B; *1957*, Table 187B; and *1958*, Table 183B.
† Estimated.

TABLE 16*

PER CAPITA ATTENDANCE AT
MOTION-PICTURE THEATERS
IN EIGHT COMMUNIST COUN-
TRIES, 1955

Country	Per Capita Attendance
Bulgaria...........	7.3
Czechoslovakia.....	12.4
East Germany......	17.2
Hungary...........	11.8
Poland............	8.1
Rumania..........	4.0
Yugoslavia........	5.7
U.S.S.R...........	12.6

* Source: United Nations, *Statistical Yearbook, 1956*, Table 183B; *1957*, Table 187B; and *1958*, Table 183B.

majority of Communist countries are in between. In Europe, Sweden has a considerable lead over the United Kingdom, West Germany, and the Netherlands (Table 17).

Two of the non-European countries of Western culture—Canada and the United States—have rates of radio receivers in use far in excess of that of Sweden, which has the highest rate in Europe, as can be seen in Table 18.

Underdeveloped countries have a very low proportion of radio receivers in use per 1000 population, as shown in Table 19.

Communist countries, except for Czechoslovakia and East Germany, have a relatively low rate of radio receivers per 1000 population (Table 20).

TABLE 17*

RADIO RECEIVERS IN USE IN SIX WESTERN EUROPEAN COUNTRIES, 1956

Country	No. (In Thousands)	Per 1000 Population
France	10,158	233
Italy	6,306	131
Netherlands	2,878	264
Sweden	2,548	348
United Kingdom	14,434	281
West Germany	14,051	277

* Source: United Nations, *Statistical Yearbook, 1957*, Table 189; *Estimates of Population, 1956*, Table 1.

TABLE 18*

RADIO RECEIVERS IN USE IN FOUR NON-EUROPEAN COUNTRIES, 1955–56

Country	Year	No. (In Thousands)	Per 1000 Population
Australia	1955	2,051	223
Canada	1956	9,050	563
New Zealand	1956	519	238
United States	1956	150,000	892

* Source: United Nations, *Statistical Yearbook, 1957*, Table 189; *Estimates of Population, 1956*, Table 1.

C. Breakup of the Extended Family and Emergence of the Conjugal Family

The decline of the extended family has proceeded—at varying rates, to be sure—in all countries of Western culture. It gave up its natural habitat when its members migrated from the country to the city. Conditions of urban living were unfavorable to its survival.

René König (1956) points out that recent research in Yugoslavia by Bicanic and in Finland by Pipping indicates that the disintegration of the extended family began in the pre-industrial period when changes in agriculture made the large family a burden instead of an asset. In Yugoslavia the precipitation of the breakdown of the extended family as a working unit was the transition from farming with two or three pair of oxen and four or five men to plowing by one man with two horses and an iron plow.

TABLE 19*

RADIO RECEIVERS IN USE IN FOUR UNDER-DEVELOPED COUNTRIES, 1954–56

Country	Year	No. (In Thousands)	Per 1000 Population
Brazil	1954	3500	61
Egypt	1956	850	36
India	1956	1076	3
Mexico	1955	2500	84

* Source: United Nations, *Statistical Yearbook, 1957*, Table 189; *Estimates of Population, 1956*, Table 1.

TABLE 20*

RADIO RECEIVERS IN USE IN SEVEN COMMUNIST COUNTRIES, 1954–56

Country	Year	No. (In Thousands)	Per 1000 Population
Bulgaria	1954	350	47
Czechoslovakia	1956	2,906	220
East Germany	1955	5,000†	299
Hungary	1956	1,587	161
Poland	1956	3,624	130
Rumania	1955	1,164	67
U.S.S.R.	1956	29,571	148

* Source: United Nations, *Statistical Yearbook, 1957*, Table 189; *Estimates of Population, 1956*, Table 1.
† Estimated.

The separation of the home from work and the move of the family from the rural village to the urban community undermined the economic bases of the extended family. Under these conditions the traditional type of husband-wife relations also changed. During the dominance of the extended family the authoritarian conception of the role of the husband prevailed. When the extended family in the city fell apart into its component units, the conjugal family emerged. It was a small group of husband, wife, and children. It was no longer a work group, with the husband taking the roles of employer, rule-issuer, and decision-maker.

At first the husband and father maintained his authoritarian position in the conjugal family in the city. He was superordinate and the wife subordinate. Decision-making remained in his hands. Children were expected to respect and obey their parents. Discipline was rigid and severe. Gradually, however, the roles of husband and wife changed from inequality to equality, and a companionship relation developed. Sociologists describe this transition as from the institutional or traditional family to the companionship or modern family.

By the family as an institution is meant that its members are held together by the external social controls of public opinion, the mores, and law. The members of the companionship form of the family are united by the internal bonds of love, congeniality, and common objectives. Other characteristics of the institutional family are authority of the husband and father, inferior status of the wife, strict discipline of the children, and emphasis upon duty. The contrasting features of the companionship family are shared authority by husband and wife, equality in the status of each, respect for the individuality of the child, and emphasis upon the personality development of members of the family.

A number of factors combined to accelerate the emergence of the companionship family. Among these was the emancipation of woman in the economic, educational, social, and political areas of her life. The separation of home and work increased the responsibility and authority of the wife in the family. The greatest single factor in raising her status in the family followed her gainful employment outside the home. This economic independence tended to give her co-ordinate authority with the husband in decision-making in the home.

The effect of two world wars was, also, to raise the status of women. They entered into jobs from which they had previously been barred. As wives they took over household responsibilities that had until then been reserved to their husbands.

The development of the companionship family has proceeded furthest in the United States (Burgess and Locke, 1953). It has, however, emerged in all countries of western Europe. It is further advanced in the more highly industrialized and urban countries than in others. In all Western countries it tends to develop in the upper middle class and to be less evident in the wage-earning classes.

Survivals of the extended family persist in all countries of Western culture. In Italy and France, with their large rural populations, its ties are still strong. In other countries the older and the younger generations maintain communication and contacts, engage in reciprocal services, and participate in reunions and family events and celebrations.

D. The Rise of Large Organizations

The trend throughout Western culture, but at a more rapid rate in some countries than others, has been toward the rise of large organizations. This trend is not confined to the economic sphere of life, although it is perhaps more marked here than in the social, recreational, educational, and political areas.

In the United States the development of organization has been so pronounced that an economist, Kenneth Boulding (1953), has written a book on the organizational revolution. Our interest here is not in the facts of organization per se but in their effects upon people in the organization.

There is, first of all, the technological organization of the factory to facilitate mass production. The assembly line sets a pace for all the workers to follow. Then there is the organization of employees at different levels of operation and responsibility. There arise the problems of co-operation, conformity, and personal integrity that confront the organization man, as pointed out by Whyte (1956).

The picture is essentially the same in nearly all the other areas of human life in modern society. The individual often feels submerged in the large organizations in which his life is enmeshed. The average person seems to count for little or nothing in the large organization. A church member feels lost in a congregation of one thousand souls. A voter feels the futility of his one ballot when over sixty million vote in a presidential election.

More serious than apathy is the conflict which arises within the person from his impulse to conform to the pressure exerted by the organization and his wish to express his own views and hold out for their adoption. The basic problem is to find means of stimulating individual initiative, self-expression, and originality and at the same time to promote the values inherent in the team play and efficiency that derive from organization.

At any rate, human beings are increasingly dependent upon organizations for opportunity for the realization of their desires. Until recently, retired people have been largely without participation in organizations and without a share in the benefits of membership in them.

E. Automation and the Increase of Leisure Time

The transition from handwork to mass production of commodities has made possible both a rise in the standard of living and a reduction in the hours of work.

Automation in all countries of Western culture, and particularly in the United States, where it has developed most rapidly, poses a threat and a promise. The threat is the displacement of workers from their jobs. This danger is greatest for the older worker who finds it difficult, if not impossible, to get re-employment. The promise of automation is a reduction of work, a rise in the standard of living, and an increase of leisure time. No country of Western culture has worked out adequate protection against the readjustment of the employees displaced by automation.

One manifestation of the increase in leisure time is the introduction of compulsory retirement at a fixed age. Optional retirement at earlier ages appears to be a partial solution of the problem of automation. We are toward the end of an era predominantly motivated by the philosophy of work. We are to enter a new age where enjoyment of leisure will increasingly take over the center of the stage.

No country of the Western world has as yet seriously faced the challenge of the changes now in progress. Evidence of public response to the new boon of more leisure is found in the increasing popularity of travel, in the enjoyment of vacations, and in the new meaning of the week end.

The trend to automation and the increase of leisure time call for new social inventions and new forms of organization to maximize their advantages and minimize their disadvantages.

F. The Conservation of Human Life

All Western cultures are concerned with the conservation of human life. They have all achieved, as compared with economically underdeveloped countries, a marked increase in life-expectancy. For our six selected European countries the average number of years of life which males and females can expect at birth is presented in Table 21. The Netherlands has the highest life-expectancy at birth of any country in the world. Four non-European countries of Western culture also have high rates of life-expectancy, as shown in Table 22.

All these rates are very much higher than for economically underdeveloped countries, as Table 23 reveals.

The life-expectancy at birth of Communist-dominated countries is intermediate between those of nations of Western culture and economically underdeveloped countries (Table 24).

The greatest success in the conservation of human life has been in the tremendous reduction in infant and maternal mortality. All countries of Western cultures have scored brilliant successes in achieving low rates of infant mortality (Tables 25 and 26). Rates are the number of deaths of infants under 1 year per 1000 live births. Similar low rates of infant and maternal mortality are reported for the non-European countries of Western culture. By contrast the corresponding rates for the economically underdeveloped countries are

TABLE 21*

AVERAGE LIFE-EXPECTANCY AT BIRTH, SIX WESTERN EUROPEAN COUNTRIES

Country	Year	Males	Fe- males
France................	1950–51	63.8	69.3
Italy.................	1950–55	63.6	67.3
Netherlands...........	1950 52	70.6	72.9
Sweden...............	1946–50	69.0	71.6
United Kingdom: England and Wales.......	1950	66.5	71.2
West Germany.........	1949–51	64.6	68.5

* Source: United Nations, *Demographic Yearbook, 1957*, Table 24.

TABLE 22*

AVERAGE LIFE-EXPECTANCY AT BIRTH FOUR NON-EUROPEAN COUNTRIES

Country	Year	Males	Females
Australia.........	1946–48	66.1	70.6
Canada..........	1950–52	66.3	70.8
New Zealand.....	1950–52	68.3	72.4
United States†....	1949–51	65.5	71.0

* Source: United Nations, *Demographic Yearbook, 1957*, Table 24.
† The rate for the United States for the white population for 1950 are male, 66.6; female, 72.4.

high, as shown in Table 27. The infant mortality rates of Communist countries, with the exception of Czechoslovakia, are closer to underdeveloped countries than they are to Western nations (Table 28).

Six trends have been chosen to give

background to our consideration of aging and its problems in modern Western societies. The first five of these are obviously interdependent: they are the change from home to factory production, the transition from the rural to the urban way of life, the

TABLE 23*

AVERAGE LIFE-EXPECTANCY AT BIRTH, THREE UNDERDEVELOPED COUNTRIES

Country	Year	Males	Females
Brazil (Federal District).......	1949–51	49.8	56.0
India............	1941–50	32.5	31.7
Mexico..........	1940	37.9	39.8

* Source: United Nations, *Demographic Yearbook, 1957*, Table 24.

TABLE 24*

AVERAGE LIFE-EXPECTANCY AT BIRTH, THREE COMMUNIST COUNTRIES

Country	Year	Males	Females
Hungary.........	1948–49	58.8	63.3
Poland...........	1948	55.6	62.5
U.S.S.R.........	1955–56	63.0	69.0

* Source: United Nations, *Demographic Yearbook, 1957*, Table 24.

breakup of the extended family and the emergence of the conjugal family, the rise of large organizations, and the growth of automation and the increase in leisure time. The sixth trend is the conservation of human life.

All these trends have effected great transformations in our style of life, in our thinking, and in our behavior. Only one of them was intended, namely, the conservation of life. The others were developments that are still continuing to shape our changing society and the personality of its members.

The net effect of these dynamic trends has had, on the whole, an adverse impact upon the aging segment of countries of Western culture. These effects will now be taken up in some detail.

III. Effects upon Aging

The total effect of these trends upon older people constitutes a paradox. The proportion of older people in the total population of countries of Western culture has increased tremendously, but their function, role, and status have declined.

TABLE 25

INFANT MORTALITY RATE, SIX WESTERN EUROPEAN COUN- TRIES, 1955

Country	Rate
France	38.6
Italy	50.9
Netherlands	20.1
Sweden	17.4
United Kingdom	25.9
West Germany	41.7

TABLE 26

INFANT MORTALITY RATE, FOUR NON-EUROPEAN INDUSTRIAL COUNTRIES, 1955

Country	Rate
Australia	22.0
Canada	31.3
New Zealand	24.5
United States	26.4

A. Prolongation of Life

More people are living beyond 65 years of age than a century ago. Exact figures are not available for all countries of Western culture, largely because of changes of political boundaries and the lack of statistical data for the earlier period. But the increase in the proportion of older persons is impressive, as can be seen from Table 29.

In one hundred years the percentage of population 65 years of age and over more than doubled in Great Britain and Sweden and almost doubled in France and the Netherlands. For the United States the estimated increase was even greater. The proportion quadrupled. Comparable data are not available for Italy and West Germany. The largest factors in the increasing proportion of people living beyond 65 has been (*a*) the great decrease in infant and child mortality, (*b*) the reduction in the death rate from communicable and other diseases of early and middle adulthood, and (*c*) the decreasing proportion of population under age 20 resulting from a declining birth rate.

In countries of Western culture people who pass the 65-year mark are living longer but not much longer than 50 or 100 years ago. At the age of 65 the expected years of life remaining for men and women are given for our six selected countries in Table 30.

Of these six countries, at age 65 the expected number of years remaining is highest for men (14.1) and for women (15.0) in the Netherlands. It is lowest for men in the United Kingdom (11.9) and for women in Italy and West Germany (13.7

TABLE 27

INFANT MORTALITY RATE, SIX UNDERDEVELOPED COUN- TRIES, 1955

Country	Rate
Argentina	62.0*
Brazil	170.0†
Egypt	148.5
India	99.9
Mexico	83.3
Venezuela	69.9

* Estimate for 1940–50.
† For 1950.

TABLE 28

INFANT MORTALITY RATE, SIX COMMUNIST COUNTRIES, 1955

Country	Rate
Bulgaria	82.4
Czechoslovakia	34.1
Hungary	60.0
Poland	81.4
Rumania	78.2
Yugoslavia	112.8

years). The range is wider for men (2.2 years) than for women (1.3 years). The highest life-expectancy at age 65 in the world has been reported for Norway (14.9 for men and 16.0 for women).

It is interesting and, I believe, significant to note that in all countries of Western culture and in almost all others the life-expectancy at age 65 is higher for females than for males. This difference might be explained as of biological origin except for a significant fact. The differences between the sexes in the number of remaining years is not uniform from country to country. It is large in some but very small in others. The largest differences in the six countries reported on above are for the United Kingdom (3.0 years) and for France (2.5 years), or 20 per cent higher for women than for men. The corresponding percentage for the United States is as high. For the other countries the differences are small, ranging from 10 to 13 months (1.1 years for Italy, 1.0 years for Sweden, 0.9 years for the Netherlands, and 0.8 years for West Germany). Evidently, the cause is not due to innate biological differences between the sexes but is to be found in environmental and social factors. Further research might well lead to significant findings.

TABLE 29*

PERCENTAGE OF POPULATION 65 YEARS AND OVER IN SIX WESTERN COUNTRIES

Country	1850	1900	1950
France.............	6.5	8.2	11.8
Italy...............		6.2	8.3
Netherlands........	4.8	6.0	7.7
Sweden............	4.8	8.4	10.3
United Kingdom.....	4.6	4.7	10.8
United States.......	2.1†	4.1	8.1

* Source: United Nations, *The Aging of Populations and Its Economic and Social Implications, 1956,* and, for Italy (1958), United Nations, *Demographic Yearbook, 1956*, Table 4.
† Estimated.

Jean Daric (1954) explains how in France the prolongation of life of older persons has differentially affected the family structure and relations in the country and in the city. In France the average duration of life increased 25 years between 1850 and 1950. The result in rural districts was a marked aging of the heads of families and managers of agricultural production. Since they had the disposition of the

patrimony, their sons had to wait much longer to obtain full control of the farm. As a consequence, the more enterprising youth migrated to the cities. The older generation tended to be resistant to modern agricultural methods.

In the city the increase of life-expectancy and the decrease in number of children has rendered the situation of aged

TABLE 30*

YEARS OF LIFE REMAINING AT AGE 65 IN SIX WESTERN EUROPEAN COUNTRIES

Country	Year	Men	Women
France..........	1952–56	12.1	14.6
Italy............	1950–53	12.6	13.7
Netherlands......	1953–55	14.1	15.0
Sweden..........	1951–55	13.8	14.8
United Kingdom..	1956	11.9	14.9
West Germany...	1949–51	12.9	13.7

* Source: United Nations, *Demographic Yearbook, 1958*, Table 31.

persons very precarious. The burden of supporting old parents falls upon a greatly reduced number of adult children. "The loosening of family solidarity and the conditions of urban life diminish the chances of being taken into the homes of their children. The city family is more and more reduced to the couple and their unmarried children. This explains why the systems of social security for the aging have arisen in the city" (Daric, 1954, p. 334).

B. The Paradox of Security and Insecurity

The security which the older person formerly had in the family is now supplied by the state. Old age and survivor's insurance or government pensions protect him against want and against disabling illness. The prolongation of life means that more people can count on living beyond 65 years and that they may live somewhat longer after they reach that age.

This security in a more favorable life-expectancy is countered by insecurity because of fear of the incidence of disabling illness in the later years. The fact is that there has been a rising curve of physical and mental disabilities in the later years of life. As measured by care in hospitals, the increase has been even greater than the increase in the number of those 65 years and over.

In terms of rates of mortality there is an increase in our selected countries of Western culture in diseases of the heart and other cardiovascular conditions and cancer (Table 31). It is generally lower in pneumonia and tuberculosis. Only in Italy, of these five countries, was there a decrease in the period 1931–49 in heart and other cardiovascular conditions. The Netherlands reported a small decrease for both men and women, and the United Kingdom noted a decrease for cancer in women.

From 1931 to 1949 large decreases were reported for tuberculosis in European countries of Western culture in the middle-aged group (45–64). Except for France, it decreased for the age group 65 and over in the five nations listed in Table 32. Pneumonia and influenza decreased markedly for both middle-aged and older persons in all five countries except France (Table 32).

One of the two major anxieties of retired people is the possibility of prolonged illness against which there is no complete protection except in the United Kingdom by the National Health Service or elsewhere by private health insurance. The second major insecurity is the fear of inflation which haunts older persons. Inflation is an economic malady which afflicts all countries of Western culture. The fig-

TABLE 31

DEATH RATES PER 100,000 FOR AGES 65 AND OVER

COUNTRY	HEART AND OTHER CARDIOVASCULAR DISEASES				CANCER			
	1931		1949		1931		1949	
	Male	Female	Male	Female	Male	Female	Male	Female
France..................	2786	2219	3793	2896	551	490	1029	760
Italy....................	3486	3376	3340	3205	491	437	754	605
Netherlands..............	2762	2980	2885	3154	1189	999	1136	977
Sweden*.................	3914	3756	5044	4970	1016	840	1081	895
United Kingdom..........	4133	3608	4399	3864	1111	886	1167	808

* For Sweden the age group is 70 and over.

TABLE 32

DEATH RATES PER 100,000 FOR AGES 65 AND OVER

COUNTRY	TUBERCULOSIS				PNEUMONIA AND INFLUENZA			
	1931		1949		1931		1949	
	Male	Female	Male	Female	Male	Female	Male	Female
France..................	126	73	150	81	507	486	549	490
Italy....................	72	63	55	37	1035	986	452	390
Netherlands..............	112	94	87	81	996	1031	458	492
Sweden*.................	104	105	78	57	978	1113	336	387
United Kingdom..........	72	63	55	37	494	474	353	296

* For Sweden the age group is 70 and over.

ures given in Table 33 are percentage increases in the cost of living from 1948 to 1956. Except for West Germany, these are all considerable rises. They markedly affect the purchasing power of everyone who is on a fixed income. For most retired persons inflation of this magnitude, unless counterbalanced by rise in pensions and insurance benefits, has disastrous consequences for their standard of living.

C. Loss of Priority by the Family

In all societies of the past and in Western countries before the industrial revolution, the extended family provided security, protection, and reciprocal services to its members. Ogburn and Tibbitts (1933) have amassed the evidence to show the loss by the family of its historic functions of economic production, care of health, leisure-time activities, religious practices, education, and protection.

The full force of these shifts has fallen heaviest on the older person. He can no longer count as a matter of right and of moral and legal obligation on economic support by his children. He is less and less likely, if widowed, to be offered a home by a son or a daughter. If ill, particularly with a chronic ailment, his children are more and more disposed to shift his care to a hospital rather than to provide a bed in their home. If lonely, he must more and more look elsewhere than to his descendants to provide companionship and sociability. In short, he must seek elsewhere for the satisfaction of his needs—financial, health, and social. In Western cultures he turns to the government or to other organizations.

D. Organizations Take Over First Place

The older person, like those in all age groups in modern society, must rely less upon the family and more on organizations for support and for the fulfilment of his desires. Organizations in Western countries are taking the primary place which the family had held from the beginning of human history.

The national government previously had seemed remote from the everyday life of the older person. It now mails to him his monthly pension or insurance check. He moves into housing specially designed for older residents which is subsidized by national, state, or municipal governments. Medical care in the home, hospital, or geriatric clinic is, in many European countries, under governmental auspices. In England, Sweden, and other nations such medical care is available to residents from infancy through old age.

In the United States, with its greater reliance on private agencies, other organizations than governmental play a larger

TABLE 33*

INCREASE IN COST OF LIVING,
SIX WESTERN EUROPEAN
COUNTRIES, 1948–56

Country	Per Cent
France	34
Italy	29
Netherlands	36
Sweden	42
United Kingdom	45
West Germany	13

* Source: International Monetary Fund, *International Financial Statistics*, Vol. 10 (October, 1957).

role than in Europe. If the individual takes the initiative in making financial provision for retirement, he relies less on making his own investments but rather more upon savings banks, building and loan associations, investment trusts, and life insurance companies. In addition, the company or organization for which he works often makes provision for pensions or annuities for its retired employees.

Data for the different countries of Western culture are available to compare the ratio of life insurance in force to national income (Table 34). Insurance-in-force figures for the United Kingdom and West Germany used in calculating the ratios represent insurance in force in domestic companies of the country, including their foreign business. For other countries, insurance in force used is on lives of residents of the country in both domestic and foreign countries. These ratios indicate that the people of less industrialized countries, such as France and Italy, rely less on life insurance than do persons in other countries. For non-European countries of Western culture the ratio of life insurance in force to national income is much higher and increasing more rapidly than for the above countries (Table 35).

TABLE 34*

PERCENTAGE OF LIFE INSURANCE IN FORCE TO NATIONAL INCOME, SIX WESTERN EUROPEAN COUNTRIES

Country	1950	1957
France............	10	16
Italy.............	8	13
Netherlands.......	51	49
Sweden...........	43	52
United Kingdom...	56	57
West Germany.....	20	28

* Source: Institute of Life Insurance and Statistical Office of the United Nations.

Health insurance in the United States more than in Europe is also a matter for private rather than for governmental organizations. The Blue Cross and the Blue Shield are the best known of many similar organizations offering payment of the medical bills of hospitals and physicians. Pioneering demonstrations in group medical care are in progress under the auspices of companies and other organizations.

The dependence of the older person upon organizations is not limited to economic support, to housing, and to provision for health care. It extends over the entire range of his interests and activities. He needs, especially, organizations through which he can realize the potentialities of utilizing the leisure conferred upon him by retirement. Certain existing organizations like the church and the schools are beginning to reorient their programs to meet the needs of older people. These institutions have an opportunity to provide for certain of the leisure-time interests of older people.

E. Leisure and Loneliness

The superabundance of leisure of older people results naturally from retirement. But many of them are not prepared for a life of leisure. They have lived in the work-oriented countries of Western culture. Work has been central in the lives of men. Housework has had a similar significant meaning for women.

Since 1900 the hours of work have been reduced from the 12-hour day to 8 hours for 6 days or $5\frac{1}{2}$ days a week. Automation promises further shortening of the work week in terms of days worked or hours per day.

Relatively few workers when they retire are prepared to use this sudden gift of free time. That is one of the reasons that at 65 when eligible for retirement benefits so many of them, especially men, desire to continue in their jobs or to find new employment.

But only a minority of men and women 65 years and over are gainfully employed (United Nations, 1957–58). France and

TABLE 35*

PERCENTAGE OF LIFE INSURANCE IN FORCE TO NATIONAL INCOME, FOUR NON-EUROPEAN INDUSTRIAL COUNTRIES

Country	1950	1957
Australia..........	42	62
Canada...........	115	146
New Zealand.......	63	88
United States......	97	126

* Source: Institute of Life Insurance and Statistical Office of the United Nations.

Sweden are tied for first place in the percentage of men economically active (36.1), with the Netherlands a close third (35.5). Fourth, fifth, and sixth places are taken by Italy (33.0), the United Kingdom (32.0), and West Germany (26.8).

A much smaller proportion of women are economically active. France has the highest percentage (13.5); the United Kingdom, the lowest (5.3). Second to fifth places are held by West Germany (9.7), Italy (8.6), Sweden (7.8), and the Netherlands (6.3).

The differences between these countries are not large and are due to a complex of factors. Among the reasons for low percentages are the degree of industrialization, the effect of eligibility for social insurance benefits, and extent of unemployment. Among the factors making for high percentages are the extent of self-employment, the prevalence of agriculture, and the proportion of small businesses.

The main point, however, is that in western Europe as well as in the United States the gainful employment of older men is on the decline. Although this country had, in 1950, 41.4 per cent of men 65 years of age and older economically active —higher than any of the six European countries—estimates are for a continuing decline.

The opportunity for remunerative work by older men and women has been decreasing in all countries of Western culture and in all probability will keep on becoming smaller. The problem then becomes how to give retired persons substitute leisure-time activities from which they will get the satisfactions other than income which they obtained from work.

Havighurst and his associates in their studies of the meaning of work and retirement indicate that other satisfactions are often as important as or even more important to the worker than income (Friedmann and Havighurst, 1954). Among these are having friends on the job, keeping busy, feeling useful, getting status, having self-respect, being creative, and being of service.

Research findings show that those who have been most absorbed in their work with few if any outside interests are those who have the greatest difficulty in adjustment to retirement. They are at a loss to know how to fill their leisure time with satisfying activities. Not being able or even interested in making new friends, they may become lonely and unhappy. The opportunity for leisure does not automatically provide activities and guarantee happiness.

The increase of leisure, instead of diminishing loneliness, may, therefore, actually augment it. Retirement from work generally means the loss of friends on the job. These may be the only or almost the only friends of the man or woman whose life is centered in work. Work was also a way of scheduling time. Withdrawal from the job leaves a void which some workers are not able to fill. The person with nothing to do becomes lonely.

Other factors enter into the increase of loneliness in modern society. The most important one, perhaps, follows from the breakup of the extended family. In the past the large group of relatives living in proximity provided a common social life for its members. The conjugal family of husband and wife and children at best assures the older person of only a minimum of social life.

The high mobility of modern society leads to the dispersal not only of relatives but of friends. The friends of childhood and of early adult life, if living, are likely to reside in other communities. Many find it difficult to make new friendships.

Townsend (1957) found in Bethnal Green, a district in East London, that 5 per cent of the old people he interviewed said that they were "very lonely," 22 per cent "sometimes lonely," and 72 per cent "not lonely." The Milan, Italy, study of older people (1291 men and 2276 women 55 and over) reports replies of "very lonely" by 10 per cent of the men and 13 per cent of the women and of "sometimes lonely" by 20 per cent of the former and 22 per cent of the latter. The statements of loneliness increase with age: at ages 60–64, "very lonely," 8 per cent of men, 13 per cent of women; at age 85 and older, 18 per cent of both sexes; at ages 60–64, "occasionally lonely," 17 per cent of men, 20 per cent of women; at age 85 and older, 24 per cent of men, 21 per cent of women (Ingegnieros, 1958). In a representative sample of 890 older persons in

California the proportion of "very lonely" varied from 57 per cent of those married but not with spouse to 16 per cent of those living with spouse only (Bond, 1954).

F. Roleless Role of the Aging

Modern economic social trends have brought losses as well as gains to all age groups in the population. But the full impact of their adverse effects has been experienced by the aging. Let us recapitulate the series of blows which struck them one after another. First, they lost their economic independence. They were demoted from the status of employer to that of employee. Their place of work was no longer the home but the factory or office. Second, in increasing numbers they had to give up rural residence for urban living. Third, they were now forced to retire from work by the decision of the employer rather than of their own free will as in the past. Fourth, they lost their former favored position in the extended family. No longer were the grandfather and the grandmother the center of the absorbing social life of their descendants but often became unwanted hangers-on, taking part by sufferance in the activities of their children and grandchildren. Fifth, deprived of the society of their family and having lost associates on the job and other friends by death or departure to other communities, they found themselves cursed instead of blessed by leisure time in abundance and little or nothing to do with it.

In short, the retired older man and his wife are imprisoned in a roleless role. They have no vital function to perform such as they had in rural society. This is doubly true of the husband, because a woman as long as she is physically able retains the role and satisfactions of homemaker. Nor are they offered a ceremonial role by society to make up in part for their lost functional role.

This roleless role is thrust by society upon the older person at retirement, and to a greater or lesser degree he has accepted it or become resigned to it. The retired person speaks of being "turned out to pasture," "put upon the shelf," or given "a rocking chair on the porch to watch the world go by." Certain stereotypes and myths have grown up in Western cultures to sanction this roleless role. They may be briefly stated as follows:

1. *Passive behavior* is the expected pattern for the older person in retirement. He should now "take it easy, loaf, and fish." He has worked so hard all his life that now he wants only to rest.

2. *Dependence* on others for advice and assistance is the natural and inevitable consequence of advancing years. Ethel Shanas (unpublished paper) has analyzed this as a reversion in second childhood to the baby role.

3. *Custodial care* in institutions is the answer to chronic illness, invalidity, and the mental disturbances common in old age. Accordingly, the proportion of older persons with physical and mental illnesses occupying hospital beds has increased faster than their percentage of the population.

4. *Withdrawal from social participation* tends to accompany departure from employment. Often the older person feels "elbowed out" of groups by subtle pressures.

5. *No preparation* for retirement is required or expected. Older persons, it is asserted, need only to relax, read, and listen to radio and television.

6. *Circulation of myths* which have no basis in fact is prejudicial to older persons. Typical of these are that older workers are unable to learn new skills and have more accidents, more absences, and less productivity than younger workers.

These stereotypes are prevalent in the public mind and are often accepted by older workers. They are the greatest obstacle to progress by society and by the older person himself. Milton L. Barron (1953) has characterized our older citizens as a minority group inasmuch as they suffer from discrimination in the same way as do racial and ethnic groups. In this sense, they are second-class citizens and are deprived of their full rights to economic, social, and civic participation.

This analysis of the roleless role of the older person is what the sociologist calls an "ideal construction." It is a conscious distortion in which attention is paid not to the average but to the extreme tendencies in the situation. The purpose of an ideal construction is to provide an instrument for the measurement of reality. In this way the roleless role of old people today is contrasted with their significant role before the industrial revolution.

The effects of economic and social trends which catapulted old people from the family-oriented rural society to the organization-centered urban society are still in operation. The aging will continue to increase in numbers relatively as well as absolutely. Years will be added to their life-span. They will still feel insecure until the double threat of prolonged disability and of inflation can be lifted. Older people will continue to depend less upon family and relatives for their support and social life and win their financial and social independence by the help of public and private organizations which are taking over first place in their lives. The increase of leisure presents a problem, first, of how to fill it and, second, of how to use it for self-expression and for community service. There will still remain the most difficult, but at the same time the most challenging, problem of solving the present roleless role of the aging by inventing new patterns of leisure activities and new roles with a functional value to the person and to society. It will be interesting to find out in our survey how far the countries of Western culture are making progress toward this objective and what we may learn from their experience.

IV. SOCIETAL CONCERN FOR THE AGING

This volume is primarily interested in the problems of aging in countries of Western culture and in what these countries are doing about them. We have seen that the extended family is no longer a cohesive economic and social unit with the capacity to give adequate care to the aging. The major responsibility for their welfare has now been taken over by government (national, provincial or state, and municipal) and by private organizations (economic, social, and cultural).

This intervention by government and private organizations has been a result of the concern of the public for the problems of the aging in the transition from a rural to an urban civilization. The chapters in this book which follow deal with societal concern for the aging in nine different areas: (1) population structure and trends; (2) employment and retirement; (3) income maintenance and medical insurance; (4) housing and community services; (5) physical health and rehabilitation; (6) mental health; (7) family structure and relationships; (8) beyond family and work; and (9) research.

A. Population Structure and Trends

In all countries of Western culture the increase in the proportion of the aging in the population has dramatized their present plight. Yet this one statistic is not of much help as a basis for shaping policies and programs for the welfare of older people. We should know much more.

We need, first, to know the position of the aging in the population structure of each country. We are interested in the relative proportions of the aging by sex to other age groups such as children, youth, early-adult, and middle-adult population.

Second, it is important to learn what the factors are that have been and now are affecting the proportion of the aging in the population. What has been and is the relative effect on the number and proportion of older people of such changes as increasing or decreasing fertility, immigration and emigration, and increase in life-expectancy?

It is necessary, in the third place, to study the trends in the proportion of the population in the different age and sex groups. The forecast of future trends depends in part upon the projection of past trends but even more upon an analysis of the factors which affect the proportion of old people in the total population.

The knowledge to be gained by a searching analysis of the structure and trends of the aging population is indispensable for an understanding of the problems of aging and in arriving at their solution. It has a direct bearing on formulating policies of employment and retirement of older workers. It is basic to the issues in income maintenance and housing in old age. It enables us to forecast the volume of care needed for physical illness and mental disorders in old age. It will affect in the future as it has in the past the nature of family organization and relationships. It is helpful in planning for leisure-time living in the later years.

B. *Employment and Retirement*

Employment, as we have seen, took on new meaning with the industrial revolution. It no longer meant working at home on the farm or in the shop under the direction of father or mother. It became typically laboring in the factory or the office, with hundreds and later thousands of employees organized into a working force by managers and supervisors.

It was in the context of this change in the nature of employment that the phenomenon of retirement was introduced. Previously in the familial stage of work there was no retirement from employment. The individual on his own volition gradually shortened his hours of work or changed from heavy to lighter work. As long as he was ambulatory he still had odd jobs or chores to do. Only with disabling illness did he stop working.

Retirement was introduced into industry along with pensions and old age insurance. It has taken various forms—optional, man-

datory, flexible, etc. The age of retirement may be arbitrary (or one fixed age for all employees) or variable.

In the United States the policies and practices of retirement are in a state of controversy, confusion, and perplexity. A good look at European experience will be helpful in getting perspective on our own problems. Information is needed on the changing patterns of employment and retirement. What are the present trends, for example, in the duration of the work life of the person and of the lengthening period of retirement? Particularly, what is the role of the older workers in the nation's manpower resources? What do they do, and where do they work? How do they differ from younger workers by occupation, by productivity, by full-time or part-time work, and by self-employment?

What are the current practices and attitudes of government and business in employment of older workers? How do older persons adjust to new technological practices and attitudes? Are they able to learn new skills? What does the future hold for the employment of the older worker?

Are retirement policies and practices moving to a consensus, or are they tending to variability to meet individual differences in the worker and to take account of diversity in requirements of the work? Are there other trends that are emerging?

The examination of conditions and trends in European countries should throw light on the shaping of employment and retirement policies and programs in this country.

C. *Income Maintenance and Medical Insurance*

European governments have had longer experience than ours in the United States in meeting the economic needs of retired persons. We, of course, had the advantage of their experience in shaping our social security legislation. Our program of Old-Age and Survivors Insurance was, however, fashioned to meet the American situation and not copied from any one European country.

Our survey of selected countries of Western culture provides the opportunity to compare differences in philosophy, policy, and practices. It should enable us to discover trends both in actual operation and in their thinking about desirable changes to be made. Especially valuable will be an examination of the recent legislation and proposals for legislation in countries like Denmark, Great Britain, Sweden, and West Germany.

It is important so far as feasible to determine how far governmentally sponsored programs are the sole source of retirement income or how much it is augmented by savings, insurance in private companies, dividends and interest, pension by employer, assistance from relatives and friends, etc.

Certain special problems of income maintenance merit particular investigation. There is permanent disability which may begin before the older person reaches the age of eligibility for insurance benefits or pensions. There is the nature and extent of assistance programs and how they articulate with and supplement insurance benefits and pensions. The income maintenance of widows, who constitute around one-half of women over 65, presents some particular problems. Then there are the questions of methods of financing old age benefits and the present and future costs of old age security to the economy.

One of our unsolved problems is that of an adequate program of insurance against medical expenses, especially those of prolonged illness which cause the aging great anxiety. For that reason European experience deserves special study. Examination needs to be made not only of the provisions of their programs but of the success of their operation.

D. Housing and Community Services

In the past in countries of Western culture the conception of housing for older persons was very limited. At first it was confined almost entirely to the indigent aging who had either no kinfolk or none who would take them into their homes. The almshouse or poor farm provided by the community was the place of last resort and no return. Old people's homes, under private and generally religious auspices, for the deserving aging were later established and carried less social stigma than the public institutions.

Today the concept of housing for the aging has broadened to include provision for all older people. It is also a more flexible concept, taking in a wide variety of forms of housing to meet the needs and interests of the aging of all social and economic classes, of all the later ages, of all conditions of health, and of all individual preferences. There is also more consideration of the residential cycle. The residential cycle emphasizes the sequence of types of housing to meet the changing needs of older persons at particular stages of health and economic status in the later years.

The survey of housing in selected countries of Western culture exhibits the present diversity of housing for older people. There is independent living in bungalows, row houses, flats and apartments, retirement towns, etc. There are communal living arrangements, with dormitories, residence halls, and several story apartment-like buildings. There are special arrangements for medical care, general hospitals, geriatric hospitals, halfway houses, convalescent homes, foster-homes, etc.

Despite the diversity of housing design and facilities for the care of the aging, one central criterion is gaining recognition, namely, that the housing arrangement must be as homelike as possible. This criterion emphasizes the values of privacy, the retention of some household possessions linking the present with the past, and the minimizing of regulations and regimentation.

Pioneering projects are appearing in various countries to enable older persons to remain in their own homes as long as possible. Homemaking services and "meals on wheels" enable physically disabled persons to stay out of hospitals and homes for the aged. The team of visiting physician, nurse, dietitian, and social worker makes it possible for many sick persons to be cared for in their own homes and thus frees hospital beds for those who require more specialized and intensive treatment. European experience can offer much of value in our plans for development of community services.

E. *Physical Health and Rehabilitation*

In recent years in countries of Western culture entirely new conceptions of the physical health of the aging are supplanting those previously held. The earlier notions tended to be pessimistic. Aging was thought of as the period of biological decadence inevitably accompanied by degenerative diseases. The emphasis was upon *geriatrics,* the treatment of the so-called diseases of old age. The prevailing attitude was one of hopelessness even among physicians. Chronic illnesses and physical disabilities were frequently termed incurable. Treatment was largely limited to custodial care and to remedial measures.

Today the goal is rehabilitation and the restoration insofar as possible of the functioning of the individual. Pilot projects have demonstrated the success of the new methods of physical re-education in cases formerly considered hopeless. Techniques have been developed of enlisting the cooperation of the patient in putting forth his full effort in relearning impaired physical activities.

The goal of physical health has become positive. One aspect of this point of view is preventive. Manifestations are modern sanitation, the protection of the water supply, sewage-disposal systems, vaccination and innoculation programs, screening projects and regular physical examinations for the early detection of disease, etc.

Another aspect of modern public health is educational. Its purpose is the instruction of the public at all ages in practices that will achieve and maintain good health. The principles of nutrition are well established but not generally known or practiced by the public. The value of exercise and recreation are well known, but modern life has diminished active participation in games and sports. Yet the maintenance of good health in the early and middle adult years is the best guaranty of its continuance in the later years.

All countries of Western culture are concerned about the health of all their citizens. It will be interesting to survey what is being accomplished in these countries in the treatment of diseases and disabilities and in programs of rehabilitation, prevention, and education for older people.

F. *Mental Health*

Mental health, up to the present time, has been considered mainly on its negative side. The chief interest has been in the care and treatment of mental illnesses, such as the psychoses and the neuroses. This direction of attention was only to be expected with the apparent increase in mental disorder which came in the wake of the industrial revolution and the growth of cities.

In the earlier period, when men and women worked as a family group on the farm or in villages and towns, there may well have been fewer mental breakdowns. But, at any rate, the extended family cared for its members in mental illness, and they were sent to the insane asylums of those days only as a last resort. Even today the admission rate to mental institutions is less from rural than from urban areas.

In countries of Western culture the last 100 years have seen a great development of the sciences of the human mind—psychology, psychiatry, and psychoanalysis. The new knowledge gained by research has led to the development of the applied science of psychotherapy.

More recently there have been discovered by medical science the so-called wonder drugs, which in experimental use have produced marked improvement in many but not all mental patients. The results already attained are promising for greater gains in the future. Mention should also be made of the demonstration of successful use of shock treatment by electricity and certain drugs.

The main point is that mental hospitals need no longer be places of custodial care. They are on the way to becoming, like general hospitals, centers for successful medical and psychotherapeutic treatment. This transition is now in progress and is somewhat further advanced in some countries than in others.

Older persons present two special problems as compared with younger people. First, many of them are suffering from senility and arteriosclerosis, which do not yield to present methods of treatment. Second, in some countries many who are not psychotic, or have only a temporary mental disturbance, unwanted by relatives or without relatives, are committed to mental hospitals.

It would seem that the first group might in the great majority of cases be better cared for elsewhere than in mental hospitals. They should be carefully screened before admission, as should also the second group of the temporarily mentally disturbed, to find out the best substitute arrangement. Our survey of mental health in countries of Western culture will attempt to ascertain the extent to which pioneering efforts are being made to reduce the load of the old on mental hospitals and secure their placement in the facility most suited to their needs.

There remains the almost untouched field of insuring the positive mental health of the great majority of older people. The approach here would seem partly psychotherapy in dealing with minor mental disturbances and anxieties. It would be partly educational in disseminating the principles of good mental health. But it would also be preventive in attacking the conditions making for frustrations and anxieties, such as fear of retirement, loss of status when retired from employment, inadequate income, and anxiety about prolonged illness and inflation.

G. Family Structure and Relationships

The small family of husband, wife, and children of modern society is in striking contrast with the large three-generation family living under one roof of the past. Yet in countries of Western culture this change in social structure took place in recent times as a consequence of the industrial revolution and the growth of cities.

First, we are interested in knowing the factors which brought about this change. Several of them have already been discussed in this chapter. They include technological changes in farming, the shift from the home to the factory as the place of work, the loss of the function of production by the family as a unit, the migration of the family to the city, and the entrance of women into industry. All these changes combined to break up the large family and contributed to the emerging of its component autonomous units of husband, wife, and children.

Second, we wish to survey the evidence of the persistence of the extended family not as a housing unit but as a network of relations that still are significant in the lives of older people. Under what conditions does the extended family survive no longer as a unit of economic production but as a unit of frequent social contacts and reciprocal services?

Third, what has been the fate of older people in their family relations as a result of these catastrophic changes? How has the breakup of the extended family as an economic unit affected their position in the family? What has been the effect of retirement from employment upon the older man and his family? How have he, his wife, and his children reacted to the impact of these experiences? What effect have they had on relations of husband and wife, of parents and their adult children, and of grandparents and grandchildren?

Fourth, what are the family relations of those detached from the nuclear family, namely, the widowed, the single, and the divorced? The widowed and the single had a haven of refuge in the extended family of the past. To what extent do they now associate with relatives, or do they lead an isolated, lonely, and unhappy life in their old age?

Fifth, what changes are taking place in family relations in adjustment to the trends of modern life? Are these adjustments further advanced in certain countries than in others?

Finally, in what ways may we in the United States profit by this survey of changing family structure and relationships in countries of Western culture?

H. Beyond Family and Work

Many older men believe that life is really finished after the work career is over. Many aging women feel that life is hardly worthwhile after they have reared a family and the children have left home to begin their careers. Yet retirement living can be viewed by both men and women as an opportunity to begin a new career.

This challenging conception of retirement is new and one that is just beginning to capture the imagination of older people and of gerontologists interested in their aspirations.

There are of course obstacles to the realization of this vision of the possibilities in retirement living. Some of these are in the minds of older people. Others are in the difficulties of setting up the objective conditions for the realization of the vision.

Preretirement attitudes hamper both men and women. Many men feel that only remunerative work will keep up their morale. They reject the idea of retirement. Many women want to continue living in the lives of their children and grandchildren. They also reject retirement as a new way of life.

There are at present no approved and generally accepted patterns of retirement living. Society and its institutions have not provided new roles to replace the old ones.

Robert J. Havighurst (1954) has outlined the basic roles by which adults gain self-expression and recognition. One of these, the work role, is lost upon retirement. In countries of Western culture the other roles—family member, citizen, church member, association member, friend, user of leisure time, and student—tend to contract for most older people. One or more of these may almost cease to exist for some aging persons. Nearly all of them change in their meaning and satisfaction for the retired person. He may feel superfluous, pushed aside, and crowded out in some groups in which he once played an active role. Upon being retired from work, he may discover that he is being retired by his family, his church, and his club. Or for one reason or another, sometimes financial, sometimes psychological, he withdraws from one or more of these roles.

One solution open to the older person is to join or to form groups with members of his own age. These are beginning to multiply in countries of Western culture. Another is for institutions such as the church and the school to re-examine their function with reference to older people and to engage in experiments designed to find vital activities for older people that will give new content to old roles in which the aging will find recognition and fulfilment.

Particularly difficult is the problem of devising substitutes for the meaning which work has had. The opportunities for remunerative employment for older men are continuing to decline. What are the activities and roles in retirement that can replace the meaning of work for retired men? Will our survey of the existing situation in European countries give us clues to the answers to this problem?

I. Research

Action for the welfare of the aging preceded the rise of social gerontology, which, as a pure science, is the study of aging in its psychological and social aspects. In fact, research in social gerontology is recent both in the United States and in other countries of Western culture. The International Association of Gerontology held its first congress only 10 years ago. This past decade has witnessed the growth of research in social gerontology.

Research in aging has now reached the point where comparison of findings and methods in different countries are of increasing value. A first step is to survey the progress of research in selected European countries to ascertain the conditions which stimulated its development. Under what various auspices have investigations been carried on, and what have been the motivations for the research? To what extent have the studies been made by individual scholars or by the organization of large-scale studies?

A second step is to discover the topics of inquiry that have engaged the attention of European scholars. Have they been mainly of practical interest related to current policies and programs? Or have they concentrated rather on topics of basic scientific concern and on gaining new knowledge of the psychology and sociology of aging?

A third step is to inquire into the contributions which European studies have made to methods of research. What have we to gain in our techniques of inquiry by our survey of investigations already made or in progress in countries of Western culture?

V. CONCLUSION

The comparative survey of aging and its problems in selected European countries is timely for the further development of social gerontology in the United States. In both European and American countries this field as a new science is fresh and of recent origin. But social action in behalf of the aging has a longer history in the Old World than in the New. For example, the recognition of governmental responsibility for action to introduce old age insurance goes

back to 1889, when Chancellor Bismarck instituted this program in Germany. Not until 46 years later by the distress of old people in the depression and the pressure of the Townsend Movement did the United States enact social security measures for its older citizens. Today, 25 years later, we are in a position to view our problems, policies, and programs in the light of the trends and developments in other countries of Western culture.

REFERENCES

BARRON, M. L. 1953. Minority group characteristics of the aged in American society. J. Gerontol., 8, 477–82.

BOND, F., BABER, R. E., VIEG, J. A., PERRY, L. B., SCAFF, A. H., and LEE, L. J., Jr. 1954. Our needy aged. New York: Henry Holt & Co.

BOULDING, K. 1953. The organizational revolution. New York: Harper & Bros.

BURGESS, E. W., and LOCKE, H. J. 1953. The family from institution to companionship. New York: American Book Co.

DARIC, J. 1953. Structures familiales comparées. *In* G. FRIEDMANN (ed.), Villes et campagnes: civilisation urbain et civilisation rurale en France, pp. 333-35. Paris: Librairie Armand Colin.

FRIEDMANN, E. A., and HAVIGHURST, R. J. 1954. The meaning of work and retirement. Chicago: University of Chicago Press.

HAVIGHURST, R. J. 1954. Flexibility and the social roles of the retired. Am. J. Sociology, 59, 309–11.

———. 1958. A world view of gerontology. *In* A survey of European gerontology. J Gerontol., 13 (Suppl. No. 1), 2–5.

———. 1959. The sociological meaning of aging. *In* Proceedings of the Fourth Congress of the International Association of Gerontology, 1, 118–28. Fidenza, Italy: Tipografia Tito Mattioli.

INGEGNIEROS, S. 1958. Aspetti gerontologici milanese. Milan: Quaderni della "Citto di Milano."

INTERNATIONAL ASSOCIATION OF GERONTOLOGY. COMMITTEE ON SOCIAL RESEARCH. 1958. Cross-national surveys of old age. Ann Arbor: Division of Gerontology, University of Michigan.

INTERNATIONAL LABOUR OFFICE. 1957. Yearbook of labour statistics, 1957. Geneva: The Office.

INTERNATIONAL MONETARY FUND. 1957. International financial statistics, Vol. 10 (October). Washington, D.C.: The Fund.

KÖNIG, R. 1956. Changes in the Western family. *In* INTERNATIONAL SOCIOLOGICAL ASSOCIATION, Transactions of the Third World Congress of Sociology, 4, 63–74. Amsterdam: The Association.

MOERS, M. 1953. Die Entwicklungsphases des menschenlichen Lebens. Ratingen: Aloys Henn Verlag.

OGBURN, W. F., and TIBBITTS, C. 1933. The family and its functions. *In* Recent social trends in the United States, 1, 661–708. New York: McGraw-Hill Book Co.

SAUVY, A. 1955. The historical and sociological basis of social policy and social problems. *In* Old age in the modern world, pp. 28–32. Edinburgh: E. & S. Livingstone.

SHELDON, J. H. 1955. The social philosophy of old age. *In* Old age in the modern world, pp. 15–26. Edinburgh: E. & S. Livingstone.

SPIEGELMAN, M. 1955. An international comparison of mortality rates at the older ages. *In* UNITED NATIONS, WORLD POPULATION CONFERENCE, Transactions of the World Population Conference, 1954: papers, 1, 289–309. New York: United Nations.

TARTLER, R. 1957. Das Alter in der modernen Gesellschaft. Stuttgart: Ferdinand Enke.

TOWNSEND, P. 1957. The family life of old people. Glencoe, Ill.: Free Press.

UNITED NATIONS. DEPARTMENT OF ECONOMIC AND SOCIAL AFFAIRS. 1956. The aging of populations and its economic and social implications. ("Population Studies," No. 26.) New York: United Nations.

UNITED NATIONS. ECONOMIC COMMISSION FOR EUROPE. 1957–58. Economic survey of Europe. New York: United Nations.

UNITED NATIONS. STATISTICAL OFFICE. 1955–58. Demographic yearbook. New York: United Nations.

———. 1956–58. Statistical yearbook. New York: United Nations.

WHYTE, W. H. 1956. The organization man. New York: Simon & Schuster.

II

Population Structure and Trends

PHILIP M. HAUSER AND RAUL VARGAS

I. Introduction

The age of a person is a unique attribute, beginning at the moment of his birth. It is unequivocally determined by the increasing passage of time and is subject to continuous increases until the person's ultimate demise.

The age of a population, or an aggregation of persons, is not so simply determined. It may be conceived as either the aggregate age of all its members, as a frequency distribution of the age of its members, or by some measure of central tendency such as an arithmetic average or a median. The age of an aggregation of persons is also unique to a population and changes with the course of time. But unless the population is a closed one, that is, subject neither to increase nor to decrease by reason of fertility, mortality, or migration, the age of a population does not necessarily increase over time. An aggregation of individuals subject to change through births, deaths, and migration may grow younger as well as older. Moreover, it is subject to different rates of growth among its various age components as a result of past as well as current changes in the components of population change. That is, past changes in migration, fertility, or mortality, in interaction with current changes in these events, can affect the age structure of a population. The "age" of a population is therefore a much more complex matter than the age of an individual.

II. Factors Affecting Age Structure

Recent studies, especially those by the United Nations, have added considerably to knowledge about the effects of changes in fertility, mortality, and migration on the age structure of a population. It has been demonstrated, for example, that declines in the death rate have contributed little to changes in the age structure of populations, as compared with declines in the birth rate, and that these respective changes have different impact on the base (lower ages) and apex (older ages) of a population. Moreover, it has been shown that the effects of changes in fertility and mortality on the age structure of a population may be both independent and interrelated, depending on the specific course and stage of population change.

In general, the reduction of fertility and mortality produces aging of a population.

A decrease in fertility produces a decrease in the number of births and of young people and an increase, therefore, in the proportion of old people. If a lower level of fertility is maintained, the age structure tends to stabilize, but with a higher proportion of old people than that of the original population. If fertility continues to drop to lower levels, the population will become older and older.

A decline in death rates can produce different instantaneous effects, depending on the ages at which mortality reduction has taken place. If the decline is uniform

29

throughout the whole life-span, there will be
no instantaneous aging or rejuvenation, but
the life-expectancy will be increased, and an
increase of older people should be expected
to occur later on. That is, aging would occur
after some considerable passage of time. If
the decline of mortality occurs in the older
ages, aging will be instantaneous, and the
population will stay old as long as the new
level of mortality is maintained, growing
older if that level is reduced even more. If
the decline in mortality is in the younger
ages, there will be an instantaneous rejuvenation of the population; but, as the life-
expectancy is increased, more people will be
kept alive to reach older ages, and aging
occurs in the long run.

The combined effect of the reduction of
fertility and mortality is inevitably the
aging of a population, and this is the situation in all the relatively aged countries of
the world.

Migration, unfortunately, is a demographic variable more difficult to measure,
and the data available are scarce and incomplete. In general, the evidence is that
the effects of migration on the aging of a
population are relatively unimportant as
compared with the effects of declining fertility or mortality. In the case of a country
of emigration, the effect would be null only
under the assumption that the migrants
constitute a representative sample of the
country's population—a random sample in
the case of large emigration. Most of the
time this is not the case, for migration is
highly selective by a series of characteristics, including age. If the median age of the
emigrants is lower than the median age of
the whole population, migration will produce instantaneous aging, especially if the
migration rate is high and mortality and
fertility remain constant. During the process there will be a trend to successive aging
and rejuvenation as the survivors of successive cohorts reach older ages. This oscillat-
ing trend can be detected, moreover, only if
the rate of emigration is quite high. If the
emigration has been highly selective by some
trait, differential aging with respect to this

trait could better be detected than total
aging of the population.

In the case of a country of immigration
the results are inverse. There would be aging
or rejuvenation only insofar as the migrants
would be younger or older than the country's population. Most of the time the median age of migrants is lower than the
median age of the population. Therefore,
the impact of immigration is reflected in an
instantaneous rejuvenation, and the aging
process is retarded. This fact is perceptible
only in countries with high immigration
rates. The selectiveness of migration, moreover, makes conclusion difficult. More research is needed in this area to permit definitive generalization.

Before focusing on trends in the age structure of the United States and selected European populations, let us examine the population structures and vital rates of various
parts of the world in the light of which our
own and European patterns of aging can be
better understood. Table 1 presents statistics relating to the age structure, fertility,
and mortality of some seventy-two countries.

As a basis for comparing the "age" of
these populations, the proportion of the
population 65 years of age and older is
shown in accordance with conventional us-
age. It may be observed that there is considerable variability in the populations of
older persons in these seventy-two nations.
The extremes are represented by Togoland,
with only 1.5 per cent of her population 65
and over, and by France, with 11.8 per cent
in this age range.

The United Nations in its analysis of the
age structure of the nations of the world has
arbitrarily defined populations as "young,"
"mature," and "aged." The young are nations with less than 4 per cent of their people 65 years and older; the mature, with
4–7 per cent; and the aged, with over 7 per
cent. It is instructive to examine the characteristics of the countries which fall into
these respective groupings.

The young countries are without exception the economically less-developed coun-

TABLE 1*

TOTAL POPULATION, BROAD AGE STRUCTURE, CRUDE BIRTH RATE, CRUDE DEATH RATE,
AND LIFE-EXPECTATION AT BIRTH FOR SEVENTY-TWO COUNTRIES IN OR AROUND 1950

COUNTRY	YEAR OF CENSUS OR ESTIMATE	POPULATION (000's)	BROAD AGE STRUCTURE (PER CENT OF POPULATION)			1950 CRUDE BIRTH RATE	1950 CRUDE DEATH RATE	LIFE-EXPECTANCY AT BIRTH, 1950	
			Under 15	15–64	65 and Over			Male	Female
France.................	1950	41,943.0	21.72	66.49	11.79	20.7	12.8	63.6	69.3
Belgium................	1950	8,639.4	20.91	68.04	11.05	16.9	12.5	62.0	67.3
Great Britain...........	1951	48,840.9	22.48	66.69	10.83	16.3	11.7	67.3	72.4
Ireland................	1951	2,960.6	28.87	60.44	10.69	21.3	12.7	60.5	62.4
Sweden................	1950	7,043.9	23.40	66.28	10.32	16.4	10.0	69.0	71.6
Austria................	1951	6,905.7	23.25	66.62	10.13	15.6	12.4	61.9	67.0
West Germany..........	1950	47,695.7	23.55	66.47	9.98	16.3	10.4	64.6	68.5
Norway................	1950	3,278.3	24.40	65.96	9.64	19.1	9.1	69.2	72.6
New Zealand (excluding Maoris)................	1951	1,822.4	28.38	62.04	9.58	24.7	9.3	68.2	72.4
Switzerland............	1950	4,814.5	23.63	66.80	9.57	18.1	10.1	62.7†	67.0†
East Germany..........	1946	17,313.7	24.92	65.80	9.28	‡	‡	‡	‡
Denmark...............	1950	4,281.1	26.34	64.55	9.11	18.6	9.2	67.8	70.1
United States..........	1950	150,696.0	27.15	64.67	8.18	23.5	9.6	65.5	71.0
Italy..................	1950	46,279.4	26.34	65.60	8.06	19.6	9.8	‡	‡
Australia..............	1951	8,431.3	27.06	64.92	8.02	23.3	9.6	66.1	70.6
Netherlands............	1951	10,264.5	29.48	62.66	7.86	22.7	7.5	70.6	72.9
Canada................	1951	14,009.5	30.34	61.91	7.75	27.1	9.0	66.3	70.8
Czechoslovakia.........	1947	12,146.6	24.34	68.08	7.58	23.3	11.5	‡	‡
Iceland...............	1950	143.6	30.85	61.63	7.52	28.7	7.9	60.9†	65.6†
Spain.................	1950	27,963.1	26.23	66.54	7.23	20.2	10.9	47.1†	53.2†
Portugal...............	1950	8,441.2	29.47	63.55	6.98	24.4	12.2	55.5	60.5
Hungary...............	1941	9,315.1	25.98	67.05	6.97	21.0	11.5	54.9†	58.2†
Soviet Union...........	1939	169,486.3	36.20	56.90	6.90	‡	‡	‡	‡
Finland................	1950	4,028.0	30.00	63.38	6.62	24.5	10.1	58.6	65.9
Greece................	1940	7,344.8	32.99	60.70	6.31	‡	‡	‡	‡
Basutoland............	1946	557.7	37.83	55.93	6.24	‡	‡	‡	‡
Union of South Africa (European)...............	1946	2,371.3	30.49	63.33	6.18	25.1	8.7	63.8	68.3
Yugoslavia.............	1951	16,339.3	30.82	63.51	5.67	30.3	13.2	‡	‡
Poland................	1949	24,160.0	28.37	66.55	5.08	30.5	11.6	55.6	62.5
Japan.................	1950	83,165.0	35.42	59.64	4.94	28.2	10.9	61.9	65.7
Peru..................	1949	7,424.5	42.08	53.60	4.32	32.3	12.5	‡	‡
Trinidad and Tobago......	1950	632.5	39.58	56.31	4.11	37.5	12.2	56.3	58.4
Haiti.................	1950	3,086.1	38.02	57.98	4.00	‡	‡	‡	‡
Israel.................	1951	1,323.9	30.48	65.52	4.00	33.0	6.5	67.5	70.5
British Guiana..........	1946	369.3	37.72	58.29	3.99	40.4	14.6	49.3	52.5
Honduras..............	1950	1,505.5	40.58	55.45	3.97	40.4	12.0	‡	‡
Jamaica...............	1949	1,374.2	35.97	60.11	3.92	30.0	11.9	55.7	58.9
Argentina.............	1947	15,828.7	30.85	26.93	3.92	25.5	9.0	56.9	61.4
Puerto Rico............	1950	2,212.0	43.12	53.08	3.80	39.0	9.9	‡	‡
Paraguay..............	1950	1,328.1	43.77	52.51	3.72	‡	‡	‡	‡
South Korea...........	1952	19,410.6	41.09	55.21	3.70	‡	9.4	47.2†	50.6†
Alaska................	1950	128.7	26.46	69.85	3.69	27.2	9.1	‡	‡
Union of South Africa (non-European)..............	1946	9,014.7	39.52	56.84	3.64	‡	‡	50.7	49.8
India.................	1951	356,798.7	37.45	58.97	3.58	24.9	16.1	32.4	31.7
Ecuador...............	1950	3,201.8	42.46	54.00	3.54	47.3	17.7	50.4	53.7
Chile.................	1948	5,621.0	37.21	59.29	3.50	32.4	15.7	49.8	53.9

* Source: United Nations, *Demographic Yearbooks.*

† In or around 1940.

‡ Data not available.

TABLE 1—*Continued*

COUNTRY	YEAR OF CENSUS OR ESTIMATE	POPULATION (000's)	BROAD AGE STRUCTURE (PER CENT OF POPULATION)			1950 CRUDE BIRTH RATE	1950 CRUDE DEATH RATE	LIFE-EXPECTANCY AT BIRTH, 1950	
			Under 15	15–64	65 and Over			Male	Female
Ceylon...................	1947	6,878.9	37.15	59.37	3.48	40.4	12.6	57.6	55.5
Turkey...................	1950	20,860.2	38.04	58.55	3.41	‡	‡	‡	‡
Mexico...................	1950	25,743.7	41.78	54.86	3.36	46.0	16.2	37.9†	39.8†
Cuba....................	1943	4,778.4	36.40	60.26	3.34	28.3	7.5	‡	‡
Panama..................	1950	755.3	41.62	55.02	3.33	33.3	9.6	50.5†	53.5†
Malaya..................	1947	2,202.1	41.29	55.50	3.21	42.0	15.8	‡	‡
Philippines..............	1948	19,233.6	44.17	52.68	3.15	21.9	8.2	‡	‡
Egypt...................	1947	18,908.4	38.07	58.83	3.10	44.4	19.1	35.6	41.5
El Salvador..............	1950	1,854.6	41.16	55.88	2.96	48.5	14.7	49.9	52.4
Angola..................	1940	3,728.3	40.41	56.66	2.93	‡	‡	‡	‡
Colombia................	1950	11,254.1	42.01	55.09	2.90	36.7	14.2	‡	‡
Costa Rica..............	1950	800.2	42.87	54.24	2.89	46.5	12.2	‡	‡
Dominican Republic.......	1950	2,135.7	44.50	52.64	2.86	37.2	10.0	‡	‡
Nicaragua...............	1950	1,056.9	43.28	53.87	2.85	41.2	10.8	‡	‡
Burma...................	1954	18,597.3	37.42	59.75	2.83	46.1	39.3	‡	‡
Algeria (Moslems)........	1948	7,554.0	43.02	54.28	2.70	39.5	‡	‡	‡
Venezuela...............	1950	5,026.8	41.96	55.38	2.66	42.6	10.9	‡	‡
Guatemala...............	1950	2,784.2	43.63	53.76	2.61	50.9	21.9	‡	‡
Thailand................	1947	17,432.1	42.32	55.10	2.58	28.4	10.0	48.7	51.9
New Zealand (Maoris).....	1951	115.4	46.49	50.97	2.54	45.1	12.1	54.0	55.9
Formosa.................	1950	7,554.6	41.41	56.09	2.50	42.5	11.3	50.4	53.7
Brazil..................	1950	51,827.8	41.86	55.69	2.45	‡	‡	‡	‡
Mozambique..............	1940	5,085.3	43.46	54.30	2.24	33.9	6.1	‡	‡
Greenland...............	1945	21.4	42.65	55.18	2.17	49.4	25.0	‡	‡
Gold Coast..............	1950	3,869.2	36.53	61.95	1.52	30.7	21.3	‡	‡
Togoland................	1950	397.4	35.45	63.09	1.46	‡	‡	‡	‡

tries of the world. They are largely in Asia, South America, and Africa and are predominantly agricultural nations. These countries include most of the world's population, for the data which are available indicate that China, with almost a fourth of the world's population, although not shown in the table, also falls into this group.

The young nations, it is to be observed, have general or crude birth rates mostly above 30 (twenty-five of the thirty-seven); and almost half above 40 (sixteen of them). The median crude birth rate of these nations, as reported, is 40. Moreover, the young nations have relatively high general death rates, although the incompleteness of death registration distorts the available data and makes a definitive statement difficult. The median expectation of life for females in this group of nations for which such data are available is 53 years.

The mature nations, by the United Nations classification, include those still in rapid industrial transition, such as the U.S.S.R. and Japan, and, in general, nations relatively favorably situated in respect of national income per head in comparison with the young nations. The Communist countries of eastern Europe are heavily represented in this group, as are also the relatively less economically developed European nations. The birth rates of these countries are relatively high, with a median of 29. The death rate is lower than in the young nations, and, although the statistics are inadequate, the median expectation of life at birth for females, reported as 64 years for the nations for which they are available, is undoubtedly indicative of better mortality conditions than obtains among the younger countries.

The aged nations in Table 1 are, on the

whole, the economically more developed nations of the world. They are entirely drawn from Europe or from areas mainly settled by Europeans in North America and Oceania. They constitute but a small portion of the world's total population. Their general birth rates, although boosted by post–World War II conditions, are relatively low, with a median birth rate, as shown in Table 1, of 20. Their death rates are also relatively low, as indicated by a median expectation of life 71 years for females. Their most important common characteristic, as will be demonstrated, is undoubtedly found in their sharing of a declining birth rate over a relatively long period of time.

It is to be noted that the United States, while among the aged nations, is fairly well down the list. With 8.2 per cent persons 65 years old and over, the United States is below the midpoint of the group. In general, it is the northern and western European nations which are the most aged.

This overview of the age structure of the nations of the world for which reasonably satisfactory data are available permits several conclusions. First, there is great variability among the nations of the world in their proportions of older persons. Second, the presence of a relatively large proportion of aged characterizes a relatively small part of the world's total population. Third, the most aged nations are the most economically advanced nations; these are, also, the nations with the lowest birth and death rates. Fourth, the problems of an aged population are relatively new problems and apparently are among the by-products of economic development which characterizes Western civilization.

In the materials which follow, we shall focus on the age structure of the United States and selected European nations and the factors associated with changes in the age structure.

III. Aging in Selected Countries

The twenty aged countries listed at the top of Table 1 have not always been aged. Aging, however, has been a continuous process in these countries, over the period for which census statistics are available. The scope of this paper and the availability of census statistics make an exhaustive analysis of the aging process in all aged countries impossible. Nine countries have been selected for consideration, namely, France, the United Kingdom, Sweden, West Germany, the Netherlands, Italy, Czechoslovakia, Canada, and the United States. Analysis of the data for these countries will serve to illustrate the process and disclose the factors which have been involved.

In the following presentation certain limitations must be borne in mind: (1) even though the countries considered possess the best census and vital statistics, the data are, nevertheless, far from adequate, and especially is this the case for the historical data; (2) because the data have improved over time, and differentially among countries, comparability for the same country, as well as between countries, at a given year is adversely affected. For these reasons the figures that are presented must be regarded as approximations. Furthermore, the incidence of wars and changes in territorial coverage of some of the countries make the figures not strictly comparable geographically in some instances. In the case of Germany, for example, all the information refers to prewar Germany, except for 1950, when it refers to West Germany only.

A. Population 65 Years and Over

Except for France and Sweden, the aging of nations is largely a product of the twentieth century (see Fig. 1 and Table 2). In Sweden the population 65 years of age and over increased rapidly between 1850 and 1900, remained on a plateau of a little over 8 per cent between 1900 and 1920, and then rose sharply again. In France the proportion of older persons rose rapidly from the mid-nineteenth century to 1890, remained at about the same level of somewhat over 8 per cent for two decades to 1910, and then resumed its increase. For the other seven selected nations, however, including the United States, the rapid increase in proportion of senior citizens 65 or over took place mainly after the turn of the century. Especially rapid in each of the nations under consideration has been the increase in proportion of older persons since 1920.

The proportion of females 65 and over, with a few exceptions, exceeds that for males over the years in each of the countries considered. Only in Italy over four census dates,

a rise over previous decades. It is not too easy to generalize about the differences in these ratios of the proportion of older females to that of older males because they result from a combination of influences, including selective migration and differential war losses, as well as differences in historical and current fertility and differential mortality in the countries.

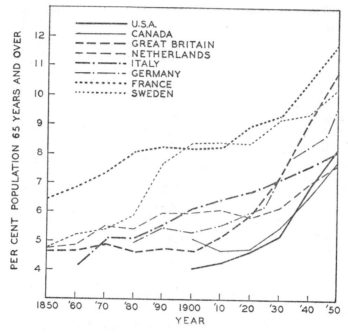

Fig. 1.—Percentage of population 65 years old and over for eight selected countries, 1849–1951

mainly before 1900, and in Canada, in 1951, does the ratio of the proportion of older females fall below that of older males. As an extreme case, almost 14 per cent of the females in France were reported 65 and over in 1950, as contrasted with less than 10 per cent males. In France the ratio of the population of senior females to that of males was 1.42. The next largest ratios occur in England (1.33) and Czechoslovakia (1.23). Canada, with a ratio of 0.99, a somewhat larger proportion of older males than older females in 1951, shows the effects of selective male immigration over recent years. In the United States the excess of older females was indicated by a ratio of 1.10, which represented

B. Relation of Older to Younger Population

An examination of the relation of older population to various age categories of the younger population reveals interesting differences among the nations studied. These relationships are presented in Table 3 and Figure 2. In the first block of this table the conventional old age dependency ratio is shown, that is, the number of persons 65 years of age and older for each 100 persons of working age, taken as the population 15–64 years old.

In 1950 the old age dependency ratios in the nine countries ranged from 11.3 in

TABLE 2*

PERCENTAGE OF POPULATION 65 YEARS OLD AND OVER BY SEX FOR NINE
SELECTED COUNTRIES IN OR ABOUT GIVEN YEAR

Country	1850	1860	1870	1880	1890	1900	1910	1920	1930	1940	1950
	Both Sexes										
France	6.47	6.89	7.41	8.11	8.28	8.20	8.36	9.05	9.35	.....	11.80
United Kingdom	4.64	4.68	4.79	4.62	4.77	4.69	5.22	6.03	7.40	8.97	10.83
Sweden	4.78	5.22	5.43	5.90	7.68	8.37	8.44	8.40	9.20	9.41	10.31
Germany†	.....	.....	.....	4.72	5.10	4.88	5.04	5.77	7.36	.....	9.27
United States	.....	.....	.....	.....	.....	4.07	4.30	5.67	5.41	6.85	8.14
Italy	.....	4.19	5.11	5.12	.....	6.16	6.50	6.75	.....	7.43	.....
Canada	.....	.....	.....	.....	.....	5.07	4.66	4.78	5.56	6.67	7.76
Netherlands	4.75	4.89	5.52	5.45	6.01	6.01	6.12	5.88	6.21	7.01	7.73
Czechoslovakia	.....	.....	.....	.....	.....	.....	.....	.....	6.60	.....	7.58
	Male										
France	6.06	6.15	7.06	7.80	7.92	7.63	7.61	8.23	8.30	.....	9.68
United Kingdom	4.28	4.31	4.44	4.24	4.31	4.18	4.63	5.40	6.65	8.03	9.26
Sweden	3.94	4.39	4.56	5.15	6.98	7.60	7.62	7.58	8.38	8.68	9.70
Germany†	.....	.....	.....	4.46	4.71	4.42	4.47	5.27	6.89	.....	8.91
United States	.....	.....	.....	.....	.....	4.03	4.21	4.62	5.35	6.67	7.75
Italy	.....	4.21	5.20	5.22	.....	6.16	6.54	6.72	.....	7.15	.....
Canada	.....	.....	.....	.....	.....	5.06	4.47	4.75	5.48	6.62	7.78
Netherlands	4.26	4.33	5.01	4.99	5.55	5.59	5.76	5.55	5.95	6.71	7.42
Czechoslovakia	.....	.....	.....	.....	.....	.....	.....	.....	6.06	.....	6.81
	Female										
France	6.89	7.23	7.75	8.38	8.65	8.74	9.09	9.78	10.33	.....	13.77
United Kingdom	5.02	5.02	5.11	4.99	5.20	5.16	5.80	6.62	8.10	9.85	12.27
Sweden	5.60	5.99	6.16	6.59	8.35	9.08	9.22	9.19	10.01	10.11	10.94
Germany†	.....	.....	.....	4.96	5.48	5.33	5.58	6.23	7.82	.....	9.58
United States	.....	.....	.....	.....	.....	4.11	4.41	4.73	5.46	7.03	8.53
Italy	.....	4.14	5.00	5.03	.....	6.20	6.45	6.78	.....	7.71	.....
Canada	.....	.....	.....	.....	.....	5.05	4.87	4.83	5.63	6.72	7.74
Netherlands	5.21	5.42	6.00	5.91	6.44	6.42	6.48	6.21	6.46	7.29	8.04
Czechoslovakia	.....	.....	.....	.....	.....	.....	.....	.....	7.10	.....	8.43
	Sex Ratio (Older Females per 100 Older Males)										
France	114	118	110	107	109	115	119	119	124	.....	142
United Kingdom	117	116	115	118	121	123	125	123	122	113	133
Sweden	142	115	135	128	120	119	121	121	119	116	113
Germany†	.....	.....	.....	111	116	121	125	118	113	.....	108
United States	.....	.....	.....	.....	.....	102	105	102	102	105	110
Italy	.....	98	98	96	.....	101	99	101	.....	108	.....
Canada	.....	.....	.....	.....	.....	100	109	103	103	102	99
Netherlands	122	125	120	118	116	115	113	112	109	109	108
Czechoslovakia	.....	.....	.....	.....	.....	.....	.....	.....	117	.....	123

* Source: United Nations, *The Aging of Populations and Its Economic and Social Implications* ("Population Studies," No. 26 [New York: United Nations, 1956]).

† West Germany in 1950.

TABLE 3*

OLD AGE DEPENDENCY RATIO AND RATIO OF POPULATION 65 YEARS OF AGE AND
OVER TO YOUNGER POPULATION GROUPS FOR NINE
SELECTED COUNTRIES, 1900–1950

Country	1900	1910	1920	1930	1940	1950
	Old Age Dependency Ratio (Persons 65 Years and Over per 100 Persons 15–64 Years)					
France............	12.5	12.7	13.3	13.8	....	17.7
United Kingdom...	7.4	8.2	9.1	10.8	12.9	16.2
Sweden............	14.1	14.1	13.5	13.9	13.4	15.6
Germany†.........	8.1	8.3	8.5	10.6	....	13.8
United States......	6.6	6.8	7.4	8.3	10.1	12.5
Italy.............	10.3	10.9	10.9	....	12.0	12.1
Canada...........	8.4	7.5	7.9	8.9	10.2	12.5
Netherlands.......	10.2	....	9.6	9.8	10.8	12.3
Czechoslovakia.....	....	....	....	9.8	....	11.3
	Persons 65 Years and Over per 100 Persons 45–64 Years of Age					
France............	40.2	40.4	39.6	41.7	....	49.0
United Kingdom....	31.6	32.4	31.4	34.4	39.9	45.1
Sweden............	49.2	48.3	48.0	48.8	43.7	44.8
Germany†.........	31.9	32.9	30.1	35.1	....	38.5
United States......	29.6	29.4	28.9	31.0	34.6	40.0
Italy.............	35.1	37.2	38.8	....	42.3	....
Canada...........	36.2	33.2	31.8	33.2	35.8	43.7
Netherlands	38.6	....	36.5	36.3	38.3	40.3
Czechoslovakia.....	....	....	....	36.6	....	36.7
	Persons 65 Years and Over per 100 Children 0–14 Years of Age					
France............	31.4	32.4	39.8	40.7	....	54.4
United Kingdom....	14.4	16.9	21.6	30.6	42.0	48.2
Sweden............	29.1	30.3	32.6	41.7	50.9	47.9
Germany†.........	14.0	14.8	22.2	31.3	....	39.4
United States......	11.8	13.4	14.7	18.4	27.4	30.3
Italy.............	18.0	19.1	21.6	....	24.2	29.7
Canada...........	14.7	14.1	13.9	17.6	24.0	25.6
Netherlands.......	17.3	....	16.7	19.0	23.5	24.6
Czechoslovakia.....	....	....	....	25.1	....	30.4

* Source: United Nations, *The Aging of Populations and Its Economic and Social Implications* ("Population Studies," No. 26 [New York: United Nations, 1956]).
† West Germany in 1950.

Czechoslovakia to 17.7 in France. The United States had a relatively low old age dependency ratio of 12.5 persons 65 and over for each 100 persons 15–64. Between 1900 and 1950 the greatest increase, absolute and relative, in the old age dependency ratio occurred in the United Kingdom. There the ratio increased from 7.4 to 16.2, or more than doubled. The next greatest increase in the old age dependency ratio during the first half of this century was that in the United States, which increased from 6.6 to 12.5, or almost doubled.

pendency during the twentieth century took place after 1930.

The old age dependency ratio is conventionally used largely for evaluating the economic burden of old age. It and the ratio of older population to other segments of the age structure have interesting social and political implications as well as economic ones. For example, the ratio of population 65 and over to persons 45–64 or to youngsters under 15 may conceivably have some implications for the conservatism of a society, for opportunity for younger persons to achieve

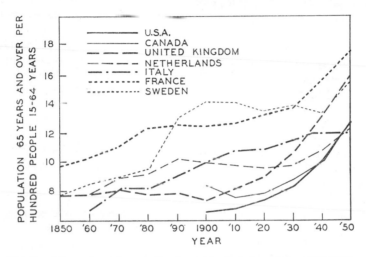

FIG. 2.—Old age dependency ratios for eight selected countries, 1850–1950

In the United Kingdom, between 1900 and 1950, senior citizens above working age increased by 8.8 persons per 100 persons of working age. In Sweden, which had an old age dependency ratio of 14.1 by 1900, the increase in the first half of the century was only 1.5 older persons per 100 persons of working age. The United States ranked second only to the United Kingdom in absolute increase in dependency between 1900 and 1950, adding 5.9 senior citizens to her population for each 100 persons of working age. It is to be observed that most of the increase in old age dependency which occurred during the first half of this century took place since 1930. Among the countries shown, seven-tenths of all the increase in old age de-

advancement, and for the patterning of many types of activities, including education, religion, recreation, and consumption. In the absence of adequate knowledge grounded on research, most of what can be said about these relationships at this time is necessarily speculative. But it is worth noting the great variations among the countries in these ratios.

In the second block of Table 3 the number of persons 65 and over per 100 persons 45–64 years of age is shown. Again France has the highest ratio, with 49 persons 65 and over, for each 100 of intermediate age 45–64. Czechoslovakia, at the other extreme, has only 37 older persons per 100 of intermediate age. The United States, with 40 older persons per 100 of intermediate age, is among the lowest of the countries in this respect, exceeding only West Germany and Czechoslovakia in this index.

The historical data indicate that France and Sweden were the first of the countries to achieve relatively large numbers of older persons in relation to those of intermediate age. In 1900, Sweden's ratio of old to intermediate population exceeded that of France, reflecting probably the results of relatively heavy emigration in the late nineteenth century. With the decline in emigration, it has actually declined since.

Throughout most of the first half of this century the United States had the lowest ratio of older persons to those of intermediate age among these nations. It was the relatively great increase in this ratio in the United States between 1940 and 1950 that placed the United States above West Germany and Czechoslovakia, as indicated above. It is possible that, in consequence, persons of relatively vigorous intermediate age were able to rise to positions of leadership more readily in the United States than in the other nations during this critical period of world history.

The ratio of persons 65 and over to those under 15 varies even more markedly than the indexes reported above. France, in 1950, had 54 older persons for each 100 children; in contrast, the Netherlands had fewer than 25; and Canada, a little over 25 aged for each 100 children. The United States had 30 older persons per 100 children in 1950. In 1900 the United States had fewer than 12 older persons per 100 children under 15; and Germany and the United Kingdom each had only 14. Most of the increase in the ratio of older persons to children among these nations which has occurred since 1900 has, except for Sweden and Germany, taken place since 1930. Over three-fourths of the increase which occurred in the Netherlands, and over half that in the United Kingdom, took place in the 20 years between 1930 and 1950. The other nations showed increases during the same period which ranged between these figures, except for Sweden and Germany.

C. Differential Rates of Increase of Age Groups

The relationships examined above arise from the difference in rates of increase among the age groupings of the populations. These are given on an annualized basis, for countries for which they could be calculated, in Table 4, which presents rates of increase (geometric rates) of persons 65 and over in comparison with rates of increase of persons under 65, by decade since 1900 and by half-century since 1850.

For each of the six countries, persons 65 and over increased more rapidly than persons under 65 during the first half of this century. With few exceptions, this also tended to be true for each country in each decade. Canada and the United States had the fastest-growing older populations between 1900 and 1950, with annual rates of increase of 2.8; France and Sweden had the lowest rates of increase in older population, 0.9 and 1.1, respectively. The fact that France and Sweden with the highest proportions of aged had slower-growing older population than Canada and the United States may seem contradictory on first examination. But the differences in rates of growth of older population is partly a result of the differences in rate of total population growth, which has been much greater in the latter than the former countries. Canada and the United States experienced total population increases of 2.0 per cent per year and 1.4 per cent per year, in contrast with France's 0.2 per cent and Sweden's 0.6 per cent per year during the first half of the century.

France and Sweden's relatively high proportion of older persons results from the fact that the rate of growth of older population in the former countries greatly exceeded that of the growth of their younger population. Although the older population also grew more rapidly in Canada and the United States, the ratio of older growth to younger growth was not so high in these countries as in France and Sweden. This is documented in Table 5, which presents the ratio of growth of older population to younger population.

Between 1900 and 1950 the rate of growth of persons 65 and over in France was over nine times that of the population under 65. In contrast, in the United States the older population grew a little more than twice as fast as the younger; in Canada, only one and a half times as fast.

Older population in Sweden grew only twice as fast as younger population in the first half of this century. But it is to be remembered, as shown above, that aging began earlier in Sweden than in the other countries. Between 1850 and 1900, Swedish

older population grew almost three times as fast (2.7) as her younger population, a rate certainly above that of the United States and Canada for that period although below that of France.

For the age structure of a population to remain unchanged, it is necessary that each age group grow at the same rate as total population growth. If the older population grows more rapidly than the younger population, the age structure changes in the direction of older age. The relationship between the rate of growth of the aged population and the younger population, or, more precisely, the departure from unity of this

TABLE 4

ANNUAL RATE OF INCREASE (GEOMETRIC) OF THE POPULATION 65 YEARS OLD AND OVER
AND UNDER 65 FOR SIX SELECTED COUNTRIES BY DECADE, 1900–1950,
AND BY HALF-CENTURY, 1850–1950

COUNTRY	RATE OF INCREASE DURING GIVEN DECADE					RATE OF INCREASE DUR-ING GIVEN HALF-CENTURY	
	1900–1910	1910–20	1920–30	1930–40	1940–50	1850–1900	1900–1950
France							
All ages..........	.20	− .10	.61	.10		.14	.18
Under 65.........	.18	− .17	.61	− .06		.10	.10
65 and over........	.41	.70	.94	1.33		.61	.93
United Kingdom							
All ages..........	.99	.46	.45	.47	.38	1.16	.56
Under 65.........	.93	.38	.32	.27	.23	1.16	.42
65 and over........	2.10	1.92	2.53	2.93	1.98	1.17	2.25
Sweden							
All ages..........	.73	.67	.39	.37	1.01	.78	.63
Under 65.........	.72	.68	.31	.35	.91	.70	.59
65 and over........	.81	.63	1.33	.57	1.95	1.91	1.06
United States							
All ages..........	1.93	1.41	1.51	.71	1.36	†	1.38
Under 65.........	1.91	1.37	1.44	.55	1.22	†	1.30
65 and over........	2.51	2.25	3.01	3.12	3.13	†	2.80
Canada							
All ages..........	3.02	2.03	1.70	1.03	1.98	†	1.95
Under 65.........	3.07	2.02	1.61	.91	1.87	†	1.89
65 and over........	2.16	2.31	3.23	2.90	3.54	†	2.83
Netherlands							
All ages..........	1.39	1.45	1.46	1.18	1.26	1.03	1.35
Under 65.........	1.37	1.48	1.43	1.09	1.18	1.00	1.35
65 and over........	1.58	1.09	1.99	2.42	2.27	1.51	1.85

* Source: United Nations, *The Aging of Populations and Its Economic and Social Implications* ("Population Studies," No. 26 [New York: United Nations, 1956]).

† Data not available.

relationship, may thus be taken as an index of the intensity of aging. Further examination of Table 5, then, permits the following conclusions. France has been aging more rapidly than any of the other five countries during the course of this century, while the Netherlands has been aging most slowly. The United States between 1900 and 1950 aged less rapidly than France or the United Kingdom but more rapidly than the Netherlands, Canada, or Sweden.

by the postwar baby boom. The irregular patterns of aging for France and Sweden attest to the complex nature of the effects on age structure of changes in fertility, mortality, and migration, especially as a result of war and depression. The actual magnitudes of the changes shown (as, for example, the great increase in the index of intensity of aging for the United States between 1920–30 and 1930–40) are affected also by census errors in reporting and especially by

TABLE 5

RATIO OF RATE OF INCREASE OF POPULATION 65 YEARS OLD AND OVER TO RATE OF INCREASE
OF POPULATION UNDER 65 YEARS FOR SIX SELECTED COUNTRIES BY DECADE,
1900–1950, AND BY HALF-CENTURIES, 1850–1950

COUNTRY	RATIO OF RATES IN GIVEN DECADE					RATIO OF RATES IN GIVEN HALF-CENTURY	
	1900–1910	1910–20	1920–30	1930–40	1940–50	1850–1900	1900–1950
France............	2.2	5.1	1.5	23.2		6.1	9.3
United Kingdom.....	2.3	5.1	8.0	10.8	8.8	1.0	5.4
Sweden............	1.1	0.9	4.3	1.6	2.1	2.7	1.8
United States........	1.3	1.6	2.1	5.6	2.6	*	2.2
Canada............	0.7	1.1	2.0	3.2	1.9	*	1.5
Netherlands.........	1.2	0.7	1.4	2.2	1.9	1.5	1.4

* Data not available.

Among the four countries for which data are available for 1850–1900, France aged the most rapidly and England the least. However, England increased her rate of aging the most between the two half-century periods considered. England's index of intensity of aging increased fivefold between the two half-century periods, while France's index went up 50 per cent, Sweden's actually declined, and the Netherlands remained at about the same level.

The index of intensity of aging by decades falls into reasonably regular patterns. As a result of the postwar boom in births, aging declined in intensity between 1940 and 1950 in comparison with the experience of 1930–40 for each of the countries for which data are available, except Sweden. In the United States, Canada, the Netherlands, and the United Kingdom the process of aging accelerated, decade by decade, until decelerated

response variability in reporting age in relation to social security developments.

D. The Process of Aging

The age structure of a population, as has been indicated above, is the result of the interplay of fertility, mortality, and migration. To the lay person it would seem that decreased mortality must be the most important factor in the aging of a population. Actually, as has been suggested above, this is not the case.

Let us examine the effects on the age structure of a population of changes in death rates and birth rates and begin with the consideration of mortality.

Crude death rates are shown, as far as the data permit, for the nine selected countries in Table 6 from 1905 to 1909. It may be observed that all these countries have experienced declines in mortality to reach the low levels shown for 1950–54, ranging from 7.5 for the Netherlands to 12.7 for France. In general, it may be stated that the death rates for these nations, all of them relatively economically advanced, are low. The differences in the crude death rates among these countries reflect differences in age structure as well as differences in mortality conditions. For example, the higher death rate in France in 1950–54 than in the Netherlands is partly attributable to the difference in the median age of these countries, 35 years and 28 years, respectively, in 1950.

per cent at age 65, in contrast with an increase of 37 per cent at birth. Roughly parallel increases were experienced by each of these Western nations during the first half of the century. However, it may be observed that the highest expectation of life at birth in or around 1950 is found in the Netherlands and the lowest in France. Moreover, the Netherlands had higher life-expectancy at birth than France throughout the course of this century. This relationship seems, but is not, inconsistent with the fact that France has, by far, the higher population of older persons.

Other conclusions of a general nature

TABLE 6

CRUDE DEATH RATES FOR NINE SELECTED COUNTRIES, 1905–54
(Five-Year Averages)

Country	1905–9	1911–13	1915–19	1920–24	1925–29	1930–34	1935–39	1940–44	1945–49	1950–54
France	19.5	19.0	19.2	17.3	17.3	16.0	15.7	17.9	13.9	12.7
United Kingdom	†	14.2	†	12.5	12.5	12.2	12.2	12.2	11.5	11.7
Sweden	14.6	13.9	†	12.4	12.1	11.7	11.7	10.8	10.4	9.7
Germany‡	18.3	14.8	†	13.9	11.9	11.0	11.9	12.2	11.0	10.6
United States	15.4	13.9§	14.5	12.0	11.8	11.0	11.0	10.5	9.9	9.5
Italy	21.7	19.3	†	17.5	16.6	14.1	13.9	14.5	11.7	9.8
Canada	†	†	†	12.3	11.1	10.0	9.8	9.8	9.4	8.7
Netherlands	14.7	13.1	†	11.0	10.0	9.0	8.7	10.3	9.4	7.5
Czechoslovakia	24.1	20.4	†	16.5	15.2	13.7	13.2	14.3	13.6	†

* Source: United Nations, *Demographic Yearbooks;* League of Nations, *Statistical Yearbook, 1940.*
† Data not available.
‡ West Germany from 1945 to 1954.
§ For the period 1910–14.

A better comparison of differential mortality among these countries is afforded in Table 7, in which life-expectancy is shown by sex at selected ages.

Life-expectancy at birth has materially improved in each of these countries during the course of this century. In the United States, for example, expectation of life at birth for males between 1900–1902 and 1949–51 increased from about 48 years to 65 years and for females from 51 to 71 years. Increases in life-expectancy at older ages have been less spectacular. For males, in the United States, for example, life-expectancy increased by 28 per cent at age 20, 11.4 per cent at age 40, and only 10.8

which may affect the structure of a population may be reached from a study of life-expectancy. Most of the gain which has been achieved in mortality has occurred at the younger ages and especially at infancy— that is, mortality under 1 year of age. Female expectation of life is greater than that of male, and the gap seems to be increasing with improvement in longevity. The "span" of life, that is, the actual length that the human body can survive, does not seem to have been increased; it is the number of people who manage to live large proportions of the span that has increased.

With these considerations in mind with respect to mortality, let us turn next to a

TABLE 7

EXPECTATION OF LIFE AT SPECIFIED AGES FOR NINE SELECTED COUNTRIES
BY SEX, IN OR AROUND 1900, 1930, AND 1950

COUNTRY AND YEAR	LIFE-EXPECTANCY FOR GIVEN SEX AND AGE							
	Male				Female			
	0	20	40	65	0	20	40	65
France:								
1898–1903......	45.31	41.03	26.65	10.46	48.69	43.59	29.10	11.47
1928–33........	54.30	43.30	27.62	10.86	59.02	47.40	31.37	12.57
1950–51........	63.60	48.40	30.40	11.90	69.30	53.40	35.00	14.40
England and Wales:								
1901–10........	48.53	43.01	26.96	10.80	52.38	45.77	29.37	11.99
1930–32........	58.74	46.81	29.62	11.30	62.88	49.88	32.55	13.07
1951..........	65.80	49.10	30.50	11.20	70.90	53.50	34.70	13.80
Sweden:								
1901–10........	54.53	45.88	30.77	12.81	56.98	47.66	32.53	13.69
1931–35........	63.22	49.44	32.50	13.15	65.33	50.55	33.54	13.71
1946–50........	69.04	52.14	33.84	13.53	71.58	53.95	35.29	14.27
Germany:								
1901–10........	44.80	42.60	26.60	10.40	48.30	44.80	29.20	11.10
1932–34........	59.86	48.16	30.83	11.87	62.81	49.84	32.33	12.60
1949–51†........	64.60	50.30	32.30	12.80	68.50	53.20	34.70	13.70
United States:								
1900–1902......	47.88	38.38	27.65	11.50	50.70	39.92	29.08	12.22
1929–31........	57.71	44.88	28.68	11.72	60.99	47.21	30.86	12.78
1949–51........	65.47	48.92	30.79	12.74	70.96	53.73	35.06	14.95
Italy:								
1901–11........	42.24	43.27	28.23	10.74	44.83	43.69	29.18	10.81
1930–32........	53.76	46.75	30.39	11.92	56.00	46.75	32.14	12.66
Canada:								
1930–32........	60.00	49.05	31.98	12.98	62.10	49.76	33.02	13.72
1950–52........	66.33	50.76	32.45	13.31	70.83	54.41	35.63	14.97
Netherlands:								
1900–1909......	51.00	45.70	29.50	11.60	53.40	46.90	30.80	12.30
1931–40........	65.50	50.80	32.80	12.80	67.20	51.50	33.30	13.30
1950–52........	70.60	53.70	34.90	14.10	72.90	55.40	36.30	14.70
Czechoslovakia:								
1929–32........	51.92	45.29	28.96	11.32	55.18	47.40	30.98	12.06

* Source: United Nations, *Demographic Yearbooks.*
† For West Germany.

consideration of fertility. Five-year average crude birth rates are shown in Table 8.

It may be seen that the birth rate has fallen in each of the countries under consideration during the course of this century through the depression thirties, during which each of the nations experienced its low point in fertility. The war period had irregular effects on the birth rate, reflecting differences in participation in the war. The postwar period produced increases in fertility for all these nations, although of varying degrees and durations.

Comparison of crude birth rates among

erful tools of analysis, namely, the "stable-population" model.

The "stable population" is the population which would result if, assuming a closed population, that is, no migration, an observed set of birth rates and death rates at each age continued to operate indefinitely. It is called a "stable" population, even though it may increase or decrease, because both its age structure and its rate of change become fixed or stable. By constructing stable populations for different combinations of birth and death rates, it is possible to determine how changes in fertility or

TABLE 8

CRUDE BIRTH RATES FOR NINE SELECTED COUNTRIES, 1905–54
(Five-Year Averages)

Country	1905–9	1911–13	1920–24	1925–29	1930–34	1935–39	1940–44	1945–49	1950–54
France.............	20.1	19.4*	19.9	18.5	17.3	15.1	14.9	20.6	19.3
England and Wales.	26.7	24.1	21.7	17.6	15.8	15.3	15.9	18.3	15.9
Sweden...........	25.6	23.6	20.3	16.3	14.4	14.5	17.7	19.0	15.5
Germany†.........	32.3	27.0	23.1	19.7	16.3	19.4	17.3	16.5§	15.8
United States	‡	‡	22.8	20.1	17.6	17.1	19.9	23.3	24.3
Italy.............	32.6	31.7	30.1	27.2	24.5	23.2	20.5	21.1	18.2
Canada...........	‡	‡	28.2	24.5	22.2	20.3	26.5	26.8	27.8
Netherlands.......	30.0	28.1	26.7	23.4	21.7	20.3	21.8	25.9	22.1
Czechoslovakia.....	33.0	29.6	26.7	22.9	19.7	17.1	20.8	22.3	‡

* For the period 1910–14.
† For West Germany from 1945 to 1954.
‡ Data not available.
§ For the period 1946–49.

these countries is, like the crude death rate, affected by differences in the age structure of the population. The data for controlling differences in age structure for international comparison are not too satisfactory and are, therefore, not presented here. The point in presenting these crude birth rates at this juncture is merely to indicate that the birth rate, as well as the death rate, has been declining in each of the nations under consideration.

With both decreasing mortality and decreasing fertility under way, which has the greater effect on aging? It is possible to obtain an answer to this question by resorting to the use of one of the demographer's pow-

mortality affect the age structure. This has been done for our purposes by constructing stable populations for Sweden and for the United States for four combinations of birth and death rates, respectively. For each country a set of high and low fertility rates was held constant, while high and low sets of mortality rates, respectively, were used with each set of fertility rates.

For Sweden the "high" fertility rates used were those for the period 1948–52; the "low" fertility rates were those for 1933–37. The "high" mortality rates were for 1931–40 and the "low" for 1951–55. For the United States the high and low fertility rates were for 1950–54 and 1935–39, respectively; and the high and low mortality rates were for 1929–31 and 1950, respectively. The results of these calculations are shown in Figures 3 and 4.

In each of these nations it is clear that variations in fertility have much more effect on age structure than do variations in mortality. With the high sets of fertility, the age structure of the stable population remains approximately the same (compare the solid and broken lines), whether high or low patterns of death rates are used. Likewise, with the low sets of birth rates, the age structure of the stable population remains about the same, whether the high or low sets of death rates are used (compare dash-

dot and dot lines). These findings are consistent with those of other studies and permit the following conclusion. Fertility is more important than mortality in its effects on the age structure of a population under the conditions of "closure" assumed by the stable population model. In the nations with the older populations, then, it is the declining birth rate more than the declining death rate that has produced the observed aging. Thus it is now clear why France, with higher death rates than the Netherlands, nevertheless has an older population. The explanation lies in the greater decline in the French than in the Dutch birth rates.

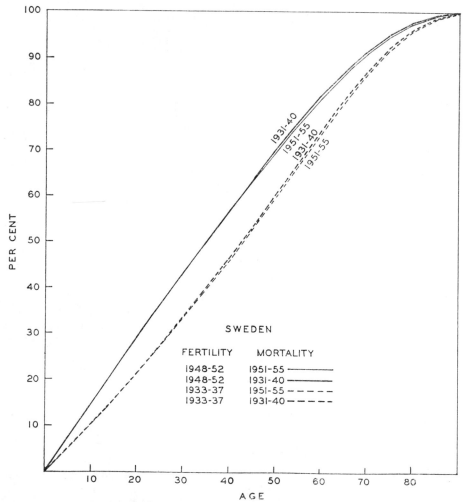

Fig. 3.—Cumulative percentage distribution of stable population of Sweden, with average fertility and mortality levels in given years.

IV. Composition of Population

A. Population Pyramids

The age structure of the selected countries in about 1950, compared with about 1900, is shown in Figures 5–12. The figures portray the results of the processes and the data described above. It is to be noted that, without exception, the 1950 age structure of the countries considered have larger older components and smaller younger components than they had in 1900. The discrepancies are greatest for France (Fig. 11) and smallest for the Netherlands (Fig. 8). The United States (Fig. 10), as may be expected,

lies between these nations in differences between its 1950 and 1900 age structure. A close examination of these pyramids gives some indication of the role of both fertility and mortality in the aging of a population, for in each of these countries aging was the result both of a shrinking base (fertility decline) and of an expanding apex (mortality decline).

B. Labor Force by Age

As a population ages, so does its labor force or "economically active" members. Of special interest in the consideration of aging

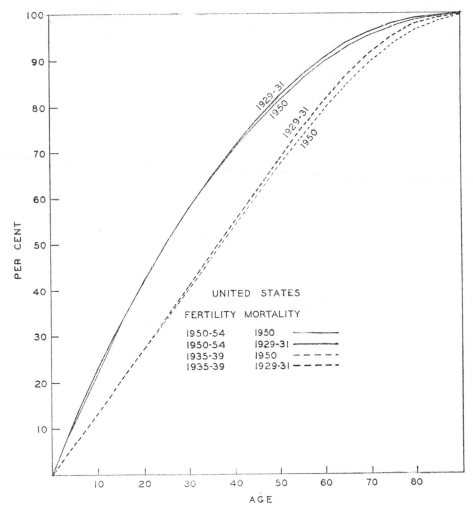

Fig. 4.—Cumulative percentage distribution of stable population of the United States, with average fertility and mortality rates in given years.

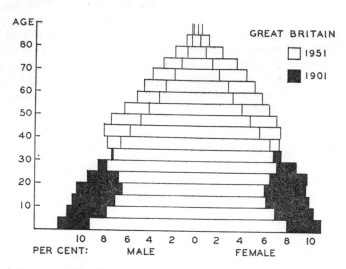

FIG. 5.—Population pyramid for Great Britain, 1901 and 1951. (Data in Figs. 5–12 from United Nations, *The Aging of Populations and Its Economic and Social Implications* ["Population Studies," No. 26 (New York: United Nations, 1956)].)

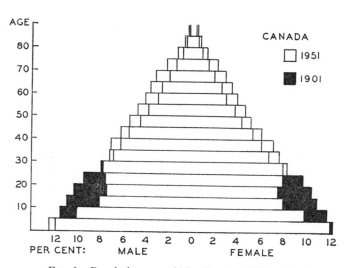

FIG. 6.—Population pyramid for Canada, 1901 and 1951

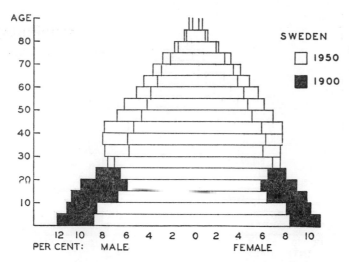

FIG. 7.—Population pyramid for Sweden, 1900 and 1950

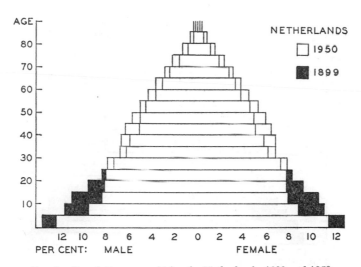

FIG. 8.—Population pyramid for the Netherlands, 1899 and 1950

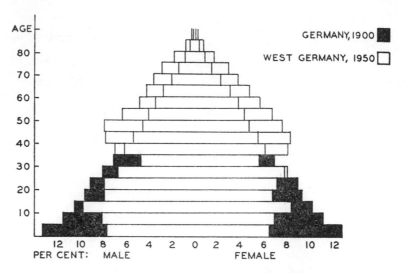

Fig. 9.—Population pyramid for Germany, 1900, and West Germany, 1950

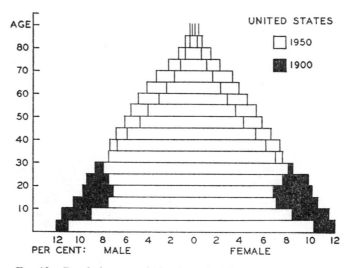

Fig. 10.—Population pyramid for the United States, 1900 and 1950

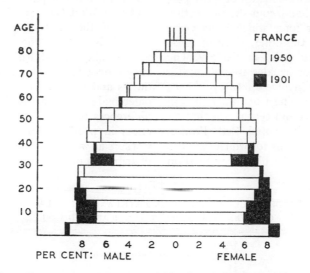

Fig. 11.—Population pyramid for France, 1901 and 1950

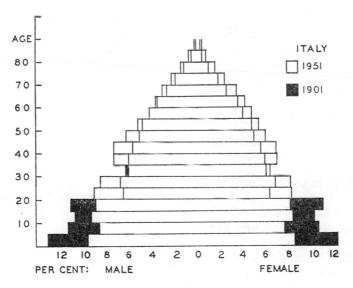

Fig. 12.—Population pyramid for Italy, 1901 and 1951

in respect to labor-force activity are the labor-force-participation rates of older persons, on the one hand, and the proportion of the total labor force which is 65 years old and over, on the other. Each of these items is shown for males in Table 9. The labor-force data for females are not considered because they involve difficult problems of comparability arising from differences in national definitions and census practices.

Again it may be noted that France, among the seven nations for which data are presented, has both the highest proportion

cally active (26.8 per cent). (This relatively low percentage is partly the result of the fact that West Germany is more urban because of the split of Germany.) In the United Kingdom, the Netherlands, and Sweden about one-third of the older males were economically active; and in the United States and Canada about two-fifths of the older males were in the labor force. These differences reflect, of course, mainly differences in provision for pensions for older workers as well as differences in urban-rural distribution of population. As will be shown

TABLE 9

MALE LABOR-FORCE-PARTICIPATION RATES AND OLDER LABOR FORCE
OF SEVEN SELECTED COUNTRIES AROUND 1950

COUNTRY AND YEAR OF CENSUS	MALE LABOR-FORCE-PARTICIPATION RATES				MALE LABOR FORCE 65 YEARS AND OVER AS PERCENTAGE OF TOTAL LABOR FORCE
	14 Years and Over	15–44 Years	45–64 Years	65 Years and Over	
France, 1946..............	85.5	92.0	89.0	54.4	7.6
United Kingdom, 1951†.....	87.9	95.8	95.4	32.0	4.4
Sweden, 1950..............	84.5	93.3	92.2	36.1	5.3
West Germany, 1950.......	83.0	93.6	89.6	26.8	3.8
United States, 1950‡........	78.9	83.4	88.2	41.5	5.5
Canada, 1951§.............	82.4	89.3	90.7	38.5	5.1
Netherlands, 1947‖........	85.1	88.4	93.5	35.6	4.0

* Source: United Nations, *Demographic Yearbook, 1954.*
† Based on a 1 per cent sample (does not include Northern Ireland).
‡ Based on a 20 per cent sample.
§ Excludes Yukon and Northwestern territories.
‖ The age groups are 14–39, 40–64, and 65 and over.

of her labor force in the older age category and the highest labor-force-participation rate for older male workers. In 1946, 7.6 cent of France's male workers were 65 years of age and over. In contrast, among these nations, less than 5 per cent of the workers in West Germany, the United Kingdom, and the Netherlands were 65 and over, and between 5 and 6 per cent of the workers in Canada, the United States, and Sweden. Moreover, in France well over half of the males 65 years and older (54.4 per cent), were in the labor force. In contrast, little more than a fourth of the male workers 65 and over in West Germany were economi-

below for the United States, agricultural workers tend to remain economically active longer than non-agricultural workers.

Thus France, the most aged of the Western nations, has the largest population of older persons among her male workers and the largest proportion, by far, of males 65 and over who are economically active. France's labor-force-participation rate for older men is one-third above that for the next highest nation and twice that for the lowest of the nations considered. These differences are in some measure the result of the fact that the data for France, 1946, are closer to the war-mobilization state than the data for the other countries. They may, however, also reflect social, cultural, and economic differences and also raise the question of whether France's older population is also a factor. That is, it is possible that, with the increasing aging of a population, older persons may have to work because of the economic pressure of the increased burden of dependency represented by a high proportion of aged persons.

V. SUMMARY AND CONCLUDING OBSERVATIONS

The "age" of a population is more complex and more difficult to determine than the age of a person. Moreover, a population may grow younger or older over time, whereas a person can grow only older. It is the interaction of fertility, mortality, and migration, past and current, that determines the age of a population at any given time. Of these factors, a declining birth rate is, in general, the most important in producing an older population, whether measured by median age or by proportion 65 years of age and older.

The continuation of declining fertility with declining mortality, characteristic of the more economically advanced nations, accounts for their relative old age. The economically less developed nations, with relatively small declines in mortality and even smaller decreases in fertility, have relatively young populations. Intermediate between the "young" and "old" nations are the "mature" countries, those now undergoing industrialization.

Among the old countries France has aged the most. In France, the other nations of the world, including the United States, may observe the prototype toward which they are moving and shall continue to move as long as their fertility and mortality decline. France, the oldest nation, with about one in nine persons 65 or older, has aged rapidly during the course of this century. Between 1900 and 1950, persons 65 and over in France increased nine times as rapidly as

those under 65. In 1950 there were about 18 persons 65 and over for each 100 persons of working age, 15–64; 49 older persons for each 100 of intermediate age, 45–64; and 54 older persons for each 100 children under 15 years of age. All other things being equal, France's age structure tends, therefore, to decrease her product per head, retard the rate of promotion of her more active workers, and produce a relatively mature environment, personal and physical, for her children.

The full personal, social, political, and economic consequences of a relatively aged population are not known. Yet there is undoubtedly a connection between France's relatively high proportion of older persons and the fact that her older workers remain economically active in larger proportion than those in other countries. The relatively large proportion of the French labor force which is 65 and over may further adversely affect her productivity. Moreover, it is possible that France may have been adversely affected, both in the economic and the political realms, by the greater proportion, and possible greater dominance in leadership, of older persons in her industrial, commercial, and political affairs. This observation must remain speculative, but it could conceivably have some role in France's economic and political difficulties in the pre- and postwar periods. Finally, it may be further conjectured that the relatively high proportion of older persons who make up the human environment of the children in France may conceivably have adverse effects on the vivacity, the adventuresomeness, the self-expression, the initiative, and the creativity of her youngsters.

The other Western nations, including the United States, are certainly faced with the prospect of continued aging. This process will be relatively rapid if the birth rate continues its secular decline, as the postwar marriage and baby booms are dissipated. In the United States, for example, the current recession has broken the postwar boom in marriages and is beginning to effect declines in the birth rate. Should the birth rate continue its downward trend, the population of the United States, the aging of which was slowed by relatively high postwar marriage and fertility rates, will continue to age at an accelerated rate. Under conditions of declining fertility and mortality all the Western nations could, within a relatively short time, approximate the age structure of France. With such an age structure they would, also, be subject, of course, to the economic, social, and political consequences of aging.

The "mature" and "young" nations of the world, while they are also subject to aging as their mortality and their fertility decline, are not likely to approximate an age structure like France's for many decades. The only factor which could change this outlook would be necessarily spectacular developments which would greatly reduce their birth rate at rates of decline greatly surpassing those of France and the other Western nations. This, for the time being, does not seem a likely event.

A final observation on national differences in aging seems in order. The world political order today is characterized by three distinctive political groups, the "free world," of which the United States is the leader; the "Communist world," of which the U.S.S.R. is the leader; and the "neutral" or "uncommitted world," of which India is probably the key nation. It is of some interest that this political division tends to coincide with the United Nations classification of nations by age. That is, the free world is made up, in the main, of the relatively old countries, whereas the Communist world includes only "mature" and "young" countries, and the uncommitted countries are virtually all "young."

If youth means vigor and age debility, the Western and free nations may be handicapped in the intense competition—economic, social, political, and perhaps military—which seems to lie ahead. But youth has not always triumphed over age, and age has many virtues and strengths not possessed by youth. The relation of age to the political question which is posed, while exciting and portentous, is, in the present state of knowledge, not known. In posing the political question, however, it perhaps makes more clear and also more dramatic the need to learn about the consequences of the aging of nations.

REFERENCES AND BIBLIOGRAPHY

COALE, A. J. 1956. The effects of changes in mortality and fertility on age composition. Milbank Mem. Fund Quart., **34,** 79–114.

DONAHUE, WILMA, and TIBBITTS, C. (eds.). 1957. The new frontiers of aging. Ann Arbor: University of Michigan Press.

HAUSER, P. M., and SHANAS, ETHEL. 1952. Trends in the aging population. *In* A. I. LANSING (ed.), Cowdry's problems of ageing, pp. 965–82. 3d ed. Baltimore: Williams & Wilkins Co.

HAWLEY, A. H. 1959. Population composition. *In* P. M. HAUSER and O. D. DUNCAN (eds.), The study of population: an inventory and appraisal, pp. 361–82. Chicago: University of Chicago Press.

LORIMER, F. 1951. Dynamics of age structure in a population with initially high fertility and mortality. (Population Bull. No. 1.) New York: United Nations.

NOTESTEIN, F. 1954. Some demographic aspects of aging. Proc. Am. Philosophical Soc., **98,** 38–45.

SAUVY, A. 1953. L'Europe et sa population. Paris: Les Éditions Internationales.

———. 1954. Le vieillissement des populations et l'allangement de la vie. Population, **9,** 675–82.

SHELDON, H. D. 1958. The older population of the United States. New York: John Wiley & Sons.

TIBBITTS, C. (ed.). 1959. Aging and social health in the United States and Europe. Ann Arbor: Division of Gerontology, University of Michigan.

UNITED NATIONS. DEPARTMENT OF ECONOMIC AND SOCIAL AFFAIRS. 1953. The determinants and consequences of population trends. ("Population Studies," No. 17.) New York: United Nations.

———. 1955. Age and sex patterns of mortality. ("Population Studies," No. 22.) New York: United Nations.

―――. 1956. The aging of populations and its economic and social implications. ("Population Studies," No. 26.) New York: United Nations.

―――. 1958*a*. The future growth of world population. ("Population Studies," No. 28.) New York: United Nations.

―――. 1958*b*. Recent trends in fertility in industrialized countries. ("Population Studies," No. 27.) New York: United Nations.

UNITED NATIONS. STATISTICAL OFFICE. 1955–58. Demographic yearbooks. New York: United Nations.

UNITED NATIONS. WORLD POPULATION CONFERENCE. 1955. Age structure and labor supply. *In* Transactions of the World Population Conference. New York: United Nations.

VALAORAS, V. G. 1950. Patterns of aging of human populations. *In* Social and biological challenge of our aging population, pp. 67–85. New York: Columbia University Press.

III

Employment and Retirement

SEYMOUR L. WOLFBEIN AND ERNEST W. BURGESS

One of the overriding and fundamental trends which has affected employment patterns in the United States, western Europe, and, in fact, virtually every industrialized nation in the world is represented by the changes which have occurred in man's span of working life during the twentieth century. A brief review of some of the forces which have impinged upon the length of working life, the social and economic context in which these changes have taken place, and the results they have generated provides a significant background to the gerontological evolution both here and abroad.

I. THE LENGTH OF WORKING LIFE

The length of time a person spends as an economically active member of the population is a function of a number of forces, all of which are highly correlated with the social and economic progress of his country. He must, in the first place, survive to an age where it is feasible for him to make his first part-time or full-time entry into the labor force; and, of course, the length of time he spends thereafter as a worker also depends in a major way on how long he lives.

At the same time, however, custom, law, tradition, industry, and business practice also play pivotal roles in determining the length of a man's working life. To the extent that a country has compulsory school-attendance laws or laws stipulating a minimum working age, the time of labor-force entry may be extended further and further into a person's teens. Technological developments and advances in science may make it necessary for a person to get more education and training before becoming a worker, with the same results in terms of delay in labor-market entry.

At the other end of the age scale, barriers or discrimination on the basis of age may cut off a person's working life. Social insurance systems and private pension plans also have a marked effect on what part of a person's older years are spent as a worker. All these major forces are, in a sense, summarized and reflected in what we call the "length of working life."

A. United States Experience

The experience in the United States can be summarized very briefly and will serve as our benchmark against which we can view the experience of other countries. In this country there has been a significant and substantial *increase* in the three primary forces which have played a vital role in shaping the social and economic trends which form the subject of this chapter as well as this volume: (*a*) life-expectancy—the total span of our lives; (*b*) work-life-expectancy—the years we spend as economically active members of our society; and (*c*) the years spent outside the labor force—as youth getting education and training and as other persons in retirement. In Table 1, in a few figures, is the story for the United States.

The fact that all three forces—life, working life, and non-working life—have increased simultaneously in the last 50-odd years represents the basic framework for the problems we are considering. Thus the increasing expectation of life is the primary generator of the "older-worker problem" to begin with. We have long passed the time, both here and abroad, where this problem referred to a comparatively small population group. In terms of sheer numbers, as well as proportions of the total population of a country, we are dealing with a significant and substantial social, economic, and political force.

the labor market. In fact, in the United States, the average American male makes his first full-time entry into the labor force between his eighteenth and nineteenth year of life. At the turn of the century, more than one out of every five youths 10–15 years of age were already workers. This trend has had a number of overriding effects on the problems we are considering— including the increasing education and training of persons when young and the subsequent results in terms of their future working lives as well as the very impact on the older person as a manpower resource in the light of delayed entry by youth.

TABLE 1*

LIFE-EXPECTANCY, WORK-LIFE-EXPECTANCY, AND YEARS OUTSIDE
LABOR FORCE, BY SEX, UNITED STATES

YEAR	MEN			WOMEN		
	Life-Expectancy	Work-Life-Expectancy	Years outside Labor Force	Life-Expectancy	Work-Life-Expectancy	Years outside Labor Force
1900	48.2	32.1	16.1	50.7	6.3	44.4
1940	61.2	38.3	22.9	65.9	12.1	53.8
1950	65.5	41.9	23.6	71.0	15.2	55.8
1955	66.5	42.0	24.5	72.9	18.2	54.7

* Source: S. L. Wolfbein, "The Length of Working Life," in *Proceedings of the Fourth Congress, International Association of Gerontology, Merano, Italy* (Fidenza, Italy: Tipografia Tito Mattioli, 1959), 3, 153–84.

Again, increasing life-expectancy, combined with the concentration of exits from the labor force during the sixth decade of life, has operated to increase the period of time spent in retirement. In the United States the average number of years spent in retirement by men more than doubled between 1900 and 1955. It is this increase in the span of life spent in retirement that brings to the fore the major questions of social insurance, income adequacy, housing, and many other related problems.

Yet the increasing amount of time spent in retirement has been matched by an equally important development at the other end of the age scale: there has been a marked increase in the age at which young persons make their first full-time entry into

It will be noted from Table 1 that part of our increased longevity has gone into an increase in the number of years spent in the labor force—into the vital span of our working lives—and part into an increase in the years spent outside the labor force. This points to a tremendously important fact which has prevailed here as well as in many other nations of the world: despite the substantial delay in entry into the work force by young people and the earlier exits by older persons, we actually put in many more years of work than did our counterparts 50 years ago. And, paradoxical as it may seem, despite these added years of labor-force activity, we spend more of our lives in retirement than did our 1900 counterparts. The answer to this seeming paradox is, of course, the added years of total life we have today.

The fact is that men today put in about a decade more of work during their lives than they did under 1900 conditions; but the data show that men really do not spend a much smaller proportion of their lives outside the labor force than they did back at the turn of the century. The longer life afforded them permits more time as workers and more time for education at one end

12 more years for working life, 10 more for education and training, marriage, and motherhood—and, of course, retirement.

To summarize briefly, the interrelationships among life, working life, and nonworking life set the basic structure of the problems of employment and retirement we are considering. In this country the trends among the three have resulted in a longer life, with more older persons in general and more older workers in particular; a longer

TABLE 2*

TRENDS IN LIFE AND WORKING LIFE, SELECTED COUNTRIES
(In Years)

Country	Time Period	Life-Expectancy	Work-Life-Expectancy	Non-Work-Life-Expectancy
Sweden.................	1816–40 1931–35	41.47 64.24	25.59 38.09	15.88 26.15
France.................	1864 1933–38	39.85 58.71	23.93 35.66	15.92 23.05
Germany...............	1871–80 1932–34	36.97 61.29	22.74 37.04	14.18 24.25
Switzerland............	1876–80 1933–37	41.86 62.59	25.91 38.06	15.95 24.53
Italy..................	1881–90 1930–32	35.40 54.85	26.40 32.92	14.00 21.93
Australia..............	1881–90 1932–34	48.97 65.26	29.80 39.00	19.17 26.26
United States (white)......	1900–1902 1939–41	49.61 64.99	30.11 39.26	19.50 25.71

* Source: G. Mortara, "Durée de la vie économiquement active suivant la mortalité," *Bulletin of the International Statistical Institute*, Part IV: *Demography and Labour Statistics*, **33** (1951), 147–74.

of the age scale and more retirement at the other.

Much the same situation is true among women, who have experienced a tremendous increase in labor-force activity since the turn of the century—the average number of years of working life among women has tripled between 1900 and 1955. Yet, as Table 1 shows, the 22 years of additional life-expectancy available to women in this country since the turn of the century has been divided almost equally between labor-force activity and non-labor-force activity:

span of working life, yielding a significantly higher manpower potential generated by the population; and a longer period spent outside the labor force at both ends of the age scale, yielding particularly significant increases in time spent in education and training to begin with and in time spent in retirement.

B. Experience Abroad

The experience we have described for the United States has characterized societies of the Western world with practically no exceptions. The particular experience of a specific country varies, of course, with its social and economic history, its mores and traditions, the impact of war and peace, etc. But the primary evolutionary forces which have impinged upon life and working life are essentially the same in Western society.

The substantial amount of materials developed by Giorgio Mortara (1951), a student of these phenomena for more than a half-century, gives rather vivid testimony on the similarity of these trends among the various nations of the world. Table 2 is illustrative.

Considering the great difference in time periods involved, as well as the substantial variations in the industrial and economic history among the various nations, the similarity in trend shown by Mortara's data is quite significant. In each of the countries, expectancies of life, of work life, and of non-work life all went up, as they did in the United States. The duration of life spent outside the labor force rose considerably, but so did the span of working life under conditions of increasing longevity.

Reflecting upon his studies of the data for forty countries, Mortara makes some points of considerable interest not only to the subject of this chapter but to some of the others in this volume. He says (translating freely from the French):

I had supposed, up to now, that the decline in mortality left unchanged the age limit of working life. But it seems to me to be evident that this hypothesis does not correspond with reality.

In effect, the decline in mortality is symptomatic of a whole group of improvements in conditions of life, which have favorably affected the work capacity of individuals and which reflects itself in the reduction in the frequency and duration of illness and in invalidism caused by ill-health.

Thus we can say that a sexagenarian, living in a country or in an age of low mortality, has a much superior capacity for work than he would would have in a country or in an age of high mortality. It would appear to be absurd to attribute the same upper age limit to working life

to an American as to a Chinese or to a Swede living today and one of 200 years ago.

In fact, the decline in mortality is accompanied by a moderate increase in the upper age limit of economically active life. This increase, without doubt, is more than sufficient to compensate for any economic disadvantage resulting from a slight increase in the ratio between the average duration of all periods of economic inactivity and the economically active period, which apparently accompanied a decline in mortality [1951, pp. 173–74].

More recently, a number of countries have been studying some of these phenomena through the use of standard actuarial techniques, resulting in a series of tables

TABLE 3*

EXPECTANCY OF LIFE AND WORKING LIFE AT BIRTH FOR MEN IN FRANCE

Year	Life-Expectancy	Work-Life-Expectancy	Years outside Labor Force
1906	46.9	32.3	14.6
1936	55.9	37.0	18.9
1946	61.6	41.0	20.6

* Source: P. Depoid, "Tables française concernant la population masculine (1906–1946)," *Bulletin of the International Statistical Institute*, Part IV: *Demography and Labour Statistics*, **33** (1951), 131–46.

of working life, similar to these constructed for the United States by this author. These tables, which permit stricter comparability from one country to another, reinforce our general conclusions, as the following brief illustrations show:

P. Depoid (1951) constructed a series of tables of working life for France, from which we abstract summary figures (Table 3) comparable to those we presented above for the United States.

The trends during the first half of this century in France parallel ours about as closely as could possibly be expected. As was true in the United States, all three of the forces being studied increased in France. The pattern of change in France has also been very similar to ours. There, too, a substantial increase in age of entry by the young and a significant decrease in age of exit from the work force by the older person have occurred. But, as Depoid (1951) points out, "despite the reduction in age of entry and earlier retirement, work-life expectancy has continued to increase under the important influence of declining mortality" (p. 140). This was exactly our comment on the trend in the last 50 years in this country.

Moving across to the other side of the world, we find a recent (1951) table of

countries are quite striking (New Zealand, 1955).

II. THE OLDER PERSON AS A WORKER

With increasing duration of life and working life, the older person has become a more and more significant factor in the manpower resources of his country. Table 4 and Chart II describe one dimension of the role of the older person as a worker,

CHART I

LIFE- AND WORK-LIFE-EXPECTANCY AND YEARS SPENT IN RETIREMENT, MALES, BY AGE, NEW ZEALAND AND THE UNITED STATES

——— U.S.A.(1950) – – – – – NEW ZEALAND (1951)

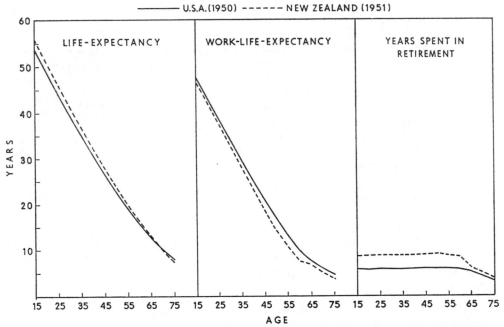

Source: Derived from New Zealand, *Table of Working Life, 1951 Male Population* (*Including Maoris*) (Wellington, N.Z.: Census and Statistics Department, 1955).

working life constructed by the government of New Zealand (1955) exactly comparable to the 1950 table for the United States. The three important factors being examined in this section are presented for both the United States and New Zealand in Chart I. Considering the many differences between the two countries (the New Zealand table, incidentally, includes the Maoris), the similarities in both levels and structural patterns by age for the two

showing the extent to which men and women in their sixth decade of life continue as active participants in the labor force in western Europe and some of the British commonwealths. Although pension and retirement systems begin to operate in many of these countries for persons in their early sixties, worker rates are relatively quite high for men between 60 and 64 years of age. For western Europe proper, the lowest labor-market participation rates for men 60–64 years of age prevail in Austria, where seven of every ten men in this age group are still active in the labor force. Worker rates for these men reach close to, and even hit, the 90 per cent mark in such nations as Norway, Switzerland, Denmark, and the United Kingdom. Similarly, for men in their later sixties—more than two of every five are still in the labor force in Austria, and the proportion goes up to a high of 75 per cent in Norway.

Women have become an important factor in the worker resources of all countries, although the more striking trends here have affected those in the age groups below 60. Still, the data show that labor-market participation among older women is relatively high, too—and, of course, much higher than a generation ago. Social and economic differences make for extremes, as shown in Table 4, indicating, for example, a labor-market participation rate of about 14 per cent for women 60–64 years of age in the United Kingdom and 40 per cent in France and Finland. But, for the rest of western Europe, worker rates for these women vary within a comparatively small range of one-

CHART II

WORKER RATES FOR OLDER MEN, SELECTED COUNTRIES

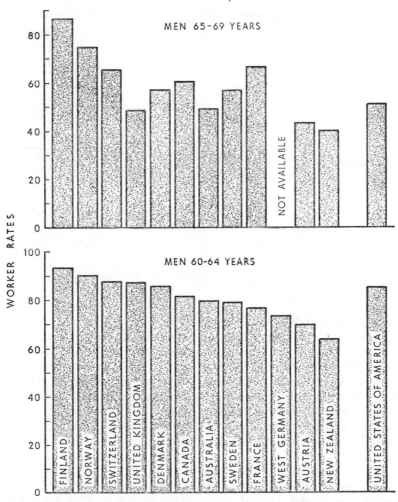

Source: Derived from United Nations, *Demographic Yearbook, 1956.* Percentage for Finland of men 65–69 years was based on high proportion engaged in agriculture and no retirement requirement for eligibility for pension.

fifth to one-quarter. Similarly, for women 65–69 years of age, anywhere between 10 and 20 per cent are still in the active labor force.

In addition to technical and conceptual differences in enumeration, the economic background of the country and the economic opportunities for older persons go a long way toward explaining the differences as well as the similarities in worker rates shown in Table 4. For example, older peo-

meaningfulness in explaining differential worker rates. They are of substantive interest in themselves as indicators of the kinds of jobs older persons hold and their relative importance in their country's economy. While these kinds of data are not generally available on a current comparable basis, Table 5 presents some information which is pertinent and again underscores some of the basic similarities and differences in the phenomena we are examining.

TABLE 4*

PERCENTAGE WORKER RATES FOR OLDER MEN AND WOMEN, SELECTED COUNTRIES

COUNTRY	WORKER RATES					
	Men			Women		
	Total	60–64 Years	65–69 Years	Total	60–64 Years	65–69 Years
United Kingdom (1951)	87.9	87.8	48.7	34.5	14.4	9.0
Canada (1951)	82.3	81.4	60.1	23.7	12.4	8.5
Australia (1947)	65.3	79.9	49.7	19.0	10.4	6.9
New Zealand (1951)	58.4	63.9	40.0	17.8	8.9	5.2
Denmark (1950)	64.5	85.9	57.5	32.2	23.6	13.0
Norway (1946)	86.6	90.0	75.4	26.9	22.5	17.8
Sweden (1950)	65.2	79.7	56.4	23.2	18.9	11.8
Finland (1950)	87.6	86.6	NA†	52.4	42.0	NA
France (1946)	85.5	76.3	66.5	46.2	40.2	31.3
West Germany (1950)	63.2	73.0	NA	31.4	21.2	NA
Austria (1951)	63.9	69.9	43.6	35.1	25.9	19.1
Switzerland (1950)	66.7	87.9	65.9	26.2	23.8	17.3
United States (1950)	78.9	79.4	59.8	29.0	20.5	12.8

* Source: United Nations, *Demographic Yearbook, 1956.*
† NA = Not available.

ple tend to stay in the labor force longer in agriculture than, say, industry. Thus at least part of the differences in worker rates between the United Kingdom and Sweden and Switzerland, for example, can be explained by the fact that only 6 per cent of the male labor force in the former nation is employed in agricultural and related pursuits as against 45 per cent for the latter two countries.

The occupational and industrial pursuits of older people are of great interest to us here, however, above and beyond their

Table 5 compares the occupational distribution of older males in the United States with the United Kingdom and Denmark, the latter two countries exhibiting some marked differences in economic base, as already indicated. In the United States about 30 per cent of these workers are in the professional, managerial, clerical, and sales categories—all in what is generally called the "white-collar group." While many of the jobs in this group are routine, a substantial proportion are in the higher ranks of the occupational hierarchy, both in status and in income. Interestingly enough, the United Kingdom and Denmark also have a high proportion of their older men in these occupations, although in these two countries the proportion is closer to 25 than to 30 per cent. Both European countries also have lower proportions in the managerial, administrative, and clerical groups and higher proportions in the sales categories than the United States.

The reader can note the other major dimensions of the occupational structure among older persons in these countries by scanning the remaining data in Table 5. Of particular interest are the differences in the importance of agriculture, the major role played by industrial and transport work, and the relative importance of the service trades in the United Kingdom. It is noteworthy that about 40 per cent of the men 55–64 years at work are in industrial and transport occupations and that from one-quarter to one-third of the men 65 years of age and over are similarly engaged.

This leads us to examine another dimension of the occupational structure which prevails among older persons. To what extent do the jobs older persons hold differ from those held by their younger counterparts? For this comparison we calculated an occupational distribution similar to that presented in Table 5 for men in the age group 35–44 years in which career development has had some chance to develop and in which the characteristic "problems of the older worker" are not yet as exacerbated (Table 6).

TABLE 5*

PERCENTAGE OCCUPATIONAL DISTRIBUTION OF OLDER MALE WORKERS, SELECTED COUNTRIES

OCCUPATION	UNITED STATES		UNITED KINGDOM		DENMARK	
	55–64 Years	65 Years and Over	55–64 Years	65 Years and Over	55–64 Years	65 Years and Over
Total	100	100	100	100	100	100
Professional and related workers	5	6	4	5	5	5
Managerial, administrative, and clerical workers	20	17	10	8	12	12
Sales workers	5	6	9	13	7	8
Farming, fishing, and related workers	19	28	8	13	29	35
Industrial workers (craftsmen, production process workers, and laborers)	37	24	30	27	36	33
Transport workers	3	2	10	5	7	4
Service	5	11	13	14	3	3
All other†	6	6	16	15	1	....

* Source: United Nations, *Demographic Yearbook, 1956.*

† Includes workers whose occupation was not classifiable elsewhere. (This amounted to almost 10 per cent in the United Kingdom.)

TABLE 6*

PERCENTAGE OCCUPATIONAL DISTRIBUTION OF MEN 35–44 YEARS OF AGE

Country	Total	White Collar	Farming	Industrial and Transport	Service	All Other†
United States	100	32	13	45	5	5
United Kingdom	100	24	7	46	9	14
Denmark	100	23	26	47	3	3

* Source: Calculated from United Nations, *Demographic Yearbook, 1956.*

† Includes not elsewhere classified.

Our point of comparison is now not only among countries but among age groups within each of the three countries (cf. Table 5). It is highly significant to note that the proportions engaged as white-collar workers (professional, managerial, and sales) are about the same for each age group. In the United Kingdom, for example, 24 per cent of the men 35–44 years of age were occupied in this category; the corresponding percentages were 23 for men 55–64 and 26 for men 65 and over. In Denmark the percentages were 23, 24, and

half again as large as for the men 35–44 years. On the other hand, the proportion engaged in industry and transport is significantly higher in each country for men 35–44 than for men 65 and over. Thus, generally speaking, the farm and factory represent the illustrations, par excellence, of the contrasting areas of economic opportunity for the older worker—both here and abroad.

One other set of data illustrates and reinforces the points made up to now. Information is available for this country and

TABLE 7*

PERCENTAGE OF MALE WORKERS ENGAGED AS WAGE AND SALARY WORKERS OR EMPLOYERS AND SELF-EMPLOYED, BY AGE, SELECTED COUNTRIES†

COUNTRY	ALL MALE WORKERS		AGE 55–64		AGE 65 AND OVER	
	Wage and Salary Workers	Employers and Self-employed Workers	Wage and Salary Workers	Employers and Self-employed Workers	Wage and Salary Workers	Employers and Self-employed Workers
United Kingdom	89	8	84	12	72	21
France	68	32	50	50	42	58
West Germany	77	18	66	33	29	69
Belgium	72	23	63	36	30	68
Denmark	71	29	56	44	42	58
Sweden	78	23	63	35	42	57
Netherlands	69	23	62‡	37‡	36	60
Switzerland	71	23	64	34	42	52
United States	78	21	70	29	59	40

* Source: United Nations, *Demographic Yearbook, 1956*.
† Where percentage adds to less than 100, remainder are either unpaid family workers or unclassifiable.
‡ Age 50–64.

25; in the United States they were 32, 30, and 29.

The major differences occur in the almost classic examples of farming and blue-collar (industrial and transport) work. In each country the proportion engaged in farming and related occupations goes up with age, while the proportion engaged in blue-collar work does the opposite (i.e., goes down with increasing age). In the United States and the United Kingdom the proportion of men 65 and over in farming is about double that for the age group 35–44; in Denmark, a more agrarian economy, the rate for the older worker is about

a number of western European nations on what proportion of workers (by age) are employed as wage or salary personnel, on the one hand, and as working for themselves or as employers of labor, on the other hand (Table 7).

In every one of the countries the proportion of men engaged as wage or salary workers is, of course, much higher than that engaged as employers or self-employed workers. However, in each of them the proportion working in their own businesses goes up with age and is highest for those 65 years of age and over. In fact, with the exception of the United States and the United Kingdom, in each of the countries the proportion engaged as employers or self-employed workers actually exceeds the wage and salary component in the 65-and-over age group. The United States and the United Kingdom are similar in their exceptions because of the relatively smaller importance of agriculture in their respective economies in terms of numbers employed.

The importance of self-employment as an area of labor-market participation for the older person is often viewed against the apparent trend in this country and abroad toward the diminishing role of this kind of employment and the increasing trend—numerically and relatively—toward wage and salary jobs. Does this point toward a gradual decline in employment opportunities for the older person?

This, of course, is a complex question and cannot be answered solely in terms of changing occupational trends. But, even within the confines of these trends, there is at least one contraindicating factor. At the same time that wage and salary employment has overtaken and exceeded self-employment, we have had another important development: the growing trend toward white-collar jobs. In this big area, as we have shown, the older worker has held his own—it is an area, in fact, where the older worker may be least disadvantaged (to put it negatively) or may have some substantial work advantages (to put it positively).

These reflections lead us to view the older person as a worker from another perspective. So far we have considered the extent to which older persons participate in the labor force and the kinds of employment they follow. To put it technically, we took some specific age-sex group, examined its labor-market participation rate and its occupational distribution, and made comparisons with other age-sex groups.

It is also pertinent to put our inquiry this way: How important is the older worker in the over-all labor-force picture of his country? For example, for what part of his nation's labor force does the older worker account? How much of the employment in a given occupation is filled by older workers?

The available data reveal that men 55 years of age and over account for the proportions shown in Table 8 of the total male labor force for selected countries in western Europe. Thus men 55 years and over account for anywhere from 14 to 19 per cent of their countries' male workers. This is significant not only as a current indicator but also in terms of historical perspective, since it was not many decades ago that the average male did not even survive to this age level.

TABLE 8*

PERCENTAGE OF MALE LABOR FORCE 55 YEARS AND OVER, SELECTED COUNTRIES

Country	Per Cent
France	14
West Germany	15
Finland	15
Denmark	17
United Kingdom	17
Sweden	18
Switzerland	19
United States	18

* Source: United Nations, *Demographic Yearbook, 1956.*

Similar calculations can also be made for a few countries on an occupational basis. Table 9, for example, shows the relative importance of the male worker 55 and over to the various occupational groups in the United Kingdom and Denmark and in comparisons with the United States. Here, again, the figures can speak for themselves. Apparently, the older worker plays an important numerical role in most occupational groups. In many of them he actually accounts for from one out of five to one out of every four male workers in the field.

This leaves us now with one last item in our general review of the older worker in the labor force—his role in the future. A good deal of work has been done both here and abroad in projecting into the future, not only in terms of anticipated changes in the manpower supply, but also in relation to future pension costs and other items.

What part of a nation's future labor force can be expected to be composed of older workers depends on a variety of social, demographic, and economic factors. The configuration of a country's population profile obviously will be a prime force. The existence of employment opportunity (or, oppositely, substantial unemployment) also plays a part. Important, too, are such questions as to whether older men will continue to display the long-term trend toward

lower labor-market participation rates, especially after age 65, and whether women will continue their trend toward higher labor-market participation in their forties and fifties.

In the United States detailed labor-force projections have been made by age and sex (Wolfbein, 1959). Without going into the details, these projections show a ten-million labor-force increase between 1955 and 1965. One of every two of these additional workers will be 45 years of age and over.

In the United Kingdom detailed projections have also been made for almost ex-

TABLE 9*

PERCENTAGE DISTRIBUTION OF MALES BY OCCUPATIONAL GROUP
UNITED KINGDOM, DENMARK, AND THE UNITED STATES

OCCUPATIONAL GROUP	MEN IN EACH OCCUPATION 55 YEARS OF AGE AND OVER		
	United Kingdom	Denmark	United States
Professional and related workers....	15	19	15
Managerial, administrative, and clerical......................	19	21	20
Sales...........................	20	17	15
Farming, fishing, and related workers......................	22	19	24
Industrial workers...............	15	16	16
Transport workers...............	16	14	8
Service workers..................	26	16	25

* Source: Calculated from United Nations, *Demographic Yearbook, 1956*.

TABLE 10*

ESTIMATED WORKING POPULATION OF
GREAT BRITAIN
(In Millions)

Age Group	1954	1964	1979
15–44.............	15.01	15.28	15.29
Men 45–64 ⎱ ... Women 45–59 ⎰	7.23	7.70	7.63
Men 64 and over ⎱ Women 60 and ⎬. over ⎰	1.07	1.18	1.47
Total........	23.31	24.16	24.39

* Source: Great Britain, Committee on the Economic and Financial Problems of the Provision for Old Age, *Report* (Cmd. 9333 [London: H.M. Stationery Office, 1954]).

actly the same period of time—1954–64 (Great Britain, Committee on the Economic and Financial Problems of the Provision for Old Age, 1954). Unlike the United States, however, where the projections assumed continued drops in worker rates among men 65 and over and continued increases in worker rates among older women, the projections in the United Kingdom assumed the same age-sex labor-market participation rates in 1964 as prevailed in 1954. Nevertheless, the United Kingdom story also points to the increasing role of the older worker (Table 10).

These projections look toward an increase of 850,000 in the labor force between 1954 and 1964. Of these, 580,000, or 68 per cent, will be persons 45 years of age and over. In other words, about two of every three additional workers during the decade would come from the 45-and-over age group.

As can be seen, the British have also prepared projections for 1979 (a quarter of a century beyond the 1954 base period), and these show an even stronger picture in terms of the role of the older worker. Over the 25 years, 800,000 of the 1,000,000 projected labor-force increase was expected to be supplied by persons 45 years and older. In fact, a full 400,000 are expected to be supplied just by men 65 and over and women 60 and over.

The Organization for European Economic Co-operation has brought together projections of the population of working age for the period 1951–71 for a number of western European countries. Abstracting from the details, we have the data given in Table 11.

It should be remembered that we are dealing with the population of working age (generally men 15–64 and women 15–59) rather than with actual workers. However, only a radical shift in rates of labor-market participation could change the conclusion that the labor force is and will grow older and that older persons will be a higher proportion of the labor force of most western European countries. Only in Germany and Austria is there a marked shift to be expected the other way among males—and this is because the older males in 1971 will represent an age cohort affected by the severe casualties of World War II.

In summary, then, the employment and labor-force picture for the present and the more or less immediate future is much the same for the Western world and the United States. The span of man's working life has kept pace with the significant increases in his total life-span, generating substantial increases in his nation's manpower potential and making the older person a prime resource in the over-all labor force and the occupational and industrial complex of his country.

III. THE OLDER WORKER AND RETIREMENT

At present there are two major ways of looking at retirement, one negative and the other positive. The negative conception of retirement is that of the giving up of gainful employment. The positive conception of retirement is that of a new way of life. The negative conception appears to dominate much if not most of present-day thinking

TABLE 11*

PERCENTAGE OF POPULATION OF WORKING AGE 45 YEARS AND OLDER BY SEX, SELECTED COUNTRIES, 1951–71

COUNTRY	MALE		FEMALE	
	1951	1971	1951	1971
United Kingdom....	34	38	32	33
Belgium............	36	37	33	32
Netherlands........	30	31	27	28
Luxembourg........	33	38	30	34
West Germany......	36	32	32	33
Denmark..........	33	35	29	31
Norway...........	32	38	36	33
Sweden...........	34	40	30	34
France...........	34	33	33	29
Italy.............	28	33	26	30
Switzerland........	34	36	31	32
Austria...........	38	33	34	33

* Source: Calculated from data in Organization for European Economic Co-operation, *Demographic Trends in Western Europe: A Report by the Manpower Committee* (Paris: Organization for European Economic Co-operation, 1956), Table VIA, pp. 25–28.

about retirement, at least in the sense that the greater good is for a person to continue to be gainfully employed as long as possible.

It is pertinent, then, to examine retirement from this standpoint and to speculate upon the long-time prospects of the relative place of work and retirement in the life and thinking of older persons. The attempt will be made to find tentative answers to the following question: (1) What is the long-time trend in retirement? (2) What are the factors, at present, making for retirement? (3) What steps are being taken to prolong the working life of older persons?

A. Trend to Retirement

The increase in retirement as a phenomenon in countries of Western culture may be seen in the figures showing the decrease of the percentage of men 65 years of age and over who were economically active in comparing the two periods around 1930

TABLE 12*

PERCENTAGE DECREASE FROM 1930–31 TO 1950–51 OF MALE POPULATION 65 AND OVER ECONOMICALLY ACTIVE

COUNTRY	MALE POPULATION 65 AND OVER ECONOMICALLY ACTIVE	
	1930–31	1950–51
Australia...............	57.0	33.2†
Belgium................	45.3	24.7‡
Canada................	55.7	38.6
Denmark...............	41.7	35.9
France................	59.4	36.1†
Great Britain...........	47.9	31.4
Italy..................	72.6	33.0§
Netherlands............	42.6	35.5‡
Norway................	53.1	42.1
Sweden................	49.8	36.1
Switzerland............	62.5	50.7
United States..........	58.3	41.4

* Source: J. Daric, *Vieillissement de la population et prolongation de la vie active* (Paris: Presses Universitaires de la France, 1948), for early years; and United Nations, *Demographic Yearbook, 1956*, and International Labour Office, *Statistical Yearbook, 1956*, for later years.
   † For 1954.   ‡ For 1947.   § For 1955.

and 1950 (Table 12). During the period of approximately 20 years each country shows a decline, in most cases a marked decline, in the proportion of those economically active. Where later figures are available, the decline is continuing. It is evident that the percentage of the retired men has increased and, barring unforeseen contingencies, will continue to increase.

B. Factors Affecting Retirement

Four factors will be considered in relation to their effect upon the percentage of older persons who are retired. Two of these

factors are societal. They are (1) the adequacy of pensions and the existence of restrictions on employment of older persons and (2) the occupational structure as it adversely affects their employment opportunities. The two other factors are individual. They are (3) the adverse state of health of the person and (4) personal preference for retirement.

ADEQUACY OF PENSIONS AND EXISTENCE OF RESTRICTIONS ON EMPLOYMENT

Dich (1959), a Danish gerontologist, has stated that "the effect of higher pensions will always be that employees retire earlier from work." Certainly, the existence of an old age pension system combined with restrictions on working beyond an arbitrarily fixed age will result in an increase in the percentage of retired persons.

Data from two sources (Great Britain, General Register Office, 1952; Brown *et al.*, 1959) in Britain enable us to perceive the drop in employment of men 60–69 years of age by successive ages. They also make possible a comparison between the country as a whole (1 per cent sample 1951 census) and an industrial area, Birmingham (medical survey 1953), during a period of full employment (Table 13).

It is significant to note that the big drop in employed older persons comes at the pensionable age of 65 both for Great Britain (24.5 per cent) and for Birmingham (18.4 per cent). The drop is less for Birmingham than for Great Britain, a fact which will be held for comment later.

In the case of older female workers in Great Britain who are eligible for pensions at the age of 60 the drop in employment takes place over three years—59, 60, 61—as seen in Table 14. It appears that the combination of restrictions on employment and the availability of pensions affect the percentage of those who retire at the pensionable age.

Dich (1959) contended that the effect of higher pensions would be to increase earlier retirement from work, but he admitted that there were no empirical data to support his theoretical analysis. Results of a recent American study provides inferential evidence (Burgess and Thornbury, 1960). A comparison is made of the replies of 1130 older employees 55–64 years of age to two statements: "If I can, I want to work full time after I am 65" and "After I am 65 I want to work part time to earn up to $1200 a year allowed by social security."

TABLE 13*

COMPARISON BETWEEN GREAT BRITAIN AND BIRMINGHAM IN THE EMPLOYMENT OF MALES 60–69

Age	Great Britain (1)	Birmingham (2)	Percentage Higher in Birmingham (2 − 1)
60.........	91.4	94.8	3.4
61.........	89.1	93.6	3.5
62.........	89.4	92.3	2.9
63.........	85.7	90.7	5.0
64.........	82.9	88.3	5.4
65.........	58.4	69.9	11.5
66.........	50.7	75.0	24.3
67.........	46.9	64.6	17.7
68.........	45.1	61.5	16.4
69.........	40.8	51.7	10.9
Total..	70.1	80.3	10.2
60–64......	87.8	92.1	4.3
65–69......	48.7	64.8	15.1

* Source: Great Britain, General Register Office, *Census 1951: One Per Cent Sample Tables*, Part I, Sec. II: *Occupations* (London: H.M. Stationery Office, 1952), and R. G. Brown, T. McKeown, and A. G. W. Whitfield, "Medical Fitness in Relation to Employment of Men Aged 60–69, in *Proceedings of the Fourth Congress, International Association of Gerontology, Merano, Italy* (Fidenza, Italy: Tipografia Tito Mattioli, 1959), **3**, 101–19.

Five companies with 829 employees offered the usual range of retirement benefits from social security and company pensions. One company provided a much higher retirement income amounting to approximately two-thirds of the average of the last 5 years' wages or salary (Table 15). These findings, if they can be generalized, give support to Dich's assumption of the effect of higher pensions on the desire to retire rather than to continue working. In all companies the preference is for part-time rather than for full-time employment.

Additional supportive evidence for Dich's assumption is the low proportion of employed males 65 and over in Belgium (24.7 per cent reported for 1947), the lowest reported in western European countries. This country requires retirement except for occasional work as a condition of eligibility for pensions. At the same time the pension

TABLE 14*

PERCENTAGE OF OLDER WOMEN EMPLOYED AT SUCCESSIVE AGES 55–64 YEARS

Age	Women Employed	Age	Women Employed
55.........	30.5	60.........	18.7
56.........	28.4	61.........	15.2
57.........	27.7	62.........	13.6
58.........	27.5	63.........	12.3
59.........	24.3	64.........	11.6

* Source: Great Britain, General Register Office, *Census 1951: One Per Cent Sample Tables*, Part I, Sec. II: *Occupations* (London: H.M. Stationery Office, 1952).

TABLE 15*

PERCENTAGE WANTING TO WORK FULL AND PART TIME AFTER AGE 65

EMPLOYMENT PREFERENCE AFTER 65	RETIREMENT INCOME	
	Five Companies (Lower Income)	One Company (High Income)
Full time...........	34.9	10.3
Part time...........	72.7	37.2

* Source: E. W. Burgess and R. T. Thornbury, "Attitudes toward Working Full Time and Part Time of Older Employees" (unpublished paper).

is relatively high—60 per cent for single persons or 75 per cent for married persons of average earnings during lifetime. The earnings for each year are revalued by coefficient reflecting cost-of-living changes (U.S. Department of Health, Education, and Welfare, 1958). The situation in Belgium may be compared with that of France, with a very low pension and no retirement eligibility for receiving it. In 1946 half (54.4 per cent) of the males 65 and over were reported as economically active (United Nations, 1956).

OCCUPATIONAL STRUCTURE AND DIFFER-
ENTIAL OPPORTUNITY FOR
EMPLOYMENT

The position of the older person in the
industrial and occupational structure markedly affects his chances of continuing in
his regular occupation after 65. Certain
types and kinds of occupations give little
opportunity for employment and thus tend
to force the older person into retirement.
Table 7 showed that for nine countries all
but the United Kingdom and the United
States had higher proportions of economically active males 65 and over who were
either employers or working on their own
account than those who were salaried employees and wage-earners.

Two countries, Sweden and the United
Kingdom, give the breakdown between employers and those working on their own
account. In both countries there was a
higher proportion of economically active
males 65 and over compared with those
55–64 among those working on their own
account than among employers (Sweden,
78.9 and 28.6 per cent higher; England
and Wales, 75.9 and 78.3 per cent higher).

Five countries report salaried employees
and wage-earners separately (Belgium,
Denmark, the Netherlands, Sweden, and
West Germany). In these countries there
were much higher percentages of all those
employed of wage-earners than of salaried
employees 65 and over still economically
active than of those 55–64 (see Table 18).
In Denmark the proportions were almost
identical. Only in Belgium is the percentage
of salaried employees among older workers
higher in comparison with those in the
55–64 age bracket.

The census of 1951 1 per cent sample
(Great Britain, General Register Office,
1952) provides data that are indicative of
the differential chances of continuing employment after 65 by twenty-seven industrial groups, as shown in Table 16. The
third column of this table indicates the
percentage that gainfully employed males
65–69 are of those age 60–64 occupational-
ly active. The inference is that this comparison is an approximate measure of the
possibility of continuing work in each industry in the age group 65–69. It will be
noted that the variability is wide, ranging
from the lowest (12.2 per cent) among
coal-, gas-, and cokemakers and workers in
chemical and allied trades to the highest
(83.3 per cent) among makers of products
not elsewhere specified. This industrial
group is composed of workers in rubber,
plastics, and molding, makers of musical
instruments other than pianos, and other
products. Five other occupational groups
with a percentage of 50 or higher employed in the age group 65–69 than in
the age group 60–64 are persons in defense services (66.3 per cent); tanners,
etc., leather-goods makers, fur-dressers
(66.3 per cent); workers in wood, cane, and
cork (65.3 per cent); agricultural, horti-
cultural, and forestry workers (56.3 per
cent); commercial, finance, and insurance
workers (56.3 per cent); painters and dec-
orators (51.8 per cent); and persons engaged in personal service (50.7 per cent).

The other occupational groups with lower chances than 40 per cent of employment
for the age group 65–69 as compared with
the age group 60–64 are: workers in metal
manufacture, engineering, and allied trades
(38.9 per cent); clerks, typists, etc. (37.0
per cent); persons employed in transport
and communication (28.4 per cent); and
other and undefined workers (25.3 per
cent).

HEALTH STATUS IN RELATION
TO RETIREMENT

Certain older employees retire from their
work or are retired by their employers because they are no longer physically fit to
continue at their regular occupation. A consideration of the health status of older persons raises certain questions. What proportion of males 65–69 are fit for full-time
employment? What proportion of retired
males 65–69 are fit for full-time employment and willing to work and are employed? What proportion of retired males

65–69 are fit for full-time employment but cannot find work? What proportion of retired males 65–69 are unfit for full-time work and what percentage of these are gainfully employed?

A searching study was made in Birmingham, England, of the relation of medical fitness to employment of 1062 men aged 60–69 inclusive. Their fitness was assessed by eleven practitioners. Of special interest are the medical findings on 458 men aged 56–69 (Brown *et al.*, 1959). Three-fourths (74.4 per cent) were reported to be fit for their original employment, and 11.6 per cent were regarded as unfit for their original employment but fit for other work (or a total of 86 per cent fit for work). Fourteen per cent were considered to be unfit for any employment. Of the 86 per cent fit to work, 63.7 per cent were employed; 4.4 per cent of the remainder wished to work; and 17.9 per cent did not wish to work. Of the 14.0 per cent unfit for any work, 1.1 per cent were employed, leaving 12.9 per cent unfit for work and unemployed. Evidently, the findings of this study

TABLE 16*

PERCENTAGE OF MALES IN GREAT BRITAIN OCCUPIED AT AGES 60–64, 65–69, AND 70 AND OVER

OCCUPATION	AGE			PERCENTAGE AGE 65–69 IS OF 60–64
	60–64	65–69	70 and Over	
1. Fishermen	2.2	1.0	2.0	45.5
2. Agricultural, horticultural, and forestry workers	78.7	44.3	46.3	56.3
3. Mining and quarrying workers	39.7	19.5	5.9	49.1
4. Makers of brick, glass, and other non-metalliferous mining products	3.0	1.4	7.0	46.7
5. Coal-, gas-, and cokemakers and workers in chemical and allied trades	4.9	0.6	5.0	12.2
6. Metal manufacture, engineering, and allied trades workers	107.1	41.7	17.0	38.9
7. Textile workers	17.8	7.4	4.2	41.6
8. Tanners, etc., leather-goods makers, fur-dressers	9.2	6.1	3.2	66.3
9. Makers of textile goods and articles of dress	8.6	4.1	4.7	47.7
10. Makers of food, drinks, and tobacco	9.8	4.2	2.2	42.9
11. Workers in wood, cane, and cork	25.9	16.9	7.1	65.3
12. Makers and workers in paper, bookbinders, printers	11.0	5.1	3.9	46.4
13. Makers of products not elsewhere specified	2.4	2.0	1.2	83.3
14. Workers in building and contracting	56.9	26.8	12.9	47.1
15. Painters and decorators	16.6	8.6	4.8	51.8
16. Administrators, directors, and managers not elsewhere specified	31.4	14.1	13.0	44.9
17. Persons employed in transport and communication	85.2	24.2	13.4	28.4
18. Commercial, finance, and insurance workers (excluding clerical staff)	83.3	46.9	41.0	56.3
19. Professional and technical workers (excluding clerical staff)	36.7	18.2	14.5	49.6
20. Persons employed in defense services	16.0	10.6	9.9	66.3
21. Persons professionally engaged in entertainment and sport	5.6	2.7	2.3	48.2
22. Persons engaged in personal service (including hotels, institutions, clubs)	47.9	24.3	17.2	50.7
23. Clerks, typists, etc.	51.4	19.0	11.7	37.0
24. Warehousemen, storekeepers, packers, bottlers	31.7	13.3	6.4	42.0
25. Stationary engine-drivers, crane-drivers, tractor-drivers, stokers, etc.	21.3	8.6	3.1	40.4
26. Workers in unskilled occupations not elsewhere specified	104.4	48.2	24.8	46.2
27. Other and undefined workers	9.5	2.4	8.0	25.3

* Source: Great Britain, General Register Office, *Census 1951: One Per Cent Sample Tables*, Part I, Sec. II: *Occupations* (London: H.M. Stationery Office, 1952), Table II.3.

indicate that, of the 35.2 per cent of the retired men 65–69 years of age, 12.9 per cent could be attributed to state of health and 22.3 per cent to other reasons. But Birmingham is an industrial area, and the period of the study was one of full employment.

Is it feasible to adapt these findings to Great Britain? The assumption will be made that the percentage of the unfit to work among males 65–69 will be the same

table that deserve comment: (1) The percentage of older men judged to be unfit for employment remains relatively low during the ages studied and only reaches a peak of one in four (23.6 per cent) at 69 years. (2) The percentage of retired men who are fit for employment but not wishing to work makes a big jump from 4.5 per cent at age 60 to 17.5 at age 65. The fact that one in every six men at age 65 takes advantage of his eligibility for a pension and, although

TABLE 17*

PERCENTAGE OF MEN CONSIDERED TO BE FIT FOR EMPLOYMENT

AGE	EMPLOYED MEN		RETIRED MEN		
	Fit	Unfit	Fit and Wish To Work	Fit and Do Not Wish To Work	Unfit
60	93.1	1.7	....	0.9	4.3
61	90.7	2.9	....	2.9	3.6
62	90.0	2.3	0.8	3.1	3.8
63	89.8	0.9	0.9	0.9	7.4
64	87.4	0.9	2.7	4.5	4.5
65	68.9	1.0	3.9	17.5	8.7
66	72.9	2.1	1.0	17.7	6.3
67	63.3	1.3	8.8	11.4	15.2
68	60.4	1.1	5.5	20.9	12.1
69	51.7	....	3.4	21.3	23.6
Total	78.8	1.5	2.4	9.1	8.2
60–64	90.2	1.8	0.8	2.5	4.7
65–69	63.7	1.1	4.4	17.9	12.9

* Source: R. G. Brown, T. McKeown, and A. G. W. Whitfield, "Medical Fitness in Relation to Employment of Men Aged 60–69," in *Proceedings of the Fourth Congress, International Association of Gerontology, Merano, Italy* (Fidenza, Italy: Typografia Tito Mattioli, 1959), **3**, 101–19.

for the whole country as for Birmingham. Under this assumption the percentage of the unfit to work will also be 14 per cent. But the percentage of retired males 60–65 for Great Britain was 51.3 instead of 35.2, as in Birmingham. Accordingly, our estimate is that about three of every eight males 65–69 in Great Britain are retired due to reasons other than health.

The Birmingham study also analyzed the percentage of men considered fit to be employed by age from 60 to 69 and by those retired and still employed. The findings are presented in Table 17. Three points emerge from an examination of this

capable, does not wish to continue working demonstrates the relation of a pension system to retirement. (3) The findings presented indicate that for retired persons in Birmingham personal preference not to work is a more important factor in making for retirement than medical unfitness for employment.

In this industrial area it is evident that there is no substantial reservoir of fit men who are willing to work in the age group 65–69. But the proportion of all men 65–69 who are unfit for employment is small. Consequently, the investigators make the point that, "if an advancement of age of retirement were considered desirable for other reasons, there appear to be no medical grounds which would prohibit it."

PERSONAL PREFERENCE

Personal preference for retirement is an omnibus category covering many different reasons other than those previously considered. In a sample of one of fifty Parisian workers who had received their old age pension a year or less, Tréanton (1959) reports that 23 per cent state that they stopped working of "their own will." Nearly half (47 per cent) gave reasons of health or fatigue, and a quarter (26 per cent) were forced to retire.

age in these occupational statuses for five European countries.

It is interesting to note the marked increase in the age group 65 and over as compared with the age group 55–64 in employers and those on own account who are still employed. Correspondingly, there is an even greater decline in the percentage still employed after 65 among salaried employees and in three of the five countries for wage-earners.

The actual numbers, of course, in all these occupational groups decline after the pensionable age. The point is that personal preference to continue working finds greater expression in continued employment

TABLE 18*

PERCENTAGE EMPLOYED BEFORE AND AFTER 65, BY OCCUPATIONAL STATUS

COUNTRY AND YEAR	EMPLOYERS AND ON OWN ACCOUNT		SALARIED EMPLOYEES		WAGE-EARNERS	
	55–64	65 and Over	55–64	65 and Over	55–64	65 and Over
Belgium (1947)	36.0	67.7	16.2	10.9	46.7	18.9
Denmark (1950)	43.7	58.1	17.4	12.7	38.9	29.2
West Germany (1950)	33.2	68.2	24.9	8.8	41.2	20.5
Netherlands (1947)	37.3	61.8	17.3	7.3	42.4	29.2
Sweden (1950)	35.8	60.8	19.2	8.8	44.3	33.4

* Source: United Nations, *Demographic Yearbook, 1956,* Table 14.

The Birmingham study (Brown *et al.,* 1959) indicates that half the men 65–69 who had retired did not wish to continue working, although the medical examination found them fit for full-time employment. This proportion would undoubtedly be smaller for Great Britain as a whole, or about one-third according to our estimate.

One way of estimating the influence of personal preference on retirement is to eliminate or at least to reduce the effect of being forced to retire. This can be done by comparing the percentage of those retiring who can determine when they retire (employers and those working on their own account) with those where the decision is made for them (salaried employees and wage-earners). Table 18 gives the percentage of men before and after 65 years of

among employers and those working on their own account than with salaried employees and wage-earners.

It is apparent that the four factors examined—the adequacy of pensions and restrictions on employment, the occupational structure with differential work opportunities, the health status of the older person, and personal preference—are all conditions making for or against retirement. Research, however, is needed to determine more precisely how these and other factors operate independently and in conjunction to affect retirement behavior.

C. The Prolongation of Working Life

In France, Great Britain, the United States, and other countries there has been a lively interest in prolonging the working life of older people. In 1948 Jean Daric published his book *Le Vieillissement de la population et prolongation de la vie active.* In it he examines the economic and social consequences of the aging of the population, analyzes the available data on aging from a special public opinion poll con-

TABLE 19*

PART-TIME WORKERS AS PERCENT-
AGE OF ALL EMPLOYED
PERSONS BY AGE

Age	Men	Women
60–64........	0.6	16.4
65–69........	2.3	17.0
70–74........	5.9	12.2
75 and over...	6.7	6.1

* Source: F. L. G. Clark, "Would Short Working Hours Prolong Employment for the Elderly?" in *Proceedings of the Fourth Congress, International Association of Gerontology, Merano, Italy* (Fidenza, Italy: Tipografia Tito Mattioli, 1959), 3, 109–19.

ducted by l'Institut National d'Études Demographiques, reviews the objections against and the arguments in favor of the prolongation of working life, and discusses the possibilities of a policy aimed at lengthening the working life of older persons.

Daric (1955) reports the findings of a survey of elderly workers in France. Special provisions to help older employees were found in only a few firms. These provisions include their placement in light work, transfer to different jobs where the hours and speed of work can be modified, assignment to special work groups, and the introduction of homework.

Abrams (1955) enumerates a few measures undertaken by governments to encourage employment of older persons, such as the setting-aside of public jobs for the elderly by Denmark, subsidies to employers hiring the aged by Switzerland, and training centers under governmental auspices in France, Italy, Belgium, and Switzerland. He recommends that the effectiveness of these measures should be evaluated.

These projects listed by Daric and by Abrams are only a few of the many attempts to provide special employment for the elderly or to improve their work skills by retraining. Other investigators have been concerned with broader changes in employment policies and practices.

F. L. G. Clark (1959) is concerned with the question, "Would short working hours prolong employment for the elderly?" In other words, can a person when no longer fit for full-time work find part-time employment? He utilizes the data of the national census of April, 1951, which reports 51,576 women and 28,467 men 60 and over as holding part-time employment. The proportion of men but not of women in part-time gainful employment increases with age, as shown in Table 19.

TABLE 20*

PERCENTAGE PART-TIME MALE WORKERS IN
TEN OCCUPATIONS BY AGE GROUPS

OCCUPATION	ALL MEN EMPLOYED IN SAME OCCUPATION		
	60–64	65–69	70 and Over
Clerks..............	1.6	4.5	10.2
Shop assistants.......	2.5	9.0	19.4
Teachers (not music teachers)..........	3.0	20.0	22.5
Caretakers..........	3.5	12.7	21.8
Farm workers........	1.5	6.4	16.2
Gardeners (mainly jobbing)..........	3.2	9.9	23.1
Warehousemen.......	0.3	1.8	5.8
Office cleaners........	6.4	20.0	36.2
Kitchen porters.......	2.2	6.7	14.2
Watchmen..........	2.3	5.5	11.5

* Source: Great Britain, General Register Office, *Census 1951: One Per Cent Sample Tables*, Part I, Sec. II: *Occupations* (London: H.M. Stationery Office, 1952).

Ten occupations account for more than half the male part-time employees in Britain according to the 1951 census (Great Britain, General Register Office, 1952). All these show increasing proportions with successive ages, although, of course, the actual numbers of men at work decrease with age (Table 20). Part-time work, at least for older men, accounts at present for only a small percentage of those still employed after 65 years of age. It is confined to a limited number of occupations. Can it be further expanded?

Part-time employment is an attractive method of prolonging the working life of older persons. It would utilize the services of many not capable of, or, if capable, not desiring, full-time employment. But Le Gros Clark (1959) is skeptical of the possibilities of overcoming the resistance in manufacturing industries to the extension of the practice of part-time employment for elderly persons. He sees, however, no reason why part-time work for older men and women should not expand considerably in many offices, shops, and retail stores, where a measure of flexibility is more feasible than in industry. He also points out that professional persons often have the opportunity of adjusting their hours of work to suit their physical convenience.

Barbara Shenfield (1955) analyzed the employment status of persons 65–69 years as shown by the 1 per cent sample report of the British census (Great Britain, General Register Office, 1952). She was interested in exploring whether industries with a relatively high or those with a relatively low proportion of older workers might be expected to absorb a considerable number of persons beyond retirement age. She concluded that "there is no immediate prospect of a substantial increase in the numbers employed who are over pensionable age" (p. 312).

The prospects for an expansion of the volume of employment for persons 65 years of age and older do not appear to be bright. The secular trend in all countries of Western culture shows a continuing decline in the proportion of the economically active of those above pensionable age. There is no evidence of the emergence of counteracting factors.

There remains the question of how great a hardship this situation will impose upon the older person. There is evidence that gerontologists would be well advised to direct their attention away from providing more employment to the problem of the older worker of pensionable age who continues to work not because he prefers to do so but because of financial necessity.

The opinion of 71 per cent of those polled in Great Britain in the world poll of 1958 reported that the old age benefits were "too low" (International Research Associates, 1958). In the countries canvassed this reply was exceeded only by Italy (76 per cent) and by France (87 per cent). Belgium, which has a relatively adequate system of benefits, has, as we have seen, a low proportion of males 65 and over employed (24.7 per cent). Reference has already been made to a comparison of the older employees of one company with a high retirement benefit system with five other companies with lower benefits, with 10.3 per cent in the former and 37.2 per cent in the latter wanting to work full time after age 65.

The proportion of older persons who continue to work because of financial pressure is large. In the 1953 investigation of the Ministry of Pensions and National Insurance (1954) the chief reason given by British workers for continuing employment beyond the minimum pensionable age was financial need (44.7 per cent). Only one in five (20.2 per cent) stated that they prefer to work. In the Birmingham study (Brown *et al.*, 1959) the proportion reporting financial need was even higher (78.5 per cent) as the reason for still working. Again only one in five (20.5 per cent) gave personal preference as their reason for being employed.

Three pressures impinge upon persons which force them to retire. These are ill-health, age restrictions, and lack of opportunity for employment.

The chief pressure forcing men and women to remain in the labor force is financial need. This problem can be met by increasing pensions or other sources of retirement income to provide an adequate level of benefits.

The optimum situation would appear to

be one in which a man or woman at 65 would freely choose without external pressure whether to continue employment or to retire. The obstacle of ill-health may be reduced by medical science and public health education. Age restrictions may be modified by scientific evidence showing that older workers are as productive as young workers (Burns and Spaeth, 1960). Opportunity for work may be obtained as those now forced by financial need to work against their will can enjoy retirement.

The present system of arbitrary employment policies and practices and of inadequate pensions is a combination of contradictions. It forces persons from financial need to continue working who would prefer to retire and others to retire who would prefer to continue working. Once practical measures are taken to end compulsion in employment and in retirement, there will be full employment for all that wish to continue working.

In this chapter we have been concerned with retirement from the standpoint of the factors influencing persons at pensionable age to retire or to continue gainful employment. In succeeding chapters other aspects of retirement and life after 65 will be considered, such as income maintenance, housing and community services, physical and mental health, family structure and relationships, and life beyond the family and work. The center of interest will shift from the opportunity of employment beyond pensionable age to providing the opportunities in retirement for a new way of life.

REFERENCES AND BIBLIOGRAPHY

ABRAMS, A. J. 1955. Discrimination against older works in various countries. *In* Old age in the modern world, pp. 291–95. Edinburgh: E. & S. Livingstone.

BROWN, R. G., McKEOWN, T., and WHITFIELD, A. G. W. 1959. Medical fitness in relation to employment of men aged 60–69. *In* Proceedings of the Fourth Congress, International Association of Gerontology, Merano, Italy, **3**, 101–8. Fidenza, Italy: Tipografia Tito Mattioli.

BURGESS, E. W., and THORNBURY, R. T. 1960. Attitudes toward working full time and part time of older employees. (Unpublished paper.)

BURNS, R. K., and SPAETH, J. L. 1960. Productivity and aging. *In* R. K. BURNS (ed.), Objective criteria of aging and determinants of retirement. Chicago: University of Chicago Press.

CLARK, F. L. G. 1959. Would short working hours prolong employment for the elderly? *In* Proceedings of the Fourth Congress, International Association of Gerontology, Merano, Italy, **3**, 109–19. Fidenza, Italy: Tipografia Tito Mattioli.

DARIC, J. 1948. Vieillissement de la population et prolongation de la vie active. ("Institut Nationale d'Études Démographiques, Travaux et Documents," No. 7.) Paris: Presses Universitaires de France.

———. 1955. Survey of the employment of elderly workers in France. *In* Old age in the modern world, pp. 295–99. Edinburgh: E. & S. Livingstone.

DEPOID, P. 1951. Tables françaises concernant la population masculine (1906–1946). Bull. Internat. Statistical Institute, Vol. **33**, Part IV: Demography and labour statistics, pp. 131–46.

DICH, J. S. 1959. The economic-political consequences of an ageing population. *In* Proceedings of the Fourth Congress, International Association of Gerontology, Merano, Italy, **3**, 77–85. Fidenza, Italy: Tipografia Tito Mattioli.

GREAT BRITAIN. COMMITTEE ON THE ECONOMIC AND FINANCIAL PROBLEMS OF THE PROVISION FOR OLD AGE. 1954. Report. (Cmd. 9333.) London: H.M. Stationery Office.

GREAT BRITAIN. GENERAL REGISTER OFFICE. 1952. Census 1951: one per cent sample tables, Part I, Sec. II: Occupations. London: H.M. Stationery Office.

GREAT BRITAIN. MINISTRY OF PENSIONS AND NATIONAL INSURANCE. 1954. Reasons given for retiring or continuing at work. London: H.M. Stationery Office.

INTERNATIONAL LABOUR ORGANIZATION. 1956. Yearbook of labour statistics. Geneva: International Labour Organization.

INTERNATIONAL RESEARCH ASSOCIATES. 1958. World poll. New York Herald Tribune, October 11–12.

MORTARA, G. 1951. Durée de la vie économique active suivant la mortalité. Bull. Internat. Statistical Institute, Vol. **33**, Part

IV: Demography and labour statistics, pp. 147–74.

NAVILLE, P. 1959. Measurement of working life and employment of older workers in France. *In* C. TIBBITTS (ed.), Aging and social health in the United States and Europe, pp. 74–95. Ann Arbor: Division of Gerontology, University of Michigan.

NEW ZEALAND. 1955. Table of working life, 1951: male population (including Maoris). Wellington, N.Z.: Census and Statistics Department.

ORGANIZATION FOR EUROPEAN ECONOMIC CO-OPERATION. 1956. Demographic trends in western Europe: a report by the Manpower Committee. Paris: The Organization.

SHENFIELD, BARBARA E. 1955. Employment prospects for older workers in Great Britain. *In* Old age in the modern world, pp. 305–12. Edinburgh: E. & S. Livingstone.

TITMUSS, R. M. 1959. Essays on the welfare state. New Haven, Conn.: Yale University Press.

TRÉANTON, J. R. 1959. Adjustment of older people to urban life in France. *In* C. TIBBITTS (ed.), Aging and social health in the United States and Europe, pp. 167–73. Ann Arbor: Division of Gerontology, University of Michigan.

UNITED NATIONS. 1956. Demographic yearbook, 1956. New York: United Nations.

———. 1958. Demographic yearbook, 1958. New York: United Nations.

U.S. DEPARTMENT OF HEALTH, EDUCATION, AND WELFARE, SOCIAL SECURITY ADMINISTRATION. 1958. Social security programs throughout the world, 1958. Washington, D.C.: Government Printing Office.

U.S. DEPARTMENT OF LABOR. 1955. Our manpower future. Washington, D.C.. Government Printing Office.

WOLFBEIN, S. L. 1959. The length of working life. *In* Proceedings of the Fourth Congress, International Association of Gerontology, Merano, Italy, **3**, 153–84. Fidenza, Italy: Tipografia Tito Mattioli.

IV

Income Maintenance and Medical Insurance

WILBUR J. COHEN

I. Brief Summary of Status of Present Programs

At the end of 1958, fifty-seven countries throughout the world had some type of government-sponsored income-maintenance program providing benefits for aged (and disabled) persons, and almost as many countries also had some type of government-sponsored medical insurance or medical service program which pays for the costs or provides medical care for all or large groups in the population, often including the aged who have retired and the disabled.

These programs are usually, but not always, nation wide in their geographical scope and, in a few cases, are universal in their application throughout the nation in that all aged persons are eligible for benefits. In some cases they may be limited initially to principal urban areas or to certain industrial or occupational groups. This is particularly true when plans are in the early stages of evolution such as in newly developing countries. In some countries the plans may not be universal in character but may cover a very large proportion of the population. The plans may be organized and administered by public authorities or may utilize quasi-governmental or non-governmental agencies. Financing may involve payroll taxes, general government contributions or subsidies, or some combination of these approaches. The principles of insurance and assistance, or both, may be used, although the former is predominant. In a few countries insurance and assistance principles may be combined in the same program.

Illustrations may also be found of countries in which old age benefits or health services are provided on a universal basis as a matter of right, with little or no reliance on the past contributions of individuals. However, not all countries with such national programs have applied the same principles equally to income-maintenance and health programs. Historical developments, traditions, culture, and economic and social developments all play a significant role in determining the evolution and type of social security institutions of different countries.

There is a wide variation in the specific characteristics of the plans used in different countries to provide income and health protection in old age. Despite the variations, there are many similarities in the plans and experiences of countries with these income and health programs which have had, and will continue to have, value and pertinence to programs and developments in the United States.

Policies and programs with respect to providing income and medical care to aged persons raise many important, complex, and controversial issues. Throughout the world individuals and organizations, voluntary and public agencies, political and professional associations, and governments, over many years, have struggled with these same basic issues.

A major factor in the development and expansion of income and health programs in Western countries in the last 75 years has been the desire of peoples and governments for some protection against the major economic and social hazards of life without recourse to charity. Out of this grew the social insurance movement in Europe, beginning in Germany in 1883, which ultimately spread to the United States in the early part of the twentieth century through workmen's compensation which provided cash wage-loss benefits and medical care for work-connected accidents.

The same kinds of problems which gave rise to the social insurance movement in Europe also ultimately resulted in the development of the same kinds of social insurance institutions in the United States. Today, as in the last 75 years, the experiences of Western countries, the United States, and other countries of the world in the social security field are interacting upon one another. The whole process in both Europe and the United States is still in a stage of growth and change. A number of divergent tendencies and forces are at work in different countries which make it hazardous to isolate the important current trends of significance for the future development of social security in the United States. It is possible, however, to record some of the more significant developments in western European countries which have had an impact upon the social security system of the United States or which may throw light on some of the current issues being discussed in this country. The following discussion attempts to highlight some selected developments and issues.

A. Extent and Character of Old Age Programs

When the United States Congress decided to establish an old age insurance program as part of the Social Security Act in 1935, there already were such programs enacted in twenty-two of the twenty-seven European countries. Germany had inaugurated such a system for invalidity and old age insurance in 1889. Denmark established a national old age assistance plan in 1891. Great Britain enacted an old age assistance program in 1908, an invalidity insurance program in 1911, and then added old age and survivors insurance in 1925. Sweden established its program, which has features of insurance, pensions, and assistance, in 1913. Only Albania, Finland, Norway, Switzerland, and Turkey, of the European countries, did not have old age benefit programs by 1935.

It is interesting to note that "invalidity" insurance (or what is called in the United States "permanent total disability insurance") in effect preceded old age insurance in both Germany and Great Britain, whereas, in the United States, disability insurance was not added to the old age insurance program until 21 years later (1956), although federal grants to the states for disability assistance to needy individuals had been added to the over-all social security program in the United States a few years earlier (1950); survivors insurance benefits for widows and orphans had been added in 1939. Governmental health insurance programs preceded old age insurance programs in both Germany and Great Britain.

When the executive branch of the United States was considering adoption of the original old age insurance plan in 1934, there were only twenty-eight countries with general old age insurance or pension programs in the world, of which twenty-two were in Europe, the other six being Australia, Brazil, Chile, New Zealand, Union of South Africa, and Uruguay. The European experience was thus the most important in the minds of the staff of the Committee on Economic Security which drew up the old age insurance plan. The most important of the European systems in 1934 were those of Germany and Great Britain, both of which then had a uniform pensionable age of 65 in their contributory insurance programs but had very different types of benefit programs, with some experience under a wide range of conditions such as war, depression, inflation, and deflation.

When the Committee on Economic Security, established by President Franklin D. Roosevelt in 1934 to draft the Social Security Act, came into being, one of the first duties of its staff was to make a survey of the main European experience in social insurance and public assistance. The report of the staff of the committee, *Social Security in America* (1937), contains a list of the staff studies made and indicates the substantial extent to which reference was made to the European experience. Of even more significance is the fact that the senior members of the policy and research staffs were familiar with the European experience from firsthand study. Thus the European experience had a pertinent bearing on a number of the policy decisions incorporated in the original 1934–35 proposals.

Since 1935, the remaining five European countries have adopted old age benefit programs. The countries, and the dates of adoption of their programs, are as follows: Norway, 1936; Finland, 1937; Switzerland, 1946; Albania, 1947; and Turkey, 1949.

Thus, as of 1958, all European countries have some old age benefit program. Counting both East and West Germany as separate countries, there are twenty-eight countries in Europe with programs. These programs usually—but not always—combine benefits for the aged, the disabled, and the widows and orphans (survivors). There are wide variations in the approach, scope, adequacy, financing, types of benefits, and administration in these programs. The experience of these countries offers a rich opportunity to the student of social security to find many variations of provisions operating under diverse conditions, with almost constant changes of provisions to meet new and changing needs.

B. Extent and Character of Medical Insurance Programs

All the European countries except Finland have some kind of government-spon-

sored medical insurance or medical service program which pays for part or all of the costs or provides medical care for all or large groups in the population, often including the aged and the disabled. A government-sponsored plan for health insurance was first established in Germany in 1883. In Great Britain a limited governmental health insurance program was established by Lloyd George in 1911. The systems spread to many countries throughout Europe and the rest of the world. The United States is almost alone among the major industrial countries of the world which do not have some kind of government-sponsored health insurance or medical care program for at least large groups of industrial workers. Some governmental measures exist for special groups in the United States, such as veterans, seamen, Indians, persons in military service, public assistance recipients, injured workmen, the mentally ill, and the tubercular. In addition, one state, California, has a government health insurance program limited to hospital insurance for employees covered under its unemployment insurance and cash sickness-benefits program.

The controversial nature of medical insurance in the United States under any kind of public auspices has led to frequent examination of the European experience by both the opponents and the advocates of various measures. There are those who claim that any kind of public responsibility for any medical care insurance inevitably leads to "socialized medicine." Great Britain is usually cited as an example for this claim, since it now has a universal, public medical-care program. On the other hand, there are those who claim that the experience of countries on the European continent demonstrates that a publicly sponsored or financed health insurance system is a bulwark against the adoption of a public medical service plan for the entire population.

It is not likely that this kind of an argument can be resolved by reference to any generalization based upon European experience. Suffice it to say that countries of varying background, and with varying economic and political ideologies—Ireland, Sweden, Spain, Yugoslavia—have some kind of health insurance program under public auspices.

Although it has not been possible to verify the statement by checking with every country, it is not believed that there exists in Europe a separate publicly financed hospital insurance program solely for the beneficiaries of the social security system such as has been proposed in the Congress of the United States (usually referred to as the "Forand Bill"). Because the health insurance and service programs of European countries deal with general groups in the population, it has not been possible to determine whether any important special arrangements have been made for the aged which are not applicable to younger persons in a group. Ireland appears to be the only country which provides for only hospital care to insured workers. An evaluation of the experience of countries providing hospital coverage remains an area for additional research. An appendix summarizes the medical-care insurance provisions for pensioners in ten western European countries.

II. Old Age Programs—General

Every old age program in every country is different from that of another country. Human ingenuity being what it is, there is most likely to be a tendency toward further variations of details in the programs for the future. On the other hand, there are some general types of programs which can be classified, if it is remembered that social institutions have many facets which prevent clear-cut classifications which do not overlap.

A. Types of Old Age and Disability Programs in the United States

Such terms as "insurance" and "assistance" are subject to varying interpretations in different countries. It might be best to see, in a general way, how these terms are used in the United States before attempting to summarize European plans.

In the United States there are five main types of old age and disability programs of public concern:

1. The contributory, wage-related old age insurance program with which is combined survivors and permanent total disability insurance. This program is operated by the federal government.
2. The state old age assistance, permanent total disability assistance, and blind assistance programs for needy individuals financed in part by federal grants-in-aid under very general federal standards.
3. State or local general assistance or "poor relief" statutes applicable to needy older people who, for one reason or another (such as premature old age or not meeting state residence or other requirements), are not eligible for federally aided old age or disability assistance.
4. Supplemental old age and disability pension plans established by employers, by unions, or by collective bargaining which, except for very general approval by the tax or insurance authorities for tax-deduction or investment purposes, are not subject to public control as to the characteristics of their financing or benefit provisions.
5. Savings or profit-sharing plans for old age and disability similar to those enumerated under No. 4 above.

B. Types of Programs in Western Europe

It is not possible to take the classification which is useful in the United States and use it for comparison with other countries without some modification. Some countries have adopted an old age program which is neither strictly "insurance" nor "assistance," in the way these terms sometimes are used in the United States. In some European countries there is a truly universal old age pension program providing benefits to everyone meeting the age and residence requirements. Among the European countries, Denmark, Finland, Norway, and Sweden have programs which provide for paying a basic benefit to all aged persons without an income or contribution test.

In some European countries there is a national pension program, but with an income test for part of the benefits. These programs have some aspects of "assistance" involved in them (in the sense this term is used in the United States), but the income tests are on a more liberal and objective basis than "poor relief" and hence do not carry the same stigma as a "means test."

These varieties of universal pension plans combine various features, or principles, of different plans. An analysis of the elements and trends in the evolution of these plans is essential to the understanding of the controversial issues involved in old age programs.

Prior to 1935, European systems of old age security were considered to be of the "classic" social insurance type or the "classic" public assistance type. As variations of each emerged, there appeared a kind of merging of insurance and assistance principles. With the introduction of the term "social security" in the United States, the expression gained universal currency to denote all varieties of plans and to cover the hybrid and universal types of plans evolving out of the early classical approaches.

From the United States, the term and the concept spread to New Zealand in 1938 and to other countries, eventually culminating in an international social security convention adopted by the International Labor Conference in 1952.

The tendency toward a blending of insurance and assistance programs in some plans was pointed out in an important document published by the International Labour Office in 1942 entitled *Approaches to Social Security*. This report noted that the world-wide experience had indicated that

social assistance is a progression from poor relief in the direction of social insurance, while social insurance is a progression from private insurance in the direction of social assistance.

If present day developments have been correctly read, social assistance and social insurance are moving ever closer to each other. As the culmination of a long evolution they may even meet and combine; until, as in New Zealand and Denmark, we can no longer say whether social assistance or social insurance predominates, but only that they possess a national system of social security [pp. 86–87].

In all European countries, as in the United States, social policy has been directed toward minimizing the extent to which older persons need to rely upon assistance. Where the programs take income into account, there has been pressure for liberalization of the income test so that the "assistance" features are minimized. The effort to minimize the role of assistance was undertaken at the end of World War II as part of the effort of postwar reconstruction. However, the inflation which developed made it impossible for the effort to succeed as fast as its proponents had hoped.

In Great Britain, for example, 72 per cent of all persons receiving national assistance as needy persons in December, 1956, were of pensionable age (65 for men and 60 for women). The overwhelming majority of these (90 per cent) were receiving assistance as a supplementation to their small insurance or pension payments. Only 10 per cent of the aged on assistance were receiving no such insurance or pension payments. The average allowance in supplementation of retirement pensions (15s. 1d.) in 1956 was approximately three-eighths of the normal retirement pension, then 40 shillings a week (in 1959 it was 50 shillings a week). The problem of supplementing social security benefits in the United States by public assistance is a growing matter of concern. The British experience indicates the importance of reviewing periodically the relationship between the benefit levels of both programs and the reasons for supplementation of the insurance benefit. In Great Britain it appears that most supplementary payments are given to meet rent. In the United States it appears that a growing proportion of supplementary payments are given to meet nursing-home and medical-care costs.

C. Equity and Adequacy in Old Age Programs

One of the persistent problems in income-maintenance programs is the application of the two principles of "equity" and "adequacy" in the construction and modification of specific benefit provisions. These principles apply primarily to the formulation of policy in contributory programs, but, to some degree, they also are applicable to non-contributory and general pension programs. Each of the old age programs in western European countries has wrestled with the conflict between these principles and the innumerable problems involved in combining or separating them in the same program.

The concept of "equity" derives from private insurance, which has played an important role in influencing the evolution of "social" insurance. This concept conceives of the individual's benefit as the annuity which would be purchasable on an actuarial basis by the contributions made by the individual or on the individual's behalf. A strict construction of this concept would be incompatible with the fundamental purposes of social insurance, since it would preclude the payment of any except the most inconsequential benefits in the initial operation of the plan and also would result in too small benefits for the lowest-paid workers.

In some countries, such as the United States, Germany, and France, "equity" considerations have loomed relatively large where individual responsibility has been stressed in a contributory program. In Denmark, the Netherlands, and Sweden this element has been negligible in their plans, while in Great Britain it has played a moderate, but subordinate, role as compared with the United States, Germany, and France.

All countries, however, are faced with the task of defining and redefining "adequacy" of benefits. Some concept of "social adequacy" is explicitly or implicitly behind every old age benefit structure. The objective may be to keep most persons off poor relief, to pay a "minimum subsistence," to provide a "basic floor of protection," or to provide a level of living compatible with a standard of "health and decency." There may be many other expressions of the objective. They may vary from country to country and from time to time in a particular country. This is one of the basic problems of an old age benefit program which is related to many social and economic factors, such as costs, incentives, cultural patterns, the standard of living of the economy, and the relationship to other institutional arrangements (private insurance, private pension plans, homeownership, and savings), to mention a few.

Reinhard Hohaus (1948), vice-president and actuary of the Metropolitan Life Insurance Company, was the first to point up the implications of these two principles in his stimulating article on "Equity, Adequacy and Related Factors in Old Age Security" published originally in the *Record* of the American Institute of Actuaries in June, 1938. He showed that private insurance, being voluntary in character, must be built upon the equity between the various classes insured or that people would drop their insurance in one group for another. Social insurance, on the other hand, being compulsory in character (as far as contributions are concerned), aims primarily at providing society with some protection against major hazards which are widespread and far-reaching enough to become "social" in scope and complexion.

Private insurance, then, tends to be adapted to the individual's need for, and his ability to afford, protection against a risk. Social insurance, on the other hand, tends to be molded to society's needs. Both programs contain elements of individual and societal needs. How both of these factors are combined and emphasized can change the program very substantially.

Different countries have blended elements of private and social insurance in various ways.

Hohaus claims that society's need is for a "minimum of protection," and he thus introduces a controversial and changing element as to what is meant by "minimum." He concludes that "private insurance would collapse if it stressed considerations of adequacy more than those of equity, so will social insurance fail to remain undisturbed if considerations of equity are allowed to predominate over those of adequacy." He says that this "need not necessarily imply that all considerations of equity should be discarded from a social insurance plan: rather the point is that, of the two principles, adequacy is the more essential and less dispensable."

What is meant by "equity" in social insurance is not a clear-cut matter. In private insurance the concept means that the individual's benefits are not less than the "value" of the contributions paid, including any interest on any reserves minus administrative costs and taking into account mortality or other relevant factors. But in social insurance it becomes difficult to determine this in view of compulsory employer contributions and direct or indirect subsidies. Moreover, whether a standard of individual or group equity should be applied is open to differences of opinion. Another view is that equity is attained if all who contribute the same amount receive the same in benefits, while beneficiaries will argue that, if benefits are not related to length of contributions or amount of earnings, a cardinal element of equity is violated.

The generality of these two concepts makes them difficult to define in specific terms in a particular country. The difference in the meaning of the concepts in different economic and cultural settings makes it impossible to compare their application in various countries. Nevertheless, the fact of the matter is that the issues raised by these concepts are inherent in the formulation and revision of old age

benefit provisions. In general, the payment of a flat benefit is an illustration of a program which may have a high degree of "minimum social adequacy," while a program providing benefits and contributions related to previous wages may have a high degree of "equity." But programs of flat-rate contributions and benefits may have a high degree of equity and also a high degree of minimum social adequacy (as, for example, Great Britain). Programs, such as those in Scandinavia, Israel, and New Zealand, which have flat-rate benefits but contributions fixed as a percentage of payroll, are illustrative of programs with a relatively high degree of social adequacy and a minimum of individual equity.

In Great Britain proposals for a wage-related benefit program (which will be discussed later) indicate a movement away from a "minimum" concept of social adequacy to a higher level. In the United States the original 1935 old age insurance law, by relating benefits to total wages and postponing the effective date of benefit payments to 1942, stressed equity considerations. The 1939 and 1950 amendments strengthened the "social adequacy" elements at the expense of "equity" considerations and also strengthened and preserved the wage-related character of the program.

In both Denmark and Sweden proposals for changing their programs to a wage-related benefit program have been considered. These proposals are still under consideration. In Great Britain the government has made such a proposal.

Undoubtedly, tradition and the difficulties of changing over to a new approach have played some part in the discussions in Denmark and Sweden. On the other hand, there is strong pressure from labor groups in Great Britain and Sweden for a change to a wage-related program. It may be noted that the U.S.S.R., Czechoslovakia, Poland, and Yugoslavia have wage-related programs and that the recent changes in West Germany are designed to strengthen and retain a wage-related system in the face of inflationary tendencies and to meet the increases in wages, productivity, and the increasing level of living.

No single, simple conclusion can be drawn from the experience in western Europe as to the changing emphasis on "equity" and "social adequacy." Too many other factors come into play to make observations or decisions on only two elements in the equation. One conjecture may be tentatively drawn from the experience both of western Europe and of the United States. If productivity and, hence, the general level of living continue to rise, then it will become necessary to re-examine the concept of "social adequacy" incorporated in the old age benefit program. The "minimum" concept may rise as the level of living rises for the economy as a whole. A decline in the standard of living through war, inflation, or population increases would raise still other issues. Thus the question of "social adequacy" of the benefit amount, and the scope of the program, may be a changing one which each generation in each country will have to decide for itself in relation to many variables.

D. The Uniform versus the Wage-related Benefit

A major issue which has resulted in basic differences in the way old age programs have operated in various European countries is whether the old age benefit should be uniform or wage-related. Expressed in general terms, this may be stated as the question whether the old age benefit should be the same amount for everyone or whether it should vary for each person in relation to an individual's past earnings. As will be shown, there are several important variations on both of these general approaches. However, the broad policy questions and experience of different countries will be discussed first, before indicating the modifications of each method which have developed over the years in the different systems.

Old age benefit programs developed out of a concern by society for the large number of persons who became aged without any independent source of income. Wages were low, and it was difficult, if not impossible, for most individuals to save a sufficient amount for their old age. Without some method of providing some regular income for aged persons, there would be much social and political discontent.

An old age benefit program involves, however, a matter of redistribution of income within any nation, as among old and young, the retired and the employed, and the higher-income with the lower-income receivers. Thus a major matter of economic and social policy had to be decided as to how much income was to be redistributed and how. This question thus touched on philosophical, economic, social, and humanitarian objectives.

A major factor in this situation was the decision of Denmark in 1891, and Sweden in 1913, to utilize a uniform rate for old age payments and for Great Britain in 1911 to pay disability and unemployment benefits on a uniform basis irrespective of wage levels. This same principle was embodied in the British old age insurance program of 1925 and has become a major distinguishing characteristic of the British programs for nearly 50 years. Although now under serious criticism in Great Britain by advocates of the wage-related philosophy, the Scandinavian and British approach was adopted in most of the British Commonwealth countries and has exerted a major influence on many other programs throughout the world.

The British approach of paying a uniform benefit each week was born in a period when wages were relatively low and wage differentials relatively narrow and when the objective of old age pensions was primarily to keep persons off poor relief of the Elizabethan poor-law type. Thus a uniform amount could meet this objective for a substantial proportion of persons. It was simple and understandable to large numbers of persons and relatively easy to administer in an era when business machines and mechanized procedures for handling complex administrative matters were unknown. But more basic than even these factors was the egalitarian belief which in part grew out of the socialist movement that all persons should be treated equally when in need. Groups of workmen, both in small groups in their local "friendly societies" and in their large national unions and political associations, ardently advocated "equal shares for all" as a method of sharing their scarcity. There was no general recognition of a society in which productivity would be increasing, wages would rise, the standard of living would improve, or inflation would be a major factor. These elements did not begin to play any major role in reshaping social security policy in most countries until after World War I and only became a matter of general recognition after World War II.

In an era of scarcity, low-wage levels, and the influence of a strong socialist movement, uniform benefits were rationalized as the most effective method of redistributing the available amount of income to the benefit of the lowest-income groups. The public responsibility for the aged was thus expressed in terms of achieving the maximum social result by assuring a "basic minimum subsistence" to the aged and leaving the individual free to supplement this meager amount from whatever other source he could. The program thus developed was a unique blending of socialist and conservative philosophies to the effect that the best method of carrying out public responsibility with the minimum cost and the least interference with other important objectives of society was to have a uniform benefit for all aged persons.

Several problems began to arise. If a country wished to have an insurance or pension program with benefits related not to an individual's need but as a matter of statutory right, it seemed necessary to finance a major share of the cost from payroll contributions. If there was also to be a uniform benefit, then it was only reasonable to have a uniform contribution, irrespective of earnings. In order that a uniform contribution would not be burdensome on the lowest wage-earners, it must necessarily be geared to, and limited by, the income of the low-income receivers. Hence there was a very restricted limit to the amount which could be derived from the payroll contributions. As the standard of living rose over the years, if flat-rate contributions were retained, it was necessary either to raise the uniform contributions, which would bear most heavily on the smallest earners, to raise a larger proportion of the costs from other kinds of revenues, to keep the level of old age benefits down, or to employ some combination of these three elements.

This is the dilemma of uniform benefit programs. In Great Britain serious consideration has been given to modification of their uniform benefit program. The Trades Union Congress and the British Labour party reversed a long-standing policy in 1957 by advocating building onto the uniform benefit program a supplemental wage-related program (Labour Party, 1957). The Conservative government in 1958 indorsed a system of graduated contributions and benefits, stating:

> The earlier analysis of the present position brings out strikingly the limitations of a flat-rate system. The developing needs of the old in a community enjoying rising standards of life cannot be adequately met by contributions which have to be fixed at a level all can afford to pay. The speed of the convoy is that of the slowest ship [Great Britain, Ministry of Pensions and National Insurance, 1958, p. 9].

The British government's proposal for a graduated contributions and benefit program suggested April, 1961, as a likely effective date. The change in the British program, if it takes place, is a significant change which, along with the changes made in the West German system in 1957, may have important repercussions in other European countries in the future.[1]

[1] Both Great Britain and Sweden adopted graduated benefit systems in 1959 to be superimposed on their existing flat-rate pensions.

The conflict over changing the Swedish system to a graduated program has resulted in major political differences in that country. Efforts to change the Swedish pension program resulted in the fall of the government in 1958.

The Social Democrats proposed a system of supplementary wage-related benefits in 1958 on top of the uniform basic benefits. The total benefit—basic plus supplementary—would amount to about 65 per cent of the individual's average income during his 15 best income years. The cost of the supplementary benefit was to be met entirely by the employer. The supplementary benefits would be automatically increased in relation to the price index.

An advisory referendum on supplementary pension was undertaken at a national election in 1957. The results were 46 per cent for the Social Democrat proposal described above; 35 per cent for voluntary supplementary pensions established by collective or individual measures and supported by the Conservatives, Liberals, and employers; and 15 per cent for a voluntary plan, administered by the government, and supported by the Agrarian party. Four per cent of the ballots were invalid.

The conflict in Sweden brings out the many different policy questions involved in developing a graduated program. To what extent should contributions for old age be compulsory? Who should contribute? How much? What effect will these decisions have on wages and the total economy?

The decision in 1935 in the United States to incorporate the wage-related principle in the old age insurance program was a vital one. As private pension plans spread, it becomes more difficult to change from a uniform program to a graduated one. The decision in the United States came at a time when there were relatively few private pension plans, and, hence, the policy and technical problems were not so difficult as they are now in western European countries.

E. Adjustments to Increases in the Cost of Living

A major problem for all kinds of old age programs occurs when prices increase, especially when they increase rapidly in a short period of time.

An increase in prices acts to decrease the value of fixed social security benefits. Individuals who are on fixed incomes feel the effect adversely. In order to adjust the benefit structure to rising prices, many social security programs have periodically raised the basic benefit level or added special cost-of-living supplements. In countries with flat-benefit structures, such as Great Britain and some of the Scandinavian countries, the increase in the benefit did not change the basic characteristics of the system. In those systems where benefits are related to wage level and length of contribution, the minimum benefits were increased (Italy and Belgium). This tends to modify the basic philosophy of the wage-related system by limiting the spread in benefits and thus tending toward the flat-rate systems.

Inflation causes serious problems for all types of systems whether they are insurance, pensions, assistance, or some combination of these, or whether they are related to wages or need or are uniform. The most important factor, of course, is that it injects new financial considerations into the program at a time when the government is having other financial difficulties. Inflation may result in a temporary or permanent increase in income to the old age system which collects contributions in relation to wages, employment, or income. This increase in income may be used, in part, as a supporting argument by those groups appealing for an increase in benefits. Where the system has some reserves, the existence of such reserves may be used by some persons as another argument for such an increase. But any increase in benefits necessitates considering long-run costs and financing methods to meet such costs.

The net effect of these and other factors

is to delay government action so that there is a lag in adjusting benefit payments to the rise in the cost of living. To overcome this, some countries, such as Denmark, Iceland, and the Netherlands, introduced automatic adjustments in the benefits to the cost of living. Despite the obvious advantages of this approach to the beneficiary, it has not received universal acceptance because of other considerations.

F. Adjustments to Changing Wage Levels and Productivity

In considering recent proposals and changes in old age benefit levels, two types of adjustments must be clearly distinquished. First is the adjustment to changes in prices. This is usually an adjustment to changes in the cost of living. Second is the adjustment to changes in wage levels. This is usually an adjustment to changes occurring both in the price level and in the productivity of the economy. These two adjustments both can be incorporated into the same program or can be separated.

Reference has already been made to countries which have incorporated a cost-of-living adjustment in their benefit structure. Despite inflation, it is significant that only a limited number of countries have included such an automatic adjustment in their laws, preferring an *ad hoc* arrangement for determining the necessary benefit and financial changes necessary as conditions warrant and by the normal processes of parliamentary debate.

The adjustment to changing wage and productivity levels is of recent origin. As best as can be determined, the idea of such an adjustment first was proposed in Sweden (Sweden, Pension Committee, 1950). Although the proposal was not accepted in Sweden, it was adopted by Germany in 1957 and has been included in the British Labour party's proposal of 1957.

Actually, the mathematical basis for such an adjustment is not complex in principle. The earnings of each individual are related to the average earnings of all persons each year. Then these indexes are averaged over a person's entire lifetime, so that his relative rank in relation to all persons would be determined. The level of earnings at the time the individual claims his benefit, along with the number of his years of coverage, would determine the individual's monetary amount of benefit. Adjustments after retirement would also be made on the basis of changes in earnings levels.

The system in the Federal Republic of Germany was basically modified in 1957. One of the more important changes made was the introduction of an automatic adjustment to reflect changes in past wage levels. This very much paralleled the proposal that had been considered in Sweden, except that the German basis goes much further because it relates not merely to future contributory coverage but also to the very extensive coverage that has existed for many decades in the past. In fact, the German system has been in operation for so many years that the working lifetime of virtually all retired persons in the population has been within the period when contribution records were maintained.

For those retiring in the future under the German system, the contribution record of all past years will be adjusted on the relative basis previously described. The benefit will then be determined from the years of coverage, the relative rank of the individual's earnings, and the current average wage at time of retirement. The current average wage is computed as the average of the first three of the four years preceding the year of retirement. Those currently retired had their benefits adjusted by a conversion table, after adoption of the law, so as to yield approximately the same result as though individual recomputation on the same basis as for future retirants had been made. There had been considerable debate as to whether benefits in force should be automatically, and more or less continually, adjusted in the future in case of further inflation and, also, if this were done, whether the adjustment should be on the basis of changes in price level or on the basis of changes in earnings level. The latter basis, it is to be recognized, would usually produce a greater increase, since wages tend to keep pace with inflation and further rise with improved productivity even if there were not continued inflation. The final law, however, does not contain any provisions for automatic adjustment of benefits in force but provides only for study of the system's financial position and of trends in productivity and earnings. Based upon recommendations made by an expert advisory council, the German Parliament increased benefits effective January 1, 1959, on the basis of employment and productivity gains since 1957 (U.S. Department of Health, Education, and Welfare, 1959).

The Netherlands has also adopted an automatic adjustment feature in its universal old age pension plan that was established in 1956 to replace a temporary plan that had been adopted shortly after the war. Since this program provides flat benefits, it is relatively easy, at appropriate intervals, to apply changes in the cost-of-living index to the benefit rate. In actuality, between the time that the legislation was enacted and payment of the first benefits, the cost of living changed sufficiently to result in a higher rate of benefit than had originally been anticipated. The financing of the plan is achieved through a tax on wages and earnings, and this is geared in with inflationary conditions, since the maximum taxable limit is similarly adjusted for changes in the cost of living.

Denmark, too, has adopted a plan involving a minimum pension payable irrespective of income or means, which is to be adjusted for changes in the cost-of-living index, just as is the so-called national pension which depends on the income of the individual. A somewhat related development in Denmark is the new provision for inflation-proof annuity contracts purchasable from insurance companies or banks. These are designed to supplement the social security benefits and so are available in only limited amounts. The premium rate is to be adjusted for changes in the cost-of-living index, and likewise the eventual annuity payments are so adjusted. Obviously, if there is a rise in the cost of living, part of the higher annuity payable will be met by the increased premiums paid. The remaining portion of the annuity, including any adjustments after entering on receipt of annuity, will come from the government. Of course, in no event will the annuity be less than that purchasable from the premiums paid.

A number of other countries that have been plagued by inflation are apparently thinking of installing some automatic built in device in their social security system to compensate for this factor. For instance, in Great Britain, the Labour party's proposal is for a general contributory plan to be added on top of the existing flat-benefit system. In the contributory portion the same general basis of automatically allowing for changes in the earnings level would be incorporated as prevails in the German plan and in the Swedish proposals.

An alternative, and somewhat more traditional, approach to the problem of offsetting inflation in the case of an earnings-related benefit program is to base the pension on the average salary during the last few years (5 or 10 years) before retirement. This approach is used by many private pension plans in the United States. This procedure may be subject to greater chances of unusual results because of ignoring most of the individual's working history. It also does nothing about changes in economic conditions following retirement. Nonetheless, perhaps because of its greater simplicity, it is being widely adopted or considered by many countries.

Ad hoc methods still remain popular in many countries. Thus, in the United States, benefits were increased on the average $77\frac{1}{2}$ per cent in 1950, by approximately 15 per cent in 1952, by about 12 per cent in 1954, and by 7 per cent in 1958. In Belgium, France, and Italy benefits have been raised by increasing the value of earnings or contributions made in early years when wages were less. *Ad hoc* methods have the advantage of being adaptable to the situation. For instance, when a certain degree of inflation occurs and some changes are possible in part due to the prospects of increased income, the legislators can take a new look at both the benefits and the financing of the system. It can then be decided by the elected representatives of the people whether benefits should be adjusted in amount or whether the available money should be used to finance new types of benefits. This is of special importance when the system is still in the process of development. From a purely political standpoint, under *ad hoc* arrangements, the legislators or administration at the time would get the credit for any changes—rather than those who originally developed the cost-of-living or other economic indexes. This consideration might be less significant in parliamentary forms of government where the legislative and executive branches are under the same control.

III. RETIREMENT CONDITIONS

Among the important conditions affecting an old age program are: (1) the age or ages at which benefits are payable to aged persons; (2) whether receipt of benefits is subject to a test of retirement, and, if so, what kind of test; (3) whether benefits are increased for delayed retirement, and, if so, by how much; and (4) whether benefits are reduced for early retirement, and, if so, by how much. These conditions affect the social adequacy of the benefits payable, the cost of the program, and other provisions of the plan. Experience of European countries with these provisions is discussed in the following pages.

A. Retirement Age

Retirement ages vary substantially among the twenty-eight European old age programs. A spread of 20 years exists between the highest and lowest retirement ages provided under general programs in Europe. The spread is 15 years for men and 20 years for women.

In ten countries the age is the same for men and women. A majority of the countries, totaling eighteen, provide a differential age for men and women. In Europe the differentials for women, where they exist, are usually 5 years below that for men in all but two countries.

Table 1 indicates that the highest retirement age is 70 and that the lowest is 50 for women and 55 for men. The infor-

TABLE 1*

PENSIONABLE AGES FOR NORMAL BENEFIT UNDER GENERAL OLD AGE PROGRAMS IN EUROPE, BY COUNTRY, 1958

Country	Men	Women
Albania	60	55
Austria	65	60
Belgium	65	60
Bulgaria	60	55
Czechoslovakia	60	55
Denmark†	65–67	60–62
Finland‡	65	65–63
France	60	60
Germany—East	65	60
Germany—West	65	60
Great Britain	65	60
Greece	65	60
Hungary	60	55
Iceland	67	67
Ireland	70	70
Italy	60	55
Luxembourg	65	65
Netherlands	65	65
Norway	70	70
Poland	65	60
Portugal	65	65
Rumania	60	55
Spain	65	65
Sweden	67	67
Switzerland§	65	63–60
Turkey	60	60
U.S.S.R.	60	55
Yugoslavia	55	50

* Source: Compiled from the following: *Social Security Programs throughout the World, 1958* (Washington, D.C.: U.S. Social Security Administration, Division of Program Research, 1958); D.S. Gerig, "Pensionable Age under Old-Age Pension Schemes," *International Labour Review*, Vol. **72** (October, 1955).

† For the minimum pension in Denmark, the age is 67 with no contributions or income test. For the national pension and supplements (subject to income test), the age is 65 for men and married women and 60 for single women. According to a law passed in 1956, these age limits will be increased by 1 year from April 1, 1959, and by 1 additional year from April 1, 1961, so that the age limits will be 67 and 62, respectively. The law contains an exemption clause whereby the age limit may be reduced to 60 years when warranted by special conditions.

‡ Assistance portion of the benefit payable to women at age 63.

§ Women workers eligible at age 63; wives at age 60.

mation from this table may be summarized as follows:

Four countries have a retirement age of more than 65 years for both men and women: two countries (Ireland and Norway) specify age 70 for all persons, and two (Iceland and Sweden) specify age 67 for all persons.

Four countries (Luxembourg, the Netherlands, Portugal, and Spain) have a uniform age of 65 years for both men and women. Thus a standard age of 65 for both men and women, which was in effect in the United States during the years 1935–56, is not the most typical in Europe at the present time.

A dual pensionable age of 65 for men and 60 for women is prescribed in eight countries (Austria, Belgium, Denmark, East Germany, West Germany, Great Britain, Greece, and Poland).

Two countries with age 65 for men have differential ages for women. One country (Finland) has 65 for men, and the assistance portion may be paid at age 63 for women. In Switzerland women workers become eligible at age 63; if the wife is age 60, the couple's pension is payable. No country in Europe (and no other in the world) has the 65 for men and 62 for women (full benefits for widows and an actuarially reduced benefit for other women) which is now in effect in the United States.

In the ten remaining countries, a uniform age of 60 is provided in two (France and Turkey); in seven (Albania, Bulgaria, Czechoslovakia, Hungary, Italy, Rumania, and Russia) a dual pensionable age of 60 for men and 55 for women is specified; and one (Yugoslavia) has 55 for men and 50 for women. The information classified separately for age by sex for the twenty-eight European countries, as of 1958, is shown in Table 2. Thus the "median" pensionable age may be said to be 65 for men and 60 for women.

In the course of many years of experience, some countries have lowered their pensionable ages, and a few others have increased them. While it is not possible to generalize about whether there currently is a definite trend upward or downward, it is clear that there has been a review of the pensionable age in many countries, and it appears that this is likely to spread to other countries.

The four countries with an age requirement above 65 have not altered it since it was first adopted: Ireland has maintained age 70 since 1908; Norway, age 70 since 1923; Iceland, age 67 since 1909; and Sweden, age 67 since 1913. An Irish White Paper in 1949 proposed lowering the age

TABLE 2*

PENSIONABLE AGE FOR NORMAL BENEFIT UNDER GENERAL OLD AGE PROGRAMS IN EUROPE SUMMARIZED BY AGE AND SEX, 1958

Retirement Age	Men	Women
70.........	2	2
67.........	2	2
65.........	14	4
63.........	....	1
60.........	9	11
55.........	1	7
50.........	....	1

* Source: Derived from Table 1. The ages tabulated for women were Denmark, 60; Finland, 63; and Switzerland, 60.

to 65 for men and 60 for women as part of introducing a contributory plan. This was not adopted in the new Irish Act of 1952, although the legislation did provide that insured workers who had paid 156 weekly contributions may receive unemployment benefits so long as they are unemployed, without limit as to duration, between the ages of 65 and 70. Sweden has studied, on various occasions, the possibility of reducing its 67 year age limit but has decided against it because of the cost involved as a result of its unusually large aged population.

Great Britain began with a uniform age limit of 70 in 1908 in its non-contributory program and reduced the age to 65 when contributory insurance was introduced in

1925. In 1940 the age for women was reduced to 60. In 1954 an advisory committee (the Phillips Report) recommended
(with the two trade unionists dissenting)
that the pension age should be raised from
65 to 68 for men and from 60 to 63 for
women. It was proposed that legislation
should provide for an increase of 1 year
in a period of not less than 5 years, with
further increases of a year at a time at
later intervals. No action was taken by the
government on this recommendation (Great
Britain, Phillips Committee, 1954).

In 1957 the British Labour party and
the Trades Union Congress advocated a
basic change in the British flat-rate contributions and benefit program. A wage-
related program was proposed. No modification was recommended in the age of
65 for men. Because women draw a flat-
rate pension at age 60, no change was suggested for this payment; but, to receive
the full basic National Superannuation pension, age 65 was proposed for women also
(British Labour Party, 1957).

The original German law of 1889 provided pensions only after age 70. The German program was initially principally an
invalidity insurance plan, and its old age
provisions were essentially supplemental in
character. Old age pensions were smaller
than invalidity pensions and were payable
only to persons over 70 who could not
prove that they were invalids. There was
much pressure to lower the age from the
start, but the cost seemed too great. The
government later found that its actuarial
estimates considerably overstated costs,
and, in 1916, it reduced the age to 65,
bringing it in line with the retirement age
fixed in 1911 in a separate program for
salaried employees.

After World War II, East Germany
adopted a sex differential of 65 for men
and 60 for women. In 1957 West Germany
adopted its new "dynamic pension" program and, along with many other changes,
provided that a woman may draw her pension at age 60 if she has worked in covered employment for at least 10 of the 20
years prior to retirement. A provision
formerly applicable only to salaried employees was also extended to wage-earners;
at age 60 an insured person becomes entitled to a pension if he has been unemployed a full year.

The Danish experience differs from that
of both Great Britain and Germany. Danish non-contributory pensions began in
1891 with a uniform pensionable age of
60. In 1922 the age for men was raised to
65, although discretion was given to pay
pensions to men at age 60 in exceptional
cases where failing health or other special
circumstances warranted. In 1948 the Danish government set up a special advisory
commission to report on whether to replace the non-contributory program with
a pension plan. The commission reported
in 1955 and, while recommending against
establishment of an insurance plan, did
recommend that the pension age be increased to 66 for men and 61 for women.
They proposed that the age be increased
from 65 for men and 60 for women in two
step-ups of $\frac{1}{2}$-year (that is, to $65\frac{1}{2}$ and
$60\frac{1}{2}$, and to 66 and 61) in 2-year intervals.
In the important revisions of 1956, a minimum pension was established for which age
67 is required. No minimum contributions
and no income test are required for this.
For the national pension and supplements
(both subject to an income test) the age,
beginning in April, 1961, will be 67 for
men and 62 for women. The ages will be
66 and 61, respectively, from April, 1959,
to March, 1961.

Denmark is thus the only European
country (and one of only three or four
countries in the world) which has raised
its pension age since it first established an
old age program. Whereas in the original
law of 1891 the age was 60 for both men
and women, by 1961 the age is scheduled
to be 67 for men and 62 for women.

B. Retirement Test

Several European countries, like the
United States, provide for payment of the

old age benefit only upon "retirement" from gainful work. Other countries provide for payment of a "pension" upon attainment of pensionable age, irrespective of retirement. It should be kept in mind that the term "pension" is not used in either the "insurance" or the "assistance" programs in the United States. This was a deliberate attempt by those who formulated the original Social Security Act to sharply distinguish these programs from the European models as well as from veterans' "pensions" in the United States which are paid entirely out of general federal revenues.

In comparing plans which have retirement provisions with those which do not, the level of benefits, the retirement age, and the type of program (whether insurance or assistance) must be considered, in addition to wage and employment conditions in the country. It is not possible, therefore, to evaluate by itself the effect of a retirement test on the old age program or the economy.

In Great Britain the question of the retirement test has been discussed and debated in recent years. The contributory pension plan was introduced in 1925, and, until the 1946 law took effect, insured persons received their old age benefit when they reached pensionable age, irrespective of whether they were working or not. The old age benefit was then a relatively small uniform amount. In 1946, based upon the recommendations of the Beveridge Report, pension payments were made conditional on retirement from work, for the 5 years between ages 65 and 70 for men and 60 to 65 for women, and provision was made for increasing the pension by adding delayed retirement credits for persons continuing to work after reaching the minimum pensionable age. At age 70 for men, and 65 for women, the benefits are paid irrespective of retirement.

Beveridge analyzed the problem as he saw it in 1942 as follows:

Pensions adequate for subsistence without other means should be given only to people who, after reaching a minimum age for retirement, have in fact retired from work. To give a full subsistence income to every citizen on his or her reaching the age of 65 or 60 would impose an unjustifiable and harmful burden on all citizens below that age.

Making receipt of pensions conditional on retirement is not intended to encourage or hasten retirement. . . . To attempt to force people to retire before their powers and desire for work fail, and to compel them by a rise in the minimum age of pensions to struggle on after their powers have failed, are two errors and injustices which should be avoided by any system of social insurance designed to increase human happiness [pars. 244–45].

The British retirement test differs in a number of important respects from that of the United States. In the first place, the British attempt to enforce bona fide retirement by requiring the individual to show he has retired from regular employment. Those persons who intend to do some work after retirement are treated as retired if the work is only occasional, inconsiderable in extent, or otherwise not inconsistent with retirement. Rather elaborate and technical rules have been established to define these terms. An independent adjudicating authority decides individual cases—initially by an insurance officer—with a right to appeal to a local tribunal and ultimately to the national insurance commissioner.

Discussion on the retirement test in Great Britain now centers around its application in any national superannuation plan with wage-related contributions and benefits. It is estimated that abolition of a retirement test in such a plan would increase the cost about three-quarters of 1 per cent of payroll. In general, the same questions of financial costs and social priorities and needs which have been the decisive elements in retaining the retirement test in the United States are being considered in Great Britain.

Conditions of employment and related economic and social factors are so different in the various European countries, and the provisions of the old age programs so diverse, that it is not possible to summarize here or to generalize about the retirement test or its absence from European programs. Almost every variety of provision can be found among the European countries.

C. Delayed Retirement Credits

Available information indicates that in 1958 eleven European countries had some type of provision which increases the old age benefit when the beneficiary delays his retirement past the normal or minimum pensionable age. These countries are Bulgaria, Czechoslovakia, Denmark, Finland, France, Great Britain, Iceland, Italy, Turkey, the U.S.S.R., and Yugoslavia.

Finland, Iceland, and Great Britain are illustrations where the uniform benefit is increased. France, Italy, and Turkey have wage-related systems in which the benefit is increased for delayed retirement. The rate of increase in the uniform benefit programs is as high as 12.5 per cent of the benefit for each year of delay in Finland (for the basic pension), 7.5 per cent in Iceland, and 6 per cent in Great Britain. In the wage-related programs the increase is 4 per cent of wages in France and 1 per cent of wages in Turkey. In France, for instance, the benefit attainable at age 60 increases from 20 per cent of wages at age 60 to a maximum of 40 per cent of wages at age 65.

A delayed-retirement credit provision is usually justified on the grounds that it encourages employment, reduces the cost of retirement to the program or to the nation, or is equitable to the contributor or beneficiary.

Experience in Great Britain and New Zealand seems to indicate that the financial inducement involved in a delayed-retirement credit does not have any appreciable effect on postponing retirement. Failing health or strength usually are the determining factors in early retirement, and compulsory retirement in a firm usually determines the particular retirement age for many persons. It is not possible to evaluate the psychological effect which delayed-retirement provisions have on encouraging older persons to work. The level of benefits and many other factors undoubtedly play a significant role.

If the delayed-retirement credit is made equal to the actuarial saving due to the postponement of benefits, there is, of course, no net saving to the old age program. Thus, in the United States, it is estimated by Robert J. Myers, the chief actuary of the Social Security Administration, that a delayed-retirement credit of about 8–10 per cent of the benefit for each year of postponement would be equivalent to the actuarial saving. But this would mean an increase in cost to the program of over 1 per cent of payroll, which is equivalent to close to $2 billion annually.

There are some who advocate repeal of the retirement test, or introduction of a delayed-retirement credit, on the grounds it would benefit the nation and the individual to continue working. This involves an analysis of both general economic conditions and the implications of employment for older persons in a work-centered society. It should be noted that this argument tends to be advanced vigorously when economic conditions are good and is of less currency in a period when economic conditions are adverse or are declining.

The argument that a delayed-retirement credit is necessary to assure "equity" to the contributor or beneficiary may be more frequently heard when the old age program is financed with payroll or earmarked taxes on the contributor. However, the relevance of the argument may depend upon other factors in the financial and benefit structure, such as whether the benefit payable to the individual already is in excess of the value of his own contributions and the "adequacy" of the benefits. Those who oppose the delayed-retirement credit, however, point out that, from an adequacy standpoint, the amount needed by a beneficiary does not depend upon the age of retirement.

In Britain the delayed-retirement credit was subject to review by an advisory committee in 1956 (Great Britain, National Insurance Advisory Committee, 1956). Current data on its operation are reported by the Ministry of Pensions and National Insurance in its annual reports. In general, it may be noted that the provision has its supporters and opponents. There is a general recognition of the practical difficulty involved in eliminating it, even by those who wish to use the savings for other improvements in the old age program which have a higher social priority. Thus, as in many other provisions in an old age benefit program, social philosophy and costs, incentives and psychology, merge together in the consideration of alternatives, and it becomes difficult to make a decision on the basis of one factor alone.

D. A Flexible Retirement Program

Some old age benefit programs provide that benefits may be paid to an individual prior to his normal retirement age if he takes a reduction in his benefit. Others provide, as we have seen, for the increase in the benefit if the individual postpones retirement after the normal retirement age. Practically every old age benefit program now provides for the payment of benefits to persons disabled prior to the normal retirement age.

These three provisions may be said to produce a condition of flexibility in a retirement program. Costs, social philosophy, and administrative feasibility appear to influence the decision as to such conditions.

E. Disability Insurance

One of the areas in which European experience and materials have made an important contribution to social security in the United States is with respect to the concepts in the formulation of disability insurance and the methods of administering it.

Disability payments, as part of a social insurance program, developed earlier and more extensively in Europe than in the United States. While in the United States some experience was derived from workmen's compensation, occupational pension and disability plans, and veterans' disability programs, in the formulation of a general disability insurance program, definitions and administrative experience in the disability provisions of social insurance were readily transferable from Europe to the United States. Although there are important exceptions to a categorical statement, the disability insurance provisions of the social security program and the comparable major provisions of European programs perhaps are closer, on the whole, in their principles, concepts, and administration than with respect to old age programs, which are more varied.

A basic document on disability insurance in the United States, *Disability among Gainfully Occupied Persons* published by the Social Security Board in 1945, relied heavily on European experience. A comparative analysis of the permanent disability insurance provisions in six selected European countries (Czechoslovakia, France, Germany, Great Britain, Italy, and Sweden) was tabulated for 1939.

The relevance of European experience was a major factor in the controversy over whether disability insurance should be added to the social security system. The minority view (two members) of the Advisory Council on Social Security to the Senate Committee on Finance in 1948, which opposed disability insurance as part of the social security program, stated:

It is sometimes claimed that other countries have blazed the way for the successful inclusion of total disability in a governmental contributory social insurance program. This type of coverage originated in central Europe. To cite Germany and Austria as examples which we should now emulate will not carry conviction in the United States. [U.S. Congress, 1949, p. 89].

IV. Attitudes toward Pension Provisions

As indicated previously, the pensionable age and level of benefits varies widely among European countries. To what extent this accurately reflects the attitudes of persons in different countries is not known.

In 1958, "World Poll," conducted by International Research Associates, asked persons in several countries concerning their views on two issues affecting older persons. The first question dealt with "the right age for retirement for a man." The replies showed that the average retirement

TABLE 3

OPINIONS ON ADEQUACY OF BENEFIT LEVELS IN OLD AGE PROGRAMS IN SEVEN COUNTRIES, 1958*
(Per Cent)

Country	Too High	Too Low	About Right	Don't Know	Total
Great Britain.	1	71	26	2	100
Denmark....	3	47	46	4	100
Sweden......	5	47	46	2	100
Germany....	2	48	37	13	100
Netherlands..	1	64	30	5	100
Italy........	1	76	16	7	100
France.......	†	87	6	7	100

* Source: *New York Herald Tribune*, October 11–12, 1958.
† Less than 0.5 per cent.

age preferred in the six European countries ranged from 66.3 years in Great Britain and Denmark to 57.1 years in France. In Sweden the average was 64.2 years; Germany, 63.4; the Netherlands, 62.5; and Italy, 60.8.

Another question asked was: "From what you know about the system of government old age benefits in your country, do you feel that these benefits are too high, too low, or about right?" The results of the poll on this question are shown in Table 3.

Several observations may be made from these results. In the northern European countries there is reasonably good agreement that the appropriate age for a man to retire is about 65. In the southern European countries (Italy and France) the appropriate age is lower. These results probably stem in part from the fact that the current age for pensions corresponds closely with the attitudes expressed. Current practice apparently influences attitudes as well as vice versa.

It also appears that practically no one in any of the countries polled considers payments to the aged too high. While a substantial proportion think the level of payments is about right, there is a larger proportion in every country who believe payments are too low.

V. Economic and Financial Aspects

The economic and financial aspects of providing income to aged persons raises many large and controversial issues. Illustrations can be taken from the European experience to document any of a number of conflicting positions which are recurrently debated. Advocates and opponents of specific policies in the United States have frequently quoted European experience in their behalf—both "successful" and "unsuccessful" experience.

Are payments to the aged a "burden" on the economy? Are reserves necessary or desirable in old age insurance? Are private pension plans desirable? Who should bear the costs of pensions? What effect do pension programs have on investments, incentives, and the general progress of the economy? These are some of the basic questions which are common to all countries with old age programs.

A. Costs of Old Age Security

Over the course of many years there has been widespread interest in the costs and the so-called "burden" of providing for the aged. A number of financial studies have been made on the expenditures for social security or for social services and for public expenditures for the aged. All these studies have many deficiencies, although they can be used for limited, specific purposes. However, when attempting to make international comparisons, it is necessary to have the total income and expenditures (public and private) on behalf of the aged, since there are different divisions of public and private responsibility for the aged in different countries. For instance, the growth of private retirement plans, in several countries, makes any analysis limited to public expenditures of very limited use. Moreover, the question of including or excluding disability, veterans', and public employee programs (and excluding survivors' benefits) makes international comparisons very difficult.

Only two studies are known which bring together all available expenditure data for the aged. Miss Lenore Epstein has published some general estimates for the United States for 1951. Brian Abel-Smith has made estimates for the United Kingdom for 1954. These estimates are of interest in showing the kinds of data which are necessary if more reliable international comparisons are to be made in the future.

The costs of a particular old age plan depend upon the level and scope of benefits and the maturity of the program. In most cases, as old age benefit programs mature, the costs increase. Thus a comparison of plans in different countries, which are in different stages of development, is of limited value.

Although the old age insurance system in the United States is 25 years old, it is still in the early stages of development. Present-day costs are below those which will eventually evolve as the program matures and the number of beneficiaries increase. Costs may also increase as the level and scope of benefits change, although relative costs may be stabilized or decline if the gross national product continues to increase.

The long-run cost of the Old-Age, Survivors, and Disability Insurance system in the United States was estimated in 1958 to cost about 8¾ per cent of payroll on a "level-premium" intermediate cost basis. This was based upon cost estimates issued in 1958 for the law as last amended in 1958 (Myers, 1958*b*).

Another difficulty involved in making comparisons of the costs of European plans is that frequently financing of old age is tied together with other social security programs in a co-ordinated financing arrangement. Finally, in countries with reserves, interest earnings may yield a substantial income.

These factors should also be kept in mind whenever comparisons are made. Too frequently, cost comparisons between European and United States programs have been made without due regard to these limitations and differences.

Obviously, old age programs cost money. And different countries have different ideas as to how these funds can best be raised. The concepts of equity and adequacy of financing and benefits vary with different countries. There is no single formula to appraise these differences or developments. Despite the material produced in recent years on the financing of old age programs in various countries, it is impossible, as yet, to make a valid comparison of different programs in different stages of evolution. Much more technical work needs to be done to make some progress in this area.

B. Sources of Funds

Policy decisions with respect to financing old age benefits have had an important bearing on policies with respect to the type and adequacy of benefits provided. Decisions as to benefits and contributions are usually tied together.

A number of the old age benefit programs in Europe are financed on a tripartite basis, that is, with contributions from employers, employees, and the government. The general programs in Austria, Belgium, Germany, Great Britain, Italy, Switzerland, and some of the smaller countries follow the "classical" tripartite financing basis. In this respect the program in the United States differs from these programs in Europe.

The European programs were originally enacted as a part of the political and social movement, at the turn of the century, to

overcome the poverty which existed. The
low wages of many persons made it difficult
to assess the full cost on employers and
employees. Hence governmental contributions were necessary to inaugurate the systems.

In addition, it was not possible to pay
full benefits to older persons who had not
contributed for their entire working lifetime, unless the employer or the government made up the deficit. Hence a governmental subsidy was adopted to mitigate the
financial impact on the employer and the
employee of the so-called "accrued liability" for past service on which no contributions had been collected.

The system in the United States is not
only self-supporting from employer and
employee contributions (plus the interest
earnings from the Trust Fund), without
any general government subsidy, but it also
provides for equal contributions from employers and employees.

In Albania, Bulgaria, Czechoslovakia,
Poland, Rumania, Yugoslavia, and the
U.S.S.R., no employee contributions are
payable. These programs all have been
modeled after those in the U.S.S.R. In
Hungary there is an employee contribution
for old age pensions—as distinct from invalidity and survivors' insurance. There are
no payroll contributions in Ireland, since
old age payments are on an assistance
basis only.

In countries where both employers and
employees contribute, their respective contributions are not always equal. In a number of countries the employers' contributions amount to a larger proportion than
those of the insured individual. This is the
case in France, Greece, Italy, Portugal,
and Turkey. In one country, Iceland, the
individual pays a larger share of the contribution than the employer—in fact, more
than double the latter.

There are several other varieties of financial arrangements. In a few countries
the financing is primarily through subsidies, or earmarked income taxes. This is
the case in Denmark, Finland, and Sweden. In Greece, Portugal, and Turkey, and
in some of the other European countries,
there is no subsidy from public sources.
France pays pensioners with low incomes a
special subsidy financed by earmarked
taxes. In Ireland the total cost is met from
governmental funds. In the United States,
while there is no subsidy from public
sources to the insurance program, the federal government makes a substantial financial contribution to the states for old age
assistance.

C. Private Pension Plans

Private pension plans have existed in
countries like Denmark, Great Britain,
Norway, Sweden, and Switzerland for more
than 50 years. Undoubtedly, there are private pension plans in other European countries, but no comprehensive report for all
European countries on this aspect appears
to have been made. Existing information
relates to programs in Denmark, Norway,
Sweden, and Switzerland as of 1952 and to
Australia and New Zealand as of 1951
(Anonymous, 1953). A recent survey by
the Government Actuary (1958) in Great
Britain presents information on British developments.

In general, the same policy questions
arising out of the existence of private pension plans appear to exist in European
countries as in the United States. The lack
in many plans of "vesting provisions"
(preserving the accrued rights of employees who quit), which tends to inhibit mobility of labor, has raised serious questions as
to the desirability of having "portable pensions" in Great Britain. Likewise, the existence and rapid growth of private plans
have stimulated vigorous opposition to increases in the benefit level, as proposed in
the recent plan of the British Labour party
for the governmental system.

Another important policy question has
been whether private plans which have benefits equal to, or better than, that required
by a governmental plan should be permitted to be exempt from or to "contract out"

of the general public system. This issue was current in Great Britain in 1957–58, where, interestingly enough, both the Labour party and the conservative government are recommending such a policy with respect to the graduated wage-related benefits above the basic minimum (50s.). This same policy was urged in 1935 in the United States by some insurance companies but, after extended discussion, was dropped by Congress and its insurance-company sponsors. Actually, such a proposal was adopted by the United States Senate (the "Clark Amendment") but was not incorporated in the final Social Security Act of 1935. Insurance companies in the United States have not favored "contracting out" in the old age benefit program since 1935 (Clark, 1959).

In general, it may be said that the sponsors of private pension plans in Great Britain and the United States tend to favor an old age benefit limited to provision for "basic needs" in retirement. On the other hand, because private pension plans tend to cover the higher income-earners and do not cover all employed persons or the self-employed, there is still pressure for improving the adequacy of the benefits for the public system for those not covered by private plans. Hence the conflict between the advocates of the two types of plans persists. The controversy tends to place employers and insurance companies on one side of the argument and the labor unions on the other side. The actuarial, technical, and policy problems thus tend to be transferred into the political arena because of the basic ideological differences as to the role of private and public responsibilities for providing income to the aged.

VI. Social Security Provisions and Rehabilitation of Older Persons

One of the significant developments in recent years in both Europe and the United States is the development of rehabilitation programs and their relationship to social insurance and social assistance programs. In the United States, rehabilitation measures have been developed in relation to workmen's compensation, disability insurance, and public assistance. To some extent, rehabilitation has been applied to older workers, but this has been, primarily, where the individual is physically disabled and has potentialities for being vocationally rehabilitated.

Existing legislation in the United States, as in Europe, appears to encourage closer working relationships among income-maintenance programs, health services, and vocational rehabilitation. In a number of countries with comprehensive social security programs which include health benefits, the vocational rehabilitation service is part of the over-all program or closely integrated, financially or administratively, with the social security system.

This problem of the extent to which vocational rehabilitation should be tied into the existing social security system presents many controversial issues. Should the rehabilitation service be tied to the administration of health, education, welfare, labor, the employment service, and pensions, or should it be independent? Should it be financed from social insurance contributions, general revenues, or both? Should rehabilitation have both a vocational and a social objective, and, if so, should they be administered together or separately?

These kinds of issues and problems are highlighted in the United States by the 1954 vocational rehabilitation amendments and the 1956 disability insurance and public assistance amendments and other proposals being considered. While the Office of Vocational Rehabilitation, at the federal level, is in the Department of Health, Education, and Welfare, along with medical care, education, and welfare services, at the state level it is tied in primarily with state departments of education. This is the result of the historical evolution of rehabilitation services growing out of the World War I interest in vocational education and retraining of veterans. The existing administrative relationship is distinctly an American phenomenon and differs sharply from the European experience.

Vocational training of handicapped persons was initiated in Europe and the United States before modern medical rehabilitation began to develop. The inadequacy of measures to eliminate or reduce the disability before the provision of vocational services frequently led to "training around the disability." Expensive and time-consuming vocational training was given handicapped persons who either were unable because of their disability to take full advantage of the training or who would not have needed it had medical rehabilitation and selective placement been available. This emphasis on vocational training resulted in many countries in a limited program that was not properly balanced with respect to the wide variety of services needed in an effective rehabilitation plan. The medical and vocational programs were frequently run as separate services with very limited co-ordination. The problem of administrative location, financing, and organizational relationships thus becomes part of larger issues dealing with the philosophy, orientation, and scope of rehabilitation services generally.

The current concept of rehabilitation as a process aimed at maximum adjustment of the handicapped, from the point of view of his total needs as an individual, has helped to bring the various services into closer co-operation in many countries. Vocational rehabilitation is no longer considered a separate service concerned only with the vocational problems as such but, rather, as an integral part of a broader program of total rehabilitation. Efforts are being made in many countries to integrate the vocational services with medical, psychological, educational, economic, and social assistance in order to facilitate the development of a well-co-ordinated rehabilitation service and to avoid a piecemeal approach to the task. The various professions which in the past worked more or less in isolation are thus linked up to make for teamwork in

the solution of the various problems caused by the disability. These developments have been instrumental in promoting vocational rehabilitation programs in which services are provided as part of a continuous process, eliminating, or at least reducing, harmful time lags between medical rehabilitation, vocational guidance, training, and placement. International standards adopted by the International Labour Organization in 1955 have encouraged developments along these lines in many countries.

In several countries without special rehabilitation acts, social insurance laws contain provisions for assistance during rehabilitation. In Belgium there is a special vocational rehabilitation fund within the sickness and disability insurance program from which assistance for apprenticeship training, including supplies and living and travel expenses, is provided. In Sweden the National Pensions Board, which is responsible for the old age and invalidity program and, until recently, also for the health insurance system, issued instructions in 1946 to all local sickness funds to the effect that steps should be taken to provide rehabilitation services to all those cases where medical care or vocational rehabilitation was considered advisable. To bring about this procedure, co-operation among the board, its local committees, and sickness funds was stressed.

It appears that health and disability benefit programs are, increasingly, being linked more closely with rehabilitation services in Europe. The tendency in many countries to bring various social security systems, such as sickness, invalidity, and workmen's compensation programs, together into a more unified administration may facilitate this process. On the other hand, the shortage of facilities for medical and vocational evaluation of those applying for cash benefits is still a deterrent in efforts to make rehabilitation services available to all claimants. The inadequacy of existing rehabilitation facilities in most countries has also been a great obstacle in this respect.

In some countries the social security agencies have actively promoted and financed rehabilitation facilities. In France, for example, the Social Security Funds have established several rehabilitation centers and also subsidized private facilities.

In the social security laws of a number of countries, as in the United States, there are provisions to the effect that failure of the beneficiary to avail himself of rehabilitation services, when such exists, is ground for suspension of the cash benefits. In Sweden, for example, the National Pensions Law of 1946 prescribes that the disability pension may be totally or partially suspended should the insured person refuse to undergo medical care or vocational training available at public expense which would be likely to reduce or eliminate his disability. In France benefits provided by the Social Security Funds for extended sickness may be discontinued if the recipient refuses to take advantage of rehabilitation services made available to him by the funds. Provisions of a similar nature exist in several other countries, such as Belgium, Finland, Denmark, and the United Kingdom.

Similar tendencies can be noted in the United States. Some states already provide that the cost of rehabilitating injured workmen should be a cost of the workmen's compensation program. Legislation covering federal civilian employees injured on the job provides for this, as does legislation for veterans. Proposals are pending to provide for payment of rehabilitation costs of insured disabled persons from the social security system, in order to provide additional funds to expand rehabilitation services to meet pressing needs.

It should be noted that the disability insurance amendments of 1956 to the Social Security Act provide that all disabled individuals applying for a determination of disability "shall be promptly referred" to a state vocational rehabilitation agency and that any individual who "refuses without good cause to accept rehabilitation services" shall have his benefits suspended. An-

other interesting feature of the 1956 law is that an individual who is working under a vocational rehabilitation plan is still eligible for his disability insurance benefit during the first 12 months he is working under such an arrangement. The purpose of such a "sheltered" arrangement is to enable the disabled individual to obtain work experience and to permit him a period of time to adapt to his new work assignment without loss of his benefit. In addition, the Federal Vocational Rehabilitation Act of 1954 provides for co-operative relationships with agencies relating to public welfare, veterans, and the employment service, among others.

Legislation passed by Congress in 1956 provided that federal funds could be used to match state expenditures for services to needy aged, disabled, and blind individuals on public assistance to help them attain self-care. Still other proposals are pending to expand the rehabilitation services for persons who are not rehabilitable for vocational purposes.

In both Europe and the United States increased attention and emphasis is being given to rehabilitation. The exchange of ideas, experience, and personnel has speeded up during the last 10 years. Through the United Nations, a co-ordinated program has been established which was adopted in a resolution passed by the Economic and Social Council in August, 1950. Various international organizations participated in the preparation and administration of this program. A comprehensive review of international experience, trends, and developments, entitled "Rehabilitation of the Physically Handicapped," appeared in the *International Social Service Review*, March, 1957, published by the Department of Economics and Social Affairs of the United Nations. Only very little seems to have been done so far to extend rehabilitation to older persons. As experience develops, we may expect somewhat greater emphasis to be given to older persons. This will require a de-emphasis on the vocational aspects and an expansion of the social potentialities of rehabilitation. While some of the European experience on administrative relationships may not be wholly pertinent or transferable to the American scene, it appears that closer co-ordination of rehabilitation with many other types of health, education, labor, and social security institutions is a most likely development in Europe and the United States.

VII. Minimum International Standards

The wide variety of old age benefit plans in operation and their frequent modifica-

TABLE 4

Countries Ratifying Old Age, Survivors, or Disability Branches of the 1952 Convention on Minimum Standards of Social Security, as of December 31, 1957*

Country	Old Age	Survivors	Disability
Denmark...........	X	....	X
Greece.............	X	X	X
Israel...............	X	X	....
Italy...............	X	....	....
Norway.............	X	....	....
United Kingdom.....	X	X	....
West Germany......	X	X	X
Yugoslavia.........	X	X	....

* In a number of instances, a country has not ratified with respect to a particular branch of social security but has a rather complete program of social security. In some cases, this arises because of inability to meet some technicality in the standards. For sources of the documents and a summary of the convention in relation to the United States program see R. J. Myers, "Minimum Standards of Social Security," *Social Security Bulletin*, 15 (October, 1952), 3–10.

tion make it impossible to compare European programs, as a whole, with the United States program. Differences in wage levels, prices, the extent of private pension plans, and similar factors make simple comparisons impossible. Even comparisons of separable elements, such as the retirement age or the relative adequacy of benefits, cannot be made without realizing that one element taken out of context is not the entire story. The apparent liberality or illiberality of a single provision cannot be judged by itself. A low retirement age might be coupled with low benefits, while a high retirement age might be coupled with high benefits. To appraise the adequacy of a program, the whole plan would have to be taken into account in its total economic and social setting. This, obviously, is a large and almost insuperable task.

The International Labour Office has attempted not only to establish methods of comparing the adequacy of different old age programs but to set standards for determining their status. In 1952 the International Labour Conference adopted an International Convention on Minimum Standards of Social Security. The convention covers nine branches of social security. Three of the branches are old age, survivor, and disability benefits—each type of benefit being counted as one branch.

At the end of 1957 nine countries had ratified at least three of the nine branches. Eight countries had ratified the old age, five the survivors, and three the disability branch (see Table 4). Although the United States has not ratified the convention, it appears that the old age and survivors insurance (but not the disability) provisions of the Social Security Act would fully meet the requirements of the convention. The United States also would meet the requirements in unemployment insurance, and, hence, it could comply in three branches of social security and could ratify the convention if it wished. There is no present indication that the United States will ratify it. The United States has taken the position that ratification of conventions which are based on provisions of state-operated programs is not constitutionally possible.

The Minimum Standards Convention contains a number of highly technical and complex provisions, including alternatives, which are used to determine whether a country meets the minimum standards outlined in the convention. Provisions are included as to the extent of coverage, the scope of the contingency, qualifying conditions, and amount and duration of benefits. Some modifications of the general standards are permitted for underdeveloped countries, special groups of workers (such as seamen, who are excluded from the convention), federal states, the treatment of aliens, and similar matters.

The two major provisions of the Minimum Standards Convention relating to old age benefits are as follows:

1. Age 65 and retirement, although a higher age is permitted if the working ability of elderly persons is considered. In actuality, therefore, the retirement age is almost completely flexible, and the figure of 65 is merely a guide.
2. Benefits for a typical worker should be 40 per cent of earnings for a man and wife of pensionable age but could be 30 per cent if a shorter qualifying requirement is made. The United States system would have to meet the 30 per cent requirement, since it has a relatively liberal qualifying condition —a maximum of 10 years (40 quarters of coverage).

For the survivors' benefits a 5-year qualifying requirement and a benefit of 30 per cent of earnings for a widow and two children are required. The United States program more than meets this requirement.

For disability insurance benefits the requirement for benefits is 40 per cent of earnings for a man, wife, and two children if the qualifying requirement is 15 years of contributions or 30 per cent if it is 5 years. Since the United States pays disability insurance benefits only to persons age 50 or over, it does not meet the standard for ratifying this branch.

The International Labour Office has also prepared suggestions for a convention on advanced standards of social security. These, however, have not been considered by the International Labour Conference up to this time (1959).

VIII. Adequacy in Relation to Program Objectives

When Sir William (later Lord) Beveridge published his famous report *Social Insurance and Allied Services* in 1942, he advocated a cautious and conservative policy on increasing the amount of the old age pension in Great Britain, stating: "It is dangerous to be in any way lavish to old age, until adequate provision has been assured for all other vital needs such as the prevention of disease and the adequate nutrition of the young" (par. 236). Beveridge's statement raises many controversial and complex issues. What is "adequate" provision for the aged and other groups in the community?

There is no single, simple objective standard for determining the long-run adequacy of all types of old age benefits. Concepts of adequacy can and do vary. Beveridge's concept of adequacy for social insurance benefits in Great Britain differs from ours in the United States. Beveridge (1942) stated that social insurance "should aim at guaranteeing the minimum income needed for subsistence . . . determination of what is required for reasonable human subsistence is to some extent a matter of judgment; estimates on this point change with time, and generally, in a progressive community, change upwards," p. 14.

It is relatively much easier to indicate in what respect particular benefits are inadequate at a given moment of time than to define "adequacy" as a timeless standard. It is easier to describe inadequacy than to determine adequacy.

Adequacy of benefit protection cannot be divorced from other objectives and characteristics of a specific program. It is important to define the objectives and characteristics of each risk and to obtain general agreement on them. Standards of adequacy among the social insurance programs in the United States differ with respect to the risk. Thus a higher proportion of wage loss is usually provided for short-term risks such as unemployment and sickness as compared with long-term risks such as old age, disability, and premature death.

Motivation is a very important factor in determining the level of benefits in social insurance. Hence in the social insurance programs in the United States there are differentials in benefits. As Professor J. Douglas Brown has said: "Differentials, as a factor in motivation, must be measured by the response they receive, not by their arithmetic. The response to a thousand dollar differential among university professors is very different from its response among big league ball players."

In our incentive economy "equity" is an important factor to be considered as well as "adequacy" in determining the level and character of social insurance benefits. Is it possible to achieve a reasonable state of equity *and* adequacy, or must one factor be achieved at the expense of the other?

Benefits in various programs are a compromise among adequacy, motivation, equity, and other factors. Among these other factors are costs, the desirability of having minimum and maximum benefits, and administrative considerations related to prompt and efficient payment of benefits.

In the legislative evolution of any program consideration must be given to the social priority of various improvements. Not all elements are of equal importance in improving the benefit adequacy of a program. In terms of adequacy of the program as a whole, there are a number of factors to be given consideration in addition to the level of benefits. Among these factors are the eligibility for benefits, duration of benefits, classes of beneficiaries, types of benefits, etc. Value judgments enter into decisions of priorities. There is no substitute for judgment in this area.

Costs are a major factor in decisions on adequacy. Innumerable proposals have been made for the amendment of the Old-Age and Survivors Insurance Program. The problem is one of evaluating each of these in terms of needs, priorities, and effects on the individual and the economy?

It is possible for benefits to be inadequate for some individuals, while they may be "too adequate" for others. The latter situation may arise when a benefit is payable under more than one program for the same risk or when allowance is made for the non-taxable status of benefits. It may not always be possible to solve the problem both of inadequacy and of "overadequacy" at the same time.

Tying the level of social security benefits *automatically* to changes in the consumers' price index raises many difficult problems. Despite the European experience, it does not appear likely to be accepted in the United States, at the present time, as a solution to the adequacy of benefit problem. In the first place, such a proposal might tend to result in the impression that the basic benefits are "adequate" and only need adjustment to the price level (although it still would be possible to have the basic benefit raised from time to time). In addition, such a proposal would be opposed on the grounds that it might act as an incentive to inflation or at least affirmatively would not encourage price stability. Finally, it provides for dealing with the benefit side of the program without simultaneously considering the cost side.

It is also doubtful whether it is yet feasible in the United States to adjust automatically various other provisions of the program to changes in economic conditions. From time to time, consideration has been given to various methods of modifying the provisions of the social security system so that the program will have an even more important anticyclical effect than it might have under the present provisions of the law. For instance, suggestions have been made for reducing the contribution rates during periods of low business activity and increasing them during periods of full employment.

Several practical problems arise in the consideration of the desirability and workability of any such proposals. Based on past experience, Congress has not been very favorable to the insertion of automatic escalator clauses into the statutes. The effect of any such provision is to delegate the law-making power to some administrative agency to determine the occurrence of specific events which affect the rights of individuals and the economy. While the discretion of the administrative agency might be almost none whatsoever, nevertheless, the effect of any such proposal might be considered a serious abrogation of the legislative authority.

While it could be argued that there would be no real abrogation of legislative authority by Congress under any such proposal, since Congress could change the law at any time, it is probable that the precedent-making effect of any such proposal would result in hesitation by Congress before enacting any such proposal. Although various escalator clauses have been considered from time to time in terms of increases in veterans' benefit and other fixed statutory payments to individuals, Congress has always indicated its unwillingness to adopt any such proposals, since it is pointed out that it is in session every year and can make the necessary adjustments in any legislation in the light of what Congress determines are *all* the relevant facts at the time.

As in the German law and the Swedish and British proposals, it would be possible to have a built-in factor in the law adjusting the maximum social insurance benefit to changes in wages.

Research and statistical efforts in the field of adequacy of benefits must proceed on a number of fronts at the same time. Based on the European experience, it is clear we will need more adequacy studies in the United States in the future, and we will need them more promptly. The problems of determining adequacy of social insurance benefits will become more complex as the various forms of private benefits expand. The level of living enjoyed by beneficiaries will be provided from more than one source of income.

A very important factor in determining the adequacy of social insurance benefits is whether medical care is financed on a prepayment basis (i.e., not out of pocket). If comprehensive medical care is afforded, the "adequacy" of cash benefits is increased. For instance, aged persons ordinarily must allocate a substantial portion of their retirement incomes for out-of-pocket medical expenses. To the extent that a larger portion of medical costs are met by prepayment arrangements, the more adequate will be their cash benefits.

Another important factor is the extent of homeownership. To the extent that beneficiaries own their own homes, or are paying for their own homes, or have substantial rental commitments, the adequacy of their benefits may be affected. Housing costs are a substantial and variable factor in the adequacy equation. (For an interesting discussion of "benefit rates and the problem of rent" see Beveridge, 1942, Part III, Sec. I). It appears that the long-run improvement in the adequacy of benefits of social insurance benefits will depend more upon relating and adjusting changes to wage and productivity increases rather than to price changes or family budget figures.

As the standard of living and productivity rises for the community as a whole, the level of all social insurance benefits and public assistance payments also should tend to rise. No one in the United States has yet devised a satisfactory formula to do this automatically. It might be possible to accomplish such improvements in benefits through the legislative process on an *ad hoc* basis, but, based upon past experience, it may not be possible to do so as promptly as would be desirable. Is it possible to do so more promptly? In order to do so, there must be more extensive data bearing on the adequacy of benefits.

Adequacy of social insurance benefits in many countries (Great Britain, Canada, and some thirty other countries) is affected by family-allowance payments. Barring a serious decline in business conditions or a marked change in attitudes resulting in more favorable support for such allowances, it does not seem likely that the United States will adopt such a program in the foreseeable future.

An advisory council on social security might well be established to evaluate periodically the adequacy of the protection afforded under all public and private security programs in the United States. Such an evaluation should take into account the effects of existing programs and various proposals on the individual, the family, and the economy. European experience could be reviewed and made available for further consideration.

In concluding this very brief review of some of the problems common to the development of old age benefit programs in Europe and the United States, the following statement by Max Lerner is of interest:

. . . Yet despite what remains to be done, America has grappled with the problem of security, sometimes with an inventiveness that has added to the European experience instead of merely imitating it. And in doing so it has passed through a revolution in action, thought, and feeling which makes its welfare structure wholly different from the America of the 1920's which most European commentators still take as their prevailing image [1957, p. 131].

IX. Summary of Major Provisions of Eleven Countries

Two documents in Part II summarize the major provisions of the old age benefit programs of eleven western European countries in outline form. These summaries were prepared by the Division of Program Research of the Social Security Administration, Department of Health, Education, and Welfare.

The eleven countries for which summaries are included are Belgium, Denmark, Finland, France, West Germany, Great Britain, Italy, the Netherlands, Norway, Sweden, and the U.S.S.R. A wide variety of provisions is included in these countries.

The information generally represents the status of the programs in 1957. One document deals with cash benefits under the old age programs; another, with medical-care insurance for pensioners.

Because of the almost infinite variety of provisions in European old age benefit programs, it is not possible to make even the simplest generalization without the possibility of some exception. For those who wish to ascertain to what extent the European systems have a certain type of provision or not, the most useful and recent clas-

sification of provisions will be found in *Old Age Insurance,* a report made at the International Social Security Association XIIIth General Meeting, London, May, 1958, by R. J. Myers and Arnold Saxer. Mr. Saxer's report contains information on twenty-two European countries.

REFERENCES AND BIBLIOGRAPHY

ABEL-SMITH, B., and TOWNSEND, P. 1955. New pensions for old. London: Fabian Publications, Ltd.

ANONYMOUS. 1953. Private pension plans in six countries. Social Security Bull., August, pp. 10–17.

———. 1959a. Social security in the Union of Soviet Socialist Republics. *Ibid.,* August, pp. 3–7.

———. 1959b. New graduated retirement benefits in Great Britain. *Ibid.,* September, pp. 4–9.

———. 1959c. New graduated pension system in Sweden. *Ibid.,* November, pp. 13–17.

BEVERIDGE, SIR WILLIAM. 1942. Social insurance and allied services. New York: Macmillan Co.

BRITISH LABOUR PARTY. 1957. National superannuation: Labour's policy for security in old age. London: Labour Party.

CLARK, R. M. 1959. Economic security for the aged in the United States and Canada, Vols. 1 and 2. Ottawa: Department of National Health and Welfare.

COHEN, W. J., and FARMAN, C. H. 1955. Social security programs throughout the world, January, 1955. Bull. Internat. Social Security A., September–October.

DE SCHWEINITZ, K. 1943. England's road to social security: from the Statute of Laborers in 1349 to the Beveridge Report of 1942. Philadelphia: University of Pennsylvania Press.

FRIIS, H. 1959. Comparison of benefits in the Danish social security legislation. Bull. Internat. Social Security A., January–February.

GERIG, D. S. 1955. Pensionable age under old-age pension schemes. Internat. Labour Rev., 72 (October), 262–82.

GREAT BRITAIN. GOVERNMENT ACTUARY. 1958. Occupational pension schemes. London: H. M. Stationery Office.

GREAT BRITAIN. GUILLEBAUD COMMITTEE 1956. Report of the Committee of Enquiry into the cost of the National Health Service.

(Cmd. 9663.) London: H.M. Stationery Office.

GREAT BRITAIN. MINISTRY OF PENSIONS AND NATIONAL INSURANCE. 1958. Provision for old age: the future development of the National Insurance Scheme. (Cmd. 538.) London: H.M. Stationery Office.

GREAT BRITAIN. NATIONAL INSURANCE ADVISORY COMMITTEE. 1956. Report of the National Insurance Advisory Committee on the question of earnings limits for benefits. (Cmd. 9752.) London: H.M. Stationery Office.

GREAT BRITAIN. PHILLIPS COMMITTEE. 1954. Report of the Committee on the Economic and Financial Problems of the Provision for Old Age. (Cmd. 9333.) London: H.M. Stationery Office.

HOHAUS, R. A. 1948. Equity, adequacy and related factors in old age security. *In* W. HABER and W. J. COHEN (eds.), Readings in social security. New York: Prentice-Hall, Inc.

HOHMAN, HELEN FISHER. 1940. Old age in Sweden. Washington, D.C.: Social Security Board.

INTERNATIONAL LABOUR OFFICE. 1936. The International Labour Organization and social insurance. Geneva: International Labour Organization.

———. 1942. Approaches to social security: an international survey. Geneva: International Labour Organization.

———. 1949. Post-war trends in social security. Internat. Labour Rev., June, July, and September.

———. 1950. Social security in agriculture. *Ibid.*, February and March.

———. 1955*a*. The financing of social security. Geneva: International Labour Organization.

———. 1955*b*. The age of retirement. Geneva: International Labour Organization.

———. 1958. The cost of social security: 1949–1954. Geneva: International Labour Organization.

INTERNATIONAL SOCIAL SECURITY ASSOCIATION. 1955. The cost of social security: 1949–1951. Geneva: International Social Security Association.

———. 1958*a*. Old age insurance. Geneva: International Social Security Association.

———. 1958*b*. Recent developments in social security. Geneva: International Social Security Association.

LERNER, M. 1957. America as a civilization. New York: Simon & Schuster.

MYERS, R. J. 1952. Minimum standards of social security: new international convention. Social Security Bull., 15 (October), 3–10.

———. 1958*a*. International trends in social security. Bull. Internat. Social Security A., 11 (January–February), 41–51.

———. 1958*b*. Old-Age, Survivors, and Disability Insurance: financing basis and policy under the 1958 amendments. Social Security Bull., 21 (October), 15–21, 39.

NELSON, G. R. (ed.). 1953. Freedom and welfare. Denmark: Ministry of Social Affairs.

ROBSON, W. A. 1957. The welfare state. London: Oxford University Press.

SELDON, A. 1957. Pensions in a free society. London: Institute of Economic Affairs.

STOCKMAN, H. W. 1957. History and development of social security in Great Britain. Bull. Internat. Social Security A., 10 (January–February), 3–71.

SWEDEN. PENSION COMMITTEE. 1950. Proposal for a general pension insurance in Sweden. Oslo: Swedish Government.

TITMUSS, R. M. 1959. Essays on the welfare state. New Haven, Conn.: Yale University Press.

UNITED NATIONS. 1952. Methods of administering assistance to the needy. New York: United Nations.

U.S. COMMITTEE ON ECONOMIC SECURITY. 1937. Social security in America. Washington, D.C.: Government Printing Office.

U.S. CONGRESS. SENATE. 1949. Advisory Council on Social Security. Recommendations for social security legislation: the reports of the Advisory Council on Social Security to the Senate Committee on Finance. (Sen. Doc. 208 [80th Cong., 2d sess.].) Washington, D.C.: Government Printing Office.

U.S. SOCIAL SECURITY ADMINISTRATION, DIVISION OF PROGRAM RESEARCH. 1958. Social security programs throughout the world, 1958. Washington, D.C.: Government Printing Office.

———. 1959. West German Parliament approves general increase in pensions. ("Research and Statistics Note," No. 1.) Washington, D.C.: Social Security Administration. (Mimeographed.)

V

Housing and Community Services

WILMA DONAHUE

Europe, like the United States, has experienced an extreme housing shortage, especially since the last world war; but, unlike the United States, it is not neglecting its older citizens in the development of housing programs to meet the shortage crisis. In keeping with their philosophy that the aged have equal rights with the young to the goods and benefits of society, the various countries, as they build housing for young families, are including a reasonable proportion of units especially designed for the aged. The United States, only now beginning to take similar account of the housing needs of the elderly, is fortunate in being able to take advantage of the longer experience of western Europe and the United Kingdom for guidance in its planning.

Before the twentieth century the policy of most European countries for housing old people was to provide communal-type, institutional arrangements for the indigent sick or frail who were without families or whose relatives could or would not care for them. The administration of these workhouses or poor-law institutions was harsh and often punitive, the environment unstimulating and custodial in nature. Medical care was minimal. Residents were forced to work for their keep as long as they were able to carry on. In general, there was much neglect which reflected the low esteem in which society held the individual unable to maintain himself in the community.

The reform in social policy toward the elderly, which began in the early decades of the present century, has resulted not only in the establishment of such measures as pension schemes and invalidity insurance but also in the development of new approaches to housing and living arrangements. This chapter will (1) provide a review of the housing trends and the means of meeting the housing needs of older people in several European countries; (2) identify the concepts and principles embodied in the housing programs and designs; and (3) describe the community services provided to make possible more effective utilization of existing housing and living arrangements as well as the newer types of housing developments.

I. HOUSING TRENDS AND FACTORS IN EUROPEAN COUNTRIES

There is a marked contrast between the countries of southern Europe and those of the more northerly countries of western Europe. In the former, housing for the elderly is still restricted largely to institutions for the indigent supported by statutory and religious organizations. Many of these are structures built one or more centuries ago which have undergone a degree of modernization. Some progress has been made in Switzerland and West Germany, but the most enlightened and vigorous reforms have taken place in the Scandinavian countries, the Netherlands, and the United

Kingdom. An assessment of housing trends, therefore, has to be confined largely to these countries. Note might be made, however, that there is evidence that France and Italy, when able to do so, will follow the current policies of the other countries.

A. An Overview

At least two major factors influenced the trends in housing older people. First was the institution of universal pension schemes which made old people financially capable of paying for their own maintenance separate from their families and outside public assistance institutions. When they were able to be independent in the selection of housing, it was natural that old people should call attention to their special needs by seeking accommodations which were designed to match their financial and physical status. The second major factor influencing housing was a new appreciation of the fact that good social health requires that members of all age groups be housed in accordance with their particular needs. Sweden has gone further than most other countries in the adoption of this principle and has declared through legislative action that old people have the same right as younger groups to share equally in all the social programs, including housing. As a result of the operation of these factors, a diversification of housing and living arrangements has come about, not only in Sweden but also in Denmark, the Netherlands, Great Britain, and other countries. Three general categories—independent housing, communal homes for the normally aged, and sheltered care institutions for the chronically ill in need of constant medical and nursing care—can be identified.

INDEPENDENT HOUSING

One housing principle, adopted quite universally in Europe and the United Kingdom, is that old people should continue to live in their own homes as long as they are physically and mentally able to do so.

Widespread acceptance of this principle has fostered diversity of accommodations to compensate for diminished physical energy and reduced financial resources, with the result that, although still limited, independent quarters have been provided in most countries through a program of (1) construction of new specially designed accommodations and (2) conversion and remodeling of existing dwellings.

In general, independent housing is designed to permit the individual the kind of privacy and freedom enjoyed by younger people while at the same time providing for ease of housekeeping and safety of movement within the dwelling space. The most common types of accommodations provided are flats and apartments in buildings of two or more stories (more often than not without elevators), motel-type apartments, and detached cottages or bungalows. These various types may be found grouped in one or more sections of the city or in special housing estates; they may be arranged in blocks within the residential areas of the community; or they may be distributed throughout the housing developments which accommodate the younger age groups. The newest old age homes, especially in the Netherlands, also often include cottages for the more able-bodied elderly.

COMMUNAL HOMES FOR THE NORMALLY AGED

One of the significant developments in housing since the last world war has been a more perceptive analysis of the need for homelike accommodations for those aged persons who may be so frail and disabled that they need oversight and some assistance with the activities of daily living but who do not need constant medical care and nursing service.

Thus, in 1947, the Swedish Riksdag adopted a declaration of principles with reference to communal homes according to which those old people in need of oversight but not requiring hospital service were to be housed in old people's homes, while those who were sick were to be admitted to hospitals and nursing homes for chronic patients or the mentally ill (Swedish Social Welfare Board, 1952). The 1957–58 Riksdag reaffirmed these principles (Berggren, 1958a) and thus encouraged the already clearly established trend of reserving old people's homes exclusively for the normally aging and of designing such homes to suppress all features conveying the impression of an institution.

The United Kingdom, likewise, has sought to serve the housing needs of frail elderly people unable to maintain their own households by providing small home-like residential accommodations. Shenfield (1957) states that in 1947 the Ministry of Health pointed out "the need to go forward with the creation of homes which would provide for about 30 or 35 elderly residents." The National Assistance Act of 1948 included legislation which placed responsibility on the local authorities to provide accommodations for the elderly which would be substitutes for normal homes.

Just after World War II the Netherlands adopted a policy of providing apartment living within old age homes for couples in need of oversight, thus reducing somewhat the institutional character of the homes (Bouwcentrum, 1955) and maintaining a semblance of homelike living for the couples.

The Europeans point out a psychological advantage in separating the housing of the frail or disabled elderly from that of the sick or mentally deteriorated old people. Dr. Ali Berggren, chief of the Division of Social Care, Royal Social Board of Sweden, compared the incidence of illness among essentially well persons living in an old age home where sick people were also housed with that occurring among a second group living in an old age home where there were no sick persons. He reported that the incidence of illness among the able-bodied was significantly higher in the former home than in the latter.

SHELTER FOR THE CHRONICALLY ILL

The chronically ill old person in Europe is most frequently housed in a large institution which is a hospital or which has a hospital-like character. The nursing home as it is known in the United States, although present, is not yet so common in many parts of Europe. Hospitals devoted entirely to geriatric patients are fairly prevalent but as an organized system are probably best developed in the United Kingdom. These hospitals provide acute care and rehabilitation services for the chronically ill. If there is no suitable place for recovered patients in the community, or if rehabilitation fails, the hospital may become a permanent shelter for them. The United Kingdom has also established a few "halfway houses" which are convalescent units halfway between hospital care and living at home. One type—rest homes—cater to the older person who is chronically sick but who does "not need the expensive service of hospital care [but does] need constant attention and help of a simpler kind and could not manage at home" (Shenfield, 1957, p. 165).

The other type—halfway convalescent homes—care for patients sent from geriatric hospitals before returning to independent living. In the latter type, the patients are in transit; in the rest homes they are likely to remain until a terminal illness. Halfway convalescent homes are not provided by statutory services, but these and the rest homes have been provided by voluntary bodies. They are not part of the National Health Services.

In several countries—Sweden, Denmark, Finland, and Germany, for example—are to be found some very large old age communities which include accommodations ranging from those for the able-bodied through those for persons requiring long-term hospitalization. Sabbattsberg in Stockholm (Mehr, 1957), De Gamles By in Copenhagen (Hjem, 1951), Tieverko Sovitetaan in Helsinki, and Richler Heemstatten in Cologne, Germany (Roggendorf,

1953), are examples for developments which include hospital and nursing units, congregate living arrangements for the frail, and private quarters for those able to care for themselves.

In the Netherlands the commercial nursing home is a common institution; and, although there is no general policy with reference to where nursing care shall be given, some old age homes make it a practice to send sick residents to be cared for in homes of this type. Although there is currently a very strong policy for abolishing the proprietary nursing homes, the Netherlands must still use them because the number operated on a non-profit basis is still too limited to meet the need. A plan for including nursing-home care as a part of the obligatory health insurance for persons with an income up to approximately 7000 guilders is expected to enlarge materially the possibilities for establishing non-profit nursing homes. There has been considerable dissatisfaction with the custodial type of care offered in many of the proprietary nursing homes, and there has also been a question of the specific place of nursing homes in the total medical-care pattern for the aged. The Dutch National Committee of Old People's Care, therefore, employed Bouwcentrum (Housing Center) of Rotterdam to carry out a study of the nursing homes and to make recommendations regarding the type of care that should be offered by these homes and to suggest detailed specifications for building and operating them. On the basis of the study, it was recommended that the nursing homes should continue to be operated independently but should include comprehensive rehabilitation services and also should be closely allied to local hospitals for direction of medical treatment (Bouwcentrum, 1955).

COMMUNITY SERVICES

Application of the principles of continuing independent living arrangements for older people as long as possible soon made obvious the fact that many people would be able to maintain their households only if they had some household help and other services brought to them. Thus, as Shenfield (1957) points out, "it is important to consider housing, domiciliary services and communal care together because a coordinated policy in the provision of all three is the only way to make the most effective use of them all, both from the point of view of the needs of older householders and from that of the cost to the community" (p. 134).

Perhaps because of the earlier and more clearly established decision to help older people continue to live independently in their own homes, most of the European countries are far ahead of the United States in the development of community services for the aged. The United Kingdom, the Netherlands, Denmark, Sweden, and, to a lesser extent, Switzerland, West Germany, and France offer a fairly comprehensive range of services; and some of the countries provide special training courses for persons wishing to prepare to serve either as volunteers or as paid workers in these programs.

The costs of the community service programs—health, home helps, food services, social, and recreational—are considered much more economical to society than the building and maintenance of institutional types of housing that would be necessary for the rather large marginal group who are now able, through relatively extensive use of these community services, to care for themselves.

Before discussing the detailed methods and programs for meeting the housing and community service needs of the elderly, consideration will be given to some of the factors which have determined the character, direction, and magnitude of the solutions undertaken.

B. Factors in Housing the Aged

The countries of western Europe have been forced to give attention to the special housing needs of older people for about the same reasons as those now confronting the United States. The underdeveloped countries will be faced with the same factors as they move on to an urbanized and technological order.

INCREASE IN NUMBER AND PROPORTIONATE SIZE

The first factor influencing the development of special housing for older people is the change in the population structure. In all countries of Western culture there has been an increase in both the absolute number of old people and the proportionate size of this age group. All projections of population trends indicate that for the next several decades the increase will continue, if, as Hauser and Vargas point out in chapter ii, the mortality and fertility rates continue to decline.

In comparison to the United States, most of the countries of western Europe and Great Britain already have a considerably larger proportion of old people in their populations. Currently in the United States 8.7 per cent of the population is 65 years of age and over. Only Italy among western European countries has a lower proportion, about 8.1 per cent, while France ranks highest with approximately 12 per cent in the upper age group. The Scandinavian countries and the Netherlands, England, and Switzerland fall between these extremes. To illustrate the projected increase in the proximate size of the older age group in the next few years, it can be noted that Sweden expects the 10.3 per cent in 1950 to increase to 14 per cent in 1970; the Netherlands predicts the 8.7 per cent of 1957 to change to 10.7 per cent by 1975 and to 11.1 per cent in 1980.

Inasmuch as the housing needs of today's older people are still inadequately met, these projected increases in their numbers for the next few years are inevitably hastening the construction of all types of accommodations for this group.

FAMILY RELATIONSHIPS

A second factor serving to increase the demand for special housing for old people is the breakdown of the extended kinship family occurring as a consequence of industrialization. As Burgess points out (chap. i), the nuclear family unit, consisting of one adult generation and its immature progeny, has become the common pattern in practically all Western cultures, although there are variations among countries in the extent of dissolution of the family structure. These differences are reflected in the housing policies.

In Italy, where societal and legal obligations to support elder relatives are still binding, the influence of the extended family remains strong; and housing which affords independent living for the older generation is almost non-existent. Usually, only institutions to domicile the indigent chronically ill are provided. On the other hand, in Sweden, England, and the Netherlands, where there has been some relaxation in the statutory and/or moral demands on children for the care of parents, it has become a national policy to provide independent accommodations and institutions with a homelike character as substitutes. Townsend (1957) in his study of Bethnal Green, a London borough, and Sheldon (1948) in his survey of Wolverhampton, England, found that family cohesion still tends to be strong among the working classes. In their study populations most older people preferred to live independently of their children but still tended to dwell in the same districts and to maintain almost daily contacts with them or other nearby relatives. The government support to local housing trusts, which provides small, congregate accommodations for those living within the district, is based on a policy which recognizes and makes possible this type of continuing family relationship. In Sweden governmental subsidization for the improvement of well-built old houses and inclusion of small pensioners' units within ordinary housing developments likewise promote the maintenance of intergenerational relationships and prevents what Mehr (1954) terms "social invalidity" of the aged.

Usually it is only in the more rural areas, where there is still some semblance of the family as a collective unit, that any significant proportion of older people wish to live in the homes of their children. In West Germany, for example, Friedeburg (1955) studied the preferred living arrangements of working- and middleclass men when they retired and reported that, while 36 per cent of those from communities of 2000 or less chose to live with their children, only 7 per cent of those from cities of 100,000 or over held such a preference.

ECONOMIC STATUS

Impetus was given to the establishment of national and local housing schemes in many countries because the incomes and pensions of old people were so meager that they were able to rent only the cheapest, and therefore the poorest, accommodations for themselves. An investigation in Stockholm in 1940 showed that, although there were very few slum areas in the city, almost all the oldest, most unsanitary, and practically doomed apartments were inhabited by elderly people. The Rowntree Committee (1947) study of housing of old people in seven areas in England likewise indicated that the aged generally lived in substandard dwellings. The committee, however, pointed out that the older person was probably housed no worse than the average individual of his class. But, as Shenfield (1957) cogently remarked, "second- and third-floor accommodation and shared kitchen or sanitary facilities, though by no means exclusively the housing problems of older people, press more hardly upon them than upon younger persons who are physically more able to cope with these inconveniences" (p. 137).

National pension rates were improved in most countries after these investigations were made; but, since the pensions are still intended only to provide a basic minimum income, the problem of being able to compete for suitable housing remains a pressing one for most old people. In the Netherlands, for example, the national pension for a couple is 1584 guilders per year; food costs alone amount to 1100 guilders. In the United Kingdom at least one-fourth of the aged require an assistance grant in addition to their national pensions and other retirement incomes; and as many as 40,000 of Stockholm's 63,000 pensioners require rent supplements.

With the building of special low-rent housing and the modernization of old dwellings, significant numbers of old people now find it possible to acquire accommodations that suit their physical needs and their ability to pay. Thus the social health of these countries has been materially improved, especially so since the housing for old people has not been at the expense of the younger group but in proportion to it.

HOUSING SHORTAGES

As a matter of fact, the general housing shortage which existed after the last world war was a major factor in promoting housing for the aged. Large quantities of dwellings had been destroyed, and this situation, coupled with a continuing increase in the general population, made necessary the full utilization of all available housing as well as the construction of new dwellings. When studies of overcrowding showed that many old people were living in homes too large for their needs, steps were taken to persuade them to seek more suitable living arrangements, thus freeing the larger homes for occupancy by families with children. For example, the Netherlands established a policy of offering a subsidy to old people to help defray costs of moving to smaller accommodations; the same step was taken by some local authorities in England. While these and other measures helped to make better use of existing housing, there was still an insufficient supply for families of all ages. The governments of the various countries, therefore, established subsidy programs to stimulate the construction of more dwelling units and to make special provision for the housing of the elderly.

Thus simultaneous construction of homes for all age groups resulted in many instances in the inclusion of dwellings for the elderly as a part of regular housing projects, thereby avoiding the segregation of the old. In the Netherlands, for example, the small one-story, motel-type pensioners' apartments built among the three- and four-story workers' flats are often seen. In England new bungalows or flats for older people are generally a part of an ordinary housing estate. Special flatlets in converted houses are provided in a number of areas. Sweden, likewise, encourages the inclusion of old people's accommodations in regular apartment houses.

ATTITUDES OF OLD PEOPLE TOWARD SPECIAL HOUSING

The habits and preferences of old people themselves are necessarily factors in schemes to provide special housing for their use, and the question naturally arises as to what proportion of the elderly in any community may be expected to make use of the independent housing and communal homes so carefully designed to meet their needs. Neither shortages of regular community housing nor incomes too low to pay for what is available necessarily lead old people to want or to accept the special accommodations which so many communities are now providing for them. Likewise, neither loneliness nor lack of nearby relatives is by any means always sufficient to create a willingness to leave the neighborhood in which roots have been established over long periods of time. Thus, however poor their present housing situation, many find it more congenial than the prospect of changing to an unfamiliar housing development or to a communal house in a neighborhood where they would be strangers.

Shenfield (1957) analyzed the preference of most older people to *keep* their old homes in contrast to a few who *seek* new housing. Three measures—pensions and rent allowances, rent controls, and security of tenure—assist old people to keep their homes, although they also tend to freeze the use of housing. Older tenants do not try to move into smaller quarters even when they can find something cheaper than the controlled rent units, because they do not save any income if they are getting a rent allowance, and they may lose this security of tenure by moving. The pattern of most old couples living in their own homes after retirement and not with their children is firmly established. It is only when considerable care is needed for elderly parents or a surviving spouse that the older person is likely to be found living in the home of one of the children.

Van Zonneveld (1956) studied the attitudes of Hollanders toward old age homes in his survey of 3000 aged residents of Groningen. Approximately two-thirds do not favor living in communal homes. Women are somewhat more favorably inclined toward this type of living than men (especially older women), and childless persons have a more positive attitude than those with children. Social class is also found to be related; those of lower classes, especially men, accept the idea of a communal home more willingly than those of the same age group from the higher classes. Income is similarly related, with those in the lower-income bracket being attracted to communal living. Health and mental status do not seem to be of importance in determining the degree of favorable attitude toward a home, except that among the oldest women subject to "fits of oppression" there is a significant number in favor of communal arrangements.

Pagani (1956) makes the observation that in Italy, where pension levels and other incomes are unusually low, "seeking admission to a public institution is a generalized solution for aged industrial workers, inasmuch as it is not unusual and involves no feelings of individual inadequacy or loss of dignity. At the same time we can state that it is not due to a lack of family solidarity but to economic insecurity." He puts his assumption affirmatively by pointing out that the retiring worker finds himself in a crisis period characterized by (1) a low level of living; (2) individual and social isolation; (3) family dependence and small personal prestige; and (4) emotional strain caused by his awareness of his dependency. By entering an institution which removes his dependency on the family and secures for him a new sense of usefulness through participation in work programs, he achieves a rational solution to the crisis. This hypothesis, it might be pointed out, neglects the women whose occupations have been those of homemakers.

The three factors which tend to predispose the elderly to enter an old age home are, according to Shenfield (1957), lack of other suitable housing (suitable for independent living), inability to manage a household any longer, and loneliness. These reasons are similar to those on which the current policies of Sweden and Denmark are based; that is, when an individual is in need of assistance with daily activities or is in other social distress, he should find a home for the aged available. In practice, the first two factors may hardly operate, according to Shenfield, except in the case of private homes taking fee-paying patients by private arrangement. The shortage of places in homes provided by statutory and voluntary bodies is such that only those who are clearly unable to manage independent living arrangements are likely to be considered for admittance.

It is more than likely, of course, that attitudes toward acceptance of special accommodations, particularly those of the communal type, are conditioned by the widely held cultural precept that older people, like others, should live independently in their own homes as long as possible. Too, in some places, rather strong vestiges remain of the societal expectation that adult children provide homes for their aged parents. It may be expected that attitude toward living in the new, special accommodations will change as their advantages become more widely recognized and as old culture patterns give way to new definitions.

In summary of this brief review of trends and factors influencing the housing of old people in Europe, it is apparent that, as in the United States, there has been a great increase in the number and proportion of old people in the population; that government and voluntary groups have attempted to meet the housing needs of both the able-bodied normally aged and the chronically ill by providing a variety of housing types and accommodations serving different tastes and offering various services; and that such assistance has been necessary because of the shift of direct responsibility from the family to the state for the care of older family members and because the income and pension status of the aged has been insufficient for them to care for all their own needs without provision of special subsidies or services.

II. MEETING THE HOUSING NEEDS OF OLD PEOPLE IN EUROPE

A more detailed comparison of ways in which the housing needs of old people are being met in Western cultures will reveal some variation in the solutions employed by different countries. In general, however, the similarities are much more striking than the differences, in part, because the economic means of the aged in all countries are limited and the national resources that are available must necessarily be shared proportionately by all age groups.

The circumstances of the elderly determine to a large extent the kinds of housing and the amounts of the various types required to provide each individual with the sort most appropriate to his situation. Further considerations include the magnitude of the need (especially with respect to the extent it is being met), the role of government and private organizations in bringing about the solution of the housing problem, the costs to society, and the charge to old people themselves. No country has as yet achieved an ideal plan, but noteworthy and, in some instances, striking progress is being made.

A. Some Characteristics of Older People Related to Housing

Although the economic status of the aged is a prime determinant of the amount and quality of housing old people can purchase for themselves, other factors less susceptible to statutory regulation may be equally important in attempts to satisfy the psychological as well as the physical needs of older people. Chief among these are family relationships and general levels of physical and mental health.

FAMILY STATUS

European sociologists do not predict that there will be a reversal in the tendency toward the breakdown of family structure, because they see the present trend as the inevitable outcome of the social structural transformations resulting from modern developments. Therefore, if the trend continues, the time will come when the family no longer serves the functions of offering shelter, care, and direct, affectional relationships to the older generation; then far-reaching social policies must be developed to supply substitutes, not the least important of which are housing and community services.

Several comprehensive surveys, made by local communities in the United Kingdom and other countries, underscore the trend toward separate living of the generations and indicate the need for independent dwellings for the elderly. The Wolverhampton study (Sheldon, 1948) showed that only 12 per cent of older people live with children; and, of these, the largest proportion is among the very old and the widowed. Shenfield (1957) also found that approximately 12 per cent of the elderly live with their children, with the propor-

tion increasing to one-third for those over 80 years of age. In the Netherlands, 11 per cent of the aged live in the homes of their children or other relatives; in France, on the other hand, 25 per cent of the single elderly and 30 per cent who still have spouses live with their children. Burgess gives a comprehensive breakdown of family relationships and responsibilities in chapter viii.

MENTAL AND PHYSICAL HEALTH STATUS

In the absence of a system of family care and protection, the health status of older people becomes a matter of major consideration in the planning of the type, number, and special features of their living accommodations. The findings presented in chapters vi and vii are pertinent to the problems being considered here.

The Netherlands recognizes four categories of old people with reference to health needs and housing: (1) the physically able who can live independently without special help; (2) the physically restricted, able to live independently with the assistance of special amenities; (3) the weak, frail, and somewhat disabled who need to reside in the residential home; and (4) the chronically or long-term ill or disabled who require nursing home care. The policy is to care for the members of the latter two categories in different homes. Current national estimates, based on a number of surveys (van Zonneveld, 1956), indicate that theoretically 10–14 per cent of the aged population are in need of accommodations which offer general care, while 3–4 per cent are in need of nursing-home care. This latter figure includes 1–1.5 per cent who are mentally ill.

In Sweden, as already pointed out, the policy since 1947 has been to utilize the old age homes for housing the frail well aged, yet an investigation made in 1950 showed that, of the 27,900 persons residing in these homes, 59 per cent were mentally disturbed, senile, or chronically ill. The latter group alone accounted for 30 per cent. On the other hand, a study of the general hospitals in Stockholm showed that 12 per cent of the beds were occupied by chronically ill old people who would be better cared for in some other type of facility.

The situation in England appears to be little different from that on the Continent. Sheldon (1948) found that 11 per cent of the Wolverhampton sample were so ill or so disturbed that they were confined to bed or to their quarters. He also estimated that 11 per cent were slightly impaired mentally, while 3.8 per cent were so severely disoriented they needed care in a mental hospital.

B. Estimated Need for Housing and Community Services

If quarters in old age homes catering to the frail and disabled are needed by an estimated 10–15 per cent, and if mental hospital facilities are required for another 1–3 per cent, it probably may be assumed that 85–90 per cent of the elderly need and can effectively use independent living arrangements especially if special personal services are provided by the community.

The need for community services for the aged is dependent upon the number of elderly people who remain in their own homes, since most service is directed to this group. How many of the 85 per cent living outside the institutional setting are in actual need of service is difficult to determine. Factors to be considered, however, are age and marital status. It is assumed that the older the individual, and particularly if he lives alone, the more and the greater variety of services needed. Yet this assumed increase in need is offset by the fact that as many as one-third of those 80 years old and over live with their children; and among those who do, there are many who have great vitality. It is probable that no general estimate of the extent of communal services needed can be made. Rather it must be a matter of local determination in relation to the age and health characteristics of the total population of the community and the availability of a full range of living accommodations.

C. Amount of Housing Provided for Older People

Although the vigorous building programs adopted by most of the European countries following the last world war resulted in the construction of a relatively large number of dwellings, the supply is still far below the estimated need. Proportionately, the shortage of independent accommodations is greater than it is for communal institutions.

INDEPENDENT HOUSING (FLATS, ETC.)

The emphasis was placed on providing pensioners' flats, cottages, etc., because of the high cost of building and operating institutions and because it was in accordance with established aims. Also, since the private accommodation is usually considered an economical way, within limits, to care for the elderly by utilizing the ability of old people to maintain their own households and to look after themselves, social planners and housing experts are undertaking to include in many building programs a significant amount of housing of proper size and design, which will make possible continued occupancy by the aged even after the appearance of considerable frailty and disablement.

Sweden, for the past two decades, has encouraged the construction of inexpensive accommodations for the aged. By 1954 between 30,000 and 40,000 pensioners' dwellings had been built, or somewhat over 7 per cent of all private units constructed since 1939. This proportion can be compared to the slightly more than 10 per cent of the population making up the pensioner group. If only the larger cities are considered, an even greater proportion of old people are housed in community-built independent accommodations. In Stockholm, for example, there were (in 1956) 9000 pensioners' flats or enough to house 14.5 per cent of Stockholm's 63,000 people aged 67 and over. When this comparison is based on families in place of single individuals, it shows an even larger proportion of the old age group living in independent dwellings.

The housing program for old people in Denmark is similar to that of Sweden except that the national government plays a somewhat smaller role. In Copenhagen, in 1951, there were about 5200 pensioners' flats, one-fourth of which were occupied by couples. Thus approximately 13 per cent of the 48,000 old age pensioners were housed in these flats (Danish Society, 1951, p. 50) and about 3 per cent more were housed in the old people's home of Copenhagen (De Gamles By). Today, in the whole country of Denmark, there are about 250,000 pensioners, and 11.5 per cent of them live in pensioners' quarters or in municipal homes for the aged.

For England it has been reported (Shenfield, 1957) that, following World War II, the proportion of one-bedroom houses (considered to be of a suitable size but not specially designed for old people) built by local authorities to all other housing built by these authorities was 8 per cent. More recent figures supplied by Shenfield show that, by the first quarter of 1958, the proportion had increased to 18.8 per cent. But, owing to the lack of provision in former years and to growing needs, about 20 per cent of all housing should be built suitable for the elderly to bring up to 5 per cent the proportion available to them. The shortage is even worse, if anything, in the provision for communal accommodations. Some local authorities have over 300 persons on their waiting lists. Out of 145 local authorities in England and Wales in 1958, there were 90 that had provided less than one bed per 1000 of the population (two beds per 1000 has been suggested to be the minimum provision required).

TABLE 1*

NUMBER OF DWELLINGS AND "EN PENSION" HOMES BUILT IN THE NETHERLANDS WITH FINANCIAL
AID OF THE GOVERNMENT DURING THE PERIOD MAY 1, 1945—JANUARY 1, 1959

| PROVINCE OR CITY | No. OF DWELLINGS | "EN PENSION" HOMES | | | | TOTAL No. OF BEDS |
| | | Extension Modernization | | New Buildings | | |
		Homes	Beds	Homes	Beds	
Groningen	1,030	9	328	16	748	1,076
Friesland	889	10	243	24	1,246	1,489
Drenthe	506	4	68	9	616	684
Overijssel	433	5	243	4	626	869
Gelderland	936	6	494	22	1,900	2,394
Utrecht	770	13	585	11	1,527	2,112
North Holland	1,736	13	358	34	2,295	2,653
South Holland	1,935	2	57	17	1,506	1,563
Zeeland	161	5	169	7	578	747
North Brabant	865	9	381	17	1,749	2,130
Limburg	546	5	344	8	751	1,095
Amsterdam	855	1	15	2	469	484
The Hague	97	. . . . .	. . . . .	3	741	741
Rotterdam	196	1	13	3	105	118
Total	10,955	83	3298	177	14,857	18,155

* Source: F. H. J. Nierstrasz (private communication, 1959)

The Netherlands, although emphasizing the importance of older people living in their own homes, has provided a proportionately smaller number of such accommodations than some other countries. Between 1945 and 1959 the Dutch built 10,955 dwellings especially designed for old people, constructed 177 old age homes, and modernized 83 existing buildings to provide a total of 18,155 beds "en pension" homes. Table 1 shows the distribution of the dwellings and old age homes throughout the country. Table 2 shows the age distribution of residents in 1950.

COMMUNAL ACCOMMODATIONS

In considering communal arrangements, it seems desirable to separate those serving only the normally aged and those which serve the chronically ill in need of hospital care. It is not possible, however, to do this satisfactorily, because even in those countries, such as Sweden, where the separation of these two groups is an established policy, there remain, for matters of expediency, some sick old people among the normally aged.

In general, however, Sweden does distinguish between the old age homes which are intended for persons who need some form of assistance but not continuous nursing care and the nursing homes which are intended for sick persons. In Stockholm in 1954 there were 1000 placed in old age homes or enough to accommodate 1.5 per cent of the pensioners in the city, and 1900 placed in nursing institutions, which accounted for another 3 per cent of the older group. By 1960 the city expects to increase the capacity of old age homes by one-half and nursing homes by about one-third. In relation to the calculated number of old persons 65 years of age and over at the end of 1960, there will be 4.4 placed per 1000 aged (Dahlström, 1956).

The Ministry of Welfare of the Netherlands reported in 1957 that approximately 40,000 of 9,000,000 (4.3 per cent) old people lived in old age homes. In Amsterdam 3.5 per cent of the aged are being accommodated in recently built institutions offering complete nursing care.

Shenfield (1957) has expressed the opinion that in England the demand for care in a residential setting which provides nursing service exceeds the supply by a significant amount. The National Old People's Welfare Council (1954a) has estimated that in London no more than 8.5 per cent of those who wish to enter communal homes are able to find space. In 1956 only 71,713 of the 6.5 million persons in England of pensionable age were accommodated in old age homes (excluding 12,000 additional places in almshouses) (Great Britain, National Old People's Welfare Council, 1956).

It appears, then, that, when an over-all estimate is made of the amount of various types of housing available, the aged, at least in several countries of Europe and the United Kingdom, have approximated their proportionate share of the total housing built over the last 20 years (a statement which could not be made with reference to the United States). Accommodations for the able-bodied, although larger in total amount, are proportionately much less numerous than are those for the sick and the disabled. In both categories, however, the supply is still far short of the demand.

TABLE 2*

RELATION OF AGE TO RESIDENCY IN OLD AGE HOMES, THE NETHERLANDS, 1950

Age	Total Population 65 and Over	No. in in Homes	Per Cent in Homes
65–69	308,714	4372	1.4
70–74	234,236	6825	2.9
75–79	147,499	8009	5.4
80–84	72,328	6504	9.0
85–90	31,714	3753	11.8

* Source: Central Bureau of Statistics.

D. Sponsorship

Traditionally, responsibility for the housing and care of older people was assumed by religious bodies in all countries of western Europe. Gradually, as the volume of need exceeded the capacity of the churches to meet it, public agencies were required to provide various forms of care and facilities. Today, government exercises principal responsibility in most countries, although its activities are usually exercised through or co-ordinated with those of local authorities, religious groups, labor organizations, voluntary associations, housing trusts, and private builders.

Rudd (1956) provides a brief but vivid review of the historical background to modern housing and care of the elderly. In essence, he points out that during the Dark Ages the monks maintained infirmaries in their monasteries where they cared for sick and abandoned old people. During the Reformation many non-monastic infirmaries were established by religious groups. The almshouses which grew out of these infirmaries represent perhaps the first involvement of government in the provision of housing for old people. Although these institutions were publicly supported, the religious influence remained strong, and many of the almshouses included a church or chapel where the old spent their time offering prayers for their benefactors. Later, under the influence of the poor laws, the public almshouses lost their religious character and took on the role of workhouse, in which poverty, considered to be the result of laziness and sin, was punished by hard work. Following the Middle Ages, the administrators of public institutions began to develop more humane attitudes toward the residents. Today there is in every country of western Europe and England, in both public and private institutions, a genuine effort to modernize the old structures and to introduce the newer concepts of good care. Thus, in Rome, one may visit an old age home by entering a little court surrounded by what appears to be an ancient structure (the law prohibits the change of external appearances for historical reasons), but the interior has been modernized to include cheerful wards, an up-to-date surgery ward, laboratories, modern kitchens, occupational therapy rooms, sheltered workshops, etc. Similar experiences are to be had in the Netherlands, West Germany, England, and Sweden.

Although governments have played an increasingly important role in providing housing for the elderly, the contributions of the church and of other agencies have remained strong. During the seventeenth century, the Dutch Reformed church and Dutch merchant corporations established many old age homes in Holland. In West Germany today, for example, there are 927 Evangelical church old people's homes, with 147,000 beds, or enough to accommodate about 3 per cent of the population aged 65 and over.

In Stockholm, near the beginning of the eighteenth century, when measures were taken to prevent distress and to eliminate begging on the part of the old, each parish was charged with taking care of its own poor. At that time communal homes were established by every parish (Erlandsson, 1954); and, in 1918, the parishes also began to build flats for old people. By 1954, they had constructed 31 blocks consisting of almost 2900 flats, 600 of which were for couples. In 1958 the Stockholm Municipal Diet voted to build another 1000 flats to be scattered through public housing developments in 69 places.

As interest in providing housing and old age homes developed, the churches and governments were joined, in some countries, by various organizations such as labor unions, foundations, voluntary associations, and limited-dividend housing trusts. Among examples in England of voluntary bodies that have had a major influence on the development of housing policies and programs in the United Kingdom are the National Corporation for the Care of Old People, which has been generously supported by the Nuffield Foundation, and the National Old People's Welfare Council, which has given leadership to the development of housing for the elderly since its inception. The Women's Voluntary Service for Civil Defense is another example of a voluntary group which has helped provide accommodations for old people needing care in residential clubs, nursing homes, and halfway houses. In Switzerland, also, Pro Senectute (Old People's Foundation) has stimulated and assisted local cantons and communities in their efforts to construct old people's accommodations.

The gradual extension of governmental and other forms of community responsibility for older people, as society has become industrialized and hence more complex, is clearly manifested in the field of housing. The role of government has become that of building and operating homes for the aged and institutions for care and treatment of the chronically ill, of providing partial and full subsidies permitting low-income older people to occupy good housing, of setting standards for housing accommodations, and of contributing leadership in giving recognition to the significance of living accommodations to the well-being of older people.

The church and other voluntary agencies continue to make important contributions by adding to the supply of housing and by providing administrative services for many homes for the aged—for some of those which are publicly supported as well as for those which are church supported. Government and voluntary agencies are frequently joined also in extending a variety of services to elderly people in their own homes. In general, the European pattern finds government agencies shouldering the principal responsibility for standard setting, construction, and financing in the area of low-income housing but often working in close partnership with non-governmental organizations and associations.

E. Financing

State subsidization of housing programs has come to be the chief instrument through which the housing circumstances of the aged are being improved in the Scandinavian countries, the Netherlands, the United Kingdom, and West Germany. As a rule, financing is shared jointly but not necessarily in equal proportions between the state and the local municipality or authority. Generally, financial aid takes two forms: (1) rent subsidies to individuals which are made as supplements to pensions or as part of public assistance grants by way of reduced rents and (2) building grants made to non-profit builders, voluntary bodies, or local authorities for the construction of independent units or of old age homes and for the modernization and/ or conversion of large old houses into smaller living units. Of course, state aid is also being made available in most countries to build long-stay hospitals to accommodate the chronically ill who need continuous nursing service. An indirect form of aid to housing is found in the subsidization of various organizations and agencies by federal and local governments to underwrite, in part, the costs of community services which make it possible for older people to maintain their own households.

Sweden affords a good example of the role of government in financing housing and community services for the elderly. Since 1939 the state has provided special grants to municipalities and communes to build independent housing for pensioners. These grants are used for (1) constructing blocks of pensioners' flats in normal residential areas; (2) including pensioners' quarters in apartment buildings designed for younger families; and (3) converting old well-built homes for occupancy by several elderly couples or single persons. The size of the state subsidies ranges from 25 to 80 per cent of building costs, depending upon local need. By July 1, 1954, the state had granted construction subsidies up to the value of 102 million kronor ($20 million) in partial support of the building of 23,100 pensioners' flats (Mehr, 1957).

The construction of communal homes as well as of the independent type of living accommodations is also subsidized in large part by the state. Each commune is required by law to provide a home for its aged residents. The larger communities may have several large homes (five are found in Stockholm), or, in the more rural areas, several communes may form a communal union and build a single home. The 2281 rural communes have thus combined to form 821 communal unions. Thus the old people of rural Sweden tend to be just as well housed as those living in urban centers—perhaps even better, since the homes in rural areas are generally much smaller and more homelike.

The rural communes also tend to make considerable use of the home-improvement type of subsidy and loan, since it is a means for improving the standard of living of old people while at the same time making it possible for them to continue to live in their old homes and/or communities. These home-improvement subsidies, made separately or in combination with loans, are payable by the state up to 8000 kronor ($1544). The local municipality assumes the remainder of the cost.

In addition to the construction subsidies, Sweden, since 1954, has had a program of municipal *rental allowances*. Every municipality decides for itself whether it wants to grant these allowances and how much they should be. The state contributes from 42 to 75 per cent of the costs, depending on the size of the tax base in each municipality. Mehr (1957) is of the opinion that these rent allowances are the most significant social-insurance reform in recent years because they mean that "pensioners no longer need deny themselves decent housing for financial reasons because the total cost of rent is covered by the allowance" (p. 6).

Community services to help old people who are independently housed are also supported in large part through the social assistance program in Sweden. Since this type of assistance is not restricted to any definite form, it can be used by municipal social welfare offices to provide any type of service needed. Thus it has been possible to develop extensive programs of household help for the aged and also to care for old people residing in their own homes or in nursing homes (Swedish Institute, 1956).

The low level of old age pensions in Sweden in relation to cost of living has been basic to the development of programs of rent allowances, construction costs, and community services. Another example of the relationship of the level of old age pensions to national housing practices and financing is found in the Netherlands. Here, where the basic pension of 1584 guilders for a couple is too low to meet even subsistence needs, the government is aiding, through subsidy programs, the building of flats especially designed for occupancy by the aged where an older couple can be maintained for 2700 guilders per year, as compared with 5000 guilders (plus an additional clothing allowance) required to keep them in an old age home, according to F. H. J. Nierstrasz, a staff member of Bouwcentrum, Rotterdam (personal interview, 1957).

England affords a further example of the participation of the national government in the provision of housing and services for the elderly. The Housing Acts of 1936 and 1948 made possible the granting of financial aid to local county councils or county borough councils for (1) building new structures for independent living; (2) conversion of old homes; (3) building communal structures; and (4) offering community services to aid those living independently. Through the National Assistance Act, England also grants rent allowances to those old people whose incomes are so limited that, despite the receipt of a pension, their means entitle them to assistance grants. The National Assistance grant is made up of two parts. One is the scale rate, a level determined by Parliament with reference to the cost of living as being a minimum subsistence payment, and, insofar as the pensioner's income falls below the scale, it is brought up to the statutory level. The second part is the rent allowance and is considered of the utmost importance. Rent controls operating since the war years have recently been abolished, and, as a result, some rents have risen.

Since 1957 about 500,000 National Assistance grants have been increased to take care of the advances in rents, the average increase being a little over 5 shillings (72 cents) per week. In this way many old people have been able to retain their homes and meet increased rent charges.

Government programs for housing the elderly are negligible or non-existent in France, Italy, and Switzerland; but West Germany is beginning to give some attention to this need. In such cities as Berlin and Hamburg, high-rise pensioner flats, usually without elevators, are being built with support from the federal government. The money is loaned to private builders at a very low rate of interest with a 40- or 50-year amortization period. Thus they can be offered at a low rental rate. The first units built especially for old people after the war allowed only 32 square feet per apartment; the size has been increased to 130 square feet now; and it is hoped that, in the near future, funds and material will make it possible to increase the size to 172 square feet. Chronic hospitals also are being built with the assistance of government funds to house the sick aged. In Hamburg, for example, a new three-story building has been added to a general hospital which serves as a central receiving point where all those admitted are screened to determine whether they should be cared for in the hospital or sent to an old age home.

Other financial resources for housing the elderly have greatly augmented the housing supply and services for the aged in most countries, since government interest and support of housing programs and community services have not excluded the participation of non-governmental agencies. No matter how much state and municipal subsidization has been available, it has never been enough in any country to provide adequately for the increasing demands. The non-governmental groups have attempted to help fill the gap and have rendered valuable aid in this respect. Since in a number of European countries there has been a willingness of governmental agencies to give some financial support to the efforts of voluntary groups, the value of government expenditures has been considerably enhanced.

In the Netherlands, housing corporations build about three dwelling units for each one built by public authorities, according to G. de Haan, staff member of Gemeentelijke Dienstvan Sociale Zaken (personal interview, 1957). The Dutch federation for the care of old people, which is composed of all top-level voluntary organizations concerned with the care of the aged, receives some financial aid from the government for its programs of research and for inspection of old age homes. There are many church-subsidized old age homes in the Netherlands, and a considerable number of the newest and most modern ones have been built recently by both Catholic and Protestant church groups. The churches are also an important source of funds for making up the difference between living costs of the aged and their old age pensions and incomes. The churches and voluntary groups, such as the Women's Voluntary Service, subsidize the community service programs, although some financial assistance often is provided by the government, especially the local municipalities. The Red Cross provides some assistance for occupational therapy programs.

The Netherlands is fairly typical of voluntary effort in other countries. In England, for example, voluntary groups, upon application, may receive financial assistance from governmental sources for building new dwellings or converting old ones. Normally, housing through voluntary effort is provided in one of these ways: the formation by local groups of special housing societies for the express purpose of establishing housing schemes for the elderly; the assumption by established voluntary agencies of the development of housing programs; and the adoption of housing as a part of the responsibility of the local old people's welfare committees. Financial assistance which is available to these voluntary groups for the construction of new housing includes (1) a £10 subsidy per year for 60 years from the Exchequer for each new one-bedroom bungalow or flat suitable for old people and (2) a maximum of 90 per cent of the capital cost of the scheme to be obtained as a mortgage through the local authority. The repayment period is for 60 years at a current rate of $5\frac{1}{2}$ per cent (Great Britain, National Old People's Welfare Council, 1956). For the *conversion of old houses,* three types of assistance are available: (1) a 50 per cent improvement grant in a lump sum; (2) an improvement grant in the form of an annual subsidy for 20 years; or (3) the obtaining of a mortgage. Encouraged recently by the government, local housing societies have been especially concerned with the conversion of existing property because it can be used in accommodating old persons in their local neighborhoods. The converted homes are frequently managed by volunteers, making it unnecessary to employ anyone beyond an overseer who may get only his living in payment. Home-help services are also provided in many English communities through the efforts and support of the local old people's welfare committees and through the Women's Voluntary Services. These services are often in addition to those supplied by local municipal authorities, although the latter are permitted to give financial assistance to voluntary groups which provide hot meals to old people living at home or operate luncheon clubs where older people may obtain meals at nominal charges.

To summarize briefly, financial support is provided by the federal and local governments of most countries. This aid may be in the form of rent allowances, low-in-

terest, long amortization loans, or outright grants. The housing may be built by municipalities, or the funds may be made available to voluntary groups or to private builders who build low rental housing. Financial aid is available for new housing, conversion, or the construction of old age homes and nursing homes. In general, programs of conversion are the least popular with government agencies. Financial assistance is generally available to voluntary groups also for providing various types of household help and care services. To the government support of both housing and community services are to be added the funds raised by voluntary agencies, the church, and labor organizations.

F. Payments Made by Old People

Government subsidization of construction of low rental housing and of old age homes is generally insufficient, however, to bring rentals within reach of pensioner incomes. Hence, in several countries, notably Sweden, Denmark, and England, the authorities find it necessary to provide rent supplements or allowances.

RENT ALLOWANCES FOR INDEPENDENT DWELLINGS

Since 1954 Sweden has had such state-subsidized rental supplements which are fixed in amount by the municipalities. The state contributes from 40 to 75 per cent of the costs, depending on the size of the tax base in each municipality. A rough average rental allowance in rural areas ranges from 150 to 180 kronor per year ($30–$36) for a single pensioner and 200 to 240 kronor ($40–$50) for a married couple. In the cities they may range from 500 to 1000 kronor ($100–$200) or even higher (Tegner, 1956). The full rent allowance, established by the municipality, is payable if the pensioner does not earn more than 1000 kronor per year if single or 1500 kronor if married. No form of retirement pension, general family allowance, sickness benefits, or assistance received from relatives or others is considered as income in calculating the amount of rental allowance to be made to the pensioner (Swedish Institute, 1956). If the income exceeds the limits set by as much as 400 kronor for single persons and 600 for couples, the housing allowance is decreased by one-third of the amount by which the income exceeds the basic 1000 or 1500 kronor, respectively. If the income exceeds 1400 or 2100 kronor, there is a further decrease amounting to two-thirds of the excessive amount.

Although the granting of the municipal housing allowances to persons in receipt of retirement incomes is left to a local decision, practically all Swedish municipalities have adopted the plan. A number of cities have added additional sums so that the pensioners' incomes meet with more than mere subsistence needs. The following quotation by Mehr (1957), mayor of social affairs in Stockholm, will illustrate how one large community has used the rental allowance provision to augment the income of its old people:

To begin with, single persons are eligible for an allowance of 525 kronor, and married couples 686 kronor. This sum has nothing to do with the cost of the dwelling, but is meant to help pay part of other living costs. The rent allowance has thus been used to improve the general standard of living for old age pensioners living in Stockholm. In addition, both single and married couples are entitled to a *sum equal to* costs of living in a dwelling, including heating costs, if any. The upper limit is normally fixed at 1600 kronor (February, 1957), but this limit is exceeded if the rent for a standard dwelling, usually one room and kitchen, happens to be higher. Rent allowances are subject to an income test . . . but are not reduced until a single person makes more than 1000 kronor a year and a married couple 1500 kronor. . . . A single pensioner in Stockholm, without any large income of his own, thus has his rent paid for him by the pension; in addition he gets 2675 kronor to pay for other living costs. Of this sum about 2150 kronor is represented by the national pension and 525 kronor by the municipal rent allowance. . . . The [rent] allowances mean

that pensioners no longer need deny themselves decent houses for financial reasons. The actual cost of housing is covered by the municipal rent allowance. As a result, pensioners are not compelled to find accommodation in pensioners' homes, but can compete with everyone else for the dwellings available on the housing market [pp. 5–6].

The pensioners' homes offer accommodations at rents fixed to cover the actual costs of operation. But, since rental allowances usually cover the total rent, there is no disadvantage to the occupants. To qualify for admission into a pensioners' home, the person must be receiving the national old age pension and either lack a suitable dwelling or the possibility of acquiring one by his own efforts. It is intended that the pensioners' flats are to be rented to persons having the least income.

It might also be pointed out that the system of rent allowances has encouraged private organizations and institutions to build dwellings for the aged, since they can count on the municipal rent allowance which makes it possible to charge rents that will cover the costs of operation.

Denmark, like Sweden, has taken steps to help cover rent payments. In 1937, by an amendment to the Danish National Insurance Act, a plan of state subsidies was established for the operation of dwellings erected or acquired by local authorities to accommodate old age pensioners (Danish Ministry of Labour and Social Affairs, 1953). Under the amended Housing Aid Act of 1951, the state pays one-half of the annual deficit incurred by the local authorities in operating approved old age pensioners' flats. This rule applies automatically to all pensioners' flats erected after July 1, 1951, and, upon application to local authorities, can be applied to those constructed at an earlier date.

The flats are rented to pensioners who are in difficult situations—financially or otherwise. The rents of the flats are fixed at amounts somewhat below the rate paid by pensioners in ordinary one- and two-room flats. The pension payable to those living in these low rental flats, however, is reduced by about 4 per cent. They have thus little, if any, economic advantage over pensioners living in ordinary flats. Nevertheless, the flats are popular because they are more modern and comfortable than the ordinary ones that can be rented at a comparable cost.

Some concern has developed in Denmark about gathering the old age pensioners in special housing projects, since it tends to isolate them and impairs their opportunity for finding occasional odd jobs with which to supplement their incomes. To meet this criticism, the 1951 Housing Aid Act provided that old age pensioners in economic need or other difficult situations could receive a subsidy for rent of accommodations in ordinary non-profit housing projects which had been erected subsequent to July 1, 1951. The subsidy reduces the rent to the level applying to old age pensioners' flats.

England, likewise, provides rent subsidies to help old people of low income meet the cost of living (Rowntree, 1947). The Parliament of 1940 established supplementary pensions for old people and widows, the cost of which is borne by the Exchequer and administered through the regional offices of the National Assistance Board. For the year ending December 31, 1957, the National Assistance Board reported that 978,000 allowances were being paid to supplement retirement pensions. The supplements are granted only to persons whose incomes are too low to meet their needs (approximately 25 per cent of old age pensioners). To the extent that a pensioner's income falls below a subsistence minimum, it may be made up by an assistance grant, and to this is added an allowance for rent. The amount of rent allowance depends upon the general rent levels of the locality and the recommendations of the local advisory committee. In most instances, the rent is covered in full. In applying the needs test, many resources are left out or taken into account only in part. The exemptions include (1) the

earnings of sons and daughters living in the household of the parent (although it is assumed each makes a contribution to the household); (2) the first 10s. 6d. ($1.50) a week of superannuation payments coming from sources other than the Exchequer; (3) the first £375 and interest on it of war savings. Additional capital does not disqualify the pensioner for a supplementary pension unless it exceeds £400 and then only on a sliding scale in relation to increasing amounts of capital. If the pensioner owns the house in which he lives, its value is disregarded entirely, and an allowance for the mortgage interest, etc., is made in place of a rent allowance.

In the Netherlands, where practically all dwellings constructed after the war were subsidized by grants either for building costs or for operating costs, rents have been kept at reasonable levels. In the case of aged couples who have incomes lower than 2520 guilders per year, or single persons whose annual cash income is below 1640 guilders, a rent subsidy of 100 guilders per year is made available if they live in postwar houses or in institutions.

In brief, it is obvious that these countries consider the principle that all old people should maintain their own households as of such major importance that far-reaching government programs of financial aid have been devised to insure that pensioners will have the means to live independently if they wish. These programs also assist the voluntary and private organizations which provide non-profit pensioner housing by insuring that the old person has sufficient income to cover rental charges.

ALLOWANCES FOR COMMUNAL ACCOMMODATIONS

The payments old people must make for accommodation and care in old people's homes are also subsidized by the state. With some modification the municipal housing allowances in Sweden apply to persons living in an old age home, so that the older person is not called upon to pay beyond the limits of his income (Swedish Institute, 1956). For example, in Gothenburg, the fees at the two most modern old people's homes are set at 6.70 kronor per day ($1.30), which makes it possible for the resident to pay them out of his old age pension and still have a sum left over for pocket money (Gothenburg Municipal Executive Board, 1957). It might be noted here that applications for admittance are handled on the basis of need and not according to income or property.

In England, where local authorities are charged, under the National Assistance Act of 1948, to provide residential accommodations for any old person in need of care and attention, the subsidy scheme has been used to some extent by local authorities to build homes themselves. But to a larger extent, the authorities have used voluntary bodies as their agents and either have contributed to the cost of establishing a home or are paying for the maintenance of residents less the amount they can pay for themselves (Shenfield, 1957). Recently, local authorities have overtaken voluntary bodies in the number of dwellings built or converted for group care of the elderly. Where local authorities pay for maintenance of pensioners in voluntary homes, the amount is usually based on the actual cost. If the resident can pay the full charge, which amounts on an average to between $7.50 and $8.25 per week, he is expected to do so. Otherwise, he pays in proportion to his resources, and the difference is made up by a grant from the National Assistance Board. But, no matter what the cost of accommodation, the pensioner is always left a certain sum laid down by regulation as personal pocket money. A similar plan is carried out in homes operated by local authorities where the average charge is about $10 per week. This is a higher figure than for the voluntary homes, because clothing and other items are not included in the charges made by voluntary groups.

As with independent housing, attempts are made to assist old people to obtain the kind of accommodations they need—in this instance, residential or communal care. The means used vary from the payment of special subsidies made directly to the individual to the fixing of rent rates at a level old people can pay from their regular pensions, with the operational deficit made up from public funds.

In summary, the social policies which have been established in the last several decades by the countries of western Europe and the British Isles reflect a full cognizance of the needs and rights of older people. Practices have been instituted to make possible the enjoyment by the aged of these rights and privileges. Government, private enterprise, and voluntary agencies are sharing with the old people in attaining an assured place in the community, either as an independent householder or as a member of a communal group. All effort is directed to helping the aged person to meet his needs as a self-supporting citizen and to remove the taint of charity from the social assistance which may be required to assist the individual to attain this status.

III. CONCEPTS AND PRINCIPLES IN HOUSING THE AGED

From their larger experience with the problems of housing relatively large numbers of old people, the Scandinavian countries and England have achieved the solutions to some of the most difficult questions confronting the United States today in its early attempts to develop a large-scale program of housing for the aged. Out of practical experience and from the results of simple survey studies of the needs and wishes of older people, these foreign countries established national policies and defined a clear-cut set of principles to guide communities in the planning and constructing of old age housing.

Reference has already been made in this chapter to a number of social concepts on which the housing principles and policies are based. These may be stated briefly as follows:

1. It is in the best interests of the economy and social health of the country to provide old people with living arrangements especially suited to their needs.
2. Industrialized society, because of its influence on the breakup of the generations, must assume some of the responsibility for the shelter and care of the aged previously supplied by the family.
3. The old age group has the right to its proportionate share of the goods and services available to other age groups in the population.
4. Mental and physical health of older people are promoted when the aged are privileged to retain active membership in the life of the community.

In Sweden a housing policy committee appointed by the Swedish minister of social welfare took the following position: "In the first place and to the largest extent possible, measures for the care of the aged should aim at assisting the aged by all available means to live independent lives in their homes as long as possible without excessive personal strain" (Ulrikoson, 1958, p. 1).

Mehr (1957) has described in some detail the policies followed in the city of Stockholm which are the same as those subscribed to on a national basis:

The goal of old age assistance in Stockholm is to provide conditions making it possible for old people to enjoy a free and independent life, to the same extent and in the same social forms as younger and middle-aged people enjoy. Essential components of this goal are, of course, economic security, dwellings, and medical service. We also need an open service which can give the aged occasional help and do odd jobs for them. Further, we must try to abolish or prevent the isolation which so easily becomes an accompaniment to old age in a modern society. "Old" and "lonely" are, alas, two words which are only too often linked together, and rightly. Various measures designed to improve the old person's contentment with his life must therefore be regarded as important factors in modern old age assistance [pp. 1–2].

The English likewise have taken a broad overview of the housing for the elderly. In *Housing for Special Purposes* (Great Britain, Ministry of Local Government and Planning, 1951) the following statement is made:

The ultimate object of all housing activity is to give the opportunity of living a full and happy life in healthy and congenial surroundings. . . . For older people it means that accommodations should be provided which enable them to take their part in the life of the community. . . . Elderly people with their greater freedom from family cares can render valuable service to the community in which they live [p. 6].

The most common dictum on housing the aging, heard everywhere in England (and also in the Netherlands and the Scandinavian countries), is that the elderly should live in their own homes as long as possible because it is more economical for the state and because the old people are happier. Admission to an old people's home should be a last resort (Moss, 1957). Currently, however, this policy is under question because it may mean that old people are kept at home under circumstances where they cannot be properly cared for except by an unreasonably heavy burden on a family, with perhaps adverse effects on young children. Also, it may be more expensive both directly in the cost of buying services and indirectly in absorbing scarce personnel.

With these objectives in mind, an examination of the various types of independent and institutional housing that are being built in various countries will illustrate the means employed to achieve the stated goals. An understanding of the social values of a country and a knowledge of the housing principles based on them make it relatively easy to predict the policies that will be adopted in consideration of such specific and major questions as uses of independent and institutional homes, size and site of housing developments, services to be included with housing, special design features needed, and programs to meet the social needs of residents.

A. Homes versus Institutions

In the United Kingdom, the Netherlands, and the Scandinavian countries, where family responsibility for the older generation is declining and where, although it may still be a legal requirement, the law is not enforced (in England it is no longer legally required), the emphasis is upon providing independent living accommodations for those able (with or without help) to maintain their own homes. Institutions are reserved for those who are so frail or disabled that they cannot manage a household any longer or who are so sick that they must have constant medical attention. Effort is expended in creating a homelike atmosphere in the institutions in an attempt to make them more acceptable substitutes for independent living and family relationships.

TYPES OF ACCOMMODATIONS

Pensioners' flats or apartment buildings are the most common forms of independent accommodations in countries that have housing programs for the elderly. As a rule, these buildings are from two to four stories high. Entrance to each flat is gained directly from the street or, in the case of upper floors, from a balcony. The flats are usually built in blocks and may include such central features as heating, assembly halls, kitchens, craft rooms, laundry, and bathing facilities. Although each block of flats has a superintendent (usually a trained nurse in Sweden and Denmark) who assists the occupants in cases of emergency and illness, complete privacy and independence of action can be maintained by the residents.

Another type of housing which is seen more often in Holland and England than in the Scandinavian countries is the small cottage or motel-type apartment. In the Netherlands these are often interspersed in short blocks or distributed among high-rise family-apartment developments. In England the cottages are sometimes designed as an integral link in the attached dwellings built for younger families; in other instances they are grouped together around a common square or garden. And in some housing developments ("estates," as the English call them) the cottages are scattered through the property. There is, as a rule, a superintendent in charge whose function is that of rent-collector and liaison between renter and local authorities. Services include heating, community clubroom, and gardening.

In the Netherlands is to be found a special type of cottage development—the *hofje* —already mentioned as a traditional form of housing first built by seventeenth-century Dutch merchants for their retired servants and workers. The inclosed court of the *hofje* offers a special charm. Located, as many of them are, in the hearts of large cities, they seem quite remote from the hustle and noise outside their walls. The attached cottages are arranged with their backs forming the solid outside walls of the square and their doors opening on the friendly central court. The *hofje* usually includes quarters for the supervisor (manager), but otherwise there is often no central service. Sometimes, however, there are, especially in modernized units, such central services as heating, kitchens, etc. The new *hofjes* of today are almost exact duplicates of those constructed several centuries ago, except that modern conveniences are now included, and sometimes meals, laundry, and home-help services are offered.

Intermediate between completely independent housing and the communal old age home is the "center system." A large communal building—the "mother" home—has small houses built around it. In case of temporary illness, frailty, or loneliness, the "mother" home provides the occupants of the cottages with such services as hot meals, cleaning, heating, laundry, and occasionally some nursing care. When the residents become too frail or lonely, they move into the central home.

Institutional or congregate living arrangements range, in all the countries studied, from the remodeled large old houses, through the institutions and the church or other voluntarily supported homes of the past, to the most modern of buildings conceived to preserve the dignity and independence of the old person. These institutions all offer central services, including dining. Many, but not all, include medical and infirmary care. Some of the ingenious architectural features developed to reduce the institutional character of the old age homes will be discussed in a later section.

The large old people's villages which have been built in several countries deserve a special note because, in spite of the fact that experience has made them more and more unpopular in Europe and the United Kingdom, there is evidence that builders and social planners in the United States are moving toward the construction of similar developments. The principle of the village is to provide for all the needs of the elderly. Thus the village includes a number of types of accommodations so that, as the individual becomes progressively more feeble, there is a living arrangement where the needed degree of care is offered. The villages usually include such central features as a dining hall, church, post office, and recreation center, and, if far removed from a community, a small shopping center. A number of these large villages have been in operation since the 1920's, and a study of them is useful in determining whether they constitute a desirable form of housing arrangement for the aged (Donahue, 1960).

PROVISIONS FOR PRIVACY

Privacy has come to be recognized as one of the major attributes of good housing for older people. Dr. Berggren, of Sweden, comments that every old person has the right and necessity to be alone as opposed to being isolated. The provision of cottages, flats, apartments, and maisonettes built for single- or two-person occupancy has as a primary objective the preservation of privacy. In the communal homes there is also increased effort to insure that each individual has a reasonable degree of privacy. The newer buildings have private rooms for single persons and couples. Older buildings are being remodeled to provide single rooms or to reduce the size of the large wards to accommodate four to six persons in place of fifteen or twenty. In some instances half-partitions are used, especially in those units where persons live who are receiving nursing care. Even in the old-time institutions which do not lend themselves to remodeling, privacy is provided by hanging curtains permanently around each bed space. Although such an arrangement seems cramped and airless, the occupants, when asked by the writer how they liked the plan, replied that they liked it very much indeed because they had a place of their own, away from the prying eyes of their neighbors.

There is also a tendency to reduce the amount of common living space provided in the communal homes and to distribute the square footage among the living quarters of the residents. Little use is made of common space generally, since the residents prefer to sit and to entertain their friends in their own rooms rather than in a public room. In order to make the single room appear to have a maximum of privacy, a small vestibule is recommended. Water closets are installed in most apartments, and in the newer buildings there are also some private baths. In older buildings bathtubs are sometimes installed in the kitchens.

The notion of privacy is expressed outside the dwellings by providing small yard-garden spaces, often shielded from the adjoining garden by a fence or solid wall. In the Netherlands, where the one-story row housing is common, each apartment has its garden opening off the living room to furnish, in good weather, an extension of space.

INDIVIDUALIZATION OF ACCOMMODATION

As much value is placed on providing a homelike atmosphere which reflects the personality of each occupant as on privacy. One way in which this is accomplished is by permitting the renter to use his own furnishings. Even in communal homes this is the practice, although the individual may be advised on the suitability of pieces and helped to have old furniture refinished and re-upholstered in suitable colors and fabrics. Sweden has perhaps gone further than other countries in reducing the institutional quality of old age homes by using different colored and patterned wallpapers and textiles throughout the buildings, gay scatter rugs (on non-slip mats), a variety of small table lamps in place of overhead lighting, a lavish number of plants, and good pictures for the walls.

B. Size of Housing Developments

If there is a single trend with reference to the size of housing developments, it is to keep them relatively small. After early experiences with large old people's villages, such as De Gamles By in Copenhagen or Riehler Heimstattan in Cologne, each of which accommodates nearly 2000 persons, it was concluded that the bringing-together and isolation from the regular community of large numbers of old people is an undesirable practice. In consequence, most housing developments of all kinds are now kept relatively small.

In Stockholm, on the basis of practical experience, it is recommended that the ideal number of flats in pensioners' blocks be 100. This size is considered "large enough to constitute a unity in regard to the staff needed to help the elderly dwellers, and small enough so that the old folk cannot dominate but will naturally melt in with the other populations in the area" (Mehr, 1957, p. 7).

With reference to the number of old people who should be accommodated in a single old age home, there is some divergence of opinion. In the Netherlands it is recommended that a home should not be built for less than 50 persons because it is not economical to operate for any smaller number. At the upper limit, 300 places are set as the maximum number, according to F. H. J. Nierstrasz (personal interview, 1957). Dr. Berggren, in Sweden, recommends that the optimum number of places in each home be from 30 to 40. Except in large cities, where the homes may accommodate from 80 to 150 persons, the number of places in each separate home is as a rule not less than 18–20 and not more than 60. In planning new old age homes, the number of places needed is estimated on the basis of 10 per cent of the number of inhabitants in the community aged 70 and over (Berggren, 1958a). In the United Kingdom the recommended number is 25–40 people, with 30 considered an ideal number. If it is desired to accommodate more than 30 old persons at one site, additional buildings, each designed for about 30 people, should be added (Great Britain, Ministry of Local Government and Planning, 1951).

It should be pointed out, however, that, although there is general agreement in most countries that on many grounds small homes are desirable for older people in communal care, there is not infrequently a gap between declared policies and actual practice. In Stockholm, for example, there is a relatively new fourteen-story all-purpose home for the aged. In the United Kingdom, in place of building to accommodate 30–40 persons, homes to accommodate 60–75 residents have been approved officially and constructed. The increase in size is justified on the grounds that in the small homes staff is hard to get and keep; thus the small home is often insufficiently staffed. With a larger staff for 60 residents, duties can be switched, temporary absences of staff can be absorbed, and the staff is more contented because they have more social life. In fact, to get and keep staff, the wishes of the staff rather than the requirements of the elderly are given preference. These are the practical considerations which tend to shape policies despite the best intentions.

C. Siting Old People's Housing

In the past, European countries and the United States made it a custom to locate homes for old people in remote spots ostensibly to shield them from noise and traffic. Today there is a unanimity of opinion that this is not a desirable practice for a number of reasons. First, it is against the wishes of old people themselves. A number of surveys of old people's housing preferences show that they wish to live close to friends and relatives, shops, and other community services rather than in isolated areas. In large cities, such as Stockholm, London, and others, where it is not possible to obtain land at permissive cost in the central part of the town, practice is opposed to principle, and new housing and conversion of existing dwellings are still located in remote areas. There is, however, considerable objection on the part of old people to moving to the pensioners' flats built in the suburbs (Goldberg, 1959).

A second consideration is that, when old people are moved into new housing located away from the area where the family members reside, they lose much of the help and companionship their children provide. In the Wolverhampton study (Sheldon, 1948), it was found that, although not sharing the same accommodations, family members often lived in such close geographical proximity that they shared their daily lives with one another and offered each other much reciprocal service. Townsend (1956) likewise, in his study of the extent and content of the individual family relationships of old people in Bethnal Green, found that, of those living alone, three-quarters of them saw at least one relative every day or every other day and received many services from them of a domestic nature. Townsend, therefore, argues that social policies for housing should maximize these enduring aspects of family life by locating dwellings for old people in proximity to that of younger families. Thus the younger and older generations need not share the same roof but can profit mutually from close association. Shenfield (1957) points out an added practical advantage of this arrangement is that it is easier to convince old people living in a too large accommodation to move to a smaller and more appropriate one if the move does not entail going to a new district far removed from contact with relatives. Where congested urban areas are being cleared and sites redeveloped at lower densities, local authorities are asked to give special consideration to enabling the old to remain in the neighborhood they know and where they have social connections and to keep them whenever possible near their families.

Another principle in selecting sites for old people's housing, which is closely related to the foregoing, is that it should be integrated with normal housing in such a way that any appearance of an old persons' colony is avoided. It is for this reason, in part, that the large retirement towns, such as Whitly Village near London, De Gamles By in Copenhagen, and others, are now looked upon with some disfavor. In Stockholm, where only a modest number of pensioners' flats are built together in any one residential area, old people have expressed some objections to living even in this degree of segregation. It is largely for this reason that the government makes aid available to non-profit builders for the provision of pensioners' units in ordinary apartment houses. The Central Housing Advisory Committee of the Ministry of Local Government and Planning (1951) in England recommends that dwellings for the elderly be sited among ordinary housing developments, but, in order to expedite the provision of some central supervision, these dwellings may be grouped together up to twenty cottages, or they may be interspersed with family dwellings but arranged so that the cottages are within easy reach of one another.

Finally, it is recommended that communal homes for the aged be located so that they are an integral part of the community. The English Advisory Committee on Housing (Great Britain, Ministry of Local Government and Planning, 1951) suggests that the hostels planned for those who are no longer able to manage a household be located in the same districts as the groups of old people's cottages and near the health centers of the public health authorities. Thus "a complete range of suitable accommodations for old people will be available to them in such a way as to insure that such changes as they have to make as they advance in years will be least upsetting to them" (p. 11).

Old people's homes are, of course, not restricted to the larger cities, especially in countries where there is a legal requirement that all old people must be provided suitable housing by the local authorities. The modern practice is to locate the old age home serving a rural area in a small village where the residents can easily mingle in the life of the community. In other words, although an old age home inevitably represents some separation of the occupants from normal residential living, an effort is made to prevent their isolation from the community.

The foregoing suggestions are those which have evolved out of a good many years of experience in a number of countries. In all instances small projects as completely integrated with the community as possible are recommended as the most desirable practice. It should, however, be pointed out that large homes and the old age village in remote areas are still being constructed. The newest old age home in Stockholm is a high-rise building of fourteen stories; in Oslo a thirteen-story building has just been completed. An announcement has recently been made (German Federal Republic, 1958) of the plans for the first "Old Age Village" at Murnaw in West Germany. It is to be built on a 30,000-square-meter tract of land on the slopes above Lake Staffelsee in the foothills of the Bavarian Alps. It is described as being in distinct contrast to the usual old age home because its "inmates" are to be given more individual care, greater freedom

of activity, and an activities program. In spite of the glowing account of the opportunities for the old people to lead independent lives in one- and two-room flats and of a research program to study the problems of aging, one must still pause to consider the advice of those long experienced in operating projects involving the isolation and separation of the aged before accepting the proposed Murnaw Old Age Village with uncritical enthusiasm.

D. Medical Care and Housing

Medical care of old people living in their own homes is little different from that of other age groups. The question is largely how medical resources are to be divided and whether special clinics and health programs for the elderly are to be developed. Chapter vi indicates the extent of these kinds of services provided by various countries.

The problem with reference to old age homes is, however, somewhat different and revolves around the question of what and how much, if any, medical service is to be provided by the home, and where, if full medical care is not provided, such service will be obtained. As already mentioned, the old age home was traditionally a place where the indigent sick aged went for shelter and care until death. There was thus established a societal expectancy that old age homes would offer life-term care. There is a lingering flavor today of this stereotype which, especially in the United States, is confusing the adoption of clear-cut policies with regard to the amount and type of medical care to be included in the services of old age homes.

HOW MUCH MEDICAL CARE?

Sweden has adopted a national policy which delineates more clearly than the provisions of other countries the roles of the hospital and of the old age home in caring for the sick aged. The Minister of Social Affairs and the Social and Medical Boards have agreed that old persons who are sick shall have the same care in the same hospitals and under the same law as all other citizens. Dr. Berggren (1958b) has expressed the Swedish position as follows:

We are now of the opinion that an old person, when he gets sick, shall have the same opportunity of a doctor's help in the ordinary hospital organization as any other citizen. But we have a great shortness of hospital beds and nursing personnel, so that for the present, and in some provinces for another ten years, we are obliged to organize home-care and sick-care to a certain extent in old age homes [p. 2].

It is clearly recognized by Dr. Berggren and others that the shortage of medical personnel already handicapping hospitals in their effort to care for the long-term ill aged makes it utterly impractical to assume that the medical service afforded residents in hundreds of old age homes goes beyond mere custodial care. In the large cities, of course, where the personnel shortage is less acute, the picture is somewhat better. In Stockholm, for example, there are five homes which combine a nursing home with an old age home and offer full-scale medical care and rehabilitation services (Dahlström, 1956).

In the Netherlands, with the new trend toward offering two types of housing—the independent dwelling for those able to maintain a household and the old age home for those who need nursing care—hospital-type care is introduced into nursing homes and excluded from old age homes.

Although considered atypical and undesirable by the Dutch, a large home in The Hague illustrates the range of care available in one of the new types of the "all-round care" homes. For the most able, there are small cottage apartments built adjacent to the large central building. The old people occupying these cottages receive no medical or nursing care except for temporary illness. For those who need continuing medical service there are several types of accommodations within the central building. The first of these is designed for occupancy by a couple of which one

member needs continuing medical care and is a self-contained apartment consisting of living-sleeping room and kitchen-dining room. A balcony offers extra space in good weather. For single persons who are still largely able to manage for themselves, there are single-room accommodations; and, finally, for those who are so ill that they need continuous hospital-type care, there is a hospital wing. Although the building includes an assembly hall, craft rooms, and recreational facilities, it has the character of a medical institution rather than that of a home, an impression augmented by the location of the morgue in the wing where the more able residents are housed. The building of this type of "all-round care" home is being discouraged also in other countries of Europe as an undesirable practice.

In England and in a number of other countries the trend is to provide a variety of housing accommodations for those who are too frail or too ill to manage households for themselves. These can be classified as follows:

1. *Residential homes* for the ambulatory who can look after their personal needs but who must have housekeeping services and some general oversight. Only temporary illness of a few days' duration can be cared for in these homes.

2. *Halfway homes* associated with geriatric hospitals for those people who need convalescent care after hospitalization and before they return to their homes and also for those who need longer-term care while they undergo physical and mental rehabilitation before discharge to their homes. Actually, there are very few of this type accommodation, and it is predicted by various leaders that there will not be much development in this direction.

   The Guilleband Committee, in its study of the structure of medical care, condemned the halfway houses as intermediate accommodations for the long-term ill in the belief that persons ordinarily cared for in them are rightfully hospital patients.

3. *Rest homes* for those who do not need hospital care but do need constant attention and help of a simpler kind. Admission to

these units usually follows evaluation in a geriatric hospital. The National Corporation for the Care of Old People has established a number of these rest homes.

4. *Long-stay annexes* for the irremediably sick. These are designed to accommodate the chronically ill and are therefore technically a part of the medical-care services (see chap. vi), as, for example, the Geriatric Unit of the Cowley Road Hospital, Oxford, or the Geriatric Hospital of the Sunderland Area Hospitals.

The housing of the mentally confused old people is a problem still of concern to the English (and all other countries, for that matter). In 1950 the Ministry of Health (1950) recommended that long-stay annexes be established for patients without marked behavior disorders as distinct from the disturbed types. The annexes, it was suggested, might be associated with mental or general hospitals or with hospitals for the chronic sick, although it would be preferable to locate them outside the curtilage of a mental hospital.

The Netherlands' Ministry of Housing and Building recently supported the preparation and publication of a report prepared by Bouwcentrum (1958) on the subject of nursing homes for the mentally infirm old people. A special committee of professional people assisted Bouwcentrum in this study and recommended that the mentally infirm (senile dementia, lightly depressive and inactive, alcoholics, mentally deficient, epileptics, etc.) should be provided separate homes and should not be cared for in a psychiatric institution or in a separate department of old age homes or institutions serving the mentally fit aged. The report says that "among other things it has been precisely the careless mixing of totally different categories which . . . has led to less desirable conditions. Moreover, the category in question requires a specific form of nursing which— partly for psychological reasons—can hardly be combined with the care of mentally fit old people." Although it is recommended that the home have a capacity for 150 per-

sons, it is emphasized that patients should be accommodated in units serving no more than 12 persons. Detailed building plans are a part of this report. (See chap. vii for further discussion of this type of accommodation and other arrangements for the senile aged.)

FINANCING MEDICAL CARE IN HOMES FOR THE AGING

One problem which is a determining factor in the provision of medical and nursing care in homes for old people is that of the cost of building and equipping medical care or hospital units and of employing a skilled staff. In fact, this cost, as much as the shortage of professional personnel, is a major determinant of the medical care policies recommended.

In Sweden, where virtually all hospitals are maintained at public expense (in 1954 the publicly subsidized hospitals had places for about 100,000 patients while private hospitals had only 2000 places), it is logical to follow a policy of offering hospital service to old people in the regular hospitals as opposed to diverting staff and equipping expensive units for old age homes (Tegner, 1956). Since the basic principle is that all citizens are entitled to the best possible care at low cost, no one is expected to be denied adequate care for lack of funds. Aged persons who have chronic illnesses of long duration will be cared for in chronics' homes, but the cost will usually be covered by benefits or will be made up by public assistance.

The United Kingdom, likewise, through the National Health Service Act, makes hospital care and the services of specialists available to people of all age groups. The hospitals in a number of areas have established special geriatric units where care on a long-term basis is available. The emphasis in these hospitals is on rehabilitation of the patients and in making the hospital service an integral part of the total community program for the aged. Such services make unnecessary the inclusion of hospital units in the old age homes. It must be admitted, of course, that the shortage of hospital beds often makes it necessary to nurse older residents in a home. Also, as more elderly and infirm persons enter homes, the need for nursing care may be extended, and "sick bays" are beginning to appear more often in communal homes. The National Health Service scheme, of course, entitles old people living independently to care by a doctor and to glasses, dentures, surgical appliances, and prosthetic devices. The patient pays certain fees for these services, but repayment can be obtained from the National Assistance Board if the recipient is too poor to pay himself.

In the Netherlands there exists a voluntary sick-insurance scheme which more than two-thirds of all the aged use. The premium is very low. Almost all residents of homes have this type insurance, which entitles them to the same health services and care as the general sick funds.

E. Design and Special Features

A number of European countries have carried out practical experiments with different designs for independent dwellings and for old people's homes. As a result, they have developed standards that have gone through a fairly extensive process of evaluation and have established some guide lines for future construction and design—in general, economy of size, easy maintenance, and a homelike quality.

INDEPENDENT DWELLINGS

The *Housing Manual, 1949* and its *Supplement, 1951,* published by the Ministry of Health (1949, 1951) in England, list the recommended designs for accommodations to house able-bodied aged persons capable of looking after themselves. In summary they are as follows:

1. Accommodations should be provided in self-contained dwellings of either one- or two-story cottages or cottage flats or on the lower floors of blocks cf flats.

2. The units should be comprised of a living room; double bedroom, entered from living room or hall; working kitchen; and combined bathroom and water closet. The bedroom may take the form of a bed recess with a separate window, in which case an additional single bedroom may be provided.

3. The recommended minimum sizes for rooms are (in square feet): living rooms, 140–60; living room and bed recess, 230–50; double bedroom, 120 (minimum); and single bedroom, 70–80.

4. Over-all sizes of dwellings are, for two persons, 450–550 square feet; for three persons, 550–650 square feet.

5. Special features include: front and back doors sheltered to prevent drafts; good thermal insulation; easy access to fuel from within the house; clear space on either side of the beds; handrail to the bath; stairs, if any, easy to climb, with handrail; fireplace in main bedroom, if a separate room; solid-fuel heater in the living room; heated towel rail in bathroom; living room with sunny exposure; bay window or veranda whenever possible; sills of windows low enough to see out of from chair or bed; water closets and bathroom doors opening outward; communal garden maintained in front of dwellings; private garden plot of personal cultivation in the rear; and central heating prepared for large blocks of flats.

A typical plan for a two-person flat having a bed recess in place of a bedroom has the following specifications:

Living room...........	14'3" × 11'3"
Bed recess.............	9' × 8'3"
Working kitchen........	7'9" × 7'6"
Bathroom with water closet...............	7' × 4'

A typical two-person, one-bedroom flat has approximately the same dimensions except that the bedroom is 11 feet, 3 inches by 10 feet, with the bathroom and halls correspondingly larger.

Ancillary accommodations are needed for the warden's flat and office, a guest apartment or two, storage space, and heating plant; and, if central dining or cooking is a feature, a kitchen and some staff quarters are included.

The external architecture of these English cottages reflects the traditional designs of the region where they are located. Usually of brick fireproof construction, they form neat rows of houses, often in a garden setting.

In Sweden, pensioner flats are typical of the public independent housing built in that country as well as in Denmark, Switzerland, and West Germany. As a rule, the pensioner flats consist of one room and kitchenette for single persons, and one room and kitchen or one room, sleeping alcove, and kitchenette for two persons (married couple, sisters, etc). The recommended floor space for new flats is 260–330 square feet for one person and 320–70 square feet for two persons. Kitchens and kitchenettes are fitted with electric ranges; cupboards and shelves are readily accessible; and refrigerators are installed in the newest kitchens. Each flat has a lavatory with hot and cold running water and a water closet. There are no private baths, but ten to twelve flats share a common bathroom, which is generally located in the basement and is large enough to permit the bathers to receive assistance when needed. Some flats have a bathwoman on duty at specified times to help the residents bathe. Bathtubs and water closets have grab bars (Mehr, 1957).

Some ordinary apartment houses in Sweden also have flats especially designed for invalids. These flats generally consist of two rooms, a kitchen, and a windowed hall. The total floor space is about 860 square feet. Doorways and corridors are large enough to permit the use of wheel chairs. Special attention has been given to the design of the kitchens. The space beneath the sink is open so that the housewife can use it while sitting down; wall cupboards are low enough to be easily reached from a wheelchair. Bathrooms are larger than usual and are equipped with stand-off grips, horizontal-bar supports, and handholds around the toilet. Other aids have been built into wardrobes, closets, doors, and windows. Electric switches

are easily reached and activated. Built-in features include linen closet, clothing rack, wardrobe, and ironing boards. According to Mehr (1957), this type of flat and these special features have given most favorable results when used for old people.

The pensioners' flats in Copenhagen, like those in Sweden, are grouped in several centers throughout the city. Their design has been described as follows (Københavns Kommunes Socialdirektorat, 1948):

In planning these centers Copenhagen has chosen a mixture of two building systems: central corridor houses and ordinary staircase houses. The first type is especially intended for the oldest and weakest inhabitants and has lifts and garbage chutes.

The flats, which are situated in detached blocks, have all sitting rooms placed in such a way as to admit full and direct sunlight. They have central heating, gas, electric lights as well as hot and cold water. Those of the occupants who cannot or who do not wish to cook their own meals may buy their dinner at a very moderate price. Most of the centers have bathing departments for common use and a feast room gratuitously placed at the disposal of inhabitants for celebrations of family as, e.g., golden weddings, etc. . . .

The flats for married couples consist of two rooms of a total area of about 46 square meters and those designated for single persons have . . . about 37 square meters and consist of one room and usually an alcove. Every flat has a kitchen, a lavatory, a hall with a built in wardrobe [p. 13].

The special housing for old people in Holland, like that in Sweden, includes experiments with various design features. A number of manuals have been issued on housing the aged (Bouwcentrum, 1955, 1958) based on careful study of old people's needs with reference to their status and physical and mental health. There is an emphasis on privacy, and many of the residential (communal) homes in the Netherlands (mandatory in the province of Frisia) have a water closet in every room or apartment, and many of the rooms include kitchenettes.

In general, all plans for pensioners'

homes emphasize compactness and special design features to make maintenance and living easier. Most of these accommodations are probably too small in scale to suit the American taste, but they are not too different from what the United States has been able to provide through its program of public housing. For example, one of the newest public housing developments, the A. Gideon Spieker Terrace in Toledo, Ohio, built in 1958, has 44 one-bedroom units (for two-person occupancy) of 530 square feet each, and 6 efficiency units of 325 square feet each. Equipment for these units includes refrigerator, electric range, cupboards, gas-burning space heater, individual water heater, bathtub with built-in seat and handrail, water closet, and lavatory. The preservation of privacy, independence, and self-support are the prime and the most valued characteristics of these designs for independent dwellings; and most old people seem to prefer to sacrifice size to any one or all of the others.

COMMUNAL HOMES

Specifications for residential hostels (old people's homes) are also given special attention in *Housing for Special Purposes* (Great Britain, Ministry of Local Government and Planning, 1951) with the following standards:

1. The building
   a) Not more than two stories high
   b) First floor—communal rooms, dining room, kitchen, residents' bed-sitting rooms, and warden's apartment
   c) Second floor—bed-sitting rooms for residents
   d) Communal rooms should face south or west and afford view of garden
   e) Bed-sitting rooms should face west, south, or southeast so each one will get some sunlight every day
   f) Rooms for single men, single women, and couples should be mixed rather than placed in separate wings
   g) If rooms are placed on both sides of a central corridor, the corridor should have natural lighting and ventilation

   h) All rooms, halls, and passages should have central heating
   i) Communal rooms should have open fires in addition
2. Bed-sitting rooms
   a) Size: single, 140 square feet desirable, 108 square feet minimum; double, 180 square feet minimum
   b) Fittings and features: wash-hand basin; built-in cupboard with hanging space and shelves; electric fire; electric bell by bed; good central light plus a bedside lamp; good natural lighting
3. Communal rooms
   a) Dining room: 15 square feet per person, with small tables in place of refectory tables
   b) Common rooms: 20 square feet per person
4. Bathrooms and water closets
   a) One bath to every 10 residents—to be used by either sex
   b) Two water closets to every 10 residents —separate for the sexes
5. Ancillary accommodations: warden's office (130–50 sq. ft.); cloakroom with water closet and basin; kitchen with wash-up, larder, storerooms, linen room, and laundry; service elevator near kitchen; staff sitting room and lavatory accommodations; staff bedrooms and warden's apartment if resident; small pantry with sink and electric kettle for use of residents; small laundry and trunk storage for residents

The modern old age home in Sweden probably represents today's most advanced thinking in the design of old people's homes. Sweden has been able to experiment with various types and features because the housing authorities there have been determined to find the most suitable and most homelike accommodations possible. The architects have become interested and are beginning to specialize in the design of old people's homes.

Some of the special features that are given attention in the design of the modern Swedish homes are outlined by B. Boustedt, architect of Kungälv, Sweden, who designed and built 35 homes for old people during 1957. The general architectural features may be summarized as follows:

1. The buildings are of fireproof construction and often made of brick. No pensioners' rooms may face north.
2. Construction is kept low but frequently includes some sections of two-story height.
3. Most are built for small numbers of single men and women. Very few accommodations are provided for couples.
4. Single rooms must have a minimum furnishable floor space of 10 square feet.
5. Each room must have a small anteroom with a hot- and cold-water basin, coat rack, and built-in wardrobe.
6. Two water closets are provided for each 8 pensioners, and bathrooms with foot baths are available in every corridor.
7. Common rooms, sitting and recreation rooms, dining rooms, and small coffee kitchens are on each corridor for the use of residents; auditoriums are provided for religious and other types of meetings.
8. Space for the administration and operation of the home also includes kitchen, laundry, offices, medical treatment rooms, nurses' rooms, and, if the staff lives in, bedrooms and sitting rooms.

There are no fixed types of plans for these homes. The design is worked out in each individual case on the basis of the type of community, nature of the terrain, and part of the country. The architect meets with the community planning committee and arranges for representatives to visit several homes to learn at firsthand the problems and their solutions. Following this experience, the architect and committee complete the plans, which include not only the design and standard equipment of the home but the furniture, textiles, art objects, pictures, plants, etc. This type of individualized planning accounts for the inherent charm of the modern Swedish old age homes.

A number of special features contribute to the coziness and homelike atmosphere that do not appear in the list of minimum standards. One of the most effective in reducing the institutional character is the treatment of corridors. A number of devices are employed to achieve short corridors with an open character. One method is to provide visual contact in the corridor at all times with furnished areas. Small sitting rooms may be used to break the length; the ends of the corridors may be made wide enough to accommodate some furnishing along one side without jeopardizing the safety of the residents. Often one side is made of glass, thus permitting a view of the garden and terrace. Other homelike features include provision of several small sitting rooms to encourage more family-like groupings of the residents; several dining rooms in place of one large room are also used to promote intimate interpersonal groupings. Floor plans are arranged so that the rooms of the residents in each part of the building are grouped for easy access to a coffee kitchen and small sitting room. Open fireplaces, fitted with gleaming copper pots, good inexpensive Swedish furniture, colorful textiles, and good art objects all add a personal quality to the building. Outside, there is usually a terrace and inclosed courtyard which offers protection from wind and the eyes of the passerby. A fountain, small pool, shrubbery, and gay lawn furniture in the summer add their touches also.

An ingenious architectural design which encompasses the principles of intimate groups, privacy, and independence is to be found in the old age home "Jarnbrottsshemmet" in Gothenburg. It was opened for occupancy in 1956 and consists of two star-buildings (each has a small central hall from which three wings lead) built side by side and connected only through the household department in the basement floor. Every star has three floors, and every floor has thirteen rooms—twelve single rooms and one double room. Each floor forms a closed unity for the fourteen old persons living there and has its own sitting room, dining room, coffee kitchen, bathroom, and balcony. The use of a star with "three arms" avoids the long corridors found in the more traditional old age homes. Rooms are furnished by the Social Board, but each person who wishes to may bring his own furniture or pieces of it. An attempt is made to vary the furniture, curtains, carpets, and wallpaper so that no room is like another. The rooms each have a small entry hall with washstand and cloakroom. There is central heating provided by the district heating center. The kitchen serves all six dining rooms in the two buildings. Two rooms in each building are set aside as medical treatment rooms for the care of temporarily ill residents. There are also hobby rooms for weaving and woodworking, an auditorium for entertainment, and a small chapel for private devotions.

The "all-round" plan for residential care, although not in accord with current Dutch policy, is being tested in the Netherlands. Moerwijk is a typical example. It is located in a southern suburb of The Hague and is operated by the Municipal Welfare Service. The architectural design is considered an experiment in combining service flats with self-contained flats and nursing department. The central building consists of a number of wings built in the shape of an H and varies from two to four stories in height. Altogether the project houses 298 residents and has room for five guests and six staff persons. The wing consists of 14 bed-sitting rooms intended for one-person occupancy each. These rooms have floor space of 118 square feet. Other wings have flats for couples, and the floor space varies from 260 to 380 square feet. The smaller flats contain a living room and bedroom; the larger ones have an added kitchenette which also serves as dining room. The hospital unit has twelve "sick bays," of which six with a total of twenty-two beds are for women, and six, with twenty-four beds altogether, are for men. There are also three isolation rooms. The common rooms include a dining room, library, auditorium with stage and seating 250 persons, billiard room, and several small sitting rooms. There are, of course, all the usual service departments. Near the main building are six semidetached houses of 470 square feet each. Three of these are for two-person occupancy and include two rooms and

kitchenette; the other three are intended for three people and have three rooms and kitchenette.

In summary, it may be pointed out that the principles, although not universally applied, of housing which are being developed in Europe and the United Kingdom take cognizance of the personal rights of the individual to freedom of choice, independency, privacy, and personal dignity. Through the medium of suitable living accommodations, the older person is able to remain a functional part of the community and to find a receptive attitude toward himself. The family is considered of major importance but is protected from being overburdened by the fact that older members have available to them accommodations outside the domain of the younger family. Finally, architectural and social planning are providing facilities and trained personnel for the rehabilitation and maintenance of health, occupation of time in interesting activities, and the satisfaction of close personal relationships.

F. Programing and Design

The foregoing discussion of design has made some reference to space allotted in both independent housing developments and communal homes for recreation, crafts, social activities, and health programs of various kinds. The impression may have been created that European houses are designed to emphasize activities of the residents. Such an impression would be incorrect, because, while this need is not neglected altogether, actually only a minimum space is assigned for use in group activities beyond passive sitting.

It is probable that this situation will not persist much longer because there is an increasing perception of the importance of what Mehr (1957) calls "leisure service for the aged," for old people living either in the community or in old age homes. In chapter ix Havighurst discusses some of the new developments in this field.

The very large old age homes do contain hobby and craft shops, auditoriums for lectures and group celebrations, television rooms, and ordinary sitting rooms. In addition, these large homes have rehabilitation centers, including occupational therapy. Special staff personnel are employed to assist in developing these programs. However, for the most part, only a relatively small number of residents participate in these planned activities, preferring apparently to engage in passively sitting out their lives. In De Gamles By, where there is a highly skilled and excellent occupational therapist, with well-equipped craft rooms and shops at her disposal, no more than 10 per cent of the residents take part in the craft program, according to Dr. Torbin Geill, medical director of the town. In other instances, where the old age homes do not cater to the sick and to those in need of rehabilitation, even less activity is found. Perhaps it is no mere accident that, as is frequently true in our country, the craft rooms are often just what appears to be left-over space in the basement turned into a hobby shop as an afterthought. The residents do not find such space easily accessible or attractive, and only a few are motivated to take part. It may be that the idea of old people leading an active existence after retirement to an old age home is still too great a departure from the stereotype that, when man is old, he must sit and rest. Most certainly, the persistent inclusion of activity rooms and intimate space for small-group functioning and the employment of skilled directors of leisure programs will gradually bring about the change in attitude which the planners in most European countries are seeking.

In the independent housing developments in England, Switzerland, the Netherlands, and the Scandinavian countries there is usually included at least one building which is open to the use of residents free of charge. A few of these are open also to older people living in the neighborhood; but, aside from the old people's clubs which are found to some extent in practically all countries now, there are few comprehensive leisure-time programs.

Perhaps a glimpse of the possibilities for such programs in countries with social policies which permit the older age group to share equally with other population groups is to be found in the plan envisaged for Stockholm in the near future (Mehr, 1957). Each group of pensioner flats usually contains (1) an auditorium where lectures, plays, and films are offered and parties are held; (2) a snack kitchen; (3) small rooms for group gatherings; and (4) hobby rooms equipped with tools, looms, and sewing machines. The city proposes to open these facilities to pensioners scattered in ordinary apartment houses. "The idea is to let the pensioners get together in a friendly informal atmosphere, where they can talk, drink coffee, do handwork, play cards, listen to lectures, watch films, or hold social evenings." In addition to the leisure-time space in the pensioners' flats, the city of Stockholm is trying to establish a network of rooms and halls throughout the city for the leisure use of old people by encouraging parish homes and the city's youth recreation centers to set aside space for this purpose. Behind the provision of space, there is an effort to encourage the pensioners to form clubs and draw up their own programs.

In the Netherlands there is already a similar policy in operation. Day centers which are open daily offer organized programs and provide space for informal socialization. More of these types of programs are planned in recognition of the need to provide activities both within the old age institutions and in the community.

G. Administration and Personnel

The character of the administration and the personnel requirements for successful management of a housing project reflect (1) the type of housing (whether individual dwellings or communal); (2) the philosophy held with reference to the rights and roles of older people in society; (3) the nature of the program offered; (4) the adequacy of funds for operation; and (5) the skills of the staff. When the goals are more than domiciliary or custodial—when there is concern for the social and psychological needs of residents as well as for their physical well-being—it may be considered that the home is under advanced management and that it is seeking to comply with the best practices of the day.

Generally speaking, most western European countries are well advanced in their desire to assist in creating good lives for the old people and with reference to staff-resident ratios, types of personnel required, and integration with other community agencies and resources. In some cases the standards are made statutory; in others they are recommended practices. In this connection, it may also be said that some of the European countries are giving world leadership in the provision of organized training programs for matrons and wardens of old age homes.

PERSONNEL STANDARDS AND PRACTICES

The staff-resident ratio in housing projects consisting only of independent living quarters is usually quite small. This represents a planned attempt to encourage old people to continue to meet their own needs, in part because the able-bodied require much less service than the frail, disabled, or ill, who are usually to be found in the institutions for the aged, and in part because there is a desire to keep costs at the lowest levels consistent with good housing practices.

In the housing estates in England, there is usually a housing manager who is responsible for management, rent collection, and liaison between the administration (local authorities, housing trusts, etc.) and the residents. In recent years there has been a tendency to appoint a warden also to give some slight care when necessary to elderly people in flats or small houses on a housing estate. There may also be assistants to do yard and maintenance work. In the Swedish pensioners' flats, which house from 200 to 250 persons, the staff is somewhat larger and includes a house-mother, nurses (probably three), and a cook if there is a common dining room. Responsibilities of the housemother are those of general administration, summoning a doctor in case of illness, arranging for admission to hospital or nursing care when necessary, and supervision of the staff. The practical nurses help the pensioners with shopping, preparation of food, housekeeping, and other chores when such assistance is required. The staff of larger homes may include a social director. All the projects, of course, have the requisite number of custodians.

The communal homes naturally have a larger professional staff because the residents require a larger measure of assistance with their daily activities of living and more frequent nursing care and rehabilitation service. In a Swedish home accommodating about 40 people (the number recommended as an ideal size) the staff is made up of the matron, who is usually a trained nurse and a graduate of the special training program for matrons of old age homes; a corps of five or six practical nurses; a cadre of household help; and a part-time occupational therapist, physical therapist, and physician. A social caseworker is not included, even in most of the larger homes, in the belief that, when such help is required, the worker from the social welfare office can supply the service.

The auspices under which a home is operated are also often major factors in determining the type, number, and responsibilities of staff members. Those under the sponsorship of large organizations usually have fixed rules and specialized management services, thus relieving the matron of business and managerial responsibilities. In the small homes under local voluntary bodies, much of the business detail, such as rent collection and property management, is carried out by members of the voluntary organizations.

The staff-resident ratio is, of course, considered an important factor in the economic and humane administration of a home. In England, in public assistance institutions which house 400–500 essentially able-bodied residents, the recommended ratio is 1 staff member to 7 or 8 residents. In the small voluntary home, where there is likely to be considerable nursing required, the ratio is 1 to 5 (Rowntree, 1947). Shortages of staff are, however, grave, and an old persons' home recently constructed could not be opened for lack of personnel.

The quality of staff is also considered in setting up standards, because it is fully recognized that the happiness of the residents and the success of the homes are as dependent upon the personal characteristics of the matron and her assistants as upon their training.

TRAINING PERSONNEL

During the last 10 or more years the rapid multiplication of the small old people's homes accommodating from 30 to 40 persons has created a severe need for qualified persons to manage them. This has led several countries, usually through voluntary agencies, to establish training courses for potential matrons and wardens.

Two examples of these courses are included here because such training is needed in the United States and is not yet being undertaken on any systematic basis. There are signs, however, that it is only a matter of time until specific training will become a requirement by licensing agencies in this country. European experience will offer guidance in the planning of this training.

England and Sweden have the most complete courses, with Sweden's being the longer and more comprehensive. The British training course offers a useful pattern, however, because it illustrates a successful joint effort on the part of agencies in planning, supporting, and offering the course. The moving force in organizing the training program is the National Old People's Welfare Council. In the past the program was assisted financially by the National Corporation for the Care of Old People, the Thomas Will Trust, and the King George VI Foundation. Today, additional grants

for the training programs are available from the education authorities.

The stated goal of the course is to develop "a cadre of enlightened people to help the elderly not only in old people's homes but in their own homes." The first course was offered in 1950 (Great Britain, National Old People's Welfare Council, 1954*b*). It is now offered to from 30 to 35 students each year. The course is 14 weeks long and is entitled "A Training Course for Matrons and Assistant Matrons of Old People's Homes." Candidates need have no special qualifications, provided they are genuinely interested in old people, but those with some knowledge of nursing or managing other types of institutions are preferred (Great Britain, National Old People's Welfare Council, 1953*a*). Women between the ages of 27 and 50 are considered the most suitable trainees. Tuition alone is £35 (about $98). The total cost to the student, including travel and living expenses is estimated at £120 (approximately $350).

The course consists of two parts: theoretical training and practical work. The first 3 weeks are spent in practical training in an old people's home (1 week each with the assistant matron, the cook, and the matron). Four weeks of theoretical training follow, supplemented by field trips for observation of various old people's welfare programs. Four weeks are then spent in practical training in the geriatric unit of a hospital, and the next 3 weeks in an old people's home. The course is completed with a final 2 days of discussion and evaluation of the experiences.

The following is a syllabus of the lectures offered during the theoretical part of the course (Great Britain, National Old People's Welfare Council, 1953*b*):

Historical Introduction (2 lectures)
   Position of older citizen in society; pension schemes; work of voluntary, religious, and governmental agencies; dissolution of poor law and its replacement by new legislation; development of old age homes before the National Assistance Act.

Legislation (7 lectures)

National Insurance Act, 1946; National Health Act, 1946; National Assistance Act, 1948; conditions of service for staff at old people's homes.

Social Background (6 lectures)

a) Old people in the community, including discussion of effects of different types of housing, old people's needs; description and evaluation of different types of old people's welfare services offered in their own homes; place of the home in the community; keeping residents in touch with activities of the district.

b) The work of the National Old People's Welfare Committee.

Household Administration (6 lectures)

a) Domestic administration—housekeeping, cleaning, heating, use of different types of heat for cooking, sanitation.

b) Office organization—records, admittance, bookkeeping, staff insurance, taxes, work and vacation assignments, license requirements, menus, wills, death, etc.

Catering and Nutrition (9 lectures)

Kitchen equipment and layout, buying and storing food, principles of preserving and cooking food, care and cleaning of equipment, essentials of good nutrition, menu planning, food service.

Elementary Psychology (4 lectures)

Understanding human behavior, changing attitudes and prejudices, improving interpersonal relationships, emotional adjustments.

Psychological Effects of Aging (3 lectures)

General approaches to old people, the nervous system in old age, general hints on handling old people.

Home Nursing for the Elderly Sick (10 lectures)

Nursing the bedfast, care of sickroom, management of patients, nursing procedures, first aid, prevention of accidents.

Occupational Therapy and Leisure-Time Activities

Kinds of activities and their use in rehabilitation of old people [pp. 2–5].

In addition to the 14-week course, the National Old People's Welfare Council has also been offering a series of short "Refresher Courses" for the in-service training of wardens and matrons from both voluntary and local authority homes. These are similar to the short courses offered by a number of educational institutions in the United States for the in-service training of nursing-home administrators. The course lasts 5 days. Tuition is £7 10s. (about $26), and this covers tuition, room, and food. Topics covered by lectures include statutory provisions for the aged, psychological effects of aging, problems of sickness, modern methods of rehabilitation, household management, catering, occupational therapy, and aids for the disabled. Each training course is limited to 25 students. Attendance at refresher courses varies from 35 to 45 persons.

The Swedish Welfare Association has been training matrons since 1908 and is today the official training agency for Sweden. The comprehensive training program requires $34\frac{1}{2}$ months to complete. Prerequisites for enrolment are: (1) age—22–30 years; (2) education—at least primary and preferably high school; (3) training and experience—in housekeeping; (4) skills—proficiency in sewing, weaving, cooking; (5) health—physician's certification of good health based on a physical examination; and (6) insurance—member of an approved sick fund (Hamrin, 1957).

The course content includes both practical experience and theoretical studies. The practical training is obtained in old age homes, general hospitals, and mental institutions.

Table 3 summarizes the schedule of training and method of meeting the costs to the student. Tuition is free throughout the 3 years.

The theory courses include lectures in the following fields: anatomy, physiology, public health, nursing and techniques, psychology, social legislation, Swedish language, mathematics, methods of occupational therapy, psychiatry, nutrition and dietetics, civics, social legislation, institutional management, and bookkeeping. Field trips to old age homes and institutions are also a part of the training program.

In the Netherlands the Committee on Training of the Dutch Federation for the Care of the Aged plans and prepares the programs for training of personnel to work in homes for the aged. Dr. R. J. van Zonneveld, chairman of the committee, reports that, since 1955, a 2-year training program for intern home-helps in residential homes has been in operation and that during this 3-year period 450 girls have passed their examinations. Refresher courses for matrons of old age homes have also been organized by provincial social welfare bureaus. Currently in the planning

is a diminishing expectancy of family responsibility for its older members. Much social legislation, therefore, has been aimed at providing substitutes for the financial support and security formerly found in the extended family setting. Old age pensions, health insurance, special rent and clothing allowances, etc., are aimed at making it possible for the elderly to live independently of their families and outside an institution. To a certain extent, these measures are accomplishing their purposes; but, to the degree that older people become frail and unable to care for their own personal

TABLE 3*

TRAINING PROGRAM FOR MATRONS OF OLD AGE HOMES AND
METHODS OF MEETING COSTS TO STUDENTS

Schedule of Courses	No. of Months	Provided to Student†
Probation—old people's home.............	1	Board and room
Theory I...............................	1¼	Board and room
Practice—old people's home..............	7	Board, room, cash allowance
Practice and Theory—general hospital......	12	Expenses reimbursed by state
Practice—mental hospital................	3	Salary
Theory II..............................	3	Defray own expense‡
Attendance—old people's home...........	4	Board and room
Theory III.............................	3	Defray own expense‡

* Source: Based on Hamrin (1957).
† The student provides own books and supplies.
‡ Can apply to the general student loan fund for help.

stage are programs to be sponsored by the Dutch Federation for the Care of the Aged for a 2-year training course for special nursing aids for the aged in nursing homes.

IV. COMMUNITY SERVICES

When old people live near their relatives or with their children, they usually receive many important personal services from them as well as the satisfactions of companionship and affectional relationships. Yet, as a part of the great complex of social and economic changes of the past decade, the family structure in almost every developed country is moving toward the nuclear unit as opposed to the extended kinship of three generations and collateral relatives as in the past. Coincidently, there

needs, to perform the normal activities of daily living, to find social contacts in the community around them—to that extent additional assistance must be provided if they are to remain free in their living arrangements and actions. Thus for approximately the last 10 years most of the countries of western Europe and Great Britain have been developing systems of interrelated and co-ordinated services to prolong the period of usefulness, health, and independent living of old people.

A. Costs of Home Services versus Cost of Institutionalization

These programs have now been in operation long enough to permit some evaluation of the extent to which they are accomplishing their purposes. In general, there appears to be agreement that old people like and want the services and that these services are keeping many older people out of old age homes and from occupying hospital beds. The question now of major concern is that of the accuracy of one of the premises on which the maintenance of the independence of old persons is based—that is, that it is more economical to provide home service for some of them than it is to maintain them in institutions.

TABLE 4*

ANNUAL EXPENDITURE OF PUBLIC FUNDS FOR
PENSIONERS LIVING IN VARIOUS TYPES OF
ACCOMMODATIONS, DENMARK, 1950

LOCATION	EXPENDITURES PER PERSON (IN KRONOR)†		
	State	Munici-pality	Total
Own home.............	1691	673	2364
Old home for the aged...	2200	2120	4320
New home for the aged..	2700	2600	5300

* Source: Based on Friis (1956).
† There are 5.18 kronor to one United States dollar.

Henning Friis (1956) has made a comparison of the relative public agency costs in Denmark per individual of maintaining an older person in old and new homes for the aged and in his own home. The results are presented in Table 4 and indicate that in Denmark it is of major economic advantage to the community to find ways of maintaining old people in their own homes.

As already pointed out, the Dutch find it more economical to give assistance to old people in their own homes than to provide institutional care for them until the time comes when daily nursing care is required. In France the home-care program for sick older people costs about 1000 francs per day as compared with 4000 francs per day for hospital care. In Sweden it is estimated to be cheaper to provide 100 hours of domestic help per month for one person than to provide a place in an old age home.

Shenfield (1957) has estimated the average costs of providing different types of services for old people and concluded that "it is worthwhile to spend up to 100 pounds [$280] per year to help keep an old person at home rather than in a home or hospital bed, and this can probably be achieved for a good deal less if family help is available" (p. 170). The basis for her conclusion is presented in Table 5. As already mentioned, however, there is now some question whether the costs would differ greatly if other expenditures of old people living at home (which may be provided by National Assistance or partly subsidized pensions) were added to the costs met directly by public services.

There appears, however, to be general agreement that under most circumstances it is economical to provide community services to help keep old people in their own homes. The other hypothesis, that old people are necessarily happier to remain inde-

TABLE 5*

ESTIMATED AVERAGE COST IN ENGLAND
OF DIFFERENT LIVING ARRANGE-
MENTS FOR THE OLD

Living Arrangement	Cost per Year (In Pounds)
Chronic hospital bed............	400
Local authority home...........	200
Halfway house.................	320–350
Voluntary body home...........	180–195
Flatlet or hostel................	600
Boarding with private family.....	130–150
At home with domiciliary services†	80–100

* Source: Based on Shenfield (1957).
† Includes home-help laundry, some hot meals, some nursing care, attention of general practitioner, and other general medical services.

pendent, has not been so well authenticated. Thus Shenfield (1957) cautions that "where, however, old people live alone and have no help from relatives or neighbors the happiest arrangement for them is not simple to decide" (p. 171). This is a matter which invites further study.

B. Types of Community Services

There is a good deal of similarity among countries in the types of services provided older people living at home. In general, they include domestic aid, health care, meals, social contacts, and educational-recreational experiences. These services are often referred to as "open-care" as opposed to the care offered in old age homes or similar institutions.

DOMESTIC AID

Household help is the most common form of service offered and is available to some extent in all the countries of western Europe. England was the first country to initiate the service, but Sweden now has an equally extensive program. In January, 1958, legal provision was made in the Netherlands to provide special home-help service to old people. Under this new plan, which is subsidized by the Ministry of Social Welfare and local agencies, home-helpers may work on an hourly wage scale and thus offer short-time or temporary assistance to old people; or, on the other hand, they may (for the first time) give service to the aged for an indefinite time when long-term assistance is required.

TABLE 6*

OPEN CARE GIVEN DURING 1956
GOTHENBURG, BY AGE

Age (in Years)	No. of Persons
Under 50	46
50– 59	127
60– 69	538
70– 79	1476
80– 89	868
90–100	76
Total	3131

* Source: *Redgörelse för den öppa aldringsvardeni Göteborg ar 1956* (Gothenburg, 1957). (Mimeographed.)

Household help for old people is, in most countries, an extension of the homemaker service developed originally to assist families in times of a mother's illness or absence from home. This has generally meant that the amount of service available to old people has been very limited, since it has been difficult to secure enough household

helpers to supply the needs of even the young families. In order to improve this situation partially, a number of countries have developed separate systems of household help for the aged.

The tasks generally performed by the domestic helpers include cleaning, cooking, light laundry, and shopping. A twice-yearly housecleaning is also sometimes included.

TABLE 7*

OLD PEOPLE DROPPED FROM OPEN CARE
GOTHENBURG, 1955
($N=3131$)

Reason Dropped	No. Dropped
Died	53
Hospitalized	353
Entered old people's home	97
Relatives took over	112
Improvement in health	128
Other	17

* Source: *Redgörelse för den öppa aldringsvardeni Göteborg ar 1956* (Gothenburg, 1957). (Mimeographed.)

In general, domestic aid is intended to offer assistance with the harder tasks of housekeeping, leaving the simpler day-to-day management of the household to the older person. The household helper may come daily or a few times a week, and each visit is usually between an hour or two in length. The helper is trained to report illness she may find to the district nurse or to the social welfare center; thus there is an extra measure of protection afforded.

As would be expected, there is an increase with age in the number of persons receiving the domestic aid. Table 6, based on the Gothenburg, Sweden, program, illustrates this point.

For the most part, open care for the aged is a long-term or permanent arrangement. Table 7 indicates that only 4 per cent (128) of the 3131 persons in the case load improved to the point where the service was no longer needed.

Another measure of the permanency of care needed is indicated in Table 8. The service in Gothenburg started in 1952, and 35 persons who initially were in the program were still receiving aid in 1956.

It appears that if the open care is designed as an alternative to institutional care, it may be expected that a majority of cases will require continuing service. The more successful the program in aiding people to continue to maintain their own households, the greater the duration of their need unless relatives can be persuaded to take over.

The laundry work done by the household helper is usually confined to personal items. The heavy work of laundering household linen (sheets, etc.) is so difficult that a number of communities and voluntary groups have developed laundry services or use of rental bed-linen service. In England, for example, the National Assistance Board

TABLE 8*

DURATION AND NUMBER RECEIVING
OPEN CARE, GOTHENBURG, 1956

Duration	No.
1 month..............	77
1–6 months..........	485
6–12 months.........	408
1–2 years............	783
2–3 years............	638
3–4 years............	349
Over 4 years.........	35

* Source: *Redgörelse för den öppa al-dringsvardeni Göteborg ar 1956* (Gothenburg, 1957). (Mimeographed.)

may give supplemental grants to old people to cover laundry costs. The importance of this service to the old people can be seen in the fact that, of 821,000 special grants made by the board, 314,000 were for laundry costs (Shenfield, 1957).

HEALTH SERVICES

As in the United States, there is a shortage of long-stay hospital beds in practically all countries. In consequence, measures have been taken to conserve the available beds for the acutely ill and to supply care for the longer convalescent periods or for the chronically ill in the home. A brief summary of these plans is appropriate here, since they constitute an important part of the community services for old people.

The most usual home health service offered is bedside care. This service is organized similarly to the visiting-nurse program in the United States. The nurse goes into the home daily or as needed and gives bedside care, medical treatment, special medications, and baths and massage and makes the patient comfortable. She may also offer counsel and guidance in health matters to the patient and his family.

Other types of home health services are now being offered as a result of the growing emphasis on rehabilitation of older people and on preventive measures. In England, for example, physical and occupational therapists visit and treat the aged blind and disabled who are in need of training in activities of daily living and of restorative occupation. Occupational interests of other elderly persons are encouraged through competitions, instruction by local educational authorities or women's institutes, guilds, etc. (Great Britain, National Old People's Welfare Council, 1958a). A chiropody service has been established in many areas by local old people's welfare committees with the support of grants from the National Corporation for the Care of Old People or from the local authorities. As of April, 1959, the National Health Services Act of 1946 was amended to allow local authorities to grant aid to voluntary bodies to provide chiropody services. The premise is that, if old people are to stay on their feet, then their feet must be kept in good shape. Chiropody service is often available at the meetings of old age clubs as well as in the homes of old people.

In addition to the organized health programs, such as the home nursing services, mobile physiotherapists and occupational therapists, mobile meals, etc., effort is made to provide remedial devices to those who need glasses, dentures, hearing aids, crutches, artificial limbs, etc.

FOOD SERVICES

Several types of food services have been developed to provide nourishing meals for impoverished old people and for those who live alone but are too frail or disabled, lack the skill, as in the case of many men, or neglect to cook properly for themselves.

The meals-on-wheels service, which began in England and has spread to a number of other countries, including the United States, brings hot, well-planned meals to the homes of selected old people. The British Red Cross Society started the first scheme and, with other voluntary agencies such as the Women's Voluntary Services and some old people's welfare committees, now support and operate the program. Candidates for this service are the bedbound who have no one to care for them, the disabled living in high-rise apartments without elevators, and those who are considered medically too frail to be able to care for their own nutritional needs.

The meals are usually planned by a dietitian and are prepared in community kitchens, in industrial canteens, at the headquarters of voluntary groups, and in the kitchens of private caterers. They are transported in insulated containers by motor (van or private car) or, in the Netherlands, by bicycle. The food is transferred to the service plate or heating pans of the old person, so that there is no actual interchange of crockery. A sample English meal includes a piece of meat or steamed fish, a boiled potato, a vegetable, and a steamed bread pudding. The number of meals delivered to an old person per week varies according to the need and availability of the service; but, as a rule, delivery is not made daily. Enough food is often taken at one time to supply a second meal.

Mobile meal services are found, in addition to England, in Sweden and Denmark, where the residents of the pensioners' flats may choose this service in preference to cooking for themselves or in instances of temporary illness. In Sweden about 8 per cent of the elderly living in their own homes receive the service.

Another form of food service found in England is the dinner club, which provides opportunity for a group of lonely old people to come together daily for at least one warm meal at a nominal cost. These are separate from the community kitchens which were a wartime measure and are now largely abandoned, where any person, regardless of age, could get a meal at a very nominal fee. Naturally, because of the cheapness of the meals, these kitchens had many old people among their clients.

In France there are day centers for the elderly—*foyers*—where old people come about 11:00 A.M. or noon to have a warm lunch. They spend the afternoon in card-playing, reading, or other activities and then go home at 5:00 or 6:00 P.M., taking a hot evening meal with them. Some of these clubs are formed in connection with the community hospital. They are often housed in separate buildings but on the hospital grounds, according to M. Renaudin, president of the Committee for the Organization of Aid to Old People (a federation of 14,000 private organizations in France). A private association, Amis des Vieux, coordinates private ventures for providing poor old people with meals. Another, the Brave Gens, helps old people by distributing food parcels (French Committee for Social Service and Social Work, 1954). The municipal Social Service Bureau, which is administered by committees of which two-thirds of the members are nominated from among people doing social work in the commune, runs communal restaurants for old people.

Large cities in the Netherlands, such as Rotterdam and Amsterdam, and some smaller communities have a meals-on-wheels service for old people. The Municipal Welfare Department buys the food and has it prepared in municipal kitchens. The Women's Voluntary Service distributes the meals four times a week to the old people.

SOCIAL ACTIVITIES

Acute loneliness is found among old people in every country. There are always some who have little or no family left and whose social resources are practically nonexistent. In addition, many are too handicapped physically or too mentally depressed and discouraged to be able to find a solution to their own loneliness. Yet they desire independence and a role in life. An almost universal problem of old people is the fear and dislike of continual dependency upon family, especially if this means taking refuge in the homes of their children, where they crowd the young family for space and interfere with its freedom of action. In chapter ix Havighurst has dealt at length with the attempts being made in various countries to provide roles for older people in which they may find satisfaction and secure ego support. The following is a brief overview of these developments as a part of the community services being made available to the aged.

The services designed to provide social relationships for the elderly include in most countries such activities as friendly visiting, old people's clubs, vacations, and short in-residence hospital visits to provide relief for young families and a change for the aged.

The friendly visiting program is essentially of the same nature as in the United States. Usually members of a volunteer organization or church group visit old people in their own homes and perform such services as writing letters, reading aloud, lending a listening ear, doing such chores as shopping, making telephone calls, etc. Old people do not pay for this service.

In the Netherlands the Union of Women's Volunteers has a visiting program and operates 250 old people's clubs. In Amsterdam about 40 per cent belong to the League for the Aged. The league, according to De Haan (private communication, 1957), provides both cultural and recreational activities for its members through a system of social clubs. In England the Women's Voluntary Service and the many voluntary Old People's Welfare Council Committees have extensive visiting programs. These visitors are instructed to call *regularly* upon their older persons and to give such help as shopping, exchanging library books, writing letters, reading, collecting pensions, and offering friendliness. They are also urged to

judge whether there is a need for services from other sources such as meals-on-wheels, home helps, gift food, blankets and bedding, and medical equipment (bed rests, etc.). The visitors may also serve old people living in hostels and old age homes.

Other types of programs which are offered in some countries to call the attention of citizens to the needs of old people at the same time offer a measure of socialization for them. In Copenhagen there is an annual "Old People's Week" sponsored by the Lutheran parishes. During this week younger families are encouraged to invite one or more older people to their homes. Out of these visits, permanent relationships are sometimes established. In France the National Committee for Organization of Aid to Old People sponsors an annual "Old People's Day," which is always the last Sunday in October. In addition to the collecting of money which is used to support services for the aged in France, the organization promotes a program of visiting. The social workers of various agencies supply the names of old people who are poor. The names are put in sealed envelopes which are distributed in public places together with an invitation urging that the old person be visited on "Old People's Day." The National Committee reports that many friendships have been formed which endure throughout the year and bring great happiness and benefit to the old.

EDUCATIONAL AND WORK ACTIVITIES

For the most part European countries have probably given less attention to the provision of educational activities directed to the elderly than has the United States. The folk schools of Denmark, Switzerland, and Sweden have older people among their clientele.

Increased attention is being given to the establishment of work programs for the aged. The Finnsbury Scheme for the Employment of the Elderly, in London, is an example. It was started by Dr. Blythe

Brooke, a public health officer, to serve the needs of patients appearing daily at the clinic requesting medical service but with no apparent illness beyond loneliness. Dr. Brooke rented an old house and advertised that work would be available for elderly people. Many of the old people who had gone to the clinic transferred to the workshop, where they worked at simple sewing, packaging, or assembly tasks for 2 hours a day. Their remuneration was 1s. an hour (14 cents). So successful was this experiment that a new building was constructed offering more space and equipment. The National Old People's Welfare Council (1958b) has recently reported on several other workshops and employment schemes for older people and lists the sources of grants-in-aid for these programs.

In France the National Committee To Aid Old People in 1950 created a homework program for old people who were unable to work normally after retirement age. Under this plan highly skilled workers make quantities of such items as children's clothes, dolls, etc. Some of the large stores in Paris and other cities have given space and a sales stand to the committee for the display and sale of these items. The old person receives 70 per cent of the profit, the store receives 10 per cent, and the committee gets 20 per cent in order to make it possible to continue the work.

OTHER FORMS OF CARE SERVICES

Night-attendance services provide persons to sit with old people who cannot be left alone during the night or to relieve relatives so that they can get enough rest to carry on the nursing of an elderly patient at home.

Foster-home care is another new service in which older people are placed as permanent paying guests in a private family. It is expected that this type of care will relieve demands for communal care, and also it is thought that foster-home care may be more economical than institutional care (Bucke, 1956).

Day centers and day clubs have been developed, where meals and other personal services, such as bathing, are provided. Most important are occupation and the opportunity to enjoy the company of others. These centers are considered valuable preventive community care for old people who might otherwise have to enter a home or hospital.

Housing management is a service which provides a manager who assists the aged person solve the practical problems of giving up old homes and settling in new ones. This service is said to increase the sense of security of older tenants and to relieve needless anxiety.

C. Eligibility Criteria for Community Service

Not all old people are presumed to require special home services, and there is great variation in the amounts and kinds needed by those who do require them. For this reason, costs are not included in the basic pension but are provided as a supplement when needed, or the services are provided without cost to the person who meets certain qualifications. Accordingly, it becomes necessary to establish rules of eligibility.

Various criteria are used. Generally, it may be said that the person must be of pensionable age unless special circumstances obtain, of low income, and usually in poor health although not necessarily sick. The usual but not universal policy is to provide the services rather than to urge reluctant families to assume responsibility for giving them.

In Gothenburg, Sweden, only such persons receive services as are eligible to a room in an old people's home or a bed in a hospital (Nordström, 1955). The services in England are made available upon the recommendations of physicians, social workers, district nurses, welfare officers, clergymen, etc. In the Netherlands eligibility is more strict; to receive help, the old person must have a medical indication of need certified by a physician. In Hamburg, Germany, the program of home care is under the supervision of doctors, who often request the services through district welfare and health officers.

D. *Sponsorship and Financing of Community Services*

Community services are sponsored and financed in a variety of ways. Usually, some government subsidization is available, and local authorities may use such funds to establish and operate programs themselves; or the local authorities may use the state subsidies and add local funds to arrange for voluntary groups to organize and manage the program. In addition, national and local voluntary agencies and foundations may underwrite the services and provide the personnel, or they may make grants to local committees on aging to set up the programs. The Red Cross in Sweden, the Foundation for the Aged (Pro Senectute) in Switzerland, the Women's Voluntary Services in England, the Union of Women Volunteers in the Netherlands, and the National Committee To Aid Old People in France are all illustrations of voluntary groups sponsoring and usually financing, at least in part, one or more types of community services for the aged.

In the Netherlands, as already noted, the Ministry of Social Welfare may make subsidies to organizations of churches and/ or private agencies which have as their objective the provision of homemaker service or household help. In such instances the federal government contributes 25 per cent of costs, the municipality 25 per cent, and the voluntary group 50 per cent plus the work.

There are two publicly supported home-helps in Sweden: one, subsidized by the state, offers assistance to families and to some old people; the other, a special home-help service for the aged supported by municipal funds, serves only old people. In 1955, all but 5 of the 1031 municipalities in Sweden had a state-subsidized home-

help program, while 441 of them also had a municipally supported scheme. Of the latter, 315 were under management of local public authorities, while 126 were being administered by private associations (Nordström, 1955). The Swedish Red Cross also sponsors and finances a national home-help service.

In England, local authorities are responsible for providing a home-help service. This scheme, originating during World War II, was made permanent under National Health Service and included old people as well as the sick and the mothers of young children. The local authority employs and pays the home-helpers. In some areas the Women's Volunteer Services administer the program for the local authorities.

In France, financial support for the home-care program is provided by the National Committee To Aid Old People, whose funds come, in turn, from collections made on the annual "Old People's Day" ($350,000 was collected in 1953, for example). Relief societies in the various communities, which usually have nurses and homeworkers already on the staff, supply the personnel.

Another source of subsidization of the home service programs is the fees paid by the older people. The rates paid are so small, however, as to be almost negligible in the total cost of underwriting a program.

In England the local authorities try to recover all or part of the cost from the household of the old family if the family has resources. Charges to the old person are based on a sliding scale. In 1948, for example, the service was free to those whose income was 26s. ($3.64) or less a week, but, when the income was as much as 38s. ($5.32), a charge of 2½d. (about 3 cents) per hour was made.

The Gothenburg fee rate in 1956 ranged from free service to 3 kronor (about 60 cents) per hour, as shown in Table 9. These figures make clear that about 80 per cent of the service is given without cost to the recipient. The total cost of the open care program in Gothenburg is reported as

2,950,565 kronor ($569,459) for 1957. Fees collected from the old age group amounted to only 165,000 kronor; municipal grants make up the remainder of the sum.

E. Amount of Community Services Provided

How well the community services succeed in meeting the needs of older people is, of course, dependent upon the number of persons reached and the quality and quantity of assistance provided each of them.

Monsieur Renaudin, president of the Committee on Organizations To Aid Old People (personal interview, 1954), reports that private organizations (relief societies) gave care to 200,000 old people in France during 1953, that is, about 4 per cent of the older population. Both domestic help and nursing service were provided in a ratio of 3 hours of home help to 1 hour of nursing service.

In Stockholm, during 1954, state-aided home help was given regularly to 4389 old persons and occasionally in 18,823 cases. This amounted to just over 1,000,000 hours of help to old people (this excludes the old people who were members of families receiving family home help and who were thus indirectly aided). Municipal home-help services reached also several hundred more persons (Nordström, 1955). In Stockholm the municipal program provided 77,500 hours of domestic aid during a year (1953), and at the same time the Red Cross offered another 32,500 hours; together the two programs served 1300 old people (Mehr, 1954). Gothenburg, another large municipality (365,000 population), did not initiate its home-help service for older people until 1952; but, by 1957, it was employing 1000 home-helpers who were serving 2000 old people (Gothenburg Municipal Executive Board, 1957).

F. Personnel for Community Service

As in any personal service, stress is placed on the quality and training of personnel employed to assist and care for old people. Characteristics of reliability, attitudes of helpfulness, discretion, and an understanding of old people are regarded as important. Assuming that this type of personnel can be recruited, questions of training, supervision of workers, standard of performance, and rate of pay then become major concerns of organizations administering the various programs. Margareta

TABLE 9*

FEE RATE PAID BY OLD PEOPLE FOR HOME HELP, GOTHENBURG, 1956

Rate per Hour (In Kronor)	No. Paying
Nothing (free).....	2249
:50..........	214
1:00..........	110
1:50..........	51
2:00..........	54
2:25..........	5
2:50..........	46
3:00..........	46
Total..........	2775

* Source: *Redgörelse för den öppa aldringsvardeni Göteborg ar 1956* (Gothenburg, 1957). (Mimeographed.)

Nordström (1955), an enthusiastic supporter of home-help service, sounds the following warning:

The home help principle is right but it has its pitfalls. We need only to consider how much harm that can be done to the good purpose by dishonest or unfit helpers, more or less consciously wasted working hours or the tendency to throw on the shoulders of the public such responsibility that has from time immemorial been the selfevident duty of relatives and neighbours.

RECRUITMENT

With these criteria for good home-helpers, recruitment of workers is usually among middle-aged women whose children have left home and who find they can now spend 2 or 3 hours a day assisting old people. The part-time nature of the jobs is conducive to employing these women with limited time. There is, also, a feeling in many countries that, because of labor short-

ages, women with full time available should
be employed in full-time jobs and not in
home-help services. The age distribution of
the home-helpers in Gothenburg (Table
10) illustrates the tendency for middle-
aged women to enter this service.

The methods of recruitment used are the
usual newspaper advertisements and circulars. Public meetings also are held to give
information and to attract prospective
home-helpers. In one Swedish community a
meeting was held for members of women's
organizations and the association of old age
pensioners. The Swedish film *We and the*

TABLE 10*

Age Distribution of Home-
Helpers, Gothenburg, 1956

Age (in Years)	No.
20–24	67
30–39	397
40–49	647
50–59	522
60–69	162
70–72	5
Total	1800

* Source: *Redgörelse för
den öppa aldringsvardeni Göteborg ar 1956* (Gothenburg,
1957). (Mimeographed.)

Aged was followed by a discussion of the
care of the aged in their homes and the
home-help service. A call for home-helpers
was made, and 30 women volunteered for
service. In another community a questionnaire was prepared and sent to 100 women.
Thirty responded to the questionnaire, and
half of them applied to become home-
helpers.

All countries report that it is difficult to
get women for housework. In Hamburg,
Germany, it has been found that only a
middle-aged woman who wants part-time
work will seek employment as a home-
helper. But, if they work as much as one-
half time, they qualify for retirement pensions, according to W. Elmer, director of
welfare service (personal interview, 1957).

TRAINING

Household assistant is a position in Europe for which young women are prepared
through a standardized training course.
Such household assistance is defined by the
Dutch as the assistance rendered by skilled,
specially trained women employed by and
working under the supervision of an organization in families where they substitute for,
assist, and instruct the housewife who, as a
result of sickness, insufficient preparation,
physical defects, or social conduct, is unable to accomplish her household tasks
suitably. This assistance is meant to support or reconstruct a healthy family. More
recently, the "household assistant to the
aged" has become more or less a specialized
field of household assistance.

The training for household assistant to
the aged requires an additional year of
training beyond the year required for the
regular household assistant. The regular
curriculum includes courses on religious
thought; family government; education
and recreation; and such home economics
courses as cooking and dietetics; sewing
and mending; and theory of laundry,
housework, budgeting, child care, and nursing. The additional year of specialized
study in preparation for working with the
elderly includes four major programs: (1)
general orientation in the old age problem,
including demography, health status and
programs, psychological and several other
aspects of aging, and social legislation; (2)
practical problems of living and working
with the aged; (3) hygiene and nursing
for the healthy aged person; and (4) handicrafts and recreational activities.

The minimum age requirement for admission to these training courses is 19
years, and most applicants are young wom-
en. Middle-aged Dutch women who work
prefer factory and office work. Those who
are married would lose status if they engaged in work outside their own homes.

In Sweden household helpers for service
to families are required to have from 3 to
15 months of training, the exact amount

depending upon previous experience. Training for household helpers to the elderly, however, is not yet extensive in Sweden. This may be the result, in part, of the fact that Swedish women, unlike Dutch women, go into household help service after their children leave home and are therefore already experienced housekeepers. A few communities offer short programs of a week or less. In Gothenburg, for example, prospective home-helpers may be given 66 hours of special training. The program is sponsored by the Public Assistance Committee working in collaboration with the trade schools and is supported by funds provided by the municipality. The course covers such topics as diet, cooking, housekeeping, home sick care, psychological and sociological problems of old people, and ethical considerations. In Shovda, another Swedish town, there is a regular training course, but the home-helpers are called together occasionally for a social evening and a lecture on the care of old people. "Information Day" is the method used by the village of Vreta Kloster to educate the home-helpers. Lectures are given by a physician, a social welfare worker, and a district nurse to inform the home-helper of available services.

The Swedish Red Cross, which has organized a home-help service, also provides courses for persons who are to work with the aged. The course consists of 42 lessons and includes lectures, demonstrations, and practical work. Topics covered are psychology of the aged, needs for proper nursing care and exercise to avoid disablement, use of occupational therapy, mental health, and organization and administration of programs of home care.

SUPERVISION AND SALARIES

The organization employing the service personnel and directing the community service programs provides the supervision of the workers. It also fixes salaries and pays the workers directly. The fees paid by the old people are turned in to the agency.

In the Netherlands the Ministry of Social Welfare (1954) has issued a detailed directive regarding the subsidization of home-help services and payment of the workers. To be eligible for a government subsidy, an organization must have a supervisor of home-helpers who is a person with at least 3 years of experience supervising homemakers and home-helpers and holds at least a 2-year certificate in social work. Salary rates for home-helpers increase annually, beginning with 1150 guilders ($303) the first year to 1750 guilders ($460) after 6 years of service.

TABLE 11*

NUMBER AND ANNUAL EARNINGS OF
HOME-HELPERS, GOTHENBURG, 1955

Annual Earnings (in Kronor)	No. of Home-helpers
5000–5500	5
4000–4999	14
3000–3999	56
2000–2999	162
1000–1999	465
500– 999	370
100– 499	345
Under 100	433
Total	1850

* Source: *Redgörelse för den öppa aldringsvardeni Göteborg ar 1956* (Gothenburg, 1957). (Mimeographed.)

Home-helpers in Sweden are carefully supervised by trained professional workers. In the case of Gothenburg, where there are 1000 home-helpers, there are, in addition to the director of the program, six full-time nurses and eight full-time trained matrons whose duties are to receive applications for help, make investigations to determine need of persons making application, select and assign the home-helper, and then to supervise the work of the helper closely through home visits and records. The housekeepers are paid by the Social Welfare Board; the rate is 3 kronor per hour; and the working time on an average is 1 hour and 40 minutes per case a day. Transportation is paid by the Social Welfare Board. The amount earned annually by the home-helpers in Gothenburg is shown in Table 11.

In conclusion, the recognition of the middle-aged woman as a person whose natural experiences as a mother and housewife especially fit her to undertake the role of home-helper is serving a dual purpose—the older people receive badly needed services, and the middle-aged woman finds a new and meaningful role when her duties as a parent are finished. Thus there is in the process of being established a new societal pattern along lines in which many more social inventions must take place if the social health of the nations is to be best served.

REFERENCES

BERGGREN, A. 1958a. Introduction to an exhibition of photo-material about Swedish old age homes. Stockholm: Royal Social Board. (Mimeographed.)

———. 1958b. A short review of the principles and programs for the care of the old aged. Stockholm: Royal Social Board.

BOUWCENTRUM. 1955. Huisvesting van Bejaarden: Verpleegtehuizen. Rotterdam: Bouwcentrum. (English text.)

———. 1958. Huisvesting van Bejaarden: Verpleegtehuizen voor Geestelijk Bejaarden ("Nursing homes for mentally infirm old people"). A5.0. Rotterdam: Bouwcentrum. (English text.)

BUCKE, MARJORIE. 1956. Foster care for the elderly. Social Service Quart., **30**, 19–22.

DAHLSTRÖM, HELGE. 1956. Some notes on the old age care in Stockholm. Stockholm: Office of Social Welfare. (Mimeographed.)

DANISH MINISTRY OF LABOUR AND SOCIAL AFFAIRS. 1953. Old age pensioners flats: report of a survey. Copenhagen: Danish Ministry of Labour and Social Affairs. (Mimeographed.)

DANISH SOCIETY. 1951. Capital of a democracy. Copenhagen: Danske Selskat.

DONAHUE, WILMA. 1960. European experience in operation and services of retirement communities. *In:* E. BURGESS (ed.), Housing for older people: the retirement community. Ann Arbor: University of Michigan, Division of Gerontology. (In press.)

ERLANDSSON, S. 1954. Untitled paper. Stockholm. (Mimeographed.)

FRENCH COMMITTEE FOR SOCIAL SERVICE AND SOCIAL WORK. 1954. French report. *In:* Seventh International Conference of Social Work. Toronto.

FRIEDEBURG, L. VON. 1955. Altersbild und Altersvorsorge der Arbeiter und Angestellten. Frankfurt: Forschungsbericht, Inst. für Sozialforschung, Universität.

FRIIS, H. 1956. Calculations of possible savings through the introduction of assistance in the home instead of institutional maintenance of the aged in Denmark. *In:* The need for cross-national surveys of old age, pp. 59–61. Ann Arbor: University of Michigan, Division of Gerontology.

GERMAN FEDERAL REPUBLIC. 1958. Village experiment. Bulletin, **6** (July 8), 8. Bonn: Press and Information Office.

GOLDBERG, L. H. 1959. Care of the elderly in Norway, Sweden, and Denmark: observations from a geriatric study tour. II. Geriatrics, **14**, 115–21.

GOTHENBURG MUNICIPAL EXECUTIVE BOARD. 1957. Social welfare policy in Gothenburg. Handelstidningen: Information Center of the Gothenburg Municipal Executive Board.

GREAT BRITAIN. MINISTRY OF HEALTH. 1949. Housing Manual, 1949. London: H.M. Stationery Office.

———. 1950. Care of the aged suffering from mental infirmity. London: National Health Service. (Mimeographed.)

———. 1951. Housing manual: supplement, 1951. London: H.M. Stationery Office.

GREAT BRITAIN. MINISTRY OF LOCAL GOVERNMENT AND PLANNING. 1951. Housing for special purposes. London: H.M. Stationery Office.

GREAT BRITAIN. NATIONAL OLD PEOPLE'S WELFARE COUNCIL. 1953a. Fourth training course for matrons and assistant matrons of old people's homes. London: National Council of Social Service. (Mimeographed.)

———. 1953b. Syllabus: fourth training course for wardens of old people's homes. London: National Council of Social Service. (Mimeographed.)

———. 1954a. Age is opportunity. London: National Council of Social Service.

———. 1954b. Training and refresher courses. *In:* Progress report for the year ending 31st March 1954, pp. 3–5. London: National Council of Social Service.

———. 1956. Memorandum on housing for elderly people. London: National Council of Social Service. (Mimeographed.)

———. 1958a. Handicrafts for older people. London: National Council of Social Service.

————. 1958*b*. Workshops and employment for the elderly. London: National Council of Social Service. (Mimeographed.)

HAMRIN, GRETA. 1957. Utbildning av föreståndarinnor för ålderdomshem. Stockholm: Svenska Socialvårdsförbundet.

HJEM, HELEN M. 1951. De Gamles By. Copenhagen: De Gamles By.

KØBENHAVNS KOMMUNES SOCIALDIREKTORAT. 1948. Københavns Kommunes Boliger for Aldersrentemodtagere. Copenhagen: Udgivet af Københavns Kommunes Socialdirektorat.

MEHR, H. 1954. The main outlines of modern old age assistance. (Paper read at the Nordic Capital Conference, Copenhagen.)

————. 1957. The housing needs of elderly people. Stockholm: Office of the Mayor for Social Affairs. (Mimeographed.)

MOSS, J. 1957. Housing the elderly. Health Horizon, Summer, pp. 30–37.

NETHERLANDS, THE. MINISTRY OF SOCIAL WORK. 1954. Scheme of regulations for subsidizing of homemakers and home-help services of 1955. The Hague: Department of Family Service. (Mimeographed.)

NORDSTRÖM, MARGARETA. 1955. Home help for old people in Sweden. Stockholm: Kungl Socialstyrelsen. (Mimeographed.)

PAGANI, A. 1956. Causes of institutionalization. *In:* The need for cross-national surveys of old age, pp. 53–58. Ann Arbor: University of Michigan, Division of Gerontology.

ROGGENDORF, DR. 1953. Die Gescheossene Altersfursorge der Stadt Köln. Cologne: Reihler Heimstatten. (Mimeographed.)

ROWNTREE, B. S. 1947. Old people. London: Oxford University Press (for the Nuffield Foundation).

RUDD, T. 1956. Caring for the elderly. London: Catholic Truth Society.

SHELDON, J. H. 1948. The social medicine of old age. London: Nuffield Foundation.

SHENFIELD, BARBARA E. 1957. Social policies for old age: a review of social provision for old age in Great Britain. London: Routledge & Kegan Paul.

SWEDISH INSTITUTE. 1956. Social benefits in Sweden. Stockholm: The Institute.

SWEDISH SOCIAL WELFARE BOARD. 1952. Social Sweden. Stockholm: Gernandts Boktryckeri.

TEGNER, G. 1956. Social security in Sweden. Tilden: Swedish Institute.

TOWNSEND, P. 1956. Family relationships. *In:* The need for cross-national surveys of old age, pp. 32–40. Ann Arbor: University of Michigan, Division of Gerontology.

————. 1957. The family life of old people: an inquiry in East London. London: Routledge & Kegan Paul.

ULRIKOSON, V. 1958. Care of the aged in Sweden. (CRRP 1957, Sec. D, Item VI-A-5; Embdesp. 763.) Stockholm: The Embassy

VAN ZONNEVELD, R. J. 1956. Socio-medical surveys. *In:* The need for cross-national surveys of old age, pp. 62–75. Ann Arbor: University of Michigan, Division of Gerontology.

VI

The Health of the Aging

VERA J. AND JEROME S. PETERSON

I. PHYSICAL HEALTH

A. Biology of Aging

Aging is regarded by the biologist as a process that begins with life of the individual cells of which the body is composed, as a process of evolution and growth, involution and atrophy. The process of aging begins at birth and is most rapid in infancy, becoming progressively slower in childhood and maturity, and affects different tissues at different rates. Involution of tissue alters anatomical structures, physiological processes, and quality of functions, in particular those of adaptability. Biological age of the various organs is not uniform and may be even more variable with advancing years and in different individuals. The graying head is not necessarily a badge of old age, nor is the smooth skin a prerogative of youth. The thymus declines in function as reproductive organs spurt into activity. Degenerative changes in articular cartilages may occur in the second decade of life, and homeostatic mechanisms which maintain a constant in-

ternal environment may become less able to withstand stress as age advances. Within a broad pattern such variations occur depending partly on genetic and partly on exogenous factors, and at any given age a particular individual represents the sum of his inheritance and environment, his traumatic and infectious experiences.

For administrative and actuarial purposes the age of 65 for men and 60 for women has been generally accepted for retirement purposes in most countries, but chronological age does not define the "old" person; and today many men and women of these ages, or even older, can in no way be considered old.

Knowledge of the normal aging process is of fundamental importance in the medical treatment and palliation of the consequences of aging. Healthy old age is a normal process of involution accompanied by a satisfactory compensation to alteration in tissue structure and function. Health in the aged is not "rejuvenation" but the maintenance of physical and psychological equilibrium with the environment. Flanders Dunbar's (1955) study of aging and illness among centenarians in the United States portrays a special group of individuals who have managed to avoid the large majority of hazards which produce illness and invalidity and to retain the capacity to enjoy life and productivity. Two centenarians in Switzerland who had lived healthy active lives, free of any disability and escaping serious illness up to the end, were re-

[1] The authors wish to acknowledge the help of the following persons who read this chapter and made valuable suggestions for revision: Professor G. A. Canaperia, Alto Commissariato, per l'Igiene e la Sanità, Rome, Italy; Dr. Maria F. Daelen, chief, International Health Section, Ministry of Interior, Bonn, Germany; Dr. Arthur Engel, director-general, Royal Medical Board, Stockholm, Sweden; and Professor Dr. P. Mundendam, director-general of health, Ministry of Social Affairs and Public Health, The Hague, Netherlands.

ported to have a multiplicity of pathological organic findings at autopsy by Vischer and Roulet (1952). The orientation of the medical profession and other disciplines to the physiological and pathological changes that come with advancing years will provide a better understanding for assessing and meeting the personal, social, and medical requirements of old age.

B. The "Normality" of Old People

If health in the aged is the maintenance of equilibrium with the environment, what is the "normal" that has to be maintained? Assessment of "normal" from an insurance point of view is not applicable to old people. Medical surveys carried out among the elderly repeatedly show that individuals who assess themselves as "normal" are frequently found after medical examination to be suffering from one or more pathological processes. The criterion of "normality" becomes the average for that age, and, the greater the age, the greater the uncertainty of what constitutes the range of "normal variability" from the standard for the young adult and, as Sheldon (1948) puts it, the more likely that the individual by sheer virtue of reaching that age must inevitably be normal. The standard, therefore, for what is normal in old age Sheldon bases on "elastic common sense," and the distinction among aged, aged and infirm, and aged with chronic illness is often slight and unstable. Medical surveys on various samples of aged populations have furnished useful information on the level of health of old people. More surveys of this kind, as well as carefully planned longitudinal studies using standard techniques, should add considerably to our knowledge of the changes that take place from maturity to senescence and of what constitutes the "normality" of old people.

CALORIC REQUIREMENT AND NUTRITIONAL NEEDS OF OLD PEOPLE

Total caloric requirement is less in the aged than in younger people because, in general, there is a decrease in muscular activity and a lowering of body metabolism. Caloric intake should be reduced to avoid the dangers of overweight in persons over 60 years of age. Sinclair (1956) has summarized the caloric requirements for the average sized person age 60 years and over as 2000 calories for men and 1750 calories for women who are sedentary; 2500 calories for men and 2000 calories for women doing light work; and 2750 calories for men and 2250 calories for women doing medium work. Observations made on the food consumption of elderly people in surveys show that old people do tend to eat less and have a lower caloric intake than active adults (Food and Agriculture Organization, 1950). Hobson and Pemberton (1955) in a survey of old people in Sheffield found that the diet they consumed supplied a daily caloric intake of 2205 calories for men and 1826 calories for women. These old people had been assessed as physically fit, and, assuming that physical fitness is related to diet, this caloric intake is adequate to meet the needs of aging individuals except where old people are working or physically very active, when caloric intake would need to be increased. A survey carried out near Sunderland, a coal-mining and ship-repairing area in England, of 1000 pensioners whose ages ranged from 62 to 97 years revealed that their caloric intake met about normal requirements on the diets they were eating, although protein intake was below the normal requirement in 37 per cent of the cases (Smith, 1957).

No marked change in diet is necessary in the absence of systemic disease or local lesions of the gastrointestinal tract. Protein and carbohydrate intake must be sufficient to maintain a state of positive nitrogen balance. Proteins are important in maintaining serum proteins and resistance to infections. Sinclair (1956) gives the daily requirements of protein as 72 grams for men and 60 grams for women. Schulze (1955) advocates 1.0–1.5 grams per kilogram body weight of protein to enlarge the range of safety for maintaining the body tissue in everyday life. Intake of vitamins and minerals must be adequate to meet the increased need of aging tissue for these substances. Calcium and iron must be sufficient to maintain normal metabolism and prevent anemia and demineralization of bone (Stieglitz, 1950). Absorption of fat may be selectively impaired to a moderate degree. It is considered better nutrition for the aged as well as the adult to reduce fat intake and to depend to a greater extent on proteins for their energy requirement. However, worthy of mention here in view of the recent literature on the relation of cholesterolemia to atherosclerosis is Sheldon's finding on the consumption of fat and a reversal in the role of Jack Spratt and his wife in the Wolverhampton survey. While 21 per cent of the female sample could not eat fat, complaining of biliousness, 30 per cent of the male sample liked, and even craved, fats, especially meat fat (Sheldon, 1948).

Animal studies suggest that reduction in calories from birth might be an important factor in preventing physiologic aging. Sinclair (1955) and others have shown that the evidence derived from animal experiments suggests that overfeeding in childhood causes early maturation and shortens life and that overfeeding after maturity increases the incidence of certain degenerative diseases that are common in old age. Stare (1956) cites experiments from Guatemala, Nigeria, and North America, to show that muscular exercise has a favorable effect on regulating serum lipids and serum cholesterol. On high caloric intake no essential gain in weight or in levels of serum cholesterol or lipoprotein occurs if the excess energy is dissipated by exercise. Stare concludes that high caloric diets are better utilized in early adulthood, when energy turnover is high, and that the same dietary habits in later adult life, usually associated with a long period of diminished activity and decreasing energy expenditure, result in an obese middle-aged individual with poor muscle tone, high serum cholesterol and B-lipoproteins, and often significant

atherosclerosis. This is the individual who in the period of advancing physiologic age after middle age shows evidence of obesity and atherosclerosis with its complications. The understanding and application of the principles of good nutrition are important in maintaining health and preventing disease with advancing age, and research in nutrition, especially as it relates to the prevention of degenerative diseases of heart and arteries, is one of the fruitful fields of gerontological research.

Although insurance statistics show that overweight is an adverse factor in attaining longevity, many obese persons survive to old age. In Sheldon's (1948) survey of old people living at home, 449 of 463 subjects had a normal level of nutrition, 3 per cent were undernourished, and 25 per cent of the women over 85 years of age were obese. In a clinical study of 450 apparently healthy patients over 54 years of age attending a consultative health center for old people in Rutherglen, Scotland (Anderson, 1955), more than 50 per cent were over ideal weight; in the survey of 1000 pensioners in Sunderland, over 75 per cent of the women were overweight (Smith, 1957). Exton-Smith (1955) states that a substantial proportion of subjects over 60 years of age, especially women, are overweight. Obesity may not be a bar to long life, but it is a liability in attaining longevity and in advancing years carries a high morbidity and mortality rate. Conditions detrimental to health accompany obesity. Hypertension is five or six times as common in the overweight as in the undernourished female. Diabetes is a frequent concurrent of overweight and, though mild in the aged, carries the threat of circulatory complications. Other conditions, such as infections of the skin, painful feet, degenerative rheumatic affections of the joints causing pain, especially in the weight-bearing joints, and dyspnea not due to respiratory or cardiovascular disease, may be aggravated by obesity and result in disabling ill-health in the elderly.

The small but significant proportion of malnutrition found among old **people** was due to restriction in activity, which makes shopping and cooking difficult, as well as to economic factors, apathy, and ignorance (Sheldon, 1948; Hutchinson, 1954; Hobson and Pemberton, 1955). As the elderly reduce the bulk of food eaten, it is necessary to see that adequate amounts of the essential foods are taken.

METABOLISM

Homeostatic mechanisms that regulate and keep the different body systems in a steady state become less efficient with advancing age, and the elderly adapt less readily to stress and changes in internal and external environment (Stieglitz, 1950). Body metabolism is usually lower in persons over 60 years of age because of a decreased energy requirement of body tissue consequent to a decrease in muscular activity. Observations by various workers reveal a significant reduction in basal oxygen consumption with increasing age. The experimental work of Shock and his associates (1955) has demonstrated that, under resting conditions, the oxygen consumption of functioning cells does not change significantly with age. A large proportion of the reduction in total basal oxygen uptake in older individuals may be attributed to the gradual loss of cellular elements which occurs with aging. Studies of oxygen uptake (Shock *et al.*, 1955) of different organ tissues, however, indicate that certain tissues may show alteration in metabolic rate with age which may not be entirely explained by loss of functioning cells. Much more research is needed to determine the part played by alteration in anatomical structure, physiological processes, and quality of functions and adaptability of aging tissues in modifying body functions.

BODY TEMPERATURE

Old people complain of cold more than younger ones. The mechanisms for preventing heat loss are less efficient in the older than in the younger person. According to Cannon (1939), the decreased abil-

ity to withstand cold in old age apparently may be due to decreased heat production. Thewlis (1954) states that in old age temperature may be below normal; Howell (1950), however, measured the temperatures of 326 healthy Chelsea male pensioners between the ages of 65 and 91 years, all ambulatory, apparently well, and not needing medical treatment, and found oral temperatures of 95.2° F.–100.2° F. and concludes that the range of normal temperature among the aged is greater than in earlier life. Bastai and Dogliotti (1938) advise taking rectal temperatures, since in the old a marked difference is found between external and internal temperatures. It is important clinically to recognize that infectious processes may appear with normal, or even low, temperatures and that in some old persons a temperature of 98.4° F. may be equivalent to 2°–3° of fever. Temperature and pulse in the early stages of bronchopneumonia may be within the normal range and cause a delay in making diagnosis and instituting specific treatment.

PULSE

Pulse rate of 335 healthy Chelsea pensioners was observed by Howell (1950), who recorded frequencies between 44 and 108 beats per minute. The mean pulse rate fell between ages 60 and 84 years but rose sharply again after this latter age. Variation in pulse rate in the old makes a pulse chart unreliable in trying to assess the onset of acute infections. Pulse rate may have no bearing on severity of an infectious process or on the ultimate prognosis of the disease. In a particular old person a pulse rate of 75 may be tachycardia.

HEMOGLOBIN LEVELS IN OLD AGE

Some degree of anemia is the usual finding among the elderly. Sheldon's (1948) inquiry into the nutritional status of 463 old people living at home revealed the presence of iron deficiency in 5 per cent of the women subjects, but no hemoglobin determinations had been done. Hobson and Blackburn (1953), in a random sample of old people, found hemoglobin levels below normal in 5.1 per cent of the males and 6.5 per cent of the females, women having lower values than men. In both sexes there was a significant downward trend in hemoglobin content of blood with increasing age. There was no significant social class difference in hemoglobin levels. In the study of old pensioners in Sunderland, Smith (1957) reports 88 per cent of the women and 55 per cent of the men in a random sample as having hemoglobin levels below 90 per cent, the degree of anemia increasing with advancing age. At the consultative health center in Rutherglen (Anderson, 1955) the second most frequent diagnosis among four hundred old persons referred by their general physician for a medicosocial assessment was microcytic hypochromic anemia. De Grailly and Destrem (1953) state that in the healthy aged the blood is characterized by a certain amount of excess globulin with a decrease in hemoglobin. Binet and Bourlière (1955) give as normal findings in the old hemoglobin values for men of 14.1 ± 1.53 g/100 g blood, and for women 13.7 ± 1.07 g/100 g blood as contrasted to normal adult values of 16 g/100 g blood in males and 14 g/100 g blood in females. Howell (1950), however, after hemoglobin determinations on 52 male and 63 female patients over 60 years of age in a chronic disease hospital who were not suffering from known anemia, chronic bronchitis, or new growths, concludes that the statement "old people are anemic" is incorrect as a general statement. He found a wide range of hemoglobin values from 12.9 g to 23.3 g/100 ml in his subjects (standard 13.8 g/100 ml = 100 per cent hemoglobin), extending in the direction of greater hemoglobin content than less. Brull (1954) states that age of itself does not lower hemoglobin and that it is necessary to exclude the presence of hypochromic anemia or pernicious anemia in aging persons.

In neither the Wolverhampton (Sheldon, 1948) nor the Sheffield (Hobson and Pemberton, 1955) surveys were the old people with low hemoglobin values being treated for anemia. As Stieglitz (1950) points out, anemia is of considerably more significance in old people, since their ability to readjust and to compensate for inadequacies declines. The content and quality of blood assume a critical role in the presence or threat of circulatory insufficiency, and hemoglobin content needs to be maintained at an optimum level. Because of the adverse effect of anemia in cardiac disease and on the course of cerebral arteriosclerosis, one simple hemoglobin determination in all old people would detect a potentially remediable cause of ill-heath (Hobson and Pemberton, 1955).

BLOOD PRESSURE

Statistical analysis of clinical material reveals an interrelationship of hypertension, arteriosclerosis, and the aging process (Grollman, 1955). Loss of elasticity of the vascular tree due to arteriosclerotic changes in the blood vessels is reflected in a rise in systolic blood pressure and a small decrease in diastolic pressure, but this is not hypertension. In the true hypertensive state there is not only an increase in systolic blood pressure but also a marked rise in diastolic blood pressure. The fundamental disturbance here is caused by an increase in peripheral resistance due to alteration in function and loss of adaptability rather than to structural change. In hypertensive cardiovascular disease there is also a concomitant rise of diastolic blood pressure with the rise of systolic blood pressure. The experimental work of Grollman indicates that hypertensive-cardiovascular disease is due to renal dysfunction. Rise in diastolic pressure occurs when the arteriosclerotic process involves the renal blood vessels and is a direct result of an interference with the normal incretory (as distinct from excretory) function of the kidney responsible for maintaining the normotensive state. In addition, abiotrophic changes causing groups of glomeruli and complete nephrons to disappear occur in the kidney in man. This process produces the characteristic irregularity of contour of the senescent kidney and also contributes to the production of hypertension of increasing severity with age.

Rise in systolic pressure alone, therefore, is not true hypertension and may be present in many subjects who feel perfectly fit and capable of normal activity. This is of extreme clinical importance in the management of old people, since the treatment of blood pressure per se may provoke unnecessary anxiety and tension. Hobson and Pemberton (1955) found no correlation of hypertension, heart disease, or high blood pressure with vertigo, tinnitus, angina of effort, clinically detectable arteriosclerosis, or size of heart by X-ray, and, in spite of an elevated blood pressure, subjects may be normally active and have a feeling of well-being. In Denmark, Norgaard (1955) determined blood pressures of 2269 elderly persons, ranging from 70 to 91 years of age, all of whom were physically active, many holding auto driver's licenses. Among males, ages 72–82 years of age, he found blood pressures of 156 ± 30 systolic, over 89 ± 20 diastolic. Among women in the same age group the mean value was 157 systolic over 89 diastolic. Male subjects 82–91 years of age had an average blood-pressure value of 160 over 83. At the Rutherglen Consultative Health Centre (Anderson, 1955) 186 out of 400 patients examined had blood pressures of 140/90 or over; and, of this number, 109 had no symptoms of headache or vertigo, while 77 had symptoms of headache or vertigo. Of the subjects with no complaints, 66 had a systolic pressure of over 170, and 13 had a diastolic pressure of over 110.

Results of blood-pressure surveys support the view that the significance of an elevated blood pressure must be assessed in light of the whole old person, his physical state, and symptoms and ability to function and that an increase in blood pressure per se should not be isolated as a target for treatment.

MUSCULATURE AND SKIN

Histological studies of normal skin of individuals at various ages have not revealed any striking differences between age groups. Except for atrophy in the epidermis and atrophic changes in the collagen fibers, there are no appreciable microscopic changes in the sebaceous or sweat glands, blood vessels, nerves, or fat in the skin of the old (Vickers and Sneddon, 1956). The skin changes that occur with aging seem to be due more to alteration of function than to anatomical changes. A gradual decrease in the secretion of the sebaceous glands gives the skin a dull and dry appearance. Senile pruritus, when not due to systemic disease, and senile dermatitis are two frequent dermatological complaints of old people and are associated with dryness of the skin. It is possible that alteration in hormonal secretion also might be a factor in producing skin changes and loss of hair or baldness. The cause of graying of the hair is not understood, but it is associated with a loss of pigment cells and is a hereditary characteristic.

In the natural aging process there is a reduction in the number and size of tissue cells with replacement by less specific elements like fat and connective tissue and a general loss of elasticity which is more obviously seen in the skin. Muscle and strength wane, and the wrinkled and flabby skin is characteristic of old age. Physical fitness and body build are some measure of musculature. In Sheldon's (1948) survey 70 per cent of the old people were in the normal and plus normal category when assessed for body build, more men than women being in these categories. The surveys of Hobson and Pemberton (1955) in England and van Zonneveld (1954) in the Netherlands show a high proportion of physically fit old men and women, in general women being less fit than men, with unfitness rate rising with age.

DIGESTION

Since the gastrointestinal tract undergoes involution and atrophy with age as evidenced by diminution in acid secretion and digestive enzymes of the stomach and intestinal canal, some impairment in function is to be expected (Stieglitz, 1950). Sheldon and others found, however, that, unless systemic disease is present, the aged follow a normal diet, enjoy food, and eat the usual foods at the usual times. Widdowson and McCance (1955) in Germany showed that old people respond to the stress of a sudden gross departure from their previous food intake qualitatively and quantitatively in the same way as young men, retaining sufficient elasticity of function to make exactly the same response whether they are faced with starvation or an abundance of food. Sheldon (1948) states that, as only 18.8 per cent of his sample had digestive symptoms, one must respect the durability of the stomach. Proper chewing and teeth are necessary for adequate digestion, but again old people show a remarkable degree of adaptability. In Sheldon's study there were no appreciable ill effects on digestion from defects of teeth. Of his sample, 38 per cent had inadequate teeth for mastication, including those who had dentures and did not use them as well as those with a few stumps or bare gums, and no digestive symptoms. The group having neither natural teeth nor dentures (14.4 per cent of the men and 7.7 per cent of the women) found no difficulty in eating even hard and tough foods on gums alone without any reflection on digestive function. Hobson and Roseman (1953) also found patients chewing on gums alone and, among the 230 old persons examined, could find no evidence that dietary intake or nutrition was affected adversely by poor dentition.

Stieglitz (1950) stressed the importance of adequate ingestion of water. Besides stimulating the flow of digestive juices which are necessary for good digestion, water is required for good bowel and kidney function to help the body get rid of the wastes of metabolism.

RESPIRATORY SYSTEM

Morphologically, there is a decrease in the elastic tissue of the lungs and tracheo-bronchial tree which leads to fibrosis, with a reduced vital capacity, and produces the emphysematous barrel chest of the old person who suffers with shortness of breath. Most old people have a cough, which varies from an occasional spasmodic cough, usually in the morning and often aggravated in the winter, to a more constant cough as age advances. In the earlier years it is probably due to cardiovascular disease which is usually fatal by the age of 74. After that age it is more likely to be a true senile bronchitis. "Chronic bronchitis" is a frequent concomitant of advancing years in western Europe, more common in England than on the Continent, and called in England the "English disease." It may become a cause of disability, and, according to Brockington (1957), its maximum mortality is between 65 and 80 years. Shortness of breath or dyspnea is a serious symptom in old people because of its effect in restricting their movement. It appears after the reserves of the body are used up, and is most frequently the result of chronic bronchitis and emphysema and cardiac insufficiency.

CENTRAL NERVOUS SYSTEM

Assessment of the central nervous system reveals a wide variation of findings which in apparently physically fit persons must set one on guard in making diagnoses of central nervous system disease. Loss of tendon reflexes, especially ankle jerks, may occur without any other evidence of cord lesions. Findings such as absent pupillary reaction, loss of superficial reflexes, absent vibration sense in the sacrum, lower limbs, and dysmetria, and patchy analgesia may be seen without any anatomical lesion to account for them and are the result of involution and deterioration in function that goes with senescence. At the Rutherglen Health Centre (Anderson, 1955) abdominal reflexes were absent in 55.6 per cent of the subjects between 55 and 74 years and in 64.6 per cent of those aged 75 years and over. Absent or diminished tendon reflexes were also noted in the absence of definite disease of the central nervous system.

Slowing of sensorimotor performance is one of the most obvious and readily detected changes that occurs in aging. Skills develop with practice and use. After maximum attainment, efficiency in performance declines with age, noticeable even in early or late middle age. This is due to changes in the peripheral organs as well as the central mechanisms of the brain (Welford, 1956). The conduction time of nerve impulses increases with age, and experiments have shown that there is a slowing in the central processes necessary to organize a complicated movement pattern (Singleton, 1955). Older people lose some of their efficiency in anticipating the planning of a series of movements and must program one movement at a time. The speed of visual perception also tends to diminish, and a greater amount of light is required for visual stimulation as age increases. Much can be done in research in industrial design and engineering to improve the efficiency of older people on the job or in everyday living at home by recognizing and providing against the limitations age imposes on performance.

The results of intelligence tests reveal a parallel between decline in intellectual and sensorimotor function with increase in age. However, there is a wide overlap in performance of younger and older individuals, many older persons scoring as well as, or even better than, the average of the younger subjects. There also seems to be somewhat less decline among the well endowed and people of superior attainments.

Older people depend to a much greater extent on sensory stimulation, particularly their eyes, in performing tasks than do younger people (Szafran, 1955). They are handicapped in situations where they are deprived of visual information and particularly when movements depend more on postural sense than on eyes. Rigidity of the ciliary muscles in older individuals causes a loss in the power of accommodation. Decline in the function of the central nervous mechanisms that give kinesthetic information subserving postural tone and orientation produces clinical problems of practical importance, notably a liability to falls. Age groups show a steadily rising incidence of vertigo, difficulty in the dark, and liability to falls, especially after 75 years. Sheldon (1948) found that, by the age of 80, 73 per cent of females and 36.3 per cent of males were affected, but this seemingly greater susceptibility on the part of women than men to falls is probably due to a greater exposure to risk arising out of their housekeeping activities. Falls are catastrophic occurrences in the lives of the elderly. They often precipitate senile decay and are one of the most pernicious "previous illnesses" affecting the health of old people.

VISION

The eye is an important organ in maintaining the old person in equilibrium with his environment, and much of the disability due to its dysfunction is readily remediable. As age advances, the individual relies more and more on visual information to reinforce proprioceptive cues, and tasks previously performed through habit or by touch alone come to require direct visual attention. Visual acuity falls with age. Studies show that a majority of old people need glasses for close work and that many who possess glasses either find them useless or are using glasses that are definitely harmful (Sheldon, 1948). An eye examination and provision of properly fitted glasses would prevent or relieve an avoidable source of disability for the elderly (Sheldon, 1948; Hobson and Pemberton, 1955).

C. Vitality of Old People

Planning for medical care is an important feature of the total program for the care of the aging population. The old do not form a homogeneous group. There are the healthy and self-reliant, the frail, the incapacitated, the chronically ill, the lonely—each group with a different need. In planning medical care for an increasing old age population, it is important to know the state of health of old people, the frequency with which they fall ill, from what causes, and what their medical needs are.

Many medical surveys have been done in a variety of communities to determine the state of health of old people living at home and have contributed to our knowledge of the health and needs of old people.

1. *Wolverhampton survey.*—This pioneer medical survey followed a social study (Rowntree, 1947) in the same community and was undertaken by Sheldon for the Nuffield Foundation on a random sample of 477 persons 60 years of age and over living at home from May, 1945, to January, 1947. The report by Sheldon (1948) is a classic document which drew attention to old people in Western society as individuals with a medical and social past and present and with definite needs that must be met if the increasing number of old people in the community is to be provided for adequately in the future.

If activity and a feeling of physical fitness are measures of the state of health, the power of adaptation in those who survive to old age must be considerable. Sheldon found in his survey of old people that many preserve a remarkable amount of physical sturdiness. When assessed in respect to state of health, 46.2 per cent of the old people were "normal." Since more than this percentage complained of particular symptoms, the old person can carry on adequately in spite of several, and sometimes considerable, complaints. More women than men were in this group. Since knowledge of "normal" at present is confined to the years of growth and maturity, and the changes and rate of change from maturity to senescence are still largely unknown, "normal," as Sheldon defined it, was based on his standard of "elastic common sense."

The group classified "normal plus" comprised 24.5 per cent of the sample, and the men and women in it showed remarkable vigor and hardiness. More men than women were in this group. Men tend to die earlier, but those who attain advanced ages are of particularly good fiber and in very good physical health.

The "subnormal" group was made up of 29.2 per cent of the sample. There was an equal number of men and women in this group. However, 62.5 per cent of the "subnormal" women were over 85 years of age, while the bulk of the "subnormal" men (81.6 per cent) were below 80 years of age. The whole group is remarkable for its persistence in carrying on in spite of severe or painful defects of health, the women especially seeming to have a tenacious hold on life and continuing to survive in spite of chronic ill-health.

In this survey only 2.5 per cent of the old people living at home were confined to bed; 8.5 per cent were confined to the house; and the movements of 22.5 per cent of the sample were restricted to the neighborhood.

Only a small percentage of the aged require medical care for sickness. The larger need of older persons is for services that will help them to remain at home in familiar surroundings where the risk of deterioration and disability is considerably less.

2. *Sheffield survey.*—Hobson and Pemberton (1955) undertook a similar survey to assess the health of a random sample of 476 persons 61 years of age and over living at home in the Sheffield area. A previous study of the social circumstances and needs of old people in Sheffield had been made by the Sheffield Council of Social Service in 1948 (Greenlees and Adams, 1950). The medical survey revealed a high proportion of elderly men and women who appear to remain more or less unrestricted in activity. Women seemed rather less fit than men (54.9 per cent of females as against 71.2 per cent of males being unrestricted in activity), and age for age there were more disabilities among elderly women than elderly men. Just over 50 per cent of the

total sample regarded themselves as fit, but only 25 per cent of them were assessed as fit by the physician after examination. In both sexes, disablement increased with age; however, in the higher age groups there was a considerable number of very fit men and women. Ill-health in old age is to some extent related to poverty. Mean disablement scores tended to be higher in those on low incomes and were significantly higher among those living in the poor neighborhoods as compared with those living in the better residential areas of Sheffield. Mean disablement scores of men who had retired did not differ significantly from scores of those still working at similar ages, suggesting that retirement usually occurred for reasons other than ill-health.

3. *Groningen survey.*—Van Zonneveld (1954) reported a survey of old people undertaken by the University's Department of Preventive and Social Medicine in the city of Groningen (Netherlands), which has a diversified population of farmers, laborers, and industrial workers. The purpose of the survey was to assess the physical and mental state of the old people and the way they adapted to their ailments, to find out how they were being cared for, and to get some idea of the best possible provision for them from a sociomedical viewpoint. Three thousand persons 65 years and over (one-fourth of the entire aged population of the city) were included in the survey. The older person estimated his own state of health, and in every age group more than 80 per cent of the men and about 74 per cent of the women had no special complaints of health. Although more women than men complained about health, the number of those who complained did not increase with advancing years, and there was no significant difference in complaints about health based on social class. Men who were still working complained less about health than those who had stopped working. About 8 per cent of those between 65 and 70 years and 40 per cent of those 80 years and over lived dependently. However, about 3.7 per cent of the

old people were in need of home help. An interesting finding was that six parents of individuals in the study were still alive at the time of the survey.

4. *Study of the aged by general practitioners in the Netherlands begun in 1953.*— Another investigation reported by van Zonneveld and Groen (1957) is still under way and covers random samples of more than 95 per cent of all the aged in the Netherlands. Preliminary information collected from 1000 forms shows that three-fourths of the men and two-thirds of the women considered themselves in a good state of health, although subsequent examination by a physician found fewer than this number in a good state of health. Within the 3 months before the investigation two-fifths of the men and three-fifths of the women had consulted their doctor, and the same proportion were attending their doctors regularly.

D. Common Disorders of the Aged

The disorders of old age do not seem to have changed with time. Hippocrates (1943) characterized old men as suffering from "difficulty of breathing, catarrh accompanied by coughing, strangury, difficult micturition, pains at the joints, kidney disease, dizziness, apoplexy, cachexia, pruritis of the whole body, sleeplessness, watery discharge from the bowels, eyes and nostrils, dullness of sight, cataract, hardness of hearing." Medical surveys show that first heart disease, then arthritis, followed by chronic bronchitis, painful feet, urinary disorders, vertigo, and defective hearing and vision are the chief causes of disability leading to restriction of motion and loss of independence of old people. The following data are derived from the Wolverhamptom survey, except where otherwise indicated, and were obtained by inquiry only from 477 old persons over 60 years of age. They reveal the disorders which occur frequently among old people.

1. *Bronchitis.*—Evidence of bronchitis was reported in 40.9 per cent of the sam-

ple, more frequently in males than females, and varied from an occasional spasmodic cough in winter to the constant cough of a true senile bronchitis in the more aged subjects.

2. *Heart disease.*—Under the method of survey the extent of cardiac illness was not accurately determinable, but 5 per cent of the sample was estimated to have cardiac defects leading them to consult a doctor. Unless the patient suffered a thrombosis with pain or edema, he did not bother to see the doctor. This was also true for patients with angina of effort and edema of the feet, who carried on, modifying their activity as was necessary, in spite of symptoms. Evans (1956) states that "patients over 70 years of age should be considered to have some cardiac impairment even though there may be no demonstrable cardiac disease."

3. *Hypertension.*—Of the sample, 9.4 per cent were under, or had been under, treatment for high blood pressure. Observations in this survey also show that rise in systolic blood pressure is compatible with a feeling of well-being and normal activity.

4. *Dyspnea or shortness of breath.*— This is a serious symptom, second in importance to senile weakness, in causing discomfort and loss of independence for old people. It is most frequently the result of respiratory embarrassment and circulatory insufficiency and is an indication of depleted body reserves. In the Groningen survey (van Zonneveld, 1954) dyspnea and a sense of suffocation were common complaints occurring more frequently among women than men and among those of lower than higher social class.

5. *Rheumatic affections.*—Over half the sample (55.4 per cent) had rheumatic symptoms, varying from twinges of muscular pain to crippling incapacity of joints. Women were affected more than men, and, because of their responsibility for housework and often the care of a family, the effect of arthritis of the knee joints, usually menopausal, was a particular hardship, especially where obesity was an added handicap. The large number of persons with arthritis of varying types and extent who were still capable of unlimited movement affirmed the endurance and determination of the aged. In classifying their sample for degree of mobility, Hobson and Pemberton (1955) remarked, "It would be a mistake to assume that all those with unrestricted activity were fit and well. It was simply a refusal to give in to the aches and infirmities of age that allowed many still to be classified 'mobility unrestricted.'" The types of rheumatic affections were (*a*) rheumatoid arthritis, which produced in some instances complete immobility of hand and wrist; (*b*) osteoarthritis of the hip and other joints; and (*c*) spondylitis. This last, a genuine phenomenon of old age which results from senile changes in the spine, is slowly progressive and sometimes so severe as to produce a doubling-up of the body. Its incidence rises abruptly after the age of 80 years. Some old people are able to carry on, but spondylitis usually causes great disability, especially when other symptoms are present.

6. *Varicose veins.*—Of the sample, 60 per cent, all under 80 years of age, suffered with varicose veins, which were an important cause of "bad legs." Ulcers were present as a complication in 5.4 per cent of these cases.

7. *Weakness.*—Although difficult to differentiate from weakness associated with cardiac disease, 12.1 per cent of the sample seemed to suffer from a true senile weakness which caused considerable incapacity. It is considered a definite clinical entity and is greater the older the age group, especially among women after the age of 75. Its importance in geriatrics lies in the increasingly serious restriction it imposes on the activity of old people as age advances.

8. *Genitourinary symptoms.*—Frequency and urgency of micturition were found in 31.5 per cent of the sample and was greater among women than men. In males it is largely due to prostatic obstruction; in

females it is the result of postpartum trauma to the pelvic floor, chronic cystitis, strain, coryza, cold weather, or senile weakness of the sphincter of the urethra. In the Groningen survey (van Zonneveld, 1954) nocturia and dysuria were frequent complaints, more frequent among men than women. True incontinence was rare among the elderly at home. Incontinence, urinary or fecal, occurring as a result of stroke, pelvic operation, or senile weakness, is one of the distressing aspects of geriatric medicine. It causes strain in the household in terms of patient care and linen care, becomes a barrier to social contacts for the old person, and is one of the most frequent reasons that lead families to seek institutional care for an aged member.

9. *Defects of vision and hearing.*—Of the sample, 6.3 per cent had normal vision without glasses and enjoyed vigorous health, and 12.3 per cent had diseases of the eye—1 per cent was totally blind, 5.6 per cent had cataracts, and many had corneal opacities. Almost 3 per cent needed glasses but did not have them, and one third of the sample found their present glasses unsuitable. Sheldon found a distinct correlation between economic level and the likelihood of having unsuitable glasses. The ignorance among old people of the true nature of glasses was evidenced by the fact that 10 per cent had come by their glasses in a haphazard way—either as a gift or inheritance or by purchase in a store simply by trying on glasses until one was found that gave a satisfactory magnification. A proper eye examination had never been done among 17.5 per cent of those with glasses. The number of old people with defective vision who possessed either useless or definitely harmful glasses indicate a service that could easily remove a source of disability for the aged.

In the Groningen survey (van Zonneveld, 1954), 87 per cent of males and 79.5 per cent of females could see well with or without glasses. In the entire sample about 1.7 per cent of the males and about 1.3 per cent of the females could see neither near nor far and used no glasses, and in the entire group 6.9 per cent of the males and 12.7 per cent of the females found their glasses of no use. More females than males had complaints referable to the eye. After the age of 80 years, only 25 per cent of the old people had no complaints of the eye or ear.

Sheldon found that 31 per cent of the sample had evidence of defective hearing. With advancing age, the efficiency of function of the inner ear declines, more so in men than women. At age 80 and over the incidence of severe deafness is 60 per cent. Tinnitus was also present in 17.8 per cent of the sample queried on this symptom. In the Groningen survey (van Zonneveld, 1954), in the oldest age group 26 per cent of the males and 32 per cent of the females had perfect hearing. The increasing association of vertigo and liability to fall, deafness, and advancing age suggests that the inner ear, labyrinth, and central connections do not wear as well as other organs. Since many old people with moderate deafness had a defect only in one ear (about 25 per cent), it would seem that one-third of the old age population might benefit from the use of hearing aids. The use of glasses and a hearing aid could frequently mean the difference between dependency and unsociability and the ability to get about and lead a useful life.

10. *Vertigo and liability to fall.*—Vertigo was present in 51.6 per cent of the sample and was greater among women than men. It may be due to changes in blood pressure, diseases of the ear, or senile degeneration of the labyrinth. Vertigo and deafness are usually associated. Of the 26 subjects who complained of tinnitus, 22 also had vertigo. It would appear that the whole labyrinthine apparatus and cochlea are prone to senile degeneration, which increases as age advances, becoming particularly pronounced at age 80.

Advancing age groups also show a steadily rising liability to falls, associated with an increasing incidence of deafness, difficulty in the dark, and vertigo. The incidence is particularly high in women—73 per cent of women over the age of 80 were liable to fall. This poses a serious clinical problem of practical importance, since falls often precipitate senile decay. Sheldon found falls the second most important previous illness affecting present health in his subjects. Howell (1956) found the chief reasons for falls among the old people he interviewed at home to be unsuspected cerebral thrombosis, degeneration of the posterior columns of the spinal cord, senile muscular weakness, vertigo, and impaired vision.

Movements of old people are handicapped in circumstances where they are forced to depend more on postural sense and less on the eye. Although there might be psychological aspects to the difficulty old people experience with their vision at night, most cases of difficulty in the dark are due to a senile failure in mechanisms serving posture and orientation, in which the labyrinth plays an important part. Szafran (1955), of Cambridge, corroborated Sheldon's observation that direct visual information is of much greater importance in middle and later life in performing tasks. Beyond age 75, mechanisms subserving postural tone are liable to fail suddenly in function. In maintaining balance, the labyrinth supplies information on the position of the body in space which is supplemented by information from the eyes, muscles, and joints of the body. In old age labyrinthine as well as central nervous system mechanisms that provide kinesthetic information decline. These changes result in an increased liability to trip over trivial objects and to greater difficulty in recovering from even slight disturbance of balance.

11. *Difficulty with stairs.*—This is not a clinical illness but is a great handicap and source of difficulty for old people. Sheldon found that 38.5 per cent of the sample had difficulty in negotiating stairs. Ascending stairs was a greater source of difficulty than descending them: 14.4 per cent had difficulty ascending stairs because of dyspnea, angina, or intermittent claudication;

5 per cent had difficulty in getting down steps, owing to diseases of the knee or hip, stiffness of leg or feet, vertigo, faulty vision, or lack of confidence; 19 per cent had difficulty both ways; and 6.3 per cent found stairs impossible to negotiate. Severe impairment of mobility was more frequently the result of recovery from stroke.

Of the women having difficulty with stairs, 78 per cent were either partially or wholly responsible for their own housekeeping, and 10 per cent of those looking after an old person had trouble with stairs. However, only half the old people having trouble with stairs were willing to leave their homes to avoid this difficulty. The Nuffield Social Survey on old people recommends that "stairs should be wide and shallow, and should have a hand rail on both sides" (Rowntree, 1947).

12. *Other disorders of the aged.*—Mortality statistics suggest that diabetes and tuberculosis are no longer major medical problems of the aged. Diabetes is a relatively mild disease in the aged and is easier to control than in the younger individual. However, its frequent association with peripheral vascular disease and the attendant complications constitutes a threat to the well-being of the aged.

Tuberculosis is not the killer it was before the successful use of chemotherapy in its control. In the Scandinavian countries tuberculosis is no longer a serious health problem, and many of the sanatoria and dispensaries that were previously required for the care of tuberculosis patients have been converted to care for old people. A program for the aged in Norway has been developed by the Old People's Health Committee. The National Tuberculosis Association, which has developed an interest in geriatry and heart disease, is an active participant of the Old People's Health Committee.

In Belgium, Clerens (1956) has pointed out the flagrant difference between morbidity and mortality rates in tuberculosis among the aged as a result of drug therapy and the potential danger of the treated chronic case as a carrier of resistant bacilli. The need in Brussels for isolating infectious cases has tripled the need for hospital beds since the war, and a greater number of these patients are over 50 years of age. The report of the Committee on the Care of the Chronically Ill and the Aged at the Ninth Congress of the International Federation of Hospitals recommended basing the need of beds for the care of chronic tuberculosis on the number of those sick, rather than the death rate, since in a number of countries the trend in morbidity does not parallel the trend in mortality (Delore, 1955, 1956a). Tuberculosis always remains a possibility in the differential diagnosis of a chronic cough in the old person. An incompletely healed foci within an apparently calcified area radiologically, or a long dormant infection, are potential sources of reinfection. When the immune mechanisms and vigor of the older person decline, these areas light up, causing active disease which requires hospitalization for treatment.

Diseases of the nervous system fall into two overlapping groups: those associated with behavioral changes, which require the help of a psychiatrist in dealing with them, and those associated with organic lesions, which fall in the domain of the neurologist. They are often secondary to vascular degeneration or to neoplastic changes in the central nervous system and account for some of the main chronic illnesses of old age. Howell (1956), in an assessment in the homes of 509 older patients awaiting hospital admission, found cerebral thrombosis or hemiplegia the commonest diagnoses, affecting 11 per cent of the old people, with senility accounting for 10 per cent of the diagnoses.

Early recognition and treatment of illnesses, especially those that might restrict movement, are important in preventing disability in the aged. Up to the age of 70 years, the pathological conditions that produce incapacity and restrict movement are the same as at all adult ages. After age 70 the chief causative factors of restricted movement are more specific symptoms of aging—weakness, vertigo, difficulty with traffic, lack of confidence, spondylitis, and sensitiveness to cold. Other conditions, such as arthritis, painful feet, defective vision, angina, and mechanical disabilities from previous accidents, may also cause great impairment of function.

Tables 1–5 show the admission or discharge diagnoses of old people from various institutions in several countries.

Social care has to be related to medical needs, and, in planning housing and other community services for the aged, it must be remembered that the people utilizing these facilities may suffer with these medi-

TABLE 1*

DIAGNOSES AMONG 400 PATIENTS 54 YEARS AND OVER ATTENDING THE CONSULTATIVE HEALTH CENTRE AT RUTHERGLEN, SCOTLAND

Disease	Male	Female	Total
Blood pressure 140/90 or over:			
(1) With no symptoms of headache or vertigo	62	47	109
(2) With symptoms of headache or vertigo	28	49	77
Blood pressure less than 140/90 with no symptoms	5	3	8
Microcytic hypochromic anemia	14	18	32
Osteoarthritis	15	16	31
Fibrositis	3	24	27
Chronic bronchitis	18	4	22
Coronary artery disease (previous coronary thrombosis)	11	4	15
Tumor—malignant	5	4	9
Intermittent claudication	10	. . . . . .	10
Valvular heart disease			
(1) Rheumatic	1	3	4
(2) Arteriosclerotic	2	1	3
(3) Syphilitic	1	. . . . . .	1
Diabetes mellitus	2	3	5
Pernicious anemia	1	2	3
Angina pectoris	1	2	3
Miscellaneous	24	17	41
Total	203	197	400

* After W. F. Anderson, "A Clinical Study of the Patients Attending a Consultative Health Center for Old People at Rutherglen, Scotland," in *Old Age in the Modern World* (Edinburgh: E. &. S. Livingstone, 1955), p. 537.

cal conditions. All measures that protect the health and preserve the mobility of old people should be developed and integrated in a program of total care to help them maintain their integrity and independence as fully functioning social individuals in the community.

TABLE 2*

PROVISIONAL DIAGNOSIS IN 4622 CHELSEA PEN-
SIONERS ADMITTED FOR TREATMENT TO THE
INFIRMARY OF THE ROYAL HOSPITAL

Disease	Per Cent
Bronchitis	13.5
Old age debility	11.6
Myocardial degeneration	9.5
Influenza	7.8
Digestive disorders	7.7
Rheumatic diseases	6.1
Other cardiovascular diseases	6.1
Central nervous system lesions	5.1
Pneumonias	3.1
Cancer	4.3
Genitourinary	3.4
Other diseases	21.7
Total	100.0

* After T. H. Howell, *Old Age* (London: H. K. Lewis & Co., 1950), p. 85.

TABLE 3*

DIAGNOSES IN 1100 PATIENTS 65 YEARS AND
OVER ADMITTED TO A GENERAL MEDICAL
SERVICE FROM 1952 TO 1956 (REPRESENTING
28.4 PER CENT OF ALL PATIENTS ADMITTED
DURING THE SAME PERIOD)

Illness	No. of Patients	Per Cent
Cardiovascular	240	21.8
Respiratory	238	21.6
Neuropsychiatric	162	14.7
Nutritional	130	11.8
Senility	117	10.6
Gastrointestinal	80	7.3
Liver, bile duct, pancreas	72	6.5
Rheumatism	61	5.6
Genitourinary	38	3.5
Skeletal	31	2.8
Blood	15	1.4
Skin	13	1.2
Endocrine	9	0.8
Others	45	4.1

* After P. Delore and P. Arnaud, "Motifs d'hospitalisation des malades âgés de plus de 65 ans," *Tech. Hosp.*, **11** (August–September, 1956), 48–53.

TABLE 4*

DIAGNOSES IN 243,730 PATIENTS 60 YEARS
AND OVER ADMITTED TO HOSPITALS
IN ITALY, 1954

DISEASE	TOTAL NO. PATIENTS ALL AGED	PATIENTS 60 YEARS AND OVER	
		No.	Per Cent
Circulatory system	87,723	33,527	38.2
Nervous system	83,431	29,768	35.6
Tumors	100,259	28,999	29.0
Psychotic disease	49,385	8,586	17.4
Skin diseases	47,929	7,972	16.6
Genitourinary system	109,913	17,931	16.3
Bones, etc.	47,966	7,091	15.0
Accidents	259,547	34,573	13.3
Digestive system	401,132	36,746	9.2
Respiratory system	179,273	15,652	8.7
Infectious	156,332	9,748	6.2

* Source: Personal communication from Professor G. A. Canaperia, 1957.

TABLE 5*

DIAGNOSES AT DISCHARGE OF PATIENTS 65
YEARS OR MORE IN SIXTEEN HOSPITALS
(JANUARY 15 AND/OR APRIL 15, JULY 15, AND
OCTOBER 15, 1954) IN THE NETHERLANDS

(*N* = 2441 Men and 2358 Women)

DISEASE	PER CENT	
	Males	Females
Malignant neoplasm	17	15
Prostatic hypertrophy	14	....
Heart	10	13
Accidents	9	13
Vascular	6	7
Hernia of the abdominal cavity and ileus	5	2
Diabetes	4	11
Gastric and duodenal ulcers	4	3
Urinary tract	4	....
Liver and gall bladder and biliary ducts	4	11
Mental	4	4
Eye	4	4
Bone and other organs of locomotion	3	6
Hypertension	2	5
Cerebrovascular lesions	2	2

* After H. J. Bronts and R. J. van Zonneveld, "The Impact of Aged Patients on Hospital Care: A Survey into Number, Length of Stay, and Diagnosis of Aged People Admitted to a Number of Hospitals in 1924, 1939, and 1954," *Ziekenhuiswezen*, **30** (October, 1957), 305.

E. Mortality and Morbidity in Old Age

CAUSES OF MORTALITY IN OLD AGE

People who survive to old age do not die of old age. They die from disease, and, as Vischer and Roulet's (1952) post mortem report indicates, usually a multiplicity of morbid processes are found on autopsy. Biological death is exceedingly rare, and, according to Gavey (1949), when this does take place, the heart is usually the primary

causes of mortality have been reduced, there has been very little decrease in mortality from disease of the circulatory system, tumors, and senility.

Also on the increase is the death rate from cancer (Table 8). The death rate of older males from tuberculosis (Table 9) had increased in three of the leading European countries reported and for females in two. Other countries showed a moderate decline. This is in sharp contrast with the

TABLE 6*

AGE-ADJUSTED DEATH RATES PER 1000 FOR AGE GROUPS 45–64 AND 65 AND OVER
BY SEX FOR ABOUT 1930 AND 1950†

COUNTRY	1930				1950			
	45–64		65 and Over		45–64		65 and Over	
	Male	Female	Male	Female	Male	Female	Male	Female
England and Wales........	16.6	12.1	90.1	70.8	14.5	8.4	81.1	59.3
Australia................	14.1	10.1	74.5	59.7	14.4	8.7	79.1	57.3
Canada..................	13.2	11.8	70.9	64.5	12.9	8.5	63.8	53.4
Netherlands....	11.7	11.4	72.6	69.4	9.1	7.2	61.8	57.6
Belgium.................	16.9	12.6	83.9	71.6	15.0	9.1	76.7	61.4
France..................	20.4	13.2	97.0	79.2	14.9	8.5	77.2	54.2
Switzerland.............	19.1	13.1	89.0	76.7	13.2	8.5	74.7	60.8
Germany................	14.6	12.1	80.7	74.4	12.6	8.6	72.2	64.6
Denmark................	12.6	12.0	73.7	71.6	10.3	8.2	67.5	62.7
Norway.................	12.0	9.9	64.6	58.3	8.9	6.5	59.4	51.7
Sweden.................	12.7	11.3	70.5	67.2	10.0	7.8	67.2	60.7
Finland................	23.3	13.8	83.6	71.3	19.5	9.3	87.0	68.8
Italy...................	15.2	12.0	80.9	73.5	12.5	8.2	66.3	58.8

* After M. Spiegelman, "An International Comparison of Mortality Rates at the Older Ages," in *World Population Conference, 1954, Papers* (Geneva: United Nations, 1954), **1**, 302.
† Adjusted on the basis of the age distribution of the total population of the United States Census of April 1, 1950.

factor. Some degree of arteriosclerosis and emphysema seems to be a "normal" finding in the aged. The risk of degenerative disease is the price of longevity. Spiegelman (1954) reports that the general death rates for both males and females 65 years and over have declined from 1930 to 1950 in the countries included in Table 6 but are still about five to six times higher than for adults 45–64. The death rate from cardiovascular-renal disease is increasing and is now the leading cause of mortality in old age (Table 7). Freudenberg (1955) has shown that in Germany, although other

mortality rate for this disease for the age group 45–64, which showed consistent declines, generally large, for both sexes and all countries. Six of the ten European countries show a drop, generally a steep one, in pneumonia, while the others show a small rise for one or both sexes (Table 10).

Cancer is becoming an increasingly important cause of mortality. The incidence of tumors increases with age. As age increases, however, the rapidity of growth and the malignancy of tumors decrease, especially after the period of highest can-

TABLE 7*

DEATH RATE PER 100,000 FROM CARDIOVASCULAR-RENAL DISEASE FROM SELECTED COUNTRIES, ca. 1931 AND ca. 1949†

COUNTRY	AGES 45–64				AGES 65 AND OVER			
	1931		1949		1931		1949	
	Male	Female	Male	Female	Male	Female	Male	Female
England and Wales........	565	443	565	359	4133	3608	4399	3864
Australia.................	509	396	785	460	3233	2775	4512	3598
Canada...................	437	409	694	395	3270	3204	4037	3643
Netherlands..............	335	366	317	263	2762	2980	2885	3154
Belgium..................	547	438	587	379	2947	2580	3449	2894
France...................	563	397	474	332	2786	2219	3793	2896
Switzerland‡.............	877	830	823	615	4632	4773	4963	4831
Germany.................			366	285			2813	2767
Denmark.................	367	321	393	275	2704	2861	3350	3468
Norway‡.................	543	461	530	403	3288	3024	3736	3582
Sweden‡.................	547	521	644	514	3914	3756	5044	4970
Finland..................	662	431	851	439	1759	1503	4055	3287
Italy....................	463	461	415	341	3486	3375	3340	3205

* After M. Spiegelman, "An International Comparison of Mortality Rates at the Older Ages," in *World Population Conference, 1954, Papers* (Geneva: United Nations, 1954), 1, 306.

† Death rates not adjusted for age.

‡ For these countries age group as indicated:

Switzerland........	50–69	70 and Over
Norway...........	50–69	70 and Over
Sweden...........	45–69	70 and Over

TABLE 8*

DEATH RATE PER 100,000 FROM CANCER FOR SELECTED COUNTRIES ca. 1931 AND ca. 1949

COUNTRY	AGES 45–64				AGES 65 AND OVER			
	1931		1949		1931		1949	
	Male	Female	Male	Female	Male	Female	Male	Female
England and Wales........	293	298	322	264	1111	886	1167	808
Australia.................	212	225	207	224	976	720	1001	750
Canada...................	197	264	227	257	839	748	1005	810
Netherlands..............	248	312	242	255	1189	999	1136	977
Belgium..................	187	239	221	234	626	592	762	679
France...................	182	194	248	223	551	490	1029	760
Switzerland†.............	549	405	482	358	1485	1100	1625	1053
Germany.................			257	263			1113	947
Denmark.................	245	303	228	268	1077	1085	1042	963
Norway†.................	390	369	307	306	1211	960	1397	1025
Sweden†.................	291	308	236	268	1016	840	1081	895
Finland..................	198	197	393	250	524	401	1303	902
Italy....................	172	186	243	206	491	437	754	605

* After M. Spiegelman, "An International Comparison of Mortality Rates at the Older Ages," in *World Population Conference 1954, Papers* (Geneva: United Nations, 1954), 1, 306.

† For these countries age group as indicated:

Switzerland........	50–69	70 and Over
Norway...........	50–69	70 and Over
Sweden...........	45–69	70 and Over

TABLE 9*

DEATH RATE PER 100,000 FROM TUBERCULOSIS FOR SELECTED COUNTRIES
ca. 1931 AND *ca.* 1949

COUNTRY	AGES 45–64				AGES 65 AND OVER			
	1931		1949		1931		1949	
	Male	Female	Male	Female	Male	Female	Male	Female
England and Wales........	151	58	104	28	73	40	81	22
Australia.................	112	44	81	18	97	45	121	29
Canada...................	90	61	56	27	99	81	80	44
Netherlands..............	82	71	42	27	112	94	87	81
Belgium..................	115	46	111	23	73	49	73	34
France...................	265	100	153	50	126	73	150	81
Switzerland†..............	187	133	83	38	199	217	124	105
Germany.................	......	......	91	30	......	......	124	69
Denmark.................	63	49	30	12	74	62	40	37
Norway†.................	136	116	68	28	138	110	83	53
Sweden†.................	120	101	55	30	104	105	78	57
Finland..................	305	170	262	67	171	112	313	121
Italy....................	129	88	91	32	72	63	55	37

* After M. Spiegelman, "An International Comparison of Mortality Rates at the Older Ages," in *World Population Conference, 1954, Papers* (Geneva: United Nations, 1954), **1,** 306.

† For these countries age group as indicated:

Switzerland........	50–69	70 and Over
Norway...........	50–69	70 and Over
Sweden...........	45–69	70 and Over

TABLE 10*

DEATH RATES PER 100,000 FROM PNEUMONIA AND INFLUENZA FOR
SELECTED COUNTRIES, *ca.* 1931 AND *ca.* 1949

COUNTRY	AGES 45–64				AGES 65 AND OVER			
	1931		1949		1931		1949	
	Male	Female	Male	Female	Male	Female	Male	Female
England and Wales........	169	96	65	34	494	474	353	296
Australia.................	102	64	47	21	489	402	374	282
Canada..................	86	68	33	18	525	621	285	262
Netherlands..............	112	96	39	33	996	1031	458	492
Belgium..................	112	83	41	20	515	487	259	220
France...................	102	68	41	28	507	486	549	490
Switzerland†..............	192	165	31	25	1225	1241	363	383
Germany.................	......	......	37	27	......	......	351	335
Denmark.................	75	66	28	24	549	578	532	554
Norway†.................	128	114	43	45	773	840	729	871
Sweden†.................	131	147	29	22	978	1113	336	387
Finland..................	109	69	45	28	247	227	278	279
Italy....................	234	165	54	31	1035	986	452	390

* After M. Spiegelman, "An International Comparison of Mortality Rates at the Older Ages," in *World Population Conference, 1954, Papers* (Geneva: United Nations, 1954), **1,** 306.

† For these countries age group as indicated:

Switzerland........	50–69	70 and Over
Norway...........	50–69	70 and Over
Sweden...........	45–69	70 and Over

173

cer mortality, and vigorous therapy should be directed against the tumor consistent with the requirements of the case irrespective of age.

MORBIDITY AMONG THE AGED

It is important to know the incidence of disease in the aged in order to plan intelligently for the medical and social services they require. Sheldon's (1948) survey in Wolverhampton showed that 29 per cent of the subjects were receiving medical at-

65 years, with rheumatism next. In the fall of 1957 a national survey on morbidity on a random sample of 75,000 families was started in Italy. This study should provide some interesting facts about illnesses and illness rates among the older aged members of these families (Canaperia, personal communication). There is a need for more morbidity studies in the general population to furnish a total picture of the nature and extent of illness among the aged. At the present time almost the only source of in-

TABLE 11*

PATIENT POPULATION,† ALL DISEASES AND CONDITIONS REQUIRING CONSULTATIONS,‡ IN EIGHT PRACTICES FOR THE PERIOD APRIL, 1951—MARCH, 1952, BY AGE AND SEX

AGE GROUP	POPULATION— ALL EIGHT PRACTICES		CONSULTATIONS—ALL PRACTICES			
			No.		Rate per 100 Practice Population	
	Male	Female	Male	Female	Male	Female
0–14.......	3,135	3,138	11,862	12,149	353	363
15–44.......	4,787	6,456	13,741	26,591	268	386
45–64.......	2,352	3,187	10,083	15,913	399	468
65 and over..	1,031	1,488	5,114	9,286	460	582
Not stated...	824	967	....	....	....	....
All ages....	12,129	15,236	40,800	63,939	336	420

* After W. P. D. Logan, *Studies on Medical and Population Subjects* ("General Practitioners Records," No. 7 [London: H.M. Stationery Office, 1953]), pp. 41 and 85.

† Patients consulting are the numbers consulting for each specified disease and are not aggregated in group totals.

‡ Consultations are the times each disease was diagnosed. They are thus overstated to a certain extent by counting each diagnosis made at "multiple diagnosis" consultations.

tention at the time of survey. Hobson and Pemberton (1955), in the Sheffield survey, found that about 47 per cent of the old people were receiving medical attention every 3 months or more often. In the general practitioners' survey in the Netherlands (van Zonneveld and Groen, 1957), 40 per cent of the men and 60 per cent of the women were receiving medical attention regularly at the time of survey. The same proportion had consulted their doctors within 3 months prior to the investigation.

In Britain the Monthly Survey of Sickness conducted by the Ministry of Health (1951–52) reports "ill defined symptoms" the most frequent complaint of persons over

formation, outside reportable diseases, on the prevalence of illness and disability is hospital records. These do not give a true picture of morbidity from all diseases, including the less serious and non-disabling illnesses, which is a prerequisite for setting up health services that will meet the overall needs of the aging.

Tables 11 and 12 give some information on the extent of illness in different age groups in two different studies. Table 13 shows morbidity by severity of illness from the Survey of Sickness study done in Britain. From Tables 14 and 15, showing consultations by age groups and by place, it is readily seen that an increasing amount of the general practitioner's time is spent in the care of the aged.

The clinical problems posed by age-linked diseases are the everyday problems in the medical practice of the family physician and will become more so as the old age population increases. An important contribution that can be made now to the medical care of the aged is to inculcate in the medical student, general practitioner, and specialist the idea that it is socially

TABLE 12*

RATES OF NEW AND RECURRENT ILLNESSES TO-GETHER WITH INCAPACITY AND MEDICAL CONSULTATION RATES ARISING FROM ALL SICKNESS, NEW AND CONTINUED, PER 100 PERSONS INTERVIEWED

	1947	1948	1949	1950	1951
New and recurrent illnesses:					
21–64 years.....	44	40	44	44	57
65 and over.....	39	39	44	42	55
Incapacity:					
21–64 years.....	161	97	112	115	233
65 and over.....	255	224	217	212	371
Medical consulta-tion:					
21–64 years.....	49	39	48	43	60
65 and over.....	73	64	72	68	88

* After "Survey of Prevalence of Sickness, March Quarter, 1951," *Monthly Bulletin of the Ministry of Health and the Public Health Laboratory Service*, **10** (October, 1951), 240.

TABLE 13*

PERCENTAGE DISTRIBUTION OF ILLNESSES BY CATEGORY OF SEVERITY (SEXES COMBINED) JULY–JUNE, 1947–48 AND 1948–49

	Se-rious	Mod-erate or Mild	Minor	Ill De-fined	Total
Aged 16–64 years:					
1947–48.....	2.2	5.4	70.8	21.6	100
1948–49.....	2.3	6.0	65.1	26.6	100
Aged 65 and over:					
1947–48.....	12.1	4.5	67.6	15.8	100
1948–49.....	11.4	5.2	63.3	20.1	100

* After W. P. D. Logan, "Illness, Incapacity and Medical Attention among Adults, 1947–49," *Lancet*, April 22, 1950, p. 773.

and economically fruitful to treat diseases in the old. The factor of age alone ought not to weight a decision against active treatment for the old person. The idea that age makes disease incurable is not tenable. It is possible to arrest, modify, or even reverse apparently irreversible changes, and every tissue should be allowed the chance of becoming restored to as near to normal a functional state as possible. Early diagnosis, active treatment, and rehabilitation may not achieve a medical cure, but they can prevent chronic invalidism and loss of personal and economic independence and reduce the demands on community resources.

TABLE 14*

CONSULTATIONS BY AGE GROUPS

Age Groups Male and Female	Total Con-sultations in One Year	Patients in Each Group	Average Consulta-tions per Patient per Annum
Up to 14 years.	24,011	6,712	3.58
15–64 years...	66,328	17,957	3.69
65 years and over........	14,400	2,696	5.34

* After R. C. Walsh, "Medical Care of Old People at Home," in *Old Age in the Modern World* (Edinburgh: E. & S. Livingstone, 1955), p. 80.

F. Assessment of Type of Medical Care Required by the Aged

It is now generally agreed that hospitalization of the older individual often leads to his physical and mental deterioration. The discovery that a great many hospitalized old people suffer from hospitalization rather than illness has introduced a new concept about the kind of service required for the care of the old, and today the cardinal principle in the care of the aged is that, in sickness or in health, old people are better off in their own homes. Medical and social services should, therefore, be designed to enable the aging individual to remain at home as long as possible. Elderly people are easily disoriented in strange surroundings, and it is impossible to give them the individual and personal attention possible at home, so that, in addition to the illness for which they were admitted to the hospital, complications develop in the wards. Rowntree (1947) estimates that, in England, only 5 per cent of old people need communal care because of increasing feebleness or actual ill-health; the other 95 per cent can live on their own or with relatives. Moreover, 70–80 per cent of the disabled can be cared for at home if adequate medical, para-medical, and social help is available. Erlandsson (1956) lists the following conditions as doing better at home with

been allocated in the National Health Service (1957) hospitals as giving reasonable hospital service with no undue strain for the treatment of chronic sick patients other than the mentally ill and mentally defective. For England and Wales in 1951, the ratio of chronic beds per 1000 general population was 1.35. To achieve this ratio, 12 per cent of hospital beds were reserved for the chronically ill. Amulree stresses especially the proper utilization of the hospital bed—"the right patient in the right bed"—as a means of increasing availability of hospital accommodation to the sick pop-

TABLE 15*

CONSULTATIONS BY PLACE IN EIGHT PRACTICES, APRIL, 1951—MARCH, 1952
(Rate per 100 Practice Population)

Age Group	All Eight Practices		Surgery				Home Visits				Other Consultations			
			Male		Female		Male		Female		Male		Female	
	Male	Female	No.	Rate	No.	Rate	No.	Rate	No.	Rate	No.	Rate	No.	Rate
0–14.......	3,135	3,138	7,123	211.9	7,223	215.6	4,136	123.0	4,287	128.0	603	17.9	639	19.1
15–44.......	4,787	6,456	11,256	219.3	20,200	293.2	1,866	36.4	5,341	77.5	619	12.1	1,050	15.2
45–64	2,352	3,187	7,375	292.0	11,154	328.1	2,100	83.1	3,785	111.3	608	24.1	974	28.6
65 and over.	1,031	1,488	3,085	277.7	3,799	238.0	1,714	154.3	4,660	292.0	315	28.4	827	51.8
Not stated..	824	967	......	.....	......	.....	.....	.....	.....	.....	.....	.....	.....	.....
All ages ..	12,129	15,236	28,839	237.7	42,376	278.1	9,816	80.9	18,073	118.6	2,145	17.7	3,490	22.9

* After W. P. D. Logan, *Studies on Medical and Population Subjects* ("General Practitioners Records," No. 7 [London: H.M. Stationery Office, 1953]), based on material taken from p. 119.

domestic help than in the hospital: sequelae of cerebral lesions without progressive paralysis, invalidity following fracture of the neck of the femur and amputations, psychic changes, blindness, and bed cases where nothing can be gained from further vigorous treatment or hospitalization.

NEED FOR HOSPITAL BEDS AS REVEALED BY SURVEYS

Lord Amulree (1953), of St. Pancras Hospital in London, estimates the need for beds of the geriatric service of a general hospital to be 0.5–0.75 per 1000 population. In England and Wales as a whole just over 1.2 beds per 1000 population have

ulation where hospitalization is really needed for active treatment.

At the Seventh International Hospital Congress, Tunbridge (1951) stated that the Nuffield survey in England revealed a need for 2.5 beds per 1000 population for the chronically ill and that more than 60 per cent of the beds in hospitals for the chronic sick were occupied by patients over 65 years of age.

The reports on accommodation needed for the care of the aged chronic sick do not always distinguish between the need for facilities for active treatment in hospital or nursing care in nursing or "old age" homes, and it is, therefore, difficult to compare needs. If the trend toward establishing special geriatric units in general hospitals extends in more countries, the need for each kind of accommodation will be more sharply defined. In Switzerland it is estimated that 4–5 per cent of persons 60 years and over need care in a home and that there is a need for 2.0 beds per 1000 population for the chronically ill (Pfister, 1951). Roth (1955) reported 25,000 persons over 65 years living in private and public homes for old people in Switzerland, where there are 7000 beds for old people in need of nursing care in homes for the chronic sick. Although there are no purely geriatric hospitals in Switzerland, eighteen hospitals have special units for the care of the aged and chronic sick. In Sweden in the acute hospitals of the Stockholm area on May 12, 1953, 31.1 per cent of 1101 patients were 60 years and over, reflecting roughly a proportion of six to seven old persons per 1000 population getting hospital care (Berg, 1954). The Swedish Hospital Committee in 1943 (Erlandsson, 1956) found 3–4 per cent of Sweden's old age population to be suffering from chronic illness and recommended expansion of facilities for chronic illness to cover 3 per cent of the aged population, or accommodations for 20,000 persons. The Riksdag in 1947 adopted a declaration of principle governing the design and maintenance of communal homes which were to be developed as real homes for normally aging persons and invalids (Swedish Social Welfare Board, 1952). Sick old people requiring special care were to be admitted to hospitals or nursing homes dealing with chronic physical or mental disease.

Studies of hospital admissions in France show that, on the general medical services of one hospital, 28.4 per cent of the patients over a 4-year period were over 65 years of age (Delore and Arnaud, 1956). In 1954–55, 35 per cent of hospital admissions to the Hôtel Dieu in Paris were more than 60 years of age and occupied 51.3 per cent of the hospital beds; 18 per cent of the admissions were more than 70 years

of age and occupied 31.8 per cent of the hospital beds. The number of beds occupied increased with advancing age (Magdelaine and Pequignot, 1957). Huet (1957), discussing the excessive occupancy of hospital beds by the aged, attributes the misuse of the facilities of the hospitals of the public assistance to the lack of appropriate community services which forces the old who are not in need of medical care in hospitals nevertheless to seek admission to them. He estimates that for old people depending on public assistance 7500 beds are necessary—5000 for the disabled and 2500 for the fit. At present there are only 3500 beds in homes for the aged, forcing old people who cannot be accommodated in homes to seek hospital admission. In view of these figures, Delore's (1956b) estimate that 20 per cent of hospital beds in France should be reserved for old people does not seem adequate under the existing organization of facilities for the aged.

There are at present in Brussels 770 beds available in the geriatric center for old people. It is estimated that the present need is 1000 beds, and, to meet population increase of old people in the future, 1500 beds will be needed (Clerens, 1956).

There has been an increase in the proportion of persons 65 years and over in the population of the Netherlands from 6 per cent in 1900 to 8.5 per cent in 1957, and it is estimated that by 1980 it will be 11.1 per cent. A recent survey on the number, diagnosis, and length of stay in twenty-one hospitals of patients 65 years and older in the years 1924, 1939, and 1954 shows an increase in the percentage of old people in the total hospital population during these years. In 1924 the percentage of people over 65 years of age in the hospitals was 7; in 1939 the percentage was 10; by 1954 it had increased to 16. The percentage increase of those 65 years and over in the hospital population was greater than the percentage increase for the same age group in the total population—the percentage of persons 65 years and over in the hospital population was 16 per cent in

1954, while the percentage in the Netherlands was 8.2 per cent. However, there is no great difference in the percentage by 5-year age groups when the distribution of aged patients in the hospitals is compared to the distribution of the total aged population of the country by the same age groups. This would seem to indicate that becoming older does not necessarily mean a greater likelihood of being admitted to the hospital (Bronts and van Zonneveld, 1957). The Groningen survey (van Zonneveld, 1954) had concluded that, considering no other circumstance but the physical and mental state of the old person, the needs per 1000 population older than 64 years are 4.3 beds in general hospitals, 34 beds in nursing homes for the chronically ill, and 153 beds in old age homes for the frail who do not need special nursing care. In addition, more beds are needed for rehabilitation. Home help is needed for 3.7 per cent of the old people. The survey found that 43 per cent of the old people were able to live independently. These figures do not differ from those calculated for the whole aged population of the Netherlands. More recently, van Zonneveld (1957) reported that 3.7 per cent of the old people of Groningen need immediate admission to old age homes and that 2 per cent need to be admitted to a nursing home.

The facts brought out by these figures illustrate the disproportionate use of hospital facilities that might occur when more suitable services and accommodations are lacking and indicate the estimated need for hospital and nursing care for the aged in several countries.

DURATION OF HOSPITAL STAY

Lord Amulree (1953) states that from one-fourth to one-third of the admissions to geriatric units will die in the first month; for the others the average length of hospital stay will be about the same as for the younger age groups. At St. Pancras the length of hospital stay on the Geriatric Service was 42 days, as against 35 days for patients on the medical, chest, and skin services. Of 894 patients admitted to the Geriatric Unit, only 77 remained longer than 6 months. The average duration of hospital stay at the Hôtel Dieu, Paris (Magdelaine and Pequignot, 1957), among all patients 70 years and over was 54.93 days, as against 19.23 days among all patients 50 years and less. The mean duration of stay on the Geriatric Service of the Hospital in Sabbatsberg, Sweden, was 1 year and 2 months, which Erlandsson (1956) considers too long for effective utilization of hospital beds. On the Geriatric Unit of the Ulleval Hospital in Oslo, Norway (Gaustad, 1956), only 5 per cent of 739 cases admitted in 1953 were still there at the end of April, 1954. In the twenty-one hospitals investigated in the Netherlands the median length of hospital stay of patients 65 years and over was 43 days in 1954, about two to three times longer than the mean length of stay of patients under 65 years of age.

The need for hospital beds and the duration of hospital stay will be reduced by the development of geriatric units for active diagnosis and treatment in connection with the general hospitals and by the creation of ancillary services and facilities outside the hospital for the care of the disabled, infirm, and chronic sick.

II. PROGRAMS FOR PROVIDING MEDICAL CARE FOR OLD PEOPLE

A. Medical Care for the Aged in Britain

This section attempts to give an idea of what several European countries are doing to provide medical care for their old age population. Health programs for the care of old people stress preventive measures and rehabilitation to prevent illness, infirmity, and disability and to keep the old at home where they do better living independent lives for as long as possible. Planning along these lines is socially and economically sound. The most extensively organized program for health and medical care in western Europe at the present time is in Britain and has been developed as part of the provision of the National Health Service (1957). Different areas in Britain have pioneered in services to the aged. For example, a laundry service was first started in Bristol in 1951 with money from the National Corporation for the Care of Old People (Walsh, 1955). In Oxford a day hospital was created to care for burdensome cases and by providing relief to exhausted families prevented a breaking-up of the family (Townsend, 1955). Buckinghamshire, in the Oxford Regional Hospital Board area, pioneered in the use of a consultant in geriatrics to serve both hospital and local authority. This resulted in the better use of existing beds and, therefore, of hospital facilities.

A survey of services available to the chronic sick and elderly in 1954–55 studied hospital and specialist services provided for old people and the chronic sick (other than the mentally ill or defective) and their relation to the services provided by local authorities in both their health and their welfare capacities (Boucher, 1957). The National Health Service provides for hospital service, preventive health service through the local health authority, and general practitioner service which enables everyone to have a family doctor. The National Assistance Act of 1948 extended the local health authority service to provide care to the sick at home.

Responsibility for the care of the chronic sick and old is, therefore, shared by hospital, local authority, and general practitioner, and their first aim is to provide adequate care and treatment of old people in their homes for as long as possible. Domiciliary services cost less than residential care or hospital care and in the long run are more economical. However, to be completely effective, home care requires full development and integration of preventive, domiciliary, and outpatient services, even when they are administratively and financially independent.

The best practices revealed by the survey were brought to the attention of those responsible for the development of services to the aged in Britain for general implementation and are summarized here.

1. *Home care* is provided by general practitioners with the co-operation of the local health authority. It takes care of all sick who do not need, or cannot benefit by, hospitalization.

2. *Hospital care* is available for the acute sick and for the chronic sick in need of active treatment. Although medical care is furnished by the hospital staff, total medical care requires the co-operation of the general practitioner and local health authority personnel. In Britain the trend has been to organize geriatric services attached to general hospitals as an integral part of the hospital. The diagnostic and consultation services of the hospital are available to geriatric patients, and all other supportive facilities are created to insure continuity of care of the elderly patient at home, in hospital, and after hospital discharge. Ideally, there should be no more than 100–150 beds in a geriatric unit (Delore, 1955; Warren, 1956a). Smaller centers located nearer the homes of the old people are being developed in relation to these larger centers to make it easier for the elderly hospital patient to retain contact with family and home. The Geriatric Service is not used as a service for incurables, but temporary admissions or regular readmissions of suitable patients are permitted where hospital accommodation exists. Temporary hospitalization of these burdensome cases relieves the strain on families and offers an opportunity for a medical checkup of the chronic patient. The standard for hospital beds, excluding the mentally ill and defective—1.2 per 1000 population—will vary depending on local factors, but, in areas where age distribution of population is normal and where effective ancillary services exist, it will provide a reasonable hospital service.

It is not the responsibility of the hospital authority to give all the medical or nursing care needed by an old person, however minor the illness or however short the stay in bed, nor does the hospital have to admit all those who need nursing care because they are entering upon the last stages of their lives.

Patients with acute illnesses or exacerbations of chronic conditions are admitted to the hospitals as emergencies. Other patients upon application for admission by the general practitioner are placed on a waiting list. The physician in charge of the Geriatric Service, alone or with the social worker from the hospital or local authority, and with the agreement of the general practitioner, who may wish to be present, visits the patient at home to determine the medical and social needs and to assign priority for admission to the hospital. The general practitioner is always kept fully informed of the findings and status of his patient. Alternatively, patients may be seen in the Geriatric Outpatient Department by the Geriatric Service physician. When the latter cannot visit the patient at home, the social worker makes a home visit to assess the social conditions before placing the patient on the waiting list, and there is a standing arrangement for regular review of the waiting list.

Either health visitor, social worker, or other officer of the local health authority makes periodic visits to those on the waiting list to reassess need for admission. The health visitor, who may be attached part time to the Geriatric Service of the hospital, maintains liaison between the Geriatric Service and general practitioner and sees that the patients on the waiting list get all the home help possible while awaiting hospital treatment. The functions of the health visitor, who is a trained nurse and midwife with sociological experience, were widely extended by the National Health Service Act, and she plays an important role in the health program for the aged.

After discharge from hospital, continuity of care is insured by notifying the general practitioner and, if the patient consents, the medical officer of health. The hospital and local authority service co-operate in providing continuing care following hospitalization. The local authorities, in their health capacity, provide home nursing, domestic help, health visitors, and other domiciliary services; in their welfare capacity they provide residential accommodation and certain domiciliary services that come under the National Assistance Act.

Other facilities that extend hospital care outside hospital premises and permit a greater use of hospital beds are:

3. *Convalescent homes,* or "halfway houses," have been useful in freeing expensive hospital accommodation and in continuing hospital care, preferably carried on by the same personnel, for the final stages of clinical rehabilitation and social readjustment. These homes or annexes for short stay are used for patients who have finished active treatment but for various reasons cannot return home immediately and are never used for direct admission of a new patient.

4. *Long-stay accommodation* for patients who cannot benefit from active treatment but who need a higher standard of nursing than they can get at home or in a local authority provision has also proved useful. Patients are first admitted to the Acute Geriatric Service for assessment before going to long-stay centers. These homes are integral parts of the Geriatric Service, sharing its personnel, and patients remain under the supervision of the physician of the main geriatric center. They admit patients confined to bed and unable to return home, patients who show mental symptoms that make it impossible for them to be with others in common rooms, and patients who can get only to a wheel chair and who cannot go to a welfare home.

5. *Day hospitals* have been useful in relieving hospital and home in the care of the chronic sick. Patients may be discharged from hospitals earlier than usual to continue treatment there, or treatment can be started in day hospitals while awaiting admission to hospital. Physiotherapy and occupational therapy are available, and rehabilitation for hemiplegics can be continued, individually or in groups. The social

contacts provided by the day hospital relieve the monotony and isolation of the lives of lonely, elderly chronics and improve their mental attitude. These hospitals have been found feasible for patients with some mental impairment, although this requires liaison with the mental hospital and co-operation with an ambulance service. By sharing in the care of a difficult sick aged member, they have rendered an important service to families.

6. *Residential care* is provided by the Welfare Authority. Residential care is provided for (1) active elderly people in need of such care; (2) the otherwise active resident during minor illnesses which may involve a short period in bed; (3) the infirm, including senile, who may need help in dressing, toilet, etc., or who may need to live on the ground floor because of inability to manage stairs, or who may spend part of the day (or longer periods during bad weather) in bed; and (4) the elderly who have to take to bed and are not expected to live more than a few weeks and who cannot benefit from treatment or nursing care beyond what can be given at home, and whose removal to a hospital, away from familiar surroundings and attendants, would be felt to be inhuman.

The small welfare homes accommodating twenty to forty residents are for those aged who can take care of the personal necessities of living and are under the direction of a warden or matron. Care is given by attendants, assisted or advised by the visiting nurse. In larger homes there is a superintendent and/or matron in charge, and care is given by a small staff with nursing qualifications or experience. They admit the more physically or mentally infirm and disabled who need greater care and supervision. Hygiene of the homes is supervised by the medical staff or medical officer of health. Residents are free to nominate their own doctor, and, in addition, a local practitioner may make one or more routine visits a week.

The welfare authority does not have to provide prolonged nursing care to the bedfast, except for those in the last stages of their lives. It is felt that the concentration of disabled and bedfast patients in "infirmary wards" attached to larger homes is inadvisable.

Old people fluctuate between infirmity and sickness, and arrangements should facilitate their temporary or permanent admission from welfare homes to hospital when health deteriorates or, conversely, the transfer from hospital to welfare homes when health improves and there are no relatives or friends to go to. The situation where a hospital patient is medically fit but cannot be transferred to a welfare home because of an apparent lack of accommodation, while at the same time residents in suitable welfare homes are waiting admission to hospital can be avoided by the appointment of a consultant geriatric physician working with the regional hospital board and the local authority and having responsibility for, as well as access to, all accommodations. Such an arrangement has proved successful in Buckinghamshire and the Oxford Regional Hospital Board area.

7. *Home medical service* has been of great value in helping to keep sick old people out of institutions and hospitals. The doctor is the team leader in this multidisciplinary approach in caring for the old at home, but, to be effective, it requires the co-operation of the statutory and voluntary organizations, doctors, nurses, social workers, and other paramedical staff.

A wide range of organizations and interested individuals, even in war years, co-operated in the development of the highly successful schemes for home medical service to be found in Britain today. The National Old People's Welfare Committee was formed in 1940 to study the needs of old people, to encourage and promote measures for their well-being, and to co-ordinate the services provided them. The committee is independent of statutory authorities, although it receives recognition and support from them, and plays an important role in the care of the aged.

Domiciliary service requires the co-operation of a cohort of social workers, ministers, relatives, and friends to assure an efficient, integrated scheme that will assist old people in remaining in their homes with comfort to themselves and without undue strain on their families.

Loneliness is a generally recognized factor in senile decay. A "visiting service" developed under the Welfare Department has done a great deal to help old people living alone. It is one of the main services rendered by local voluntary committees and brings to the old the community services available to them. Next to being visited, the three most common needs of old people are help with meals, laundry, and chiropody. Civic restaurants offer cheap, hot, balanced meals to pensioners in arrangement with owning authority, welfare authority, and voluntary organization. "Meals-on-wheels" for the housebound are organized by the Women's Voluntary Society, British Red Cross Society, or Salvation Army, and a hot meal is brought to the housebound at midday once, twice, or six times weekly. Laundry is often the last straw that forces families to seek institutional care for their aged, especially incontinents. Laundry help is provided through voluntary organizations, sometimes collaborating with municipal authorities. In some boroughs of London linen is collected in containers three times weekly and returned quickly. Linen and night clothes kept by the district nurse are available through a lending service. Automatic washing machines with special facilities for drying and ironing are set up in accessible places so that old people or their families can, for a small charge, do their own laundry. Chiropody is not yet included in the services provided by the National Health Service but is of great value in keeping old people ambulant and independent. Voluntary effort with the co-operation of the local chiropodists, and some help from the local authority, has in some areas provided cheap, or free, service to pensioners. Service is also given through clinics, and, for

those who cannot get out, a home service is available (Evans, 1955; Walsh, 1955).

Holidays at seaside for those who would benefit from them are arranged by the Old People's Welfare Committee. Some five thousand social clubs in the country—and more are envisioned—have also been developed by the Old People's Welfare Committee with the co-operation of doctors as a means of providing many services that help to keep the old out of hospitals.

More and more of the general practitioner's time is being spent in the care of aged patients. The average number of consultations per patient per annum for the 65-and-over age group is greater than for any other age group, and, as the population ages, the number of older patients in the general practitioner's practice will increase. Logan (1953) reports the study of consultations by age groups in eight representative practices in England and finds that in the 65-and-over group the average number of consultations per patient per annum is 5.34 as compared to 3.69 for the 15–64-year group and 3.58 for the group under 15 years (Table 14). The Ministry of Health's (1951–52) surveys on the prevalence of sickness also reveal a greater number of consultations among persons 65 years and over than in younger age groups (Table 12). Old people should be provided with a family doctor who can see them at home, and a geriatric physician should be available for consultation at the patient's home or at the clinic to assess the need for admission to the Geriatric Service of the general hospital or other accommodation.

Nursing help of various kinds, such as simple dressings, bed care, and injections, can be provided at home, and a state-registered or state-enrolled nurse or male or female practical nurse may be employed to give this service. Health visitors (who in Britain are public health nurses and act as counselors and health educators but are not responsible for practical nursing service) see that the old get the services they need (Lamont, 1953). Night attendants have proved helpful in giving night care and affording relief to families from the burden of steady care.

Some of the medical aids that help the old person at home to preserve his independence are eyeglasses, dentures, hearing aids, trusses and surgical appliances, multi-leg walking sticks for the disabled, eating utensils with built-up handles, combination knife and fork to permit hemiplegics to eat unassisted, elastic shoelaces and long shoehorn to aid arthritics, and long-handled combs (Warren, 1955).

Mechanical aids and safety devices can be provided to help the old person in independent living and to protect him in his environment (Walsh, 1955). Rails along staircases or ramps over staircases, handles by stairs and lavatory, adaptations of kitchen equipment, shelves, etc., to overcome disabilities from arthritis, hemiplegia, and other defects, and loan of bedpans, commodes, crutches, wheel chairs, and special beds (from local authority or British Red Cross Society) support the old person and allow him to manage for himself. All safety appliances and measures, such as non-skid mats and polish, fire guards, and adequate lighting of dark corners, should be employed to protect the aged from injury.

Transport facilities and ambulance service must be available to enable the old person to utilize the medical and social resources of the community and to benefit from home medical care.

8. *Outpatient services* for the ambulatory and non-resident sick make it possible for the elderly to remain home and also benefit from medical care. Besides functioning as a consultation service for general practitioners, the outpatient department classifies the sick and finds those cases needing social welfare services, hospital admission, or medical care and serves as a center for chiropody, physiotherapy, and other auxiliary services. It treats cases amenable to therapy on an outpatient basis and follows patients who after discharge from hospital still require treatment at home or in welfare homes. By continuing care after hospital discharge, disability can be prevented and hospital readmission avoided. It also offers a means of early therapy which may arrest deterioration and eliminate need for hospital admission. Attendance at geriatric clinics in Great Britain increased from 6988 in 1950 to 18,401 in 1955 (Great Britain, National Health Service, 1957). The outpatient department can be used for patients awaiting admission to hospital, the general practitioner still continuing surveillance of his patient. An efficient appointment system to reduce waiting time and the co-operation of the local authority in running an ambulance service are requisites for an effective outpatient service.

Physiotherapy and occupational therapy services can be provided through clubs, day hospitals, and outpatient departments and permit the discharge of patients from hospitals earlier than would otherwise be possible. Treatment, especially rehabilitation of hemiplegics on an individual or group basis, can be continued in these centers. Physiotherapy and occupational therapy are important measures in relieving pain, in preventing or delaying deterioration, and in helping to maintain or restore independence of the old person in his home or in an institution.

B. Medical Care in Sweden

Basically the same trends in the development of medical care for the aged are seen in Sweden as in England. The number of people older than 65 years in 1950 was about 720,000, or 10.2 per cent of the whole population; in 1955 the numbers had increased to 800,000, or 11 per cent of the entire population. It is estimated that the number of aged increases by 15,000 every year and that in 1970 the number of persons 65 years or older will be 1,020,000, or 13 per cent of the entire population. In spite of this increase in the so-called non-productive, dependent maturates of the population, the level of life has improved in Sweden. Not only have better food, better housing, and better medical care made it possible for the aged to look after themselves but the tradition of family and neighborly help, respect for personal liberty, and sense of community responsibility for the individual have always helped the majority of old people to spend their old age in their own homes. Here the care of the aged is the responsibility of the municipal authority, and the community tries primarily to make it possible for the aged to manage for themselves in their own surroundings so that the majority of the aged do live outside institutions. A pension system whereby everyone from the age of 67, regardless of economic class, receives a pension makes it possible for old people to get along without other pecuniary assistance. However, where need can be shown, the local authorities, subsidized by the state, may grant a further amount for rent.

The increasing number of aged creates an ever increasing demand upon the resources of social health care. It is estimated that about 20 per cent of the aged older than 65 years need permanent care of some sort (Engel, personal communication). Hospitals and nursing homes are used where permanent care or treatment are needed. Municipal homes for the aged are meant only for those who, though not actually sick, cannot manage for themselves alone or even with occasional domestic help. About 4.5 per cent of the aged over 70 years are cared for in homes for the aged. The Riksdag in 1947 removed the homes for the aged from the Public Assistance Authority and designated them to be used as real homes for normally aging persons and invalids in need of permanent care. Sick old persons and others requiring special care were to be admitted to hospitals or nursing homes for chronic illnesses or mental disease. However, lack of facilities for the care of the chronic and mentally ill has made it necessary for the homes for the aged to continue to shelter some of these cases.

Homes for the aged now come under the Social Aid Act and are the responsibility of the Royal Social Board. Subventions from the state to the municipalities has furthered a program of new building and modernization of old institutions. The homes for the aged are open institutions where the aged may live if he wants and needs to do so. They are attractive abodes where the old person may have his own furniture and personal belongings if he wishes and for which he pays a fee, predetermined by the municipalities. In 1954 there were about 1350 homes for the aged, with 37,000 beds. Although building and modernization of old buildings are creating additional beds, the relative number of beds is decreasing, owing to the increase in the number of old people. In 1950, excluding homes for the chronic and mentally sick, there were 75 beds per 1000 persons over 70 years of age as against 99 beds per 1000 persons over 70 years in 1938. However, as other means of treatment are enlarged to meet the specific medical needs of the old, the prevailing number of beds in these homes seems sufficient.

In Sweden special home help for old people was first started in 1950 with the pioneering work of the Red Cross at Upsala and has rendered a valuable service in making it possible for many old people to remain in their own homes (Nordström, 1956). Home help service now covers the whole country, although it is further advanced in some parts such as Stockholm, Göteborg, and Malmö. The need for additional beds in homes for the aged has been lessened by this service. It has moreover provided the kind of care that old people prefer in a manner that serves their interest best at a lower cost to the community. The home-help services are organized and financed by different agencies—for the old by the local authority or the Red Cross; for invalids or chronic sick (including usually a number of aged) by the provincial council responsible for medical care; for families by the local authorities. Home-help services are available to all people regardless of economic status, but, where the individual or family is able to pay for the service he does so, not directly to the helper but to the agency responsible for running the service.

Home helpers are housewives or mature women with free time to give to this service. They clean, wash up, buy and prepare food, or help with dressing, personal hygiene, walks. They get some general instruction from the agency organizer or district nurse but receive no special training. Those who work among the sick aged are given a short course of 50–100 hours in sick care through the Red Cross. On the other hand, training of matrons for the homes for the aged is organized by the Swedish Social Care Association at state expense for about 3 years, the greater part of the time being spent in institutions.

In 1952 the minister of social affairs appointed a committee to survey the problem of health care for the aged. The committee's report was published in 1956 (Sweden, 1956), and the Riksdag of 1957 passed a bill which in principle adopted the conclusions reached—namely, to support and strengthen measures in the field of old age pension, housing, and domestic help to allow the old to live independently; to increase the number of institutions for old people with chronic illnesses and to reserve the homes for aged for those who are not actually sick but who are in need of constant care; and to intensify research in aging.

The Swedish Parliament passed a law in 1951 which established in principle the right of every citizen to receive free medical care under a national insurance plan, but economic developments within the country have not permitted its full realization.

Medical care service for the old is at the debut of organization in Sweden, and the formula best suited to its needs is still a matter of discussion. At the present time medical care is the chief responsibility of the provincial councils or governments, although the top authority and supervision over the care of the sick belong to the State or Royal Medical Board. However, the state has actually taken over only a small part of the care of the physically ill, practically limited to the university teaching hospitals. The state does furnish the greater part of the care of the mentally ill. Hospitals are the responsibility of provincial councils and provide hospital care for old people. The Royal Medical Board is responsible for the care of the mentally ill old person. The Royal Social Board is responsible for homes for the aged and medical care of old people. Since the Royal Social Board has no full-time doctors on its staff, difficulty and delay sometimes arise in distributing the medical cases falling under its jurisdiction. The old person, presenting symptoms of various chronic illnesses and disabilities, often suffers from the delays that occur before a proper classification and placement is made. There is not as yet organized home medical care in Sweden, although a visiting nurse service is available.

In the summer of 1950 Erlandsson (1956) started a geriatric service in the hospital at Sabbatsberg, Stockholm, where a home for the aged has existed since 1752 (Hilleboe, 1955). Projects to establish geriatric medical services in connection with hospitals, ambulatory medical care, and centers for preventive treatment and to increase and make more effective home help are under way.

Although there is a difference of opinion as to who should sponsor geriatric units and, consequently, as to whether they should be attached to hospitals under the county or provincial council or to homes for the aged under the municipal authority, there is general agreement on the urgent need to expand the number of beds in suitable hospital facilities for sick old people (Kindstrand, 1947; Birch-Lindgren, 1956). Erlandsson estimates the need for 20,000 beds, covering 3 per cent of the aged population, to take care of the chronically ill and to be divided (although allocation is difficult) between the geriatric service and infirmaries or rest homes for sick old people.

In Sweden serious thought and careful planning are going into creating a scheme of old age maintenance, adapting the results of gerontological research and the experience of others, to meet the problem now and in the future. Erlandsson distinguishes three groups of old people who require different kinds of care. The first comprises aged persons in good health or persons who are infirm and best cared for in their own homes or in homes for the aged. In the second group belong aged persons who are acutely ill and who should be given medical care at home or in the hospital. The third is a group composed of aged persons with chronic illnesses or persons who are continuously ill and cannot be cared for at home and for whom long-term care in a geriatric unit attached to a general hospital will be necessary. Whether the geriatric unit is part of a large hospital or a small unit close to the patients' homes, it should be equipped with all the facilities for diagnosis, treatment, and rehabilitation and should have easy access to the various specialty consultations and services that might be required. In addition, the geriatric unit should offer an opportunity for education of the medical and nursing personnel in the care of the aged and should encourage and carry out research in the problems of geriatry.

Pedicure, hearing tests, and the provision of free hearing aids, the loan of wheel chairs and other hospital equipment to the patient at home through the Red Cross, and laundry service have helped the elderly to remain at home. A "meal-on-wheels" service organized by the Red Cross, restaurants, or homes for the aged delivers daily in some communities to old people living at home.

C. Medical Care in France

In France the problem of the care of the aged is serious, since this country has, along with Belgium, the highest proportion of old people in its population in western Europe. The proportion of persons over 65 years in France in 1900 was 8.4 per cent, in 1950 it was 11.4 per cent, and it is predicted that by 1980 the proportion of persons over 60 years in the population will be 18.5 per cent (Daric, 1948, 1956). The greatest cost in care of the aged is the cost of caring for the sick and disabled. At present, the care of the aged is still primarily the responsibility of families. Few specialized services have been developed in the community. Although there are homes for the aged, they have not enough accommodations, and they do not give the aged infirm and chronic sick the medical care they need. An inquiry into the status of old people in the north of France revealed an over-all insufficiency in all types of services for the aged, including housing and hospitalization (Gosset, 1953; Covalt, 1956). Public hospitals furnish medical services on an outpatient basis, and some have day centers where old people can enjoy warm food and companionship. Voluntary agencies, frequently under religious auspices, provide some services to old people, and on National Old People's Day funds which go to pay for housekeeping help, nursing, meals, and other services are collected by voluntary society agencies. Old age assistance benefits are low, and as yet there are few special housing facilities for the aged. Following the war, unstable economic conditions and inflation, low wages, the increasing number of women working outside the home who could no longer care for an aged parent, and the weakening of filial ties have all contributed to the plight of the old person in France.

Programs for the aged must be geared to the economy of the country. One of the plans for the medical care of the aged presented by Huet to the General Assembly of the Advisers of Health at Dijon in 1955 recommends the organization of health care at local levels and suggests establishing in each commune a municipal bureau of social welfare (Wibaux and Huet, 1956). These bureaus of social welfare would maintain contact with the old in their homes and with geriatric services attached to general hospitals and could assign cases to hospitals for medical care. The geriatric hospitals would have attached to them convalescent homes, or "halfway houses," where patients could be sent before returning home, and which could be used as a base for sending patients to summer vacation homes or to give temporary lodging during cold weather. They are envisioned also as having a rehabilitation center to train patients socially and professionally, so that they can return to live in their homes and perhaps even to do some work later on. Study and evaluation of patients for eventual retraining for possible work later on should be done in the geriatric hospital with the aid of an inspector of work and a social assistant. The plan also provides special accommodation to which the geriatric hospitals can send patients after discharge—such as homes for the retired old, homes for the chronically ill, disabled, and bedridden, and homes for senile dements, as well as follow-up facilities for continuing medical supervision. These facilities would enable the geriatric hospital to make the optimum use of its beds for the active treatment of the sick old person.

The scheme stresses particularly the organization of home care. Domestic help, ancillary services, and outpatient services should be developed to keep the old out of hospitals and homes for the aged. Providing a midday meal in a restaurant and at home in the evenings and creating clubs and recreational facilities, especially in towns where life is more complex and the old person may be more isolated from neighborly contacts, are measures that will allow the aged to carry on in his own home.

In this plan the geriatric unit is the principal peg in the system of aid to the aged. This unit of 120–50 beds is visualized as being attached to a regional hospital, under the control of the regional geriatry service, and having two medical and one surgical services along with complete up-to-date facilities for diagnosis, treatment, and research. It should be staffed by specially trained medical personnel and social

assistants and have a small school of nurses attached to it.

D. Medical Care in the Netherlands

The care of the aged in the Netherlands is regarded as the concern of society as a whole, and several studies of the aged population have already been mentioned. In 1949 a national committee for old people's care was formed by the Netherlands Association for Social Work and the Netherlands Association for Gerontology to study and correlate information on the problems and needs of old people.

Investigations of rural and urban communities have shown a need for old age homes and nursing homes for the aged. Some provision for the care of old people has existed for a long time in the Netherlands. Since the thirteenth century the church has maintained *hofjes,* or old age homes, some of which have been modernized and are still in use. In Zutphen, over a century ago, homes where the old were housed, fed, and clothed were established by rich merchants and landowners, and in Amsterdam one of these homes has been in existence since 1610. Many of these accommodations are small cottages in attractive settings, and nursing care is sometimes provided for the sick aged. In the latter part of the eighteenth century, homes for the old were built by the municipal authorities, and today a variety of establishments supported by church, municipal, or voluntary agencies cares for the aged, including invalids and the chronically ill. Some of the larger homes may have modest hospital facilities, and occasionally the smaller homes may have an infirmary. Separate facilities are provided for cases of senile dementia (Watkins, 1951).

There are no country-wide figures available on accommodations for old people or for the aged chronic sick. A survey of 812 non-private homes conducted in February, 1950, showed that 29,563 persons 65 years or older were housed in these homes. Of these old people, 8.3 per cent were permanently bedridden, 28.7 per cent were more or less invalided, and the remaining 63 per cent were still capable of looking after themselves. Private homes do not come under statutory regulations, and statistics on them can be obtained only where regulations exist. However, the tendency is to bring these homes under governmental control, and now in several large cities and in two provinces regulations do exist so that the government will be able to exercise some control and establish requirements which should be met by the nursing homes. In The Hague, in January, 1958, there were 125 nursing homes for a total of 3758 sick, disabled, and incapacitated persons 60 years of age and over. Five of these homes are administered by the local government and care for 995 persons, 32 are church institutions and care for 1652 persons, and 88 are privately run homes caring for 1111 persons. Of the total number of aged, 1282 (34.1 per cent) were permanently bedridden, 1770 (47.1 per cent) were partially bedridden, and 706 (18.8 per cent) were ambulatory. The treatment given in practically all these homes is confined to simple care and nursing. Although the sick funds of the national health insurance are gradually extending their coverage, they do not as yet provide for care in nursing homes (Mundendam, personal communication).

In 1953 the Federation of Nursing Homes for the Chronic Sick, which aims at a regular control of nursing homes and a state-controlled training of personnel, was founded. The federation receives a subsidy from the central government, and about 45 homes with a total of 2000 beds are members. A Roman Catholic organization of nursing homes has been established recently.

Since the middle 1920's housing developments have begun to make provisions for the aged, either in small units in large projects, which keep the old person near the family, or in dwellings designed particularly to meet the special needs of old people and where nursing care may be given to the sick in his room or in an infirmary. In the new architectural development of building a town within a town in a circular plan, a nursing home or hospital toward which the elderly gravitates as he comes to need more and more sick care is placed in the center of the community.

The national health insurance in the Netherlands started with sick funds to provide general practitioner's service and drugs and are gradually extending their provisions. All persons below a certain income level (6900 florins per year), or four-fifths of the population of the country, are covered by the sick fund and are registered with a general practitioner who gives the first medical care (van Zonneveld and Groen, 1957). Many agencies co-operate to care for the aged, and much social work is being done among old people. The social workers have no special training in the problems of the aged, but it is felt that some training is desirable and should be provided. The village nurse and private organizations give home nursing and help with shopping. The various Cross societies participate actively in providing home help, and in eight towns the Union of Women Volunteers has organized "meals-on-wheels" and "friendly visiting." In Zutphen, the Union of Women Volunteers and the Cross Society help old people with their personal hygiene, saving on the use of nursing time for this service. Much mutual aid is also given among the old to one another (Gijsbers, 1956).

At the present time there is no national plan for providing special medical care for the aged. All sick persons are looked after by general practitioners, and the elderly sick are accommodated in the available community hospital facilities. There are no geriatric departments or other special provisions for aged people, and the number of chronic-sick aged people in hospitals is comparatively small. Hornstra, investigating the need for nursing-home care on the Isle of Schouwen-Duiveland in 1953, estimated that 2 per cent of the people over 65 years of age needed care in nursing homes. Schreuder, in the agricultural region of southwestern Frisia, found 2.3–4.2 per cent of the old required accommodation in nursing homes. Among the 3000 old people in the Groningen survey, 3.7 per cent needed immediate admission to old age homes and 2 per cent to nursing homes. In Rotterdam an inquiry among 5800 old people revealed that 5.4 per cent needed nursing care and 22 per cent general maintenance (van Zonneveld, 1957). However, in general, although many old people need care in nursing homes, they are unwilling to leave their homes to enter communal homes, even when the latter are better for them sociomedically.

E. Medical Care in Belgium

Of all the countries of western Europe, Belgium has the highest proportion of old persons in her population, and on the basis of the census of 1947 it is estimated that in 1977 the proportion of persons 65 years of age and over will be at least 15 per cent.

It is recognized that the needs of the aged well, the infirm, and the chronically ill are different and that a different type of service will be required for each group. The community is not concerned with those in favorable material circumstances. Belgium has a tradition of sick care and homes for the aged based on charity, and public or private hospices have always sheltered the indigent. In 1925 a commission for public assistance was established in each commune to provide welfare assistance, medical service at home, drugs, and hospital care to the indigent, and under this program of assistance the aged received help at home in money or in kind and care or hospitalization in case of illness. Those needing special care because of the infirmities of age were placed in special institutions or hospices provided by the commission or by private and religious organizations.

The hospices did not make congenial homes for the aged, and the limitations and undesirability of this type of care were recognized. In 1949 a memorandum from the Ministry of Public Health and the Family called for the renovation and modernization of archaic institutions into pleasant, comfortable homes where old people would find a more cheerful and homelike atmosphere. A subsidy of 60 per cent was offered to encourage this work, and under this stimulus 38 homes were modernized, and 35 new homes were constructed.

In 1955 in Belgium there were 548 institutions with a total of 30,948 beds for the old, divided among 236 private institutions having 13,133 beds and 312 welfare homes with 17,815 beds. In addition, there were 83 religious communities with 972 homes, and other special groups, such as the sailors and displaced persons, also have their own homes for the aged.

The buildings of privately run homes are also being modernized to provide attractive, comfortable surroundings for the aged. Residents in homes are admitted at full or half-rate, or without charge, without any distinction in the accommodation accorded the individual, the Commission of Public Assistance being responsible for the amount the individual is unable to pay. Pensioners pay for their accommodation from their pensions but are allowed to retain a third for personal use, and pocket money is given to the indigent. A medical examination is done on admission, and provision is made for periodic medical examination of all residents.

A program of building of homes especially designed for the comfort and convenience of old people has been started. In the new buildings single rooms and apartments for married couples have been built in pavilions of 30–50 beds in pleasant surroundings. They are self-contained and equipped with amenities that will aid the aged to live independently in comfort and with facilities for recreation and with an infirmary to care for the sick. They are located near urban centers within easy access of transportation to facilitate visiting among residents and relatives and friends. An example of this type of housing for the aged has been constructed by the Intercommunale of Social Work in the region of Charleroi, near Brussels, and consists of 240 beds in pavilions of 50 beds each.

The ill aged will require more specific medical care, and the trend, supported by the Ministry of Public Health and the Family, is to establish centers of geriatry for the care of the acutely and chronically sick aged. These centers will provide medical and surgical care and will include such specialist services as eye, dental, chest, cardiac, X-ray, and neuropsychiatry and physiotherapy consultations and treatment. They will be equipped with laboratories for clinical research and a center for rehabilitation and will be in close contact with the medicosocial services which the aged will need. They are planned as centers for active diagnosis and treatment where a patient will spend a minimum of time in the hospital and will be promptly discharged as soon as the hospital is no longer his proper place. In this setup the rehabilitation center will play an important role in re-education to prevent disability and to upgrade existing incapacities so that the old person will be able to manage the essential needs of daily living for himself. Patients attending the rehabilitation center remain under regular medical supervision, and recreational activities and occupational therapy are integrated into the rehabilitation program.

At present there is a center of geriatrics at Charleroi with about 80 beds, and the Intercommunale of Social Work of the Region has a project for a hospital of 600 beds for the aged acute and chronic sick. At Duerne a special hospital for the chronic sick has recently been opened, and it is independent of the nursing home which is in this area. Projects are under way for the construction of other centers at Louvain, Tirlemont, and Antwerp.

The aged well and the aged infirm who can still manage to look after themselves fairly adequately will get along at home if provided with some conveniences and help. Special housing, home help, domiciliary care, and other social services have enabled many old people to live in their own homes. "Meals-on-wheels," help with laundry, and foot care have been started in some areas, and plans to extend these services to a larger number of old people have been made.

Public interest in the welfare of old people has been stimulated through programs of information and education by official and voluntary organizations, and funds are collected which help to support some of the services for the old during an annual Week for the Aged (Belgium, Commission de Co-ordination de l'Office d'Identification, 1957a, 1957b).

F. Medical Care in Italy

Italy also faces the problem of an increasingly larger aging population. In the nineteenth century, migration drained her of her younger adults, and even today the younger adults seasonally migrate to find employment in other countries or live temporarily outside their country, returning to spend their old age. Since World War II, Italy has been facing pressing social, political, and economic problems. Her sociomedical resources have gone into providing for the needs of all ages, so that, although the problems of population aging concern her, no special facilities have been developed for the aged.

The care of the healthy aged is not a community problem. Maintenance of traditional and close family links has preserved the status of the old in the pattern of family life. There are throughout Italy 1761 institutes devoted to the care of old people which accommodate 83,680 aged; an additional 400 institutes care for other categories of people but also have rooms for old people (Canaperia, personal communication). Many of these institutes are centuries old, originally established through the bounty of wealthy families but now depending mainly upon contributions from local municipal and provincial administrations for their maintenance. An important percentage of these institutes is attached to, and run by, some religious order. Others are directed by municipal and provincial administrations.

Many of these institutes preserve a proud tradition of service to the aged. Since its beginning in the fourteenth century, S. Lorenzo in Venice has always allowed its guests to have their own rooms and kitchenette with their own furniture and personal belongings. Others are more rigid in their administration, but there is a trend toward the new concepts of caring for the aged. Plans for modernizing the old buildings of these institutes into more comfortable dwellings and transforming their large dormitories into smaller rooms with one, two, or four beds are under way.

The administrators of these institutes have founded the Italian Gerontological Association, which publishes a monthly journal dealing with the problems of geriatrics and organizes seminars and conferences for administrators, social workers, and others employed in the care of the aged.

Most sick old persons are cared for in the wards of general hospitals. Italy is only at the beginning of a movement toward the development of special care of old people in general hospitals, and only a few hospitals have geriatric wards. Besides the general hospitals there are special hospitals, *cronicari*, for the care of the chronically ill for whom there is no hope of rehabilitation. The *cronicari* are less well equipped than the general hospitals and comprise 9892, or 5.3 per cent, of a total of 188,285 available beds in Italian hospitals. However, the majority of patients aged 60 years and over are cared for in the wards of general hospitals. In 1954, of a total of 1,821,000 patients admitted to general hospitals, 243,730, or 13.4 per cent, were 60 years or older (see Table 4).

G. Medical Care in the Federal Republic of Germany

Germany also faces the problem of an increasing number of old people in her population. The proportion of persons 65 years and over was 4.8 per cent in 1880, 7.5 per cent in 1939, and 10 per cent in 1955, and, by 1972, it is estimated that this age group will comprise 13 per cent of the population (World Health Organization, 1955). Germany has had for a long time a scheme of sickness insurance (*Krankenkassen*) under which medical care is provided to a large proportion of the population. Of a total of 7,499,522 persons receiving medical care under this scheme, 350,183 were aged 60 years and over in 1955 (Germany [West], Statistisches Bundensamt, 1955).

Homes for the aged existed in Germany before the war. In 1955 there were 2384 welfare homes for the aged in West Germany with 111,000 beds, and there are many plans for the construction of additional homes for old people. In Hanover the church home mission plans two homes for aged married couples. At present there is an awakening interest on the part of religious, governmental, and voluntary organizations in providing care and services to old people. In 1954 an "Age Academy" was formed under the auspices of the church in Hemer (Rhineland/Westphalen) and, in co-operation with state, welfare, medical, and voluntary organizations, organized discussions on all phases of the problems of the aged which should stimulate creation of facilities and services that old people need. A center of activity in behalf of the aged is in Frankfurt, and a great deal of public interest has been aroused in providing sociomedical care for the aged (Pastor, 1957).

III. Rehabilitation

Rehabilitation is the logical third step following prevention and curative measures in a program of total medical care for the aged. In Western countries during the past decade there has been a surge of professional and public interest in rehabilitation as an essential part of the total effort to solve the social and economic problems that medical progress has created. Persons who a few decades ago would have died from acute communicable diseases now live but in later years acquire disabling illnesses. Each year medical advances are made that prevent death but leave the survivors with severe disabilities. Until medicine provides specific answers to the problems of diseases of the heart and circulation, arthritis, and other chronic diseases a dynamic co-ordinated program of total rehabilitation, physical and social, will be necessary to train these survivors to live as effectively as possible within the limits of their capacity (Rusk, 1956b). As Rusk points out, the problems of chronic diseases can be met not by building more facilities for care but by utilizing, and creating wherever possible, abilities of the disabled. Rehabilitation exploits fully what capacity is left to restore function, physical and psychological, and to return independence, dignity, and meaning to the life of the disabled. It protects community resources and allows the best use to be made of hospital beds and patient-care institutions and services.

Much of the disability and ill-health of old people is the result of medical neglect. Now that the mathematical chance of surviving to old age has increased, a more positive approach to the incurable diseases of this period of life is needed to avert the personal frustrations and community problems that accompany physical disability and mental ill-health. The medical profession is beginning to realize that old people do respond to treatment and can recover function to a surprising degree. Until recently the tendency has been to protect the old person, because of age and frailty, from a battery of diagnostic procedures and therapeutic armamentaria. Geriatric medicine must combat this attitude if a considerable number of old people are to be saved from disability and from occupying hospital beds for a long time and overcrowding hospital facilities. The average number of days of hospitalization is twice as long among persons over 65 years than among those under 65 years (Rusk,

1956b). Chronic illness and disability in old persons call for active medical treatment and rehabilitation if they and the community are to be spared the consequences of neglect.

Rehabilitation begins with the beginning of medical treatment, either at home, in the outpatient department, or in the hospital ward. Medical treatment has significant purpose when the patient is considered as a whole. The recovery of physical function in a damaged organ may be incomplete medically, but, if the aged patient can resume his usual life and do what he needs and wants to do, and can maintain a state of physical, psychological, and social harmony with his environment, then he has recovered and is in a state of health within the flexibility of Sheldon's definition "normal for age." For example, various surveys have shown that, in reply to questions assessing physical fitness and health, a surprising number of old people rate themselves in a good state of health, only to be classified after medical examination as not being healthy. It appears that, as long as the individual is able to function adequately in his environment, he does not consider his heart disease or residual paralysis as reasons for assessing himself in a bad state of health.

It is important to undertake physical, psychological, social, and environmental assessment of the patient's condition and needs before beginning rehabilitation. This can be done through the co-operative effort of doctor, social workers, and nurses and should, ideally, begin in the home before the patient's admission to the hospital or geriatric unit.

A psychological assessment is extremely valuable, since the success of any rehabilitation measure depends perhaps even more on the patient's emotional adjustment and psychological makeup, and his desire to get well, than on medical results. Knowledge of his background is valuable in understanding and treating him, and a social and environmental assessment gives a picture of the patient and his illness in the light of his domestic and family life. This is essential for rehabilitation which includes the recovery of domestic and family relationships disturbed by illness.

Rehabilitation can be carried out in hospitals, clinics, convalescent homes, clubs, and even in the patient's home, according to the facilities for caring for the aged developed in each country. Patients must participate actively in their treatment. Contrary to general belief, old people do not like to be overprotected and coddled and are capable of, and desire, much more activity and independence than they are usually allowed.

Rusk distinguishes three groups of patients who need rehabilitation: (1) the obviously handicapped—patients with hemiplegia, arthritides, fractures, amputation, and neuromuscular disease; (2) the chronically ill without signs of a manifest disability—chronic cardiacs, chronic pulmonary disease; and (3) the elderly person who is not obviously ill but whose physical fitness is impaired so that he is unable to perform his everyday functions without difficulty (Rusk and Dacso, 1956). The latter group is, perhaps, the most neglected medically among the aged and the one which will benefit greatly from some form of rehabilitation therapy.

Rehabilitation is an essential part of hospital treatment and should begin whenever a healthy old person first becomes a sick patient. After assessing the need for admission to the hospital, the patient should be prepared psychologically for the change in environment which may cause confusion, incontinence, and physical disorientation. In all events, hospitalization should be undertaken with proper respect and all due care. Treatment should begin as soon as possible after admission and continued actively until the maximum result has been achieved and no further benefit can be expected from a continued hospital stay, and then the patient should be discharged without delay (Exton-Smith, 1955). Immobilization in bed results in physical and psychological complications and is to be avoided. Ward routine should be modified for each patient after the acute stage of his illness has passed to preserve and restore physical and social capacities. The accepted reasons for keeping patients in bed are not valid for the elderly (Amulree *et al.*, 1951). At the Sabbatsberg Hospital every patient must be out of bed for some time every day, and many ingenious devices and adaptation of equipment have been utilized to help the old people do for themselves (United Nations, 1952; Hilleboe, 1955). Rails in halls, slings over bathtubs, low beds, special wheel chairs that can be propelled with one hand, high chairs with high rounded arms and backs to support old bodies that spend so much time seated, and many other personal tools help the old person to take care of himself. Learning ability even of those in the eighties is remarkable. Many have been able to learn a new language or to relearn speech that has been lost after a cerebral accident as well as to weave or knit. In Copenhagen, at the Old People's Town, older patients are also urged toward early ambulation even if frail, feeble, and disabled (Hilleboe, 1955). Early ambulation eases the strain on the nursing and hospital staff and helps to increase the patient's self-confidence.

While in bed the elderly should have skin and toilet care, and position should be changed frequently. Passive exercises, putting the joints through a maximum range of movement at least once daily, should be done to prevent loss of muscle tone or stiffness and deformity of the joints. As soon as possible active exercise requiring active participation on the part of the patient should begin. Later communal exercises in a gymnasium provide social contacts and help to maintain mental alertness and stimulate greater physical activity as well as save the therapist's time.

Occupational therapy is another important adjunct in testing and restoring skills lost through illness or adverse psychological reaction to the restrictions of advanced age or enforced retirement. After training in the activities required for daily living, the elderly may be able to return to his former independence, and many women may even be able to take up again their domestic and household tasks. Occupational therapy dispels boredom, stimulates alertness by developing new interests, hobbies, and talents, and may become the means of providing economic independence for some elderly persons. Success and pride in achievement build up self-confidence and help to maintain the individual's social integration.

Howell (1950) prescribes group remedial exercise in the gymnasium for his arthritics. Every effort is made to stimulate interest in exercises and games, and the old people often find themselves doing much more than they realized themselves capable of doing. Howell alternates occupational therapy, on wards for the bedfast or in the workroom, with exercise days. For movements of the shoulder joints heavy rug looms are employed. Table looms are used by patients needing to exercise movements of elbows, wrists, fingers, and knees. Making knotted woolen rugs on a stringed frame or more complicated and strenuous basketwork is used as a good exercise for arthritic fingers. Knitting is forbidden, since it requires so little movement that ankylosis often occurs while doing it. The old-fashioned treadle sewing machine exercises stiff ankles, and leather work and sewing aid in keeping joints supple. Helping with ward routine gives the patient the satisfaction that comes from performing a job whose usefulness to the ward community can be immediately appreciated and is a first step to the realization that personal independence is possible for him.

The potentialities for rehabilitation of the chronic sick are great, and patients selected after thorough examination, diagnosis, and classification respond to suitably graded programs. A group-training course organized by the United Nations (1952) lists the following four principles of rehabilitation in the aged: (1) an active regime from a mental and physical point of view within the capabilities of the patient;

(2) precise diagnosis and etiology of the disease; (3) an energetic graded regime; and (4) occupational therapy to maintain and improve the patient's zest for living.

The rheumatic diseases, circulatory disturbances, central nervous system lesions such as hemiplegia, dietetic deficiencies, and some psychological states are amenable to improvement on appropriately graded regimes. Since rehabilitation procedures are based on physical activity, the status of the circulatory system and response to exercise should be carefully assessed at the beginning and throughout the period of therapy.

Exercise plays an important role in maintaining the efficiency of the body, and both functional capacity and tolerance to exercise can be increased with training. Well-compensated cardiacs are capable of a surprising degree of activity, and they should be encouraged to participate in all programs which will help to maintain and increase their capacity for activity and work. In economic situations which absorb them, aged compensated cardiacs are able to work satisfactorily under medical supervision when selectively placed under favorable conditions in regard to kind and hours of work, opportunity for rest, difficulty of travel, and other stress factors involved.

Hemiplegia is one of the most common disabilities treated by rehabilitation. The hemiplegia may be due to cerebral hemorrhage or more usually to cerebral thrombosis, which may result in a variable clinical picture. Since the elderly may also have general cerebral arteriosclerosis, both factors must be considered in the physical and psychological assessment, especially when the patient seems difficult and unco-operative. The clinical picture and response to medical treatment must be evaluated in relation to the extent of brain damage, which will also influence the final capabilities of the patient. Two-thirds of the patients surviving the initial shock learn to walk again. Rusk found the average training time for his hemiplegics to be 6 weeks. An analysis of the first 1000 stroke cases from Bellevue showed that, after an average training time of 7 weeks, 900 patients were ambulatory and able to meet the needs of daily living and outside institutions and that 400 were able to go back to some kind of gainful work. The average age of the patients was 63 years, and the average time from stroke to beginning of treatment was 9 months (Rusk, 1956a). Abramson (1955) reports among his patients in New York City less than 2 per cent of patients unsuitable for rehabilitation, while 80 per cent could be trained to care for themselves completely, the average age of the older group being 62 years.

Both Howell (1950) and Exton-Smith (1955) stress the necessity of beginning rehabilitation of the hemiplegic soon after admission to hospital. Immediately after onset good nursing and general care are essential. Infection may cause confusion and simulate a picture of mental disturbance, and anemia may also retard recovery. Later treatment depends on the specific local function to be improved. A wide range of exercises, equipment, and mechanical aids for suitably guided movements in learning to stand and walk, the Guthrie-Smith sling for restoring function of the shoulder joint, and speech therapy to overcome language disturbances help patients relearn lost function and make the necessary readjustments for living independently in their environment.

What can be done to reduce disability is demonstrated by an experiment by Howell. He asked 56 bedridden patients at St. John's Hospital, "Why can function not be performed?" and in 3 weeks was able to get 49 up, and in 2 months 36 were discharged. By grouping ambulatory hemiplegics, mobile arthritics, and convalescent pneumonias by functional recovery rather than structural lesion in cheerful wards, he was able to encourage independence and release nursing service to more needy wards (Howell, 1950).

Marjory Warren (1955), reporting on the treatment of 18 double amputees admitted to the Geriatric Unit of the West Middlesex Hospital, discusses the rehabilitation and management of these patients and shows the effectiveness of new methods of treatment adapted to the special problems presented by individual patients and the importance of regular medical follow-up. Of 18 double amputees of the lower limbs, 11 were educated to walk on pylons, and 5 could climb stairs.

The statistical results of rehabilitation in the Old People's Town in Copenhagen show the importance of beginning rehabilitation as early as possible in ambulant geriatric clinics (Porsman, 1955). The Old People's Town accommodates old people who can look after themselves and others who need more medical and nursing care. It has a general department for residents partially able to look after themselves and an infirmary for bedridden patients. Porsman reports the results of rehabilitation of 325 patients admitted to the infirmary from July 1, 1952, to January 1, 1954, and concludes that "the results would be considerably better if treatment were commenced before the patients were disabled to such an extent that admission to a hospital is necessary." Of 26 patients with rheumatoid arthritis who were bedridden at the beginning of rehabilitation treatment, only 3 were fit enough to be discharged to the General Department or Nursing Department of the Old People's Town or to their own homes, and, of 50 patients with fractures of the lower extremities also bedridden at the beginning of rehabilitation, the corresponding discharges were 22. Dementia was the most frequent reason for the failure of rehabilitation because these patients were unable to co-operate. Porsman ascribes the dementia in some cases to the feeling of patients that their doctors had "given them up" and also to the leaving of familiar homes for an old age welfare institution.

IV. Preventive Measures

Stieglitz (1949) has said that, "if increased longevity is associated with health and useful vigor during the declining years, it may be an immensely valuable asset especially if these potentialities of the elderly are wisely developed, guided and utilized." This goal can be achieved through promotion of health, prevention, curative treatment, rehabilitation, and research.

Health promotion and prevention aim to save the old from a state of "medicated survival" so that the average man of 75 in the future will maintain as maximum a degree of alertness and vigor as is biologically and physiologically possible. This preparation for old age must begin before the onset of old age. Churchill has said that all the world can be young but that, to come there, one must begin on the way early.

A. Good Nutrition

Heredity and nurture are important in longevity. At the present state of knowledge, preventive measures can be more realistically applied to the exogenous and environmental factors of aging. The evidence, largely based on animal experimentation, of Sinclair (1955) and others suggesting that overfeeding in childhood causes early maturation and shortens life and that overfeeding after maturity increases the incidence of certain degenerative diseases that are common in old age emphasizes the role of nutrition from the earliest years of life. Good nutrition is important in building good body tissue, and a nutritionally adequate diet from childhood on is reflected in the structural and functional adequacy of aging tissues. Premature physiological aging can be prevented by applying the principles of good nutrition.

B. Preventive Health Centers

Preventive health centers should also be an integral part of medical-care programs for the aged. Early recognition and early diagnosis of morbid processes are important in preserving the health of the aged. The report of the Committee of the Care of Chronic Illness and the Aged at the Ninth International Congress of Hospitals at Lucerne in 1955 recommended a further study into the creation of preventive medical centers in the framework of the general hospitals and geriatric services (Delore, 1955). These centers can carry on health education to advise the middle-aged person how to preserve his health and prepare sensibly for advancing years. They can also do periodic medical examinations to assess health and prevent illness and disability, to detect and treat early deviations from the "normal," and to control disease processes that are not curable.

Wibaux (1956) places the responsibility for preventing disabilities of old age upon each individual. He states that no individual has the right to illness and impotence which will necessitate care and help for which society has to pay, so it is his obligation to keep himself well and protect himself from accidents. He suggests a first preventive health examination at the age of 50, when advice for health protection based on the findings of the examination should be given. A second examination should take place at age 60, when the individual is urged to follow a strict regimen of health care; and a third examination should be mandatory at age 70, when it is absolutely exigent that advice and treatment be followed. The pressure of modern life usually does not allow for radical modifications in the pattern of living, and the old, if well, will find it difficult to accept changes that are not immediately and specifically directed toward correcting an existing abnormality. Continued effort must be made to get the young to realize the goals and value of periodic health examinations and to form attitudes which will carry over into old age.

The ages given by Wibaux are already too late to begin preparation for avoiding the physical and psychological hazards of aging, but they suggest good stopping points for health assessment to prevent infirmity and disability arising out of conditions that might be uncovered by periodic examination. Rolleston (1922) has written: "Where the ideal of prophylaxis of infections and of other causes of morbid action is attained, a healthy old age and physiological death without attendant disabilities and horrors should be the common lot of man, instead of being somewhat exceptional in the case of the first, and extremely rare as regards the final act."

Preventive health examinations are being done through health and welfare centers in Oslo, and instruction and retraining for later years are begun at age 50 (Delore, 1955). The Consultative Health Centre in Rutherglen, Scotland (Anderson, 1955), for people over 54 years was started in March, 1952, with the basic idea of integrating "available services for old people in an endeavour to keep them in a sound state of physical, mental and social well-being." The functions of the center are listed below and serve as an illustration of the services and guidance possible in a preventive center:

1. To act as a source for the spread of information relating to the promotion of health and the prevention of disease.
2. To compile a register of the elderly living within the district.
3. To examine healthy old people at routine intervals and to wage a search for early and unsuspected disease.
4. To integrate treatment with the social environment through care and aftercare work.
5. To reduce the demand on hospital beds to a minimum.
6. To provide a citizens' advice bureau for old people.
7. To carry out research into the aging process.

C. General Education of the Public

An important preventive measure in geriatrics is general education of the public in matters of health protection. Although the childhood of the already aged is beyond reach, knowledge that a happy childhood is the best security for old age is good health education for the parents of today and will benefit the young who will arrive at the end of the life-table some day. Attention has been drawn to the possibility that character formation and emotional development in the early years of childhood influence adjustment to others in old age (Lamont, 1953). Mental attitudes in old age reflect attitudes of earlier life. To maintain the mental health of the aged, it is important to start early in acquiring and keeping alive indoor and outdoor interest, cultivating and nourishing friendships, and developing the proper balance among work, rest, and recreation. The old as he relinquishes the active pursuits of maturity must be reoriented to accept his new status which carries new values and potentialities. Education of the young directed to molding an attitude which accepts old age as a normal part of the social pattern for which they assume responsibility now, and a status to which they can look forward in the future, will create and strengthen a society which provides security in old age.

Dissemination of information to the public on the problems of old age, on the services available to old people, and on how to obtain such services is as important an aspect of health education as stimulation of the state and responsible authority to provide wisely and adequately for the old.

D. Gerontological Research and Professional Education

Gerontological research must be stimulated and supported in order to advance our knowledge of the biology and clinical manifestations of aging as well as the diseases of particular significance in later life, such as cardiovascular diseases and cancer, and of how to provide health care to the aged.

Professional education also must recognize the needs of geriatric medicine and provide the training that doctors, nurses, social workers, and other paramedical workers will need if they are to fulfil their function in the program of care for old people. The single unit best equipped to practice preventive geriatrics and geriatric medicine is the general practitioner, for steadily more and more of his professional time is occupied in the care of the old. The students of medical and allied professional schools must be oriented to the geriatric aspects of their courses, and, where indicated, the curriculums should include courses that deal with the specific problems of geriatric medicine.

Since medical care of the old is only one phase in the over-all need of the aged, all preventive measures in the field of health, housing, employment, and social security must be co-ordinated and integrated to achieve a maximum of result at a minimum cost to private and public funds. Not only must the medical care of the old be treated as a whole but his total care must be related to the aggregate of his medical, social, and economic needs.

V. Conclusion

Increasing interest in gerontological activities on the part of individual countries (as well as international organizations) reflects the growing concern of countries in the increasing proportion of aged persons in their populations, and conferences and studies into the nature and extent of the problem and the best means of meeting it are being undertaken or planned. Among recent meetings in which several countries have participated may be mentioned the Advisory Group on the Public Health Aspects of Aging of Populations held by the Regional Office for Europe of the World Health Organization in Oslo in July, 1958 (1959b); an Expert Committee on the Mental Health Problems of Aging and the Aged held by the World Health Organization in Geneva in September, 1958 (1959a); and a Seminar on the Individual and Social Importance of Activities for the Elderly held under the auspices of the European Office of the Technical Assistance Administration of the United Nations in Königswinter, Germany, in October, 1958 (1959).

The conclusions reached at the technical discussions of the Fifth Session of the Regional Committee for Europe of the World Health Organization summarize the trend in the medical care of the aging population in European countries. Home care is emphasized as being the most desirable and to be encouraged whenever it is medically possible in terms of all the specific health and social services previously enumerated. Adequate home care and, in fact, the entire program of sociomedical care can be achieved only through the wholehearted co-operation of medical, voluntary, and official or government bodies on all levels of administration and implementation of services. Hospitalization, when necessary, should be for active diagnosis, treatment, and rehabilitation and should be geared to achieve the maximum therapeutic benefit in a minimum of time and with a view to returning the patient to his usual environment in the same, or a higher, level of health so that he may be able to maintain a fairly independent existence or to get along with a minimum of help.

The old need the same facilities of high-quality care as the young for both acute and chronic diseases. In order to assure care of high caliber for the chronically ill old, without unduly burdening existing hospital facilities, special geriatric services may be required. The geriatric service is envisioned not as a place for permanent care but as an active service where a considerable number of patients (up to 70 per cent) should be ready for discharge in 6–7 weeks.

REFERENCES AND BIBLIOGRAPHY

ABRAMSON, A. S. 1955. Rehabilitation in geriatric practice. Canad. M.A.J., **72**, 327–34.
AMULREE, (LORD) B. W. S. 1953. The formation of a geriatric service. Tech. Hosp., **8** (May), 22–25.
AMULREE, (LORD) B. W. S., EXTON-SMITH, A. N., and CROCKETT G. S. 1951. The proper use of the hospital in the treatment of the aged sick. Lancet, **1**, 123–26.
ANDERSON, W. F. 1955. A clinical study of the patients attending a consultative health centre for old people at Rutherglen, Scotland. *In*

Old age in the modern world, pp. 534–40. Edinburgh: E. & S. Livingstone.

BASTAI, P., and DOGLIOTTI, G. C. 1938. Physiopathologie de la vieillesse et introduction à l'étude des maladies des vieillards. Paris: Masson & Cie.

BELGIUM. COMMISSION DE COORDINATION DE L'OFFICE D'IDENTIFICATION. 1957a. Les problèmes de la vieillesse, Vol. 1: En Belgique. (Cycle de conférences présentées aux réunions de travailleurs sociaux de la Commission de Coordination, septembre 1955—juillet 1957.) Brussels.

———. 1957b. Les problèmes de la vieillesse, Vol. 2: À l'étranger. (Rapports présentées aux journées internationales d'études organisées par la Commission de Coordination, 7–11 novembre 1956.) Brussels.

BERG, G. 1954. Befolkningsutveckling och sjukvardsbehov i Stockholms lan. I. Svenska Lakartidningen, 51, 1097–1121.

BINET, L., and BOURLIÈRE, F. 1955. Précis de gérontologie. Paris: Masson & Cie.

BIRCH-LINDGREN, C. 1956. À propos des projets de création de divisions hospitalières pour le traitement des maladies des vieillards et des maladies chroniques en Suède. Tech. Hosp., 11 (March), 65.

BOUCHER, C. A. 1957. A survey of services available to the chronic ill and elderly in 1954–55. London: H. M. Stationery Office.

BROCKINGTON, C. F. 1956. Short history of public health. London: J. & A. Churchill.

———. 1957. Introducing chronic bronchitis. National Association for the Prevention of Tuberculosis (London), 20, 134.

BRONTS, H. J., and VAN ZONNEVELD, R. J. 1957. The impact of aged patients on hospital care. A survey into number, length of stay, and diagnosis of aged people admitted to a number of hospitals in 1924, 1939, and 1954. Ziekenhuiswezen, 30, 305–14.

BRULL, L. 1954. Problèmes de gériatrie. Rev. méd Liège, 9, 202–5.

CANNON, W. B. 1939. Ageing of homeostatic mechanisms. In E. V. COWDRY (ed.), Problems of ageing, pp. 623–41. Baltimore: Williams & Wilkins Co.

CLERENS, J. 1956. Problèmes de gérontologie. Tech. Hosp., 11 (May), 28–30.

COMFORT, A. 1956. The biology of senescence. London: Routledge & Kegan Paul.

COVALT, NILA K. 1956. European approach to rehabilitation of older people. J. Am. Geriatrics Soc., 4, 235–41.

CREW, F. A. E. 1954. Progress and future developments affecting the care of the elderly. In The care of old people: report of the Seventh National Conference. London: National Council of Social Service.

DARIC, J. 1948. Vieillissement de la population et prolongation de la vie active. ("Institut Nationale d'Études Démographiques, Travaux et Documents," No. 7.) Paris: Presses Universitaires de France.

———. 1956. Problems of the aged in Europe. In European seminar on social services for the aged, Liège, 1955. Geneva: United Nations.

DELORE, P. 1955. Rapport de la IIIᵉ Commission d'Étude et de Recherches (b): soins aux malades chroniques et aux vieillards. IXᵉ Congrès International des Hôpitaux (Lucerne, 29 May–3 June, 1955).

———. 1956a. Résumé of the work of the Committee To Study and Investigate the Care of the Chronically Ill and the Aged: report presented by the president to the IXth Congress of the International Federation of Hospitals in Lucerne in 1955. Tech. Hosp., 11 (January), 26–27.

———. 1956b. The old in modern society. Ibid., June, pp. 15–17.

DELORE, P., and ARNAUD, P. 1956. Motifs d'hospitalisation des malades âgés de plus de 65 ans. Tech. Hosp., 11 (August–September), 48–53.

DUNBAR, FLANDERS. 1955. The long-lived: ageing and illness. In Old age in the modern world, pp. 412–20. Edinburgh: E. & S. Livingstone.

DURAND, J. D. 1955. Demographic background in developed and under-developed countries. In Old age in the modern world, pp. 32–36. Edinburgh: E. & S. Livingstone.

ERLANDSSON, S. 1956. Les infirmités de l'âge avancé et ce qu'elles réclament comme organisations médicales. Tech. Hosp., 11 (February), 32–36.

EVANS, F. T. 1956. Anaesthesia for the elderly. In W. HOBSON (ed.), Modern trends in geriatrics. London: Butterworth & Co.

EVANS, G. 1955. Comprehensive care of old people: the role of the local authority welfare department. In Old age in the modern world, pp. 84–95. Edinburgh: E. & S. Livingstone.

EXTON-SMITH, A. N. 1955. Medical problems of old age. Bristol: John Wright & Sons.

FOOD AND AGRICULTURE ORGANIZATION. 1950. Report of the Committee on Caloric Requirements. ("FAO Nutritional Studies," No. 5.) Geneva: United Nations.

FREUDENBERG, K. 1955. Mortality trends by ages over a period of eighty years in Germany. *In* World Population Conference, 1954, Papers, Vol. 1, Meeting No. 2, pp. 77–88. Geneva: United Nations.

GAUSTAD, V. 1956. Project for organizing hospital and home services for the aged in Oslo. Tech. Hosp., 11 (March), 40–43.

GAVEY, C. J. 1949. The cardiology of old age. Lancet, 2, 725–36.

GERMANY (WEST). STATISTISCHES BUNDENSAMT. 1955. Gesundheitswesen: Statistische Ergebnisse 1955. Statistik der Bundesrepublik Deutschland, Vol. 174. Wiesbaden.

GIJSBERS, A. 1956. Symposium on home services. *In* European seminar on social services for the aged, Liège, 1955. Geneva: United Nations.

GOSSET, A. 1953. Les vieillards en établissements hospitaliers: l'amérlioration du sort des gens âgés. Journées Régionales d'Études Organisées par la Délégation Régionale du Nord de l'Alliance Nationale contre la Dépopulation. Collection Informations Sociales. L'Union Nationale des Caisses d'Allocations Familiales. Paris.

GREAT BRITAIN. NATIONAL HEALTH SERVICE. 1957. Geriatric services and the care of the chronic sick. London: H.M. Stationery Office.

GRAILLY, R. DE, and DESTREM, H. 1953. Physiologie générale, diététique et comportement de la vieillesse. Paris: Masson & Cie.

GREENLEES, A., and ADAMS, J. 1950. Old people in Sheffield. Sheffield: Council of Social Service. 1950.

GROLLMAN, A. 1955. The interrelationship of hypertension, arteriosclerosis, and the ageing process. *In* Old age in the modern world, pp. 517–19. Edinburgh: E. & S. Livingstone.

HILLEBOE, H. E. 1955. Geriatric services in Denmark, Norway, and Sweden. Geriatrics, 10, 541–48.

HIPPOCRATES. 1943. Loeb Classical Library, Vol. 4. London: Heinemann.

HOBSON, W., and BLACKBURN, E. K. 1953. Haemoglobin levels in a group of elderly persons living at home alone or with spouse. Brit. M.J., 1, 647–49.

HOBSON, W., and PEMBERTON, J. 1955. The health of the elderly at home. London: Butterworth & Co.

HOBSON, W., and ROSEMAN, C. 1953. A dental survey of a group of old people living at home. Brit. Dental J., 94, 208.

HOWELL, T. H. 1950. Old age. London: H. K. Lewis & Co.

———. 1953. Our advancing years. London: Phoenix House.

———. 1956. Basic problems of the aged and chronic sick. J. Am. Geriatrics Soc., 4, 224–34.

HUET, J. A. 1957. The impact of illness of aged people on the economy of Parisian hospitals. *In* Proceedings of the Fourth Congress, International Association of Gerontology, Merano, Italy, 3, 366–74. Fidenza: Tipographia Tito Mattioli.

HUTCHINSON, B. 1954. Old people in a modern Australian community. Melbourne: Melbourne University Press.

IRVINE, E. D. 1954. Medical aspects of aging. *In* Living longer: some aspects of the problems of old age. London: National Council of Social Service.

KINDSTRAND, W. 1947. Den geriatriska enheten som form for aldringsvård och varför? Social Medicinsktidskrift, No. 4 (April), p. 145.

KRAG, C. L., and KOUNTZ, W. B. 1950. Stability of body function in the aged. J. Gerontol., 5, 227–35.

LAMONT, D. J. 1953. The role of the health visitor in the care of the elderly. M. Officer, 92, 162.

LOGAN, W. P. D. 1953. Studies on medical and population subjects. ("General Practitioners Records," No. 7.) London: H.M. Stationery Office.

MAGDELAINE, M., and PEQUIGNOT, H. 1957. Les besoins d'hospitalization des vieillards et leurs causes. *In* Proceedings of the Fourth Congress, International Association of Gerontology, Merano, Italy, 3, 398–404. Fidenza: Tipographia Tito Mattioli.

MINISTRY OF HEALTH AND THE PUBLIC HEALTH LABORATORY SERVICE. 1951–52. Monthly bulletin: survey of prevalence of sickness, 10, 11, 81, 162, 239; 11, 11, 86, 127, 272.

NORDSTRÖM, MARGARETA. 1955. Home help for old people in Sweden. Stockholm: Swedish Social Welfare Board. (Mimeographed.)

NORGAARD, A. 1955. Blodtrykket hos aldre personer med fuld førlighed. Nord. med., 53, 311–13.

PASTOR, A. P. VON. 1957. Neue Ziele der Alterspflege und Altersfursorge in Deutschland. Ztschr. Praventivmedizin, 2, 257.

PFISTER, H. O. 1951. Chronic invalids. *In* VII International Hospital Congress, Brussels, 1951. London: International Hospital Federation.

PORSMAN, V. A. 1955. Statistical results of rehabilitation in "The Old People's Town" in Copenhagen. *In* Old age in the modern world, pp. 571–74. Edinburgh: E. & S. Livingstone.

ROLLESTON, H. D. 1922. Some medical aspects of old age. London: Macmillan & Co.

ROTH, J. 1955. Old age insurance and welfare in Switzerland. *In* Old age in the modern world, pp. 62–65. Edinburgh: E. & S. Livingstone.

ROWNTREE, B. S. 1947. Old people. London: Oxford University Press (for the Nuffield Foundation).

RUSK, H. A. 1956*a*. Sick people in a troubled world. Laryngoscope, 66, 1094–1112.

———. 1956*b*. Rehabilitation: an international problem. *In* Proceedings of the Second International Congress of Physical Medicine, Copenhagen, 1956.

RUSK, H. A., and DACSO, M. M. 1956. Rehabilitation in the aged. Bull. New York Acad. Med., 32, 725–33.

SAUVY, A. 1955. Age and society: the historical and sociological basis. *In* Old age in the modern world, pp. 28–32. Edinburgh: E. & S. Livingstone.

SCHULZE, W. 1955. Protein metabolism and requirement in old age. *In* Old age in the modern world, pp. 122–27. Edinburgh: E. & S. Livingstone.

SHELDON, J. H. 1948. The social medicine of old age. London: Oxford University Press (for the Nuffield Foundation).

SHOCK, N. W., WATKIN, D. W., and YIENGST, M. J. 1955. Metabolic aspects of ageing. *In* Old age in the modern world, pp. 127–37. Edinburgh: E. & S. Livingstone.

SINCLAIR, H. M. 1955. The dangers of overfeeding. *In* Old age in the modern world, pp. 106–13. Edinburgh: E. & S. Livingstone.

———. 1956. Nutritional problems of the elderly. *In* W. HOBSON (ed.), Modern trends in geriatrics. London: Butterworth & Co.

SINGLETON, W. T. 1955. Age and performance timing on simple skills. *In* Old age in the modern world, pp. 221–31. Edinburgh: E. & S. Livingstone.

SMITH, R. C. F. 1957. The effect of social problems on the lives of old age pensioners. M. Officer, 97, 303–8.

SPIEGELMAN, M. 1954. An international comparison of mortality rates at the older ages. *In* World Population Conference, 1954, Papers, Vol. 1, Meeting No. 2, pp. 289–309. Geneva: United Nations.

STARE, F. J. 1956. Nutrition and the geriatric patient. J. Am. Geriatrics Soc., 4, 744–50.

SIR HALLEY STEWART TRUST and NATIONAL OLD PEOPLE'S WELFARE COMMITTEE. 1954. Over seventy: report of an investigation into the social and economic circumstances of one hundred people over seventy years of age. London: National Council of Social Service.

STIEGLITZ, E. J. 1949. Geriatric medicine: the care of the aging and the aged. 2d ed. Philadelphia: W. B. Saunders Co.

———. 1950. Nutrition problems of geriatric medicine. J.A.M.A., 142, 1070.

STRÖM, A. 1956. An investigation of the living conditions and health of 1389 persons aged 70 years or more in Norway. J. Gerontol., 11, 178–84.

SWEDEN. 1956. Swedish government's public investigations. Stockholm: Department of Social Affairs.

SWEDISH SOCIAL WELFARE BOARD. 1952. Public assistance in social Sweden. Stockholm: The Board.

SZAFRAN, J. 1955. Experiments on the greater use of vision by older adults. *In* Old age in the modern world, pp. 231–35. Edinburgh: E. & S. Livingstone.

THEWLIS, M. W. 1954. The care of the aged. 6th ed. St. Louis: C. V. Mosby Co.

TOWNSEND, G. W. H. 1955. Making the most of institutional accommodation for the elderly. *In* Old age in the modern world, pp. 76–80. Edinburgh: E. & S. Livingstone.

TUNBRIDGE, R. E. 1951. Problems of prolonged illness. *In* VII International Hospital Congress, Brussels, 1951. London: International Hospital Federation.

UNITED NATIONS. 1952. Diseases of old age. *In* Modern methods of rehabilitation of the adult disabled: report of a group-training course organized by the U.N. with co-operation of the WHO and the ILO. ST/TAA/Ser. C/4, pp. 49–51.

———. 1959. European seminar on the individual and social importance of activities for the elderly (UN/TAA/SEM/1958/Rep. 3.) Geneva: United Nations.

VAN ZONNEVELD, R. J. 1954. Health problems of the aged. Assen: van Gorcum & Co.

———. 1957. Socio-medical investigations for

the benefit of the accommodation of the aged. J. Gerontol., **12**, 441–42. (Abstract.)

VAN ZONNEVELD, R. J., and GROEN, J. 1957. A comprehensive study of the aged by general practitioners. *In* Gerontological research of the National Health Research Council of the Netherlands Foundation for Applied Research at The Hague and the II Medical Service. Amsterdam: Wilhelmina Gasthuis.

VICKERS, H. R., and SNEDDON, I. B. 1956. Skin changes in the elderly. *In* W. HOBSON (ed.), Modern trends in geriatrics. London: Butterworth & Co.

VISCHER, A. L., and ROULET, F. C. 1952. Observations on two centenarians. Arch. path. Anat., **321**, 652–63.

WALSH, R. C. 1955. Medical care of old people at home. *In* Old age in the modern world, pp. 80–84. Edinburgh: E. &. S. Livingstone.

WARREN, MARJORY W. 1955. The management of the early double amputee. *In* Old age in the modern world, pp. 562–70. Edinburgh: E. & S. Livingstone.

———. 1956a. Le rôle d'une unité gériatrique dans un hôpital général. Tech. Hosp., **11** (February), 37–38.

———. 1956b. The geriatric approach. *In* European seminar on social services for the aged, Liège, 1955. Geneva: United Nations.

WATKINS, E. 1951. Housing for the aged: report of WHO fellow: three months' study tour, United Kingdom, the Netherlands, Denmark, and Sweden. Geneva: World Health Organization.

WELFORD, A. T. 1956. Psychological aspects of ageing. *In* W. HOBSON (ed.), Modern trends in geriatrics, pp. 69–105. London: Butterworth & Co.

WIBAUX, R. 1956. Les régimes du vieillard. Bull. Acad. méd., **140**, 532.

WIBAUX, R., and HUET, J. A. 1956. Mesures médico-sociales à prendre en faveur des gens âgés. Tech. Hosp., **11** (January), 36–38.

WIDDOWSON, E. M., and McCANCE, R. A. 1955. The response of well-nourished old men to starvation and of under-nourished old men to unlimited food. *In* Old age in the modern world, pp. 113–22. Edinburgh: E. & S. Livingstone.

WORLD HEALTH ORGANIZATION. 1955. Public health implications of the aging of populations: conclusions of a WHO meeting, based on a summary report on the technical discussions of the Vth session of the Regional Committee for Europe. Chronicles of WHO, **9**, 339–41.

———. 1959a. Mental health problems of aging and the aged: Sixth Report of the Expert Committee on Mental Health. ("WHO Technical Report Series," No. 171.) Geneva: World Health Organization.

———. 1959b. The public health aspects of the aging of the population. (EURO-112.) Copenhagen: Regional Office for Europe, World Health Organization.

VII

The Mental Health of the Aging

ROBERT W. KLEEMEIER

I. Introduction

Mental health is difficult to define. Although it refers most directly to a state of being of the individual, it can be used with broader connotation. Surrounding it is an aura implying a positive approach to mental illness, a concern with prevention of mental disease, and an interest in the adjustment process of the individual as well as in community conditions which influence individual adjustment.

Good personal mental health is associated with the absence of mental distress, with good adjustment, feeling of well-being, high morale, and happiness. In the final analysis, however, it is not an absolute condition. Rather it refers to the relative success of the individual in dealing with his own emotional stress as shown by the quality of his interpersonal relationships, the relative effectiveness of his stress-reducing behavior, and his attitudes and self-concepts. Intellectual capacity is also related—not that the possession of great ability is the prerequisite for good mental

[1] I am particularly grateful to the following, who gave me great help in my search for information on which to base this chapter: Dr. Yves Porc'her, Hôpital Henri-Rousselle, Paris; Dr. R. J. van Zonneveld, National Health Research Council, T.N.O., The Hague; Dr. A. Querido, director of public health, Amsterdam; Mr. Henning Friis, Ministry of Labor, Copenhagen; Dr. A. Berggren, Royal Social Board, and Mrs. Kate Wennerlund, Sociala Nämnderna, Stockholm; and the staff of the University of Bristol Library. There are many others to whom I am almost equally indebted.

health, or even insures it for that matter. On the other hand, nevertheless, mental deficiency is not compatible with good mental health.

At the opposite end of this multidimensional continuum lies mental illness and the incapacitating disorders of character and personality. Mental health, to a greater extent than physical health, is a condition in which interdependent social, psychological, and medical factors exert apparent influences. Thus in the broad sense of the concept every chapter in this book deals with some important aspect of mental health, because social and economic factors as well as physical health create or relieve stress, thereby changing for better or worse conditions affecting the individual's mental health. It is obvious, therefore, that a more limited approach is necessary in the present discussion of the mental health of the aged in various western European countries. To aid in this delimitation, the following analysis of the criteria of mental health status of a society is given.

A. Mental Health of a Society Seen in Three Ways

Social mental health can be considered from at least three distinct vantage points (Kleemeier, 1957a, 1957b), each of which relate to different sets of criteria:

1. Social mental health may be presented as the aggregate mental health of the individuals who compose the society. Criteria aimed at evaluating this would be derived from the

enumeration of individual adjustment characteristics.

2. Social mental health may be viewed as a community or social process. Here the approaches of the community to the problem of mental health would be sought. Treatment and custodial institutions, legal and social processes of control of mentally ill persons, and activities of the mental health professions would all fall within the purview of this concept.

3. Cultural patterns, levels of socioeconomic status, environmental factors, and social attitudes of a community undoubtedly affect mental health to a far greater extent than we are now clearly able to say. It would be reasonable, nevertheless, to attempt to describe social mental health in these terms.

Ideally, a survey of mental health of the aged in western European countries should result in a systematic exploration of all factors related to these three sets of criteria for each country under study. Unfortunately, this is too large a job to undertake at present for several good reasons. In the first place, it would involve a tremendous amount of original research, for relatively little of the required information is to be had for the asking. In the second place, it would require a degree of international coordination of effort that could be achieved only after long and careful planning, much experience in working together, and considerable dedication to the worthwhileness of the goal. Steps in this direction have already been taken, but at best these are preliminary.

MENTAL HEALTH CONSIDERED AS THE
AGGREGATE MENTAL HEALTH
OF INDIVIDUALS

In terms of this criterion we should study the incidence of mental disease in relation to the place of its occurrence—in short, the epidemiology of mental illness. Many of the basic data have been and are being currently compiled by hospitals and state agencies, but these are subjected to surprisingly little analysis and study. When the data are made available on a national basis, we find that they have been gathered for specific administrative purposes, invariably making cross-national comparisons extremely tenuous at best but more often impossible. In the following sections some such comparisons will be made, but, in general, the best that we can hope to do is to gain general impressions from available statistics and to proceed from this to our own conclusions as cautiously as possible.

Hospital census data are at best difficult to interpret; certainly, they cannot be used in our present state of knowledge as an index of the national aggregate mental health. One obvious reason for this is that hospital admissions depend upon the number of hospital beds available, and these vary as markedly from country to country as they do from state to state in the United States. With respect to the aged the inadequacy of this criterion is particularly apparent. In most western European countries the feeling exists that the mildly psychotic, aged person does not belong in the mental hospital but rather in a separate institution which may or may not be associated with a mental hospital. In both England and Denmark the view is expressed that legal certification procedures are being used to overcrowd the mental hospitals with old patients at the expense of the admission of younger patients. The Netherlands is in the process of building nursing homes for this group of patients. Sweden has an announced policy of separating the physically ill and psychotic from among the residents of its homes for the aged, making them the responsibility of the health agencies rather than that of social welfare. Such differences in this approach to the mentally ill aged make impossible the assessment of the aggregate mental health of old people through the use of hospital statistics.

However, an exemplary Swedish study of the incidence of mental illness in the entire population of a small rural area covering an extended period of time has been carried out (Larsson and Sjögren, 1954). Unfortunately, there appears to be no European counterpart of the Gruenberg epidemiological studies of senile mental illness in New York State (New York State Department of Mental Hygiene, 1955). Only when many such systematic samples of entire populations are studied will we be able to make reliable national and cross-cultural comparisons of aggregate mental health status. Even then, unless common criteria are adopted, it will be difficult to arrive at meaningful comparisons (Kleemeier, 1957a, 1957b).

MENTAL HEALTH AS A COMMUNITY OR SOCIAL PROCESS

Just as mental health can be considered as the aggregate mental health of individuals, so it can be thought of as a community or social process. From this point of view the criterion of community success in dealing with mental health problems is in actuality the effectiveness of its agencies in bringing about the rehabilitation of the mentally distressed (Joint Commission on Mental Illness and Health, 1956).

Specifically, this suggests that the criteria of social mental health are established by the rehabilitation rates of psychiatric and other community facilities designed to serve the needs of distressed people. The mental health functions of many community organizations—schools, churches, hospitals, clinics, physicians, social agencies—would thus come within purview.

Rehabilitation rates, even if they could be reliably established, would, however, be only the ultimate concern; for these are dependent upon prior social, medical, and even legal processes. A thorough survey of all these factors even in a restricted community would be a formidable task and quite impossible at present internationally, for even the tools and methods for doing such research need fashioning and development. Nevertheless, some information of the sort required is available, and profitable use can be made of it.

In the countries included in this survey great concern is evidenced over the release and rehabilitation of mental patients. All are worried over the increasing demands for psychiatric hospitalization and the strains that are being put upon overtaxed and antiquated hospital systems. France feels acutely its need for more hospital space and has given the expansion of facilities the first priorities. Denmark and to some extent the Netherlands are also engaged in building, but all recognize that this is not enough; somehow the number of admissions must be cut or the treatment facilities improved in efficiency so that more patients can be served without excessive, burdensome expansion of plant and staff.

The Netherlands has pioneered in outpatient services, and Great Britain sees hope for the future primarily in this direction. Already in England and Wales the mounting tide of hospitalization seems to have been stemmed, and during the past few years the number of hospitalized mental patients has been slowly dropping, although new admissions continue to rise in number.

Related to this vigorous and positive approach to the treatment of mental disease is the turning-away from reliance upon legal commitment and certification of patients. In some countries in the survey voluntary hospitalization is the rule rather than the exception. With this de-emphasis upon compulsion, more and more wards are being unlocked, and some hospitals, even those with unselected patients, have no locked wards at all.

In this concern with overcrowding thought has been given to the place of the aged patient in the mental hospital. Majority opinion is that he does not belong there if he cannot profit by the program of active therapy which should be offered by the mental hospital. Attention is, therefore, being paid to the setting-up of nursing homes, as in the Netherlands, or hospital annexes in Denmark, and day hospitals in Great Britain. No country has as yet put into action a system which has completely taken care of this problem, although some programs are under way.

Certainly, the place of the home for the aged, the geriatric hospital, and other institutional and quasi-institutional settings must be established in reference to the total mental health problem. The separation of the mentally frail aged from the "normal" aged person is sometimes difficult and in fact is often thought to be both unnecessary and undesirable. In many countries old people's homes care for many such individuals. Denmark would be ill prepared to accept in its mental hospitals at present all the mentally frail aged residing in its old age homes. Even Sweden, though she has tried, has not yet made the separation complete. Elsewhere there is strong feeling that mental frailty in the aged is largely a problem of geriatric medicine, with only incidental psychiatric overtones.

MENTAL HEALTH AS CULTURAL, ENVIRONMENTAL, ECONOMIC, AND SOCIAL FACTORS

We cannot escape recognition of the fact that an individual's way of life affects in important ways his mental health. Whether or not mental illness, in any of its forms, can ever be considered as the exclusive product of emotional stress arising in the day-to-day conflicts of life, there can be no denying that stress does affect the course of such illness (Kleemeier, 1958). Surely, a survey of mental health would be incomplete without consideration of this factor and the circumstances in the culture which produce it. With reference to old people, the stress attendant upon such age-related conditions as the breakup of the home and family, reduction of income upon retirement, illness, difficult or inappropriate physical surroundings, and others would be of transcendent interest. This, however, is an area in which relatively little research has been done, although, as other chapters in this *Handbook* attest, we are not without information about the basic economic and social conditions which affect the aged. What is lacking, however, is knowledge of the ways in which mental health of the aged is influenced by these conditions.

Having emphasized the importance of these factors, the necessity for research into the nature of the relationship remains if prevention of mental breakdown is to be accepted as coequal with cure as a primary goal in mental health endeavors.

B. The Community and the Mental Hospital

Health is not exclusively a medical province, although it might be argued that illness is. In mental health the lines of medical hegemony are even more indistinct than in what might be considered as purely physical health. This is of course apparent if the threefold classification of social mental health criteria described above is accepted. We cannot escape, however, the fact that the major focus of mental health activities are at present medically oriented, with primary emphasis upon cure rather than prevention. Thus the major mental health resources of the community are the various medical and closely allied professions that exert their therapeutic efforts through clinics, hospitals, and similar agencies. In the following survey, therefore, these traditional mental health resources are emphasized.

Nevertheless, this is not a story of isolated institutions and insulated professionals. Within the first post–World War II decade great awareness of the plight of the mentally ill developed in western Europe and North America. This interest both resulted in and was stimulated by the organization of mental health associations which grew apace in Europe and America during these years. In America they were perhaps more vocal and involved interested lay people to a larger extent, but the core of individuals with professional interest in mental health about whom the European associations grew certainly exerted important influence in their various countries. The efforts of the World Federation of Mental Health and of United Nations agencies continue to improve mental health conditions on a world-wide basis.

In this work the World Health Organization, a United Nations agency, has played an important part by convening groups of experts from various countries to discuss specific public health problems. From one of these expert committee sessions came a report on the place of the mental hospital in the community which has stimulated much progressive thinking (World Health Organization, 1953). In it the idea of the community mental hospital is set forth, and this new and total approach to mental illness is described.

The community mental hospital breaks sharply with traditional nineteenth-century concepts of segregation and custodial care of the mentally ill. In principle this approach has received warm acceptance by responsible mental health authorities in western Europe, but this does not mean that old ways have been abandoned there, any more than in the United States; but, certainly, the spirit of the community mental hospital idea is influencing current planning. Acute awareness of its implications are felt in England, the Netherlands, Denmark, and other countries, and, in some of these, firm steps in the direction of its realization have been taken. America has not been left in the backwash of these developments but has contributed to them in both practice and theory. However, these concepts are new and still developing, and much is to be learned by the ways in which they are applied in various countries.

THE AGED PATIENT

While the advantages of the community mental hospital and other advanced practices are not limited to any one age group, there is reason to believe that as a group the aged present sufficiently different problems to warrant special consideration. No uniform approach to the care of the senile demented patient has yet appeared, although with increasing frequency the suggestion is encountered that special institutions be provided for them. Interest is gathering in this area, and expectations for imaginative developments are not likely to be disappointed, but the moment of fruition has yet to arrive. What these expectations are will be suggested in the following sections of this chapter if the future can be judged from current developments in western Europe. Certainly, the time has arrived to give mental health problems of the aged serious and productive consideration.

II. FRANCE

There appears to be no aggressive attack directed at the specific mental health problems of the aged in France. Considerable effort and attention are being given, however, to the expansion and modernization of the mental hospital system and to the improvement of medical and social services to patients. The over-all plan for the betterment of mental health services and the rehabilitation of the hospital system has been formulated and in operation since 1953. In spite of persistent financial difficulties, considerable work has been carried out under this program. New hospitals have been built, and others have been modernized and enlarged; but antiquated institutions are still the rule, and, by the advanced standards of space requirements per patient established by the Ministry of Health, overcrowding is common.

Although no special efforts have been directed to the aged and senile patient, it is apparent that he presents an as-yet-unsolved problem to the mental health authorities in France just as he does in most other regions and countries. The Ministry of Health (1953, 1956) planning reports, which are presented in some detail below, point out that older age groups are not overrepresented in the hospital population and, therefore, cannot be held responsible for the present crowded conditions of the hospitals. There apparently is, however, a growing tendency to reduce the admission rate of aged patients by means of a more careful screening. This trend is to be seen in other European countries, but unfortunately it is not always accompanied by a clear-cut policy covering the care and follow-up of individuals so rejected.

A. The Organization of Mental Health Services

The Ministry of Health well recognizes that the treatment of mental disease is a many-sided process. Thus it is assumed that the complete mental health program begins with a case-finding agency or clinical center which may also offer outpatient in a neighboring department or in an appropriate private institution. As a result of this law in January, 1953, there were 90 such psychiatric hospitals; by 1957 these had increased to 101. Table 1 shows the number and capacity of these institutions in 1953 and their growth under the operation of the developmental plan instituted in 1953.

With the exception of the hospitals built or remodeled since 1953, the typical French mental hospital is old and vitally in need

TABLE 1*

INVENTORY OF BEDS FOR MENTAL PATIENTS IN FRANCE AS OF
JANUARY, 1953, AND UPON COMPLETION OF 5-YEAR PLAN†

TYPE OF INSTITUTION	JANUARY, 1953			UPON COMPLETION OF PLAN		
	No.	Optimum Bed Capacity	Maximum Bed Capacity	No.	Optimum Bed Capacity	Maximum Bed Capacity
Autonomous hospitals..............	7	5,853	7,641	7	6,755	8,554
Departmental hospitals..............	52	35,009	45,724	61	45,323	56,238
Psychiatric quarters of general hospitals..	11	4,435	5,790	13	5,192	7,108
Private psychiatric hospitals...........	20	13,903	18,062	20	14,638	19,071
Total for psychiatric hospitals.........	90	59,200	77,217	101	71,906	90,971
Neuropsychiatric services of general hospitals (40 per cent of total beds)......	......	....	800	......	....	1,100
Private clinics.......................	58	....	2,920	......	....	2,920
Total............................	......	....	80,937	......	....	94,991

* Source: Ministry of Health, "Plan d'équipement sanitaire: lutte contre les maladies mentales," Part I (Paris, 1953), and "Deuxième plan d'équipement, 1958–61: hôpitaux psychiatriques," Part I (Paris, 1956). (Mimeographed.)
† Does not include family colonies.

treatment. This is followed by a hospital system, with adequate provision for all necessary forms of specialized treatment, and, finally, a mental hygiene clinic to continue follow-up and necessary psychiatric care for the released patient.

MENTAL HOSPITALS

The mainstay of the mental health service of France is the psychiatric hospital in its various forms. The present system is dated from 1838, when each department of France was required by law either to maintain its own psychiatric hospital or to arrange for the treatment of its mentally ill of expansion and modernization. As indicated in Table 1, there are four different types of institutions utilized by the various departments for the great majority of mental patients:

1. *Autonomous psychiatric hospitals.* These institutions, founded centuries ago, through gifts, bequests, and ancient ownership of land are able to operate independently of departmental supervision and are related administratively only to the central national authority. Although no new hospitals have been added in this category, some increase in capacity has been effected since 1953.

2. *Departmental psychiatric hospitals.* Sixty-one departmental hospitals were in operation

in 1957. Eight of these were constructed under the 1953 plan, and two additional ones, not so financed, were placed in service during this period. Since one hospital was closed during this same time, the net increase was nine hospitals, or over 10,000 beds, in the years covered by the construction program.

3. *Psychiatric sections or annexes of general hospitals.* These have increased in capacity since 1953 but do not account for a major share of total capacity.

4. *Private psychiatric hospitals functioning as public institutions.* These hospitals, mostly operated by religious orders, have entered into contractual agreements with several of the departments to furnish necessary psychiatric hospital service. In 1953 eleven departments which had no mental hospitals fulfilled their needs in this way, and a number of other departments used this arrangement to care for patients they were not able to place in their own institutions. Although the increase in capacity of this type of institution was slight, they remain an important source of hospitalization.

FAMILY COLONIES OF THE MENTALLY ILL

At the close of the last century, following principally the experience of Belgium and Scotland, the Department of the Seine created in a village some miles from Paris a system of care for certain types of the mentally ill which permitted them to enjoy nearly normal community living under conditions of considerable liberty. Though legally certified and technically under psychiatric hospital jurisdiction, these patients are put under the care of private individuals living in the community who lodge and feed them in return for a per diem allowance provided by the state.

The "family colony," as it is called, is provided with a centralized medical service which is able to care for patients during periods when temporary hospitalization is required. In addition, visiting nurses keep the patients under surveillance.

A number of advantages are claimed for the system. Important among these is the almost total liberty it allows the patient and the fact that he may have gainful employment within the limits of his ability and under the supervision of the physician.

The therapeutic benefits derived from this regime and the relatively low cost of care have contributed to its apparent success.

In practice, patients are not supposed to work for the family with whom they live but are usually employed by neighboring farmers to help with chores. There is variety, however. One woman patient has for a number of years given private English lessons to children, and another has carried out simple clerical duties in a small office. Although a precise breakdown of the age of these patients is not available, many of them are in their fifties and sixties.

Growth of the colonies has been steady but not spectacular. Some years after the founding of the first colony a second was opened at Ainay-le-Château, about 25 miles from the original one at Dun. At present the two colonies serve about 1800 patients of the Department of the Seine. Although expansion of the colonies is anticipated, none is reported during the period since 1953. Part of the difficulty with the project lies in the fact that it can serve effectively only a rather select group of patients. They must be individuals who do not need a closely supervised therapeutic regime, who are not likely to be dangerous to themselves or others, and who are willing to remain voluntarily in these communities located for the most part several hundred miles from their homes. Because close care and supervision are not possible, one authority felt that they were unsuitable for the aged patient, although perhaps very satisfactory for the aging, physically healthy, chronic cases who are otherwise qualified for such placement.

Neuropsychiatric services of general hospitals.—These services do not receive patients who are legally certified and committed as mentally ill. It is estimated that about 40 per cent of the capacity of these units is devoted to the care of psychotic patients treated in open wards. The remaining capacity is placed in the service of non-psychotic individuals requiring treatment for various neurological disorders and for neurosurgery. Since it would appear that only about 700 or 800 beds in these services are utilized for the less severe mental illnesses, their contribution to the total resources is quite small.

Private clinics.—Similarly, these institutions make only a small contribution to total mental health treatment resources. They serve primarily patients drawn from upper economic groups who prefer not to go to public institutions. Twelve of the 58 clinics or hospitals are permitted to take legally certified patients, but these account for almost half the beds in this category. Since there are somewhat fewer patients (*ca.* 2500) than beds, these institutions do not share the general overcrowding.

DETERMINATION OF THEORETICAL SPACE NORMS

It will be noted in Table 1 that both optimum and maximum bed capacity is given. In arriving at these figures, the actual number of beds as such was ignored, and estimates were made upon the basis of theoretically determined space requirements per patient. When these norms had been determined, they were then applied to floor area available for patient use in existing institutions in order to fix both the optimum and the maximum capacity. These norms were also applied in the building of new hospitals; however, in this case it was insisted that only optimum standards be used.

In arriving at these norms, it was clearly recognized that mental illnesses are not "bed" illnesses. Mental patients do not necessarily live in the same rooms in which they sleep, and consequently they need more floor area than do patients of ordinary medical and surgical hospitals.

The Ministry of Health feels that so-called medical techniques, indispensable though they may be in certain instances, are insufficient in themselves to effect the restoration of the mental patient to the society which has already rejected him. Resocialization of the mentally ill can be fully accomplished only through the organ-ization of the social life of the psychiatric hospital with this objective in view. Therefore, projected mental hospital plans for France must include, in addition to refectories and sleeping places, dayrooms where patients may meet together for recreation and for therapeutic work programs. These must be sufficiently numerous so that reasonably small and intimate patient groups may be formed.

In addition, it was held necessary that certain patients have rooms or cubicles for themselves. Ideally, about 25 per cent of the patients should be provided with this type of accommodation, and 5 per cent was taken to be the absolute minimum.

Applying these theoretical considerations to the space needs of fifty patients, the following estimates were obtained: (*a*) 12 rooms or cubicles of 108 square feet each; (*b*) 38 beds in a ward in groups of 3, 4, or 6, with 8 as an absolute maximum, this ward to cover a surface area of approximately 2450 square feet, or about 65 square feet per patient; (*c*) a dayroom for various purposes (meetings, lectures, occupational therapy, etc.) totaling in area about 2690 square feet, or about 54 square feet per patient; (*d*) a refectory, distinct from the dayroom, with an area of about 540 square feet.

Thus the total area deemed necessary for fifty patients is 7000 square feet, or about 140 square feet each. In providing for minimum standards, the dayroom area was diminished to 32 square feet per patient, and the individual rooms from 108 to 98 square feet for 5 per cent of all patients instead of 25 per cent (France, Ministry of Health, 1953, Part I). New construction is designed according to the optimum norms given above, with the exception that 98 square feet was accepted for the individual rooms because it was felt that at this reduced figure it would be impossible to introduce a second bed into the room and thereby destroy it for its intended purpose. The provision of these rooms for 25 per cent of the patients was retained.

CERTIFICATION AND COMMITMENT

Although certification and commitment procedures are still governed by the provisions of the law of June 30, 1838, long practice and familiarity with the system give it a flexibility that is not immediately apparent. Until 1921 all admissions to mental hospitals were effected only through legal means. However, in that year, the Hôpital Henri-Rousselle in Paris began admitting patients for treatment on a voluntary basis without certification. The practice has grown since then.

nomenon, for such overcrowding has been a chronic condition. It is more than interesting to note that in 1940 more than 110,000 patients were being treated in psychiatric hospitals. This number is greater than the patient population in 1955. Since considerable expansion and modernization had already been undertaken by the later date, it is obvious that great overcrowding was characteristic of the prewar years.

The terrible conditions during World War II were responsible for the great drop

TABLE 2*

RATE OF GROWTH OF PSYCHIATRIC HOSPITAL POPULATION
IN FRANCE, 1946–55

Year	Population of France (in Millions)	Population under Treatment in Psychiatric Hospitals	Rate of Hospitalization per 1000 Population	Admissions (First Admissions, Transfers, and Readmissions)
1946	40.2	65,623	1.63	. . . .
1947	40.7	67,972	1.66	. . . .
1948	41.2	75,315	1.82	. . . .
1949	41.6	80,095	1.92	. . . .
1950	41.9	85,659	2.04	. . . .
1951	42.2	92,496	2.19	. . . .
1952	42.1	97,000	2.30	54,076
1953	42.4	100,141	2.36	57,711
1954	42.7	103,409	2.42	59,896
1955	43.0	105,492	2.45	63,520

* Source: Ministry of Health, "Plan d'équipement sanitaire: lutte contre les maladies mentales," Part II (Paris, 1953), and "Deuxième plan d'équipement, 1958–61: hôpitaux psychiatriques," Part II (Paris, 1956). (Mimeographed.)

Under the legal provisions two kinds of commitments are possible. The first is voluntary in name only and refers to a procedure whereby the family of the patients seeks and obtains the hospitalization for him. The second is involuntary in the sense that the prefect of the department, or, in Paris, the prefect of police, may order the hospitalization of persons thought to be a public menace by reason of mental illness.

OVERCROWDING IN MENTAL HOSPITALS

A comparison of Tables 1 and 2 shows clearly the extent of overcrowding in French mental hospitals. This apparently is not simply a post–World War II phe-

in the number of patients between 1940 and 1946. Deaths from hunger and cold reduced the patient population by thousands. Hunger was not the exclusive lot of the patients. The medical director of one large hospital in Paris tells of fainting from hunger three times in the streets during this time of deprivation. Reduced consumption of alcohol may also have contributed to some extent to the lessening of the patient load during this time. Certainly, the reluctance of families to send mentally ill members to hospitals where conditions were known to be difficult prevented the replacement of patients lost through death and discharge.

An analogous situation occurred during and after World War I. Then depopulation of the mental hospitals could be largely attributed to the influenza epidemic which occurred during the late years of the war. In 1920 there were 64,888 patients under treatment in the mental hospitals. In the ensuing years the population increased as follows:

1921....	66,497	1925....	75,580
1922....	68,912	1926....	77,013
1923....	71,052	1931....	88,427
1924....	73,151	1939....	103,307

CAUSES OF ACCELERATED GROWTH OF
MENTAL HOSPITAL POPULATION

It has been popular in France to attribute the rapid increase in the number of mental patients to increased incidence of alcoholism and to disproportionate representation of the aged in the hospital population. The Ministry of Health feels, however, that neither of these factors is at present responsible for the overcrowding to any great extent. Although alcoholism and psychoses with alcoholism account for a high percentage of admissions (9.44 per cent of all female admissions and 40.93 per cent of male admissions in 1955), only a relatively small percentage of the total number of days of hospitalization can be attributed to this cause (6 per cent in 1954 for both sexes combined) because of the high discharge rate. Since the aged are represented in the hospital population in almost exactly the same percentage as their occurrence in the national population, this source of crowding is also largely discounted. More will be said on this point below.

The factors held mainly responsible for the increase are as follows:

1. *Improvement of case-finding services.* Such services did not exist to any great extent before the war. Early case-finding, which leads to early cure and release, has caused a notable increase in the number of patients under treatment, particularly voluntary and outpatients.

2. *Changes in public attitude.* Greater public understanding of mental illness has resulted in increased acceptance of treatment and to a lessening of prejudice against mental hospitals. This acceptance has been aided by the development of the newer therapies.

3. *Increased scope of treatment.* Demand for psychiatric treatment for mental disturbances such as personality disorders, perversions, etc., which were never before hospitalized in France, has led to a perceptible increase in demand for beds, particularly for patients who exhibit antisocial behavior and whose conditions are often medicolegal in nature.

4. *Changed social conditions.* The difficult living conditions of today often make it impossible for families to retain mentally frail parents in the home. At another time this would have been commonplace.

5. *Growth of French population.* This factor in combination with others listed here quite naturally increases the number of mental patients.

6. *Reduction in mortality rate.* Although the number of patients released as cured or improved during their first year of treatment has increased and the mean duration of stay of these patients has decreased, a dramatic decrease in mortality rate since the war has to a large extent prevented a reduction in total patient population.

The figures used to support the last of the above items are most interesting. A study of the mean duration of stay of patients in eleven psychiatric hospitals showed that the proportion of patients released as cured or improved within a year of admission increased from 34.3 per cent of all admissions in 1934 to 42.5 per cent in 1946, and at the same time the mean duration of stay for these patients decreased from 136 days to 95 days. Furthermore, the percentage of those released cured or improved after a period of *over* a year increased from 8.2 in 1934 to 9.5 in 1946. Similarly, study of another group of psychiatric hospitals showed that, in 1951, 39.8 per cent of patients admitted during that year were released as cured or improved during the same year.

Opposed to these trends toward lessening hospital population is the evident decrease in mortality. In 1934, in the eleven hospitals mentioned above, 36 per cent of the patients present on January 1 plus those admitted during the period died within a year. In 1946 this had been reduced to 16.9 per cent, and by 1951 it was *only 4.3 per cent*. This reduction in mortality rate was, as might be expected, related to an increase in the number of days of hospitalization for those patients who do die in the hospital. This marked reduction in mortality is attributed to progress in general medical therapeutics. The net effect tends to increase the hospital population (France, Ministry of Health, 1953, 1956).

B. Causes of Diminution of Annual Increment in Hospital Population

Inspection of Table 2 shows that the psychiatric hospital population exhibited an annual increment of about 5000 patients for the period 1946–52, but for the period 1952–55 this increase appears to be no more than 3000 per year. This slackening of net increase cannot be attributed to any lessening of morbidity, for it can be seen that admissions actually rose during this period.

Several reasons are advanced by the Ministry of Health to account for the lessening of the annual increase in population in the face of the increased demand for service from the mental hospitals. Principally these are the utilization of new medical therapies and improvement of operating conditions of the mental hospitals. For several years an active program designed to effect this improvement has been under way. These measures have been directed mainly at improving and augmenting the physical equipment of the hospitals and particularly to increasing the number of medical and other personnel. Specifically, with reference to the latter factor the following developments have taken place:

Psychiatrists (médecins-chefs). In 1952 only 194 psychiatrists were employed in all the French mental hospitals. By September, 1956, this number had reached 279. A shortage is still being felt, and psychiatrists are not equally available to all French hospitals.

Interns (internes). While these are apparently training positions, they greatly augment available medical services. It is intended that each medical service shall have at least two of these posts. They have increased in number from 250 in 1952 to about 450 by October, 1956.

Social workers (assistantes sociales). In 1952 only a few hospitals had social workers attached to their staffs. The number is growing, however, and by 1956 most hospitals were able to have at least one worker.

Medical secretaries. By relieving physicians of much clerical and many routine duties, medical secretaries increase the medical effectiveness of the psychiatrist. In 1956 about 70 per cent of the hospitals had medical secretaries.

Nursing personnel. Shortages have been felt in this area. In 1952 there was not more than one nurse to every twenty-five patients. At the end of that year a recruiting campaign was instituted which proved very effective in some hospitals but scarcely altered the situation in others. It is safe to say that a shortage still exists.

Other factors have also served to ameliorate the progressive growth of psychiatric hospital population. These include the introduction of medical techniques (use of electroencephalograms, laboratories, etc.) as well as activity programs for patients (occupational therapy, recreational activities, etc.). Improvements in food and clothing and in living conditions in general have also done much to improve the atmosphere of the hospital and to facilitate the readjustment of the patient.

This program of active treatment and social rehabilitation has been demonstrably effective. In Ville-Evrard, on the outskirts of Paris, the average stay of discharged patients in 1948 was over a year; by 1956 it had been reduced to 4 months. At the beginning of the experimental period the hospital had 550 patients and admitted 100 new patients a year. By 1956 the number of beds had been reduced to 270, but the hospital gave care to 600 new patients a year. Furthermore, the proportion of patients being kept indefinitely in the hospital was reduced from 50 to 7 per cent (World Health Organization, 1957*b*).

C. The Aged Patient

In 1952 the Ministry of Health conducted a study of the aged in psychiatric hospitals in order to examine possibilities of transferring some of them to hospices. The results of this inquiry are presented in Table 3.

From this table it will be noted that during the year under investigation a total of 35,521 patients (not including outpatients and those under age 18) were admitted to French psychiatric hospitals. Of these, 5479 patients were age 65 or older,

to be encouraging. It is considerably less so for the older patients. Nevertheless, when one takes into account the total number of patients leaving the hospital for all reasons during the year of their admission —for improvement in health, transfer to hospice, and death—it becomes apparent that an almost equal proportion of each age group remains in the hospital at the end of the year. The reason for this is, of course, the higher mortality rate of the older patients.

For this reason it is felt that the older

TABLE 3*

PSYCHIATRIC HOSPITAL POPULATION OF FRANCE, BY AGE

	18–65 YEARS			66–75 YEARS			OVER 75 YEARS			TOTAL		
	Male	Female	Total	Male	Female	Total	Male	Female	Total	Male	Female	Total
1. No. of patients admitted in 1951....	15,294	14,748	30,042	1215	2223	3438	604	1437	2041	17,113	18,408	35,521
2. No. admitted and released in same year (1951):												
a) Cured or improved	6,196	6,318	12,514	363	529	892	103	163	266	6,662	7,010	13,672
b) Placed in hospice.	238	171	409	59	51	110	24	48	72	321	270	591
c) Deceased........	384	353	737	204	281	485	207	247	454	795	881	1,676
3. No. patients in treatment, June 1, 1952	33,168	38,654	71,822	2982	6914	9896	898	3266	4164	37,048	48,834	85,882
4. No. of above (3) likely to be placed in hospice............	508	894	1,402	274	840	1114	145	470	615	927	2,204	3,131
5. Deceased during 1951	1,132	1,006	2,138	508	882	1390	420	1055	1475	2,060	2,943	5,003

* Source: Ministry of Health, "Plan d'équipement sanitaire: lutte contre les maladies mentales," Part II (Paris, 1953). (Mimeographed.)

representing 15.3 per cent of the total admissions for the year.

We note further that 41.6 per cent of the patients admitted under the age of 65 are released as cured or improved during the same year. For patients in the 66–75 age group this percentage is still relatively high (i.e., approximately 26 per cent). However, for patients over age 75 the proportion released cured or improved is only 13 per cent of the admissions.

From these figures it is evident that, although the chances of early cure or improvement decrease with age, they are still sufficiently high in the 66–75 age group

age groups do not overcontribute to the swelling of the total mental hospital population. There is, however, other evidence to support this contention.

If the proportion of the aged in the mental hospitals is compared with the proportion of the aged in the total population, remarkable similarity between the two figures is found. Thus the proportion of patients over age 65 in the psychiatric hospitals on June 1, 1952, in relation to the total hospital population over age 18 was established as 16.4 per cent. The same calculation made for the entire population of France for January 1, 1953, yields a percentage of 16.02. While this proportion may vary from institution to institution, it is quite obvious that the proportion of the aged in the mental hospitals is almost identical to their proportion in the total French population.

As the proportion of aged in the total population increases, it appears that the proportion in the mental hospitals keeps pace. In 1954, 17.4 per cent of the adult population of France (not including children under 18 years) was over age 65. The same age group comprised 17.76 per cent of the adult mental hospital population during this year.

1. *Decrease in admission rate for aged.*— It is significant to note, however, that, in spite of this slight increase in the number of aged in the mental hospitals, a noticeable drop is detected during this period in the *admission rates* of the aged. In 1951 we see that 15.3 per cent of the total admissions over 18 years of age were aged 65 or older (Table 3). By 1954 this figure had been reduced to 12.53 per cent. It is felt that this diminution may be directly attributed to the adoption of a more vigorous screening program aimed at denying admission to those aged patients who cannot be aided by psychiatric therapy.

This tendency is to be seen elsewhere, notably in Italy, but what remains as yet unclear is the final disposition of these cases. Certainly, in the broad sense they remain mental health problems and cannot be dismissed as such simply because they do not qualify for hospitalization on purely medical and psychiatric grounds.

2. *Sex differences.*—The close parallel between the proportion of the aged in the national population and the hospital population does not hold if the statistics are analyzed by sex. This may be seen from Table 4.

Thus it is evident that the mental hospitals have a somewhat larger number of aged females and a slightly smaller number of males than would be expected from the proportion of these age groups in the general population. There is some evidence to believe that the proportion of hospitalized females is increasing while the proportion of aged men remains about the same. This phenomenon, however, seems also to apply to the sex ratio for patients between the ages of 18 and 65.

On June 1, 1952, there were 37,048 male patients in the mental hospitals of France and 48,834 female patients. In 1951, however, the number of adult female admissions hardly exceeded male admissions. Thus it is difficult to explain this difference of nearly 11,000 patients on the basis of a sex difference in morbidity.

Nor is the explanation likely to be found in sex differences in responsiveness to treat-

TABLE 4

PERCENTAGE OVER AGE 65 IN ADULT POPULATION AND ADULT MENTAL HOSPITAL POPULATION, FRANCE, BY SEX

	PERCENTAGE OVER 65	
	Women	Men
Adult population of France..	18.6	13.4
Adult mental hospital population....................	20.8	10.5

ment. When we consider the number of patients admitted and released during the same year in relation to total admissions, no important differences between men and women can be found.

The probable explanation lies in the fact of the higher male death rate, particularly in the later years, as can be seen from the figures given in Table 5. Thus it appears that the prolongation of life through improved medical care and more favorable living conditions coupled with the lower female death rate may be the major factors contributing to the overrepresentation of women in the mental hospitals.

3. *Proposals to meet problems of aged patient.*—Any of the plans and proposals now under way to improve the care of the mentally ill in France will benefit all age groups. The most important steps have al-

ready been initiated, and these are directed at alleviating the painful overcrowding which besets so many hospitals.

In recent years it has not been rare for some hospital populations to equal 150–200 per cent of the estimated capacity. Thus the Marchant Hospital at Toulouse, with a maximum capacity of 373 beds, had 854 patients under treatment on June 15, 1955. On the same date the Maison Blanche, a hospital of the Department of the Seine, had 3066 patients for a maximum capacity of 1969 places.

Such crowding means that every available space must be used to accommodate patients. Beds may be placed in refectories,

TABLE 5

MORTALITY RATE OF MENTAL HOSPITAL PATIENTS, FRANCE, BY AGE AND SEX

PATIENTS' AGE GROUP	MORTALITY RATE (PER CENT)	
	Male	Female
18–65	2.5	2.3
65–75	16.7	14.8
Over 75	34.2	17.1

dayrooms, and corridors and on stair landings, while in the wards the space alloted for each bed is an irreducible minimum. France is not unique in this condition, for many parallels can be found in the United States and elsewhere.

To improve this situation, much renovation of physical plant is essential. Modernization of sanitary equipment, heating plant (some hospitals did not have central heating as late as 1958), kitchens, and laundries is being provided for in plans already under way. These improvements are deemed absolutely essential if patients are to receive effective treatment. Only in this way, it is felt, can an adequate mental health service dedicated to cure rather than to custodial care of patients be established.

In making its recommendations, the Ministry of Health utilizes the ratio of

mental hospital beds to total national population set up by the Expert Committee on Mental Health of the World Health Organization (1953). This ratio of 3 beds for each 1000 of the national population means that by 1961 France should have 134,400 beds. This figure is based upon an estimated total population of 44,800,000 for the year 1961. In presenting its argument, the Ministry indicates that in 1953 England and Wales already had a ratio of 3.7 beds per 1000 population and that the ratio in Switzerland had already reached 4 beds per 1000. In the United States during the same year, of 41 states reporting, 9 had fewer beds than required by the WHO ratio, but the remainder ranged up to twice the recommended number, with New York, the most populous state, leading with 6.36 beds per 1000 patients (U.S. Congress, 1957a).

If the estimated need of 134,400 beds is accepted, reference to Table 1 shows that, by 1961, France will still need more than 40,000 additional beds to accommodate adequately its mental hospital population even after the completion of its first plan of construction and modernization. This figure is based upon maximum capacity estimates. In order to give each patient the optimum amount of space, over 62,000 beds would have to be provided in addition to those available at the completion of the first plan.

In comparing the French estimate of its own hospital needs with the actual statistics of other countries, great care must be taken. It will be remembered that the French Ministry of Health draws a clear distinction between the number of patients and the number of beds. Elsewhere this distinction is not commonly made. Thus France is *literally* providing beds for a far larger number of patients than either the optimum or the maximum capacities of her mental hospitals are estimated to have.

It is properly recognized that, urgent as is the need for additional hospital space, the answer to overcrowding is not simply to provide more beds. With this in mind, an entire mental health program is envisioned, one part of which has direct reference to the problem of the aged and others have at least indirect bearing. Briefly, these proposals and recommendations are:

1. Improvement of living conditions in the hospitals to provide an atmosphere in which modern therapeutic methods can be most effective.
2. Organization of a program aimed at preventing alcoholism and for the outpatient care of alcoholics. (That the first part of this campaign at least is under way is evident from the many posters one sees in Paris urging moderation in drink.)
3. The provision of special services for bedfast aged patients either in annexes of the psychiatric hospitals or in other accommodations related to the hospital.
4. The development of mental hygiene consultation services in order to permit the early release of patients to the care of these services.
5. The extension of family colonies and the creation of family placement services not only for convalescing patients but also for certain types of chronic patients. These latter two proposals have been under serious current consideration, but the full realization of the proposals can be effected only after a number of years.

III. The Netherlands

The Netherlands is a small country with a population about one-quarter that of France, yet it would be singularly inappropriate to refer to it as a tiny country. Highly industrialized, its ports are among the busiest in the world. A progressive country, its compact size and predominant urban character, as well as traditional patterns of social organization, have left their imprint upon the nation's developing approach toward its mental health problem. In this its methods are advanced and effective, and many are beyond the experimental stage. This does not mean that planning and implementation are complete but rather that developmental directions are clearly indicated.

A. Patient Population

Tables 6 and 8 give us some idea of the nature and composition of the mental hospital population of the Netherlands. From Table 6 we note that the total number of patients is just over 33,000. Since the estimated national population in December, 1956, was 10,957,040, it is apparent that there are about 3 mental hospital patients for each 1000 persons living in the Netherlands. This, it will be recalled, is the normal ratio for western European countries adopted by the WHO Expert Committee (World Health Organization, 1953).

Unlike France, the total mental hospital population is quite evenly divided between the sexes, with a very slight predominance of male patients. In this ratio the sex composition of the total Dutch population is reasonably well reproduced, although in actual fact there are slightly more females than males in the nation (50.2 per cent females and 49.8 per cent males).

A marked shift in the sex ratio occurs, however, in patients aged 60 and older. Here once again is seen a relatively high proportion of women, with approximately five female patients for every four males. The situation is almost the exact reverse with patients under age 60, among whom there are approximately six men for every five women.

The disparity in numbers between older men and women cannot be attributed to differences in first-admission rates, for in Table 7 it may be seen that the rate for men aged 60 and above is actually greater than that of women. While an almost equal number of male and female patients are admitted annually, this ratio is not maintained consistently over the entire age range. Thus more males are admitted under the age of 40, but in the age group 40–59 years the number of female admissions substantially exceeds that of males.

Table 8 suggests that a partial duplication of the French experience may account for the larger number of female patients in the aged group. Here we see that, even though more older women than men are released from the mental hospitals, this factor is more than compensated for by the higher male death rate in this age group. While this may not be the complete explanation for the preponderance of aged women patients, it is one which readily commends itself and is supported by experience elsewhere.

From Table 7 it can be seen that 16.6 per cent of all first admissions come from the age group 70 years and older. These figures, when compared to the percentage of this age group in the total population, indicate to some extent the overrepresentation of the aged among the hospitalized mentally ill. Thus in December, 1956, only 5.0 per cent of the male population was aged 70 and above, and only 5.6 per cent

of the female population fell within this age group. Both sexes together, aged 70 and older, comprise 5.3 per cent of the population. This age group is, therefore, admitted to Dutch mental hospitals at approximately three times the rate which would be expected from its proportion in the total population. Since not all of the mentally ill reach psychiatric institutions, admission figures and hospital-population statistics are conservative estimates of both the extent of mental illness and the contribution of older age groups to the nation's mental ill health.

B. Certification and Commitment

The great majority of mental patients in the Netherlands enter the hospital volun-

TABLE 6*

MENTAL HOSPITAL POPULATION OF THE NETHERLANDS
BY AGE AND SEX

AGE	MEN		WOMEN		TOTAL	
	No.	Per Cent	No.	Per Cent	No.	Per Cent
Under 60.....	12,740	54.0	10,843	46.0	23,583	100
60 and over...	4,378	45.2	5,315	54.8	9,693	100
All ages.......	17,118	51.4	16,158	48.6	33,276	100

* Source: *Medical Chief Inspection for Mental Health* (The Hague, January 1, 1957).

TABLE 7*

FIRST ADMISSIONS TO MENTAL HOSPITALS IN THE NETHERLANDS
BY AGE AND SEX

AGE GROUP	MEN		WOMEN		TOTAL	
	No.	Per Cent	No.	Per Cent	No.	Per Cent
0–14.............	289	6.4	167	3.9	456	5.2
15–34.............	1709	38.1	1457	34.3	3166	36.2
40–59.............	1251	27.9	1482	34.9	2733	31.3
60–69.............	464	10.3	466	11.0	930	10.6
70 and older.......	776	17.3	678	15.9	1454	16.6
Under 60..........	3249	51.1	3106	48.9	6355	100
60 and older.......	1240	52.0	1144	48.0	2384	100
Total..........	4489	51.4	4250	48.6	8739	100

* Source: *Medical Chief Inspection for Mental Health* (The Hague, January 1, 1957).

tarily for treatment. In Amsterdam, because of its highly effective program of social psychiatric service, which will be described in detail below, the proportion of involuntary or certified patients is approximately 5 per cent of the total admissions (Querido, 1948–49). Elsewhere in the country the proportion is greater, but involuntary admissions do not exceed 25 per cent of total admissions.

Under certain circumstances a patient may be placed under observation for a period not longer than 6 weeks in order to determine the advisability of committing to hospital. This provision is rarely used. It is estimated in Amsterdam that perhaps thirty patients a year are treated in this manner.

Release from the hospital is generally readily obtained and is encouraged as soon as it is thought the patient will be able to adjust to home and community life. Readmission rates consequently tend to be high, accounting for about 20–25 per cent of the total annual admissions.

Dr. A. Querido, professor of social medicine and director of Amsterdam's Central Office for Public Health, explains that hospitalization is presented to the mentally ill patient exactly as it is presented to patients with somatic illnesses requiring extensive hospital treatment. His condition is discussed with him honestly, and the need for hospitalization is thoroughly explained. In some instances the patient is encouraged to go to the hospital so that he can see for himself the kind of place it is. This approach to the patient is but part of a total pattern of social treatment designed to effect the patient's early return to society as a useful and well person. It has drastically reduced the necessity of resorting to compulsion in order to provide treatment for the mentally ill.

C. Admission of Senile Patients

In Amsterdam aged patients who are mentally disturbed are admitted first into a segregated geriatric ward of a general hospital. Here their care and treatment are under the direction of an internist rather than a psychiatrist, and the first objective is to treat any aberrant physical conditions which may present themselves. Experience

TABLE 8*

RELEASE AND MORTALITY RATE OF MENTAL HOSPITALS IN THE NETHERLANDS

AGE	MEN		WOMEN		TOTAL	
	No.	Per Cent	No.	Per Cent	No.	Per Cent
Released during year:						
Under 60.........	2781	50.5	2720	49.5	5501	100
60 and over.......	558	47.1	627	52.9	1185	100
Total released...	3339	49.1	3347	50.1	6686	100
Died during year:						
Under 60.........	241	55.9	190	44.1	431	100
60 and over.......	970	54.1	824	45.9	1794	100
Total deaths....	1211	54.4	1014	45.6	2225	100
Releases plus deaths:						
Under 60.........	3022	50.9	2910	49.1	5932	100
60 and over.......	1528	51.3	1451	48.7	2979	100
Total releases plus deaths.......	4550	51.0	4361	49.0	8911	100

* Source: *Medical Chief Inspection for Mental Health* (The Hague, January 1, 1957).

has shown that the correction of physical dysfunction in these cases frequently results in a remission of mental symptoms.

Only a relatively small percentage of these patients are ultimately sent to the mental hospital, and these are usually seriously disturbed organic cases. Of the remainder, about one-third are able to return home after treatment in the geriatric ward, one-third are sent to nursing homes for care, and about one-third die within 8 months of admission. The usual reluctance of the general hospital in accepting senile cases has largely disappeared, because patients are not deposited in their wards for indefinite periods utilizing space that could more usefully be given to acute cases. Knowledge that the hospital is functioning as part of an integrated plan which enjoins inaction and indeterminate stay has opened general hospital doors to the senile patient.

EARLY DIAGNOSIS AND SOCIAL TREATMENT

Much of what is best in the mental health services in the Netherlands can be illustrated by the operation of the Department of Mental Hygiene in Amsterdam. While this service originated in attempts to meet the demands which pressing medical needs were making upon badly strained resources following World War I, subsequent success of the empirical measures taken then has led to the establishment of a basic, underlying theory which supports the general applicability of the approach (Querido, 1948, 1948–49).

ORIGINS

Early in the 1920's the city of Amsterdam adopted a centralized system of assigning patients to hospital. This action received the full co-operation of the city's medical practitioners, because shortage of hospital beds not only was creating a delay in the treatment of patients but was forcing the physician to expend a considerable portion of his time searching for vacant beds and making necessary arrangements. Although this centralized system applied only to patients who could not pay for full hospitalization, its effects were widespread, since about 90 per cent of all patients needed assistance in the payment of fees.

The centralized system was never a simple clerical operation but was integrated into the newly established Medical and Health Department of the city. Doctors were assigned to this service and were always on duty not only to assist with the requests for hospitalization but also to operate an emergency first-aid service.

From the very beginning a psychiatrist was attached to the service in an advisory capacity. His principal function was to help in the assignment of patients to the city's four hundred psychiatric beds or to mental hospitals elsewhere in the country with which the city maintained contractual arrangements.

Gradually this function extended until it became established as the Department of Mental Hygiene, with a very active role in the community's mental health services. Its principal functions were twofold: (1) assisting and supervising the "socially unfit" (chronic mild psychotics, older mental defectives, and others needing permanent nursing and supervision) to function to the best of their capacity in the community and (2) maintaining a program of preventive care for patients who might otherwise be hospitalized and supervising the post-care of former mental patients.

PSYCHIATRIC FIRST AID

With the consolidation of these two functions and with the necessary increase in psychiatric and social personnel to carry them out adequately, a new and unique service began to develop. This has been called "psychiatric first aid." While not a wholly appropriate term, it does emphasize the most important feature of the service, that is, at the first sign of "mental disturbance" or of "peculiar behavior" the Department of Mental Hygiene is called, and the psychiatrist on duty responds, not simply with advice, but with his presence *at the scene of the incident.*

The latter point is most significant. The patient is not taken to the hospital or observation ward (or, indeed, the police station), where he is examined in private and in isolation by the physician. Rather the psychiatrist sees him where the precipitating episode occurred. The physician is able to see members of the family or other participants in the social crisis almost at the time of its occurrence and in the social and physical setting in which it took place.

After examination the psychiatrist may decide that hospitalization is best for the patient, but experience has shown abundantly that many cases once considered impossible to handle without hospitalization can with appropriate social-psychiatric direction be treated best at home. Careful reception and observation of new patients in the mental hospital or psychiatric ward are standard procedures in many states and countries, but, as Professor Querido points out, the purpose of such procedures is to determine how best the *hospital* can serve the patient. The principle inherent in psychiatric first aid is, however, the determination of the course of treatment best for the patient. Thus, while hospitalization *may* ultimately be chosen as the best alternative for the patient, it is only one of several available methods of treatment.

Social-psychiatric case histories are kept on all patients contacted and treated by the department. Approximately 50,000 of these are in a file which is consulted routinely by the psychiatrist on duty before he responds to a call. Often with this assistance he is able to approach the disturbed individual fully briefed about past episodes and treatment, so that decisions can be made quickly and intelligently.

Favorable past experience with this service has led to its ready acceptance; consequently, emergency calls for service may originate from many sources. The physician may feel the need for consultation and advice concerning his patient, or the family of the disturbed person may call directly in time of need. The police have learned to depend upon the services of the Department of Mental Hygiene and in certain cases are required to seek its aid. Thus the psychiatrist is called in immediately if mental unbalance is suspected, if a sex offense is involved, and, of particular interest to this discussion, in *all cases where the offender is above the age of 70*. This co-operation has the obvious advantage of relieving the police of responsibility for medical decisions. Since the psychiatrist's decision may contraindicate arrest and detention, respect for and understanding of his approach and recommendations by the police are essential.

Years of successful operation of this system has gradually led to the centralization of information about Amsterdam's mentally disturbed. Housing authorities, public assistance workers, as well as the Labor Exchange Office refer cases of suspected mental aberration to the Department of Mental Hygiene for attention in the knowledge that appropriate action will be forthcoming. Psychiatrists in private practice welcome this assistance, because most of them received part of their training in the department and understand its aims and methods.

Concern with the problems of the senile aged consumes a major share of the attention of Amsterdam's mental health services. Although this is only one interest in a program which has far-reaching activities covering such varied problems as emotionally disturbed and mentally defective children, industrial mental hygiene, and even venereal disease, it is an area in which active planning and development are taking place.

The numerical extent of this interest can be gauged by looking at the program of patient home supervision operated by the department. Individuals cared for under this program are persons who would otherwise be institutionalized, but, because of the psychiatric and social support they are receiving, they are able to live with their families or independently. Some of these are patients released from mental hospitals to the home supervisory care; others are cases for whom hospitalization had been requested but not carried out. These patients are not, strictly speaking, under medical treatment, but they do receive regular visits from the psychiatrist or the psychiatric social worker. The family is taught to live together, and social assistance of various sorts is given if indicated.

Amsterdam, a city of close to one million in population (870,000 in 1956), has 3000 of these patients under home supervisory care. When this number is added to the 2500 patients in mental hospitals (1958), a potential hospitalization rate of about 5.5–6 mental patients for each 1000 residents is obtained. This approximates the rate of New York State, which is the highest in the United States. The savings in hospital space and operating costs of this program are made obvious by these figures.

About 20 per cent of the patients under home supervision (about 600) are senile and mentally frail aged people. Some of these are placed in small nursing homes where some form of occupational therapy may be available for them. The great majority of these homes are privately operated, and the Mental Hygiene Department is not entirely satisfied with the quality of care they are able to offer. Certainly, it is felt that these homes are insufficient in number.

1. *Plans for care of aged mental patients.* —Senile psychotic patients are at present crowding Dutch mental hospitals and are compromising the effectiveness of these institutions in treating acute cases in need of intensive therapy. Amsterdam is, therefore, in the process of constructing four nursing homes, each with a capacity of 150 beds, designed to provide a high quality of care suited to the needs of these patients. These will not necessarily increase Amsterdam's total nursing-home bed capacity by the full 600 beds, because some of this capacity will undoubtedly replace a proportion of the existing 2000 beds now in use in the city.

Each of the proposed nursing homes is to be located in a populous central area of the city near a general hospital which will serve the medical needs of the residents. The 150 patients will be housed in five similar units designed to accommodate 30 patients in four rooms, each with a maximum of 8 patients. Every unit will have two adjoining recreation rooms, and a garden is considered as essential for each home. In addition, the homes will have a central room for physical therapy, one for occupational therapy, and a large recreation room where all residents may congregate. Some staff living quarters will be provided, but these will be kept to a minimum.

The staff envisioned for these homes include five fully qualified nurses assisted by thirty less fully trained individuals. In addition, there will be two physical therapists, one occupational therapist, and a physician to attend to the medical needs of residents on a part-time basis. One of the nurses would be in charge of operating the home. In her selection, factors of personality and attitude will be given fully as much consideration as professional qualifications.

Amsterdam is not alone in its planning and construction of nursing homes. Dr. P. Piebenga, chief inspector for mental health for the Netherlands, estimates that there is a national need for about 7500 such beds. Consequently, plans are under way for the construction of 50 homes each with a capacity of 150 beds. Work on this program has barely begun, and an early completion is not anticipated.

2. *A comprehensive program: consultation centers.*—Important though it is, the construction of nursing homes is but one facet of the Amsterdam program. Equally significant is the establishment of specialized consultation centers for old people. One of these centers is already in existence, and a minimum of three more is planned. Full development of the program, however, awaits the construction of the nursing homes, for reasons which will become apparent below.

As indicated in Figure 1, the consultation service is in reality the center about which the entire program revolves. Here is the place toward which the aged in need of help and advice turn when problems arise. Through this center social, medical, and psychiatric assistance is made available, and through its efforts the entire resources available in the city are brought to bear efficiently and expeditiously upon each person's difficulty.

It is interesting to note that in this scheme the mental hospital as such is not mentioned. The reason for this can be inferred from the Dutch position that the great majority of the aged mentally ill should be cared for outside the mental simple) governmental form to advice on personal problems. A major objective of the center is to attract as many of the aged as possible to use its services casually, so that the good rapport thus established will enable the center to come to early assistance as more serious threats to the mental and physical well-being of the individual arise.

Should a mental or emotional crisis occur, arrangements would be made for the individual to enter the observation ward of the general hospital, where proper treat-

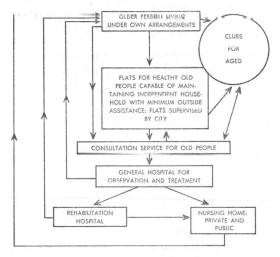

Fig. 1.—The Amsterdam plan for a community-wide approach to the alleviation of mental health problems of the aged.

hospitals, thus freeing these institutions of much of their custodial obligations and allowing them to devote their energies more fully to the treatment of acute psychotic cases. This does not mean that the senile patient is subject to psychiatric neglect but rather that, because of the relatively large numbers of these patients and their peculiar needs, they are better served in specialized settings.

Reference to Figure 1 shows that the aged person receiving consultation services can be assisted through a variety of channels. The consultation center itself may offer valuable support, assistance, and advice. Help may be extended in many ways— from the filling-out of a mysterious (yet ment would be instituted and appropriate disposition of the case be studied. If rehabilitation is indicated, as in the case of stroke, accidental injury, crippling of the joints, etc., the patient may be sent to the rehabilitation hospital for treatment and training. From here he may be able to return to his home and perhaps be maintained there under some supervision, or placement in one of the available nursing homes may be necessary.

The nursing home is indeed a key feature in this system. It is first a guaranty to the various treatment facilities that acceptance of an aged patient does not carry with it the obligation for long-term care, for such care will be undertaken by these institutions. So important are these homes to the functioning of the plan that the setting-up of more centers in Amsterdam is awaiting the completion of the nursing-home building program.

The primary objective of the consultation centers is not, of course, the placing of frail, aged people into various kinds of institutions and homes; rather it is the marshaling of all community resources to prolong the independence of the older person.

3. *Clubs.*—Organized clubs for the aged have an important place in the over-all mental health program. While the activities and functions of the clubs are valuable in and of themselves, the Department of Mental Hygiene finds them extremely useful as a device for early case-finding. As Dr. Querido says, membership "puts a handle" on the older person so that the various services available to the individual can be quickly brought to bear in the event of trouble. Participation in club activities puts the individual in contact with others who naturally become interested in his welfare. Absence from club meetings may be noticed, inquiries can be made, and, if necessary, help can be sent. Changes in health or behavior may become apparent early and corrective measures suggested and encouraged.

In Amsterdam there are about 120–30 clubs for the aged, with a combined membership numbering in the thousands. In general, programs are simple and uncomplicated. Meetings are held several times a week, usually in quarters provided by another organization, often a church. Of course, club membership is considerably larger than actual attendance. The exact number of clubs and their membership is not known, but for all of the Netherlands estimates range between 1000 clubs with a total membership of 50,000 to 1500 clubs with 100,000 members. Dr. R. J. van Zonneveld, of the Gezondheidsorganisatie T.N.O., believes that the actual figures lie somewhere between these two estimates.

D. Personnel

There are in the Netherlands about 350 psychiatrists. Many of these are in private practice, and a great number combine private practice with work in the mental hospitals and various governmental services. Some 40 of the 55 psychiatrists practicing in Amsterdam contribute a portion of their time in order to give psychotherapy to ambulatory patients of the various treatment centers of the city. They are compensated for these services by grants from the municipal Public Health Service to the treatment center. A shortage of psychiatrists exists, and it is estimated that the number in private practice in Amsterdam could be doubled to meet existing needs.

In spite of shortages in numbers, the services of psychiatrists are fairly evenly distributed throughout the country and equally available to all citizens. In Amsterdam in 1955 there were 22 treatment centers at polyclinics located in the city to treat ambulatory patients under the health insurance system. Each of these centers has a psychiatrist attached to its staff.

The city's mental hygiene service usually has 12 psychiatrists attached to it, plus 4 or 5 psychiatrists in training. Twenty-five psychiatric social workers complete the professional staff in this service. Some psychological services are provided through the university. It is felt that the use of psychiatrists in the mental hygiene service is efficient and economical. One psychiatrist working in this service is believed to be "more effective than the whole personnel of a fifty-bed ward" (Querido, 1948).

A national shortage of nurses for psychiatric patients exists and is an important contributing factor to the 12–15 per cent overcrowding that is thought to exist in the nation's mental hospitals. In early 1958 some pavilions in hospitals were standing idle because of the lack of nursing personnel. Easing of this shortage would enable the present hospital capacity to be increased by 1000 patients. In Amsterdam the present nurse-to-patient ratio in psychiatric hospitals is 1 to 7 or 8. Hopes are expressed that this can be reduced to 1 to 3½ or 1 to 4. For purposes of comparison, it is interesting to recall that this ratio in French hospitals in 1952 was approximately 1 to 25.

E. The Mental Hospital Annex

The provision of specialized services for the aged mental patient is not being held in abeyance while awaiting the completion of the national program for nursing homes. An example of what is being done is provided by Rotterdam's mental hospital at Poortugaal. This hospital in recent years was able to acquire a little-used quarantine station located some miles from the main hospital on Rotterdam's busy harbor. Here was established an annex for about 50 male and 50 female patients.

Direction of the annex remains in the hospital's hands, and medical service is provided by a hospital physician who visits the annex daily. The local operations and program are under the direction of a nurse in charge. In spite of the distance, meals are prepared in the kitchen of the main hospital and transported by truck to the annex.

The annex buildings are well situated on the busy harbor and are of low construction. Separate wings are provided for men and women. Both sections contain several large common rooms where patients engage in various forms of occupational therapy. Surrounding the buildings are grounds which may be used by the patients under supervision during summer months.

Products of occupational therapy are sold, and each patient is "paid" in tobacco or similar items for his contribution to the work. For men, in particular, tasks are provided for even the very severely handicapped. For example, one group was engaged in pulling threads from loosely woven scraps of cloth. These threads when wadded together became the waste which engine operators use to wipe their oily machinery. Other more capable men used strands of rope to fabricate chair and stool seats. Women's tasks seem less varied and are largely restricted to handwork.

In all, the annex is bright and clean. The residents give the impression of being well cared for and contented. In this perhaps it typifies the Netherlands approach to the mental health problems of the aged—thorough, imaginative, and therapeutically sound. The Dutch are vigorously aware of the challenge of an aging population. Their attack on its attendant problems has many fronts, and, while their program is still developing, its major objectives are well within sight.

IV. DENMARK

A visitor to the psychiatric wards of Copenhagen's Bispebjerg Hospital is struck by the apparent crisp efficiency of its operation, the absence of locked doors, the sparkling cleanliness, and the relative preponderance of patients who have reached the mature years of life. Crowding, however, is not evident, although Denmark shares this problem with other western European countries. Only later, upon visiting the two wards for senile patients set up in adjacent temporary wooden buildings, does the nature of the problem and the steps taken to achieve partial solution become obvious.

Faced with an increasing number and proportion of long-term patients, the hospital sought relief to pressing space problems by temporarily housing aged, mildly psychotic individuals in these one-story buildings located just a few paces from the entrance to the main psychiatric wards. Although used longer than anticipated, these wards are slated for early replacement by two new nursing homes for senile patients to be constructed within the city of Copenhagen.

These temporary quarters have served their purposes well, not only by releasing space in the main wards for active treatment of acute patients, but also by giving the aged patients a more appropriate therapeutic environment. That they have not fully solved the space problem is indicated by the fact that early in 1958 a waiting list of about twenty-four aged persons existed for places in these two wards. Some patients must wait for as long as 12–18 months for entry. Admission priority is based upon the medical, psychological, and social needs of the case.

The necessity for central convenient location of these segregated nursing homes for aged mental patients has been demonstrated by the Bispebjerg Hospital experience. Dr. Carl Clemmesen, chief of the hospital's Department of Psychiatry, found that during a 1-year period these patients had an average of nine visits from family members or friends every 10 days. At the same time, similar aged patients in another of Copenhagen's institutions some 30 miles from the city itself received practically no visitors. Obviously, the new nursing homes will be built within the city in accessible locations.

A. Mental Health Interest in Denmark

In Denmark all psychiatric hospitals, with only two exceptions, are under the administrative direction of the State Mental Health Service. The exceptions are the hospital operated by the city of Copenhagen for its residents and one private institution. A realization that development of the mental hospital system had come to a standstill during World War II and the years preceding it led in 1952 to the appointment of a commission by the Danish Ministry of Internal Affairs to study the situation and to make the necessary plans for improvement. As a result of the work of this body a reorganization program involving the extension and modernization of the mental hospital system was started in 1953.

The final report of the commission was published in 1956 (Denmark, Ministry of Internal Affairs, 1956; Strömgren, 1958). It is interesting to note that the formation of the commission and the resultant development plans came about in large measure in response to popular demand sparked by considerable public discussion of the needs of the mental hospitals. Realization that new approaches to therapy for mental patients would be compromised, if not denied, by acute lack of space in the psychiatric hospitals led to an emphasis upon elimination of hospital overcrowding as the major focus of the task.

B. The Hospital System and Its Needs

Table 9 gives the average daily number of patients in psychiatric hospitals admin-

TABLE 9*

AVERAGE DAILY NUMBER OF PATIENTS UNDER TREATMENT IN INSTITUTIONS ADMINISTERED BY THE DANISH STATE MENTAL HEALTH SERVICE, APRIL 1, 1950, TO APRIL 1, 1951[†]

	No. of Patients	Rate per 1000 in the Districts Considered[‡]
Mental hospitals.....	5461	1.55
Nursing homes.......	1242	0.35
Family care.........	917	0.26
Total............	7620	2.17

* Source: Ministry of Internal Affairs, *Betænkning afgivet af kommissionen af 29. marts 1952 vedrørende Statens sindssygevæsen* (Copenhagen: Statens Trykningskontor, 1956).

[†] Does not include Copenhagen hospitals.

[‡] Based upon a population of 3,513,170, excluding Copenhagen (November 7, 1950).

istered by the State Mental Health Service for the period April 1, 1950, to April 1, 1951. This figure does not include patients in St. Hans Hospital, which is operated by the city of Copenhagen, or in the private mental hospital alluded to earlier. The former hospital, located outside the city proper, cares for some 2200 patients, while an additional 350 beds are maintained in wards of Copenhagen hospitals. The population of the city is approximately 1,200,-00U (LeMaire, 1956).

The rate of 2.17 patients for 1000 population is based upon a provincial population (excluding Copenhagen) of approximately 3,500,000 inhabitants. This rate was considered by the commission as a clear indication of insufficient hospital space, particularly in view of higher ratios achieved by other countries with which comparisons were made.

At the time of the report Denmark's provincial psychiatric hospital needs were served by seven hospitals varying in size from about 250- to just over 1000-bed capacity. All but two of these, however, had average daily treatment loads during 1950–51 ranging between 829 and 1046 patients. Thus the average provincial Danish hospital was, as shall be seen later, larger than the commission thought for best therapeutic results.

Table 9 also shows that *nursing homes* and *supervised family placement* serve a minor, but still substantial, share of the total number of patients under treatment. The former, since the patients they serve are primarily seniles and mild chronic schizophrenics, are of particular interest to us. Not all hospitals have these homes associated with them, and further extension of these units is contemplated.

C. Increased Demands for Hospital Space

The Danish commission has attempted to account for the increase in demand for mental hospital space in a way similar to that adopted by the French Ministry of Health in their investigations reported earlier in this chapter. It is not surprising that many of the conclusions in the two studies are almost identical.

In the commission's report three related groups of factors were studied. These were: *population factors, morbidity* or *incidence of mental disease,* and *hospital factors.* Recommendations with reference to hospital development grew out of this analysis.

POPULATION FACTORS

Three aspects of population have particularly important bearing upon psychiatric hospitalization trends. The first, of course, is the size and growth trend of the total population; second, the age structure of the population; and, finally, the rural-urban ratio and the nature of the trend toward urbanization. Age structure and rural-urban ratios are important because incidence of mental disease varies with both. Tables 10 and 12, as well as Figure 2, not only show clear-cut age differences in incidence of hospitalization but also indicate age influence upon type of disorder encountered.

We have already noted in Table 9 a hospitalization rate for mental illness in provincial Denmark of 2.17 patients per 1000 population. For various reasons the commission felt that a ratio of 2.50 per 1000 must be accepted as the absolute minimum.

Failure to increase the number of beds between 1940 and 1950, owing to the stringencies of the occupation and the aftermath of war, actually led to a decrease in capacity relative to population during this period. In order to make up this lost ground, 800 new beds would have been required in 1950, and an additional 350 beds would have been necessary to reach the desired proportion of 2.50 per 1000. Taking into account that modernization will require the elimination of some of the existing capacity, it is estimated that 5200 new beds must be provided by 1970 in order to meet and maintain the above standard by that time.

This assumption is based upon the further assumption that the demand for mental hospital beds will remain unchanged. Increasing urbanization in Denmark, however, may lead to a mounting demand for space because city hospitalization rates tend to exceed those of rural areas. In Copenhagen in 1950, for example, there were 3.2 mental patients for every 1000 inhabitants of the city, and similar experience is to be expected in other urban areas of Denmark. In 1950 the urban and rural populations were about equal, but present trends seem to indicate that by 1970 approximately 60 per cent of the population will live in city areas. This development, therefore, should accentuate the demand for hospitalization.

AGING OF THE POPULATION

Another population factor likely to influence the estimates of need for mental hospital space by 1970 is increasing age of the total population which Denmark shares with other western European and North American countries. Table 10 and Figure 2

no less than 35 per cent. At first conjecture it would seem entirely reasonable to account for this rapid shift in age structure of the hospital population by the disproportionate admission of aged people. The commission believes that this may indeed have occurred to some extent in the city of Copenhagen, but it finds little to support the hypothesis in the experience of the state psychiatric hospitals as indicated by the data presented in Table 11. While these

TABLE 10*

HOSPITALIZATION RATES BY AGE FOR PATIENTS UNDER TREATMENT
IN STATE MENTAL HOSPITALS OF DENMARK

AGE	NO. OF PATIENTS PER 1000 INHABITANTS IN				POPULATION ESTIMATED JULY 1, 1954[†]
	1937	1942	1947	1952	
Under 15	0.01	....	....	0.01	....
15–19	0.19	0.22	0.21	0.30	306,400
20–24	0.88	0.72	0.60	0.66	287,000
25–29	1.65	1.36	1.07	0.91	296,700
30–34	2.64	2.12	1.71	1.61	318,800
35–39	3.72	3.26	2.33	2.35	301,700
40–44	4.25	3.78	3.21	2.98	314,500
45–49	4.71	4.48	4.16	3.76	294,900
50–54	4.45	5.07	4.58	5.15	264,200
55–59	4.36	5.11	4.62	5.62	234,800
60–64	4.05	5.09	4.80	5.78	193,400
65–69	3.82	4.27	4.41	5.66	161,700
70–74	3.52	4.25	4.32	5.75	121,600
75–79	3.02	3.89	4.50	6.13	80,500
80 and over	2.10	3.35	3.95	6.69	58,500
Total	2.05	2.13	1.96	2.19	....

* Source: E. Strömgren, "Mental Health Service Planning in Denmark," *Danish Medical Bulletin*, **5** (1958), 1–17, as adapted from Ministry of Internal Affairs, *Betænkning afgivet af kommissionen af 29. marts 1952 vedrørende Statens sindssygevæsen* (Copenhagen: Statens Trykningskontor, 1956), Table 3, p. 14.

† *Annual Epidemiological and Vital Statistics, 1954* (Geneva: World Health Organization. 1957), Table 2.

show clearly not only the influence of age upon rate of hospitalization for mental disorder but also the rapid rise since 1937 in these rates for older people. As the proportion of aged in the population increases, it is inevitable that the trend will be reflected in the mental hospital.

That this has occurred is indicated by the fact that in 1937 approximately 20 per cent of Danish psychiatric hospital patients were 60 years of age or older, but by 1952 this proportion had increased to

figures are from one hospital only, the commission believes that they are typical.

What is believed, therefore, to account for the increased aging of the hospital population is not selective admission but rather a cut in the death rate, particularly among chronic aged patients. Supporting this is the fact that the aged patients at Aarhus are not in the main suffering from the senile psychoses but rather are primarily schizophrenics who have grown old in the hospital. This point is further illustrated by the growing proportion of long-stay patients in all state hospitals. In 1937, patients who had been in the hospital 10 years or more were 35 per cent of the total, but by 1952 this group had increased to 51 per cent.

Inspection of Figure 2 shows not only an increasing rate of hospitalization of aged people since 1937 but also a decreasing rate for younger age groups. Since it is unlikely that there is any decrease in morbidity in the latter group, the explanation lies at least in part in more effective treatment of mental illness in younger people. The commission expresses the suspicion, however, that hospital overcrowding may be responsible in some measure by restricting the number of young admissions.

MORBIDITY

Predictions of future trends in mental illness depends upon a number of factors not the least of which is the influence of therapy upon the course of the various illnesses subsumed under this broad and general term. Intelligent predictions must be carried out, therefore, with substantial knowledge of the incidence of the common types of mental diseases and of the way they are likely to be affected by both cur-

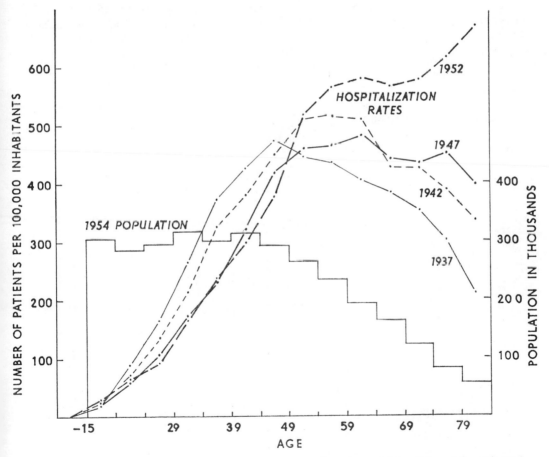

Fig. 2.—Hospitalization rates for patients under treatment in state mental hospitals and the estimated (1954) population of Denmark, by age. (After Erick Strömgren, "Mental Health Service Planning in Denmark," *Danish Medical Bulletin,* **5** [1958], 14, Table 3; and World Health Organization, *Annual Epidemiological and Vital Statistics, 1954* [Geneva: The Organization, 1957], Table 2.)

rent and developing therapeutic methods. For this reason the Danish commission conducted a study of all cases under treatment in one of the country's major mental hospitals. Partial results of this study are presented in Table 12.

TABLE 11*

ADMISSION OF PATIENTS AGED 60 AND OVER TO A DANISH STATE MENTAL HOSPITAL (AARHUS) FOR THE PERIOD 1910–50

Year	All Admissions	Admissions over Age 60	
		No.	Per Cent of All Admissions
1910	104	12	11.5
1915	142	13	9.2
1921	233	30	12.9
1925	221	21	9.5
1930	266	26	9.8
1935	252	28	11.1
1940	359	53	14.8
1945	515	69	13.4
1950	619	52	8.4

* Source: Ministry of Internal Affairs, *Betænkning afgivet af kommissionen af 29. marts 1952 vedrørende Statens sindssygevæsen* (Copenhagen: Statens Trykningskontor, 1956), Table 4B, p. 148.

The major objective of this investigation was to determine what, if any, factors were operating in the case of each patient which might influence his early discharge. These included kind of treatment being received, possibilities for the use of as yet untried therapies, physical condition of the patient as it might affect his response to treatment, age, sex, diagnosis, and other factors.

At first glance perhaps the most surprising finding is the low incidence of senile psychosis in the hospital population (Table 12). This is the less remarkable when it is recognized that the population under study does not include patients assigned to nurs-

TABLE 12*

DISTRIBUTION OF PATIENTS UNDER TREATMENT IN A DANISH STATE MENTAL HOSPITAL (AARHUS) ON JANUARY 28, 1953, ACCORDING TO AGE AND DIAGNOSIS

Age	General Paralysis	Senile	Epilepsy	Other Organic	Schizophrenia	Manic-Depressive	Reactive Psychosis	Neurosis	Psychopathy	Alcoholism	Drug Addiction	Mental Deficiency	Total
10–14							1	1					2
15–19					4	5	2	2				2	15
20–24					14	4	3	2	2			1	26
25–29					19	2	4	1	4			2	35†
30–34			1	2	30	5	4	1	7	2		3	55
35–39			2		49	9	7	2	6	3	3	2	83
40–44			4	5	47	21	10	1	4	2	1	4	99
45–49	2		2	1	65	13	7	3	5	2		4	105‡
50–54	2	1	1	2	67	15	6	2	5	1	1	1	104
55–59	8	5		3	49	20	2	1	2	1	2	1	94
60–64	8	4	1	1	49	21	2					1	87
65–69	2	6		2	22	20						1	53
70–74		14			11	14				1		2	42
75–79		11			3	2							16
80–84		10			3								13
85–89		7											7
90–94					1								1
Total	22	58	11	16	433	151	48	16	36	11	7	24	837
Per cent	2.6	6.9	1.3	1.9	51.7	18.0	5.7	1.9	4.3	1.3	0.8	2.9	100

* Source: Ministry of Internal Affairs, *Betænkning afgivet af kommissionen af 29. marts 1952 vedrørende Statens sindssygevæsen* (Copenhagen, 1956), Table 7, p. 150.

† Includes three forensic examinations.

‡ Includes one forensic examination.

ing homes or to family care. It is assumed that a great proportion of the former group of patients at least would fall within this diagnostic category. The investigators assume, however, that the proportion of seniles is likely to increase in the future because no effective therapy has as yet been found for this group and because the present successful treatment of intercurrent physical diseases serves to increase the length of hospitalization.

It is felt that modern therapeutic procedures will in all probability effectively reduce the number of cases in only two categories: general paralysis and reactive psychoses. Since these two combined comprise only about 8–9 per cent of the hospital patients, not much relief from overcrowding can be expected from this quarter. Danish planners conclude that it is "unreasonable to expect psychiatric therapy, however much it may advance in the next ten years, to decrease the demand for psychiatric hospital beds."

HOSPITAL FACTORS

Mental hospitals, like department stores, offer a service to the public. And, like department stores, their acceptance by the public depends upon a number of factors among which two are prominent: location and quality of service offered. Danish planners attempted to assess the possible influences of both of these factors upon future use of hospital services. Experience had already abundantly shown that admission frequency varies inversely with distance from the hospital; that is, patients more frequently tend to come from regions immediately surrounding the hospital than from more distant areas. Since it was felt that the building of relatively small units, more or less evenly distributed in population centers throughout the country, was the most desirable way to proceed with expansion of the hospital system, consideration had to be given to possible effects this distribution might have on utilization.

Similarly, it was known that crowded conditions with insufficient staff to give prompt treatment and attention affects adversely the hospital's reputation and inevitably its utilization. Since it is impossible to assess accurately the influence of these two factors, it was decided to base the quantitative estimate of hospital needs upon the expected and projected increases in the total Danish population. As a hedge against possible error, however, a flexible building program was adopted, which could be achieved best by operating small units. This plan was favored both for the additional therapeutic values offered and because of its adaptability.

Recalling that the Danish Mental Health Service operates three different types of care (i.e., mental hospital, nursing home, and family care), attention was given to possible future trends in the distribution of patients among these three. From experience in regions in which all three types of care are offered, no major change in the proportion of hospital population vis-à-vis the combined total of the other two forms of care was anticipated.

It was anticipated, nevertheless, that in the future fewer homes would be available for family care and, additionally, that the newer forms of therapy would demand that some patients formerly placed in nursing homes and with families as mild chronic cases could now be treated successfully in the hospital proper. Since these trends could be a matter only of conjecture at best, the ratio of 70 per cent hospital patients and 30 per cent for family and nursing-home placement was retained. However, it was thought most desirable to place the nursing homes close by the controlling hospital so that necessary therapeutic supervision could be easily maintained.

D. Plans for Development

The commission's study led directly to the formulation of broad plans for improvement of the State Mental Health Service. Six of the seven existing mental hospitals were to be thoroughly modernized and the seventh to be converted into a nursing home. Twelve new hospitals and seven new nursing homes were planned. In all, over $50 million are to be spent in carrying out the program—no mean expenditure for a country of only 4,500,000 population.

In arriving at its recommendations, the commission carefully considered three aspects of the mental hospital in relation to the perceived needs of the nation. These were the function of the hospital in relation to the total medical armamentarium, its size, and its placement in the community. Departing from the traditional pattern of large and expanding hospitals, it was decided that the ideal size for new mental hospital units would be from 300 to 350 beds. It was believed that units of this size were large enough to offer well-rounded treatment and would permit the establishment of the several necessary types of wards within its structure.

The small size of the units also made possible the placing of these projected institutions close by existing and anticipated general medical hospitals. The feeling was strong that general medical and psychiatric hospitals should be near each other so that clinical knowledge and experience, as well as the therapeutic facilities, of the two types of institutions could be brought to bear on the patient's needs. This opinion was so generally held that in 1948 the plans to build one mental hospital were scrapped because the site selected was 2 miles from the nearest general hospital. It was said not only that the distance was too great between the site and the general hospital but also that the latter was too small to fulfil the anticipated demands for services.

PSYCHIATRIC HOSPITALS OR PSYCHIATRIC CLINICS AS A PART OF GENERAL HOSPITALS?

The Expert Committee of the World Health Organization referred to earlier discussed the feasibility of limiting future mental-hospital development to clinics or sections of general medical hospitals. While seeing many advantages to this arrangement, they did not feel that these units supplanted the needs for separate psychiatric hospitals. In a similar way the Danish planners faced this problem and arrived at a not-too-dissimilar solution.

The attitude toward general hospital psychiatric wards was very favorable, and experience with this arrangement proved entirely satisfactory. In one provincial general hospital where this arrangement was tried it was discovered that the number of patients treated annually increased in both the psychiatric wards and the medical and surgical wards, although the number of beds remained unchanged after the integration of the formerly separate units. This increase in bed utilization came about because patients hospitalized for somatic reasons received prompt psychiatric care when it was required, and similarly mental patients when necessary were given early and expert treatment for physical disorders. This combined therapy led to early discharge of many patients who otherwise might have occupied beds for needlessly extended periods of time.

Nevertheless, abandonment of psychiatric hospitals or turning them into isolated chronic institutions was rejected for several reasons. Among these is the fact that psychiatric clinic patients and hospital patients are not identical and that considerable need exists for the kind of care that is offered by the mental hospital. It was further feared that clinics might tend to attract too great a proportion of professional staff already in short supply, thereby tending to downgrade psychiatric hospitals to secondary institutions suitable only for chronic and intractable patients.

Taking the entire critical situation into account, it was decided that the first plan must adopt as its primary aim the building of new psychiatric hospitals. In addition, the commission stated that it fully realized the importance of providing all general hospitals with psychiatric assistance and considered it as a matter of course that steps are to be taken to this end. But the commission felt that this important object must, everything considered, be secondary. It should in this connection be noted that when the new psychiatric hospitals are built as neighbors to or as parts of the general hospitals, they will of course serve as psychiatric clinics for the acute cases admitted to these [Denmark, Ministry of Internal Affairs, 1956].

SEPARATE UNITS FOR CHRONIC TREATMENT

Since psychiatric hospitals are designed to give active treatment of various sorts to patients suffering a number of different disorders, it is unwise and uneconomical to occupy large portions of these hospitals with chronic patients for whom only limited treatment is required. Therefore, the commission proposed to build new ward homes to supplement the nursing homes already in existence to care for these patients, most of whom are seniles. These homes are to be built according to hospital standards so that no suggestion of therapeutic neglect is given to either patient or family.

Each home is to be limited to 250 patients, who will live in wards of no more than 24 patients each. Some single rooms will be provided, and no room will be occupied by more than 4 patients. Buildings will all be constructed on one floor, with each ward having direct access to gardens, which are considered as part of the treatment facilities of the home. The buildings will be connected for ease of communication and so that common supervision can be provided to several wards at once (Guttersen, 1956; LeMaire, 1956).

One of the ward homes designed by the city architect of Copenhagen is intended for mentally confused senile patients too ill for placement in a home for the aged yet who should not be placed in a regular mental hospital. A notable feature of this structure is its circular design, which provides a central protected garden area for the patients (LeMaire, 1956).

PLACEMENT OF MENTAL HOSPITALS AND NURSING HOMES

Figure 3 gives the location of Denmark's present and proposed mental hospitals and nursing homes. Denmark's population of about 4,500,000 puts it roughly in the same class as Massachusetts, Indiana, Missouri, and North Carolina. Since it is composed of a peninsula and a number of islands, it is difficult to estimate the effective distances between the various parts of the country; however, some idea of size may be obtained by noting that the straight-line distance between Copenhagen and Aarhus is about 90 miles and that a flight of about 200 miles in any direction would be sufficient to encompass the country. Most such flights would spend a considerable portion of their journey over water.

E. Mental Hospital Staff

MEDICAL STAFF

The ordinary Danish mental hospital has about eight physicians on its staff, although the full complement is often difficult to maintain. A medical superintendent heads the unit, assisted by two senior assistants. The remainder of the medical staff consists of "junior psychiatrists" who stay with the unit for periods of 1–5 years.

Work loads in recent years have placed heavy burdens on the medical staff which could not be effectively lessened by the addition of more junior staff. Since the medical superintendent bore the brunt of much of the work increase, it was decided to increase the number of medical superintendents and thereby decrease the size of units.

NURSING

In the past, Danish nurses served 6 months in a psychiatric hospital in addition to their 3 years of basic training in order to qualify as psychiatric nurses. At present a 4-month training course is offered to them in a psychiatric hospital during their 3 years of basic training.

Fully trained psychiatric nurses form,

however, only a portion of the nursing staff, which is augmented by male and female nurses who have received a year of training in a psychiatric hospital but no other formal nursing training. In male wards in particular the products of the 1-year courses outnumber the fully trained nurses. This situation is not likely to change in the near future, but improvement in teaching of this group can be expected.

OTHER PROFESSIONAL STAFF

Additional specialized personnel is beginning more and more to assume responsibility in the total therapeutic process of the hospital. Among these are occupational therapists, physiotherapists, social workers, and psychologists. While occupational therapy is still largely carried on by nurses, specially trained occupational therapists are being added to the staff. Much occupational therapy is aimed at keeping patients busy in the most advantageous way during their period of hospitalization; however, during recent years this work has been increasingly directed into channels likely to be useful to the patient upon his discharge. Extension of this idea has led to patients being given vocational training opportunities outside the hospital in preparation for release.

Existing and planned Institutions of the State Mental Health Service in Denmark.

	Hospitals		*Nursing homes*
1. Hjørring	10. Augustenborg	1. Aalborg	10. Hvedholm
2. Brønderslev	11. Middelfart	2. Visborggaard	11. Sorø
3. Aalborg	12. Odense	3. Randers	12. Holbæk
4. Viborg	13. Nykøbing Sjælland	4. Viborg	13. Hillerød
5. Aarhus	14. Hillerød	5. Dalstrup	14. Gladsakse
6. Horsens	15. Herlev	6. Raamosegaard	15. Ballerup
7. Kolding	16. Glostrup	7. Aarhus	16. Stege
8. Esbjerg	17. Taarnby	8. Vejle	17. Sakskøbing
9. Vedsted	18. Vordingborg	9. Odense	

In addition, a hospital is planned in the Faroe Islands.

FIG. 3.—Existing and planned institutions of the State Mental Hospital Service in Denmark. (From Erick Strömgren, "Mental Health Service Planning in Denmark," *Danish Medical Bulletin*, **5** [1958], 22.)

In the main, social work has been carried out by nurses who have had some special training for this work. More and more, however, trained social workers are being hired to carry out this function.

An increasing demand for the services of psychologists has also been felt; this profession, however, is in such short supply that most psychologists in the mental hospitals are fully occupied with diagnostic testing. In some child psychiatry units, nevertheless, they take part in therapy, but at present this is rarely the case with adults.

F. The Aged Patient

Danish mental hospitals do not feel that the admission of senile patients now provides them with any special problems. They believe, however, that pressure can develop before many years. It has already been noticed that an appreciable number of residents of homes for the aged and ordinary nursing homes exhibit sufficiently marked signs of confusion and mental aberration to make reasonable their placement in a psychiatric hospital. Should this be done, however, fearful overcrowding of the hospitals would come immediately into being.

Such a course of action is not envisioned, nor does it seem necessary, for most mental disorders of this type can be adequately handled in these non-psychiatric institutional settings. When more acute phases develop characterized by marked confusion, agitation, and delirium, then psychiatric hospitals must be prepared to receive these patients. On this point the commission says:

One might consider the establishment of special wards in the psychiatric hospitals as well as special units within the larger homes for the aged, equipped for the care of more pronounced psychiatric disorders. Psychiatrically trained personnel must in that case be employed and such units should be supervised by fully trained psychiatrists [Denmark, Ministry of Internal Affairs, 1956].

It is obvious from this discussion that Denmark is not following a policy of rigidly separating the mentally ill aged from the more or less normal population in its homes for the aged. With this point in mind, it may be well to examine briefly that portion of Denmark's population which resides in her homes for the aged.

HOMES FOR THE AGED

In 1955, Danish municipalities and community councils were operating a total of 563 homes for the aged. As shown in Table 13, over 14,000 individuals lived in these institutions, and all but 741 of them were state pensioners. Not included in Table 13 are the substantial number of old people (some 4000) who live in homes or institutions supported by private foundations or organizations (Denmark, Ministry of Labor and Social Affairs, 1957a).

Although Denmark had in 1955 accommodation in homes for the aged for about one in twelve of its 200,000 old age pensioners and offered many services designed to enable them to live independently, it was, nevertheless, felt that some expansion would be necessary in the number of homes for the ill aged. It is not suggested that this program be integrated with the system of nursing homes proposed by the Mental Health Service.

G. Mental Deficiency and Age

Mental deficiency is generally considered to be a problem of childhood, and indeed it is common parlance to refer to the mentally deficient of all ages as "children." Inspection of Table 14, which gives the age distribution of the mentally retarded under the care of Denmark's Østifternes Åndssvageanstalt, shows clearly, however, that these individuals are represented in every age group including those above 70. Even though the latter are relatively few in number, they do present a special gerontologic problem.

STATE RESPONSIBILITY FOR CARE

For many years the community has assumed the responsibility for the care of this particular group of mentally handicapped. As is apparent in Table 14, about 50 per cent of these individuals are maintained in institutions, the remainder being placed under supervised extramural care.

In the last column of Table 14 the percentage of each age group being cared for in an institution is given. These percentages are highest between the ages of 3 and 14 and over the age of 50. This suggests that older mentally deficient persons, particularly those above the age of 50, are less likely to be suitable candidates for supervised extramural care than are younger adults.

Responsibility for the mentally deficient in Denmark rests with two separate administrations covering more or less separate geographic areas. Each has approximately one-half of the total number of the mentally retarded under its care. Since the statistics in Table 14 are for only one of these administrative units, it is necessary to double the figures presented in this table in order to estimate the total number of mentally deficient persons under supervision in the country.

The accumulation of patients in the older age groups apparently does not stem from

TABLE 13*

NUMBER OF RESIDENTS IN DANISH HOMES FOR THE AGED BY
AGE AND TYPE OF CONTROL†

| | OWNED BY LOCAL GOVERNMENTS | | | PRIVATELY OWNED | | |
AGE	I Metropolitan Copenhagen	II Provincial Towns	III Rural Communities	II Provincial Towns	III Rural Communities	TOTAL
60–64	52	115	130	1	25	323
65–69	198	435	508	4	53	1,198
70–74	445	1037	1066	10	77	2,635
75–79	593	1659	1666	28	102	4,048
80 and over	1026	2917	2393	45	168	6,549
Total	2314	6163	5763	88	425	14,753

* Source: Ministry of Labor and Social Affairs, *Alderdomshjemmene og deres beboere* (Copenhagen, 1957), Table 10. p. 12.
† Does not include some 4000 residents in homes supported by private foundations and trust funds.

TABLE 14*

MENTALLY DEFICIENT INDIVIDUALS UNDER SUPERVISION OF
ØSTIFTERNES ÅNDSSVAGEANSTALT, DECEMBER 31, 1953

Age (In Years)	Male	Female	Total	No. In-stitutions	Per Cent of Age Group
0– 2	23	28	51	13	25.5
3– 6	186	131	317	191	60.3
7–14	592	410	1002	645	64.4
15–19	496	354	850	471	55.4
20–29	874	721	1595	618	38.7
30–49	1141	1077	2218	1016	45.8
50–69	383	363	746	452	60.6
70 and over	44	46	90	63	70.0
Total	3739	3130	6869	3469	50.5

* Source: Henning Friis, *Personer under Østifternes Åndssvageanstalts forsorg* (Copenhagen, 1955), Table 4, p. 15.

excess admission of older persons, since only 5 per cent of the 6869 patients shown in Table 14 were admitted after the age of 40, and only 109 of the entire group reached 50 years of age before admission. Since a total of 836 individuals were 50 years of age or over at the time of the survey, it is apparent that the majority of older patients were admitted to supervisory care earlier in life. The overcrowding to be expected from the older age groups among the mentally retarded quite apparently results from the aging of the population under supervision rather than from new admissions.

behind Denmark. Thus, in 1955, 12.1 per cent of the Danish national income went for social expenditures and services; Sweden followed with 11.6 per cent; Finland, with 10.5 per cent; Norway, with 9.1 per cent; and Iceland, with 8.9 per cent (Conference of the Ministers of Social Affairs of the Northern Countries, 1957).

Table 15 shows how these countries compared in 1954 in terms of the number of beds available for the treatment of the mentally ill in psychiatric hospitals and clinics. Here we see that Sweden has the highest number of beds per 1000 population of all the northern countries. If we use

TABLE 15*

MENTAL HOSPITALS AND PSYCHIATRIC CLINICS
IN THE NORTHERN COUNTRIES, 1954

	Denmark	Finland	Iceland	Norway	Sweden
1. No. of beds	10,309	9,977†	240‡	6,614	29,425§
2. Beds per 1000 population	2.34	2.35	1.56	1.95	4.07
3. Admissions during year	19,688	10,731	141	2,948	19,091
4. No. of patients treated during year	29,452	20,482	426	11,579	....
5. No. of days treatment (in 1000's)	3,518	3,610	104	2,998	11,814
6. Percentage occupancy	97	99	119	124	‖
7. Population (in 1000's)#	4,405	4,245	154	3,392	7,230

* Source: Conference of the Ministers of Social Affairs of the Northern Countries, Samordnad nordisk statistik rörande social-lagstiftningen (Stockholm, 1957).
† Does not include 3015 beds in municipal wards.
‡ Does not include beds in small unauthorized institutions.
§ Does not include private institutions.
# Estimated from lines 1 and 2 above.
‖ See text for 1955 estimates.

V. SWEDEN

Of the five northern countries—Sweden, Denmark, Finland, Iceland, and Norway—Sweden is the largest in population and area. Her seven and a quarter million people are approximately one-third the combined population of these five countries; within her boundaries lies 36 per cent of the land area (World Health Organization, 1957a).

Along with the other nations in this group, Sweden shares a progressive social outlook. In percentage of national income devoted to social expenditures, which cover outlays for various health services including mental health, she ranks a close second

"percentage occupancy" as the basis for judgment, both Denmark and Finland appear to have just enough beds to cover their immediate needs. On the same grounds, Iceland and Norway evidence considerable overcrowding, reporting 119 and 124 per cent occupancy. While Sweden reports no comparable statistic, overcrowding is felt to exist even though in terms of beds per 1000 population it is considerably over the World Health Organization norm of 3 beds per 1000 and commands an even more impressive lead over most other western European countries (Conference of the Ministers of Social Affairs of the Northern Countries, 1957). We do know from another source, however, that in 1955 the Swedish state mental hospitals reported 117 per cent occupancy, and the mental hospitals of the three largest cities reported 102 per cent occupancy for the year. The high figure for the state mental hospitals was felt to be somewhat exaggerated, since certain reserve beds were not taken into consideration (Sweden, Royal Medical Board, 1957).

A. Mental Hospitals

Public health and sick-care activities in Sweden are either operated or controlled by public authorities. This work is under the general direction of a cabinet minister, while administrative responsibility is vested in the Royal Medical Board, which has direct control of the state mental hospitals, along with numerous other administrative, supervisory, and promotional functions.

The main part of the administration of health and sick care has been delegated to local authorities. The twenty-five county councils and six county boroughs see to it that the sick receive necessary hospital care. The county council districts correspond to the twenty-four counties, one of which is divided into two districts. These districts are indicated in Figure 4 by capital letters and by the six small black circles for the county boroughs. The care of the mentally diseased, however, has been taken over almost completely by the state; only the three largest cities (Stockholm, Gothenburg, and Malmö) have their own independent organization. The various state mental hospital districts are designated in Figure 4 by the numbers *1* through *18* (Sweden, Royal Medical Board, 1957).

In 1954 the mental hospitals of the state and of the three largest cities had a capacity of 25,597 beds, municipal and private hospitals 910 beds, and homes for the mentally diseased 4829 beds (Sweden, Central Bureau of Statistics, 1956). Since 1951 the municipal and private hospitals have diminished in capacity, although the total number of beds in the three combined re-

sources increased during the period 1951–54 by 904 places (see Table 16). Most of this small gain can be attributed to the rise in capacity of the homes for mentally diseased.

In Table 16 a comparison of the number of beds available for the treatment of somatic and mental illnesses is given for the years 1951–54. It is evident from these data that about one-third of Sweden's hospital beds are devoted to the treatment of mental disease and that during these years the slight relative increase in total capacity did nothing to disturb this ratio materially. That this trend has been going for at least a quarter of a century is shown in Figure 5, in which the number of beds for somatic illnesses is compared graphically with the number of beds for mental disease and mental deficiency.

OTHER PSYCHIATRIC BEDS

Table 16 does not include the 747 psychiatric beds in general hospitals and similar establishments which were in use in 1954 (Sweden, Central Bureau of Statistics, 1956). Nor does it include the 1104 beds in Sweden's twenty-one special institutions for the treatment of alcoholics. In 1954 these *Alkoholistanstalterna*, as they are called, admitted 1432 patients, of whom 384, or 27 per cent, were above the age of 50; only 2.7 per cent, however, were 65 or more years old. From the age distribution of admissions for the years 1947–54 it is evident that the vast majority of admissions into these institutions come from the age group 30–64, with the heaviest representation in the years 30–49. Alcoholism is not an evident problem of the aged in Sweden (Sweden, Central Bureau of Statistics, 1956).

HOMES FOR THE AGED

In addition to the above, in 1954 there were 752 beds in "approved wards for the insane" in Sweden's 1357 homes for the aged. These are apparently diminishing in number, for in 1952 and 1953 they averaged 853 beds. This downward trend is somewhat accentuated by lessened use of these wards, for during the same 3-year period percentage occupancy dropped from 97 to 91 (Sweden, Central Bureau of Statistics, 1956). This trend is to be expected in view of Sweden's policy of reserving its old age homes exclusively for relatively well aged individuals who need minimum assistance in day-to-day living. In following this policy, all chronic cases, including mentally ill, are made the responsibility of the Ministry of Health and its various agencies. Arrangements for their treatment must be

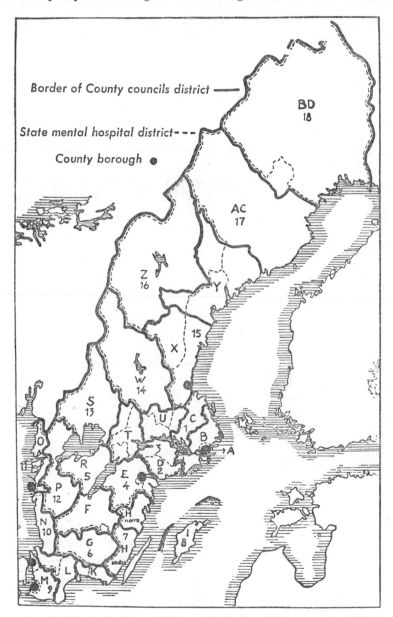

Border of County councils district ———

State mental hospital district - - -

County borough ●

BD
18

AC
17

Z
16

Y

15

X

W
14

S
13

U
C
1

O
T
3
B
A

R
5
D
2

II
E
4

P
12
F

N
10
norra

G
6
7
H

I
8

L
K

M
9

Fig. 4.—Principal districts for health and sick care in Sweden. (After Royal Medical Board, *Allmän Hälso-Och Sjukvård, 1955* [Stockholm: Kungl. Medicinalstyrelsen, 1957], p. 30.)

TABLE 16*

HOSPITALS FOR SOMATIC AND MENTAL ILLNESS IN SWEDEN, 1951–54

(Capacity in Number of Beds)

	No. OF BEDS				INCREASE
	1951	1952	1953	1954	
Hospitals for somatic illnesses..............	58,994	59,906	61,020	61,895	2901
Hospitals for mental illnesses..............	30,432	30,657	30,870	31,336	904
Total hospital beds....................	89,426	90,563	91,890	93,231	3805
Percentage of total devoted to mental illnesses.	34	34	34	34	0

* Source: Central Bureau of Statistics, *Statistisk Årsbok för Sverige*, Vol. 43 (Stockholm, 1956), Table 300, p. 254.

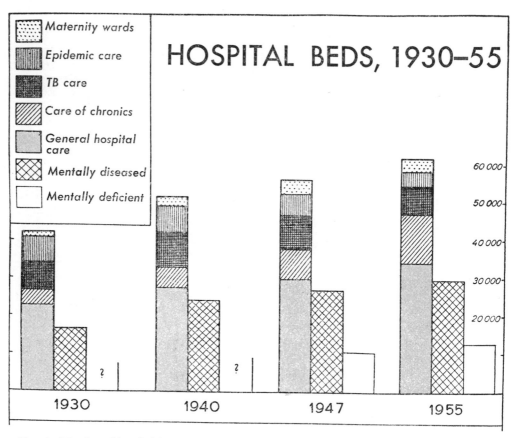

FIG. 5.—Number of hospital beds in Sweden by type of care, 1930–55. (After Royal Medical Board, Sweden, *Allmän Hälso-Och Sjukvård, 1955* [Stockholm: Kungl. Medicinalstyrelsen, 1957], p. 30.)

made outside the community homes for the aged.

While complete separation is difficult to achieve, this policy has allowed the Social Ministry to develop plans and assist in the construction of community homes for the aged which have no suggestion of hospital atmosphere. Most, however, do contain special facilities for the treatment of short-term illness, and a few have rather large sections devoted to the care of the chronically sick, but these are not typical. An example of the latter is Stockholm's splendid new Stadshagsgården, which houses 206 aged persons in a most modern and handsome building. Over half of the capacity of this home is devoted to individuals in need of very close medical and nursing attention.

COSTS

Care of the mentally ill and mentally deficient accounts for a major share of Sweden's expenditures for public health and care of the sick. Of a total of 1119 million kronor ($212.61 million) spent in 1954 on the various health services of the state and local governments, almost 20 per cent went for the care and treatment of the mentally ill. In 1954 this amounted to 217 million kronor ($41.23 million), of which all but 40 million were contributed by the state, the remainder coming from county councils and from towns outside county councils. Between 1951 and 1954 costs of these services rose sharply. In the former year the outlay was 151 million kronor ($28.69 million), indicating an increase of 44 per cent in the space of 4 years. During the same period total spending for health services, which in 1951 was 815 million kronor ($154.85 million), rose by 37 per cent, an increase which, though substantial, was clearly surpassed by the steeper rise in mental health costs. It should be noted that all cost figures given here include both operation and construction expenditures (Sweden, Central Bureau of Statistics, 1956).

B. Census Enumeration of Mental Illness

In each of Sweden's decennial censuses during the period 1860–1930 information concerning the number of blind, deaf-mutes, mentally diseased, and mentally deficient persons was gathered. In these enumerations statistical records of mental hospitals and institutions for the mentally deficient as well as reports of municipal and provincial medical officers were consulted. An additional and most important source of data was the local population records, which for more than 200 years the parish vicars have been required by law to keep. In these records are entered on a household basis each parishioner's name, occupation, birth record or date of entering the parish, marital status with appropriate dates, and date of death or of leaving the parish.

In addition, special records are kept of the blind, deaf-mutes, the insane, and mentally deficient. These records of the mentally ill are based upon the vicar's personal knowledge of the individual plus what other supplementary knowledge he can get from mental hospitals or other institutions to which the parishioner may be sent, from physician's reports, and from the records of other parish vicars. This is no frivolous record, and a great deal of effort in the past has been expended to insure accuracy. Reporting to the vicar of cases of mental illness or deficiency is legally binding upon physicians, certain other officials or administrators, and the heads of families. Similarly, when a patient is considered as fully recovered, the appropriate notation is entered upon his record. One reason for the scrupulousness of this official record is that, according to Swedish law, persons mentally diseased or deficient may not enter into marriage except with special medical sanction (Larsson and Sjögren, 1954).

These parish records have provided valuable material for census enumeration and genetic research alike, although special care and knowledge are required in their use.

They are, however, becoming less and less exact in view of a growing tendency not to report cases of mild psychoses even though admission to hospital for treatment has been effected.

There are several reasons for emphasizing this matter of parish records. It shows, for example, the very special way in which

TABLE 17*

Mental Deficiency and Mental Disease in Sweden According to Domicile, Sex, and Age, December 31, 1930

Group	No. of Persons Affected per 1000 of the Population in the Group			
	Rural Sweden		Whole of Sweden	
	Mental Deficiency	Mental Disease	Mental Deficiency	Mental Disease
Total population....	3.5	4.5	2.9	4.5
Sex:				
Men.....	3.8	4.5	3.2	4.5
Women...	3.2	4.5	2.5	4.6
Age (in Years):				
0–10....	1.0	....	1.0	....
10–15....	3.5	....	3.3	....
15–20....	4.5	0.5	4.0	0.5
20–30....	4.7	3.2	3.7	2.9
30–40....	4.3	6.8	3.2	6.4
40–50....	4.2	8.7	3.1	8.5
50–60....	3.9	9.9	2.9	9.6
60 and over...	2.7	8.6	2.2	8.8

* Source: T. Larsson and T. Sjögren, "A Methodological, Psychiatric, and Statistical Study of a Large Swedish Rural Population," *Acta psychiatrica et neurologica Scandinavica*, Suppl. 89 (1954).

mental illness has been regarded in Sweden and, particularly, the peculiar legal position of mental diseases which have traditionally set them apart from other illnesses. Equally important for our purposes here, it explains how Sweden was able to accomplish a reasonably accurate decennial census enumeration of mental disorders which was more than a recapitulation of hospital records.

In the census of 1930, the last in which an enumeration of mental disorder was made, in addition to consulting parish records, the head of every household was required to answer questions concerning the occurrence of certain defects. It was felt that a higher level of accuracy was obtained in this census than in any of the previous ones in which data on mental health were gathered. This census revealed 27,841 mentally diseased persons, 17,571 mental defectives, and 4349 epileptics (falling sickness) in a population of 6,142,191 persons (Larsson and Sjögren, 1954).

RURAL-URBAN PREVALENCE

In Table 17 some of the results of this census are presented. Considering all age groups, it appears that no difference in prevalence of mental disease exists between rural Sweden and the rates for the country as a whole. This finding is in marked contrast to the usually reported higher urban incidence of hospitalization for mental illnesses. It is a most important finding because it lends substantive support to the hypothesis that higher urban *hospitalization* rates may be associated with those conditions of city life which make it more difficult to tolerate the mentally ill in the home, plus other factors which tend more often to promote hospitalization in cities than in sparsely settled rural areas—nearness to clinics and hospitals, multiple sources of medical attention, etc. Conversely, the identity of the rural prevalence ratio with that of the entire country contraindicates any influence of the supposed differences between urban and rural living pressures in causing mental breakdown.

C. Mental Disorder and Age

Also clearly indicated in Table 17 is the association between prevalence ratio for mental disease and aging. For the groups above age 40 the incidence rate per 1000 is almost twice the national average. It should be noted that the census figures give only the rate for those affected with mental disorder at the time of the enumeration and, therefore, do not include any individuals previously affected and considered cured.

The mental deficiency rates, unlike those for mental diseases, tend to diminish from the thirties onward. Since mental deficiency is most likely to be incurred as a genetic or traumatic arresting of the developmental process, the great majority of cases are to be found in childhood. Since new cases are seldom discovered after adolescence or early adulthood, the lessening in rate during middle age and beyond reflects the excess in mortality of this group. Nevertheless, the age groups beyond 60 are represented, indicating that the aging mental defective cannot be ignored simply because he represents a lesser proportion of the total problem.

The relatively low prevalence ratio of mental retardation reported for the early ages is unquestionably artifactual and results from underreporting in infancy and childhood. The somewhat higher prevalence for rural Sweden as compared with the entire nation may result from selective factors operating in the rural-urban migrations of families with mentally defective members and perhaps, to a small extent, from a slightly greater frequency of consanguineous marriages in isolated rural communities (Larsson and Sjögren, 1954). The latter factor appears to be associated to some extent with mental deficiency in offspring.

D. Mental Hospitalization and Age

The rapid rise in the number and proportion of aged in Sweden's mental hospitals can be illustrated by the experience of St. Lars Mental Hospital at Lund (Hagnell, 1954). As seen in Table 18, in the 70 years from 1883 to 1952 the percentage of patients over the age of 60 increased from 5.4 of a total patient population of 1451 to 20.3 of a population of 4876. This means that beginning in 1883 a twelvefold increase in numbers of this age group occurred in the course of seven decades. Total hospital population increased during this time not much more than threefold. The figures for the last decade are, if anything, an underestimation of this top-heavy age distribution, for, in 1952, 29.3 per cent of the male patients and 26.8 per cent of the female patients were over 60 years of age.

Figure 6 documents the not surprising fact that this increase in aged patients cannot be accounted for by the general rise in the percentage representation of their age group in the general population. The distribution of first admissions over age 60 by diagnosis is given in Table 19. The 246 older patients shown here were among the 1028 patients of all ages admitted to St. Lars during 1951–52. Forty-seven per cent of these patients upon admission were diagnosed as suffering from a senile mental disorder: senile psychosis, 34 per cent; psychosis with arteriosclerosis, 12 per cent; and presenile psychosis, 1 per cent. An additional 26 per cent were diagnosed as af-

TABLE 18*

NUMBER OF PATIENTS IN ST. LARS HOSPITAL, LUND, SWEDEN, FOR THE PERIOD 1883–1952

	PATIENTS		
		Above 60 Years	
DECADE	Total No.	No.	Per Cent
1883–1892.....	1451	79	5.4
1893–1902.....	1172	92	7.8
1903–1912.....	727	70	9.6
1913–1922.....	990	110	11.1
1923–1932.....	2801	262	9.4
1933–1942.....	4124	573	13.8
1943–1952.....	4876	992	20.3

* Source: O. Hagnell, "Psychosis in the Aged, an Increasing Psychiatric Problem," *Nord. Med.*, 51 (1954), 738.

fective psychosis: depressive, 22 per cent, and manic psychosis, 4 per cent. Of the remainder, 15 per cent were classified as schizophrenia and 12 per cent as suffering from other diseases.

An interesting sidelight on this aspect of psychiatric care is the additional fact that at the time of admission two-thirds of these

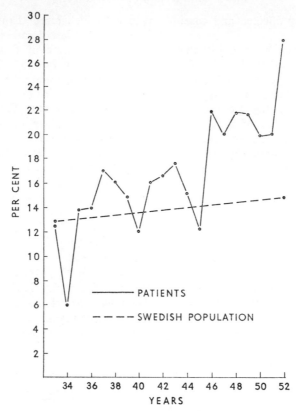

Fig. 6.—Percentage of patients over age 60 of the total number of patients of St. Lars Hospital and the percentage of the total Swedish population over age 60 for the years 1933–52. (After O. Hagnell, "Psychosis in the Aged, an Increasing Psychiatric Problem," *Nord. Med.*, **51** [1954], 738, Fig. 2.)

TABLE 19*

DISTRIBUTION OF AGED PATIENTS ADMITTED TO ST. LARS HOSPITAL,
LUND, SWEDEN, DURING 1951–52 BY AGE AND DIAGNOSIS

Age	Senile Psychosis	Psychosis with Arterio-sclerosis	Depressive Psychosis	Schizophrenia	Other	Total	
						No.	Per Cent
60–64	1	2	26	14	14	57	23
65–69	11	14	20	14	13	72	29
70–74	23	4	6	6	11	50	20
75–79	27	8	2	4	2	43	17.5
80–84	13	2	. . . .	. . . .	1	16	6
85–89	7	. . . .	. . . .	. . . .	. . . .	7	3
90–95	1	. . . .	. . . .	. . . .	. . . .	1	0.5
Total	83	30	54	38	41	246	. . . .
Per cent	34	12	22	15	17	. . . .	100

* Source: O. Hagnell, "Psychosis in the Aged, an Increasing Psychiatric Problem," *Nord. Med.*, **51** (1954), 739.

patients had some complicating somatic disease and that one-half of these were cardiovascular disorders. This fact suggests that the greater the numbers of aged in the mental hospital the greater will be the demands for general medical and surgical services if the challenge of these complicating physical conditions is to be met.

Sjögren (1954), in a survey of 3000 cases treated in the years 1940–51 in the women's department of Gothenburg's Lillhagen Mental Hospital, found that 25 per cent of all first admissions could be attributed to neuropsychiatric geriatric diseases.

Figure 7 furnishes further documentation of the increasing demands made by older people upon the resources of Swedish mental hospitals. In the period 1931–55 the proportion of first admissions over age 60 at *onset of disease* rose from 8.7 to 19.7

per cent for men and from 10.4 to 22.6 per cent for women. While these figures are for the state hospitals and those of the three largest cities, this would comprise the great majority of the first admissions in the country.

Sweden, however, has not felt up to this time that the mental health problems of the aged are uniquely urgent. Dr. Hans Curman, secretary of the Swedish Association for Mental Health, says that, in the past, gerontologic aspects of mental health have not been stressed but that the necessity for such emphasis in the near future is foreseen. Should this emphasis be adopted as a part of the program of the association, its promulgation would be in highly effective hands, for the main work of this group has been the carrying-on of valuable educational work reaching professional and lay groups alike. Particularly important

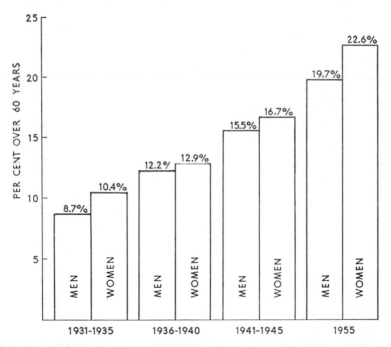

Fig. 7.—Percentage of first admissions to the state mental hospitals and those of the three largest cities of Sweden who were age 60 or older at the time of onset of disease for the period 1931–55. (After T. Larsson and T. Sjögren, "A Methodological, Psychiatric, and Statistical Study of a Large Swedish Rural Population," *Acta psychiat. et neuro. scandinav.*, Suppl. 89 [1954], p. 160, Table 41; and Royal Medical Board, *Public Health and Sick Care in Sweden: Annual Report of the Royal Medical Board, 1955* [Stockholm: Kungl. Medicinalstyrelsen, 1957], p. 140, Table 30.)

has been its work in building up a library of mental health films and promoting them throughout Sweden (Nyblaeus, 1956).

All in all, Sweden's great concern for the welfare of her aged, plus her imagination and willingness to meet the needs of this segment of her people, leads one to predict with confidence that no important aspect of the mental health of her aged subjects will long be neglected.

VI. UNITED KINGDOM[1]

Great Britain is acutely aware of the many problems which a modern, forward-looking nation must solve in order to meet adequately the mental health needs of its citizens. In Britain the satisfaction of these needs lies primarily within the province of the state-operated health services in which mental health interests are but part of a many-sided responsibility. This means that expenditures of both money and energy in the field of mental health must be viewed as part of an integrated effort to maintain the health, both physical and mental, of the entire nation.

Increasingly, the mounting numbers of aged is cause for special attention to be directed toward this segment of the population, but here again, with few exceptions, geriatric problems are not singled out as being uniquely different from those of other age groups. This approach, of course, has several advantages, the most conspicuous of which is the potential diversity of medical skill and facility which can be brought to bear upon mental and physical illness in the aged.

SCOPE

In spite of administrative integration, mental health services remain a distinct sphere of activities and responsibilities within the state health services. That their

[2] Almost without exception the discussion in this section refers to the situation in England and Wales; however, the picture would not be materially changed if it had proved possible to pay more detailed attention to Scotland, Northern Ireland, and the smaller units within the United Kingdom.

share of the burden imposed upon the nation's health resources is very large cannot be denied, but it is difficult to be precise. We do know, however, that, of the 481,710 staffed hospital beds allocated to all departments of the National Health Service (England and Wales)[2] on December 31, 1955, a full 44 per cent were placed at the disposal of the mentally ill and the mentally deficient. One-third (157,870) of all these beds were for the mentally ill alone (Great Britain, Ministry of Health, 1957a).

This is, of course, only one way in which the impact of mental illness on the health services can be pictured. If we consider the number of *different* inpatients treated during the year by mental and other hospitals, it becomes apparent that, because of the much lower turnover of mental patients, they are relatively far fewer than would be anticipated from the number of beds they occupy. One indication of this low turnover may be obtained by comparing the average duration of stay by different types of patients. In 1955 for selected hospital departments these durations (in days) were as follows: general medicine, 22.2; general surgery, 13.7; obstetrics, 12.1; chronic sick, 172.5; mental deficiency, 4123.2; mental illness—LMTA,[3] 552.1; and mental illness—other, 103.9.

These figures show clearly that, apart from the tremendous number of people under treatment for mental illness, the long period of their hospitalization adds a unique dimension to this problem. Since these comprise all but about 2 per cent of those receiving care, it is apparent that the mean duration of stay for the mentally ill patient is about $1\frac{1}{2}$ years (Great Britain, Ministry of Health, 1957a).

COSTS

While the relative costs of mental illness are not readily available, some indication of the importance attached to the improvement and expansion of service in this area

[3] The initials LMTA refer to those patients treated under the Lunacy and Mental Treatment Acts.

may be obtained by noting the share of capital resources available to regional hospital boards which has been allocated to mental and mental deficiency hospitals. For the period 1948–56, of the total capital expenditure of these boards, 23.9 per cent was spent on mental institutions. In 1955–56 it amounted to 34.3 per cent of total capital expenditures. Of the more than $160 million (£58,309,747) allocated for England and Wales during the entire period, more than $23 million (£8,311,586) was spent on mental hospitals and almost $16 million (£5,639,666) on mental deficiency hospitals (Great Britain, Ministry of Health, 1957a).

In general, these capital expenditures have been made for the upgrading and modernization of existing hospitals. Funds have been allocated by the Ministry of Health to improve ward layout and equipment, modernize catering arrangements, and enhance equipment and treatment facilities (Great Britain, Ministry of Health, 1957a).

That a constant effort must be made to better and modify existing hospitals to meet present-day patient loads and therapeutic demands is obvious in view of the great age of most hospitals. The Minister of Health in his report for the year 1955 noted: "Most of the existing mental hospitals were built in the nineteenth century and the last new one was opened as long ago as 1933 so that, though additions have been made to those already in existence, most hospitals reflect the past insistence upon segregation of patients from the community either through their isolated situation or the height of the walls around them" (Great Britain, Ministry of Health, 1956, p. 124).

OVERCROWDING

In view of the above statement it is not surprising that overcrowding exists. At the end of 1956 there were 138,215 patients in *designated mental hospitals,* but by "recognized space standards" there was room for only 121,213 beds. This meant that an average overcrowding of 14 per cent could be found throughout these institutions (Great Britain, Ministry of Health, 1957a).

This figure, however, represents some improvement over previous years. In 1955 overcrowding was estimated to be 14.8 per cent, in 1954 it was 15.6 per cent, and in 1953 it had been 15.7 per cent. Thus, while a fairly substantial space deficiency exists, if present trends continue, considerable relief of this condition may be expected within a reasonable period of time (Great Britain, Ministry of Health, 1955).

Mental health authorities are not being stampeded into an all-out campaign to construct new hospitals to relieve the shortage of space, although some building to this end has been effected. Rather the major objective is the reduction of the number of patients in mental hospitals by exploiting all possibilities for lessening the intake of new patients, shortening the stay of patients in hospital, and developing new methods of treating or caring for patients outside the confines of the traditional mental hospital. As we shall see, efforts in these directions have not been without success, and current developments along these lines in Britain merit close attention.

NURSING SHORTAGE

While a nursing shortage is said to exist, this apparently contributes in only a very small way to the bed deficiency. At the end of 1954 there was an average of one nurse to every 6.6 beds in designated mental hospitals. Although some dissatisfaction was felt with this ratio, lack of staff accounted for the loss of only 765 beds which otherwise might have been in service in mental hospitals. In order to rectify this condition, local recruitment campaigns for nurses were instituted in 1953, with most of the efforts being directed toward the recruitment of staff for mental and mental deficiency hospitals. While immediate results were negligible, it was felt that long-range effects will prove the effort worthwhile (Great Britain, Ministry of Health, 1955).

NUMBER OF MENTAL PATIENTS

Table 20 gives the number of patients under treatment for mental disorder in England and Wales at the end of 1954 and 1956. Only those patients whose hospitalization was effected under the terms of the Lunacy and Mental Treatment Acts, 1890–1930, are included in this table. Since, as we have seen above, more than 97 per cent of the mentally ill hospital patients are cared for under this act, Table 20 represents almost the entire mental hospital population.

versal is not then the result of any slackening in the trend toward increases in the numbers of the mentally ill but must be explained by procedural and therapeutic changes within the hospitals themselves.

VOLUNTARY TREATMENT

Under the Lunacy and Mental Treatment Acts, 1890–1930, patients who make valid written application for treatment in mental hospitals "designated" under the provisions of those acts may be received as voluntary patients. These statutes also

TABLE 20*

NUMBER OF PATIENTS UNDER TREATMENT FOR MENTAL DISORDER
UNDER LUNACY AND MENTAL TREATMENT ACT (ENGLAND
AND WALES), DECEMBER 31, 1954 AND 1956†

	Voluntary	Temporary	Certified	Total
Male:				
1954.........	16,350	100	48,345	64,795
1956.........	19,142	130	44,432	63,704
Female:				
1954.........	21,014	243	66,092	87,349
1956.........	25,927	267	59,582	85,776
Total:				
1954.........	37,364	343	114,437	152,144
1956.........	45,069	397	104,014	149,480

* Source: Ministry of Health, *Report for the Year Ended 31 December 1954* (London: H.M. Stationery Office, 1955) Table A, and Ministry of Health, *Report for the Year Ended 31 December 1956* (London: H.M. Stationery Office, 1957), Table A.

† Does not include mental deficiency.

Perhaps the most significant fact presented in this table is the slight but still perceptible decrease in the total number of patients under treatment at the end of 1956 when compared to the same period in 1954. In 2 years time a drop of 2664 patients was experienced in these hospitals. This fact is the more interesting when viewed in the light of the information contained in Table 21, which shows that during this same period the number of direct admissions increased from 76,650 to 88,542 patients. Thus, even though 11,892 more patients came in in 1956, the total number of patients in the mental hospitals at the end of the year was 2664 less than at the end of 1954. It is obvious that this re-

make provision for the compulsory admission of patients under procedures now known as certification, which "were introduced, from the late eighteenth century onwards, to authorize the detention of patients in institutions, hospitals and private homes" (Great Britain, Royal Commission on the Law Relating to Mental Illness and Mental Deficiency, 1957, par. 255). At the time these laws were first introduced, they were thought of primarily as safeguards to prevent the unwarranted detention of sane persons.

The Royal Commission on the Law Relating to Mental Illness and Mental Deficiency (1957) devoted an important share of its energies to the consideration of the various problems associated with certification. Criticism of this legal procedure was twofold: (1) that certification itself has decidedly ill effects upon both the patient and his relatives and (2) that some individuals who are not of "unsound mind" are improperly detained. While the great bulk of the testimony received was directed at the former, the implications of the latter seem to refer more specifically to the situation of the infirm aged and senile person. The facts behind this criticism are not particularly sinister but relate to the commonly accepted practice of obeying as mandatory a judicial order to admit a patient.

CERTIFICATION OF AGED

With the abandonment of the poor law in 1948, the power to order infirmaries and institutions operating under that law to receive the senile aged was lost. Evidence placed before the Royal Commission led it to report:

As a result, at a time of general shortage of accommodation, greater pressure can now be brought to bear on mental hospitals to admit a patient, provided he is of "unsound mind," than on other hospitals or residential homes. There is some evidence that . . . this has contributed to a tendency to use the compulsory powers contained in the Lunacy Acts to admit to mental hospitals patients who, though mentally ill or infirm, are not necessarily in need of the special facilities of a mental hospital. We are thinking here not only of those patients who might be equally well cared for in a geriatric or chronic sick hospital or in an old person's home, but also of those patients whose mental disturbance is clearly part of a terminal illness before death who might be cared for equally well in a general hospital. It may well be that the mental hospital is the best place for some such patients; but we consider it an abuse of compulsory powers to use them as a form of pressure on one particular type of hospital only to admit patients who could be equally well cared for elsewhere [Great Britain, Royal Commission on the Law Relating to Mental Illness and Mental Deficiency, 1957, par. 259].

In other sections of the report it is emphatically stated that the commission received no evidence to support the allegation that old people not suffering from mental disturbance or deterioration were being admitted to mental hospitals. Nor did the commission support the view that old people should not be sent to mental hospitals, for, in its opinion, the aged could benefit from the skilled attention that could be offered in these institutions. It did, however, think it wrong to admit individuals who could not be helped by hospital treatment or to retain others fit enough to leave, simply because there was nowhere else to go. It was felt, nevertheless, that this was often the case.

TABLE 21*

DIRECT ADMISSIONS TO ALL TYPES OF CARE
FOR MENTAL DISORDER DURING 1954
AND 1956 (ENGLAND AND WALES)†

STATUS	1954		1956	
	No.	Per Cent	No.	Per Cent
Voluntary....	55,220	72.1	69,479	78.5
Temporary....	1,174	1.5	1,504	1.7
Certified......	20,256	26.4	17,559	19.8
Total......	76,650‡	100.0	88,542	100.0

* Source: Ministry of Health, *Report for the Year Ended 31 December 1954* (London: H.M. Stationery Office, 1955), Table D, and Ministry of Health, *Report for the Year Ended 31 December 1956* (London: H.M. Stationery Office, 1957), Table B.

† Does not include mental deficiency.

‡ Including 46,612 first admissions (19,899 males, 26,713 females) representing 13.8 (males, 12.5; females, 15.0) per 10,000 of the population (aged 16 and over) of England and Wales.

The commission recommended that, while compulsory powers should be retained for restricted use when necessary, all hospitals should be free to admit patients informally. Certain procedural changes were recommended which should do much to eliminate the objectionable features of certification. The term itself—"certification"—it hoped would fall into disuse along with all its derogatory connotations.

While it had been argued that different procedures should be applied in the admission of senile patients, the commission did not think it desirable for any one age group of patients or for any one form of illness or deterioration to be dealt with in a special manner. Specifically, the commission felt that the law should not prevent a mentally ill patient from entering the hospital informally (i.e., without being subject to detention), even though he may not be able to make valid application as required by the Lunacy Act. It should be assumed that he is content to enter the hospital for treatment unless he positively objects. Patients who are admitted voluntarily or informally should not be required to sign admission papers or to give formal notice of intention to leave.

TABLE 22*

AVERAGE ANNUAL INCREASE (OR DECREASE) BY STATUS OF PATIENT, 1952–56, INCLUSIVE (ENGLAND AND WALES)

STATUS	AVERAGE ANNUAL INCREASE OR DECREASE		
	Total	Male	Female
Voluntary........	3184	1276	1908
Temporary.......	10	....	10
Certified........	−2912	−1131	−1781

* Source: Ministry of Health, *Report for the Year Ended 31 December 1956* (London: H.M. Stationery Office, 1957), Table A.

RISE IN VOLUNTARY ADMISSIONS

In essence the commission aimed at liberalization of the law and at bringing its provisions in line with modern therapeutic principles and practices. Inspection of Tables 20, 21, and 22 will show that, even under the Lunacy Acts, a very high, and growing, percentage of patients are classified as voluntary. Between 1954 and 1956 the proportion of voluntary patients in England and Wales increased from 25 to 30 per cent of the total under treatment (Table 20). In 1954, 72.1 per cent of all admissions were voluntary, and by 1956 this had increased to 78.5 per cent (Table 21). That this trend is stable is indicated in Table 22, which shows that for the period 1952–56 there was a mean annual in-

crease of 3184 voluntary patients under treatment in England and Wales and a mean annual decrease of 2912 certified patients.

PRIVATE PATIENTS

Most mental patients in England and Wales are cared for under provisions of the National Health Service, but a small percentage of the total are private patients. At the end of 1956, of the 149,480 patients under treatment, 4086 were classified as private patients. While most of the latter were in mental hospitals vested in the Ministry of Health, almost equal numbers were in registered hospitals, and much smaller numbers were distributed in various other kinds of accommodation, such as licensed houses, nursing homes, naval and military hospitals, and private single care (Great Britain, Ministry of Health, 1957a).

MOVEMENT OF PATIENTS

Table 23 gives an analysis of mental-hospital admissions and discharges in England and Wales for 1956. These figures show a drop in the number of patients in residence during the year from 150,856 on January 1 to 149,480 on December 31. While this is a very slight decrease in total number of patients, it assumes considerable significance when viewed as a part of the continued reduction in the number of patients already referred to above.

Table 24 complements Table 23 in that it relates the status of the discharged patients (i.e., whether voluntary, temporary, or certified) to the degree of improvement effected during hospitalization. The cases enumerated in the two tables are the same with the exception that patients discharged from three institutions included in Table 23 are deleted from Table 24. Superficial examination of the latter table might lead one to conclude that chances of recovery are unrelated to status or even that certified patients had a slightly better chance of recovery than voluntary patients, that is,

25.4 per cent recovery for voluntary patients versus 33.3 per cent for certified. Closer inspection of the data, however, reveals the error of this impression, for these percentages refer only to the rate of recovery of discharged voluntary and of certified patients considered as separate groups. When one takes into account all discharged patients during the year, it is apparent that the great majority (86.3 per cent) have voluntary status. Considering the facts, as given above, that voluntary patients comprise 30 per cent of the patients under treatment and 78.5 per cent of all admissions, the favorable position of this group as regards recovery seems obvious. In fact, the number of voluntary patients discharged as *recovered* alone exceeds the entire number of discharged certified patients in 1956.

TABLE 23*

MOVEMENT OF MENTAL PATIENTS: SUMMARY OF ADMISSIONS, DISCHARGES, AND TRANSFERS FROM ONE FORM OF CARE TO ANOTHER AND DEATHS DURING 1956

	Total	Males	Females
Resident on January 1, 1956....	150,856	64,339	86,517
Direct admissions:			
Total.....................	88,542	36,211	52,331
Not previously admitted...	50,405	21,221	29,184
Other....................	38,137	14,990	23,147
Indirect admissions...........	781	384	397
Total...................	240,179	100,934	139,245
Discharged and departed:			
Total.....................	76,481	31,230	45,251
Recovered...............	20,237	7,555	12,682
Relieved................	47,742	19,508	28,234
Not improved............	8,109	3,962	4,147
By operation of law.......	393	205	188
Transferred (under order) to			
other care.................	877	436	441
Died.......................	13,341	5,564	7,777
Remained at December 31, 1956.	149,480	63,704	85,776
Total...................	240,179	100,934	139,245

* Source: Ministry of Health, *Report for the Year Ended 31 December 1956* (London: H.M. Stationery Office, 1957), Table B.

TABLE 24*

ANALYSIS OF DISCHARGES FROM MENTAL HOSPITALS, ENGLAND AND WALES,† BY STATUS AND CONDITION ON DISCHARGE

	No.	Per Cent Recovered	Per Cent Relieved	Per Cent Not Improved	Total
Total...........	71,990	26.4	63.3	10.3	100
Voluntary.......	62,106	25.4	63.8	10.8	100
Temporary......	371	33.1	58.5	8.4	100
Certified........	9,513	33.3	60.0	6.7	100

* Source: Ministry of Health, *Report for the Year Ended 31 December 1956* (London: H.M. Stationery Office, 1957), Table B.
† Excluding Bethlem and Maudsley hospitals and Broadmoor Institution.

A. Geriatric Problems of the Mental Hospital

While recent annual reports of the Ministry of Health do not give a complete age analysis of patients under treatment, some information on age structure is given in specific research reports on single hospital populations or on groups of hospitals. We know, however, from the *Survey of Services Available to the Chronic Sick and Elderly, 1954–1955,* that 30 per cent of the residents under treatment in mental hospitals at the beginning of 1955 were aged 65 or over and that 20 per cent of the new admissions were in this age group (Boucher, 1957).

In 1938, however, only 17.5 per cent of the population of former county and borough mental hospitals was over this age. By 1948 this proportion had risen to 23.9 per cent of the total population. This age group is thus considerably overrepresented in the hospital population, for in 1938 only 8.7 per cent of the total population of England and Wales were older than 65; by 1948 this had risen to 10.8 per cent and reached 11.42 per cent in 1954.

Early in 1952, Cook, Dax, and Maclay (1952) published in the *Lancet* a study of the geriatric problem in mental hospitals. This investigation has more than passing significance because it had appeared earlier, in a somewhat different form, as a report of an *ad hoc* Geriatric Committee to the Royal Medico-psychological Association. The existence of this report indicates the concern of this body with the psychiatric problems associated with the aged mental patient.

These investigators point out that, because of conditions related to World War II, the total mental hospital population fell by 3135 patients between 1938 and 1948. This situation was largely brought about by the loss of hospital beds during this period. In spite of the decrease in the overall number of patients, the age group above 65 years increased by 7674 persons. This resulted in a fall of 10,809 patients under

age 65, which could not be accounted for by lack of suitable patients in this age group. The reason for this relates to the custom, already referred to above, of interpreting certification as a mandatory order to admit patients to hospital. Hospitals were, therefore, forced to turn away voluntary patients in order to take those who were certified, and these tended increasingly to fall in the aged, senile group. It was to prevent exacerbation of this situation that the recommendations of the Royal Commission concerning certification were made (see above).

This was not felt, however, to be the only reason for the rise in the age of the hospital population. Diminished accommodation in special institutions for the aged and less facilities for the care of the aged in the community were also considered contributing factors. It was estimated that in the Southwestern Metropolitan Region (London), with a mental-hospital population of 10,200, 743 (25 per cent) of the 2991 patients over age 65 could be cared for in institutions other than a mental hospital. This number is 7.3 per cent of the mental hospital population of the entire region. In the Southeastern Metropolitan Region in 1948 the proportion of the aged in mental hospitals who could be cared for in geriatric beds or beds for the chronic sick was estimated to be even higher.

In addition to the above, familiar reference is made to altered social conditions which decrease the number of families willing or able to take care of the chronically ill aged in the home. It was felt that many aged mental patients could be discharged if there were a woman relative at home to care for him or her; but in England, as elsewhere in western Europe, this condition is more difficult to meet today than formerly.

DISCHARGE, DEATH, AND AGE

Cook and his associates (1952) followed the history of all the patients over age 65 admitted to six mental hospitals during

1947. The disposition of these cases over a 2-year period is shown in Table 25. The total capacity of the six study hospitals was about 11,500 beds, and the 510 patients over age 65 admitted to them in 1947 represented 7 per cent of all patients in this age group admitted to the mental hospitals of England and Wales in 1947.

period 1952–57. The picture presented by the Cook data and the picture in Table 27 are not conflicting, although the latter shows a higher rate of discharge for aged patients. Whether this is actual or artifactual is difficult to ascertain; however, it is quite possible that it may reflect the shift apparent in Table 26. Here a slight

TABLE 25*

FATE OVER A 2-YEAR PERIOD OF PATIENTS AGED 65 AND OVER
ADMITTED TO SIX MENTAL HOSPITALS, 1947

FATE	MALE		FEMALE		TOTAL	
	No.	Per Cent	No.	Per Cent	No.	Per Cent
Total admissions in 1947........	167	100	343	100	510	100
After 6 weeks:						
Dead..........	45	27	50	14	95	19
Discharged.....	20	12	27	8	47	9
Remaining.....	102	61	266	78	368	72
After 6 months:						
Dead..........	60	36	86	25	146	29
Discharged.....	42	25	118	34	160	31
Remaining.....	65	39	139	41	204	40
After 1 year:						
Dead..........	70	42	101	29	171	33
Discharged.....	52	31	140	41	192	38
Remaining.....	45	27	102	30	147	29
After 2 years:						
Dead..........	80	48	120	35	200	39
Discharged.....	60	36	148	43	208	41
Remaining.....	27	16	75	22	102	20

* Source: L. C. Cook, E. C. Dax, and W. S. Maclay, "The Geriatric Problem in Mental Hospitals," *Lancet*, February 23, 1952, pp. 377–82.

The ratio of men to women admitted to the six hospitals was 1:2.05, while for all admissions in England and Wales in 1947 it was 1:1.68 for patients aged 65 and over. For the first six weeks of hospitalization the male death rate was about twice that of the female rate; thereafter this difference was diminished, but the male rate remained higher. At the end of two years only 20% of this group remained in hospital, and of the remainder one-half had died in hospital and the other half had been discharged. Throughout the period the women maintained a higher rate of discharge and a lower death rate [Cook *et al.*, 1952, pp. 378–79].

In Tables 26 and 27 and in Figure 8 discharge data are given on admissions to English and Welsh mental hospitals for the

but noticeable trend in the direction of the early release of patients can be observed in the triennium 1952–54. As may be seen in this table 72.7 per cent of all patients admitted to designated hospitals during 1952 were released within 12 months. This number was increased by about 2 per cent in 1953 and by an additional 2 per cent in the following year so that in 1954 a total of 76.7 per cent of admissions were released within a year of their entrance into hospital.

If we consider only patients under the age of 65 at the time of admission, early release has remarkably little relationship with age. Figure 8 shows graphically how closely clustered are the four age groups under age 65, while those over age 65 trail behind with scarcely more than half the rate of release at each of the selected intervals. Yet here, too, the percentage is not inconsiderable—indeed, it is surprisingly large—for more than two out of every five patients over the age of 65 admitted during 1953 were released within the year.

Just as the discharge rate was highest during the first 6 months, inspection of Table 25 shows that death rate is also high during this period and in fact is particularly high during the first 6 weeks. Thus, in this series, within 6 weeks after admission to a mental hospital approximately one out of every five patients over the age of 65 died. If we calculate the ratio of deaths expected for the general public to those occurring in this age group within 6 weeks

of admission, we find a ratio of 1:24, which means that for every death expected in the general public twenty-four would be expected in this particular group during this limited time. Thereafter, this ratio improves markedly; from 6 weeks to 6 months it is 1:3.8 and progresses to 1:1.3 for the next 6 months (Cook *et al.*, 1952).

B. Recommendations

1. Short-stay units.—This experience with both death and discharge rates led Cook and his associates to recommend the establishment of short-stay units to receive and retain patients for the period in which the greatest number of deaths and discharges occur. They feel that these units should not be larger than about twenty-five beds and should be attached to the geriatric

TABLE 26*

PATIENTS ADMITTED TO MENTAL HOSPITALS, ENGLAND AND WALES,† DURING
1952, 1953, AND 1954 ANALYZED BY LENGTH OF STAY ON DISCHARGE

YEAR OF ADMISSION	TOTAL NO. OF ADMISSIONS	PERCENTAGE OF YEAR'S ADMISSIONS DISCHARGED WITHIN—							TOTAL NO. OF DISCHARGES (12 MONTHS)
		1 Week	1 Month	2 Months	3 Months	6 Months	9 Months	12 Months	
1952.....	62,258	3.7	20.8	38.9	49.8	65.0	70.1	72.7	45,234
1953.....	67,422	4.0	22.5	41.6	52.5	67.4	72.2	74.8	50,444
1954.....	71,699	4.3	23.8	43.9	54.9	69.3	74.2	76.7	54,979

* Source: Ministry of Health, *Report for the Year Ended 31 December 1956* (London: H.M. Stationery Office, 1957), Table B. Excluding Bethlem and Maudsley hospitals and Broadmoor Institution.

TABLE 27*

PATIENTS DISCHARGED WITHIN 12 MONTHS OF ADMISSION FROM AMONG ADMISSIONS
DURING 1953 TO DESIGNATED MENTAL HOSPITALS, ENGLAND AND WALES†

PROPORTION OF PATIENTS ADMITTED IN 1953 WHO WERE DISCHARGED WITHIN—	AGE					ALL AGES
	Under 16	16–24	25–54	55–64	65 and Over	
2 months of admission..........	37.8	40.6	48.4	42.0	22.9	41.6
3 months of admission..........	49.7	51.2	60.4	53.9	29.8	52.5
6 months of admission..........	72.0	73.0	76.5	68.4	38.7	67.4
12 months of admission..........	82.4	84.0	84.3	75.3	43.8	74.8

* Source: Ministry of Health, *Report for the Year Ended 31 December 1956* (London: H.M. Stationery Office, 1957), Table I.
† Excluding only naval and military hospitals and patients in single care.

section of larger general hospital centers. The optimum period of stay should be from 6 weeks to 6 months, with the mean length of residence of about 3–4 months.

2. *Long-stay units.*—For most of the patients who remain after the expiration of the time limit set on the short-stay units, transfer to larger units (two hundred beds or more) associated with general or psychiatric hospitals would be effected. This type of accommodation would be under the clinical supervision of a psychiatrist but would serve the somewhat confused, amnesic senile person rather than chronically noisy patients or those likely to be disturbing to others. While most patients would be admitted from the short-stay units, some undoubtedly would enter directly.

3. *Temporary measures.*—Because of high costs, the *ad hoc* committee did not believe that its suggestions could be imple-

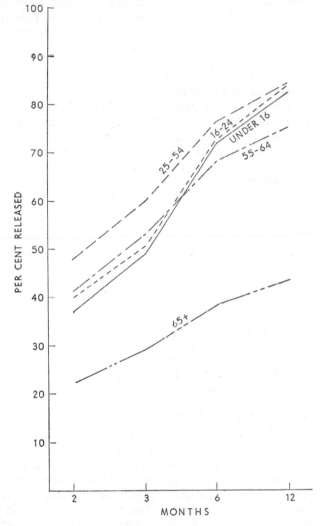

Fig. 8.—Patients discharged within 2, 3, 6, and 12 months of admission to designated mental hospitals in England and Wales in 1953. (After Ministry of Health, *Report for the Year Ended 31 December, 1956*, Part II [London: H.M. Stationery Office, 1957], p. 122, Table I.)

mented immediately and, in view of this, offered alternative suggestions. Considering the urgency of the situation the committee felt that as a temporary measure the mounting demands for mental-hospital service from the aged should be met by putting the maximum number of beds possible in old people's wards even though it caused overcrowding. This step was clearly recognized as retrogressive, but the gravity of the situation was felt to be ample justification. The committee points out that such a move was economical; it costs less to treat sixty patients in two rather than in three wards. If forced to overcrowd, the senile patient was the least likely to be affected; they are more resistant to common infectious illnesses, and their narrower interests and restricted movements made them less demanding of space.

A similar attitude of resignation was expressed by Clark (1956) in an article describing, among other functions of the mental hospital, the place of geriatrics in English psychiatric institutions. The mental hospital, he said, functions as a geriatric hospital largely by default of other agencies. The confused and ill aged are brought to the mental hospital, "always unwillingly," where after a bit they settle down. In not too long a time a fair proportion die, while some recover but have no place to go. He continues:

Our society, it has been said, has decided that a mental hospital is a fit place for old people to die in. The staff can only comply, and do their best to meet this demand by providing pleasant wards, good food, kindliness, and good physical nursing to ease the last days of these unfortunate people. But the work absorbs a great deal of their limited time [p. 1005].

This expression immediately drew a sharp attack from J. A. R. Bickford, medical superintendent of De la Pole Hospital, York, who believes that aged patients should be treated in a well-organized geriatric unit but who recognizes that these are in short supply. He asks why senile patients should be sent to mental hospitals rather than to general hospitals? Why is it more improper for a general hospital to be overcrowded than a mental hospital? His answer goes immediately to the practice of certification as applied to old people, and his criticism is the same as that of the Royal Commission reported above. Old people, he says, can be ordered to the mental hospital, and thus overcrowding is legalized. "For some strange reason the walls of a mental hospital are thought to be capable of infinite expansion, and the agreement on this between the community and its elected and paid representatives in local and central government is universal" (Bickford, 1956).

C. The Chronic Mental Patient

Bickford's opinion was an informed one based not only upon his hospital experience but upon specific study of the problem (Bickford, 1954). Of some 450 men at De la Pole Hospital, other than those on admission and convalescence wards, 384 had been in the hospital for periods shown in Table 28.

TABLE 28

NUMBER OF YEARS' STAY IN
HOSPITAL FOR 384 MEN

Years	No.
2– 4	63
5– 9	87
10–14	46
15–19	63
20–24	37
25–29	38
30–39	29
Over 40	21
Total	384

Why, he asks, are the results so bad? Basically, he believes the reasons to be twofold: psychiatrists are spread too thinly in the chronic wards and not enough money is allocated for mental hospitals. The doctor in the chronic wards will have hundreds rather than tens of patients. In 1954 the cost per week for a mental patient was likely to be not more than $14 (£5), while for the general patient it would usually be $28 (£10) per week and more in sanitoriums and maternity hospitals. Of this sum, $5.60 (£2) would have been set aside for medical treatment for general hospital patients but only $0.56 (4 shillings) for mental hospital patients.

Bickford is also critical of the physical conditions and standard of living of patients in chronic wards—lack of privacy, limited space, inadequate activity programs, and other conditions all too commonly associated with mental hospitals in all countries. These conditions are contrasted with those which greet the newly admitted patient. These receive the best of treatment and are assigned to modern, well-fitted, comfortable wards. However, if the patient is not cured in 6 months, he is still treated with kindness, "but skill and energy are tacitly withdrawn. He becomes a chronic patient."

In bleak chronic wards psychiatric attention will be relatively less frequent. Doctors will see 30 patients on admission wards for half their time and perhaps 200 chronic cases for the other half. Or perhaps one physician will spend full time looking after 30 patients in admission wards, while a colleague will attend 400–500 chronic patients. Bickford does not believe that new admissions need the disproportionate amount of time given them, largely at the expense of chronic cases. This is naturally a controversial point, but Bickford accepted his own challenge in an unambiguous way by introducing marked changes in the therapeutic regimen in his own hospital.

Behind these changes and the urgency in making them is the belief that remission can be expected in most chronic mental disorders as a part of the natural history of the disease. Included in these expectations are both the schizophrenic and the senile patient. Remission in the case of the former may take anywhere from 10 to 50 years, but Bickford has faith that it will occur; therefore, he believes that the patient must be taught in the hospital to live with his strange delusions and experiences in preparation for his return to society. While these may persist, the patient may learn to behave in such a way that he need not be kept hospitalized. Even the restless, violent senile rarely remains this way for more than several weeks. Bickford believes that he, too, can be returned to the community sometime after this initial phase.

Although notable efforts are made to increase the livability of the ordinary chronic ward, these are too often shallow and without deeply felt therapeutic objectives. Occupational therapy, social clubs, frequent entertainment, games to watch and play, excursions, and instruction in painting and sculpture, while basically good, are in danger of becoming ends in themselves. Bickford believes that this is particularly true of occupational therapy, which can under such circumstances become, from the point of view of treatment, "quite meaningless and absolutely useless."

All hospitalization must aim at fitting patients for discharge, never allowing them to adopt the attitude that they may remain indefinitely. Chronic patients, too, must be fitted to return to home and work. To achieve this end, an active and imaginative program for chronic patients was set up at the De la Pole Hospital characterized by meaningful group activity. Instead of assigning the majority of patients to useless cleaning duties, they were cleared from the wards morning and afternoon to take part in planned therapeutic activities, leaving the actual ward work to a small crew of co-operative patients to whom this work offered a realistic challenge. Non-co-operative and hallucinated patients also went to work in groups and were given definite objectives. Week-end visits home were instituted in order to give the patient (and his relatives) experience in living outside the hospital. Within 6 months every patient in these chronic wards was receiving some active treatment every day.

WIDESPREAD USE OF NEW APPROACH

The De la Pole Hospital experience is not an isolated one. In 1955 the Ministry of Health reported that, in addition to the development of new physical and chemical therapies, as well as psychotherapy, there had been a revival of interest in social re-education which had been "equally important for the long-stay patient." This approach has been incorporated into the concept of the *therapeutic community,* and this in turn has become the goal toward which many hospitals are oriented. More and more hospitals are adopting "techniques of habit training as the first step in the rehabilitation of the more chronic and deteriorated patients (Great Britain, Ministry of Health, 1956).

UNLOCKING THE WARDS

Creation of the therapeutic community is hampered by the locked wards and security precautions traditionally associated with mental hospitals. The unlocking of these doors is a major convulsion through which the hospital must go to achieve fully the permissive atmosphere sought in hospitals aspiring towards this goal.

"On June 5, 1956, I opened the last closed ward at Hatton, so that now any of our 1,380 patients is free to walk out of the place if he wants to do so," writes Medical Superintendent E. S. Stern (1957) of the Central Mental Hospital, in Hatton. In this hospital there is no main gate to be locked and no porter there to guard it if there were.

Hatton is not a special hospital, for it shares the problems faced by ordinary British mental institutions—overcrowding, a shortage of nurses but fortunately a low staff turnover, and an unselected group of patients. The process of opening wards was a gradual one carried out largely on the initiative of the superintendent. It depended upon educating the staff and securing their co-operation. No wards were opened until the staff was ready to accept the idea. As the program gained momentum, it gained supporters, and instances arose in which the ward staff requested the unlocking of doors with no prompting from above.

The most difficult wards to open were those for senile and demented patients who were likely to wander off and get lost. The only serious accident, in the early phases of this experiment, was with one of these patients. Liberation of the wards is bought at the expense of greater attention paid and interest given to the patient. With greater freedom, patients leave the wards to spend time in more congenial places and thus indirectly relieve to some extent overcrowding.

Hatton is not unique; other hospitals are completely open, and many have only a few locked wards. While there are problems associated with this liberal practice, escape from hospital is not a major difficulty. Many hospitals report that patients seem to have less desire to escape when free to do so.

D. Future Hospital Planning

The influence of these new concepts of treatment and of mental hospital function is being felt in the planning for future British mental health needs. If patients can be rehabilitated and if the community is willing to accept mental patients as it does other sufferers, then the segregation of the mental hospital from the community is unnecessary and undesirable. The British people seem to accept this generalization as an abstract principle, but there is some hesitancy when it is applied or perhaps toward the way in which it is applied. In Bristol, for example, plans to use a large residential dwelling as a hostel for selected adult mental defectives had to be abandoned because of protests of residents of the neighboring area who feared that potential child molesters would be included in the patient group. This objection was not considered as a final deterrent to the project, but it led to exploration of new locations.

Nevertheless, current thinking rejects the isolation and segregation which have characterized the treatment of the mentally ill in the past. Most mental hospitals in Britain were built during the last century and reflect in their isolated locations or their fortress-like structure the then prevailing views toward mental illness. These attitudes cut both staff and patients from the community and, in and of themselves, were damaging both to the patient's well-being and to the quality of professional care he received. The large tracts of land once thought indispensable are no longer considered necessary. This change should enable new hospitals as they come into being to be placed side by side with general hospitals in urban areas (Great Britain, Ministry of Health, 1956).

But the building of new hospitals does not loom as the central core of Britain's mental health planning. Where building is needed, more often it will take the form of short-stay psychiatric units of general hospitals. Provision of special geriatric units should lessen the need to expand facilities for the care of chronic patients in mental hospitals. The possibilities for discharging aged patients after treatment will be explored and expanded. The most promising development, however, is the way in which the mental patient is being reached with treatment and service in the community itself.

E. Community Services

Recognizing that successful treatment of the mental patient involves co-operation among the hospital, the family, and the community, in a growing number of instances community health services and mental hospitals have integrated their efforts in treating the mental patient. At Oldham, for example, a city of over 120,000 population in the industrial Midlands, all patients with mental disorder are seen by a psychiatrist acting for both the regional hospital board and the local health authority before or instead of being sent to mental hospitals. Day hospital services and a mental health team, including the services of a clinical psychologist, are available. At Nottingham the superintendent of Mapperley Mental Hospital supervises the mental health serv-

ice of the local health authority and is helped by a team of social workers drawn from both the staff of the hospital and the local health authority. Instances abound in which the mental hospital staff and the local authority co-operate in the treatment of individual patients.

F. Treatment

Mental patients may be divided into three types: those who may be treated outside the hospital, those who need only a short period of hospitalization, and, finally, those who may be expected to remain in hospital for a long period of time. The well-organized mental health service attempts to satisfy the therapeutic demands of all three groups with appropriate procedures and facilities. To hospitalize patients who could be treated as outpatients or to retain patients in hospital beyond the requirements of their treatment not only may be uneconomical but also may be detrimental to the patient. In England and Wales the attempt is being made to apply imaginatively this conception of treatment not only to relieve pressure on overcrowded institutions but also to secure solid therapeutic advantages for the patients.

1. *Outpatient treatment.*—The outpatient method of dealing with mental patients is becoming increasingly popular: attendance as psychiatric outpatient clinics rose from 523,218 in 1950 to 714,014 in 1955, increasing the following year to 762,072. These measures not only have served to reduce admission rates but, in addition, have hastened the return of the hospitalized patient to the community—not to speak of the advantages to the patient, who is spared the difficult transitions into and out of hospital (Great Britain, Ministry of Health, 1956, 1957*b*).

2. *Domiciliary visits.*—In view of our earlier discussion of work being carried out in the Netherlands, it is interesting to read the following in the 1956 annual report of the Chief Medical Officer for England and Wales:

The value of domiciliary visits has been much extolled in recent years especially as a result of the work of Dr. Querido in Amsterdam. Clearly it is an advantage for the psychiatrist to see the patient in his own surroundings, and to be able to assess for himself what is happening in the home; this may well indicate a line of treatment which would not be apparent in the consulting room [Great Britain, Ministry of Health, 1957*b*].

This accolade does not presage the uncritical adoption of the Amsterdam plan, but it does indicate a willingness to examine the relative merits and disadvantages of the system. Reservation concerning costs in money and time is expressed, but a wait-and-see attitude is adopted. Meanwhile, the number of domiciliary visits or house calls increases—from 5597 in 1950 and 11,229 in 1955 to a 1956 total of 18,416 (Great Britain, Ministry of Health, 1956, 1957*b*).

G. Day Hospitals

Some patients, if occupied and supervised during the day, can remain in the home during the evening and at night; others may be able to work or look after themselves during the day but need care and attention at night. Neither group needs full-time hospital care, and it is for them that so-called day hospitals and night hospitals have been developed. Experience with these has been favorable, and in 1956 there were seventeen in England and Wales, with more being planned (Great Britain, Ministry of Health, 1956).

Two factors of importance must be considered in the establishment of day hospitals: location and administrative control. Ideally, the day hospital should be placed where it can be easily reached by the patients it serves; thus it must be in a central urban area serving a catchment district which, according to British thinking, should not extend more than 5 miles in any direction from the hospital. The second point, somewhat controversial, is whether the day hospital should be associated with a mental hospital or should be entirely separate.

The advantage of the former in terms of making available trained staff and facilities is obvious, but the forbidding association with the mental institution makes acceptance of this form of treatment more difficult for some patients.

For the simple geriatric day hospital independent operation is seen as having no special disadvantage; however, more comprehensive centers require more specialized staff and facilities. If the independent unit attempts to meet all these needs, its character changes, and its costs of operation mount. It is felt, however, that the value of the day hospital to both the community and the mental health service is dependent upon the simplicity of its function and that these functions can be met by four different types of services: *day centers, day hospitals, geriatric day hospitals,* and *comprehensive day hospitals.* All these are small; the number of patients, it seems, should not number more than thirty.

1. *Day centers.*—These centers would be concerned primarily with aftercare of mental hospital patients and with their rehabilitation. Individual and group psychotherapy might be offered; social activities would be fostered through organized social clubs and other activities. Although its main function is to ease the transition from inpatient life to normal community living, some neurotics might be treated at the center. The Bromley Day Hospital has experimented with the introduction of a very few disturbed patients with the convalescing group. Since active physical treatment is not offered by these centers, this service to acutely disturbed patients must be approached cautiously.

2. *Day hospitals.*—This type of unit, attached to a mental hospital, would serve primarily early-treatment patients with good prognosis, although it would also be used to receive patients from the mental hospital who were not quite suitable for the day center or outpatient care. Active treatment would be offered, and for this reason close attachment to a bedded hospital is essential. This arrangement also enables

quick transition to inpatient care should this become necessary.

3. *Geriatric day hospitals.*—Much seemingly irreversible mental disorder in the aged results from the deterioration of personal habits and living standards induced by physical frailty. Failure to receive some attention and help during the day leads to such a stage of delapidation that mental hospitalization, always against their will, is forced upon the ailing aged person as a last resort. Once in hospital, the family, if there is one, rarely seems able to accept the patient back. To meet the needs of such patients, the Cowley Road Day Hospital, Oxford, was established (Cosin, 1954).

This unit, a proved success, was set up as a part of a general geriatric service rather than being made an exclusive psychiatric responsibility. Each patient, however, receives attention for both his physical and his mental needs. To insure this, he is given what Dr. Cosin calls a "dynamic quadruple assessment"; this includes a thorough evaluation of his physical pathology, his psychological and sociological condition, and his residual physical disabilities. This is done in order to achieve as complete rehabilitation as is possible.

As would be expected, the Oxford unit has close hospital links for both inpatient and outpatient treatment. It is under full medical control, with consultant psychiatric advice. It aims to maintain the patient in the community, living independently. To achieve this, the day hospital shares responsibility for the patient with the family and the community on the well-founded assumption that frail aged people are hospitalized permanently, because of the inability of the family to take complete, 24-hour-a-day care of the patient. By sharing the load with the family, the patient may be maintained outside the hospital with greater happiness for himself and at less expense to the community.

Most day patients require a short period of hospitalization as an inpatient in order to carry out the assessment procedures mentioned above. The decision to accept the day-hospital patient after discharge as an inpatient is made in staff conference by the clinician, the psychiatrist, the medical social worker, and the superintendent occupational therapist. However, not all patients come from the hospital, for some are referred directly by the general practitioner. Close relationships are maintained with the department of physical medicine, because many old mental patients suffer from painful physical disability. Treatment available through this department is particularly important for the confused patient who has suffered from a cerebrovascular accident.

Patients are brought to the day hospital from their own homes by transport provided by the local authority or by a volunteer hospital car service and are collected in the same way at the end of the day. Not all patients come every day or even for full days, the number of days attendance being determined by individual needs.

Some patients are assigned to physiotherapy before taking part in occupational therapy, which may be prescribed on an individual or a group basis. Group work may not be advisable for all; patients with chronic anxiety states or affective psychosis are often given a small corner and quiet, uncomplicated work to do. The occupational therapist gives reassurance and support to all. The medical social worker may interview the patient while he engages in occupational therapy rather than in the office. This approach supplants the hurried interview with the physician or social worker in more formal surroundings.

4. *Comprehensive day hospitals.*—This type of hospital is still in its experimental stage, and its potential contribution to mental health services is under scrutiny. An example is the Marlborough Day Hospital, where groups of short- and long-stay patients are accepted and where an outpatient service is offered to both adults and children. Physical treatment is given in addition to group and individual psychotherapy. The addition of a night hospital to such a

hospital would enable it to offer a full 24-hour service. At this point the question of limits of service and perhaps a redefinition of function enter the picture, but experimentation is not yet complete in this country, and change is to be expected in the various methods of taking care of patients outside the mental hospital.

5. *Aftercare.*—According to the National Health Services Act, the aftercare of discharged mental patients is made the responsibility of the local authority. This function, however, has not been well developed or organized. Even in London, where the most extensive work has been carried out, it is estimated that no more than 5 or 10 per cent of the discharged mental patients are followed by this service (Bickford, 1956).

6. *Hostels and social clubs.*—As described elsewhere in this book, Great Britain has a well-developed system of clubs for pensioners and for old people. The problem of loneliness, not only for the aged, but for all age groups, is discussed and publicized in the press and on radio and television. The National Old People's Welfare Council and the National Association for Mental Health have studied its implications and have directed a portion of their programs toward its mitigation. It remains a problem.

The Ministry of Health believes that loneliness is associated in an important, if not in a fully understood, way with mental illness, and the Ministry is, therefore, interested in any steps taken to combat this condition. Particularly, it feels the need for hostels and social clubs for discharged patients but offers no extended program as yet whereby this end may be achieved on a broad national basis.

H. Expectations

British attitudes toward mental health are in flux, and traditional methods of dealing with the problem of mental illness are subject to criticism. In this climate widespread change is inevitable. Dr. Donald McI. Johnson, Member of Parliament for Carlisle, writes in the press that the improper admission of patients is one of the greatest problems confronting mental hospitals in Britain today (Johnson, 1958). Though always legally correct, he charges that in too many cases the basis for hospitalization is medically and psychiatrically unsound. He supports his argument by referring to the Amsterdam system, which has been discussed earlier in this chapter, and to the Worthing experiment, in which the effectiveness of intensive outpatient services in the reduction of hospital admissions is demonstrated (Carse *et al.*, 1958). General adoption of similar services throughout Britain, he believes, would save upward of $28 million (£10,000,000) annually and produce therapeutic results vastly superior to those presently obtained. Unquestionably, much can be learned by observing the steps taken in Great Britain during this period of critical self-examination and change.

VII. UNITED STATES

In the United States the major responsibility for the care of the mentally ill lies with the individual states. Therefore, in spite of great national population, the mental health problems faced by each state are more nearly comparable in magnitude to those of the smaller European countries than is at first apparent. And for this reason, too, the pertinency of European experience to American mental health problems should not be underestimated.

Because several surveys covering much of the available information on the mental health of the aged in the United States are still current, it is unnecessary to go into great detail in this section (Council of State Governments, 1955; Tompkins, 1955; National Committee against Mental Illness, 1957); however, a brief overview of the American situation will be helpful for purposes of comparison with the European countries already touched upon in this chapter.

A. How Much Mental Illness?

Apart from the statistics furnished by mental hospitals, it cannot be said that we have any extensive knowledge of the actual incidence and prevalence of mental illness for any sizable region of the United States. Hospitalization rates are available, and these show the tremendous variation among the states in the amount of hospitalization provided for the mentally ill (Council of

THE AGED IN MENTAL HOSPITALS

In the United States, as in Europe, the aged constitute a major proportion of the mental-hospital population. In 1950, 25 per cent of all United States mental-hospital patients were over 65 years of age, although only 8.1 per cent of the total population was over this age (Council of State Governments, 1955). Here, again, marked differences between states appear, as is apparent from Figure 9. Thus Louisiana and

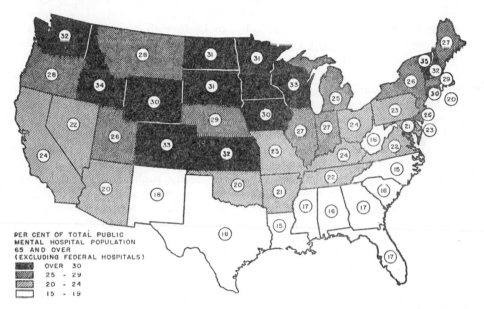

PER CENT OF TOTAL PUBLIC
MENTAL HOSPITAL POPULATION
65 AND OVER
(EXCLUDING FEDERAL HOSPITALS)

OVER 30
25 - 29
20 - 24
15 - 19

Fig. 9.—Percentage of total public mental hospital population aged 65 and over in the United States in 1950. (From Council of State Governments, *The States and Their Older Citizens* [Chicago: The Council, 1955], p. 76.)

State Governments, 1955). In forty-one states reporting in 1953, mental hospitalization rates ranged between 1.5 patients per 1000 total state population (Tennessee) to 6.36 per 1000 (New York). Over a quarter of these states had rates in excess of 5.0 per 1000, and almost another quarter had rates below 3.0, the modal interval being 3.00 and 3.99, with fourteen states falling in this category. Thus hospitalization rates in the United States tend to be somewhat above the western European countries reported on earlier in this chapter.

North Carolina, with only 15 per cent of their patient population older than age 65, may be contrasted with thirteen other states in which these proportions are two or more times as great.

Interstate differences are even greater if we consider only first admissions to mental hospitals. In 1950 Colorado had 46.9 per cent of its first admissions to state and county mental hospitals over age 65, followed by Iowa with 33.7 per cent and New York with 33.4 per cent. These three states were the highest in this respect; at the other end of the scales were North Carolina, with 12.5 per cent; Alabama, with 11.9 per cent; and, finally, Louisiana, with only 10.9 per cent of its first admissions above age 65 (Council of State Governments, 1955).

Unquestionably, the highest first-admission rates are for patients above the age of 65, and this may be attributed entirely to the steep rise in the incidence rates for psychoses of the senium (senile psychoses and psychosis with cerebral arteriosclerosis). These rates begin to accelerate at age 40, rise sharply at 50, and zoom upward at 60. In the latter age group a first-admission rate of 2.0 per 1000 population is reached—higher by far than the maximum reached by any other mental disorder for which hospitalization is sought (Collins, 1955). Of interest is the fact that all other major categories of mental illness show declining incidence in the later years of life.

Yet, in spite of the high proportion of the aged under treatment in mental hospitals and the very high admission rates for senile psychotics, it is wrong to conclude that hospital overcrowding may primarily be attributed to this type of patient. Actually, as might have been anticipated from the Danish hospital statistics given in Table 12, and from the high death rates for aged new admissions discussed elsewhere in the chapter, the number of beds occupied by senile psychotic patients is surprisingly low. Thus, while 22.9 per cent of patients in Pennsylvania state hospitals were above age 65, only 7.7 per cent were senile psychotics; and in New York, with 33.4 per cent of admissions above 65, only 12 per cent of the mental patients were senile or arteriosclerotic psychotics. It is apparent from these figures that a substantial number of the aged mental patients are those hospitalized during the earlier years of life and who remain there until the end of their days. Nevertheless, the number of old people in mental hospitals is great; in 1950 a total of 141,346 patients were 65 or more years of age. This is just over 1 per cent of the total population in this age group (U.S. Congress,

1957*b*), and, as pointed out earlier, it is approximately one-quarter of the total number of mental-hospital patients.

B. How Adequate Are Facilities?

OVERCROWDING

Perhaps the most frequently voiced problem of mental health in the United States today is the overcrowding of mental hospitals. The years following World War II saw a phenomenal growth in the population of mental institutions. Overcrowded to begin with, the situation in state hospitals, which care for over 87 per cent of all mental patients in the nation (U.S. Congress, 1957*a*), became very pressing indeed. This situation stimulated the building of some new hospitals and increases in the capacity of others, but perhaps of greater importance is the fact that the states were forced to conclude that custodial hospitalization would never provide a solution to the costly problem of mental illness. It was recognized that, in order to cut down the length of stay of mental patients in hospital and to lower the new admission rate, more and better trained personnel would be necessary and new ways of treating mental illness would have to be discovered. This encouraged the state governments to assume increasing responsibility for training and research in mental health (Council of State Governments, 1953; Kleemeier, 1956*b*).

However, training and research programs are still behind the need, and overcrowding is still the rule. By the mid-1950's the National Association for Mental Health reported that mental hospitals had only about 56 per cent of the number of beds needed to give good patient care (National Committee against Mental Illness, 1957). When one considers that in 1955 the average daily hospital census of patients was 740,295 and that there are about 600 mental hospitals in the United States, the almost staggering dimensions of this problem become apparent (National Committee against Mental Illness, 1957).

COSTS

New construction and the remodeling of state hospitals are still major items of expense. In November, 1955, a survey of state governments revealed that a total of $750 million had been appropriated for new construction, additions, and renovations to mental hospitals (National Committee against Mental Illness, 1957). By June 30, 1956, 96 mental hospitals had been erected with the assistance of the federal government through the provisions of the Hill-Burton Act at a construction cost of $86,310,458 (National Committee against Mental Illness, 1957). These great amounts of money can hardly be deemed to represent a niggardly attitude on the part of responsible authorities, yet the expenditures are generally considered inadequate for immediate and long-range needs.

One index of the adequacy of patient care is the per capita cost. In 1956 the maintenance expenditure in public mental hospitals in the United States was, on an annual basis, only $1,190.32 per patient, or about $3.26 per day. These ranged from a high of $2,012.23 for the District of Columbia to $670.74, or about $1.84 per day, for Tennessee (National Committee against Mental Illness, 1957). These costs may be compared with Bickford's (1954) estimate of $2.00 for the daily per capita expenditure for mental patients in Britain, but differences in costs and wages between the two countries make it difficult to transform these indexes into meaningful estimates of standards of care. In both countries there is agreement that this amount is insufficient for the needs of modern therapy.

STAFF

What constitutes an adequate hospital staff depends upon both qualitative and quantitative considerations, with the latter, being the more objective, the easier to specify. The American Psychiatric Association (APA) has done this in establishing its standards of care (Table 29). These stand-

ards, however, must not be confused with actuality; in 1951, for example, only ten state mental hospitals in the entire country met the APA standard ratio for physicians, and in this same year these hospitals averaged only one psychologist to every 1,241 patients (Council of State Governments, 1953). In 1955, state hospitals had an average of only one physician to every 201 patients and one graduate nurse to every 82 patients (National Committee against Mental Illness, 1957). Thus it is apparent that

TABLE 29*

NUMBER OF PATIENTS FOR EACH OF SEVERAL TYPES OF PERSONNEL AS RECOMMENDED BY THE APA

Type of Personnel	Admission and Intensive Treatment Services	Continued Treatment Services	Geriatric Services
Physician..........	30†	150	150
Clinical psychologist...........	100	500	....
Registered nurse..	5	40	20
Occupational therapist..........	100	500	250
Attendant (all types).........	4	6	4

* Source: National Committee against Mental Illness, *What Are the Facts about Mental Illness in the United States?* (Washington, D.C.: The Committee, 1957).

† Read as follows: One physician for every 30 patients on admission and intensive treatment services; etc.

shortages in trained personnel exist and that these must be corrected before mental hospitals can perform their function in a completely satisfactory way.

C. Is the Psychiatric Hospital the Proper Place for the Aged Mental Patient?

If he is clearly ill mentally, unmanageable, and likely to remain so for an extended period, the answer to the question posed on the above heading is undoubtedly "Yes." On the other hand, as we have seen earlier in this chapter, there is a tendency for the helpless, ill, older person to be placed in the mental hospital because there seems to be no other place ready to take him. Concern has been expressed in England and Denmark about the number of aged admitted to mental hospitals who might be more appropriately placed in another setting. In France and Italy the number of aged new admissions has been reduced simply by excluding cases whose condition would not warrant mental hospitalization. The same problem has been met in the United States, and various approaches to it have been adopted. Dorothy C. Tompkins (1955), in the opening paragraph of a study of the senile aged in the United States, says:

There are thousands of aged persons in mental hospitals because there is no other place for them. They are called senile, unadjusted, elderly, or emotionally labile. They overburden the facilities for care of the mentally ill and their special treatment needs cannot be met in this kind of environment.

The protest has been made that the commitment of the aged, mentally frail person is the expression of a growing sociologic trend reflecting the inability of the family to care for the chronically helpless person in the home. However, even if we accept as a premise the inability of the modern home to carry the burden imposed by a senile family member, it still does not follow that the mental hospital is the necessary institution to provide the essential care. In Connecticut, for example, a broad program of rehabilitation for the "unadjusted elderly" has been instituted in order to relieve overcrowded conditions in mental hospitals (Tompkins, 1955).

Other states have adopted the same hard-minded attitude of France and Italy and closed their doors to the non-psychotic aged. California announced a policy of discharging from state hospitals patients "merely affected with harmless chronic mental unsoundness" to responsible relatives or to the proper local county authorities. The application of this standard to admissions in 1954 resulted in 500 fewer new mental patients over the age of 65 than in 1953 (Tompkins, 1955). Two other states, Maine and Missouri, have also adopted laws designed to avoid admissions of aged patients who do not need the psychiatric care of mental hospitals (Council of State Governments, 1955).

Minnesota's experience with the "senile problem" is particularly interesting. Various well-publicized improvements in facilities and care of aged mental patients resulted in an overloading of the state hospitals with between 600 and 700 patients who could be more properly cared for in facilities other than a mental institution. In an attempt to correct this condition, the state initiated efforts designed to make the local communities and the patients' families assume more responsibility for their care. To this end recommendations were made for legislation to enable the state to charge relatives or, in the event of their inability to pay, the local communities from which they came. Local communities were also encouraged to build appropriate nursing homes or other similar institutions to provide for the needs of the mentally frail, dependent person (Tompkins, 1955).

Progress is reported from the largest state, New York; but here, too, problems abound:

An experimental geriatric building . . . was authorized by the 1953 legislature; segregation in the State mental hospitals in separate geriatric or infirmary services is now close to achievement; and the research unit of one State hospital is being reorganized to devote its entire attention to arteriosclerotic and senile changes.

The realities of the situation in New York State are suggested by the fact that Supreme Court Justice Benjamin Brenner disclosed recently (1954) that he had "reluctantly" certified four elderly sane persons as mentally ill to get them the custodial care they needed [Tompkins, 1955].

More documentation could be added to support the simple conclusion that there exists nationally in the United States a shortage of facilities to provide care for the mentally frail and helpless aged person at a cost which he and/or his responsible relatives can afford. This has led the state mental hospitals reluctantly to fill this need when other alternatives cannot be found. Although this type of patient is found in large numbers in state hospitals, this number is not sufficiently large to account for all existing overcrowding.

D. What Is Being Done To Improve Care of the Mentally Ill Aged?

In the above sections some of the steps taken by the states have already been mentioned. No clear pattern seems to have emerged as yet from the welter of policy changes, legislative acts, and various building and other programs that have developed through the past decade. Many of the states are, however, taking responsible action. Thus funds have been made available by the state of Connecticut to assist private, non-profit hospitals to improve their standards of care and for the development of home-care programs, protective workshops, foster-home programs, etc., in local communities.

Following the experience and example of Dr. Querido in Amsterdam, Dr. Maurice E. Linden, director of Philadelphia's mental health division, has begun in that city a program of psychiatric and social work counseling aimed at maintaining in the home patients who might otherwise be institutionalized. Earlier, while at Norristown State Hospital, Dr. Linden (1956) found that a variety of medications used in conjunction with an active program of group therapy brought therapeutic benefits to a wide age range of patients, including the elderly.

EFFECTS OF TREATMENT ON HOSPITAL POPULATION

In the United States, as in England, an arresting of the post–World War II upward trend in mental hospitalization is beginning to be experienced. Again increases in rate of discharge rather than decreasing admissions seem responsible. Between April, 1955, and April, 1956, New York State found a 23 per cent increase in discharges from its mental hospitals. New York's mental health commissioner writes: "For the past 10 years, our hospitals have been growing by about 2,000 patients each year. On March 31, 1956, however, there were 500 fewer patients in state hospitals than on March 31, 1955" (National Committee against Mental Illness, 1957).

Similar experiences were reported in 1956 by a total of thirty-four states and the District of Columbia. Nationally, for the first time in history, state mental hospitals showed a decline in population. The reduction of about 7000 patients, while seemingly small, must be viewed in the perspective of an average increase of 10,000 patients every year since 1945 (National Committee against Mental Illness, 1957).

This improvement cannot be attributed to any single factor, but certainly the tendency for state legislatures to provide more money so that more intensive treatment is possible and that more medical personnel is available stands high in any listing of responsible agents. Thus in 1956 the ratio of full-time state hospital employees to patients was 3.6; this was just about double the 1945 ratio of 6.8 patients for every employee. The 1956 daily expenditure figure of $3.26 per patient was more than three times that of 1945. Between 1945 and 1955 great increases were effected in the number of medical and other professional personnel in the state hospitals, which, along with widespread use of tranquillizing drugs, enabled a number of top-ranking state mental hospitals to discharge from 65 to 80 per cent of their first admissions. This is a remarkable achievement in view of the fact that early in the 1950's only 40 per cent of state mental hospital patients were discharged within 5 years of admission (National Committee against Mental Illness, 1957).

While undoubtedly better facilities and care have improved the lot of the aged mental patient, the reduction in hospital population has not come from this group. For example, the rate for cerebral arteriosclerotic patients falls well below the average for all mental patients. In 1952 only

18 per cent of such patients were discharged within 5 years of admission, and 70 per cent died within this period (National Committee against Mental Illness, 1957). Wholly satisfactory solutions to the problems presented by the aged mental hospital patient are yet to be found.

TRENDS AND DEVELOPMENTS

Recommendations directed at improving the mental health of the aged fall into four major classes: (1) improvement of traditional facilities plus the development of newer types to provide better care for the dependent aged; (2) better provision for various kinds of supportive and rehabilitative services; (3) more and better trained personnel to deal with social and medical needs of aged; and (4) research into social, psychological, and medical aspects of aging (Council of State Governments, 1953, 1955; Kleemeier, 1956a; Linden, 1956; National Committee against Mental Illness, 1957; U.S. Congress, 1957a, 1957b, 1957c). Thus the report of the Council of State Governments suggests the development of a number of different kinds of facilities as alternatives to mental hospitals for the aged (Council of State Governments, 1955). These include day care centers, manifold home-care services, foster and boarding homes, old age and nursing homes, "halfway houses," and geriatric centers.

It is not simply that a shortage of these facilities and services exists, but of equal or greater importance is the general lack of awareness that such services and institutional settings can be fashioned into an effective apparatus for the alleviation of mental and physical distress of the aged. The latter is largely a matter of education, training, and effective applied research. Fortunately, steps have been taken in this direction which should not only provide trained experts with special interests and skills in gerontology but also, by providing courses in colleges and universities, help create a body of gerontologically informed

laymen who can be counted upon to support efforts to improve the situation of the aged in society.

The United States has much to learn about the care and treatment of its mentally frail aged, but it has much to teach also. The current picture is sometimes depressing, but progress is being made and should continue at an accelerating pace. Certainly, the research efforts under way should point to bright future development, but with a steadily mounting population of aged people there is no time for complacency.

REFERENCES

BICKFORD, J. A. R. 1954. Treatment of the chronic mental patient. Lancet, 1, 924–27.
———. 1956. Certifying the old. *Ibid.*, 271, 1105-6.
BOUCHER, C. A. 1957. Survey of services available to the chronic sick and elderly in 1954–1955. ("Ministry of Health Reports on Public Health and Medical Subjects," No. 98.) London: H.M. Stationery Office.
CARSE, J., PANTON, N. E., and WATT, A. 1958. A district mental health service: the Worthing experiment. Lancet, 1, 39–41.
CLARK, D. H. 1956. Functions of the mental hospital. Lancet, 271, 1005–9.
COLLINS, S. D. 1955. A review of illness from chronic disease and its variation with age, sex, and season, with some trends. J. Chronic Dis., 1, 412–41.
CONFERENCE OF THE MINISTERS OF SOCIAL AFFAIRS OF THE NORTHERN COUNTRIES. 1957. Samordnad nordisk statistik rörande sociallagstiftningen ("Co-ordinated statistics of social welfare in the northern countries"). ("Nordisk Statistisk Skriftserie," No. 4.) Stockholm: The Conference.
COOK, L. C., DAX, E. C., and MACLAY, W. S. 1952. The geriatric problem in mental hospitals. Lancet, 1, 377–82.
COSIN, L. 1954. The place of the day hospital in a geriatric unit. Practitioner, 172, 552–59.
COUNCIL OF STATE GOVERNMENTS. 1953. Training and research in state mental health programs. Chicago: The Council.
———. 1955. The states and their older citizens. Chicago: The Council.
DENMARK. MINISTRY OF INTERNAL AFFAIRS. 1956. Betænkning afgivet af kommissionen af 29. marts 1952 vedrørende Statens sinds-

sygevæsen. ("Betænkning," No. 165.) Copenhagen: Statens Trykningskontor.

DENMARK. MINISTRY OF LABOR AND SOCIAL AFFAIRS. 1957a. Alderdomshjemmene og deres beboere. ("Arbejds- og Socialministeriernes Økonomisk-Statistiske Undersøgelser," No. 23.) Copenhagen.

———. 1957b. Old people's home in Denmark and their residents in 1955. Copenhagen: Social Science Adviser to the Ministry. (Mimeographed.)

FRANCE. MINISTRY OF HEALTH. 1953. Plan d' équipment sanitaire: lutte contre les maladies mentales, Parts I–IV. Paris: Ministry of Health. (Mimeographed.)

———. 1956. Deuxième plan d' équipment 1958–61: hôpitaux psychiatriques, Parts I–IV. Paris: Ministry of Health. (Mimeographed.)

FRIIS, H. 1955. Personer under Østifternes Åndssvageanstalts forsorg. ("Arbejdsog socialministeriernes Økonomisk-Statistiske Undersøgelser," No. 20.) Copenhagen.

GREAT BRITAIN. MINISTRY OF HEALTH. 1955. Report for the year ended 31 December 1954, Part I. London: H.M. Stationery Office.

———. 1956. Report for the year ended 31 December 1955, Part II. London: H.M. Stationery Office.

———. 1957a. Report for the year ended 31 December 1956, Part I. London: H.M. Stationery Office.

———. 1957b. Report for the year ended 31 December 1956, Part II. London: H.M. Stationery Office.

GREAT BRITAIN. ROYAL COMMISSION ON THE LAW RELATING TO MENTAL ILLNESS AND MENTAL DEFICIENCY. 1957. Report, 1954–1957. London: H.M. Stationery Office.

GUTTERSEN, A. G. 1956. Ideas underlying Danish hospital planning. Ment. Hospitals, **7**, 21.

HAGNELL, O. 1954. Psykoser hos äldre människor, ett växande psykiatriskt problem ("Psychosis in the aged, an increasing psychiatric problem"). Nord. med., **51**, 737–42.

JOHNSON, D. McI. 1958. New deal lies ahead for mentally sick. Bristol Evening Post, February 5, p. 2.

JOINT COMMISSION ON MENTAL ILLNESS AND HEALTH. 1956. First annual report. Cambridge, Mass.: The Commission. (Mimeographed.)

KLEEMEIER, R. W. 1956a. An analysis of patterns for group living for older people. *In*

I. L. WEBBER (ed.), Aging, a current appraisal, pp. 167–79. Gainesville: University of Florida Press.

———. 1956b. A program for mental health training and research in Florida: the annual report of the Florida Council on Training and Research in Mental Health. Jacksonville. Florida State Board of Health. (Mimeographed.)

———. 1956c. Training needs in psychosocial gerontology and the problems of mental health in the elderly. Orange Park, Fla.: Moosehaven Research Laboratory. (Mimeographed.)

———. 1957a. Criteri per la misurazione della salute mentale. Longevitá (Milan), November–December, pp. 190–98.

———. 1957b. Criteria for measuring social mental health of an aging population. Gior. gerontol. **5**, 1097–1102.

———. 1958. Somatopsychologic effects of illness in the aged person. Geriatrics, **13**, 441–49.

LARSSON, T., and SJÖGREN, T. 1954. A methodological, psychiatric, and statistical study of a large Swedish rural population. Acta psychiat. et neurol. scandinav., Suppl. 89.

LeMAIRE, L. 1956. Plans for psychiatric institutions in Denmark. Ment. Hospitals, **7**, 22–27.

LINDEN, M. E. 1956. Public policy and mental problems of the aging. *In* NEW YORK STATE JOINT LEGISLATIVE COMMITTEE ON PROBLEMS OF THE AGING, New channels for the golden years, pp. 77–80. (Legislative Doc. No. 33.) Albany, N.Y.: The Committee.

NATIONAL COMMITTEE AGAINST MENTAL ILLNESS. 1957. What are the facts about mental illness in the United States? Washington, D.C.: The Committee.

NEW YORK STATE DEPARTMENT OF MENTAL HYGIENE. 1955. Technical report of the Mental Health Research Unit. Ithaca, N.Y.: Syracuse University Press.

NYBLAEUS, I. 1956. The mental health film service of the Swedish Association for Mental Health. World Ment. Health, **8**, 35–36.

QUERIDO, A. 1948. Early diagnosis and treatment services. *In* The elements of a community mental health program: proceedings of a round table at the 1955 annual conference, pp. 158–81. New York: Milbank Memorial Fund.

———. 1948–49. Experiment in mental health. Social Service, **22**, 125–30, 169–71.

SJÖGREN. H. 1954. Neuropsykiatriska sjukdomar i presenium och senium. Nord. med., **52**, 1083–91.

STERN, E. S. 1957. Operation sesame. Lancet, **272**, 577–78.

STRÖMGREN, E. 1958. Mental health service planning in Denmark. Danish Med. Bull., **5**, 1–17.

SWEDEN. CENTRAL BUREAU OF STATISTICS. 1956. Statistisk Årsbok för Sverige ("Statistical abstract of Sweden"), Vol. **43**. Stockholm: The Bureau.

SWEDEN. ROYAL MEDICAL BOARD. 1957. Allmän Hälso- och Sjukvård, 1955 ("Public health and sick care in Sweden: annual report of the Royal Medical Board, 1955"). ("Sveriges Officiella Statistik.") Stockholm: Kungl. Medicinalstyrelsen.

TOMPKINS, DOROTHY C. 1955. The senile aged problem in the United States. ("1955 Legislative Problems," No. 1.) Berkeley: Bureau of Public Administration, University of California.

U.S. CONGRESS. SENATE COMMITTEE ON LABOR AND PUBLIC WELFARE. 1957a. Studies of the aged and aging, Vol. **2**: Health and health services. Washington, D.C.: Government Printing Office.

——. 1957b. Studies of the aged and aging, Vol. **9**: Research demonstration and training. Washington, D.C.: Government Printing Office.

——. 1957c. Studies of the aged and aging, Vol. **11**: Fact book on aging. Washington, D.C.: Government Printing Office.

WORLD HEALTH ORGANIZATION. 1953. The community mental hospital. ("Technical Report Series," No. 73.) Geneva: World Health Organization.

——. 1957a. Annual epidemiological and vital statistics, 1954. Geneva: World Health Organization.

——. 1957b. Fifth WHO expert committee on mental health. World Ment. Health, **9**, 20–21.

VIII

Family Structure and Relationships

ERNEST W. BURGESS

I. THE FUTURE OF THE EXTENDED FAMILY

Older people, before the industrial revolution, experienced their main satisfactions in life through their membership in the extended family. They found in it security, response, and recognition. In their role of advice-giving and assistance to their adult children, they performed a vital function.

A. Economic and Social Trends

But the effects of economic and social trends in the last 100 years has been to

[1] Grateful acknowledgment is given to those who generously assisted the author in the preparation of this chapter: Gerhard Baumert, DIVO-Institute, Frankfurt am Main, Germany; Ali Berggren, Royal Social Board, Stockholm, Sweden; Ugo M. Colombo, Public Assistance Department, Milan, Italy; Siegfried Gebauer, Bundesministerium für Familienfragen, Bonn, Germany; Maria Hagemeyer, Oberlandesgerichsdirektorin, Bonn, Germany; Alastair Heron, Department of Psychology, University of Liverpool, England; Salvatore Ingegnieros, Milan, Italy; A. Kaan, Amsterdam, The Netherlands; Lars Ögren, Swedish Institute of Public Opinion Research; Angelo Pagani, Institute of Public Assistance, Milan, Italy; Max Rheinstein, Law School, University of Chicago, Chicago; Helmut Schelsky, Hamburg University, Hamburg, Germany; Rudolf Tartler, Hamburg University, Hamburg, Germany; Peter Townsend, Department of Social Science, London School of Economics and Political Science, London, England; Jean-René Tréanton, Centre National de la Recherche Scientifique, Paris, France; Elmo C. Wilson, International Research Associates, Inc., New York; Robert J. van Zonneveld, National Health Research Council, T.N.O., The Hague, Netherlands; Angela Zuccino, School of Social Work, Rome, Italy.

decrease the economic function of the extended family and at the same time to change the role and status of older persons. Several of these trends described in chapter i which particularly affected the aging in their family relationships will be briefly recapitulated.

1. *The change from home to factory production* meant the sharp separation of work and the family which had previously been united. Both the large and the small family groups lost their function as units of economic productivity. Older as well as younger persons were now usually employees rather than employers. Women also left the home to work in factories and in offices.

2. *The development of the urban way of life* supplanted the earlier rural patterns of behavior. The country had been a favorable environment for the older person and for the extended family which he headed. The city, with its smaller home accommodations, its residential and social mobility, its rapid tempo, its impersonality, and its individualism, provided the objective conditions for the independence of the nuclear from the extended family.

3. *The rise of large organizations* in society provided a substitute for the extended family. The security in employment and retirement which the person had previously enjoyed in the extended family, he now found increasingly in large organizations—economic, social, cultural, and political. The company and the labor union

gave him security in his job. The government organized and administered unemployment insurance, workmen's compensation, permanent disability insurance, Old-Age and Survivors Insurance, and old age assistance. For his activities and social life the older person could now turn to radio, television, and motion pictures conducted by large commercial organizations, to parks and museums operated by public or private agencies, or to clubs under the auspices generally of private but increasingly of public organizations.

4. *Automation and the increase of leisure time* were manifested only in part by the institution of voluntary and compulsory retirement. Retirement raised the question of how older people were to plan and prepare for the new leisure. It provided the conditions for a new career for older people largely independent of their children and grandchildren.

5. *The conservation of human life* had resulted in spectacular decreases in diseases of infants and small children and marked declines in communicable diseases of early and middle adulthood. As a consequence, the proportion of people living beyond 65 had doubled since 1850 in European countries of Western culture. The care of the aged as well as all sick persons had been in the home by members of the immediate and extended family, but now the older ill person was treated in the clinic, the hospital, the nursing home, or other community facility.

What have been the effects of these changes upon the structure of the extended family and the relations of its members? Will it survive or perish? If it survives, what form will it take? Students of old age and the family in different countries of Western culture point out the changes affecting the extended family.

Sauvy (1955) emphasizes the role of the geographical dispersion of the family, or at least of the family in the wide sense of the word:

The increase of communication and the growth of urbanization separated the genera-

tions. The young family frequently lived in the town while the old father was left in the country. Later the town family, now grown old, found itself in turn separated from the children, at least from the point of view of housing.

Professional dispersion was added to geographic dispersion. The family ceased to work as a family; the man went off to work in one factory, the wife in another—and solidarity suffered.

The geographic dispersion of the family was accompanied by a *decrease in parental authority*. This decrease, which was part of the general pattern of enfranchisement, was accompanied by an emancipation of the wife and children [p. 29].

Sir Geoffrey King (1955) points to the change from the agricultural to the modern industrial community:

In an agricultural or peasant community old people tend to remain until the end as useful members of a family group carrying out such tasks as their strength and circumstances permit, in return for which they are looked after and provided with board and lodging. Modern ideas have disrupted this way of life. No one in these days would dare publicly to advise young married couples to live with their parents. In the old days sons and daughters used to take jobs or marry in the neighbourhood of the family home. Nowadays mobility of labour is the cry and sons may have to go long distances in search of work. These are no doubt the inevitable results of the modern industrial community [p. 37].

Burgess (1955) has expressed the American point of view:

In the rural neighbourhood of the past, social relationships were kinship centered. Naturally, where familism predominated, the role of grandparents was clearly defined. Their power was great and their status was high. In the urban way of life, family and kinship relations more and more take second place to associations with persons selected on the basis of occupational and avocational interests and similarity of ideas and values. Family and kinship ties still persist, but they are no longer central and vital. The result is that the older person feels dethroned and devalued in the realm of family relations where he once reigned supreme. He can no longer count on the role of patriarch in ordering the destiny of his children and grandchildren. He cannot even be sure of being venerated and respected. In short, he has lost his old role of dominance and has not yet found a new one [pp. 50–51].

Kooy (1957), a sociologist engaged in a study of changes in the Dutch nuclear family, states:

Hofstee shows that the bonds between nuclear and extended family weakened, which implied that the extended family as a living unit shriveled. This individualization [of the nuclear family] has not yet reached the same phase everywhere in Holland. In bourgeois circles it began early, already before the French Revolution. Among the laborers and the agrarian population we find the first signs of it much later, but among the agrarian population in the coastal provinces [the northern and western parts of the country] the process started in the nineteenth century, while it has hardly begun in this moment among the farmers of the sandy soils. Yet we find the same trend everywhere, in all regions and in all circles: the nuclear family becomes a more autonomous unit in its relations with the extended family and the local group.

Baumert (1957) asserts that changes in family structure are producing new relationships between the generations:

The situation of old people has been strongly affected by social and economic changes in recent times. Changes in family structure and living not only affect the status of aging parents but brings about new relationships between the generations, the young who would be modern and the old who have lived their lives in relation to older family patterns.

The problems involved not only concern the aging parents but concern in different ways their children and the families of their children. Institutional ties tend to weaken, patriarchal concepts lose their force, and the status of the individual rises, even in the family.

"The separation of the generations has become a generally accepted pattern," said Myrdal and Klein (1956) in their study of women in Western countries.

There has been some controversy, particularly in England, as to factual evidence on the present status of the extended family. This has led, at least in part, to the making of several intensive studies on the nature of family structure in its relation to the kin and the neighborhood. One of these, by Peter Townsend on *The Family Life of Old People,* is specifically devoted to the family relationships of aging persons in Bethnal Green, a working-class district of East London. A second investigation, by Young and Willmott on *Family and Kinship in East London,* reports on family relations of the middle-aged both in Bethnal Green and upon migrants to a suburban housing estate. A third study, by John M. Mogey on *The Family and the Neighbourhood,* deals with the effect on family relations of the move from a working-class to a residential neighborhood. A fourth project, by Elizabeth Bott on *The Family and Social Network,* analyzes in great detail twenty families of different occupational levels both in their conjugal roles and in their familial and social networks of contacts.

All these writers emphasize the persistence of the extended family among the English working class as a unit of social relations and mutual aid. As will be seen later, Young and Willmott (1957) and Mogey (1956) note the change in the frequency and nature of social contacts as the nuclear family moves from the working-class district to a new residential suburb. No other country of Western culture has such a wealth of available material on family structure and relationships as they affect older members, and these sources will be drawn on heavily in our survey of the changes in the family relationships of aging people.

B. Adaptability of Family Structure

Family structure has always shown great flexibility in its adaptation to different economic and social conditions. Among preliterate and historical peoples it has exhibited a high degree of variability. It has taken different forms according to number and sex of spouses as monogamous, polygamous, polyandrous, and group marriage. The extended family has been organized in different ways and has varied by patrilineal and matrilineal descent and by patrilocal and matrilocal residence. Systems of land tenure, with their various provisions for the inheritance of property, have also shaped the structure of the family.

For purposes of our survey of family structure and relationships in countries of Western culture our discussion will be limited to three types of the family: (1) the patriarchal extended family on the farm and in the towns; (2) the maternal extended family in urban industrial neighborhoods; and (3) the autonomous nuclear family of urban residential districts.

1. *The patriarchal extended family.*— The extended family was once the prevalent form in all human societies. It is universal among primitive peoples in two general types, the maternal and the paternal. Among peoples of ancient civilization, and still today in oriental countries, it took the form of the large patriarchal family with authority and decision-making in the hands of its head, usually the oldest male member. Le Play (1935) regarded the patriarchal form as the best representative of the family, since "it has a stable and permanent relationship with its fireside, it is faithful to traditions and it establishes its married children near the homestead in order to watch over them and to preserve them" (pp. 98–99). Marriages of sons and daughters were arranged by parents for reasons of economic and social status rather than according to the personal inclinations of the young people.

The patriarchal form of the extended family was an economic unit of production both in farming in the country and in carrying on trades in the town. As skill and discipline became more important in agriculture and in the crafts, the large patriarchal form was replaced by the semipatriarchal type of the extended family. In France this took the form of the "stem-family," to use a term applied to it by Le Play (1935). It operated under a system of land tenure which guaranteed the inheritance of an estate, family name, and

traditions from generation to generation. He applied this name to "the family which maintains a homestead for its immediate members and sends the other members elsewhere to make their own living."

When the father died, the oldest son inherited the family estate by the law of primogeniture. The latter in France had the obligation to support his unmarried brothers and sisters on the ancestral farm. It was his duty to help his sisters make advantageous marriages. He also had a responsibility to his brothers for their professional education or for getting them placed as apprentices. The homestead remained a haven to which his brothers and sisters might claim shelter. (A critique of the point of view of Le Play has recently been made on the basis of research upon the evolution of the French rural family [see Lefebvre, 1953].)

Le Play saw this stable form of family structure threatened by industrialization, the growth of the cities, and the rise of individualism. He advocated a social policy that would preserve the small patriarchal family as a stable unit of society.

2. *The maternal extended family.*—According to the studies by Mogey (1956), Townsend (1957), and Young and Willmott (1957), the maternal extended family exists in an urban neighborhood with three characteristics: (*a*) it is a working-class industrial district in which its inhabitants work and live; (*b*) it is a *closed* neighborhood in the sense that practically all the social activities of the inhabitants are carried on within its boundaries; and (*c*) couples, when they marry, tend to settle close to their parents, especially to those on the maternal side.

The outstanding features of the maternal extended family are:

a) The nucleus of the maternal extended family is constituted by the grandmother, her daughters, and granddaughters.

b) Men visit relatives but less frequently than do the women. Husbands and wives enjoy much of their recreation and social life independently of each other. The usual forms of recreation for men are drinking and visiting friends in the local pub, engaging in some sport, and attending public athletic matches.

c) Women spend their free time visiting with their mother, sisters, and other relatives (Bott, 1957). One local man sized up the difference between husbands and wives: "Men have friends; women have relatives." He added, "Women don't have friends; they have Mum."

d) A system of mutual help in time of need is carried on by the grandmother, daughters, sisters, and granddaughters.

e) In the small families within the extended family there is a strict separation of the conjugal roles of husband and wife. The husband controls the money and does not tell the wife what he earns. He gives her the housekeeping allowance customary in the neighborhood. A good conjugal relation is one with harmonious division of labor rather than with joint activities and shared interests.

The maternal extended family suffers defections when any married couple moves out of the neighborhood. For example, Bethnal Green has lost within recent years nearly half of its population by migration to suburban areas.

3. *The autonomous nuclear family.*— The nuclear or conjugal family is the predominant form in residential areas of the city. Bott (1957) describes this type of family as having a joint conjugal role relationship associated with a loosely knit network. It has developed under the following four conditions: (*a*) the place of work of the husband is not in the local neighborhood but at some distance from it; (*b*) there is little sociability with neighbors, the majority of friends of the residents living outside the area and frequently being widely scattered; (*c*) few, if any, relatives live in the same or adjoining neighborhood but are often widely dispersed over the city; and (*d*) residential and social mobility is high; couples, when they marry, tend to reside in other neighborhoods.

Prominent characteristics of the autonomous nuclear family are (*a*) that equal authority is shared by husband and wife; (*b*) that the division of labor between husband and wife is flexible and roles are easily reversed; (*c*) that compatibility of personality and complementary differences are regarded as desirable by the couple for a happy marriage; (*d*) that nearly all friends are joint friends of husband and wife; (*e*) that there is a minimum of social control by friends and neighbors; and (*f*) that leisure-time activities are largely together, with emphasis upon entertaining and being entertained by friends.

This rapid survey of the three types— large patriarchal extended family, maternal extended family, and nuclear or conjugal family—suggests certain generalizations.

The patriarchal extended family has almost disappeared from countries of Western culture. Survivals may still persist in isolated rural areas (see pp. 277–81). It also sometimes develops where the owner of a family business employs his sons and perhaps sons-in-law and especially if also all the component nuclear families live near by or, as is sometimes the case, occupy apartments in the building belonging to the patriarch.

The maternal extended family appears to be still well intrenched in homogeneous working-class neighborhoods where the residents are employed by local industry. It is most stable where at least three or four generations have been born and reared in the same locality. The departure of couples to residential suburbs loosens their membership in this type of extended family. These mobile conjugal units tend to become autonomous and to take on the characteristics of the residents of the new residential neighborhood.

The autonomous nuclear family has the characteristics which seem adapted to the urban way of life. Husband and wife no longer seek their chief companionship outside the home—the husband with friends and the wife with relatives—as in the maternal extended family. They find it with each other. They select friends not from those who live in the same block but on the basis of common tastes, interests, and similar backgrounds who are likely to reside in other neighborhoods. They are freed from the control of kin and neighbors.

The autonomous nuclear family seems destined to be the family of the future. It is still in the process of evolution. Its central value is companionship of husband and wife and of parents and children. It recognizes increasingly the sharing of authority by the spouses and their equality in status. It is a product of the effects of the economic and social trends of the times.

In this transition from the extended to the nuclear family what becomes of the relations of aging parents to their children? How have the relations of grandparents and grandchildren been affected? What changes take place in the relations of the aging husband and his wife? What are the family relations of those unattached to the nuclear family—the widowed, the single, and the divorced—who in the past could find refuge in the extended family? What changes of adjustment in family relations are taking place to conditions and trends of modern life?

Data bearing on the answers to these questions will now be presented.

II. AGING PARENTS AND THEIR ADULT CHILDREN AND GRANDCHILDREN

The changes in the relations of aging parents and their adult children and grandchildren will be discussed under the following heads: (*a*) support of parents by their children; (*b*) aging parents living with adult children; (*c*) parent-child relations; and (*d*) grandparent-grandchildren relations.

A. Support of Parents by Their Children

In the past in all countries of Western culture there was a moral and a legal obligation for adult children to support needy parents. There was also the expectation on

both sides of mutual help and care in times of illness and disability. The system of reciprocal services among relatives was particularly strong among the members of the extended family. The feelings of obligation on the part of adult children to support and care for aging parents has declined with the establishment of social insurance and of medical and other community services.

ITALY

The influence of the extended family is stronger in Italy, where the moral obligation of adults to support older relatives in need is binding, than in any of our other five European countries of Western culture. The strong sentiment of kinship makes for their willingness to support aging parents and other older relatives. The Italian law gives sanction to these feelings which express the solidarity of the extended family. It permits older persons, if needy, "to claim aid from children and grandchildren, from sons-in-law and daughters-in-law and from brothers and sisters" (Colombo, 1958, p. 26).

In general, this obligation to support parents is recognized and fulfilled. But particularly in cities there is evidence that familial attitudes and sentiments are weakening. The director of the Department of Public Assistance in Milan (Colombo, 1958) states: "I can certify that very often some old and needy parents prefer to renounce aid from their descendants rather than to occasion painful and inhuman contests. What father can agree to claim in the court against his children? Family duty, in this matter, is admirable only if spontaneous."

FRANCE

The French law is similar to the Italian statute requiring adult children and adult grandchildren to support needy parents or grandparents. Support of indigent parents and grandparents is recognized as a moral obligation, and it is rare that children seek to evade this duty. Sometimes a needy older person may have three children, and only one is giving support. The worst situation for older people is to have no family and also to be in poor health.

THE NETHERLANDS

The law requiring adult children to support needy parents is well enforced in the Netherlands. The legal provision that grandchildren be liable to the support of grandparents is in the process of being repealed and is no longer enforced. Old age assistance officials state that there is some difficulty at times in getting children to contribute to the support of their needy parents. But often, when the situation is explained, they will agree or even offer to make regular payments. There is some public sentiment developing against requiring children to make contributions for the support of their parents (personal communication from Dr. A. Kaan, 1957).

WEST GERMANY

Each district in West Germany has a social office for matters like old age assistance. The social worker investigates the need of the older person who applies for assistance and then goes to the next of kin to find out his ability and willingness to give support. If the recommended payment is not made, the matter is taken to court. Parents are becoming more loath to claim support from their children (personal communication from G. Baumert, 1957).

The extension of old age assistance to rural areas under the Association of Farmers provides for benefits at 65. This means that older persons will no longer be dependent on their children for support, and this should lead to an earlier transfer of the farm to the oldest son.

Older people in rural areas are reported to be happy and relieved at the prospect of obtaining insurance benefits. In the past there were frequent quarrels and disputes over the support money due the aged farmer who had given up the management of the farm. Sometimes the question of amount of support depended on the attitude of the daughter-in-law, and this was a cause of anxiety to the old people.

ENGLAND

The United Kingdom is the one nation of our six countries of Western culture which has abolished legislation requiring adult children and other relatives to support aging parents who are in need. It has also the most highly developed program of medical and community services for the infirm and the aged. It is, therefore, all the more interesting and significant to report findings of studies of care received by old people from relatives, since it is freely given and not under legal compulsion.

Where the extended family still flourishes, as in Bethnal Green, Townsend (1957) reports that older persons and their families (whether living together or apart) engage in a system of reciprocal services. In the Bethnal Green sample the aging obtained help not only in illnesses but when needed in shopping, cleaning, washing, and cooking. Regular help in these or other household tasks was received by 68 per cent of the aging and occasional help by 21 per cent. Only 11 per cent received no help. The old people reciprocated when able. Townsend reports that, except for those living completely alone, 91 per cent of women and 60 per cent of men did some daily or weekly service such as daily shopping, preparation of meals, looking after grandchildren, or occasional service. Only 13 per cent of the old women and 40 per cent of the old men undertook no regular personal or domestic help for others. This family system of reciprocal care is centered in an old woman and participated in much more by her, her daughters and daughters-in-law, and sisters and nieces than by male relatives.

B. Aging Parents Living with Adult Children

In all countries of Western culture a minority of aging parents still live with their adult children. It is, however, important to distinguish those cases where the grown-up children live with their parents and those where the aged couple live with their adult children.

Where the grown-up children live with their parents, the older generation takes the dominant role. The aging mother, if physically able, is in charge of the housekeeping. This arrangement proves more satisfactory to the older generation than to the young married couple. In general, it works better if the daughter and her husband live with her parents than when the couple live with the husband's parents.

If the aging individual or couple live with a married son or married daughter, the arrangement is generally difficult on both sides. It is likely to be especially frustrating to the older generation, who frequently feel in the way and useless. In certain families, particularly those of higher income, a room with at least limited housekeeping equipment is provided the old father and mother or widowed parent.

ENGLAND

Townsend (1957) states, on the basis of a 1 per cent sample, that at least 40 per cent of persons 60 years of age and over in Great Britain in 1951 were living with unmarried or married children or both. A study showed that in 1947 almost 50 per cent of old people in Wolverhampton were sharing a home with their children (Sheldon, 1948).

In Bethnal Green, Townsend (1957) found that 42.8 per cent of a sample of 203 people of pensionable age and their children were living together. But less than a fifth—19.2 per cent—lived *with* their married children. If only those with surviving children are considered, the corresponding percentages are somewhat higher —52.1 and 23.3.

The attitudes against aging parents and their married children living together is much stronger than might be expected from the percentage who actually reside with them. In Bethnal Green, for example, only 10 per cent of older parents with sur-

viving children were in favor of it. Of those living together with their married children, only 33 per cent approved of the arrangement (Townsend, 1957). They gave as their reasons against it the desire for independence, privacy, and non-interference in the lives of their children. They also emphasized the danger of conflict with the children's spouses. There seemed to be several reasons why married children and parents lived together. Older people more often lived with married daughters than with sons. Sons or daughters who were only children were more likely to continue to live with parents after marriage; widowed more than married older people resided with married children. The preferred arrangement frequently expressed was to live near but not with the married children.

Of those with surviving children, 52 per cent lived with children and 33 per cent had children living within a mile—a total of 85 per cent living with them or living not more than a mile away. Fifty per cent of all the children lived within a mile. Only 11 per cent lived outside London.

With children who lived nearby contacts were frequent. Old people saw 26 per cent of their sons and 45 per cent of their daughters daily. For at least once a week or more but not daily the corresponding figures were 42 per cent and 33 per cent. Not seen at all during the year were 4 per cent of the sons and 2 per cent of the daughters (Townsend, 1957).

WEST GERMANY

Many older parents live with children or vice versa, partly because of the housing shortage due to destruction of buildings during World War II and partly to the influx of refugees from Poland and East Germany. A survey by DIVO-Institute,[2] Frankfurt am Main, reports that 36 per cent of older men and 38 per cent of older women live with at least one child. If these percentages are calculated only for those

[2] DIVO, Gesellschaft für Markt-, Meinungs-, und Sozialforschung (an organization for market, opinion, and social research), Frankfurt am Main.

with children, they rise to 42 and 46, respectively.

In the DIVO-Institute survey older people were asked the question, "With whom do you live in the household?" Their answers were classified as shown in Table 1. The differences in response by the sexes is marked. Only 13 per cent of the men but 30 per cent of the women live alone. Nearly one-half of the men (47 per cent) and one-fourth of the women (24 per cent) reside with spouse only. In addition, 19 per cent of the men but only 9 per cent of the women live with spouse and others (children, children in law, grandchildren, other relatives, and non-relatives). The proportion living with children is about the same, or 29 per cent of the men and 32 per cent of the women. But 15 per cent of the men and only 7 per cent of the women live with spouse and children. By contrast, only 14 per cent of widowers but 25 per cent of widows are living with their children.

Older and younger people in the country often work and live together. They have one kitchen and eat at one table. The grandmother takes care of the young children.

When the old father feels physically failing, he turns over the management of the farm to his son. Often he delays this change until he is 70 or over. The son who is carrying on the major farming activities cannot do anything without the approval of the older man.

Since he is the owner of the farm, the father has a strong influence on the selection of mates for his grandchildren. In one case an old farmer disapproved of the marriage of a granddaughter to a young man from the next village because he did not have "enough ground underfoot." The girl did not marry this suitor.

The new insurance system for farmers may relieve the situation by inducing farmers to retire when they reach 65. The son will take over management of the farm at an earlier age and introduce new methods of agriculture which his father opposed.

In Germany there is now a strong trend for older people to live by themselves. They wish to become independent of their children, and this is encouraged by the recent liberalization of old age insurance, and this trend is also welcomed by their married sons and daughters. There is a growing tendency for the aged couple to remain in their home and for the children at marriage to move into new housing.

TABLE 1*

ANSWERS TO QUESTION, "WITH WHOM DO
YOU LIVE IN YOUR HOUSEHOLD?"

ANSWER	PER CENT	
	Men	Women
Alone	13	30
Only with spouse	47	24
Only with spouse and children	11	4
Only with spouse, children, and children-in-law	1	2
Only with spouse, children, children-in-law, and grandchildren	3	1
With spouse and other relatives or non-relatives	4	2
Only with children	6	11
Only with children and children-in-law	2	5
Only with children and children-in-law and grandchildren	4	7
With children and others	2	2
With other relatives or non-relatives	3	8
Not stated	4	4
Total	100	100

* Source: DIVO-Institute, Frankfurt am Main.

The custom of parents and adult children living together in West Germany is still characteristic of rural areas. The Darmstadt Community Survey (Baumert, 1954) reports that the three- and even the four-generation family was found in 42 per cent of all full-time farm families in the area studied. This type of large household, however, was present in only 16 per cent of the part-time farm families, in 9 per cent of non-farm units residing in rural communities, and in 5 per cent of families living in the city. DIVO-Institute reports that only 8 per cent of older people live in the three-generation family for their sample. The extended family in the rural area has the locus of authority and influence in the grandfather.

FRANCE

In 1946 a nation-wide poll on aging was made (Girard, 1948) which covered 904 persons retired or pensioned, of whom only 23 per cent were under 60 years, and 1561 employed individuals, of whom 14 per cent were over 60 years, with the remainder being 20–59 years old. In answer to the question, "Are you living alone or with your spouse or are you living with your children?" the following responses were received from retired or pensioned persons with children: alone, 40 per cent; with children, 39 per cent; and no reply, 21 per cent.

Employed persons with children were asked, "Do you intend to live alone later on or with your children?" They gave the following replies: alone, 50 per cent; with children, 23 per cent; and no reply, 27 per cent.

The large proportion of non-replies in the two groups makes it difficult to interpret the findings. At any rate, a large percentage of retired or pensioned older people and their children are living together.

Tréanton (1959) reports that, of 101 subjects with a child living in Paris in his sample of aged workers, the child in 48 instances resided in the same dwelling or house as the parent and in 22 other cases in the same neighborhood or district.

But the younger generation in the city follows the principle that the generations must have different homes. In the lower class the ties are strong between the generations. The older person in the city seldom lives with the children. In Paris the young people have very small houses, and most of the cases of living together are of young people living with parents. Seldom do the parents reside with their children. The rents are under control at fixed prices. Old people keep their flats, and, since it is almost impossible to get housing, the young

people who marry cannot find accommodations. So they move in with their parents. "Young couples dislike living with their parents or 'in-laws' which the housing shortage forces them to do; they do not hesitate to sacrifice their comfort in favor of their independence" (Ceccaldi, 1954).

There are two differences between France and the United States: there is close proximity of the two generations in France and there is low geographical mobility. People do not want to leave their province because of the difference in type of living among the provinces. France, composed of areas of different types of nationalities, has different styles of living.

In the country the traditional custom of married children living with parents is still maintained (Ceccaldi, 1954), and farming is an extended family affair. Agricultural economy rests on "family stock," including three generations and sometimes more, "placed under the almost patriarchal authority of the owner aided by at least one of his children, generally the eldest, who will succeed him, by the spouse of the latter, and by their children." Even in rural France the large-family ties are relaxing; in their place is the development of friendship and neighborly relations and mutual aid.

ITALY

The study of older persons in Milan yields data on the proportion of men and women 65 and over who are living with their children. The living arrangements are shown in Table 2. The percentage of the older people living together with their children is 37 for the men and 45 for the women. These percentages are quite close to those reported for England and West Germany, and they would undoubtedly be higher for all Italy, with its large rural population.

Gini and Caranti (1954) report that the housing shortage after World War II forced many young couples to double up with their parents. From 1948 to 1950, of 100 couples in Rome with known street address at marriage, less than 30 went to reside in their own dwelling, about 40 went to the husband's home, and a little more than 30 took up residence in the wife's home. In certain rural areas of Italy joint households are formed by married children living with their parents. The paterfamilias maintains his authority, although he is out of touch with recent agricultural techniques. "As he grows old he is usually helped by the oldest son, or by the one most able in business. The wife directs the housework and is often at odds with the daughter-in-law because of the diversity of habits and the general differences in view of the generations" (Gini and Caranti, 1954, p. 358).

THE NETHERLANDS

In the Netherlands the obligation to offer a widowed mother or father a home is generally recognized in the cities as well as in the country. The son or daughter will ask a parent or parents, "Do you want to live with us?" There has been some tendency to have the aged father rotate in his stay with the different children. This is particularly true if he is a nuisance and if the children feel that they must share the burden.

At present in the cities and generally in the country the nuclear family of husband, wife, and children (called *Gezin* in the Netherlands) is the predominant form. But there still remain survivals of the traditional three-generation family in eastern parts of the country. Hofstee and Kooy (1956) point out that in the isolated rural region along the German boundary the traditional household may contain (*a*) several nuclear families; (*b*) a nuclear family and one or more individuals who are not members of a *Gezin*; (*c*) two, and possibly more, nuclear families and one or more individuals; and (*d*) two or more individuals.

Hofstee and Kooy obtained data on the structure of the household on 497 farms at Winterswijk, situated near the German border. Of these, 252 were cases of the

nuclear family, and the remaining 245 were classified as traditional families. In 125 of the traditional households a married couple lived together with the parents-in-law, and in 100 cases a married couple and a father or mother of the husband or wife resided together. A nuclear family and uncle were found dwelling together in 14 cases and a nuclear family and an aunt in 6 cases. The old idea of primogeniture still prevailed, with the eldest son inherit-

TABLE 2*

LIVING ARRANGEMENTS OF 831 MEN AND
1127 WOMEN 65 YEARS AND OVER
MILAN, ITALY

WITH WHOM LIVING	PERSONS 65 YEARS AND OVER (PER CENT)	
	Men (*N* = 831)	Women (*N* = 1127)
Alone......................	7.6	20.3
With spouse................	45.4	18.6
Spouse and one or two children.	20.1	8.0
With son..................	3.0	11.0
With daughter.............	6.1	13.4
With children.............	1.7	3.0
With married children........	6.1	9.9
With one or two relatives......	4.8	9.3
With others................	2.6	2.8
No reply..................	0.2	0.1
Total....................	100.0	100.0

* Source: S. Ingegnierus, *Aspetti gerontologici Milanesi* (Milan: Commune di Milano, 1958), Table 7.

ing the farm. He accepts the duty to compensate the other children and "to bring his parents to their end."

Outstanding features of the traditional household are as follows: (*a*) the education of the child is conducted by his parents, his grandparents, and by his unmarried uncles and aunts living in the household; (*b*) if the young married couple live with the husband's parents, his wife has to subordinate herself to his mother as the mistress of the household; (*c*) if the young married pair live with the wife's parents, the husband has to subordinate himself to her father, "who will claim to be the 'farmer' until his last gasp of breath"; and (*d*) the married person who lives with his or her parents is likely to be kept in the position of a "child" until his old age. At present tensions are developing in the traditional family because of the conflict between the old forms and norms and the wishes and desires of the younger generation resulting from contact with modern culture.

SWEDEN

The national opinion study of older people (57–67 and over 67) provides data on living with children and attitudes toward this housing arrangement (Sweden's Institute of Public Opinion Research, 1956). Of those 57 and over, 6 per cent report that they live with children. But this proportion is only 3 per cent for the age group 57–67 but jumps to 11 per cent for the age group over 67.

In answer to the question, "Do you think it is all right for a person over 65 to live with his children?" 29 per cent of those 57–67 years of age and 38 per cent of those over 67 years of age give favorable replies. The corresponding percentages for those opposed are 39 and 32. The others are doubtful. When, however, persons are asked the housing arrangement they would prefer, only 2 per cent of them 57–67 and 3 per cent of those over 67 reply "with or near children." The desire to live independently is very strong in Sweden.

C. Parent-Child Relations

In the extended family the relations between the older and younger generations are close and satisfying. The aging parents are the authority to whom the son and daughter, even after marriage, turn for advice and with whom they are generally in regular and intimate contact.

Relations of parents with daughters and sons.—In working-class neighborhoods the relations between parents and their married daughters are stronger than those between parents and their married sons. Young and

Willmott (1957) present statistical evidence to support this generalization.

A greater proportion of both youngest and only married daughters live with parents.
Married women live nearer to their parents than do married men.
Married women see both fathers and mothers more often than married men see their parents.
Married women see their mothers more often than their fathers.
Married women living nearer see their mothers more often than those living further away.
Men see their mothers-in-law more than women see theirs [pp. 220–21].

The strongest relation in the extended family is that between "Mum" and her married daughters. As soon as the married daughter leaves work to have children, the ties with her mother are greatly strengthened. In fact, she seems often to be much more a member of her mother's family than the mistress of a new family. Young and Willmott (1957) speak of the great triangle of adult life as "Mum-wife-husband." Often there is avoidance of the mother-in-law by the son-in-law. Of 26 married men in their sample, they found 17 drawn into the extended family of the wife and 9 who stayed out of it. One "Mum" spoke of the latter as "out-laws" in distinction from "the in-laws" (Townsend, 1957).

The relation between the older mother and her own son is a close one. He visits her regularly but generally without his wife.

Townsend (1957) sums up most of the characteristic features of the relationship between aging persons and their married children and children-in-law as "the special tie between mother and daughter, the way married sons visited their parents unaccompanied by their wives; the tactful avoidance of children-in-law; the tensions between in-laws, particularly between husband and mother-in-law; and the close relationship between maternal grandmother and grandchild" (p. 85).

Frequency of seeing children.—Four European studies present data on the number of contacts of older persons with their children.

Townsend (1957), in his study of Bethnal Green, gives the most exact breakdown on the frequency of children's contacts with older people (Table 3). He observes that children may be divided into three groups by the frequency of contact: intimates (seeing each other every day or nearly every day), week-enders, and holiday companions (those living at a distance but attending weddings, funerals, and golden-wedding anniversaries). He also notes the regularity of the visits between parents and children.

The survey of attitudes of older persons conducted by the Swedish Institute of Public Opinion Research reports findings for

TABLE 3*

FREQUENCY OF CONTACT WITH
SONS AND DAUGHTERS

GREAT BRITAIN

Frequency	Per Cent
Daily	36
Not daily but at least once a week	38
Not weekly but at least once a month	17
Not monthly but at least once a year	7
Not seen	3

* Source: P. Townsend, *The Family Life of Old People* (London: Routledge & Kegan Paul, 1957).

TABLE 4*

FREQUENCY OF CONTACT WITH
SONS AND DAUGHTERS

SWEDEN

Frequency	Per Cent
Daily or nearly every day	59
At least once a week	20
At least once a month	12
Not monthly but at least once a year	9

* Source: Swedish Institute of Public Opinion and Research, *På Äldre Dagar* (Stockholm: The Institute, 1956), Question 15a.

men over 67 on the frequency of seeing their children (Table 4). These findings agree in general with the data from Bethnal Green on the frequency of contacts of parents and children, although the answers were recorded somewhat differently.

Even more detailed findings for a nation-wide sample of 366 older men and 455 older women in West Germany are reported by DIVO-Institute, Frankfurt am Main (Table 5). As in the other studies, the percentages are for those with living children or stepchildren. These figures correspond rather closely with those from England and from Sweden. They also indicate only small differences between men and women.

TABLE 5*

FREQUENCY OF CONTACT WITH
SONS AND DAUGHTERS

WEST GERMANY

FREQUENCY	PER CENT	
	Men	Women
Often because live with children or stepchildren	42	46
At least once a week	29	30
At least once a month	11	12
At least once every 6 months	8	5
Once a year	4	2
Only every second year	2	1
Generally none	1	1
None	2	2
Total	99†	99†

* Source: DIVO-Institute, Frankfurt am Main.
† Differs from 100 owing to rounding error.

TABLE 6*

FREQUENCY OF CONTACT WITH
SONS AND DAUGHTERS

FRANCE

Frequency	Per Cent
At least once a week	59
From time to time	32
Rarely	9

* Source: J. R. Tréanton, "Adjustment of Older People to Urban Life in France," in C. Tibbitts (ed.), *Aging and Social Health in the United States and Europe* (Ann Arbor: Division of Gerontology, University of Michigan, 1959), p. 172.

Tréanton (1959) in his study of old age pensioners in Paris secured data on frequency of contact between children and the 101 parents who had at least one child living in Paris (Table 6). The frequency of contact of older persons in Paris with their children is less than that given for England, for Sweden, and for West Germany. Over two-thirds of the children live with or near their parents (48 per cent in the same dwelling or the same household and 22 per cent in the same or nearby district).

The findings from these four separate studies in different countries support the conclusion that family contacts are frequent in European countries of Western culture and play a part in maintaining family relationships between the older and the younger generation.

Ceccaldi (1954) reports the decline of gatherings of the extended family. They occur "only during vacations and for the great religious festivals: Christmas, Easter, baptisms, first communions, marriages, funerals; anniversaries are generally celebrated in a more intimate circle."

Effect of residential mobility on contacts. —This system of family relations is disrupted when a family moves from a long-established working-class neighborhood into a better residential district. Distance greatly diminishes social contacts and upsets the customary program of reciprocal services. "Mum" loses her traditional role and central place of authority and dispenser of advice.

Twenty miles away from Bethnal Green is the new housing estate of Greenleigh, to which many residents of East London have migrated. Bethnal Green has lost nearly half its residents to this and other residential suburbs on the outskirts of London. What have been the effects of this movement of population on family and on husband-wife relations? Young and Willmott (1957) interviewed 47 former Bethnal Green residents to find the answer.

The original decision to move was a hard one. The attractions were a fine new house with a garden, with fresh air and space to play for the children. But, from the opening of the Greenleigh estates until 1956, 26 per cent of the tenants had moved back to the East End.

The move to the suburbs weakened the extended family and strengthened the husband-wife relationship, and a companionship relation developed. There is the distance, the time, and the cost of trips. The average number of contacts is cut to one-seventh for the wife and to nearly one-fifth for the husband. The husband's contacts are higher than the wives' because many return daily to work in Bethnal Green.

Because of the higher cost of housing and transportation to work, the husband economizes by giving up or reducing his drinking and his attendance at the pub and at sporting events. Husband and wife stay home at night and watch television, which is in two-thirds of the homes instead of one-third, as at Bethnal Green. A smaller proportion at Greenleigh have relatives to care for children at time of confinement of wife.

Drinkwater (1959) in his study of 550 working- and lower-middle-class women aged 45–60 discovered evidence of the transformation which he believes is now taking place in England in the relationships of older women to married daughters. His respondents were members of women's clubs, which indicated that they were already detached from or never were members of the extended family. These older women as a group expressed feelings of resentment and hostility to the recently married. They spoke of these "welfare-state marriages" or "postwar marriages."

They had bitter comments on their rejection by their daughters on marriage epitomized in the statement: "We never treated our mothers in the way we are treated by our children. We may have differed from them, but we *respected* them. We did not leave them in the lurch and then set ourselves above them." Drinkwater explains the sources of this attitude: (1) the expectation of the mothers to play the "Mum" role of confidante and adviser to their daughters after marriage; (2) the frustration of this expectation because of the new relation of companionship and partnership in marriage in which the wife turned to the husband rather than to her mother; (3) the prosperity and the services of the welfare state, which enabled the daughter to start her married life on a material plane higher than that attained by the mother until after many years of marriage; and (4) the outmoding, in the eyes of the modern generation, of the advice which the mother could give. In short, the traditional "Mum" role was passé, and the mothers in their later years were left without a function in the lives of their daughters.

Drinkwater's findings are questioned by Townsend on the ground that they were obtained from special groups of women who were members of clubs and not from a representative sample. He also notes that views publicly expressed in a club are very different from those voiced by a person in his own home.

The relation of father and grown-up son had never been so close as mother and daughter or even so close as mother and son. It had perhaps been closest where the son followed in the same occupation as the father. Bosanquet (1906) points out that before the industrial revolution a general pattern was the succession, sometimes for generations, of father and son in the same business or trade. This transmission of skill and "know-how" in the family line has been steadily diminishing. At present the rapid obsolescence of methods of work still further lessens the value to the son of the father's occupational knowledge. In present-day England the role of the older man as authority and advice-giver to his son has declined to the vanishing point.

The extended family as a cohesive social unit seems on the way out. This process is hastened in England by the policy of housing authorities to give preference in the new housing developments on the basis of need. They do not take into account family relationships or attempt to resettle the extended family as a group project. Probably "Mum" would oppose any such move. The alternative would be to remodel the old dwellings on the East Side.

Perhaps we should use the term the "kinship network" (Bott, 1957) to describe the relations of older persons with relatives where there is no extended family or where it has ceased to exist. In this way each person would have a kinship network that would generally be unique to him and not fully shared by other persons.

D. Grandparent-Grandchildren Relations

The increase in the proportion of older persons in the population of countries of Western culture living beyond age 65 means that in 100 years the chances of a child's having a grandparent have doubled. The decline in fertility during the same period results in a smaller number of grandchildren. In completed families the average number of children was more than cut in two in Bethnal Green in one generation (from 5.8 children for marriages in 1900–1909 to 2.5 children in marriages in 1920–29). The corresponding decline in Great Britain was 32 per cent (or from 3.4 to 2.3 average number of children) (Young and Willmott, 1957).

ENGLAND

In the Bethnal Green sample, Townsend (1957) reports that 14 per cent of old people lived in a three-generation home. But married couples almost invariably constituted separate households and had their own kitchen.

Almost all the old people (93 per cent) with children had at least one or more living in Bethnal Green. There was a total of 908 grandchildren.

Although grandparents had been strict with their own children, they were generally lenient with grandchildren. This was observed by Townsend (1957) and by Young and Willmott (1957), who also studied family life in Bethnal Green. The latter offer an interesting explanation of the difference in the role of the grandparent and the parent in relation to the child.

They note that parents are the authorities for the children, with the primary responsibility of teaching them right conduct. The grandparents are more easygoing. They state that the generalization of Ratcliffe-Brown about the relationship of grandparents and grandchildren in Africa as one "of friendly familiarity and almost of social equality" surely applies to Bethnal Green. But parents often feel that the grandparents are too indulgent.

Grandparents in Bethnal Green performed many services for their grandchildren. (The average age of becoming a grandmother or a grandfather was 53 and 55 years, respectively.) Sixty-three per cent of grandmothers regularly would help in taking them to school, giving them meals,

TABLE 7*

OLDER PERSONS WITH ONE OR MORE
GRANDCHILDREN, WEST GERMANY

NO. OF GRANDCHILDREN	PER CENT	
	Men	Women
One..........................	11	12
Two or more.................	59	56
None........................	24	27
Respondent had children....	(15)	(18)
Respondent had no children..	(9)	(9)
Not stated..................	6	5
Total....................	100	100

* Source: DIVO-Institute, Frankfurt am Main.

and looking after them when their parents were at work or went out in the evening. Twenty per cent of grandfathers would regularly baby-sit or bring grandchildren from school or go with them on trips to the park (Townsend, 1957).

The important role of the grandmother in the rearing of children can hardly be overemphasized. The first grandchild, particularly the eldest child of the oldest daughter, was the object of special attention and affection by the grandmother. Often the grandmother was as much concerned with the care of young children as the mother. Sometimes the grandmother would have main charge and occasionally full charge of a grandchild. This close relationship of the grandmother with grand-children helped markedly in maintaining and extending the ties of the extended family.

WEST GERMANY

Over two-thirds of older persons have one or more grandchildren (70 per cent of the men and 68 per cent of the women), according to the DIVO-Institute survey. The detailed figures are given in Table 7.

"In his relationship with his grandchildren a German may be freer and more indulgent than with his own children; he behaves more like the American father, and is more relaxed, reciprocal and joyful. Possibly this is due to the fact that he is not responsible for the education of his grandchildren; he depends on his son to be the stern father and an example to them" (Schaffner, 1948).

The grandmother still has a function in the possibilities of caring for the grandchildren. Her care of the grandchildren may lead to conflict if she is with them every day. If she tries to raise or educate them, tension is likely to arise with her daughter or daughter-in-law. In a mutually satisfactory arrangement the grandmother looks after the children when the parents lack the time or when they go out for the evening or on a holiday trip.

The progress of technology and the introduction of laborsaving devices into the home have limited the former activities performed by the grandmother for her children and grandchildren. In the past, if a stocking had a hole, the grandmother would darn it; now, with nylon, this cannot be done. This illustration symbolizes the way in which technological advances diminish the household function of grandparents.

It can, of course, be argued that some technological changes provide new chores for grandparents—such as taking children to the cinema, viewing television with them, or mending their roller skates or toy shotguns. The real question is to determine the net effect of technological inventions.

FRANCE

There is a close relation of grandparents with grandchildren if they live near each other. Parents often send their children for the night to the grandparents, who are happy to have them. They do this when they want to go out for the evening or when the wife is sick or pregnant. When grandparents are living in the provinces, grandchildren are sent to them for the holidays. Well-to-do grandparents often build a house in the country and count on having their grandchildren with them during the holidays. The parents may then be free to take short trips without the children. Because of their peasant origin, many city workers send their children to the ancestral peasant home for the holidays.

THE NETHERLANDS

The celebration of birthdays is important and is the occasion for family reunion of grandparents, children, and grandchildren.

III. HUSBAND-WIFE RELATIONS

A. Economic and Social Trends

Husband-wife relations in northwestern European countries are in a process of change. Certain of these changes are the result of economic and social trends. Others are those that come with advanced years and especially with retirement from work.

FRANCE

The Latin system of husband-wife relations is general and persists with little or no change. The husband has the conception of being the master. The wife never makes decisions but lets the husband make them. No real change in authority is taking place.

Where the wife works with the husband, she is under his complete authority. On the farm the paternalistic system of authority governs the members of the family. This system is also very frequent in small businesses. The ideal objective is for a young man to obtain a small business in which his wife often works with him. She is thus in continuous contact with him but under his authority.

ENGLAND

In working-class families in an industrial residential neighborhood the relation of husband and wife typically seems to be that of competitive co-operation rather than companionship. The aging husband finds companionship not so much with his wife as with friends at work or in the pub or at sporting events. The wife experiences companionship with her daughters and female relatives more than with the husband.

The data from Bethnal Green give support to this theory. Wives seldom knew what the husbands earned. Only seven of thirty-four wives who were asked knew the husband's earnings. On her part the wife does not often tell the husband what her income is from lodgers, from payments by children living in the home, or from contributions from children and relatives living outside (Townsend, 1957).

The traditional division of roles is for the husband to be the sole or chief breadwinner and to be consulted on any crucial decision and for the wife to have full charge of the domestic economy. Their social life is also segregated. The leisure time of the husband is spent in going to pubs, sport grounds, and clubs with brothers or work mates. In her free time the wife joins her daughters or sisters in attending movies or clubs. The sexes are also segregated in old people's clubs or in outings.

B. Retirement and After

What changes take place in the relations of husband and wife after retirement from work? Retirement (or the acceptance of a job of lower status) is a crisis for husband and wife. There is the reduction in income which generally requires drastic cuts in expenditures. In all countries of Western cultures there is the loss of status of the husband in the home and in the community. This drop in prestige and in self-respect varies from country to country and by class position.

ENGLAND

Husbands in Bethnal Green looked ahead to retirement with anxiety and fear. Therefore, they continued working as long as they could at their old job and took new employment even at a lower wage. Their status in the home and in the community was lowered when they retired and even when they changed to a part-time or full-time job of an unskilled type and less pay. The men continued to work as long as they could and then retired or were retired because of their health. Only 9 per cent retired from full-time work with choice as their sole reason (Townsend, 1957). The others generally tried to find lighter jobs.

Retirement lowered the husband's standing in the family. He felt keenly the loss of income, the boredom of nothing worthwhile to do, the feelings of uselessness and not being wanted, and the fear of becoming a burden on his children and other relatives. He had no substitutes for the satisfactions which he had obtained from work. He lost his friends at work and felt snubbed by old friends in the community. He had made no plans for retirement.

Employed women retired from work at an earlier age than men and more frequently by choice. They did not feel giving up their jobs as keenly as men because they had a useful function to perform in the home and because employment was seldom as absorbing an activity as it was typically for men.

In general, life goes on in the Bethnal Green family the same after as before retirement. There is little change in the proportion of men who assist the wife in household tasks. The amount of help a husband gives his wife depends largely on the absence of daughters in the home or within a five-minute walk (Townsend, 1957). Husband and wife generally pursue their sep-

arate social interests rather than engage more in joint activities. They do not seem to get closer together after retirement.

Indeed, there may arise new sources of friction. Minor irritations increase because of reduced income and the often unwelcome presence of the husband in the home. He feels keenly his loss of standing with his wife and children. One in five of the married women disclosed marked marital conflicts. Part of these may be due to sexual dissatisfactions, especially in cases of the frigidity of the wife due to infirmity.

THE NETHERLANDS

The older man on retirement does not lose status to the same degree as in certain other countries. This is due in large part to the respect paid to old age. It is customary for young people to give up their seats in streetcars to older men and women.

WEST GERMANY

There is no expectation that the older person after retirement should be very active (Baumert, 1957). The traditional philosophy is that a woman should grow old gracefully and reduce her activities. The expectation of the lower-middle and upper-lower classes is that the retired man should have a hobby and should work a little in his garden. He should meet with his little club (*Stammtisch*) at a table in the restaurant or *Bierstube* where he and his friends usually sit.

The extended family is at the center of interest of older persons. The retired person maintains his associations with relatives, particularly with his children and grandchildren.

IV. THE WIDOWED, THE DIVORCED, AND THE SINGLE

So far we have considered the family relations of the married and those living with their spouses. Little or no attention has been paid to single persons, the widowed, and the divorced, nor has there been any discussion of the childless couples who cut across the married, the widowed, and the divorced. Old age and retirement bring special problems to these groups of the aging population.

A. The Widowed and Desolation

The widowed constitute a high proportion of persons 65 years and over in Western countries as indicated by Table 8. In all six countries the proportion of widows is much higher than of widowers. It is over twice as high in France and Italy and nearly double in the United Kingdom and West Germany. In the Netherlands and Sweden the percentage of widowers is only one-third less than that of widows.

The proportion of widowers is remarkably the same for the six European countries for which statistics are available. By contrast the proportion of widows varies widely from 42.0 per cent in Sweden to 57.9 per cent in France. This difference is partially to be explained by the fact that France has a lower proportion of males 65 and over in the population (40.3 per cent) than Sweden (46.7 per cent). Probably, husbands killed in World War I contributed to this excess in percentage of widows. The two countries that were not involved in this war have the lowest percentage of widows 65 and over (the Netherlands, 44.1; Sweden, 42.0).

The two chief crises in the life of a woman in the later years occur when children leave home and when her husband dies. Widowers remarry, but the majority of older widows remain husbandless.

Where the external maternal family survives with "Mum" at its center, the marriage of children is not a catastrophe to the older woman so long as they remain in the neighborhood. Her tie with her daughter is even stronger than before. She now has a satisfying function for her later years in relations with her daughters, sons, and grandchildren. The crisis occurs when the extended family breaks up and the dyad relation of companionship of the married pair develops.

In Great Britain just under one-half of the women 65 years and over (48.7 per cent) are widows, and one in four of the men in this age group are widowers. The proportion, of course, is lower in the age group 65–69 and increases with age. A main point of interest is the question of who suffers more in widowhood, the man or the woman. Measures of the effects of bereavement may be found in changes in contacts with children, in self-reports of loneliness, and in mortality and suicide rates.

1. *Contacts with children.*—The Bethnal Green study indicated that the widowers saw their sons and daughters less often

TABLE 8*

PERCENTAGE WIDOWED OF POPULATION
65 AND OVER IN SIX COUNTRIES

Country	Year	Male	Female
France............	1954	23.7	57.9
Italy.............	1951	25.4	54.8
The Netherlands.....	1947	28.4	44.1
Sweden...........	1950	26.8	42.0
United Kingdom.....	1951	25.5	48.5
West Germany......	1950	28.8	56.0

* Source: United Nations, *Demographic Yearbook, 1958*, Table 6.

than married men saw their children. Widows, however, had slightly less frequent contacts than married women with their daughters but about the same with their sons (Townsend, 1957).

2. *Loneliness.*—In the Bethnal Green study 46 per cent of widowed people said that they were very or sometimes lonely, as compared with 27 per cent in the total sample. Townsend (1957) found that loneliness was related definitely to desolation, particularly by the loss of a spouse. He shows that the feeling of loneliness varies directly with the recency of bereavement. The percentage of those reporting loneliness is 93 within 4 years of death of spouse, 50 within 5–10 years, and falls to 27 after 10 years (or the same percentage as for the total sample).

Tréanton (1959) found in his study of

retired men in Paris that 41 per cent of the widowed as compared with 20 per cent of the married felt isolated to some degree.

In a representative sample of 890 older persons in California 40 per cent of widows stated that they were often lonely, as compared with 16 per cent married and living with spouse only (Bond, 1954).

TABLE 9*

DEATH RATES PER 1000 FOR MARRIED AND
WIDOWED OLDER PERSONS
GREAT BRITAIN

AGE	MALES		FEMALES	
	Married	Widowed	Married	Widowed
62........	27	37	12	17
67........	42	52	25	27
72........	63	76	42	46
77........	96	116	72	80
82........	147	175	113	131

* Source: Great Britain, Registrar General, *Decennial Supplement for England and Wales, 1951.*

3. *Death rates.*—The general death rate is higher for the widowed than for married persons in old age. The statistics given in Table 9 are from the Registrar General's Decennial Supplement for England and Wales, 1951. At every age the death rate is higher for the widowed than for the married and is much higher for widowers than for widows.

4. *Suicide rate.*—Comparative suicide rates are not available by country by age, sex, and marital status. Special studies of suicide indicate that they are higher among the widowed, the single, and the divorced than among the married (Cavan, 1928; Dublin and Bunzel, 1933). Thus they may be taken as an indication of the conditions of life of members of these groups that lessen their hold on life. The suicide rate (for the year 1955) for men was higher in the age group 65 and over as compared with the age group 45–64 (Table 10).

In England and Wales, France, and the Netherlands the suicide rate for males increases markedly after 65. In Sweden and

West Germany the increase is relatively small. The suicide rate for women is uniformly much lower than that for men. Except for France and the Netherlands it is only a little higher after 65. In fact, for Sweden it is somewhat lower.

All these data—fewer contacts with children (for the widower), more loneliness, higher death rate, and higher suicide rate—indicate the effect of the broken family relation upon the happiness and personal adjustment of the widowed. The incidence of these indicators is much higher for widowers than for widows. This fact strongly suggests that it is much harder for the widower than for the married man to make successful adjustments to the retirement crisis.

TABLE 10*

SUICIDE RATE PER 100,000 BY AGE AND SEX
IN FIVE COUNTRIES

COUNTRY	MALES		FEMALES	
	45–64	65 and Over	45–64	65 and Over
France.............	49.2	71.0	13.9	18.4
The Netherlands.....	15.5	32.2	10.5	15.0
Sweden.............	52.3	57.3	14.7	12.5
United Kingdom....	25.7	43.5	16.7	17.4
West Germany......	45.9	51.1	21.9	22.5

* Source: United Nations, *Demographic Yearbook, 1957*

B. The Single, the Divorced, and Isolation

The two smallest groups by marital status are the single and the divorced older persons. While a minority of them live with relatives, the majority live alone. The data available on the single and the divorced in old age are largely limited to their numbers in the population, their isolation and loneliness, and their care by welfare agencies.

THE SINGLE

The percentage of single men and women in the population 65 and over varies considerably in the different selected countries of Western culture (Table 11). Sweden has the highest rates of single men and single women and France and West Germany the lowest. The proportion of single women tends to be almost double that of single men except for Italy and the Netherlands, where it is about 50 per cent greater. In all six countries the percentages of divorced is low for men and women and somewhat lower for males than females.

In Bethnal Green (Townsend, 1957) many single persons were drawn into the three-generation family. In the sample in the study most of the single persons had siblings. Half of these lived with or near a brother or sister. A special 20 per cent census sample of Bethnal Green gave 39 per cent of single women over 60 as compared with only 1 per cent of married women of the same age living with brother or sister. Frequently the single person lived in the old home after the death of parents and received attention and care from a married sister. The percentages of brothers and sisters seen daily and weekly by single persons was three to five times higher than the percentages seen by married or widows with surviving children.

TABLE 11*

PERCENTAGE SINGLE OF POPULATION 65 YEARS
AND OVER IN SIX COUNTRIES

Country	Year	Male	Female
France...............	1954	6.4	10.5
Italy................	1951	7.1	11.5
The Netherlands.....	1947	9.0	13.2
Sweden.............	1950	12.9	20.9
United Kingdom.....	1951	9.0	16.6
West Germany......	1951	4.4	8.5

* Source: United Nations, *Demographic Yearbook, 1958*, Table 6.

When single siblings were drawn into the three-generation family, they often gave more service than they received. They might even take over roles like those of provider, mother, grandmother, or housewife. In these cases they had close relations with siblings, nephews, and nieces.

There are the isolated single persons who have few if any kinship ties. They com-

prise about 40 per cent of the bachelors and spinsters in Bethnal Green. Studies in England (Sheldon, 1948) and in the United States (Bond, 1954) indicate that high proportions of the single as well as the widowed report themselves as lonely.

The death rate per 1000 population of single men is higher than for married men, as shown by the data from the Registrar General's *Decennial Supplement for England and Wales, 1951* (Table 12). The

TABLE 12*

DEATH RATE PER 1000
SINGLE OLDER MEN

UNITED KINGDOM

Age	Single	Married
62.........	34	27
67.........	50	42
72.........	72	63
77.........	108	96
82.........	162	147

* Source: Great Britain, Registrar General, *Decennial Supplement for England and Wales, 1951.*

differences between single and married men are large but somewhat smaller at the ages shown in the table than the differences between the widowers and the married. The sudden crisis of widowhood seems more adverse to health than the problems faced by the single person.

The death rate for single women is practically identical with that for married women at each age.

Whatever measure of personal maladjustment is taken—isolation, loneliness, death rate, or suicide—gives findings indicative of the social disadvantage of the single state. These consequences may be averted when the single person maintains contacts and relations with members of his family like brothers and sisters, nieces and nephews.

THE DIVORCED

The persons 65 and over who are still divorced are a small and selected group. They comprise only a small percentage of those ever divorced, most of whom have married again. The great majority of them have been divorced for many years. Except for the minority who have children, their status is in some ways much like that of a single person.

The percentage of the divorced in the population is higher in some countries than in others (Table 13). Sweden has the highest rates of those divorced both for men and for women. The United Kingdom, where it is still difficult to obtain a divorce, has the lowest rates for men and women.

Where statistics are available, the divorced are found to have the highest percentage of the lonely. In one study the lonely comprised 48 per cent of the divorced, 40 per cent of the widowed, and

TABLE 13*

PERCENTAGE DIVORCED† PERSONS 65 YEARS AND OVER IN FIVE COUNTRIES

Country	Year	Male	Female
France................	1954	1.1	1.7
The Netherlands........	1947	1.2	1.4
Sweden...............	1950	1.8	2.3
United Kingdom.......	1951	0.2	0.2
West Germany........	1951	0.5	0.6

* Source: United Nations, *Demographic Yearbook, 1958*, Table 6.
† "Divorced" includes those separated for the Netherlands and for West Germany.

34 per cent of the single compared with 16 per cent of those living with spouse only (Bond, 1954). The suicide rate is also the highest for the divorced as compared with all the other marital statuses.

Cavan (1928) interprets the low rates of suicide with the married as compared with the widowed and the divorced as owing "to the relatively greater degree of incorporation into an intimate group which they experience." She continues:

Membership in a family group not only provides opportunities for expression of wishes otherwise difficult to obtain, but also acts as a means of control over the member. The widowed and divorced are in a particularly trying condition because their habitual life organization has been destroyed and they often suffer in addition from grief, and, in the latter case, perhaps social disgrace [p. 319].

V. SOCIAL POLICY AND THE FAMILY

The changes in family relations as they affect the aging have been presented for the selected countries of Western culture. In recent years there has been an increasing number of studies of old people in relation to their family life. Have the research findings of these inquiries implications for social policy? What are the current trends in social policy as they react upon the family relations of older persons?

Three countries have been the most concerned about the aging in their family relations. These are Great Britain, West Germany, and Sweden. In a fourth country— Italy—attention is being given to the potentialities of the institutional care of the aged.

A. Great Britain

Studies by Sheldon (1955), Townsend (1957), and Young and Willmott (1957) show that the program of welfare housing is undermining the extended family. They call for changes in housing policy and procedures that will enable the three generations to live close to one another.

Dr. Sheldon, in his study of Wolverhampton (1948), was the first to give detailed statistics of the proximity of the old to relatives. He found that in at least 20.5 per cent of his sample the older persons and their relatives living separately functioned as one family.

Townsend (1957), in his study of Bethnal Green, documents the reciprocal services of the older and younger generation. He shows that older persons with daughters and other female relatives made the least claim on health and welfare services. He calls for a social policy that would keep the family together if only because of the lower cost to the state. Older people want better housing, but they do not wish to be separated from relatives or to be uprooted from their old and familiar neighborhoods. He recommends more conversion of old houses, both small and large, and more new building of old people's "flatlets" and bungalows inside the city. He believes that "there is no justification for an attempt to supplant the family with State services" (p. 203). Such services as needed should give support to the family. Among his concrete recommendations for strengthening family relations are giving priority in allocating housing to the wishes of members of extended families to live near each other; the setting-up of a comprehensive family help service to include care for the isolated and handicapped old; granting allowances for the constant attendance of the bedridden and housebound; and integrating institutions for the old into the community and making them more homelike. The general principle is "to prevent old people from needlessly becoming wards of the State, by helping them to be cared for in their own homes and, whenever possible, by their families (p. 203).

Young and Willmott (1957) also advocate a policy of building new housing around existing kinship groups. They assert that the sense of loyalty to one another among the inhabitants of a place like Bethnal Green is not due to buildings. It is due far more to ties of kinship and friendship which connect the *people* of one household to the *people* of another. In such a district community spirit does not have to be fostered; it is already there. If the authorities regard that spirit as a social asset worth preserving, they will not uproot more people but build the new houses around the social groups to which they already belong.

Shenfield (1957), who recently completed a review of the social provisions for old age in Great Britain, has made recommendations to carry out what might be called a policy of housing kinship groups. She favors a mixed development. Individual or small groups of dwellings suitable for older persons would be placed among other types of housing, and some smaller dwellings suitable for older people might be introduced into large estates of three-bedroom houses. Then, too, "a granny-plus" flatlet might be added to some existing housing.

It will be of interest to learn to what extent these implications from research on the significance of kinship relations for the care and happiness of older people will affect future housing policy in Great Britain. There is no question but that the present housing policy is accelerating the decline of the extended family in working-class districts of British cities.

It should be recalled that Great Britain has abolished the legal obligation of adult children to support their needy parents. This places the question of economic contributions of children to parents purely in the realm of moral responsibility and filial sentiment. Recent studies in England have shown that the best guaranty of reciprocal services is having the older and younger generations live in proximity.

B. West Germany

As we have seen, the three-generation family of the patriarchal type still survives in rural parts of Germany. The Minister of Family Affairs advocates the strengthening of the family in part by restoring the role of the father and the effectiveness of extended family ties. Some students of the family (Schaffner, 1948) perceive tendencies in this direction; others (Wurzbacher, 1951; Schelsky, 1953; Baumert, 1954) point out that the long-term trends are the same in Germany as in other countries of Western culture. Baumert (1954) analyzes the changing roles of aging parents and their adult children and recommends that society and the state should take action to support the emerging companionship family.

Family households in which three generations live together or in which the other relatives of the wife or the husband are included comprise a smaller and smaller percentage of all households. With this appears a whole series of consequences: the ties with a larger circle of relatives become looser, the small family of the spouses with their children becomes more and more confined to itself, and the mutual dependence of this small unity of members living together becomes greater. No longer does the wife expect of the husband only that he provide well for the family and uphold its reputation; the husband no longer expects only that the wife manage the household efficiently and offer him a pleasant home life. Both expect of each other, in stronger degree than in a more institutionalized relationship, emotional affection.

A modification in the role of the children also takes place because the meaning of children in the consideration of the parents, so far as it concerns the future of the family, has somewhat narrowed, owing to economic and social circumstances. For many families, especially for those of the higher social strata, the meaning of children rested on the fact that they would be heirs of the property and traditions of the family; for families of the lower strata, that they would later play a role as caretakers of the old parents. Often education in the family was especially directed to this point, and the children were prepared for this role. On the one hand, however, the inheritable property of the family became smaller and smaller and, consequently, the institution of inheritance less meaningful. For this and many other reasons the idea of family traditions tends to vanish. On the other hand, the care of the old is taken over by the state more and more, or by other institutions, and thereby the meaning of the children as later providers is decreased. Accordingly, there also appears, especially with the smaller number of children in the family, emotional affection as a more determinate factor in the foreground without entirely suppressing the other factors.

Through the steady decline of the patriarchal concept, the place of the old in the family circle also experiences a modification, more perhaps through the taking-over of the care of the aged by other institutions. Earlier it was customary for the old parents to live in the household of one of their children and to be cared for by this one, perhaps with the common support of all the children. Today the old more often manage their own household and live on a pension. Families have given up the duty of the support of the old people. On the other hand, the aged, when their support is not furnished by property, as is more and more the case today, are independent of their children through pensions or public support.

The increasing occupational activity of married women may work in general against the loosening of the ties between parents and grandparents. This comes about because in many cases the care of the household and of the children by the grandmother makes it possible for the wife to enter a gainful occupation outside the home. The position of the old in the circle of the modern family is further strengthened through the economic independence of the elderly persons who receive pensions and therefore are not burdens on the family budget when taken into the family household. The general trend, however, is toward the financial and social independence of the old, with a weakening of ties with their children and grandchildren (Baumert, 1956).

It should not be the task of a present public policy to attempt a restoration of the former type of family life; rather, public policy should promote the development of new forms of family partnership adapted to today's economic and social conditions (Baumert, 1954).

C. Sweden

In her book *Nation and Family,* Alva Myrdal places a social policy for the aging family and the individual in the context of a social philosophy of the welfare state. She perceives the competition between the children, the potential producers of the future, and the old, whose productive life is behind them. The economic burden of support of the young and the old falls upon the younger- and middle-aged adults, who are the producers of the present.

In adjudicating this competition, Myrdal

tends to side with the children (1945). She believes, for example, that new housing should be for new families with children and that old housing should be reconditioned for the old, especially since they are accustomed to the old type of housing. She points out that the Population Commission, with its interest in children and the future, stopped the first proposal for new housing for the old in 1937. But 2 years later the Riksdag voted a grant for the erection and reconditioning of dwellings for pensioners. She predicts that, although rational considerations should support the program in the interest of larger new housing for families with children, the natural sentimentality about the old and their voting power will win out.

Myrdal attributes the provision of social security by government to the old and other handicapped persons as a result of the breakup of the three-generation family, which in the past offered protection to all its members. Government was the one organization large enough to take over this function. She also recognizes that social security for the old frees the nuclear family from heavy handicaps to its success and happiness. If legal responsibility of the adult children to support aging parents was enforced, it would place obstacles in the way of their marriage and especially be a deterrent to having children. She believes that it is necessary to develop "a complete scheme for the maintenance of old people before the new era in social policy can focus on children and family" (p. 344).

Myrdal has pessimistic reflections on the political and economic effects of the increase in proportion of the older segment of the population. She points out that old people in Sweden, because of life-tenure and seniority, control important administrative positions in public life. She refers to census findings that persons over 50 years of age owned 69.5 per cent of all wealth and that those over 60 owned 43.5 per cent, although their percentage in the population was only 22.4 and 12.8, respectively. Both because of greater power and greater numbers at the ballot, she feels, the old will win the contest between the age groups. She fears that "it will become more difficult to be young in a society controlled by the aged" (p. 89).

Guiding principles for the welfare and independence of older people have been formulated by an official committee and have been approved by the Riksdag:

A committee of parliamentary members and experts appointed by the Minister of Social Affairs in 1952 to report on the care of the aged in Sweden submitted its findings and recommendations in 1956. On the basis of this report, a bill was introduced which the Riksdag approved on December 4, 1957. The bill presented a survey of the findings and proposals of the committee and called for the Riksdag's approval of directives for the future development of the care of the aged which the Minister of Social Affairs had drawn up. These directives re-emphasize the guiding principles which governed developments in the past ten years and aim at continuing improvements in line with these principles.

"In the first place and to the largest extent possible, measures for the care of the aged should aim at assisting the aged by all available means to live independent lives in their own homes as long as possible without excessive personal strain," the committee stated in its report.

The most important condition for attaining this goal is to meet the old people's economic needs. In this respect, the Minister of Social Affairs pointed out, important progress has been made through the implementation of the new legislation on national pensions in 1948, with subsequent amendments, and on compulsory sickness insurance in 1955, as well as through full employment, which enables older people to earn an income until they reach retirement age and sometimes even thereafter.

Consequently, public measures for the benefit of the aged are no longer relief of mass poverty but must meet the aged population's special requirements of housing, personal attendance, and service. Housing of adequate standard is essential to enable aged people to live by themselves and to reduce the pressure on the resources of the municipal homes for the aged and other establishments, the com-

mittee pointed out, emphasizing the importance of adequate housing facilities from the
humanitarian and economic points of view.
[Adapted from statement by Dr. A. Berggren
of the Royal Social Board, Stockholm.]

The Social Democratic party in Sweden
seems determined to apply this policy to
income maintenance. It introduced a bill
in the Riksdag to provide insurance benefits equal to two-thirds of the highest 15
years of a worker's wage. Its defeat led to
the election in 1958 in which the Social
Democrats increased their seats in the
Riksdag but fell short of a clear majority.
By securing votes from the smaller parties,
they could remain in office and perhaps
enact this legislation.

Even without this new proposal, Sweden
and Great Britain have gone further than
other countries in providing houses and
other services that enable older people to
live independently of their relatives if they
so desire.

D. Italy

Angelo Pagani (1958), a sociologist and
gerontologist, has raised the question of
the importance of residential institutions
in the care of the aged. On the basis of
careful observation of the residents of an
Italian institution in Milan (Institute In-
abilia Lavoro dell'E.C.A.), he has outlined
an inquiry not only of the personal causes
but also of the influence of economic and
social conditions determining institutionalization.

He points out that in Italy seeking admission to a public institution is not unusual and carries with it no feeling of individual inadequacy or loss of dignity. It
is not the result of the absence of family
solidarity but rather of economic insecurity.
The urban industrial worker at the end of
his working life faces a crisis characterized
by (1) a low level of living; (2) individual
and social isolation (the loss of the natural
community on leaving the factory); (3)
family dependence, low personal status,
and moral and cultural dependence; and
(4) a difficult emotional situation due to

his awareness of his dependence. Admission to a public institution means a rational solution of his problem and an improvement of his position: (1) his new relationships insure an apparently independent life and put an end to family dependence and (2) his participation in shared
work gives him again a feeling of usefulness.

"Rejected by society, the aged find, or
aim at finding, in the institution the element of a complete society. . . . Entry into
a new community of equals causes an en-
richment of social life counterbalancing the
negative effects of institutionalization, such
as loss of full independence and removal
from home life" (p. 54). In short, Pagani
views the residential institution, at least
in Italy, as meeting the economic and social conditions facing the urban industrial
worker and as solving his personal needs.

It may well be, as Pagani suggests, that
the residential institution at present is
more adapted than other types of care for
the aged to the Italian situation. Nevertheless basic research on the significance
and potential of institutional care of the
aged versus other forms of housing is highly desirable in all countries of Western
culture.

In Italy at present only 3 per cent of
persons 65 and over live in institutions. As
Colombo (1958) points out in his book
*Principles and Organization of Social Wel-
fare,* the extended family still provides
them with the main source of support and
social life. Old people, in the large majority, live together with their children and
grandchildren. If physically able, they are
yet useful for factory and domestic activities and, for this reason, are closely
incorporated into the family unit. This situation is more evident in rural areas and
in small centers but differs somewhat in
the cities. Especially in the largest cities
many old people cannot, for various reasons, live with children and relatives and
prefer to have an independent home, sometimes very small and simple. Often living
conditions are difficult, and they are

obliged to rent an attic or a room under the staircase. But in Italy, as elsewhere, this trend for an autonomous life is strong and is increasing as housing programs are developed.

These brief statements of social policies for the aging obviously are not adequate to represent the trend of thinking about the care of older persons in these four countries. They do, however, present contrasts of emphasis upon directions of social action and so may be helpful in attempts to formulate or to reformulate national policies for the aging in countries of Western culture.

VI. Conclusion

In this chapter the family structure and relationships of older people have been discussed in the context of economic and social change. Under the impact of industrialization and urbanization the three-generation family has disintegrated as a household and as a unit of economic production. At first, however, it continued as a closely knit social unit. But now, with the development of new relationships between the generations adapted to the conditions of modern life, it is being transformed into a social network.

REFERENCES AND BIBLIOGRAPHY

ADORNO, T. W., FRENKEL-BRUNSWICK, ELSE, LEVINSON, D. J., and SANFORD, R. M. 1950. The authoritarian personality. New York: Harper & Bros.

ARENSBERG, M., and KIMBALL, S. T. 1940. Family and community in Ireland. Cambridge, Mass.: Harvard University Press.

BAUMERT, G. 1954. Deutsche Familie nach dem Krieg. Darmstadt: E. Roether Verlag.

————. 1956. The changing role of family members. *In* Studies of the family, **1**, 275–76. Tübingen: J. C. B. Mohr.

————. 1957. A pilot study concerning the family and old age in Germany. (Unpublished paper.)

BOND, F. A., BABER, R. E., VIEG, J. A., PERRY, L. B., SCAFF, A. H., and LEE, L. J., JR. 1954. Our needy aged: a California study of a national problem. New York: Henry Holt & Co.

BOSANQUET, H. 1915. The family. London: Macmillan & Co.

BOTT, ELIZABETH. 1957. The family and social network: roles, norms and external relationships in ordinary urban families. London: Tavistock Publications, Ltd.

BURGESS, E. W. 1955. Human aspects of social policy. *In* Old age in the modern world, pp. 49–58. Edinburgh: E. & S. Livingstone.

BURGESS, E. W., and LOCKE, H. J. 1953. The family: from institution to companionship. New York: American Book Co.

CAVAN, RUTH S. 1928. Suicide. Chicago: University of Chicago Press.

CECCALDI, D. 1954. The family in France. Marriage & Family Living, **16**, 326–30.

COLOMBO, U. M. 1954. Principii ed ordinamento della assistenza sociale. Dott. Antonio Giuffré, Editore.

————. 1958. Budgetary surveys. *In* The need for cross-national surveys of old age, pp. 22–26. Ann Arbor: Division of Gerontology, University of Michigan.

DARIC, J. 1953. Structures familiales comparées. *In* G. FRIEDMANN (ed.), Villes et campagnes civilisation urbaine et civilisation rurale en France, pp. 333–35. Paris: Librairie Armand Colin.

DRINKWATER, R. W. 1959. Some role problems of women in middle life and their implications for subsequent adjustment. *In* Proceedings of the Fourth Congress, International Association of Gerontology, Merano, Italy, **3**, 452–59. Fidenza: Tipografia Tito Mattioli.

DUBLIN, L. I., and BUNZEL, BESSIE. 1933. To be or not to be: a study of suicide. New York: Harrison Smith & Robert K. Haas, Inc.

GINI, C., and CARANTI, E. 1954. The family in Italy. Marriage & Family Living, **16**, 350–61.

GIRARD, A. 1948. Résultats d'une enquête par sondage sur l'âge de la retraite. *In* J. DARIC, Vieillissement de la population et prolongation de la vie active. Paris: Presses Universitaires de France.

GORER, G. 1955. Exploring English character. London: Cresset Press.

HOFSTEE, E. W., and KOOY, G. A. 1956. Traditional household and neighborhood group: survivals of the genealogical territorial pattern in eastern parts of the Netherlands. *In* Transactions of the Third World Congress of Sociology, **4**, 75–79. London: International Sociological Association.

HORKHEIMER, M. 1936. Autorität und familie. Paris: Librairie Felix Alcan.

HUTCHINSON, B. 1954. Old people in a modern Australian community. Melbourne: Melbourne University Press.

INGEGNIEROS, S. 1958. Aspetti gerontologici Milanesi. Milan: Commune di Milano.

KING, G. 1955. Policy and practice. *In* Old age in the modern world, pp. 36–45. Edinburgh: E. & S. Livingstone.

KÖNIG, R. 1946. Materialen zur Soziologie der Familie. Bern: A. Francke.

KOOY, G. A. 1957. Changes in the Dutch nuclear family's position and character in the twentieth century. (Unpublished paper proposed for International Family Research Seminar.)

——. 1960. Social system and the problem of aging. Paper given at Seminar on Aging and Mental Health, Fifth International Congress of Gerontology.

——. 1960. The rural aging in the Netherlands. Paper given at Fifth International Congress of Gerontology.

LEFEBVRE, H. 1953. Structures familiales comparées. *In* G. FRIEDMANN (ed.), Villes et campagnes: civilisation urbaine et civilisation rurale en France, pp. 327–33. Paris: Librairie Armand Colin.

LE PLAY, P. G. F. 1935. Method and sociological facts. *In* C. C. ZIMMERMAN and M. E. FRAMPTON (eds.), Family and society, pp. 98–99. New York: D. Van Nostrand Co.

MOGEY, J. M. 1956. Family and neighbourhood: two studies in Oxford. London: Oxford University Press.

MYRDAL, ALVA. 1945. Nation and family: the Swedish experiment in democratic family and population policy. London: Routledge & Kegan Paul.

MYRDAL, ALVA, and KLEIN, V. 1956. Women's two roles, home and work. London: Routledge & Kegan Paul.

PAGANI, A. 1958. Causes of institutionalization. *In* The need for cross-national surveys of old age, pp. 53–58. Ann Arbor: Division of Gerontology, University of Michigan.

RODNICK, D. 1948. Postwar Germans, an anthropologist's account. New Haven, Conn.: Yale University Press.

SAUVY, A. 1955. The historical and sociological basis. *In* Old age in the modern world, pp. 28–32. Edinburgh: E. & S. Livingstone.

SCHAFFNER, B. 1948. Fatherland: a study of authoritarianism in the German family. New York: Columbia University Press.

SCHELSKY, H. 1953. Wandlungen der deutschen Familie in der Gegenward. Dortmund: Ardey Verlag.

SHELDON, J. H. 1948. The social medicine of old age: report of an inquiry in Wolverhampton. London: Oxford University Press.

——. 1955. The social philosophy of old age. *In* Old age in the modern world, pp. 15–26. Edinburgh: E. & S. Livingstone.

SHENFIELD, Barbara E. 1957. Social policies for old age: a review of social provision for old age in Great Britain. London: Routledge & Kegan Paul.

SLATER, E., and WOODSIDE, M. 1951. Patterns of marriage: a study of marriage relationships in the urban working classes. London: Cassell.

SWEDISH INSTITUTE OF PUBLIC OPINION RESEARCH. 1956. På Äldre Dagar. Stockholm: The Institute.

TARTLER, R. 1960. The older person in relation to family community and societal factors. Paper presented at Seminar on Aging and Mental Health, Fifth International Congress of Gerontology.

TOWNSEND, P. 1957. The family life of old people. London: Routledge & Kegan Paul.

TRÉANTON, J. R. 1959. Adjustment of older people to urban life in France. *In* C. TIBBITTS (ed.), Aging and social health in the United States and Europe, pp. 167–73. Ann Arbor: Division of Gerontology, University of Michigan.

VAN ANDEL, J. C., and VAN ANDEL-RIPKE, O. 1953. Oud worden in deze tijd. Man en vrouw rondom en boven de zestig. Met een bijdrage van P. J. Bouman over het historisch en sociologisch aspect van de problemen van de ouderdom. Utrecht: Erven J. Bijleveld.

WURZBACHER, G. 1951. Leitbilder gegenwärtigen deutschen Familienlebens. Dortmund: Ardey Verlag.

YOUNG, M., and WILLMOTT, P. 1957. Family and kinship in East London. London: Routledge & Kegan Paul.

IX

Life beyond Family and Work

ROBERT J. HAVIGHURST

I. GENERAL APPROACHES TO THE SOCIAL PROBLEM OF AGING

All the Western societies appear to have followed the same general course in deal-

[1] The author wishes to acknowledge with many thanks the friendly assistance of the following persons in the preparation of this chapter: Dr. Ali Berggren and Miss Maud Helling, Royal Social Welfare Board, Stockholm; Lars Ögren, Swedish Institute of Public Opinion Research; and Dr. Bengt Rundblad, Department of Sociology, University of Uppsala, *Sweden;* Dr. Henning Friis, adviser to the Ministry of Social Affairs, and Rudolf Conrad, director of social welfare, Copenhagen, *Denmark;* Dr. Johannes Roth, secretary, Stiftung für das Alter, Zurich, *Switzerland;* Dr. R. J. van Zonneveld, National Health Research Council, R. Wentholt, Ministry of Social Affairs, C. W. van Dam, secretary, Dutch Federation for the Care of the Aged, and Mr. Streuer, director of the Roman Catholic National Federation for Welfare of the Aged, The Hague; and Dr. Frank, chairman of the Bureau for Social Welfare of the Dutch Reformed Church, Utrecht, *The Netherlands;* Dr. Jean-René Tréanton, Centre d'Études Sociologique, and M. Sadoun, associate director, French Institute for Public Opinion Research, Paris, *France;* Frau Dr. Hannah Behrends, Sepp Groth, Sociographic Institute of the University, and Dr. Ludwig von Friedeburg, Institute for Social Research of the University, Frankfurt; and Dr. Rudolf Tartler, Sociological Institute of the University, and Dr. Klaus Riegel, Psychological Institute of the University, Hamburg, *Germany;* and Allen Sanderson, director, Calouste Gulbenkian Foundation, F. Le Gros Clark, Nuffield Foundation, Peter Townsend, London School of Economics and Political Science, Marjorie Bucke, National Old People's Welfare Council, and Dr. Mark Abrams, research director, London Press Exchange, London; and Bertha James, chairman, Old People's Welfare Committee, Chislehurst-Sidcup, Kent, *England.*

ing with the social problem of old age, though each society has applied the general solution in a way which is specific and characteristic of that society. At first the problem is conceived as an economic problem, and the solution is some sort of pension to alleviate the poverty of many older people.

Next, the conception of the problem is broadened to include the matter of comfortable living arrangements for older people. This aspect of the problem arose because more and more older people were living apart from their adult children and often had to live in the oldest and poorest dwellings of the community. Since the general problem of housing was coming to be considered a social problem, and public-financed housing was being built for younger people, it was natural to consider the needs of older people also for public housing. Moreover, many older people who could afford to pay for good housing created a demand for living quarters especially adapted to their needs and wishes. The problem of housing for older people is not yet met as adequately as the problem of assuring adequate income, but it also is on the path of solution.

The third stage in recognition and solution of the social problem of old age is to conceive it as a psychological problem for the individual older person who needs ego-supporting relationships and activities to help him meet the attacks on his ego which arise from (*a*) the lessening of his physical

vigor and attractiveness; (*b*) the lessening
of his mental efficiency; (*c*) the lessening
of his satisfactions gained from his work;
and (*d*) the loss of spouse or relatives or
friends.

This third stage is generally reached in
a society only after the first two have been
worked through. When the first two stages
have progressed to the point where it is
clear that there still remains a social problem of old age, people are ready to recognize and attack the third aspect of the
problem—that of ego support for older
people. They then recognize that older people have a need to be needed—a need to
have a respected place in the eyes of others
and to be doing something which is interesting and significant in one's own eyes.

Only a few societies have reached this
third stage of social gerontology, though
there are far-seeing, sensitive individuals
in all societies who have discerned the need.
It has been defined by the leading social
gerontologists in Sweden, the country which
has the keenest sense of society's responsibility for the individual and of the individual's responsibility for society. In a
talk at a United Nations conference in
1955, Helge Dahlström, director of the
Swedish Social Welfare Office, put in one
paragraph these three stages or tasks of
social gerontology:

> Our basis for the measures for the aged is
> the conception that old people should be given
> the possibility to live a free and independent
> life to the same extent and with the same social
> amenities as the other age groups in society.
> To realize these aims, it is at first necessary
> that old people should have financial security.
> . . . Furthermore, and, in the second place, the
> old people must have access to good and appro-
> priate dwellings and a social service which cre-
> ates the possibilities for them to live in their
> own homes as long as possible. There also are
> to be measures which will help to make their
> lives pleasant and which break through the iso-
> lation from the outside world which so very
> easily becomes the lot of old people.

A few pioneering attempts to solve the
social problem of old age at this third level

may be seen in several modern Western
societies. These pioneer projects vary a
great deal from one society to another,
partly because they are experimental in
nature and partly because they depend so
much on the "national character" of a society. While Western societies have much
in common in their economic and political
evolution, they differ among themselves in
psychosociological characteristics and, consequently, tend to differ in the ways they
meet the psychological aspects of the social
problem of aging. Thus, in comparing Western societies, we shall see rather marked
differences in the ways they attempt to
meet the problem of ego support, although
the differences are minor when one compares Western societies in general with
other large groups of societies.

A. Social Roles of Adult Life

To make a clear, comparative study of
the ways various countries attack this third
aspect of the problems of aging, we have
adopted the concept of *social role* as our
major intellectual instrument. We shall
compare several social roles of older people
in the various Western societies.

The social life of a person can be described in terms of his performance of a
number of social roles. A social role is a
pattern of behavior which is taught by a
social group and is expected by the group
of those of its members who are in a certain social position. Thus a man may have
the roles of worker, husband, father, citizen, etc., while a woman may have the
roles of wife, mother, citizen, worker, etc.
When filling a particular role, a person behaves according to certain social expectations and is judged by the society in accordance with his fulfilment of these expectations.

For example, it is sometimes said of a
man that "he makes a good father" and
of another man that "he makes a poor husband." This means that the first man is
living up to the expectations of his society
as he fulfils the role of father, while the

second man does not fill the role of husband adequately in the eyes of the people around him in his society.

The social life of an adult can be fairly well depicted by a description of his behavior in the following roles: worker, spouse, parent, homemaker, club or association member, friend, citizen, church member, user of leisure time, and student. If he fills these roles well, according to the expectations of his society, he is *judged* to be a socially competent person, and he *feels himself* to be a competent and successful person. This latter fact is important for our argument. A member of a society takes into himself the social expectations and expects of himself the kinds of behavior that the society around him expects. Sometimes he sets for himself a "lower" or a "higher" standard than that of the society around him, but his expectation of himself is always clearly and visibly related to the social expectations which impinge upon him.

It should be possible, with this concept, to describe what a society expects of people as they grow older and also to judge how well they meet these social expectations. It should also be possible to compare the lives of older people in various societies in this way.

For this particular chapter we shall exclude from consideration the roles of worker and of spouse, parent, and homemaker. These are dealt with in the chapters treating work and family relationships. We shall consider, then, the following roles: club or association member, friend, citizen, church member, user of leisure time, and student.

There is an inevitable decrease in competence and in satisfaction with the worker role as a person grows older. Fortunately, the family roles remain important sources of ego support, especially for women. But, especially in urban societies, older people are thrown more and more upon the roles beyond work and family for satisfaction. If they fill these roles well, they are likely to be happy and well-adjusted people.

From the early sixties to the late seventies the satisfaction and happiness of most people depend on the competence with which they fill several of these roles. After this, as they enter the final period of life, their physical energy and/or their mental acuity fade enough to cause them to disengage themselves from the active roles of life, to find a "rocking chair," and to survey the world from its vantage point. Very few can happily find a rocking chair in their sixties.

In this chapter we shall consider each role in two aspects: what society expects of older people in this role and how well older people actually fill the role. As far as possible, we shall do this for each of the societies under consideration.

Actually, we shall have to be content with only preliminary and tentative descriptions in most cases, because there are not many scientific studies available on these topics. Consequently, we shall have to rely upon the impressions of acute observers in the various societies. This chapter, therefore, must be regarded as tentative in its conclusions and open to considerable correction by more careful studies which may be made in the future.

It will also be noticed that we have included in our list of social roles one—or maybe two—which has little importance for a great many people. The least important, from this point of view, is that of student. While this is an important role for children and young people, it is not generally regarded as important for older people. Furthermore, the role of user of leisure time is not a clearly defined one, as far as social expectations go, in most modern social groups. But it is included here because of its potential importance in the Western societies if present social trends continue to develop.

B. Roles of the Elderly Change in a Changing Society

Between 100 and 150 years ago the modern industrial countries emerged from a stage in which they were all pretty much alike in respect to the life of older people. They were predominantly rural countries, though England in particular already showed the beginnings of urbanism. In those rural societies the functions and the status of older people were quite similar and centered around the family and its economic life. There were economic and family roles which were *functional*—that is, which were useful to the society and meaningful to the individual. The old person was always useful as long as he could be active in the work of the family. As a grandparent, he had a useful set of functions. He could respect himself and be respected by others. The roles outside work and the family had relatively little significance and involved relatively little time in the rural areas, though they generally had more significance in the growing cities.

As a *citizen* the older person continued the interests and activities of his middle age. These were negligible for women, who did not have suffrage and who were not expected to be active in civic matters. For men the civic activities were limited to a few property owners, professional workers, and a small number of leaders of labor. Many ordinary men did not possess the right to vote.

As a *club or association member* there was little opportunity for the common man or woman. Such people did not belong to associations. There were no associations of older people as such. But the few middle- and upper-class men who belonged to clubs or to learned societies retained their memberships as they grew older and probably gained a good deal of satisfaction from them.

As a *church member* the individual had the consolations of the church, which were important for older people. But there were few or no active roles to be performed by the ordinary layman, regardless of his age.

The role of *friend* was a satisfying one for those who had friends outside the family. They could get together for visits—the women in their homes and the men in neighborhood meeting places, such as the tavern, the general store, and the local park in warm weather. There were, however, no practice of finding and making new friends and no arrangements for promoting the formation of new friendships.

There was no concept of *leisure-time activity* as a social role. Men did not retire from work until they were forced to do so by failing powers, and, consequently, they did not have abundant time and energy for leisure activity. Women did their traditional handwork if they could sew and use their fingers. People did not deliberately seek *new* leisure activities as they grew older.

The notion of the older person as a *student* was quite foreign. There was no idea of studying to prepare for something new in one's later years. Only those who had been students all their lives continued to be students in their old age.

OLD AGE 100 YEARS AGO

To summarize the facts about older people 100 years ago, we find that their position in society was much the same in all of western Europe. They were expected to work as long as possible and to continue to be whatever they had been in middle age. When this was no longer possible, they were supposed to live quiet, secluded lives. They were not a recognizable social group or a recognizable social problem. If there were tragedies, as there certainly were, they were quiet, lonely tragedies.

CHANGING SOCIAL CONDITIONS

As the industrial revolution gathered speed, and the cities grew at the expense of the rural villages and open countryside, a number of factors conspired to make major changes in the lives of older people. In the economic sphere the size of the group who had their own independent business, land, profession, or trade decreased, and the size of the group increased who were employed by industry, commercial organizations, and the state.

These wage-workers lost their jobs as they grew older, and they could not at first retain any power over the matter of whether they should work or not. Then, as the workers organized and grew more powerful, they were able to trade their rights to a job for rights to a pension, which gained them a measure of economic security but left them with no active economic role.

In the urban family the older people lost much of their economic function, while the normal tensions between them and their adult children increased owing to unsatisfactory living conditions and the growing uselessness of the older generation in the family. Therefore, older people preferred to live in their own quarters, apart from their grown children, if this was possible. And the number of older people living alone, without a spouse or other relative, increased in the urban areas.

At the same time the proportion of older people increased in the population, growing from 2 or 3 per cent to 8 or 10 per cent, if the proportion 65 and over is considered. Within this group the ratio of the sexes changed somewhat, with an increasing proportion of women and a much increased proportion of widows.

These changes were most striking in the industrialized areas. In the rural areas the social changes were much slower, and today the roles of older people in rural communities are still much like they were 100 years ago.

C. Social Policy for Old Age

In the modern urban-industrial society decisions are made by the society as a political and a social entity which affect the lives of old people. A modern society has a *social policy for old age*. This was not true of the earlier society, with its rural and pre-industrial characteristics. There was no need for a policy for old age in such a society because there was no problem of old age. There were economic functions for all able-bodied people, and there were traditional roles which fitted the economic functions. Old people were not plentiful, and they were seldom "in the way." If they became ill or infirm, they were cared for as a duty by the family or, in special cases, by charitable institutions. There was no stated social policy and no code concerning the lives of older people.

The modern society is more conscious of its older people and of their presence as a factor in the society's well-being. They may constitute a positive or a negative factor. Economically, their presence is both favorable and unfavorable, as the economists are discovering. In the family roles their functions are both positive and negative.

Society adopts a set of procedures for dealing with the economic and family roles of older people so as to increase the positive factors and reduce the negative ones. This set of procedures is the result of a social policy.

Generally speaking, there are two alternative social policies for old age. They are the opposite ends of a continuum, and societies range themselves between the two ends.

The one extreme might be called the policy of *autonomy*. In this case the older person is expected to preserve his independence, freedom of action, and initiative as nearly as possible as it was at his peak of autonomy, which comes in the middle years in modern societies. He is expected to exercise a maximum of choice about his life. This policy must operate in the light of the fact that people generally become less able to exercise independence as they move into old age. They have lower efficiency as workers, their health is impaired, and they may lose economic independence. The current social policy is to *supplement their resources* in such a way as to preserve and enhance their autonomy. This policy encourages individual saving, homeownership, employment as long as possible, and active leisure pursuits such as gardening and travel. It seeks to strengthen the institutions which protect autonomy—the local community, small private business, private pension systems, the single-family home. It argues that a great good is associated with the need to *look after one's self* in one's old age, even though it may be difficult to do so. This policy would use specialists in the study and treatment of older people in such a way as to assist personal initiative on the part of older people.

At the other extreme is the policy of *passivity for the individual.* Here it is assumed that the aged individual cannot care for himself in his later years and cannot guarantee his old age security by planning and saving in his middle age. The modern society is too complex for him to meet autonomously. The solution is for the state to provide financial security through a general old age pension and to provide other forms of assistance to meet his non-financial needs. This policy would build up a staff of specialists in the care of older people—doctors, nurses, social workers, housekeepers, club leaders, and counselors —whose function it is to make old age as comfortable and enjoyable as possible for people.

To most readers this policy of state aid with individual passivity would have little appeal, while the policy of autonomy, with supplemental state assistance on a minimum basis, would have a considerable appeal. But the policy of autonomy can rightly be criticized as unrealistic, if it is carried very far, in a modern industrial society. In such a society the average person has little experience of autonomy in the economic sense. He has little or no control over his income. He saves little or no money unless he is required to do so by a compulsory insurance program. His leisure activities are mainly passive and are determined for him by others who control the mass-entertainment media. Consequently, such a person can hardly be expected to become suddenly autonomous at the age of 65.

In fact, the modern industrial societies are all working out a policy somewhere between the two extremes and generally toward the autonomy pole. If a considerable degree of autonomy in old age is desirable, then probably the roles of association member, friend, citizen, and user of leisure time deserve special attention. For through these roles the older person is more likely to achieve or preserve autonomy than through the work role, where most older people have lost control of their destiny. The family roles, however, remain as areas for the exercise of autonomy and, indeed, almost as battlegrounds in the struggle for autonomy on the part of older people. In his family life the older person strives to maintain old functions or to discover new ones which will give him satisfaction, and he does this with a minimum of assistance or involvement on the part of other institutions, such as the state.

II. Comparing Old Age in Modern Societies

The purpose of the remainder of this chapter is to compare the experience of older people in various Western nations with respect to the roles of living outside work and family relations. This will be done in two steps. The situation of older people will be described in each country, with special reference to the roles mentioned above. In the concluding section the roles will be taken up, one by one, and the various countries will be compared with respect to each role.

A. Sweden

The Swedish old age population has for over 50 years been proportionally one of the largest in Europe. At present approximately 11 per cent of the population are over 65. Although one of the later northern European countries to become industrialized (after 1870), the population conditions in Sweden have been similar to that of England and France.

Relatively early Sweden adopted a system of social security for old people, which is one of the more complete and complex in Europe. It grants a flat old age pension at age 67 to everyone, regardless of his means, and the amount is relatively liberal. There is a current program for increasing the old age pension which, relative to the cost of living, will make it the highest in the world.

Sweden has also moved far ahead of most other countries in providing adequate housing for older people, especially people of small means. The housing policy has the following principles:

1. A person should have a maximum of autonomy in choosing and caring for his own home.

2. Most older people want to live in the neighborhood to which they have grown accustomed. The "home-help" and "meals-on-wheels" services help them to live in their own home, quasi-independent, as long as possible.

3. In the state program of public financed housing, old people should get their fair share.

4. For those with limited financial means there is a housing subsidy.

Thus Sweden has made relatively great progress in meeting the material needs of older people. The need for autonomy, or ego support, is also widely recognized and often spoken of by social welfare officials. In the municipal Old People's Home in Stockholm, for instance, every resident has his name and apartment or room number on a wall directory at the entrance, just as though he were a tenant in a first-class apartment house.

The state appears as an active partner in almost all schemes to improve the conditions of life for older people. Yet the state does not dominate people in Sweden. It acts as an enabling agent to put into effect the social will, which is friendly toward old people.

The society is hospitable to the concept of social and civic activity for older people, who are specifically encouraged to be active in clubs and associations, to join study circles, to travel, to take an active interest in the affairs of the day, and to develop hobbies.

At the level of ego support, or autonomy, Sweden is working experimentally in a number of ways. But here the state must by its very nature go slowly, since its purpose is to encourage personal autonomy rather than a passive acceptance of society's favors.

Sweden illustrates the fact that there is a certain tension—not to say conflict—between a policy of promoting the material welfare of older people through pensions and public housing and a policy of promoting autonomy. The Swedes are aware of this and attempt in their state welfare programs to favor a policy of autonomy.

In the following sections the factual material comes mainly from an unpublished report entitled "På Äldre Dagar" of an interview study made in June, 1956, of a national sample of people over 56 by the Swedish Institute for Public Opinion Research. The material concerning expectations about older people comes from interviews held by the writer with social welfare workers and social scientists in Sweden.

ROLE OF CLUB OR ASSOCIATION MEMBER

The Swedes think of Sweden as a land of democratic associations. They expect persons to belong to associations, not only to trade unions or professional associations, but also to any of a variety of others, which are organized for purposes of social welfare, temperance, education, etc.

From a study of participation in associations, it appears that about 25 per cent of the population aged 57 and over belong to associations other than a trade union or political organization. There is not much difference in extent of membership in ordinary associations between those aged 18–56 and those aged 57 and over (Table 1).

There is a falling-off in active participation in associations as people grow older. Thus, as shown in Table 2, about 28 per cent of those aged 57–66 attend association meetings as often as once a month, while this proportion drops to 21 per cent for those over 67.

There is a considerable verbal desire for more participation in organizations, as shown in Table 3.

Associations in Sweden seem to be more business-like and more "earnest" than in the United States. Associations for the purpose of sociability are not common; but the Old Age Pensioners Association seems to serve this purpose to some extent.

TABLE 1*

MEMBERSHIP IN SWEDISH ORGANIZATIONS

(Excluding Trade Unions and
Professional Associations)

(Per Cent)

ORGANIZATION	AGE	
	18–56	57 and Over
Political:		
Farmers party.............	4	4
Liberal party..............	2	2
Social Democratic party.....	9	6
Conservative party.........	3	4
No political.................	82	84
Christian (free church).......	7	9
Temperance.................	5	5
Sports.....................	13	1
Red Cross†.................	9	14

* Source: Swedish Institute for Public Opinion, "På Äldre Dagar" (unpublished report, 1956).
† The Swedish Red Cross has a relatively active program in local communities.

TABLE 2*

ATTENDANCE AT SWEDISH ASSOCIATION
MEETINGS

(Excluding Trade Unions and
Professional Associations)

(Per Cent)

ATTENDANCE	AGE	
	57–66	67 and Over
At least once a week..........	5	4
At least once a month.........	23	17
At least once a quarter........	14	8
At least once a half-year.......	6	5
At least once a year..........	5	3
Less than once a year.........	40	55
No answer..................	7	8
No. of respondents...........	(349)	(285)

* Source: Swedish Institute for Public Opinion, "På Äldre Dagar" (unpublished report, 1956).

It seems probable that Sweden has a wider participation of working-class people in mixed-age associations than does the United States. This is partly because of the popularity of temperance and Red Cross societies, which appeal to people of lower-middle and working-class status, and partly to the fact that the "free churches" are treated as associations in Sweden, since everybody is nominally a member of the state church, and the "free churches" are relatively small religious societies (Methodists, Baptists, Jehovah's Witnesses, Salvation Army, etc.) with voluntary membership.

TABLE 3*

DESIRE FOR MORE PARTICIPATION IN
ORGANIZATIONS, SWEDEN

("Would You Like To Be a Member of Any of
the Following Organizations, in Case You
Are Not Now a Member?")

(Per Cent)

Organization	Total Sample Aged 57 and Over Saying "Yes"
Labor union or professional...............	9
Christian (free church)..	9
Red Cross.............	8
Temperance...........	7
Housewives'...........	5
Political..............	4
Sports................	1
Other.................	2

* Source: Swedish Institute for Public Opinion, "På Äldre Dagar" (unpublished report, 1956).

The Swedish Red Cross is a popular association, with greater membership among people over 57 than under this age. Apparently, the Red Cross has somewhat greater citizen participation in Sweden than it does in other countries. It has taken a special interest in problems of older people and has been instrumental in recruiting and training home-help assistants and in providing "meals on wheels" for older people in many communities.

The "old people's club" movement seems to be just getting started in Sweden. In

1957 there were fourteen old age clubs in the homes for old age pensioners in Stockholm. There was also a new chess club for older people. Probably, clubs of this type are just beginning to grow rapidly.

The Old Age Pensioners Association is a very active reality and provides a type of old people's club activity. It has a dues-paying membership of at least 105,000 of a total of 700,000 pensioners and publishes a good monthly magazine. While people of all social positions belong to the association, the leadership is drawn largely from the Social Democratic party, and the membership probably has a relatively high working-class proportion. The association took an official position on the recent national referendum on old age security which agreed with that of the Social Democratic party, but active Social Democrats pointed out that many of the individual members of the association would vote for other positions. In any case, the political position of the national organization seems to leave the social and other activities of the local associations unaffected. On the local level the Old Age Pensioners Association seems to be mainly a social group with some common welfare functions. For instance, in the city of Uppsala (80,000) the association holds monthly meetings in the People's House, with an attendance of about 1000. There is a lecture, or movie, or some such feature with a mixed educational and entertainment value, and then the people drink coffee and have a good time. The women of this association have a number of sewing groups which meet in private homes or elsewhere in local neighborhoods. Once a year there is a fair for money-raising purposes. The officers of this association tend to be persons formerly active in Social Democratic circles, although Uppsala is a university town, with many middle-class people.

There is another old age association composed of persons who feel that the Old Age Pensioners Association is too close to the Social Democratic party.

ROLE OF FRIEND OR INFORMAL GROUP MEMBER

The Swedes have a saying, "Heaven in this world is to be alone when I want it; Hell is to be alone when I don't want it." Informal friendship relations in Sweden are regarded by older people as rather difficult to establish. The Swedes have an outer appearance of reserve which makes it difficult for them to make casual friendships.

Furthermore, there is a considerable "social distance" in Sweden among people of different social classes. This is symbolized by the fact that a person with a fairly high status generally has a title of some sort— "Doctor," or "Professor," or "Director"— and is addressed in the third person. "What does Doctor want to eat for dinner?" A person without a title is simply called "Herr" and thus is constantly reminded of the social distance between him and other people. This serves to maintain distance among members of the different social classes in spite of an ideology of political democracy.

The old people's associations, whether conducted by the Old Age Pensioners Association, by social workers under the auspices of the local social welfare office, or by churches, have more the function of promoting informal social relations than of acting as formal associations with programs and projects. As such, these organizations appear to fill an important function in the lives of Swedish older people. The social welfare boards are making a conscious attempt to encourage informal social relations in the pensioners' apartments by designing them with lounges at accessible places which seem to *invite* people to come out of their private apartments and to associate with others.

Swedes of the middle class do a good deal of touring, especially older people. There are a number of summer tours arranged by travel agencies and by individuals which take Swedes all over Europe. For example, a hotel in Merano, Italy, receives several groups each season for periods of 4 or 5 days; the people are mainly elderly women who come in pairs or small groups of friends.

Informal meeting places for older people are found in Swedish towns and cities— coffeehouses for the men who can afford it, parks and reading rooms for all kinds of people. There are also several Swedish spas (Medevi, Luka, Ramlösa) which are much frequented by older middle- and upper- class people. Then, too, certain towns are popular with middle- and upper-class peo- ple as good places to live in retirement. This is true of Uppsala and Lund, pleasant university cities, to which people often go to live in retirement.

potential political force which has the lead- ers of all parties interested. No doubt a considerable block of votes could be in- fluenced by the organized older people in their own interest. Consequently, all par- ties tend to agree on political questions affecting older people directly, such as the current proposal to increase the basic old age pension.

There is not much prestige for older peo- ple in politics as such, the leadership in political organizations generally going to young and middle-aged people. A number of older people who were political leaders now get satisfaction from leadership in the Old Age Pensioners Association.

TABLE 4*

SWEDISH PEOPLE EXPRESSING "STRONG" OR "STRONGEST"
INTEREST IN WORSHIP AND RELIGION
(On a Five-Point Scale of Interest)

	AGE						
	11–18	19–28	29–36	37–55	56–61	62–70	71 and Over
Percentage of people ex- pressing interest......	6	7	6	15	25	32	45

* Source: Swedish Institute for Public Opinion, "På Äldre Dagar" (unpublished report, 1956).

ROLE OF CITIZEN

Older people are expected to be active citizens, and their behavior indicates that they retain their civic interests. Answering the question whether they voted in the last election, people aged 57–66 indicated a proportion of 91 per cent voting, which was about the same as for those of middle age. There was a slight falling-off to about 85 per cent voting when over the age of 67.

As Table 1 indicated, older people have a slight tendency to vote more conserva- tively than middle-aged or younger people. But this may reflect a decrease of conserva- tive political strength in recent decades rather than an actual change in the politi- cal convictions of the present older people. The Old Age Pensioners Association is a

ROLE OF CHURCH MEMBER

People are generally expected to attend church more regularly and to be more in- terested in religion as they grow older. The evidence of Table 4 indicates that this ac- tually takes place to a considerable ex- tent, with substantial increase of interest in religion and worship after the age of 56. This table does not tell whether the people have individually become more interested in religion or whether the present older generation reflects a greater interest in re- ligion on the part of younger and middle- aged people a generation ago.

Individual older people do not get much chance for leadership in church organiza- tions. However, the churches give more op- portunity to older people for leadership than do other organizations, as can be seen in the fact that 4 per cent of church members over 57 were officers, compared with 2 per cent of Red Cross members over 57, 1 per cent in political organizations, and 1 per cent in the Red Cross.

Much of the general activity of the churches is directed toward older people (sewing circles, visiting done by pastors, etc.). Many of the free churches, also, have built old age homes for their older members. Among the people who were active as "visitors" in the state church, 47 per cent were over 57 in 1955, while 39 per cent of the free-church visitors were also over 57. Nevertheless, the extent of church activity and interest in social problems of old age appears to be less than in the Netherlands and the United States.

ROLE OF USER OF LEISURE TIME

It is a generally accepted proposition in Sweden that healthy old people (like people of other ages) should be active and need active kinds of recreation. The tennis-playing of the aged King Gustav was a symbol of this attitude. The term "hobby" is used respectfully in Sweden, whereas it has a slightly scornful connotation in some other countries.

The social welfare boards have "hobby rooms" in their old people's homes, with occupational therapists to teach people weaving and other arts. The tradition of home arts and crafts is supported officially by the social welfare boards. In the new pensioners' apartments there is talk of establishing hobby rooms, and the leaders of the People's House organization speak of furnishing such rooms in their buildings.

As will be seen in Table 5, older people actually tend to spend more time in passive things, such as reading and radio-listening, although an impressive 40 per cent of the people aged 68–73 say that they work more on hobbies than they did when younger. When asked what the things were for which they had "insufficient possibilities," the older people in the public

opinion study expressed dissatisfaction with possibilities for travel (18 per cent) and going to movies (12 per cent).

According to Table 6, old people retain or increase their interests in newspaper-reading, literature, gardening, travel, and music up to the age of 70. In the more demanding intellectual operations of playing chess, solving problems, etc., they lose interest after 60.

One very popular leisure activity in Sweden is the football pool, a form of government-administered lottery, and between a

TABLE 5*

INCREASED ACTIVITIES OF RETIRED
SWEDISH PEOPLE

("Since You Have Retired, What Have
You Done More Of?")

(Per Cent)

	AGE			
	Male		Female	
ACTIVITY	68–73	74 and Over	68–73	74 and Over
Listen more to radio.	52	61	67	66
Read more books....	43	52	27	24
Work more on hobbies	42	23	40	21
Go to church more...	5	10	47	10

* Source: Swedish Institute for Public Opinion, "På Äldre Dagar" (unpublished report, 1956).

third and half of the people aged 57–66 participate once a month or more (Table 7). The answers to the question, "If you should win 75,000 kronor, what would you do with the money?" are given in Table 8.

ROLE OF STUDENT

Adult education has been popular in Sweden since the development of folk high schools in the last century. Recently, there has been a new wave of interest, this time in a small "study-circle" type of educational activity, quite different from the earlier formal lecture type of educational program. The state will provide a partial subsidy for any study circle with five or more members. There were 37,920 study circles in 1952–53 and 48,096 in 1954–55. Assuming an average membership of ten to a study circle, this gives 480,000, or 10 per cent of the population age 20 and over. Of the study circles, 20,000 are sponsored by the Workers Adult Education Associa-

tion, an independent organization affiliated with the Social Democratic party. Thus they reach many working-class people. Of persons 57 years old and over, 2 per cent belong to study circles, with interests mainly in "cultural" subjects, such as literature, and in current social problems. The vocational training function of the

TABLE 6*

SWEDISH PEOPLE EXPRESSING A "STRONG" OR "STRONGEST" INTEREST IN CERTAIN ACTIVITIES AT VARIOUS AGES

(Per Cent)

AGE	ACTIVITY					
	News	Reading Good Literature	Listening to Music	Gardening	Travel or Reading about Travel	Solving Intellectual Problems, Chess, Etc.
11–14......	19	8	41	10	31	18
15–18......	27	11	47	6	34	13
19–23......	31	14	42	14	36	18
24–28......	44	19	40	14	35	16
29–36......	43	18	35	24	35	14
37–45......	44	20	36	26	36	16
46–55......	63	22	53	45	45	19
56–61......	56	18	33	36	24	16
62–70......	56	15	33	34	25	9
71 and over..	43	9	28	22	9	8

* Source: Swedish Institute for Public Opinion, "På Äldre Dagar" (unpublished report, 1956).

TABLE 7*

PARTICIPATION IN THE FOOTBALL POOL, SWEDEN

("Do You Buy Pool Tickets? If So, How Often?")

(Per Cent)

FREQUENCY	AGE	
	57–66	67 and Over
Every week..............	28	12
Twice a month...........	5	5
Once a month or less......	16	9
Never..................	51	72

* Source: Swedish Institute for Public Opinion, "På Äldre Dagar" (unpublished report, 1956).

TABLE 8*

PROBABLE USE OF FOOTBALL-POOL WINNINGS, SWEDEN

("If You Should Win 75,000 Kronor, What Would You Do with the Money?")

(Per Cent)

PROBABLE USE	AGE	
	57–66	67 and Over
Travel..................	10	4
Buy a home.............	25	18
Live in better style.......	10	17
Improve living quarters....	13	11
Give it to children or relatives..................	11	29
Give part or all to charity.	3	11
Save it.................	22	14
Invest in a business.......	2	0
Pay some debts..........	5	1

* Source: Swedish Institute for Public Opinion, "På Äld Dagar" (unpublished report, 1956).

study circle for younger people does not have much significance for older people, as can be seen in Table 9.

Generally speaking, adult education even in its modern and more attractive form has no great appeal to older people in Sweden. But there is discussion, now, of developing study circles and discussion groups dealing with preparation for retirement. This will probably be given a trial in Sweden. Also, some study circles for older people are now being started which are more social and less intellectual in program than the usual study circle. The sponsor of one of these says that it should be called a "satisfaction circle" rather than a "study circle."

B. Denmark

The Danish old age population is similar in proportion to that of Switzerland and Germany. It has been growing more slowly than that of Sweden, France, and Great Britain. At present approximately 10 per cent are over 65.

The Danish system of social security is one of the more adequate ones. All Danish citizens of 67 years or more (exclusive of civil service pensioners) are entitled to a national pension of a fixed amount, with a supplement where need can be proved.

Public housing for older people has been provided by many of the towns of Denmark, as well as by Copenhagen, on a scheme whereby the central government pays half of the cost and the local community pays half. There are about 370,000 old age pensioners in Denmark, and about 30,000 of them live either in public housing "pensioners' flats" or in municipal old people's homes.

Recently there has been some criticism of the policy of segregating old age pensioners in special apartment buildings, and, consequently, the Danish government has adopted a plan for paying rent subsidies to old age pensioners who live in non-profit housing projects, no matter where they are located. In general, it can be said that the state has made liberal provision for income

and housing for older persons who need help in Denmark.

With respect to ego support, there is relatively little going on in Denmark, though people are beginning to talk about it. There are four agencies or groups that have expressed an interest in and claim to be doing something about helping older people to find more meaning in life. These four are the church, the municipal social welfare agencies, private welfare agencies, and the old age pensioners' associations. It is too early to say which of these organizations will find ways of working effectively on behalf of older people.

TABLE 9*

REASONS GIVEN FOR STUDYING BY OLDER AND YOUNGER SWEDISH PEOPLE

(Per Cent)

REASON	AGE	
	18–56	57 and Over
To improve vocational performance.............	24	9
To prepare for an examination...................	1	0
For pleasure or because of personal interest........	56	68
Other reasons............	10	3
Cannot answer...........	9	20

* Source: Swedish Institute for Public Opinion, "På Äldre Dagar" (unpublished report, 1956).

ROLE OF CLUB OR ASSOCIATION MEMBER

Like the Swedes, the Danes do not have many organizations for purely social purposes. They have associations for serious purposes—mainly economic and political. The Danes do not have such strong temperance societies, "free-church" societies, and Red Cross societies as the Swedes, and consequently the Danes participate less in associations than the Swedes. However, a Dane who is an association member tends to retain his membership as he grows older, except that he reduces his activity and interest in his trade union.

In recent years there has been some growth of old people's clubs. Two old age pensioners' associations have been formed. A voluntary organization known as the Society for the Care of Lonely Old People (Ensomme Gamles Vaern) was founded in 1952, and the Lutheran Welfare Society has started a movement in the Danish state church to organize work on behalf of old people.

To date the activities of these organizations have remained on a highly informal level. A typical church program consists of visits by the pastor and members of a group of visitors to older members of the parish, with coffee hours in the home of the pastor for the older people. Much of the success of the program depends on the pastor's wife.

TABLE 10*

ANSWERS TO QUESTIONS BY SAMPLE OF 1200 DANISH PERSONS 60 AND OVER BY PLACE OF RESIDENCE

(Per Cent)

Like To Spend Time with—	Copenhagen	Provincial Towns	Rural and Semirural
Other old people.....	28	32	48
Young people.......	22	12	7
Both groups........	50	56	45

* Source: Danish Gallup Institute, 1951.

The Society for the Care of Lonely Old People is privately supported and works mainly in Copenhagen. It has ten "winter rooms" in Copenhagen, which are social centers under the direction of volunteer middle-class women. Some 4000 people come to these centers for entertainment and for coffee and pastry, for which they pay a small fee. During the four summer months the society operates a rural colony which accommodates 440 people for two-week vacation periods. In the course of the summer there are two gatherings in Tivoli (the famous amusement park in the center of Copenhagen) each for 1000 old people; and there is a Midsummer Eve festival.

A poll by the Danish Gallup Institute in 1951 was taken on a sample of 1200 men (65 and over) and women (60 and over).

The question was asked, "Whom do you like best to spend your time with?" The answers to this question are given in Table 10. These figures may indicate that the rural older people have a more stable and "normal" social life. They have their friends of their own age as well as their families of mixed ages. The older people in the city may be striving harder to keep "young and active."

ROLE OF FRIEND OR INFORMAL SOCIAL GROUP MEMBER

In Denmark most social activity among friends takes place in the home rather than in clubs or public places. Consequently, those older persons who live with their families tend to see their friends in their homes. On the other hand, those who live alone, in pensioners' flats and other similar lodgings, generally have relatively little informal social activity with friends.

THE ROLE OF CITIZEN

The Dane is expected to retain his interest in civic affairs as he grows older. To help him in this, a number of old age pensioners' organizations have recently sprung up. Two of them are the Folkepensionist-Foreningen, founded in 1939, and the Folke og Invalidepensionist-Foreningen, founded in 1945.

These organizations have potential political power, and they also provide a certain amount of informal social relationship through serving coffee after their meetings. Leaders of these associations are older people.

ROLE OF CHURCH MEMBER

The Danes generally take their state church for granted, with the older people more loyal in attending and taking communion. Older people have a good deal of prestige in the churches and tend to retain their position on the church councils.

An attempt was made, a few years ago, by the church to organize and hold religious services in the old age pensioners' flats, but this was discouraged by the municipal Department of Social Welfare on the ground that it might infringe on the privacy of the residents. It was said by an official of the Welfare Department that such an attempt might be regarded more favorably now.

USE OF LEISURE TIME

The Gallup Poll of 1951 asked the older people whether they find the day to be tedious. The day was seen as going easily by 82 per cent, while 8 per cent said that it varies, and 9 per cent said that it drags. The usual daily activities are listed in Table 11. The residents of Copenhagen were more likely to read, take walks, listen to the radio, and play cards than were the town and rural people.

For most of the people their present activity is something they have done for a long time. But 15 per cent started needlework or some other handwork after retiring, 10 per cent started reading or listening to music, 18 per cent started cardplaying, and 55 per cent of those taking walks have started it since retiring. In all cases, these are percentages of those who now engage in the activity. New pleasures or joys mentioned by the older people were grandchildren (31 per cent) and the Lord, the church, and the Bible (10 per cent).

There is not much development of facilities for hobbies of older people. Some of the pensioners' flats have rooms in the basement for arts and craft activities, but few of them are in use. Sometimes these rooms have been made into an extra apartment. At the great municipal Old People's Home in Copenhagen (De Gamles By) there is an excellent occupational therapy unit. The program is aimed at helping the individual (1) to feel accepted by the therapist and others; (2) to feel useful through making useful and salable things; and (3) to form social relationships with the therapist and others. Thus this is essentially an ego-support program. Apparently, its success depends on its direction by a professionally trained person; older people are not

likely to do this kind of thing on their own initiative.

ROLE OF STUDENT

Older people are welcome to take part in adult education activities for mixed-age groups of all kinds, for example, the municipal evening schools and workers' education classes. There is no movement to provide group counseling or discussion for people in preparation for retirement.

TABLE 11*

ACTIVITIES OF RETIRED PEOPLE IN DENMARK

(Percentage of Those Replying to the Question, "What Are Your Main Activities?")

Activity	Women	Men	Total
Looking after the house, garden, poultry, etc....	44	40	42
Needlework, domestic industry..............	58	2	33
Reading..............	30	38	33
Walking, riding a bicycle.	7	24	15
Visiting................	12	14	13
Working for money......	4	14	9
Radio-listening.........	5	6	5
Card-playing...........	2	4	3
Other activities........	5	18	11
Total†.............	167	160	164

* Source: Danish Gallup Institute, 1951.
† Some respondents gave more than one answer.

THREE CASES

The paucity of statistical data on the experience of older people in Denmark may be relieved by the following accounts of interviews with three older people, all residents of pensioners' flats. As will be seen, there is a considerable range of socioeconomic status among those who are eligible for residence in such flats.

Mr. Hansen—in the town of A——.— This town has built two pensioners' homes, one for couples and one for single people. The two buildings are adjoining and house about thirty people. A matron is in charge. The houses are set in a grassy park across the street from the school building.

Mr. Hansen is in his seventies and has been in his one-room apartment for 5 or 6 years. He is a bachelor and has knocked around the world, having worked in Argentina and California as a dairy worker. In 1936 he came back to Denmark and operated a small farm, but later he sold out and did odd jobs until he could work no longer. His older sister was already in this home, and he followed her.

He has belonged to no organizations and says that most people do not belong to organizations other than trade unions. He belongs to the local old age pensioners' association, which meets two or three times a year for social occasions. He enjoys these meetings. He does not know who the officers are and says that the association has no political program. Mr. Hansen enjoys religious services held alternately in this home and the one in a neighboring village a mile away. He often walks over to the other home for their service. They usually serve coffee afterward.

Mr. Gravesen.—Mr. Gravesen is 80 years old. With his wife he lives in a two-room pensioners' flat in Copenhagen. He was a barrel-builder before his retirement at age 69. When he and his wife became unable to look after their old home, they moved to this flat, where they have very little housekeeping to do. They get a hot meal every noon from a mobile kitchen that serves pensioners' flats. He belongs to no associations and dropped his union membership when he retired. He goes to church occasionally. He does not belong to an old age pensioners' association. He has done no handwork since he retired. He likes to read the newspapers and chat a bit with his neighbors. He sees his grown children and their families occasionally.

Mrs. Jensen.—Mrs. Jensen speaks good English. She was the daughter of a landowner in Jutland, who sent her to a boarding school in Copenhagen when she was a girl. She has traveled a great deal and spent five years in Boston and New York. She has a married son and a married daughter in Copenhagen, both of whom are fairly well to do. Both are now building summer homes, and she has just re-

turned from a month's visit with her daughter.

Mrs. Jensen is an amateur artist and has a nephew who studied art in Paris. She bought some of his watercolors, just in order to encourage him. Being 85 years old and unable to manage a place of her own, she feels lucky to have this flat with its services. Her only wish is that she had a small bedroom. She has not been used to sleeping in her living room. Being on the third floor, she enjoys the view from her window of a park and football field across the street.

Mrs. Jensen never belonged to any associations and does not wish for this now. She has her own personal religion and does not feel a need for a church. She reads a little and does needlework. She says, "I like to have something in my hands." She does not care much for radio, except for news and good music.

C. Switzerland

Switzerland is a conservative society, with a strong rural tradition that is guarded jealously. In 1950 only a third of the population lived in urban places. Yet the fact is that Switzerland is steadily becoming more urban and more industrial. The labor force has changed from 36 per cent engaged in agriculture and forestry in 1888 to 15 per cent today. (These figures refer to those who have been or are active in the labor force.) Meanwhile the proportions of people in commerce, transportation, and the professions have more than doubled. The proportion of pensioned persons has more than tripled.

While the society has been changing, the population structure has been changing also, with now almost 10 per cent of the people over 65. Among women, widows and unmarried women outnumber the women who have living husbands two to one in the age group over 65, while married men living with their wives outnumber widowers and single men two to one. Thus there is a large group of people, mainly women, who are pretty much alone in the world.

There is a small old age pension which goes to everybody and which is supplemented by old age assistance grants on the basis of a means test. The maximum grant is far below that of the Scandinavian countries.

In the rural villages older people have continued to have an economic and family function. They can do their share of the work of splitting wood, cutting hay and drying it, digging potatoes, and keeping the tools in repair. A farmer ordinarily holds title to his property until his death, and he usually lives in his own house with a grown child and grandchildren.

The life of an older person has not changed much in the last 100 years in the Alpine villages. But the cities have witnessed the usual urban changes. Older people tend to live by themselves; they are retired from work and have little to occupy their time.

ROLE OF CLUB MEMBER

Club life is not generally regarded as necessary for older people, and, with the exception noted below, people are expected to drop out of clubs as they grow older. Thus, in a study made in a peasant village, 14 of 37 women over 60 had been club members, but only 3 were now active. Among men over 65, 16 of 23 had been club members, but only 2 were now active.

There is the beginning of an old people's club movement in the Zurich area, with four clubs. The largest of these has been formed by Migros, a co-operative society, in connection with its Adult Education Center. Founded in 1953 with 100 members, this club has grown to 500 members, with an average attendance of about 180 at the weekly meetings. This club has a retired teacher as its principal officer. There are only 80 male members. Meetings are held in the Adult Education Center, with the lounge and buffet always open for card-playing, conversation, and coffee-drinking. The club membership is a mixture of

social classes. The women knit and put together a Christmas box for "the poor people in the mountains." There is a bus tour twice a year to summer resorts, as well as weekly excursions in the Zurich area. Recently, a group paid a visit to a new church built in "modern" style. They sang hymns together and had a wonderful experience in the sanctuary. This club is self-supporting.

According to the club president, it is difficult to get new things started. "The inertia of people is tremendous," he says. They tried fitting up a workshop for the older people, but few of them came. As a rule, they do not go in for study courses. A few take part in the regular adult classes run by the society.

The president of the club believes that older men have the greatest difficulty adjusting to life in the city. They tend to become "fifth wheels," without function. The best thing for them is a part-time job. The club keeps a list of men who want employment and succeeds in finding jobs for some of them.

Zurich contains about 55,000 older people. Perhaps 2 per cent of them have some contact with a club for older people.

In the rural villages there are no clubs for older people, but the local pastor or priest generally organizes a monthly afternoon meeting, except in the summer, when people are busy with household work. He leads a devotional service, which may be followed by refreshments. Since the church leadership tends to operate in an authoritarian manner, the old people themselves do not manage these affairs.

ROLE OF FRIEND, OR INFORMAL GROUP MEMBER

The friendship role is not highly developed. Women do not get much opportunity to leave their homes. Men are more likely to meet in a park in warm weather. Those who can afford it may have a favorite coffeehouse or tavern. Thus, in a city of 40,000, the retired middle-class business and professional man may be found either

at the "Three Kings" or "The Star." In
the study of a peasant community previously referred to, the women seldom went out,
but some of the men went to a *Stammtisch*.
One man said that his wife sent him to a
tavern "to find company," while the grandchild of another man said, "On Sunday he
goes to the tavern."

ROLE OF CITIZEN

Older men are expected to take a mild
interest in civic affairs. Women do not vote
in Switzerland, a fact which reduces the
political power of old people, since there
are more women than men in the older age
group. There is no political activity of
older people as such and no organization
of old age pensioners.

In this connection the French-language
part of Switzerland may be moving toward
a greater degree of civic activity. Thus recently the organization called Vert Au-
tomne, which keeps up the *Wanderwegen*
(footpaths) in eastern Switzerland, has recruited several hundred older people to
work part time on the upkeep of foot paths.
Although they may get a small amount of
pay, the older people see this mainly as a
means of being useful to the community.

ROLE OF CHURCH MEMBER

People tend to go to church services more
faithfully as they grow older, and those
who have been leaders in the local church
council may retain their positions of leadership as long as they wish to fill an active
role. However, the principal church activity for its older members as such is the
monthly service already mentioned.

ROLE OF USER OF LEISURE TIME

In the rural villages and in the farm-
houses the older people use their leisure
time by doing simple work around the
home. They enjoy looking after household's
cats, dogs, and birds and caring for the
chickens. Most older women do needlework. Within the family there is some
card-playing, the favorite game being jass.

Among the 60 older people interviewed in
the peasant village, 5 women and 2 men
played cards a great deal. The majority of
people read the newspapers and listen to
the radio. Somewhat over half of the older
women and men go for walks, especially
on Sunday.

In the cities the time is more likely to
hang heavily on the hands of older people.
But they also busy themselves as much as
possible with gardening, handwork, and
taking walks.

ROLE OF STUDENT

The role of student is not expected of
old people, and few of them take part in
adult classes. There is no educational program of preparation for retirement.

CONCLUSION

It might seem that older people in Switzerland lead a dreary life compared with
those in Sweden or England, for example.
But this probably is not true of those in
the villages and country, where they retain
the functions of the elderly in an agricultural society. In the cities their life probably is somewhat dreary. At least the people in the social work profession believe
that there is need for programs aimed at
helping older people find some meaning in
life.

The Swiss society Pro Senectute is now
paying more attention to the problem of
ego support for urban old people. In addition to its function of providing homes and
other material assistance to the needy aged,
it operates a visiting service. Inevitably,
older people in Switzerland will look increasingly for meaningful activity outside
the work role and outside the family circle.

D. West Germany

Germany differs from the other Western
countries in one important respect: she
has lost two world wars within the twentieth
century, with the result that the economic
cost has been borne largely by today's older

people, in addition to their personal loss of sons and husbands. In 1923–25 there was a ruinous inflation that wiped out the savings of most ordinary people, and in 1945–48 there was an inflation terminated by currency reform that confiscated the largest part of the savings of the "small people."

Thus old age has come to have the connotation for Germans of poverty and misery. But this is juxtaposed with a tradition of respect for authority, which is generally associated with old age and especially with the elderly man as head of a family. Some 10 per cent of the population in West Germany is over 65, and this will increase to perhaps 12 per cent in the next 10 years. Berlin now has 14 per cent over 65.

Interviewing a sample of working-class and lower-middle-class people aged 20–64, Friedeburg (1955) found that 75 per cent of these people thought that the economic situation of old people receiving social security benefits in Germany today was "bad" or "very bad," while only 2 per cent thought that it was "good." When asked whether they expected old age to be a "good" or "bad" time for them, 19 per cent thought that it would be a "good" time; 29 per cent thought that it would be "not so good"; 10 per cent thought that it would be "bad"; and 43 per cent could not say. Recently, the economic situation of the elderly has been somewhat improved by a new pension law which brings nearly everybody into the social security system and which has raised the level of payments somewhat.

Germany established the first system of social insurance in Europe, and consequently the people have had a long time in which to become accustomed to the state as an agent for their economic welfare. Perhaps for this reason as well as others, the German people generally appear to accept and adopt a more passive attitude toward their old age than do people of other countries. They accept retirement from work as a matter of course, and in a recent study of public opinion they indicated that the preferred average age for retirement was 63.4. They accept a system of government-supported pensions and favor its extension to practically all people.

However, one rather small group of people appears to have a different attitude toward old age. These are the people in the "independent" occupations—law, medicine, small private businesses, and certain skilled trades. They have not in the past been covered by social security laws. A recent study of these people indicates that they have managed to get along in the difficult periods of the current century remarkably well. They continue to work as long as possible, generally until 70 or 75. They may have private insurance or annuities. In case of serious difficulty they secure help from their families or other private sources. They may be described as the most "autonomous" of old people in Germany.

The need for housing of the elderly is rather poorly met in Germany, mainly because so many houses were destroyed during the war that an acute housing shortage has existed for all segments of the society. Nevertheless, there is a tradition of several centuries of old people's homes, and this type of housing is rather plentiful. Thus, in 1956, there were 729 Evangelical church old people's homes in West Germany, with 147,000 beds, or enough for about 3 per cent of the population over 65.

In postwar years there have been a few pensioners' flats erected at public expense in such cities as Hamburg. These are similar to those in Denmark but are not so numerous.

The urban-rural contrast of living arrangements is striking in Germany. For example, Table 12 compares the living arrangements of people in a rural peasant community with that in a non-homeowning section of a large city. This table shows that the three-generation family is quite common in the village but almost non-existent in the city. A study comparing living arrangements of people over 65 in several different types of communities gave the following results concerning the percentages of older people living in a three-generation family: rural village, 55; workers' suburb of a city, 53; new middle-class suburb of a city, 19; a community of refugees from Soviet-occupied areas, 16; and a rented-house area of a large city, 13.

Taking all West Germany, 26 per cent of people over 65 were living only with a spouse in 1950, while another 13 per cent were women living alone, and 5 per cent were men living alone. The preferences of men aged 20–64 concerning living arrangements are reported, as shown in Table 13, by Friedeburg. Here the urban-rural contrast is visible again, with 47 per cent of the rural men preferring to live alone with

their wives, as compared with 80 per cent of the city dwellers. If older people do not have a function in the family, it is regarded as desirable for them to live apart. For instance, one elderly lady used to darn the stockings of the family. She now lamented her loss of function, saying, "Now they have nylons, and there is nothing for me to do."

Since there has been more research on social aspects of old age in Germany than in the other Continental countries, we will report more fully on Germany, remembering that the social situation is about the same for elderly people in West Germany as in Switzerland and Denmark, though their economic situation is at present somewhat worse. The need for ego support of older people, however, is beginning to be talked about in Germany, though it is believed that the needs for economic security and for comfortable housing are somewhat more pressing.

In considering the experience of older people in Germany, it is well to remember that Germany is a heterogeneous country, with people from several different culture streams. Therefore no generalization about "German" expectations or social roles is likely to be equally true of all sections of the country. For instance, the North Germans are reputed to be a very serious, industrious, and work-minded people. For

TABLE 12*

LIVING ARRANGEMENTS OF THE POPULATION IN TWO TYPES OF GERMAN COMMUNITY

(Per Cent)

Living Arrangement	Non-home-owning Section of Large City	Rural Peasant Village
Living together as married couples, with or without children.	50	55
Living in three-generation families.	4	43
Broken families: living alone, with non-relatives, or one-sided family (e.g., mother with children).	46	12

* Source: Sepp Groth, *Soziale Welt* (Göttingen), **4** (1953), 205 ff.

TABLE 13*

LIVING ARRANGEMENTS PREFERRED BY MARRIED GERMAN WORKING-CLASS AND LOWER-MIDDLE-CLASS MEN WHEN THEY RETIRE

(Per Cent)

LIVING ARRANGEMENT	POPULATION OF PLACE OF RESIDENCE				
	Under 2000	2000–4999	5000–19,999	20,000–99,999	100,000 and Over
With children.	36	33	16	12	7
With friends and relatives	3	. . . .	5	1	1
With wife.	47	54	63	71	80
Entirely alone.	3	6	7	4	4
No answer.	11	7	9	12	8

* Source: L. von Friedeburg, *Altersbild und Altersvorsorge der Arbeiter und Angestellten* (Frankfurt orschungsbericht, Inst. für Sozialforschung, Universität, 1955), p. 63.

them, work is likely to be the principal axis of life, and the psychological significance of their work is likely to be different from that of the Rhinelanders. The latter are reputed to like a kind of work that brings them in contact with other people. They are more likely to enjoy the life of social groups than the more individualistic northerners.

ROLE OF CLUB OR ASSOCIATION MEMBER

There is a saying in Germany that, "when three Germans get together, they found a society." It is not clear whether this is more true of Germans than of other national groups, and similar statements are current concerning others. But it is true that Germany has a large number of organizations for men and some for women and that these are not limited to middle-class people. The social expectation is that people will continue to take part in the formal associations of their adult years, but with some decrease of interest and activity.

There appears to be a slight decrease of club activity after about age 60. Reigrotzki (1956)[2] found in his adult sample that 60 per cent of the men over 60 and 34 per cent of the women were members of some organization (including church societies), compared with 73 and 37 per cent of the entire adult group. Men belonged to 1.68 organizations on the average, and women to 1.28. Neuloh (1956–57), in his study of retired miners, found that two-thirds of them claimed to be as active as ever in organizations, while 20 per cent said that they had withdrawn from associations, often because of lack of money. In Neuloh's group, 45 per cent said that they still attended trade-union meetings with some regularity, while Reigrotzki, in his national sample, found that trade-union membership for men dropped from 28 per cent of those aged 45–59 to 12 per cent of those

[2] Erich Reigrotzki, of the Institut für Demoskopie, Allensbach, Bodensee, made an interview study of a national sample of adults in 621 communities, with 3246 interviews, in 1954. A good part of the data reported here is from his study.

over 60. It appears that Neuloh's miners in the Ruhr area kept up their union activity more than the average trade-union member and, in addition, took part in associations for gardeners, small-animal breeders, and for amateurs of sport and hobbies.

When it comes to clubs for older people, the German experience is just beginning. There are a few old people's clubs in the larger cities, but they are generally new and experimental. There is no organized club movement for older people, and the writer could find no instance of a club organized by and for older people. The closest approach to this is in West Berlin, where a substantial program of social centers has recently been established by the social welfare authorities. In these social centers a number of interest groups have developed, led by older people. For instance, one of them has nine such interest groups (literature, music, etc.).

At present it would appear that such old people's clubs as do exist in Germany are generally organized by social workers and that they serve as places for informal social activity for older people. They are not much like the formal self-governing associations of the middle-aged group.

In summary, it may be said that formal associations are of significant value to older people in Germany, who tend to retain their membership in them as they grow older. These associations are mainly for urban people. Men get more value from them than women do. Working-class people enjoy them as well as middle-class people.

ROLE OF FRIEND OR MEMBER OF
INFORMAL SOCIAL GROUPS

As in other countries, the informal social relationships of older people are regarded as desirable, but not much is done to promote them. The striking exception to this statement is provided by the experimental program of social centers established in 1957 in West Berlin. Thirty centers have been set up there by the social welfare authorities. At first they were open to all elderly people regardless of their economic status, but they were so well patronized that rules were drawn up giving preference to people who were in special need of them —usually working-class people. These centers seem to provide a place for informal association with other people for "passing the time." Men play cards and smoke and talk; women do handwork and talk.

The old people's clubs which have been started by social workers in other cities also seem to serve the function of providing a place and a stimulus for friendship activities. The same thing can be said of the Quaker neighborhood centers in several German cities, which serve the entire age range in a neighborhood, but usually have an informal old people's group. The social center movement is thus getting a trial in Germany, but whether it will work out remains to be seen, since earlier attempts at developing social centers for all ages in the public housing units have not succeeded. The quarters designed for social centers have generally been turned into living quarters. The writer visited some of the housing projects for elderly people built by the city of Hamburg. These do not have room for communal social activities; they are simply pleasant apartment buildings in which each elderly couple and single person have their own quarters but are not encouraged to develop a community social life.

It is generally supposed that men get more out of informal social activities than do women and that they need this more. The woman is busy with her household work and may get time to gossip with her neighbors. But her husband, if he does not have work, is likely to mope around the house and to get in her way. So she sends him out to talk with his cronies in the park, if it is good weather. When he can afford it, he goes to the neighboring *Stammtisch* to read the papers, talk with friends, and drink beer or coffee. If he cannot afford this, he spends the good weather out in the sun in a park or on a bench by the river.

In bad weather he may seek a warm room, such as a free reading room in a library or a newspaper office.

Germany has not developed any "old people's resorts" like the Florida communities or Torquay on the south coast of England. One reason is that there are no really warm winter resorts in Germany, and another is that there are not many older people who can afford such a trip. Still, one can see a substantial number of elderly people in the once-fashionable spas of Germany in the summer. For those who can afford it, the annual visit to a spa provides a pleasant outing and offers some opportunity to make friends and to be with friends.

In general, it seems that informal friendship activity is not an important source of satisfaction to many older people in Germany. It is perhaps more important to the elderly people of the villages and to a minority of people, mostly men, who have retained their earlier habits of frequenting social clubs and meeting places and have enough money to meet the expense of continuing these habits.

ROLE OF CITIZEN

The German public accepts the activity of older people in politics and respects the wisdom of old age. The age of Chancellor Adenauer is not regarded as a handicap. Some of the older Social Democrats and trade-union leaders continue to be quite active.

Reigrotzki (1956) found a small dropping-off in voting and political activity after age 60, but it was very small. Older women are more likely to cease voting than older men. Neuloh's study (1956–57) of retired miners in the Ruhr area found that 40 per cent were actively interested in politics. Eighty per cent knew their local mayor's name, and many knew him personally. Ten per cent of these men have an unpaid office in the political life of the community. It appears, then, that there is more interest in civic affairs by older people in the industrial than in the other areas and that there is more interest in domestic politics than in the national or international variety.

There is a Vereinigung der Rentner ("Union of Pensioners"), with headquarters in Frankfurt, and organized groups in several other cities. It is not nearly so active as the ones in Scandinavia.

ROLE OF CHURCH MEMBER

The general expectation in Germany is that, as people grow older, they will attend church more often and become more religious in their attitudes. However, they are not expected to take a more active part in church leadership simply because they are growing older. In the Protestant churches there are local church councils which provide lay leadership. A person serves on the council as long as he is able and willing. He is not arbitrarily retired on account of his age. But people are seldom recruited for new positions on a church council if they are already old.

The actual data on church attendance, according to Reigrotzki's study (1956), indicate that people 60–79 attend church more regularly than any other age group. It is also striking that men in the older age bracket attend church more often than women, which reverses the sex differences that appear in the earlier ages. It is not clear just what this means. There may be more old women who are invalids and unable to attend church, or the self-reports of the two sexes may differ in accuracy.

Although the church leaders in Germany are just beginning to become concerned about the problem of old age, they are much more concerned with youth problems. For instance, a Frankfurt newspaper published two leading articles on the typical city church as seen by the clergyman in the spring of 1957. One article was by a Protestant and the other by a Catholic clergyman. Both had churches in suburbs of large cities, with mixed socioeconomic populations. Both men recounted the work of a typical week. Both accounts were full of comments on the youth program, for which there was a special assistant. The Catholic pastor did not mention the old people at all. The Protestant pastor spoke of a small group of older members who gathered in the parish house once a week for coffee and of another group with pietistic leanings who consisted mostly of older people and who met for a weekly prayer meeting in the church. On the other hand, in 1956 there was a meeting of church leaders on the subject of the church's responsibility for work with older people which resulted in a series of conclusions and recommendations, including a program of counseling, of social activities, and of interest in the economic welfare of the older people.

ROLE OF USER OF LEISURE TIME

It is not expected in Germany that older people will discover or develop new leisure activities or that they will be strenuously active in such things. An exception to this general statement occurs in the case of some upper- and upper-middle-class people who specialize in certain types of conspicuous leisure activity such as travel, studying genealogy, collecting, painting, and joining groups which are interested in local history.

It is expected that older women will do handwork and that older men will sit and talk with their friends. In addition, it is expected that certain leisure habits of earlier years will be intensified, such as gardening and raising small animals.

In practice, people seem to continue the leisure activities already started and to intensify some of them. For example, Neuloh (1956–57) reports that there is much interest in small-animal raising by older people in the Ruhr region, especially of goats. Also the miner traditionally had his pig and insisted on having a pigsty in the new postwar model houses. Among Neuloh's retired miners, 67 per cent had gardens on their own land or on rented land, with 100–800 square meters of surface. Friedeburg (1955) found gardening to be the favorite anticipated leisure activity of his sample aged 20–65.

Table 14 shows what people expect to do with their spare time when they retire. Table 15 reports the preferred leisure activities of adults of all ages.

TABLE 14*

ANSWERS TO QUESTION OF NATIONAL SAMPLE OF GERMAN MEN AGED 20–65†

("What Do You Expect To Do When You Retire?")

(Per Cent)

Do gardening or raise small animals...	44
Go for walks........................	33
Follow leisure interests (art, radio, science, reading, etc.).................	31
Work for extra income..............	11
Work around the house; make myself useful..........................	11
Total........................	130‡

* Source: L. von Friedeburg, *Altersbild und Altersvorsorge der Arbeiter und Angestellten* (Frankfurt: Forschungsbericht, Inst. für Sozialforschung, Universität, 1955).

† The percentages given in the table are based upon the 51 per cent who gave specific answers to the question; the 49 per cent who did not give specific answers are omitted. The men in the sample were from the working class and the lower middle class.

‡ Some persons gave more than one answer.

ROLE OF STUDENT

Adult education is fairly well developed in Germany through the folk high schools, and a small proportion of older people enrol in these institutions for courses in "cultural" subjects. There is no adult education for old people as such, though there is some talk of experimenting with discussion groups on problems of retirement. Those older people who have led a life of scholarship, whether in teaching or in research, are welcome to go on with this work even after they retire with a pension.

E. The Netherlands

The Netherlands has experienced a relatively recent industrialization and has maintained a high birth rate which has kept the proportion of aged people at the lowest level of all the northern European countries. The proportion of people over 65 changed from 4.7 per cent in 1849 to 8.5 per cent in 1957. The ratio of women to men aged 65 and over has decreased from 1.27 in 1849 to 1.10 in 1947—an un-

TABLE 15*

PREFERRED LEISURE ACTIVITIES OF GERMAN PEOPLE

("If You Had More Money and Time, What Would You Do with Them?")

(Per Cent)

ACTIVITY	MEN					WOMEN				
	18–24	25–29	30–44	45–59	60 and Over	18–24	25–29	30–44	45–59	60 and Over
Travel.............	59	65	59	55	40	65	68	63	50	41
Entertain neighbors.	5	8	7	13	9	6	11	10	11	13
Read..............	23	38	25	23	23	28	34	31	29	23
Go to theater......	22	36	25	26	17	41	38	37	26	25
Spend time with family...........	15	40	47	52	40	35	43	51	48	42
Handwork, hobbies.	27	30	24	27	18	39	42	37	25	22
Political activity....	8	7	7	9	10	1	4	2	1	3
Take part in church activity..........	4	8	6	12	16	6	9	10	15	21
Do more in local community activity...	5	3	7	6	11	7	7	8	13	16
Play sports.........	50	44	20	17	5	31	18	14	6	......
None of these......	4	3	5	9	24	5	4	7	13	22
No. of respondents	(195)	(158)	(463)	(437)	(324)	(230)	(215)	(648)	(538)	(269)

* Source: E. Reigrotzki, *Soziale Verflechtungen in der Bundesrepublik: Elemente der Sozialen Teilnahme in Kirche, Politik, Organisationen und Freizeit* (Tübingen: J. C. B. Mohr, 1956).

usual trend. In the Netherlands there are relatively fewer elderly widows than in other countries. Among women aged 65 and over, there are almost as many women living with their husbands as there are widows.

A state old age pension without a means test has been in force since 1957.

The remarkable thing about the life of older people in the Netherlands is the extent to which they are organized into associations. Because of the religious and political heterogeneity of the people, combined with the strength of their religious ties, there are a large number of associations of older people. About 35 per cent of the older people are Roman Catholic; 41 per cent are Dutch Reformed; 7 per cent belong to the "Reformed" Dutch Reformed Church, which is more conservative in its theology; and 10 per cent claim no church ties. There is, finally, a small liberal group called "humanists."

The religious divisions are so important in the eyes of the Dutch people that they have their own radio associations and programs. As a matter of course, they run their own schools. Moreover, they have their own training schools for social workers and their own old age associations.

ROLE OF CLUB OR ASSOCIATION MEMBER

Although the Dutch do not think of themselves as "club-minded," they have made more use of clubs for older people than probably any other country. In fact, it appears that clubs are more general in Holland than in most countries. The ordinary Dutch community has its football club and clubs for gardeners, pigeon-raisers, photographers, amateur dramatists, and fishermen. There is generally a large "association of housewives." In one particular community of 60,000 inhabitants, thirty brass bands turned out for a community festival. Thus clubs or associations of various types and sizes are very common in the Netherlands.

These clubs have a fairly wide social class range of members, with their greatest numbers from the lower-middle and upper working classes. Upper-middle-class people are less likely to be club-minded. The director of a university institute commented on the club activities of the concierge of his building. When asked how he was going to spend the next week end, this man said: "Oh, we've got the Anglers' Club this evening, and then tomorrow afternoon the Football Club has a game; and I shall have to talk over Garden Club purchases of fertilizer with a committee on Sunday. There's always something to do."

Men belong to associations more than do women. The latter are expected to be at home or possibly to attend women's associations. Persons do not drop out of associations merely because of age, though they often resign because of expense or because, as they grow older, they lose interest in a particular club activity.

Old people's associations.—There are four major associations of older people in the Netherlands. Three of them are neutral in religious matters (Bond voor Staatspensionnering, Algemene Nederlandse Bond voor Ouden van Dagen, and Federatie van Bonden van Ouden van Dagen). The fourth (Unie van Diocesane Bonden van Gejaarden en Gepensionneerden in Nederland) is related to the Roman Catholic church. These four associations work together in the national Contactorgaan van Samenwerkende Organisaties, and they all have in their program the improvement of the material position of the aged and the stimulation of good recreation. Probably 300,000 of the Netherlands' 950,000 people over 65 pay dues to one of these organizations, receive its monthly or quarterly journal, and attend one or several meetings a year.

As for office-holding, 3.9 per cent of a national sample said that they now hold office in an association, with church and social organizations the most popular.

Old people's clubs.—The four general associations mentioned above have as a major activity the sponsorship of clubs for older people and probably account for a total of about 1000 clubs. The number has been growing very rapidly since 1954. Moreover, there is quite a number of old people's clubs related to the Dutch Reformed and the Conservative Reformed parishes, without a separate organization. A number of other organizations which do not consist primarily of older people support and conduct old people's clubs. For instance, the Union of Volunteer Women conducts 150 clubs, the Salvation Army has a club program, and the Protestant Christian Women's League sponsors clubs. It is estimated that probably 100,000 Dutch people are now members of old people's clubs, or about 11 per cent of the population over 65.

A major reason for the relatively large development of clubs in Holland is the fact that many local municipalities will pay about half of the running expense of a club through a system of grants approximately matching the fees paid by members themselves. The members generally pay about 10 cents (Dutch) a meeting. The municipality subsidizes a club in proportion to its attendance. Other expenses, such as those of furnishing the club quarters, may be paid by the church organization or other sponsoring groups.

Possibly another reason for the success of old people's clubs is that most of them are backed by church organizations, which in the Netherlands have vigorous programs for the social welfare of their people. There is a committee on the welfare of the aged in each major denomination and in each major district which is constantly looking for opportunities to develop clubs and other activities. These committees *for* the aged should be clearly distinguished from the associations *of* the aged.

Nature of clubs.—In the Netherlands there is general agreement that clubs should not exceed fifty members. Some organizations set a limit at twenty or thirty, while others allow a club to grow to a hundred members but do not expect an attendance of more than fifty at a meeting. Clubs usually meet once or twice a week, in the afternoon, often in a room in the

parish house of the church. The program is informal, with cards, films, phonograph recordings, occasionally a talk, and exchange of books. Excursions may be arranged, and there may be joint meetings with other clubs.

Leadership is provided by the members themselves or by middle-aged people who volunteer their services; especially in the Roman Catholic organization the principle has been adopted that leaders both of local clubs and of the Old People's Association should be themselves older people. Thus some clubs are run by older people for themselves, while others are run by middle-aged people for older people.

Most clubs have *more men than women* in active participation. This is different from the clubs in most other countries. When asked to account for this difference, Dutch informants generally remark that club work is regarded as a man's activity in the Netherlands. Most clubs adhere to a principle of mixed membership. There are a few women's clubs, such as the successful farm women's clubs in Friesland. One explanation given for the predominance of men in the clubs is that the Netherlands has relatively fewer widows than other countries, and widows are more likely to join clubs than are women with husbands.

The clubs show a leaning toward a working-class composition. Trade-union members seem to gravitate easily into clubs as they grow older, and trade-union leaders are likely to become club leaders. The Catholic Old People's Association was founded by Catholic trade-union leaders. Even today, middle-class Catholics are said to hesitate to join their Old People's Association.

One way to broaden the base of membership is to develop several clubs sponsored by a given church in a community. This has happened in Utrecht, which has twenty clubs under the auspices of the Reformed church, the various clubs tending to consist of people of like social station and similar interests.

There are more old people's clubs in

cities and towns than in the rural villages, where the old people are not so much recognized as a group apart but fit into the normal family life.

Upper-middle- and upper-class people rarely belong to clubs for old people. They meet in their own types of social clubs, which are not divided along age lines but in which older people usually have the leading positions. But these clubs have a limited significance in the social lives of upper-middle- and upper-class people. On the whole, they use their homes as a basis for their social relations. There are only a few English style social clubs in the Netherlands, such as De Grote club in Amsterdam and De Witte in The Hague.

ROLE OF FRIEND OR INFORMAL GROUP MEMBER

To a considerable extent the old people's clubs provide a basis for informal, friendly relations. Supplementing them are a few social centers, such as the one sponsored by the United Volunteer Women in Arnhem. Here a building, staffed by UVW members, is open all day.

Old men often have favorite meeting places in a park, on benches near a harbor, or in a cafe.

Generally speaking, old people are not expected to make new friends easily, and it is thought that older people suffer from social isolation as they grow older. But some persons do make new friends in the clubs. The physicians who collected the data for van Zonneveld's (1960) study rated the people whom they knew as lonely and/or withdrawn in 19 per cent of the cases of men and 24 per cent of women (preliminary report on the first 1000 cases).

Table 16 shows how the regular social contacts, with friends and families, are related to age.

ROLE OF CITIZEN

Older people are expected to become less interested and less informed on civic matters and to be "set" in their political opinions. The old people's associations have a potential, if not an actual, political significance. They are capable of providing a good many votes on a proposition of special interest to older people. For example, the Algemene Nederlandse Bond voor Ouden van Dagen, which is neutral in a religious sense, had 74,000 members in 1957, in 225 local sections. Its official purpose is to promote a better housing and financial position for the elderly and good leisure activities.

More explicitly political is the Bond voor Staatspensionnering (Association for

TABLE 16*

PEOPLE HAVING REGULAR SOCIAL CONTACTS IN THE NETHERLANDS

(Per Cent)

Age	Face to Face	By Correspondence
65–69	80	42
70–74	76	38
75–79	73	35
80–84	73	31
85 and over	71	23

* This table is from a public opinion study made in 1951–52 by interviews with a quota sample of 11,304 people in 155 communities. The women's sample was biased toward women without husbands (see J. Diedrich, *Report of a Survey of Older People, 1951–52* [Amsterdam: Bureau voor Marktanalyse en Sociografisch Onderzoek, 1955]).

a State Pension), with 160,000 members in 1957, not all of whom are old people, a monthly newspaper, and meetings of local branches one to three times a year. Having achieved its goal of a general state pension for the aged, it now works for adequate housing, greater recreational facilities, provision of adult education, and the improvement of the morale of the aged.

ROLE OF CHURCH MEMBER

It is expected that older people will become more religious and more faithful in church attendance, and this does happen except for a decrease of attendance after age 75, as can be seen in Table 17. The attendance at most churches is heavily weighted toward the older ages. Older people get some opportunity for service to the church through retaining leadership positions until they are fairly well along in years. The Reformed church has a rule that pastors must retire at 65 and lay officers at 70.

ROLE OF USER OF LEISURE TIME

The most effective influence on older people's use of their leisure time in the

TABLE 17*

REGULARITY OF CHURCH ATTENDANCE AMONG OLDER PEOPLE IN THE NETHERLANDS

(Per Cent)

Age	Male	Female	Both Sexes
65–69........	52.4	53.9	52.8
70–74........	49.4	44.2	47.7
75–79........	43.3	39.5	42.0
80–84........	34.6	25.0	30.7
85 and over...	21.7	14.3	18.6

* This table is from a public opinion study made in 1951–52 by interviews with a quota sample of 11,304 people in 155 communities. The women's sample was biased toward women without husbands (see J. Diedrich, *Report of a Survey of Older People, 1951–52* [Amsterdam: Bureau voor Marktanalyse en Sociografisch Onderzoek, 1955]).

TABLE 18*

USE OF FREE TIME BY OLDER PEOPLE IN THE NETHERLANDS

(Per Cent)

Type of Activity	Men	Women	Both Sexes
Gardening, helping on farm.............	32.0	6.5	25.0
Handwork, hobbies...	8.0	66.8	24.2
Games, music, etc....	20.8	9.5	17.7
Sports—active (fishing, etc.)..........	20.0	3.7	15.5
Reading............	6.8	10.1	7.7
Raising animals......	6.6	2.9	5.5
Smoking............	4.5	0.1	3.3
Study, administration	1.3	0.4	1.1

* This table is from a public opinion study made in 1951–52 by interviews with a quota sample of 11,304 people in 155 communities. The women's sample was biased toward women without husbands (see J. Diedrich, *Report of a Survey of Older People, 1951–52* [Amsterdam: Bureau voor Marktanalyse en Sociografisch Onderzoek, 1955]).

Netherlands is probably the old people's clubs, though, of course, the leisure activities of middle age continue as they do in other countries. People are expected to do fairly much what they have been doing, only more of it, as they grow older. The men tend to garden, fish, and play cards; the women, to knit. Table 18 shows the principal free-time activities as reported in Diedrich's (1955) survey. In van Zonneveld's study (1960), 45 per cent of men and 41 per cent of women reported that they had at least one hobby. Thirty-seven per cent of the men said that they were still working, though many of these were officially "retired," and 48 per cent said that they did *not* enjoy retirement.

Although reading was not mentioned often as a special interest, when a direct question was asked, 12 per cent of people

TABLE 19*

PREFERENCES OF OLDER PEOPLE AMONG RADIO PROGRAMS IN THE NETHERLANDS

(Per Cent)

Type of Program	Male	Female	Both Sexes
Church service.......	29	54	36
News..............	35	13	28
Light music.........	18	19	19
Plays..............	6	5	5
Classical music......	4	5	4
Readings...........	4	3	4
Sports broadcasts....	2	0	1
Children's choir......	1	2	1

* This table is from a public opinion study made in 1951–52 by interviews with a quota sample of 11,304 people in 155 communities. The women's sample was biased toward women without husbands (see J. Diedrich, *Report of a Survey of Older People, 1951–52* [Amsterdam: Bureau voor Marktanalyse en Sociografisch Onderzoek, 1955]).

over 65 said that they read "much" and 33 per cent said that they read "regularly." Listening to the radio was reported as "much" by 8 per cent and/or "regularly" by 35 per cent. Preferences among radio programs are listed in Table 19.

ROLE OF STUDENT

Older people are welcome in adult-education activities for groups of mixed ages, but there are few adult-education activities planned for older people. A few industrial concerns are beginning to take an interest in preparing their employees for retirement.

F. Great Britain

Great Britain has one of the most mature populations in the world, being exceeded only by France and Belgium in the proportion of people over 65 years of age. England's population has aged very rapidly during the present century, having more than doubled its proportion in the over-65 group.

Aging has been recognized as a social problem for a considerable time in Britain, primarily as a problem of social welfare. The first surveys of the status and problems of older people were made in England. In response to the findings of widespread loneliness as well as of need for financial assistance and physical care, there has developed a considerable social apparatus. Several social services help meet these various needs, such as the Home Help Service and the district nursing and welfare services.

Britain has invented a social instrument for the welfare of the aged in the form of the Old People's Welfare Committee, organized on a local community, a county, or a regional basis. The committee consists of representatives from voluntary and statutory bodies concerned with the elderly. Sometimes there is a social worker as the organizer and executive officer. Legislation of 1948 permits a local governmental authority to pay the salary of an organizer and to provide modest grants for the work of an Old People's Welfare Committee. In 1958 there were 1339 committees, but only a minority of communities provided for a paid staff member.

The old people's welfare committees work together through the National Old People's Welfare Council, with headquarters in London. This council issues bulletins and has several national committees to promote clubs, housing and home services, and the training of volunteers for work with the aged. Funds from the King George VI Foundation have been used to pay for training courses, with an enrolment of over two thousand persons.

The National Old People's Welfare Council (1955) has issued a circular to old people's welfare committees, with suggestions for the following services:

Friendly visiting—Bringing needs of the elderly to the notice of voluntary societies and statutory authorities—Making known to the old people themselves help available—Social and other clubs—Assisting enquirers to find accommodation—Housing—Communal homes— Boarding-out Chiropody Laundry — Night Attendance Schemes—Meals: mobile services and lunch clubs—Handicraft and other classes —Publicising or initiating occupation or employment schemes—Mobile Library Services— Aids for infirm, sick and handicapped persons— Holidays—General information and advice— Club Conferences—Conferences and meetings for voluntary workers—Old People's Days or Weeks—Transport by cars, specially adapted vehicles or wheel chairs—Film shows and recreation for the housebound and in clubs—Shopping, reading, preparing house for return of old person from hospital and other individual services.

To see how a committee operates under favorable circumstances, we may use as an example the Old People's Welfare Committee of Hammersmith, one of the central-western sections of London, which has a considerable working-class population. This borough has a total population of about 120,000, of which about 13,000 are over 65, with a ratio of women to men of almost two to one. The Old People's Welfare Committee started as a private organization during World War II and now has eight members from the Hammersmith Borough Council, eight members from voluntary service organizations, and a councilor as chairman. A full-time executive secretary, or organizer, is paid by the council, which provides between £4000 and £5000 for the work of the committee. This committee sponsors the following services for older people: mobile library service, reduced rates for cinema and concert tickets and on boot and shoe repairs, homecraft and handicraft classes, counseling service, foot clinic, friendly visiting, hairdressing service at reduced rates, legal advice, mobile meal service, luncheon clubs, radio-receiver loan, housing information, and holiday excursions.

The general British experience is that people under 70 tend to be fairly autonomous and respond to facilities which enable them to plan and act for themselves, while people over 70 tend to be more passive, asking for little more than to enjoy their last years in peace, and more content to make the best of their circumstances rather than to alter them. But this generalization must be qualified by considerations of socioeconomic status—the higher status people being more autonomous—and by considerations of personality differences. Some of the single and widowed women over 70 are quite active and autonomous.

A survey made by the National Federation of Community Associations showed some of these things. To a questionnaire sent out in 1954, ninety-nine community associations reported on what they were doing to assist old people to continue a normal community life. In general, it was indicated that older people are seldom active in the affairs of the association but that they are likely to be involved in the activities of people of their own age. Some of these groups are quite autonomous under the leadership of older people. For instance, one association reported that "our Good Companions are very independent and entirely run their own affairs." Another report stated: "Our Old Age Pensioners Association, which was organized by and is an activity of the Center, retains almost complete independence. They are so strong and active that their other name is the Youth Club."

On the other hand, other associations reported apathy on the part of older people, even when strong efforts were made to provide programs for them. One report said:

Perhaps the answer to our particular problem lies in the fact that the Old-Age member that we get is the residue of the Industrial Revolution. They have all had to work long hours for very little money in the Heavy Steel Industries or the Mines and, without being unchristian and uncharitable, I think it is fair to say that all they ask is that you leave them alone to play dominoes until the undertaker calls for them. Many of them are barely literate—they can just read a newspaper, but seem to have no understanding of the problems of the day and do not want to be bothered to learn.

ROLE OF CLUB OR ASSOCIATION MEMBER

In Britain the role of association member is an important one for adults. Members of the upper and upper-middle classes are likely to belong to social clubs as well as to civic organizations, and they retain their membership after they retire from work. Minor leadership positions often go to older men. There also are workingmen's clubs, often with their own premises and sometimes meeting in taverns. The workingmen's club is often quite important in the life of an older workingman.

Old people's clubs generally attract women and men of working-class and lower-middle-class levels. About three-fourths of the members are women, a contrast with the Netherlands, where the relative number of club members is about the same but where men outnumber women.

In Britain there were estimated to be about 6000 old people's clubs in 1957, as against 4000 in 1954. Assuming an average membership of 75, this gives a total of 450,000 club members in a population of about 5,000,000, or 9–10 per cent. Townsend (1957) has estimated that 10–11 per cent of old people are members of clubs and cites one city (Ipswich) where 20 per cent are members. Remembering that women outnumber men three to one in old people's clubs (and also that women outnumber men in the old age population), it may be that as many as 15 per cent of older women are club members and possibly 6–8 per cent of older men. There are also a number of ex-servicemen's clubs and women's clubs which have a large old age membership.

Nature of old people's clubs.—Most old people's clubs are organized and led by middle-aged members of voluntary organizations, such as the Women's Voluntary Services or the British Red Cross, or are organized and sponsored by the local Old People's Welfare Committee. However, there are also a number of clubs run by older people, including those which are organized and operated by the Old Age Pensioners Association, where the leadership is in the hands of pensioners. The Federation of Old Age Pensioners has a political program, while the clubs sponsored by the Old People's Welfare Council do not. In a particular area in Kent, there are six clubs sponsored by the FOAP and twelve by the OPWC. Here the Old People's Welfare Committee is 10 years old and consists of representatives of organizations with an interest in old people, including a representative of the old people's clubs and a representative of the Old Age Pensioners Association. The first club was started in 1947. Average attendance is about 75, of a membership of from 80 to 100. Meetings are held weekly. Each of the OPWC clubs has a clergyman sponsor and may meet in the church hall though the church does not sponsor the club. Each club has the headmaster of a local primary school as an adviser, who arranges for children of his school to take part in the club's Christmas festival, etc. The local municipality gives the OPWC a small fund which it divides among the clubs at the rate of about £5 a year. Members usually pay 4*d.*–6*d.* a meeting. Club members are generally working-class people. Some have a little money, and others receive money from their children. In this community, 90 elderly people paid 11 guineas for 2-week lodging on a vacation tour to Paignton, a summer resort, in 1958.

Another example of club structure is given by the town of High Wycombe, with about 4000 people over 65, and ten clubs with 700 members, or about 18 per cent of the older group. Here there are three women's clubs, three men's clubs, and four mixed clubs. Six of these meet in church halls, two in British Legion halls, one in a community center, and one (a mixed club) in a tavern or public house. There is no Federation of Old Age Pensioners in High Wycombe, though there is one in a neighboring town. The Old People's Welfare Committee is made up of representatives of several agencies, including the Central Aid Society, a private welfare organization of long standing in the community. Leaders of the clubs are mainly people in their fifties. There has been no change in leaders, except in the case of the oldest club (12 years), whose first leader moved out of the community. Each club has its own visiting committee, which organizes visits to club members who are ill.

The club structure in a London borough is illustrated by what exists in Hammersmith. Here the old people's clubs are under the supervision of the community recreation officer, an unusual arrangement. There are ten clubs, of which eight meet in church halls, one in a school in a housing project, and one in a rented hall. Sponsorship is provided by the Red Cross, the Women's Voluntary Services, the Old Age Pensioners Association (two clubs), and churches. They meet once or twice a week in the afternoon. Membership in the clubs is concentrated among women—and among the more active women. Thus, in a study of a sample of 100 people over 70 in this borough, Miss Slack (1954) found that 13 of 69 women were club members, while none of the 31 men belonged to a club. Of the women, 11 were widowed or single, and all belonged to clubs with mixed membership. Seven of the women were members of two clubs. Forty-one persons in the sample were homebound and thus could not get out to club meetings. The other principal reason given by non-members for not joining a club was "lack of interest" or definite "dislike" of clubs.

The old people's club movement has

grown rapidly in England in the last 10 years and may be reaching its peak at something like a membership of 20 per cent of the older people in a particular community. Limits are set by the fact that people under 70 do not join such clubs readily, that people who are homebound cannot get to club meetings, that men do not join as readily as women, and that middle-class persons are not so likely to join.

of bringing older people together to enjoy friendly association. Related activities, usually sponsored by old people's welfare committees, are holiday tours, luncheon clubs, and visiting committees. The luncheon club seems to be a British invention, mainly found in London or other metropolitan areas. For example, Hammersmith has three luncheon clubs, frequented mainly by men, and serving an average of 200

TABLE 20*

RELATIONS WITH FRIENDS, GREAT BRITAIN
(Per Cent)

RELATIONS WITH FRIENDS	MEN (65 AND OVER)		WOMEN (60 AND OVER)	
	Married	Widowed and Single	Married	Widowed and Single
At least one regularly visited or visiting in the home†	20	17	25	44
At least one regularly met outside the home†	44	66	14	5
None seen regularly	36	17	61	51
No.	(41)	(23)	(57)	(82)

* Source: P.Townsend, *The Family Life of Old People* (London: Routledge & Kegan Paul, 1957).
† At least once a month on the average.

ROLE OF FRIEND OR INFORMAL
GROUP MEMBER

Townsend (1957) studied older people in Bethnal Green, a borough of London occupied mainly by manual workers. He found that more than half the women did not visit or receive visitors from a friend as often as once a month. Men were better off, as is shown in Table 20. Some made friends through old people's clubs, and some through the churches. In this sample 72 per cent said that they were not lonely; 22 per cent, that they were sometimes lonely; and 5 per cent, that they were very lonely. Ten per cent had three or less social contacts a day on the average, that is, they saw three or less people in a customary or prearranged way at home or outside.

As is the case in other Western countries, the old people's club is mainly a way

people a day. Elderly men frequent the public parks, and in bad weather they are likely to congregate in the reading room of the local library.

A description given by Townsend (1957) of a one-day outing of old people from Bethnal Green illustrates the type of informal group activity that appeals to a large number of working-class people:

About 400 old people from Bethnal Green went in 11 coaches to Brighton for a day. The day was grey and cold. Everyone appeared to be early. One woman of seventy-five had been ill the day before and had passed a sleepless night. This did not prevent her coming on the outing. En route the coaches hummed with talk, large and small. At Brighton the 400 made their way, in slow-moving groups, to the end of the central pier, where they were to have lunch in one of the large, showy pavilions. Bystanders were told, "We're from good old Bethnal Green." There was much teasing and flirting, mutual sympathising over infirmity and health and the inadequacy of pensions, and proud stories were told about children.

The men, many of them in white silk scarves and caps, mostly gathered together in groups away from the women, partly, perhaps, because they seemed to be under-represented in numbers. One had a box camera and was at pains to take good photographs. During the midday meal only the nearest score of people or so could hear the speeches and the great majority continued eating or talking in complete innocence of the words of welcome. After the meal a long queue formed outside a sweetshop and great quantities of rock [candy] were bought for grandchildren, grandnieces and nephews. The afternoon was free and the old people seemed to do much the same as any other group of people let loose in a seaside resort, except that they did it a good deal more slowly. They tried the promenade railway, the slot machines in the amusement arcades, the shelters and deckchairs along the front, the souvenirs, the ice-cream and the postcards depicting little red-nosed men with drooping moustaches and fat women with large buttocks. People accompanied and talked to each other because they were sisters or cousins, or neighbours or children's neighbours or friends from schooldays.

A dozen of the women joined arms in one of the arcades and danced riotously up and down to the tune of "Oh, Susanna, don't you cry for me, for I come from Alabama with a banjo on my knee." At the centre of one of the larger groups was a white-haired, thin woman carrying a paper umbrella and wearing one bright red and one bright blue stocking, a multicoloured dress under her coat and a Robin Hood cap. A final hour or two was spent on the pier during which vast quantities of fish and chips were consumed in the pavilion. On the way home the eleven coaches stopped at a wayside pub. Some bought flowers for their daughters from a man outside and many thronged the bar. Several of the women danced to an accordion, one of them capering about with a large ostrich feather trembling from her head and deliberately raising the hem of her skirt to reveal a pair of long, white frilly bloomers stitched with blue ribbon. In general the women seemed to have far more bounce and energy than the men. Throughout the journey the coaches bulged with a roar of Victorian and Edwardian music-hall songs. The words voiced the preoccupations and interests of working-class families. Most people seemed to know by heart scores of these songs [pp. 127–29].

For people of upper-middle- and upper-class station there are informal association possibilities in their homes, in social clubs, and at vacation resorts. Certain towns in southern England have concentrations of older people both as year-round residents and/or vacation visitors. The towns of Torquay, Bournemouth, and Bath are noted as places for retired people to live. At Torquay the organization known as "The Good Companions," with 300 members, has a social center open six days a week.

Another type of organization promotes friendship and informal association as a by-product. This is the old people's workshop, which has been developed in a few places as a means of providing some earning opportunities to older people. The workshop at High Wycombe was opened in 1955 under sponsorship of the OPWC, with its main object "to provide the Old People of the Town and District with some occupation in pleasant surroundings and the opportunity to meet others. The remuneration is and always has been of secondary importance." A small building was turned into a workshop, and jobs were solicited from local business and industry. In the summer of 1957 there were twelve men and about forty women working at five different jobs. In addition to paying for the upkeep of the premises and for tea, the earnings, when divided equally among the workers, amounted to about a shilling an hour for a 4-day week. The people work in a relaxed fashion, with time out for the midday meal and for tea and conversation.

ROLE OF CITIZEN

The older person in Britain is expected to retain but not to increase his civic interests. A few older people maintain leadership in local community politics, though old age does not in itself give them an advantage. The English believe that older people are more conservative, but this has not been proved, although it is known that more older people vote for the Conservative party. In a study of voting behavior in a mixed district in Bristol, mainly residential, Milne and Mackenzie (1954) came to the conclusion that "the Conservatives draw their solid support from women, the middle class, and older people." Within a given social class the older people had more of a tendency than the younger to vote Conservative. A public opinion survey made in 1951 in Birmingham gave the results shown in Table 21, indicating that older people are more likely to call themselves "Conservatives." But there is no direct evidence that present-day older people have changed their political views in the moderate direction as they have grown older.

There is a certain amount of political activity by the Federation of Old Age Pensioners. This organization sponsors a number of old people's clubs and has a political program aimed at getting a standard old age pension of £3 a week. Leaders are themselves elderly people, generally thought to have a leaning toward the Labour party.

ROLE OF CHURCH MEMBER

Not more than half of the adults in Britain attend church, and, as shown in the Birmingham sample reported in Table 22, there is not much change with age. Those older people who do attend church sometimes find leadership roles available to them, and they often assume useful activity in carrying on the program of the church.

TABLE 21*

POLITICAL SELF-REPORTS IN RELATION TO AGE IN
THE BIRMINGHAM AREA

(Per Cent)

POLITICAL PREFERENCE	AGE			
	16–29	30–44	45–59	60 and Over
Conservative..................	30	38	41	50
Liberal......................	7	4	7	8
Labour......................	36	37	27	18
Doubtful....................	11	11	10	9
None or no answer...........	16	10	14	14

* Source: Unpublished data from Mark Abrams, research director, London Press Exchange.

TABLE 22*

CHURCH ATTENDANCE IN RELATION TO AGE IN THE
BIRMINGHAM AREA

ATTENDS CHURCH OR CHAPEL	AGE			
	16–29	30–44	45–59	60 and Over
Regularly....................	15	13	14	19
Occasionally.................	30	32	33	33
Never or rarely..............	55	55	53	48

* Source: Unpublished data from Mark Abrams, research director, London Press Exchange.

The churches themselves are much used as meeting places for old people's clubs, and many clergymen have active relations with a club; but very few churches explicitly sponsor programs for older people. One exception to this rule was noted in Hammersmith, where the Baptist church makes a definite effort to attract older people who are not in other churches. There are some religious radio services rather popular with older people.

ROLE OF USER OF LEISURE TIME

While the British rather expect a man to retire from his work at about 65, there is no clearly defined role for the older person as a user of leisure time. The upper-class person has been more or less leisured all his adult life and is expected to go on fairly much as in the past. The working-class man is expected to be tired and to be happy with little or nothing to do. For the middle-class man the expectations are even less clear. Women of the working class or the middle class are expected to go on keeping house much as usual.

Among manual workers there is a tendency to continue the use of their skills in such a way as to earn a small amount of money. Often a man will take his tools to his own home and perhaps set up something in his garden. For example, he may raise small animals or birds for sale, or a shoemaker may continue to do a small amount of shoe-repair work.

Hobbies are acceptable, and training in handicrafts is generally available. But relatively few men start something new along this line as they grow older. Most women have handwork to do. What people over 70 do with their time in the London borough of Hammersmith is reported in Tables 23 and 24. Reading and listening to the radio are most prevalent for the men, and these plus playing cards and doing handwork are characteristic of the women. When they leave their homes, the women spend most of their time in public

TABLE 23*

USE OF TIME BY PEOPLE OVER 70 IN HAMMERSMITH, 1953

(Per Cent)

Activity	Men (N = 31)	Women (N = 69)
Reading....................	29	59
Listening to radio............	27	53
Playing cards...............	3	14
Gardening, or tending window boxes....................	12	11
Keeping pets................	12	11
Odd jobs about home........	4	0
Handwork or hobbies........	2	28
Watching television..........	0	2

* Source: Kathleen M. Slack, *Over Seventy* (London: National Council of Social Service, 1954).

TABLE 24*

PLACES VISITED BY PEOPLE OVER 70 IN HAMMERSMITH, 1953

(Per Cent)

PLACE VISITED	REGULARLY		OCCASIONALLY	
	Men (N = 31)	Women (N = 69)	Men (N = 31)	Women (N = 69)
Park or public garden..........	8	8	5	9
Church......................	1	11	6	11
Tavern (public house)..........	3	2	7	1
Cinema......................	0	4	5	14
Theater......................	1	1	2	5
Sports, old-time dancing........	2	2	0	0
Public lecture................	0	1	1	0

* Source: Kathleen M. Slack, *Over Seventy* (London: National Council of Social Service, 1954).

parks or at church, while the men substitute a tavern for church. These tables refer to working-class people.

When the leisure activities and interests of older people are compared with those of younger people, it develops that older people generally tend to narrow their interests and particularly to spend less time and do fewer things away from home. Tables 25 and 26 show how the reading interests of older people tend to become constricted.

The reduction in reading among older people may be partically due to their having less education than the present generation of younger people.

ROLE OF STUDENT

Older people are welcome in adult classes, but they do not attend in large numbers. A study of the students in adult-education classes in the Manchester area in 1947–49 showed that the proportion of

TABLE 25*

NEWSPAPER TOPICS OF MOST INTEREST TO ADULTS IN THE
BIRMINGHAM AREA BY AGE

(Per Cent)

TOPIC	AGE			
	16–29	30–44	45–59	60 and Over
Local news...................	59	65	73	61
Party politics..................	32	52	55	44
United Nations and cold war....	32	50	54	43
Cartoons and comic strips	54	48	39	32
Cooking and running the home..	35	43	40	40
Football.....................	41	40	44	27
Trade and employment.........	31	43	47	29
Women's fashions..............	42	40	32	22
Films and film stars...........	50	36	26	12
Birds........................	33	30	29	21
Dance music..................	31	19	10	6
Racing.......................	17	17	19	12
Concert music.................	16	17	18	17

* Source: Unpublished data from Mark Abrams, research director, London Press Exchange.

TABLE 26*

AVERAGE NUMBER OF PUBLICATIONS "LOOKED AT" PER ADULT IN THE
BIRMINGHAM AREA, 3 MONTHS, 1956

NO. AND NATURE OF PUBLICATIONS	AGE				
	16–24	25–34	35–44	45–64	65 and Over
8 national dailies.............	1.56	1.53	1.40	1.45	1.19
10 national Sunday papers......	2.43	2.39	2.36	2.20	1.71
17 general weeklies...........	3.25	2.74	2.45	2.21	1.48
19 women's weeklies..........	1.61	1.35	1.26	1.12	0.87
9 general monthlies..........	0.76	0.72	0.68	0.60	0.35
17 women's monthlies..........	1.10	0.92	0.90	0.89	0.55

* Source: Unpublished data from Mark Abrams, research director, London Press Exchange.

people over 50 ranged from 12 to 32 per cent, as is shown in Table 27. Another study of a national sample of people showed that 9 per cent of the people aged 45–59 had attended within the preceding week a class or society or club or political meeting. This percentage decreased with age.

At present the adult-education authorities are experimenting with groups to discuss problems of retirement. The National Old People's Welfare Council has established a group of people to study the matter of preparation for retirement, and a movement of considerable importance may be getting under way.

TABLE 27*

STUDENTS IN ADULT-EDUCATION CLASSES IN MANCHESTER DISTRICT BY AGE, 1947–49

(Per Cent)

SUBJECT	AGE		
	Under 30	30–49	50 and Over
International affairs..	25	49	26
History.............	13	55	32
Sociology and social philosophy........	21	52	27
Literature..........	15	53	32
Appreciation of music	41	47	12
Psychology..........	47	37	16
Biology.............	31	52	17

* Source: W. E. Styler, *Who Were the Students?* (London: National Institute of Adult Education, 1950.)

G. France

France presents a marked contrast to the other countries included in this survey. Although France has the greatest proportion of older people in the population, there seems to be less feeling that old age is a problem than one finds in most other countries. Perhaps this is due to the combination of a relatively large rural population and to the strength of the French family.

Nevertheless, some people do observe evidence that old age may be both a personal and a financial problem. Tréanton (1957) studied a sample of former wage-earners in Paris who had commenced to draw their old age pension during the previous year and found that 32 per cent said that they felt "isolated." A study of a national sample of people over 65 showed that 25 per cent were living alone, and 32 per cent of Tréanton's Paris sample were living alone. There was a considerable overlapping between the group who lived alone and those who said that they felt "isolated."

Old age brings economic distress to some 30 per cent of older people, if we may so interpret the finding of the 1949 national survey of the Institut Nationale de la Statistique (1950), in which the interviewers rated the standard of living of 7 per cent of the old people as "miserable" and 26 per cent as "difficult." The old people rated themselves as 6 per cent "miserable" and 37 per cent in "difficult" condition. Of those who were in "miserable" circumstances, 76 per cent had no savings and 7 per cent had used their savings during the year. Of those in "difficult" circumstances, 58 per cent had no savings and 24 per cent had used their savings during the year.

It is probably reasonably accurate to say that there is as much financial need among older people in France as in other countries. Although there is a general old age pension, its purchasing power has been reduced by inflation in spite of periodic increases in the pension rate.

France has the lowest retirement age of all the Western nations. Sixty years is generally regarded as an appropriate retirement age, and the old age pension becomes available at that age. However, the pension is substantially larger for those who retire at a later age, and, according to a survey made in 1956, 43 per cent of the men aged 65–69 were still working full time, and 21 per cent of those aged 70–79 were employed. Most of these people were farmers or other self-employed people, as can be seen in Table 28. Some of those ostensibly retired worked part time in a kind of "black" occupation that allowed them to earn a little money while they still drew their pensions.

Retirement means a diminution of social participation, especially in the cities. Tréanton's subjects were likely to say, "I have good friends at the factory; but you know how it is in the city, we all live distant from one another. When I quit working, I quit seeing them." Others complained that the reduction of income caused them to lose their friends, because they could no longer afford to pay for the little things required for sociability.

as important ones in assisting people without depriving them of their individual initiative.

In Paris alone there are perhaps five hundred local associations giving assistance to the aged, most of them church related. The national associations with an interest in the aged appear nearly all to be church related, with the exception of several associations of retired workers, such as journalists, musicians, and actors.

TABLE 28*

OLDER WORKERS IN FRANCE BY OCCUPATION, 1956

OCCUPATION	MEN		WOMEN	
	No. Aged 65 and Over (in Thousands)	Percentage Following Principal Occupation	No. Aged 65 and Over (in Thousands)	Percentage Following Principal Occupation
Farmowners....................	508	42	652	14
Farm laborers..................	140	20	124	3
Owners of business and industry...	302	40	352	26
Professional workers and managers of business and industry........	202	21	82	7
Clerical workers................	148	12	122	3
Manual workers................	482	18	376	13
Artists, clergy, army, police.......	70	17	4	50
Domestic service................	50	32	366	16
Never employed................	18	....	948	....
Total......................	1920	28	3026	10

* Source: Institut Nationale de la Statistique et des Études Économiques, "A Sampling Study of the Economic Situation of Aged Persons," *Bulletin mensuel et statistique*, N.S., Suppl., juillet-septembre (Paris: Presses Universitaires de France, 1950).

There are a number of associations for assistance to the aged in French cities, though not nearly so many as there are of old people's welfare committees in England. These associations generally look to the welfare of aged people in economic need or in need of medical assistance. The leaders of these associations, and the social workers who work in the privately supported social agencies, believe that the government should refrain from doing much more than providing the economic base for a reasonable standard of living and that church and other private social agencies should work to preserve the autonomy of the individual. They regard their roles

The Conference de Saint Vincent de Paul, a men's organization, pays special attention to work with old people. There are several hundred local branches in the Paris area alone.

The Petits Frères des Pauvres, a laymen's organization, works systematically for the aged, providing meals, organizing holiday excursions, etc.

The Dames de Charité, with perhaps 100,000 local groups in France, is an organization principally of middle-class women which assists the needy aged with visits and material aid.

The Association Louise de Marillac, consisting of young working women, is affiliated with the Dames de Charité. There are 120 groups in the Paris region, with 4000 members.

The Filles de Charité is an order of nuns which gives guidance to church women's organizations in their work with the aged.

The organizations listed above are all Roman Catholic, but in a list of forty-five organizations which work for the aged in Paris and its surroundings, there are a number of non-Catholic groups, including the Delegation Générale des Diaconats Reformes, the Ligue Universelle du Bien Public, and the Société Philanthropique.

The writer's impression is that practically all the work done on behalf of older people in France is regarded as welfare work and is aimed at people in material need. Thus the problems of economic support and of health and housing are met by welfare organizations, private or public. The problem of ego support is recognized, but very little is done explicitly about it, especially for people not in financial need. Indeed, France with her unique type of individualism, may conclude that people can only be autonomous in old age if they are pretty much left to themselves and their families.

ROLE OF CLUB OR ASSOCIATION MEMBER

The role of club or association member is fairly common in France, and it is an acceptable role for older people. The older people engage in clubs of mixed ages; for example, there are many local lawn-bowling groups which consist mainly of middle-aged and older men.

Often the older man drops out of a club because his pension does not permit him to pay the costs of such participation. Still, Tréanton (1957) in his study of newly retired older people in Paris found that 25 per cent of them belonged to associations. He included church societies but not church membership itself as an associational membership. In his sample there were a number of people who had formerly belonged to associations but had dropped out.

Associations of fishermen are found with special frequency in small cities and villages.

There is considerable difference between the sexes with respect to club membership, the French women generally not belonging except to church societies.

Clubs for older people seem to be unthought of by French social workers. When the writer asked about them, a social worker said, "Old people do not like to be with old people. Anyway, the Frenchman is an individualist and does not care to have a club thrust on him."

ROLE OF FRIEND OR INFORMAL GROUP MEMBER

Recognizing that there is a problem of loneliness for older people, social workers have experimented with social centers where people can come for companionship. This has been done in Paris and in some provincial cities. The rooms tend to be used in bad weather; but there is no positive program attached to them. Often they are used for the serving of meals to needy old people. In Lyon there are some twenty such rooms, each with space for about fifty people. After lunch at noon, the rooms are kept open as social centers. Public funds may be used by a municipality for such a "foyer de vieillards."

Vacation tours and vacation periods are organized by welfare organizations, often using the facilities of a children's camp at times when the children are not there. There is in Paris an organization known as Vacances des Personnes Âgées, which specializes in arranging excursions for older people.

Middle-class older people are likely to keep their friendship relations within their homes, and one may find cliques of men and women who play cards together.

Middle-class women, whether married or widowed, are not likely to go away from home very often. It would be almost unthinkable for an elderly French widow to go on a bus trip with other elderly women to the Alps, for example. But this would be regarded as quite a natural thing for Scandinavian women of similar social status.

Elderly French men are likely to have a favorite *bistro* where they meet their friends and talk and read the papers. When such a man cannot go any more because of poor health or lack of money, life is hardly worth living for him.

ROLE OF CITIZEN

The Frenchman has a passion for party politics. His formal and informal associations are related to his politics. He sees

into a Fédération Nationale des Associations des Vieux de France et des Territoires Associés. At present this organization is not politically powerful.

ROLE OF CHURCH MEMBER

As can be seen in Tables 29 and 30, there is a slight tendency for older people to be more religious than middle-aged ones. Women are much more often devout in their religion than are men. There is not much opportunity for older people to take leadership roles.

TABLE 29*

RELIGIOUS OBSERVANCE IN FRANCE, BY AGE, 1952

(Per Cent)

AGE GROUP	DEVOUT†		NOMINAL‡		NO VISIBLE PRACTICE§		NO PRACTICE	
	Men	Women	Men	Women	Men	Women	Men	Women
20–34........	25	37	27	40	12	12	36	11
35–49........	25	44	27	30	13	13	35	13
50–64........	22	48	24	26	15	18	39	8
65 and over...	28	52	25	21	13	19	34	9
All ages...	24	44	26	30	13	15	37	11

* Source: "La France est-elle encore catholique?" *Les Français ont la parole* (Paris: Presses d'Aujourd'hui, 1952).
† Devout = Mass regularly; confession more than once a year.
‡ Nominal = Mass only and often irregularly.
§ No visible practice = Occasionally prays outside church.

the basic divisions of society in political terms. This continues as he grows older. If he is a trade-union member, he belongs to a union with a particular political color, and this union probably has a division for its retired members. For instance, the Union des Vieux Travailleurs de France is associated with the CGT, a leftist labor organization, and has about 300,000 members who pay nominal dues and receive a monthly newspaper called *L'Écho des vieux*. There are similar organizations allied to the CGT-FO (Socialist) and CFTC (Christian) unions.

There is a politically neutral association of older people with a rather small membership, the local associations being banded

ROLE OF USER OF LEISURE TIME

The French are widely thought of as a leisure-minded people, and, with their relatively early age of retirement, they might be expected to get great satisfaction from their leisure. If this is true of elderly people, it is not because they seek active leisure pursuits. The statistics from surveys indicate that the older people spend more time at home (Tables 31 and 32), more time in visiting friends, in gardening, and in resting, than do the younger adults. They do less traveling and take fewer vacation trips (Table 33).

Although they say they enjoy reading and listening to radio, they actually read somewhat less than younger adults. One study found that 24 per cent of older people do not read a newspaper, which is twice the size of the group of non-readers at the middle adult age.

Finally, the older French people do not feel the pressure of time as keenly as the younger ones do. It appears that they find it convenient to slow down and take life more easily than they did during middle age (Table 34).

ROLE OF STUDENT

There is very little adult education in France in the English or Scandinavian or American sense of the term. It would be unthinkable in France for an older person to "take a course" in something. Trade-union educational activity is directed toward the younger workers. Educational preparation for retirement is not regarded as holding much promise in France.

TABLE 30*

RELIGIOUS BELIEFS AND PRACTICES IN
FRANCE, BY AGE, 1948

Age Group	Believe in God	Believe in Immortality of the Soul	Attended Church Last Sunday or Sunday Before
21–29.........	62	55	35
30–49.........	67	59	37
50–64.........	70	61	41
65 and over...	71	62	39

* Source: This table and Tables 31–34 are taken from various issues of *Sondages: Revue française de l'opinion publique*, 1948–53

TABLE 31*

"WHAT DID YOU DO ON EASTER?"

(Per Cent)

Age Group	Church in Morning	Church in Afternoon	Amusement	Rest or Work
20–34......	35	7	54	4
35–49......	35	9	51	5
50–64......	34	7	54	5
65 and over.	38	14	43	5

* Source: *Sondages: Revue française de l'opinion publique* 1949.

TABLE 32*

"WHAT DID YOU DO ON SUNDAY, JULY 11, 1948?"

(Per Cent)

ACTIVITY	AGE GROUP			
	20–34	35–49	50–64	65 and Over
In the Afternoon				
Amusement away from home..........	38	30	28	25
Sport in the open air.................	26	24	16	12
Made or received visits..............	11	11	15	19
Rested............................	7	9	13	15
Walked in garden...................	1	3	5	4
In the Evening				
Amusement at home.................	33	34	42	40
Amusements away from home.........	29	21	14	8
Made or received visits..............	13	10	7	6
Rested............................	11	16	19	28

* Source: *Sondages: Revue française de l'opinion publique*, 1949

TABLE 33*

"WHICH AMUSEMENT DO YOU PREFER?"

(Per Cent)

AMUSEMENT	AGE GROUP			
	20–34	35–49	50–64	65 and Over
Reading	18	23	28	32
Radio	18	24	24	27
Plays	25	19	14	7
Receptions	14	17	17	17
Going to the country	8	9	12	11
Sport competitions	3	3	1	1
Dancing	13	4	1	0
Other amusements:				
Went away for vacation (1949)	53	45	40	23
Played cards				
Often	17	21	17	14
Rarely	42	36	35	28
Never	41	43	38	58

* Source: *Sondages: Revue française de l'opinion publique*, 1949.

TABLE 34*

"DO YOU FEEL THE NEED OF BEING ON TIME?"

(Per Cent)

AGE GROUP	FOR WORK	FOR TRAIN OR BUS	FOR MEET- ING OR AP- POINTMENT	DO NOT FEEL SUCH A NEED	DO NOT CARRY A WATCH	
					Men	Women
18–34	47	20	9	11	27	36
35–39	47	21	8	16	28	43
40–64	29	22	5	26	25	52
65 and over	11	22	7	48	27	39

* Source: *Sondages: Revue française de l'opinion publique*, 1953.

H. United States

The United States has recognized a social problem of old age only during the last two decades. As recently as 50 years ago the United States was predominantly agricultural, with a lower proportion of older people than northern Europe had had in 1850. But the population aged rapidly after 1920, and urbanization came on apace, with its consequent effects upon the family structure.

Almost at the same time, the American people became conscious of the financial problem of old age, of the housing problem, and of the problem of ego support. A national program of social security was adopted in 1936 and, with subsequent developments, now includes the vast majority of people in a contributory old age insurance scheme. Also a program of assistance to needy old people was developed in the various states during the 1930's and is used to supplement the contributory old age pension where needed.

The problem of ego support or of finding meaning in the later years has had major attention both by social welfare workers and by sociologists and psychologists. Typically, the American solution of this problem has been to find ways of helping older people to remain socially and mentally active. It has been assumed that a person will be reasonably happy if he continues to keep active and succeeds in finding substitute activities for the things he must give up as he grows older.

On the other hand, it has been found that many older people are quite content to relax their hold on life, to disengage themselves slowly from interaction with people and institutions, and to assume more and more the role of a passive onlooker. These people make less demands upon others for ego support, though they still need it, and part of the American problem is to find out how to get ego support in its less obstrusive forms.

Looking at the American scene, we can discern an emerging solution of the problem of ego support for people in the age range 60–75, when most people are active enough and healthy enough to want to maintain the level of their earlier social and intellectual life. The solution consists of a slow tapering-off of the work life and of the social and civic activities connected with middle age and a concomitant building-up of a slower-moving life with friends and others who are also growing older. For this purpose people seek formal and informal activities more and more with people their own age. This solution takes various forms, depending on the social status of people and/or their particular personal interests and family situations.

There has been more study of the roles and status of older people in the United States than in other countries. Consequently, we can give a more objective description of the expectations which apply to older people and of their behavior in relation to these expectations.

For a description of the expectations concerning the behavior of older people we shall rely mainly upon the "Study of Public Opinion concerning the Roles of Older People" (Havighurst and Albrecht, 1953). In this study a cross-section of adults of all ages was asked to judge the desirability of each of a list of 96 activities in which older people might engage. From their responses it was possible to give each of the 96 activities an "approval score," which indicated the degree to which it was considered to be desirable for older people.

The specific findings of this study will be applied in the several role areas to be discussed presently. In general, the study showed that older people were expected to taper off slowly from the high point of middle-aged activity. Their activities were regarded permissively as long as they were not too strenuous and too competitive with middle-aged people. Anything which seemed to indicate social isolation and mere vegetation was strongly disapproved. The most preferred activities for older people were in the home, in the church, and in informal friendship groups and associations of older people. Men were expected to be more active than women, especially in the role of citizen.

ROLE OF CLUB OR ASSOCIATION MEMBER

The following "approved" activities define the accepted role:

> Keeps up with clubs as much as when he was younger.
> Is president or secretary of a club with membership of varying ages.
> Joins an organization limited to older people.
> Is a regular attendant at club meetings, but not active as a leader.

"Disapproved" activities are:

> Does not belong to clubs and is not interested in them.
> Visits with and joins organizations of younger people only.
> Still belongs to one or two clubs but no longer attends meetings.

In actual behavior there is a tendency to drop out of clubs as older persons get into the sixties. Some do this because they are tired, and others because they cannot afford the expense. But there are some associations which hold their older members quite well. For instance, in the small midwestern community of "Prairie City," reported in the book *Older People,* 33 per cent of the Methodist Women's Society were over 65, and 31 per cent of the Daughters of the American Revolution were over 65. One of the men's fraternal associations had 43 per cent of its members over 65. American fraternal associations are likely to retain their members in old age because they generally provide certain insurance benefits for them.

In "Prairie City," 28 per cent of the people over 65 belonged to clubs and attended frequently, while another 14 per cent were only nominal members and never attended. The proportion of club members varied by social class from 100 per cent of upper-class men to 50 per cent of upper-middle-class men down to none of the men in the lowest class on a five-class scale. Among women, the proportions varied from 100 to 20 per cent. Women were more likely to belong to clubs because many of them belonged to church women's societies, while there are few such societies for men. In this study business organizations and labor unions were defined as "associations."

A survey of a sample of retired people in two Florida cities was reported by Webber (1954). He found that 54 per cent of the retired people in Orlando attended club or association meetings at least once a month, while 37 per cent of those in West Palm Beach did so. Women attended meetings more than men, and people of higher status more than people of lower status. The community of Orlando is a favorite place for retired people, with 13.4 per cent of its population aged 65 and over in 1950. In this community, participation in clubs and associations is probably at a maximum. Nearly all the participation was in organizations for people of mixed ages, but no doubt many of these organizations actually consisted largely of older people.

In a study of a national sample (strongly biased toward the middle class) Cavan and her associates (1949) found that about 35 per cent of the older men and about 40 per cent of the older women attended two or more club meetings a month.

The data we have been discussing deal with participation in clubs and associations which generally are open to adults of all ages. In addition, there is a lively degree of activity in old people's clubs, and it is growing rapidly, though it does not approach the degree of activity in associations of mixed ages.

It is possible to make a very crude estimate of the proportion of older people belonging to old people's clubs in certain states where surveys have been made. Such surveys have been made in the states of Iowa, North Carolina, and New York. In Iowa there were, in 1957, 74 clubs in 44 communities with 5900 members, or about 1.5 per cent of the state's population over 65. In North Carolina, 64 clubs were discovered in 1954, with about 3000 members, or 1.4 per cent of the population over 65. In New York a 1957 survey showed about 24,000 older people attending old people's clubs and social centers, which is between 1 and 2 per cent of the state's population over 65. The city of Cleveland had 67 clubs in 1957, with about 3000 members. This is about 3 per cent of the population over 65.

These places have a relatively extensive development of old people's clubs. Consequently, it seems reasonable to estimate that about 2 per cent of the people over 65 in the United States are members of clubs of older people, which is considerably less than the proportions in Great Britain and the Netherlands.

The old people's club movement is growing rapidly in the United States. For instance, four-fifths of the clubs in New York State have been founded since 1950. There was a national convention of senior citizens' clubs in New Orleans in 1957, with the host club in New Orleans celebrating its tenth anniversary. The 1958 meeting of these groups was held in St.

Louis and moved toward forming a national organization.

There is a tendency for old people's clubs to band together into city or regional organizations. For instance, the Senior Citizens Association of Los Angeles County is made up of 90 clubs and maintains a downtown office. Another example is the Council of Senior Citizens Organization of Schenectady, New York, with 8 clubs and a membership of 6000.

The ratio of women to men in old people's clubs seems to be generally about three to one. There are a few men's clubs, mainly of middle-class men.

Sponsorship of old people's clubs in the United States varies a great deal from one state to another. In North Carolina most of the clubs are sponsored and led by staff members of community recreation departments, which are also active in many other places. In other states there are many other sponsoring agencies, including public libraries, the Salvation Army, churches, women's organizations, and boards of education. The Jewish churches have been especially active in establishing "Golden Age" clubs. A considerable group of clubs have been initiated by older people themselves and are led by members of their own age group. This is most likely to be the case with clubs of middle-class membership, such as the Fossils, of Washington, D.C.; the Hyde Park Seniors, of Chicago; the Borrowed Time Club, of Lakewood, Ohio; and the Mora (Men of Retirement Age) Club, of Bethlehem, Pennsylvania.

While a good deal of the impetus for clubs and senior centers has come from organizations such as those mentioned above, there is now developing a movement for community councils on aging, analogous to the British old people's welfare committees. Two states, Massachusetts and Louisiana, have laws which permit a community to spend tax money to support such councils. In Massachusetts more than a hundred councils have been formed. California and New York have a good many community councils of this sort.

There is no highly organized national association, though there are several small organizations of this type. The American Association of Retired Persons offers a group hospital and surgical expense insurance program, plus a bimonthly magazine, *Modern Maturity*. The Senior Citizens of America, which has been led by retired educators, publishes a magazine called *Senior Citizen* and is politically neutral. There are also a number of Townsend Clubs which have continued to exist mainly as social clubs after the decline of the Townsend Movement before World War II.

ROLE OF FRIEND AND INFORMAL ASSOCIATION MEMBER

The role of friend is a highly acceptable role for older people, although it is known that many older people do not make new friends easily. Activities highly approved by public opinion are:

Goes out and visits with other people the same age a great deal.

Keeps up by mail or telephone or by personal visits with a large number of friends.

Spends more time than formerly in visiting friends, and writing them.

Visits friends and receives visits in his (her) own home.

Spends several hours a day at club or lodge rooms with old friends.

Activities disapproved are:

Goes visiting relatives or friends for long periods of time.

No longer entertains groups of friends at home.

Has lost touch with former friends.

Very seldom visits with friends though able and has some.

Lives a quiet life with no social contacts other than husband or wife.

In spite of this approval of friendship activities, only 7 per cent of the sample in "Prairie City" had close-knit friendship clique relations, while another 18 per cent had loose group relations, such as giving and receiving invitations to dinner or to parties. By far the majority—71 per cent—had only scattered social contacts, such as greetings to acquaintances at church or casual conversations with people in parks or taverns. Another 4 per cent were quite isolated.

To help people acquire friends or at least to enter into pleasant social relations, the major method is the social center, or senior center, usually a large room or a clubhouse which is open all day, with a variety of facilities for informal amusements, such as games, reading, music, arts and crafts, and usually a noontime meal service. Generally, such a center is sponsored by a community group with some such name as "Senior Citizens Council."

The earliest of these centers were established shortly after World War II. Pioneers were the Hodson Center in New York City and the San Francisco Senior Center. A number of Jewish community agencies have established such centers, and the other churches are doing likewise, with such examples as the Kundig Center (Catholic) in Detroit and the senior citizens centers sponsored by the San Francisco Council of Churches (Protestant). The United Automobile Workers in Detroit operate retired workers' centers.

City recreation commissions have used fieldhouses in the public parks for social centers, and presently a few cities, mainly in California and Florida, are building centers expressly for the use of older people. The majority of existing centers are run as social welfare ventures for the underprivileged segment of the older population. Exceptions are the centers in existence or being built in the retirement communities of the South and the Southwest, which draw a group of people who range in social status from upper-middle to upper working class. In two of Chicago's middle-class suburbs, senior citizens centers have recently been established.

An example of a center which appeals to people of all socioeconomic groups is Little House, in Menlo Park, California. Sponsored by Peninsula Volunteers, Inc., a women's organization, Little House has a building constructed especially for the use

of older people in a public park. Membership totals 1250 persons over 50, with an average age of 67. The activities are divided into basic categories: economic, recreation, education, physical and mental health, and community participation.

Generally speaking, the people of upper- and upper-middle class status, if they are in good health, keep up their earlier friendship associations and make new ones by going on tours and visiting places where other people like themselves are to be found.

ROLE OF CITIZEN

Civic activity is accepted as desirable for older people, though they are expected to make way in positions of leadership for the younger ones. Activities approved in the "Study of Public Opinion" are:

Reads political news and votes regularly.
Campaigns actively for his political party.
Accepts minor civic responsibility, such as membership on committees.
Has a leading position in civic life; is chairman of important committees.
In general, carries on in his civic life much as he has done in middle age.

However, the following activities are regarded with slightly less than full approval, though not with outright disapproval:

Runs for high state or national office.
Runs for a minor political office.
Is an interested observer, but not active in civic affairs.

Apparently, the public does not want older people asserting themselves as vigorously in political competition as if they were in middle age. Yet it is a well-known fact that men elected to state and national legislatures have little difficulty being re-elected when they are in the seventies and occasionally in the eighties. Senator Theodore Francis Green of Rhode Island is, at 92, the oldest man ever to serve in the United States Senate.

The "Prairie City" study showed that 15 per cent of older people displayed active interest or leadership in civic affairs, while another 62 per cent voted regularly but did little else of civic consequence.

Outside the political arena, in the nonpolitical affairs of city and state and nation, older people are likely to continue in positions of prestige well beyond the age when they retire from business. This is shown in Table 35, which gives the age distribution of the community leaders in Kansas City. In all except positions of business leadership and leadership of welfare agencies, the people in their seventies were overrepresented, while people in their sixties were overrepresented in all areas of leadership. A good many of the elderly women are said to be "tea-pouring and money-giving widows," but nevertheless these women undoubtedly draw a good deal of ego support from the attentions they receive.

The opportunity to serve as leaders in civic affairs is pretty much limited to people of middle- and upper-class status. It is certainly important as a means of ego support to the minority who have it. Recently a number of senior service organizations have been founded to increase this opportunity. Examples are the Senior League of Hartford, Connecticut; the Cleveland Senior Council; and the Cedar Rapids, Iowa, Senior Men's Bureau of the Chamber of Commerce. The Cleveland Senior Council, for example, was formed by some retired businessmen with the aim of putting their experience to use by the community. They have helped a local college to set up a money-raising campaign, and several of them were recruited to lead a pre-retirement program for one of the city's industries. Two counseled a social agency on its accounting and business practices. In 1957 the council had 150 members paying dues of $10 a year, with an office and a part-time executive secretary.

A member of the Senior Men's Bureau of the Cedar Rapids Chamber of Commerce described his feelings about his participation by saying, "Now I again have

TABLE 35*

AGE AND CIVIC LEADERSHIP IN KANSAS CITY, MISSOURI, BY AGE GROUPS
(Per Cent)

CIVIC ACTIVITY	AGE GROUP			
	30–49	50–59	60–69	70 and Over
Men				
Art and music patrons	18	41	25	16
Trustees of educational institutions	17	30	33	20
Directors of welfare agencies	29	38	20	13
Chamber of Commerce members	29	34	29	8
Civic promotion leaders	22	41	28	9
Governmental board members	26	39	25	10
General age distribution	55	21	15	9
Women				
Art and music patrons	30	24	28	18
Museum leaders	11	31	25	23
Directors of welfare agencies	37	40	18	5
General age distribution	51	22	16	11

* Source: Richard Coleman, *Civic Participation and Leadership* ("Preliminary Report" [Kansas City, Mo.: Community Studies, Inc., 1955]).

the chance to pay my civic rent." Service at a less prestigeful level is given by people in senior citizens' associations, as, for example, in the following summary of the work of the Los Angeles County Senior Citizens Association by its president, Mrs. Marjorie Borchardt: "You visit the sick and discouraged; you sew, knit, crochet hundreds of articles for children in hospitals and orphanages; you stuff envelopes for the March of Dimes, the Cancer Society, the Tuberculosis Association; . . . and all along with this service to others, you are taking the responsibility for better government by activity in politics."

At present there is no strong political organization of older people. There was one, however, during the depression of the 1930's, when the Townsend Movement, with several thousand local Townsend Clubs, became powerful enough to indorse and assist in electing a substantial portion of the members of the national Congress. This movement grew out of economic distress and lost its political punch when the Congress adopted old age pension laws and when economic conditions improved. But, even during the good economic conditions of the postwar period, a political program for higher payments to older people in the state of California was sponsored by the California Institute of Social Welfare and almost succeeded in winning a state election.

There were some small unions of old age pensioners during the 1940's, but they, too, are now weak or non-existent. The fact is that both major political parties have vied with each other in liberalizing social security programs for older people, and there is not now enough economic distress among older people to give rise to a political movement. In 1958, thirty-two of the then forty-eight states had commissions or committees on aging, appointed by the governors or set up by the legislatures. In the presidential campaign of 1956, Adlai Stevenson, the losing candidate, advocated the establishment of a government bureau for older persons (analogous to the existing Children's

Bureau and the Women's Bureau). President Eisenhower has established a Federal Council on Aging composed of government officials from several departments whose work impinges upon the problem of aging.

ROLE OF CHURCH MEMBER

It is generally regarded as suitable for people to become more interested in religion and more devoted to church as they grow older. Activities approved in the "Study of Public Opinion" are:

Goes to church regularly.
Reads the Bible or prayer book every day.
Has become more interested in church and religion in recent years.
An active leader in church.
In general, keeps up his church activities or increases them as he grows older.
Gets a great deal of comfort from religious belief and church attendance.

Disapproved activities are:

Has nothing to do with church.
Has become a scoffer at formal religion as he grows older.
Never attends church but speaks of himself as a church member.
No longer feels obliged to attend church regularly.

It is true that people become somewhat more interested in religion as they grow older, and their attendance at church becomes somewhat more faithful until about the age of 70, when illness and feebleness cut down their attendance. At this age the proportion who listen to religious services on the radio goes up. However, there is no radical change in religious habits between middle and old age.

Opportunity to achieve or to retain positions of prestige in the church holds up pretty well through the sixties, but few men and women keep positions of importance into the seventies. In "Prairie City," 2 per cent of the older people had leadership responsibility, and 61 per cent had frequent and active participation. In the national study reported by Cavan and her colleagues (1949), about 45 per cent of the men and 55 per cent of the women attended church once a week or oftener.

The Jewish churches have been pioneers in the development of programs for the ego support of their older people, through "Golden Age" clubs and social centers. Catholic and Protestant churches have been moving slowly in the same direction. For example, in 1956 the Florida Council of Churches held nine 1-day institutes on "The Church and the Senior Citizen." Still, the usual thing is to expect the regular life of the church to serve the older members. Thus, in a midwestern city of 400,000, of 130 Protestant churches, 5 had explicit programs for older people in 1955. The Methodist church has recently started to publish a quarterly journal called *Mature Years* for its older members.

ROLE OF USER OF LEISURE TIME

The American public expects old people to enjoy their leisure if they know how to do so. Activities approved in the "Study of Public Opinion" are:

Goes to a warm climate every winter.
Goes on a trip around the world.
Goes in for some special interest, such as gardening, cabinet-making, collecting, painting.
Plays games with a group of friends regularly.
Goes to the theater or movies regularly.
Reads several hours a day.
Listens to the radio several hours a day.
In general, gives more time and energy to recreation than during middle age.
Very active and interested in hobbies: makes them his chief interest in life.
Relaxes and finds interest in life through observing the younger generation.
Still dances and seems to enjoy it.

Disapproved activities are:

Never leaves home town or neighborhood on trips or visits.
Sits in a favorite chair for hours without doing anything active.
Is content to sit and watch the world go by.
Does nothing, just sits around.

It is clear that an active use of leisure time is favored, although relaxation is permitted as long as it does not seem like vegetation. In terms of actual performance, however, very few older people live up to the expectation of active leisure participation. In the "Prairie City" study only 2 per cent were rated high on an activity scale, defined as follows:

Has a variety of recreational interests and activities which keep him busy. Takes initiative in planning recreation for himself and others. May give talks or write articles. Known as a person with well-developed special interests. Has gained prestige thereby.

Sixty-one per cent lived a role described as follows:

Has some active recreations which he carries on individually or with others. Still has time on his hands, however. May play indoor or outdoor games—bowling, croquet, shuffleboard, golf. Writes letters, may read widely. Crochets, knits, quilts, gardens, does crossword puzzles, works on collections.

These people do three or four of the things mentioned, plus listening to the radio and visiting with friends. Thirty per cent followed essentially passive recreations, such as radio, reading, and watching the world go by with some interest. Seven per cent were vegetating.

In the "Prairie City" study the middle-class and upper-class people had far greater leisure activity than the working-class group. Table 36 shows the frequency of participation in the various leisure activities by the older people of "Prairie City." The relatively simple ones of reading, radio-listening, and visiting lead the list.

In the United States there have been a number of studies of what older people would like to do with their free time, with the result that at least half of most samples say that they have no wish for further activity. Those who do indicate a desire to do other things generally suggest arts and crafts and travel, followed by a great variety of other activities. There have been a number of books written on how to carry on a recreation program for older people, with such titles as "Fun for Older Adults" and "Recreation for the Aging."

ROLE OF STUDENT

There are no definite expectations about older people in the role of student. It is known that people's performance on intelligence tests decreases slowly with age, but it is expected that older people can learn if they want to. They are welcome to participate in adult-education courses, but very few do so.

TABLE 36*

LEISURE ACTIVITIES OF OLDER PEOPLE
IN A SMALL CITY

(Per Cent)

Activity	Men	Women
Radio-listening...............	82	82
Reading.....................	73	71
Visiting....................	56	73
Gardening...................	51	40
Sewing, crocheting, etc........	0	60
Taking automobile rides.......	42	45
Letter-writing...............	18	45
Movies.....................	16	31
Playing cards, etc............	20	25
Clubs and lodges.............	11	33
Community and church work...	11	31
Travel.....................	9	14
Golf and other sport..........	20	4
Woodworking, etc............	13	0

* Source: R. J. Havighurst and Ruth Albrecht, *Older People* (New York: Longmans, Green & Co., 1953).

However, a number of older people's organizations have educational programs. For example, the Hyde Park Seniors of Chicago have a class in painting and offer a variety of instruction in handicrafts. Quite a few public libraries have forum programs or discussion groups that are primarily for older people. The Cleveland Public Library sponsors the "Live Long and Like It Library Club," which was started in 1946 and now has some 700 members. The Drexel Home for the Aged in Chicago is experimenting currently with two study-discussion groups, one on "World Politics," and the other on "Current Issues

in American Life." The Los Angeles School System has a group of offerings for older people under its adult-education program.

In these programs the older person is a student with other old people in an ordinary educational course. In contrast to this, the principal educational emphasis at present is on preparation for retirement, with a number of agencies using a variety of methods with people in the age range 55–65. The most highly developed program of this sort is entitled "Aging in the Modern World" and was conducted by the Division of Gerontology of the University of Michigan. The program is intended to consist of ten meetings of a small group, which might be organized by a business, a library, adult school, university extension service, labor union, club, church, or community center. There is a guidebook for leaders and a handbook for group members containing nine essays on the following topics which are each to be discussed in one meeting:

Aging as a Modern Social Achievement
Middle Age: New Prime of Life
The Human Machine at Mid-Life
Aging in Earlier Cultures
New Family Roles in Middle Age
Curiosity, Comprehension, Creativeness
The Challenge of Citizenship to Middle Life
Participation through Organization in Middle Life
Creating the Climate for Adult Growth

There is also a book of readings supplemental to the topics in the handbook and three films. The purpose of this program is to help individuals understand themselves and their situation in life better and then to plan for their retirement.[3]

A different program, emphasizing more practical preparation for retirement, has been developed by the University of Chi-

[3] The guidebook, the handbook, and the book of readings were originally prepared by the Division of Gerontology of the University of Michigan for The Fund for Adult Education under the editorships of Clark Tibbitts and Wilma Donahue. The three parts have now been published in one volume by Prentice-Hall, Inc., under the title *Aging in Today's Society.*

cago Industrial Relations Center for use by business and industrial corporations in organizing discussion groups for their older employees. Burgess *et al.* (1958) studied the people who come into such groups in the companies which are using this program and concluded that the program for executives should be different from that for employees of lower-middle and working-class status.

A number of business and industrial corporations now provide leaders for preretirement study groups, using a program similar to those already described. In Cleveland a recent survey found that five companies had study groups, while about forty companies had a counseling program for individual workers.

In Minneapolis the Hennepin County CIO Industrial Union Council offers preretirement courses to its members in the 55–65 age group. In 1958 the United Automobile Workers gave preretirement courses in their summer schools.

There are two principal aims of the preretirement courses. One is to give the individual assistance in taking stock of himself and in planning how to spend his retirement. The other is to bring the individual into a group of people with common problems and common anxieties about growing older, so that he becomes more able to look at his problems objectively, knowing that his concerns are similar to those of other people and not signs of abnormality in himself.

The role of student is most readily accepted by middle-class people, who have had more experience with it, than by working-class people. However, the experiments with educational programs for workers seem to indicate that these people also have something to gain from student activities.

III. Conclusions

The purpose of this chapter has been to make a descriptive comparison of the ways in which older people get ego support in various Western countries, without evalua-

tion of the success of people in any of these countries.

We cannot say that ego support is better achieved in one country than another. To make such a statement would require two things: (1) much more adequate information than we now have and (2) the comparative evaluation of ego support coming from various sources. For example, France and Switzerland may seem to be lacking in social machinery (clubs, social centers, etc.) for ego support, but they may provide more of the traditional forms of it through the family.

The goal generally agreed upon in all these countries is a considerable degree of *autonomy* for older people, in contrast to *anomie* and *apathy*. Autonomy, in contemporary Western society, is gained and maintained by performing certain *self-preserving* and certain *socially valuable* functions.

It is not so easy for older people to perform these functions in an urban, secular society as it was in the traditional agricultural society of western Europe. Then the older person had a sort of social usefulness which is still found in the older European peasant, who looks after the domestic animals, tends the garden, repairs the hand tools, and takes care of the grandchildren. At the same time the elderly peasant takes care of himself. This person has the autonomy of being a functioning member of a family which is an economic unit. Though bound to the family in space, he nevertheless is autonomous. The old German lady who complained that she could no longer serve her family by darning their stockings because they now wore nylons was saying in effect that she had lost her function in the family and no longer felt that she counted. Therefore she was losing her autonomy.

When the old person is in danger of losing his function in the family, he tries to become autonomous by living independently, by keeping his job as long as possible, by striving to associate with younger people, and, in general, by doing things which

symbolize autonomy. The problem of Western urban society is thus to help people to
preserve their autonomy or even to enhance it, while at the same time acting
through the state to provide economic security and protection against social isolation. This is not easy to do. The state is
always in danger of doing too much as well
as in danger of doing too little for the
individual.

Therefore people who are working with
and for older people must understand and
respect what the German Committee for
the Welfare of Old People has as its motto,
"Der alter Mensch ein Subjekt ist, und
nicht ein Objekt," "The Old Person Is a
Subject and Not an *Object*"—to be handled as a sack of vegetables by the employees of the state.

In what ways, then, does the older person function in the various social roles
outside of work and family? Does he find
ways to function which enable him to preserve his autonomy?

A. Club or Association Member

In all Western societies the old person's
retaining of club participation is approved,
but in all of them he tends to give up this
participation because it costs him too much
money or too much energy and because he
comes to feel that he is not welcome. Probably the greatest participation of older people in associations of mixed ages is found
in the United States, the Netherlands,
France, England, and Germany, with lesser
participation in Sweden, Denmark, and
Switzerland.

In the case of participation in old people's clubs, the Netherlands and Great
Britain give the greatest opportunity, followed by the United States. Then come
four countries which are just beginning to
experiment with old people's associations:
Sweden, Denmark, Germany, and Switzerland. Finally, France has very little club
activity in old people's groups.

Generally, people of lower socioeconomic
status get the most help from old people's

clubs, though middle-class people participate to some extent in the United States,
the Netherlands, Switzerland, and Sweden.

Women take part more frequently than
men by a ratio of about three to one in all
countries except the Netherlands, where the
ratio is just reversed, men being much more
active in old people's clubs than women.

B. Friend or Informal Group Member

It is highly approved that older people
should have many friends and spend much
time with friends, particularly with people
of their own generation. However, older
people tend to constrict their social life
space, allowing old friends to drop away
without making new ones. The most is
done in the United States to help people
retain and develop this role, partly through
the existence of retirement communities in
warm climates and partly through the provision of social centers for older people. In
the second place with respect to social facilitation of this role are Great Britain,
the Netherlands, and Sweden. Next come
Switzerland, France, Germany, and Denmark.

C. Provision of Facilities for Social Relations

Since the conduct of old people's clubs
and social centers requires physical facilities, leadership, and money, there must be
some agency or agencies to provide these
things. In general, there are four possible
types of agencies to do this. They are:

1. *Social welfare agencies—private and
public financed.*—The private agencies consist of women's organizations, old people's
welfare committees, and senior citizens'
committees. The public agencies consist of
social welfare boards. A problem for these
agencies is to find space for their projects,
since they seldom have rooms or buildings
of their own.

2. *Community adult-education and recreation associations—private and public
financed.*—These include YMCA's, schools,
and public recreation agencies. In Sweden

a special institution is the Peoples House, which maintains a building for social and educational purposes. These agencies nearly always have space to offer, but often they do not have leadership to give, unless they are public agencies with a professional staff.

3. *Churches.*—These agencies have space but often lack trained leadership for work with older people. The Jewish churches in the United States are an exception in this respect, for they are generally well staffed for this kind of work.

4. *Old people's organization.*—These are strongest in Sweden, the Netherlands, and Great Britain. They tend to be led by older people with experience in political leadership and have a national organization. Finance is their main problem. In the United States there are a few old people's organizations with middle-class leadership and mainly middle-class composition. They are organized on a local basis.

D. Role of Citizen

Participating as citizens in political and community life, old people are expected to remain interested and to show little diminution of activity. However, functioning in this role does not give much ego support to the average person, because he has never been very active in it, and he cannot now increase his activity. Some upper-class and middle-class people have secured prestige in political and civic activities in middle age, and they are likely to continue to get ego support in this role beyond the time when their occupational role loses its value to them.

As members of a political pressure group, old people may get a considerable amount of ego support, feeling that they are working effectively on their own behalf, while a minority of them also get the prestige of leadership. This source of ego support is greatest in Sweden, Great Britain, and the Netherlands. It has a medium value in Denmark and Germany and little importance in France, Switzerland, and the United States.

E. Role of Church Member

The role of church member is generally regarded as an especially favorable one for older people both because it gives them a chance at social participation and because it gives them spiritual support. However, there is relatively little opportunity for older people to serve as church leaders. There is some tendency for the urban churches in all Western countries to recognize the social problem of aging and to undertake to increase the ego support for older people. This tendency is most pronounced in the Netherlands. Switzerland, Denmark, and the United States occupy a middle position in this respect, while Sweden, France, Great Britain, and Germany show the least evidence of it.

F. User of Leisure Time

In all the countries an active, creative use of leisure time by older people is respected and even admired, but it is not expected that many older people will accomplish this. Rather it is expected that older people will be happy if they can "take things easy" and engage in relatively passive leisure activities for which they have always had a preference but not always enough free time. Greater activity in leisure pursuits is to some extent expected and found in the United States, Great Britain, Sweden, Germany, and Denmark, possibly in that order. More passive use of leisure is found and expected in France, the Netherlands, and Switzerland.

Most older people become less and less active, physically, socially, and mentally, and this is reflected in their use of leisure. The statistical studies of leisure-time pursuits show that in all countries people increase their preferences for reading, radio-listening, visiting, and handwork for women. They do not go in for demanding types of intellectual activity. In Switzerland, Germany, the Netherlands, and Denmark there seems to be a strong preference for gardening, raising small animals, and taking walks. Travel is mentioned as a desirable thing especially by Swedes and Germans, though American middle-class older people probably actually do more traveling than any other old age group.

The evidence about the possibilities of older people developing new interests in handicrafts and hobbies is not clear. Some studies of preferences indicate that many people would like to learn new things of this sort; but in practice the projects for teaching handicrafts and for developing hobby interests seem to have been successful only in a limited group of middle-class people.

The possibility of gaining ego support through a more stimulating use of leisure appears to be good and is being explored vigorously in Great Britain and the United States especially.

G. Role of Student

Although the role of student is accepted in public opinion as a good one for older people, it is not really expected, nor is it explicitly provided for in the European countries. Older people are welcome in adult-education courses, but few of them appear. In the United States there is a little more effort to develop study and discussion groups and workshop training for older people, but this could not be said to be well established. On the other hand, there is in the United States a growing movement for study courses and discussion groups aimed at helping people in late middle age to prepare better for their old age.

H. Social Status and Ego Support

In all the countries studied it appears, in regard to social status and ego support, that:

1. Upper- and upper-middle class people have more opportunity for ego support in their later years and are more in need of it. They are more autonomous in an urban society than are lower-status people; and they preserve their autonomy better.

2. Working-class people are the targets of major efforts by private and public social agencies in programs for ego support.

3. Rural people have the least need of programs of ego support, because they have families and functions that provide them with a substantial measure of it.

Autonomy appears to be enhanced under the following conditions: (*a*) a person retains important functions of middle age (this is common in rural societies and occurs when an urban person retains his role as worker); (*b*) a person is a member of a family in which he has a significant function (this is more common in rural than in urban societies); (*c*) a person has high economic status (this enables him to do autonomy-preserving things, many of which cost money); and (*d*) a person has opportunity for free social interaction with a variety of people under a variety of circumstances (this occurs most frequently for upper-class and upper-middle-class people).

I. Principles of Ego-Support Policy

It appears that a social policy aimed at ego support will do the following things in a modern society: (1) increase opportunities for free social interaction through encouraging the efforts of older people to function in the roles of club member, friend, and church member; (2) help older people to retain their functioning in the roles of worker, citizen, and church member; and (3) aid older people in preserving or discovering active and stimulating leisure activities, partly through education.

REFERENCES AND BIBLIOGRAPHY

Aging. A monthly news bulletin issued by the United States Department of Health, Education, and Welfare.

BURGESS, E. W., COREY, L. G., PINEO, P. C., and THORNBURY, R. T. 1958. Occupational differences in attitudes toward aging and retirement. J. Gerontol., **13**, 203–6.

CAVAN, RUTH S., BURGESS, E. W., HAVIGHURST, R. J., and GOLDHAMER, H. 1949. Personal adjustment in old age. Chicago: Science Research Associates.

CENTRE NATIONAL DE L'ÉDUCATION SANITAIRE, DÉMOGRAPHIQUE, ET SOCIALE. 1952. La Sante de l'homme. (Monthly Publication No. 75.) December. Special issue on problems of aging. Lyon: The Centre.

DIEDRICH, J. 1955. Report of a survey of older people, 1951–52. Amsterdam: Bureau voor Marktanalyse en Sociografisch Onderzoek.

FRANCE. INSTITUT NATIONAL DE LA STATISTIQUE ET DES ÉTUDES ÉCONOMIQUES. 1950. A sampling study of the economic situation of aged persons. Bull. mensuel de statistique, N.S., Suppl. juillet-septembre. Paris: Presses Universitaires de France.

———. 1956. Conditions of living of aged persons. Bull. hebdomadaire de statistique, No. 431 (August 4).

FRIEDEBURG, L. VON. 1955. Altersbild und Altersvorsorge der Arbeiter und Angestellten. Frankfurt: Forschungsbericht, Inst. für Sozialforschung, Universität.

GREAT BRITAIN. NATIONAL OLD PEOPLE'S WELFARE COUNCIL. 1955. Old people's clubs. London: The Council.

GROTH, S. 1954. Das Alter in Aufbruch des Daseins. (Soziografisches Institut, Universität, Frankfurt, Neue Druck und Verlagsgesellschaft.) Frankfurt.

HAVIGHURST, R. J., and ALBRECHT, RUTH. 1953. Older people. New York: Longmans, Green & Co.

INSTITUT FRANÇAIS D'OPINION PUBLIQUE. Sondages: revue française de l'opinion publique. Paris.

INSTITUTE FOR RESEARCH IN SOCIAL SCIENCE. 1956a. A manual of organization: clubs for senior citizens. Chapel Hill: University of North Carolina.

———. 1956b. Recreation for the aging in North Carolina. Chapel Hill: University of North Carolina.

KARRENBERG, F., and BISMARCK, K. VON. 1956. Das Lebensrecht des alter Menschen. ("Kirch im Volk," No. 20.) Stuttgart: Kreuz Verlag.

LENHARTZ, L. 1958. Altersprobleme des Selbständigen grosstädtischen Mittelstandes. Stuttgart: Ferdinand Enke Verlag.

MILNE, R. S., and MACKENZIE, H. C. 1954. Straight fight: a study of voting behavior in the constituency of Bristol North-East at the general election of 1951. London: Hansard Society.

NEULOH, O. 1956–57. Die Situation der Alter Bergleute. (Progress report in files of the Sociografic Institute at Frankfurt.)

NEW YORK STATE JOINT LEGISLATIVE COMMITTEE ON PROBLEMS OF THE AGING. 1957. Brightening the senior years. Albany: The Committee.

REIGROTZKI, E. 1956. Soziale Verflechtungen in der Bundesrepublik: Elemente der sozialen Teilnahme in Kirche, Politik, Organisationen und Freizeit. (Schriftreihe des UNESCO–Instituts für Sozialwissenschaften Köln.) Tübingen: J. C. B. Mohr.

SLACK, KATHLEEN M. 1954. Over seventy. London: National Council of Social Service.

TARTLER, R. 1957. Das Alter in der modernen Gesellschaft. Stuttgart: Ferdinand Enke.

TOWNSEND, P. 1957. The family life of old people. London: Routledge & Kegan Paul.

TRÉANTON, J. R. 1957. L'adaptation des personnes âgées à la vie urbaine. *In* Proceedings of the Fourth Congress, International Association of Gerontology, Merano, Italy, **3**, 518–26. Fidenza: Tipografia Tito Mattioli.

UNION SOCIALE. Journal of the Union Nationale Interfédérale des Œuvres Privées Sanitaires et Sociales. Paris. (This journal of the union of private welfare societies has frequent articles dealing with problems of aging.)

VAN ZONNEVELD, R. J. 1960. Health conditions of the aged in the Netherlands.

WEBBER, I. L. 1954. The organized social life of the retired: two Florida communities. Am. J. Sociology, **59**, 340–46.

X

Research on Aging

JOHN E. ANDERSON

I. INTRODUCTION

One of the striking characteristics of aging is its obviousness to the ordinary, casual observer. In this respect it is like growth. However much we need science to supply information as to process and underlying causes, we do not need science to tell us that children grow or that people age, as both happen before our very eyes. Moreover, it is apparent that some persons grow old more rapidly than their peers, while others preserve their capacities until late ages. But, ultimately, if they live long enough, all persons require care in greater or less degree. In the sense both of progressive change and of the need for care, the problems of the aging are universal and are encountered in every society. But some societies, more particularly primitive ones, place less emphasis upon time and upon age than do the more industrialized societies in which people live by the clock and divide themselves by age categories.

In visiting various countries, one cannot but be impressed with the fact that the same human problems appear in culture after culture, more particularly in highly organized and complex industrial cultures, and are met in one way or another. On examining the methods of meeting the problems, similarities also appear regardless of the names they are called or the social institutions in which they find a place. So also with the science and practice of gerontology.

[1] In reading this chapter, note that this presentation is neither a complete summary nor a detailed analysis of the psychological and social research now going forward on older persons in Europe. Because of its concern with trends in research, it presents the impressions of an American who attended the International Congress of Gerontology and the International Congress of Psychology in 1957 and who thereafter visited a number of centers and talked with various governmental and university people. Involved also was some correspondence to clear up points.

This chapter was intended to cover designed research projects within psychology, sociology, and other social sciences that relate to the problem of aging. Medical, biological, and clinical studies were not to be included. Not to be covered were the social statistics collected by governments, since these are covered in other sections of this volume. What are covered are planned studies which seek data upon samples of older people in some defined fashion: by interview, questionnaire, observation, or experiment. The chapter seeks to give the American student an impression of the range and variety of work going forward in Europe and some impression of the way in which research is organized in terms of the available facilities. For the more specific results the reader should await the appearance of the scientific papers based upon the investigations which are described.

May I express my cordial thanks to the many persons in Europe who helped me from time to time in gathering material for this report and my regret that I cannot mention them all. Misinterpretations are not to be traced to them but to myself as an information channel. In particular I wish to thank A. T. Welford, L. Farrer Brown, Alastair Heron, Torsten Husén, James Inglis, Suzanne Pacaud, Jean-René Tréanton, Klaus Riegel, H. Thomae, Henning Friis, and R. J. van Zonneveld, all of whom either gave me substantial time or sent me substantial material.

In any survey of ongoing or projected research within a number of countries, some account must be taken of the position attained by scientific endeavor in those countries. This is especially true of the psychological and social sciences, in which tradition favors a speculative and theoretical approach, while modern emphasis is upon an empirical or experimental approach. In spite of much interchange of method and results, the scientists within each country work toward the solution of their own problems in their own way. At an international congress a visiting scientist is impressed by the scientific sophistication of some countries as compared with the more primitive research done in others. Each group within a culture area seems to move through its own historical development as it goes from the successful solution of simpler problems to the attack on more complex ones.

In early research on aging, emphasis went to the biological and medical aspects. The former arises as an interest area because students of lower organisms with short life-cycles see aging as characteristic of the entire life-cycle and seek to understand it as a significant part of the life-process. Because medicine is intrusted with the direct care of old people, physicians become interested in what happens to aging patients. And the prolongation of life by conquering disease and disability changes medicine itself and thus forces concern with aging and particularly with chronic illnesses. Hence interest in the biology of aging and the medical care of older people antedates interest in psychological and social care and seems to be farther along in its development in most countries, including our own.

A. The Evolution of Behavioral and Social Sciences

As background for the approach to psychosocial gerontology, we should consider three interrelated phenomena in the history of scientific thinking.

MOVEMENT TOWARD EMPIRICISM

The first dichotomy contrasts philosophizing about human behavior with an empirical approach through observation and experiment. In the history of human thinking mankind took a very long time to become empirical and to observe natural phenomena systematically. It took still longer to arrive at the point at which conditions or experimental and control techniques were deliberately set up to secure data. This development occurred first in the physical and natural sciences and later in the behavioral and social sciences.

In some European cultures the behavioral and social sciences are still dominated by earlier conceptions, with emphasis on philosophy and theory. Moreover, among scholars there is a wide range of persons with divergent interests. Some prefer to stay in an ivory tower and manipulate symbols, while others go out into the world of objects and relations and secure basic facts upon which to build their conceptions. Often there is a tradition, especially within universities, that understanding is improved by being remote from life rather than immersed in it. Continental Europe seems still to have much discussion on the theoretical and philosophical level, especially among university men. This is more apparent in sociology than in psychology, with its stronger empirical tradition. In Great Britain and the United States, as contrasted with the Continent, the empirical tradition with regard to both psychological and social problems is strong.

TAXONOMY VERSUS EXPLANATION

The second dichotomy relates to the cataloguing and describing of changes with age versus the explanation of change by an analysis of the underlying factors responsible for it. It has long been noted that in those sciences which concern themselves with living systems, beginning efforts toward understanding involve classification and description of the many variants that occur among individuals and species. Gradually, these observations are supplemented with specifically designed experiments set up to test particular hypotheses. More understanding emerges. At some point in history the experimental approach almost replaces the taxonomic approach. But in a later stage naturalistic and ecological studies reappear, and thereafter science moves forward with a parallel interest in classification and in experiment.

In the field of psychological and social gerontology, this dichotomy also emerges. We deal with an aging life-system with all its internal and external relations. We have a large concern with documenting the changes in this system as they occur, and we need such documentation not only for assessment purposes but also for stating the significant scientific problems. From taxonomy we move on to the factors that produce change and ask why one person changes more rapidly than another, how the rate of change can be modified, and how the system can be improved.

One particular aspect of taxonomy deserves special emphasis, namely, the area of social statistics about older people. Every nation in our Western culture collects statistics about its people and, in doing so, breaks down the results in terms of age, sex, status, occupation, etc. Generally, the more industrialized the country, the more statistics. It would be possible, also, I think, to show that, as science advances within a country, statistics advances also.

It is obvious that, in order to secure a comprehensive view of the aging and the aged in terms of their limitations and potentials, we need a wide variety of data collected by and from many different sources. We need social statistics and government reports to picture the extent of the problems put to society by the aging population. We need surveys of the needs of older people classified by age, sex, and socioeconomic status and of the current practices of meeting these needs. We need clinical reports and case histories as a source of exploratory material to aid in the design of investigations. As social problems arise, various breakdowns of the available statistics can be made in order to bring information to bear upon current practical problems. And, of course, good descriptive statistical material may be analyzed at any time after it is collected on the basis of hypotheses to arrive at scientific generalizations.

But it is also clear that, in order to build a sound framework of understanding and practice, we need designed and organized research that moves in to solve specific problems and to give specific answers to the questions raised by the other methods. If at a time these may seem to be in the ascendant, we still must not neglect the observational, naturalistic, or ecological methods which record the behavior of older persons in their habitats and establish the relations of their needs and actions to their environments, since these methods supplement and check all others. Science moves forward by a multiple attack; methods are its tools; the outcomes are conceptualizations or generalizations that enable us not only to control and predict behavior but also to modify stimuli and situations in a desired direction to meet practical purposes.

AGING PROCESS VERSUS ELDERLY PERSONS

The third dichotomy relates to the orientation of thinking and research about the understanding of the nature and process of aging as contrasted with concern about the methods of caring for aging persons once the changes have occurred.

Heron (1957) has pointed out that there are two kinds of psychology in approaching the problems of older people. One is the psychology of the aging process, which is concerned with understanding what is happening within the organism and in the organism's relationship to its surroundings. This is science in a traditional sense. The other is the psychology of the elderly person. Given older people as we find them, what can we discover about them and what can we do in the practical sense to improve their lot? How can we provide them with good care? How can we motivate them to learn and how do they learn? These are very different types of problems in terms of purpose or goal.

The problems of the elderly as such can be met either on the basis of practical experience or by measures which are the outcome of scientific knowledge. European countries, with their old populations, have been facing the problem of aging persons for a long time. On a practical level, using what might be called "social trial and error," substantial programs of care and many institutions of one type or another have been developed for older persons. These have made possible the partial solutions of problems. It is also clear that the advances of modern medicine are operating throughout the whole of Europe to prolong life and thus create larger problems of care. The principle of retirement is likewise being more widely applied and everywhere creates the problem of how the state can deal with unproductive persons in their declining years.

The prolongation of life and the cessation of productivity well in advance of death create psychological and social problems that do not arise in societies composed of younger persons. And psychology and sociology as academic subjects are now directed mainly toward a young population of students and have in the past been primarily concerned with the adjustment of children, adolescents, and young adults. Everywhere there arises a need for turning the attention of scientists and the new personnel they are training within these fields to the problems of the aging process and to the care of elderly people. Once a number of investigators go to work on various problems, there emerges a substantial body of empirical data and of generalizations upon which much of the practice in dealing with the psychological and social problems of older persons can be based. It is also clear that our societies,

American as well as European, are committed to a research approach, because all alike are seeing the world in which they live transformed by science.

B. Study of Participation of Various Countries in Meetings and in Publication

In order to furnish the reader a background with which to approach the research going forward in various countries and to make some comparisons between biological and medical research and psychological and social research, various analyses were made of the number of countries participating in the Third and Fourth International Congresses of Gerontology and of the fields and areas of gerontology covered by the papers presented at the congresses and represented in the "Index to the Current Periodical Literature" in the *Journal of Gerontology*. In addition, an analysis was made of the increase in the literature on gerontology over time.

NUMBER OF COUNTRIES REPRESENTED AT THE INTERNATIONAL CONGRESSES

An analysis was made of the articles, abstracts, and titles published in the *Proceedings* of the Third Congress of the International Association of Gerontology in London and of the abstracts and titles published in the *Program* of the Fourth Congress of the International Association of Gerontology at Merano and Venice, Italy, by the number of countries from which those presenting material came. The results are presented in Table 1.

More countries were represented at the Merano conference by papers of all types than at the London conference. While every country represented had papers in biological and medical research, papers in the psychological, social, and economic areas were confined to fewer countries.

Another analysis is presented in Table 2, which shows the order of areas of interest in terms of the number of papers which were presented from various countries. For all countries the contributions in the bio-logical and medical field outnumber those in the psychological and social field. No attempt was made to correct the crude figures for size of the population or the number of scientific investigators in each country. A correction that might well be made would be one for the country in which the congress was held, as this gives local workers some advantage. However, the major point of the table is that the great bulk of psychological and social in-vestigations are carried on in the United States and in Great Britain.

There is also some difference in the rela-tive emphasis placed on gerontology in Europe as compared with the United States. If we group all the papers presented by countries other than the United States together, at the London conference 67 per cent and at the Merano conference 78 per cent were in the biological and medical field. The corresponding figures for the psychological and social field were 33 per cent for the London Congress and 22 per cent for the Merano Congress. But for the United States the figures for the biologi-cal and medical field were 55 per cent at the London Congress and 61 per cent at the Merano Congress as compared with 45 per cent for the psychological and social field at the London Congress and 39 per cent at the Merano Congress. This suggests that at the present time there is within the American culture, as contrasted with western European culture, somewhat more emphasis upon psychosocial geron-tology.

AREAS OF INTEREST AT INTERNA-TIONAL CONGRESSES

A breakdown was also made of the papers presented at the Third and Fourth International Congresses at London and Merano, since this gives some idea of the range and character of the present inter-ests within the field. The results are pre-sented in Table 3.

Approximately half the papers presented at both congresses were concerned with re-search in the biological and medical field. When to these are added the papers on

TABLE 1

PAPERS AND NUMBER OF COUNTRIES AT THIRD AND FOURTH INTERNATIONAL CONGRESSES

AREA OF INTEREST	No. OF COUNTRIES	
	Third Congress (London)	Fourth Congress (Merano)
Biological and medical re-search...................	15	20
Medical care..............	5	14
Psychological research.......	4	7
Sociological research........	0	3
Social care................	5	8
Social statistics............	4	4
Economic statistics.........	3	6
All psychological and social..	9	13
Papers in any area..........	15	20

TABLE 2

ORDER OF INTEREST IN AREAS BY COUNTRIES

COUNTRY	BIOLOGICAL AND MEDICAL		PSYCHOLOGICAL AND SOCIAL	
	Third Congress (London)	Fourth Congress (Merano)	Third Congress (London)	Fourth Congress (Merano)
United States.........	49	63	41	40
United Kingdom.......	38	26	26	25
Italy.................	7	84	0	13
Netherlands...........	2	10	1	1
Germany.............	1	9	1	4
France...............	6	8	1	2
Switzerland...........	4	3	3	0

medical care, about two-thirds of all papers are in the medical field. Adding the psychological, social, and economic divisions, we find that about one-third of the papers are covered. Another breakdown is found in the last three items in the table, which show that over half the papers at each congress are devoted to research, about one-tenth to statistics, and about one-third to practical problems of care, either medical or social.

LANGUAGES IN WHICH ARTICLES ON GERONTOLOGY APPEAR

By an analysis of entries in the classified bibliography in the *Journal of Gerontology* for Volumes **6–12** (1951–57 inclusive) in which the system of classification remained

TABLE 3

AREAS OF INTEREST AT INTERNATIONAL CONGRESSES

AREA OF INTEREST	THIRD CONGRESS (LONDON)		FOURTH CONGRESS (MERANO)	
	No.	Per Cent	No.	Per Cent
Biological and medical research	99	51	162	46
Medical care	21	11	87	26
Psychological research	15	8	24	7
Sociological research	0	0	9	3
Social care	41	21	36	11
Special statistics	6	3	4	1
Economic statistics	14	7	21	6
All biological and medical	120	61	249	73
All psychological, social, and economic	76	39	94	27
All research	114	58	195	56
All statistics	20	10	25	7
All care	62	32	123	37

constant, a study was made of the languages in which material in the psychological and social fields was published. It was thought that trends might appear with time, but these did not appear, except that, in Volume **6** (1951), 90 per cent of the articles are in English and only 10 per cent

in other languages, whereas from Volume **7** (1952) onward approximately three-fourths of the articles are in English and one-fourth in other languages. The percentages for the entire period covered are: English, 78; French, 6.5; Italian, 4.5; German, 3.4; and all others (Japanese, Spanish, Russian, Portuguese, etc.), 7.5. When this analysis was first undertaken, it

TABLE 4

ABSTRACTS ON AGING BY PERIODS

Volume and Year	Average Total Abstracts per Year	Average No. of Abstracts on Aging per Year	Percentage of Total
1–7 (1927–33)	4704	6.29	0.14
8–14 (1934–40)	6270	10.00	0.16
15–21 (1941–47)	4555	23.71	0.53
22–29 (1948–54)	7362	80.86	1.09

was hoped that it could be made by country of origin rather than by language of publication. However, it soon became clear that the references did not contain enough information to make this possible. Going back to the original articles was out of the question.

INCREASE IN SCIENTIFIC INTEREST IN AGING WITH TIME

In order to discover the nature of the changes in our interests in aging over time, an analysis was made of the proportion of entries which relate to aging in the yearly index of the *Psychological Abstracts*, which has been published since 1927. The twenty-eight volumes were divided into four 7-year groups, and the proportions of references to aging to the total number of abstracts were calculated for each 7-year period. The results are presented in Table 4.

It should be noted that, since this yearly index contains cross-references to all appropriate entries, the numbers are always greater than those for the abstracts placed in the section "Maturity and Old Age." These index figures are probably underestimates since failure to note an entry is more likely than is overentry.

Although the proportions are small, the rate of growth is rapid when compared with other areas. While the absolute numbers of abstracts in the "Infant, Adolescent, and Family" area have increased during the same period, the relative number of proportion has remained unchanged (Anderson, 1956a). Moreover, references to aging increased about eight times, while the total number of abstracts increased one and one-half times. The increase is from 0.14 of 1 per cent to 1.09 per cent over a 27-year period.

As an indication of the current rate of interest we obtained the percentage of papers at the two most recent large psychological meetings. At the Fifteenth International Congress of Psychology, held in Brussels in 1957, of 256 communicated papers, 7, or 2.7 per cent, were concerned with the problem of aging. Of these, 6 were by European and 1 by American authors. This percentage is not much different from that at the 1957 meeting of the American Psychological Association, at which, of 542 contributed papers, 13 (or 2.4 per cent) dealt specifically with problems of aging.

In connection with the data on the articles on psychology, the question might well be raised as to what this proportion should be under ideal conditions. In my study of the proportion of references in *Psychological Abstracts* devoted to various scientific fields over a period of time, I found for most fields a substantial stability. Two phenomena seem to occur. One is that a field develops and moves up to sort of a high point and then remains stable over a long period of time. The other is that particular areas of interest develop for a short time, command the attention of substantial numbers of persons, and then drop out. The field of "Child Psychology" is very stable, and over the 28-year period the proportion of articles devoted to this field has been very constant in relation to the total field. The field of "Gerontology" was a very minor field, with almost no

interest when the *Abstracts* were begun. It has steadily increased with a slow and gradual growth, and that suggests permanence. But I have no answer to the question as to whether 2, or 5, or 10 per cent of the articles should be devoted to gerontology.

Another time comparison may be made. The Shock bibliography which appeared in 1951 lists 18,036 abstracts in gerontology for the world between 1900 and 1948, while *Supplement One, 1949–1955* lists 15,983. The rate per year from 1900 to 1948 was 360, while the rate per year from 1949 to 1955 was 2283, or six times as great. While these figures, which could be further broken down, are not, strictly speaking, comparable, they do show the great shift in scientific interest in all areas of gerontology. In the Introduction to the *Supplement,* Shock (1957a) points out that in 1948 there were four journals in the world devoted to gerontology, whereas in 1957 there were seventeen.

In the second edition of *Trends in Gerontology,* Shock (1957b) makes an analysis of progress in the whole field in various ways but does not, as would be desirable for our purposes, compare the psychological and social field with the biological and medical field. It is clear, however, looking at his data, that scientific interest in gerontology is not confined to one nation, one world area, or one discipline.

Shock (1957b) also analyzes the changes in the goals and content of research in gerontology and finds a shift from descriptive studies of age changes to experimental and designed studies that seek to answer more fundamental questions. He also finds a marked increase in the number of laboratories that are devoted to research on aging and an increase in the support of research on aging by grants and in the availability of experimental material in the form of animals maintained throughout the life-span. Although he is considering the entire field, he does point out that in the area of psychological and social studies proportionately more research is being done on stratified samples of the population and on people living out in the community rather than people in institutions. All this adds up to much greater sophistication in the scientific sense in stating problems, in securing samples, and in designing studies.

SUMMARIES OF CURRENT RESEARCH

Recently, several surveys of the psychological and social research on aging in Europe have appeared, of which the most comprehensive is that of Welford (1958b) in the supplement to the April, 1958, issue of the *Journal of Gerontology*. In fact, this entire supplement presents a series of papers given at a special symposium on "A Survey of European Gerontology" held at the Tenth Annual Meeting of the American Gerontological Society in Cleveland, November, 1957. Shock (1957b), in the second edition of *Trends in Gerontology*, presents a brief description of various laboratories in Europe, with emphasis, however, mainly on biological and medical research. Heron (1957) has a brief discussion of the present status of research on psychological changes with age. The most recent summary of gerontological research (mainly American) to appear in the *Annual Review of Psychology* is that by Birren (1960). The report of the Bethesda Conference on the *Psychological Aspects of Aging* (Anderson, 1956b) also summarizes many research studies (mainly American) in the area of psychological and social behavior and suggests future problems.

For a comprehensive survey of research and extensive bibliographies the reader may consult the other *Handbooks* in this series published by the University of Chicago Press under the auspices of the Inter-University Council of Social Gerontology. The first, edited by James E. Birren and entitled *Handbook of Aging and the Individual: Psychological and Biological Aspects,* presents a systematic and complete summary of the state of our present knowledge in the psychological area including personality and adjustment. The second

Handbook, edited by Clark Tibbitts and entitled *Handbook of Social Gerontology: Societal Aspects of Aging,* covers the social and economic areas.

For access to specific research studies either past, present, or future, the reader should consult the various comprehensive bibliographies (Shock, 1951, 1957a), the "Index to Current Periodical Literature" in the *Journal of Gerontology,* and the indexes or abstracts within special fields such as those in the section on "Maturity and Old Age" in Psychological Abstracts. A new abstract journal entitled *Gerontology and Geriatrics* appeared in 1958 under the auspices of the Excerpta Medica Foundation of Amsterdam, which maintains an international medical abstracting service.

II. RESEARCH IN VARIOUS COUNTRIES

We may now turn to a brief description of research projects in various European countries.

A. United Kingdom

Any presentation of the work on aging in the United Kingdom within the limited space available in this chapter will of necessity be inadequate and will either omit some projects or barely mention others. At the Third International Congress, as shown in Table 2, there were twenty-six papers and at the Fourth International Congress there were twenty-five in the psychological and social fields from Great Britain. When compared with other countries, the United Kingdom is then a large producer of papers on aging.

For a decade or more there has been a constant flow of papers, monographs, and books dealing with all aspects of aging—medical, biological, psychological, social, and economic—largely because of the interest of the Nuffield Foundation, which has served both to support research in this area and to catalyze the work of others. In addition, prior to the organization of the foundation and parallel with it, Lord Nuffield made other grants which reveal his personal interest in the problems of older people. The Andrews and Brunner book (1955) gives an account of Lord Nuffield's life and of his many benefactions.

Briefly, the foundation was established in 1943 with £10,000,000 to further (1) the advancement of health and the prevention of sickness by medical research and teaching; (2) the advancement of social well-being by scientific research and the improvement of education; (3) the care and comfort of the aged poor; (4) the advancement of education; and (5) such other charitable purposes as shall be declared by Lord Nuffield or the vote of the trustees. Note the broad definitions of the tasks set for the foundation and the great flexibility of its conception.

Over the years the foundation has devoted its largest sums to the "care of old people." It also set up the first general program for systematic investigation of the problems of aging. It has, in addition, supported much research in other areas of medicine, biology, and the social sciences as well as research in the physical sciences and in agriculture. Grants have been made throughout the United Kingdom. Included in the grants for fundamental research in the biological, medical, and social sciences have been specific grants for research on aging, in addition to those for the care and comfort of the aged poor. Also included in grants for medical research have been grants for studies of the diseases of old age. The foundation also established Nuffield Gerontological Research Fellowships.

In 1947, as a result of a report by the Rowntree Committee, the foundation established the National Corporation for the Care of Old People, which, in addition to funds from the foundation, secures contributions from other sources either for specific programs or for administering benefactions. The corporation has worked closely with other bodies and has stimulated other societies and local authorities. It not only has made grants to voluntary societies providing homes for old people but has built such homes itself. More re-cently it has shifted much of its emphasis from building homes to non-residential clubs and welfare activities. Still more recently it has undertaken long-term studies to assess the needs of old people within an area and to provide services in that area as a demonstration of what can be achieved. Thus the studies of the corporation have a very practical slant when compared with those of the foundation.

It should be noted, however, that the foundation's concern with older people, though bulking large throughout its program,[2] does not constitute its entire program, which is broad enough in scope to include almost any research or practical field that looks toward human betterment. Moreover, the foundation program has opened up areas of research and practice and then, as needs and scientific interests have changed, has shifted emphasis.

Many of the studies of British origin briefly described or listed in the Welford (1958b) survey of psychological and social gerontology in Europe were financed by the Nuffield Foundation. This report covers measures of human capacity, experimental studies of human performance, employment and retirement, and social and economic problems and has a bibliography of citations to current work. In the psychological area the studies on aging and skill (Welford, 1951, 1958a) are the outcome of the research of the Nuffield Research Unit into Problems of Aging at the Psychological Laboratory, Cambridge, which has recently closed its program. At the present time a number of studies in the social field are under way through grants from the foundation, of which only a few may be mentioned as indicating trends:

1. A study of the economic cushions which people carry forward with them into retirement has been started by Utting at Cambridge. He is attempting to determine the amount of clothing, household equipment, property of all sorts, linens, silver,

---

[2] See Case Study No. 13, pp. 448–56, for a fuller account of the work of the foundation in the field of aging.

etc., possessed by persons over 65 years, in order to determine the resources available to meet aging. At present this study is in the pilot stage in order to formulate techniques. If the techniques can be developed and the co-operation of older persons obtained, it is expected that this study will be extended to other communities.

2. The studies of aging in various industries and of the opportunities for elderly workers, some of which have been reported by Le Gros Clark, are being continued. This type of study is carried on in one industry after another and covers various factories, business firms, trading organizations, etc. Special studies are being made of women in industry and of retired women. Studies are also being made of provisions for retirement and the manner in which retirement is being met by aging men and women. This is a whole program of studies to illuminate the working conditions and the pre- and postretirement conditions of workers of all types. It seeks to answer questions about elderly workers such as "Who are you?" "What are your opportunities?" "What part-time opportunities for employment are there?" "Could more opportunities be developed?" etc.

3. At the University of Bristol there is a unit for research on the employment of older workers supported by a grant from the Nuffield Foundation. A study of the age structure in the engineering industry has already been published. The purpose of the project is to identify aging effects in industry and to find methods of minimizing them, not so much to solve employment problems as to reduce wastage of workers when jobs become too demanding. The technique is primarily that of the field study. The theoretical problems raised by the field studies are then studied in the laboratory. One experimental study using pursuit-tracking behavior seeks to determine age changes in performing continuous tasks which involve "short-term storage," while another is concerned with the effect of age on the monitoring of movement. In-

volved in these studies are Murrell and Griew.

4. At the London School of Economics, Townsend, Titmuss, and Abel-Smith are making an extensive study of the factors of all types which lead older persons to enter institutions and to live in them. Some emphasis goes to the types of relations maintained with the person's family outside the institution. Analysis is also being made of the institutional organization and pattern of functioning in homes for the aged, nursing homes, and other types of institutions. The investigators are concerned with the problem of what leads to the decision to enter an institution and, after the person is in the institution, what the effect of institutionalization is. Involved also is some study of the homes and environments from which institutionalized persons come.

5. The projects under the auspices of the National Corporation for the Care of Old People involve surveys by means of interviews, which are made by welfare workers. These seek to determine the needs of older persons and the best ways of meeting them. This corporation is asking questions as to the gaps in the present program of service and how the gaps are to be met. It studies the work of private as well as public agencies and the clientele reached by each. At present one study had been completed in Andover, and projected studies are to be done on samples in Nottingham and Sussex.

In England some studies are going forward with government support within operating agencies. Often these involve academic co-operation. For instance, the National Assistance Board, which handles two-thirds of the aged in Britain, surveys the needs of older people. The Ministry of Labour has set up an Advisory Council on the Employment of Men and Women and is concerned with the arbitrary age at which employment ceases.

Specific governmental support for research on aging comes from the Medical Research Council, which usually supports units attached to university departments or medical schools and sometimes supports individual workers by direct grant. Recently, the Medical Research Council has formed a "Group for Research on the Occupational Aspects of Aging," which is attached to the University of Liverpool, with L. S. Hearnshaw, professor of psychology, as honorary director, and Alastair Heron as full-time deputy director. The objectives of the new group are as follows: (*a*) experimental studies of the psychological concomitants of normal changes with age in the main perceptual modalities, the present emphasis being on vision and hearing; (*b*) studies of various aspects of psychological "rigidity" (these include examination of both intellectual and emotional aspects of this problem and of its relevance to industrial training and retraining procedures); and (*c*) investigation of attitudes toward aging and its consequences as held by those concerned and by others of various ages and occupational status.

During 1958 this group, in addition to laboratory studies, carried out a survey of aging in over thirty manufacturing firms representing a wide variety of industrial activities. One objective of this survey was to lay the foundations for intensive studies of particular occupational problems of aging wherever possible of a longitudinal as well as the familiar cross-sectional kind. Attention was also given to the development and study of "education for retirement" programs.

In addition to the active research going forward in Britain on "normal" old people, there is interest in elderly patients in the research departments of mental hospitals. For example, in the Department of Psychology of the Institute of Psychiatry in Maudsley Hospital, a series of studies deal with psychological functions in elderly patients. These started with attempts to study the relations between cognitive difficulties, memory impairment, and brain damage in psychiatric patients over 60 years of age. Studies of learning, of memory functions, of the capacity to reproduce designs, and of memory disorders have re-

sulted or are in process. These studies under Inglis not only are of interest in connection with psychiatric patients but also have significance in terms of methods and results for the study of normal aging.

In concluding this all-too-brief summary, may I express appreciation of the richness and variety of the approaches made in Britain to the study of older people.

B. France

In France a series of major research projects on the psychology of aging are being carried on by Suzanne Pacaud, who reported at the Third International Congress on the age relations of a number of psychological variables on four thousand subjects between 12 and 55 years. She was concerned, first, with age changes in memory and in intellectual and psychomotor functions and, second, with the effect of education upon the decline of these functions. In process now is a study of the factorial structure of these psychological abilities as a function of age. She is presently extending this series of researches upward in the age scale and, in collaboration with Professors Laugier and Piéron and with Dr. Coumétou, is making psychological and sociological studies on persons between the ages of 55 and 75 years. In addition, she has completed integrating experimental results on the age relations of a number of physiological functions in co-operation with Professors Laugier, Piéron, and Bourlière and with Dr. Coumétou. These interrelated studies represent an ambitious program.

The Centre de Gérontologie was established in 1957 under the sponsorship of the Association Claude Bernard, a nonprofit organization concerned with the development of biological and medical research in the Paris hospitals. F. Bourlière, professor of gerontology at the Paris Medical School, is the director of the Center, which is organized under four sections: biological, physiological, psychological, and socioeconomic. The main researches now in progress are: In *biology and physiology*, (1) a longitudinal research on two hundred subjects between 45 and 95 years of age to determine the influence of nutrition on the aging of some physiological functions; (2) a parallel study on the same subjects on the variation, with aging, of the thresholds of gustative perception; (3) research on the aging of skin, evolution and involution of metabolism, and the effects of aging on the liver regenerative function; and (4) other research on aging in the field of biochemistry and pharmacology. In *psychology*, (1) differential aging in a homogeneous population of teachers; (2) psychomotor-task measurement in a general population of aged people; (3) interest inventories for the aged; and (4) differential aging in a population of bicycle fans. In *sociology*, (1) a study of attitudes before and after retirement in a sample of teachers in Paris and (2) a pilot study on the causes of the higher rate of masculine mortality in the population over 60.

J. R. Tréanton, of the Institut des Sciences Sociales du Travail of the University of Paris, is making a study of the adaptation to retirement of 270 persons who have had their retirement pensions 1 year or more and who continue to live in Paris. A preliminary report of this study was given at the Fourth Congress. He obtained information on the level of economic life, the adaption to urban living, the kind and frequency of their social relations (including those with the family), the expectations and aspirations for the future, and the general attitudes toward retirement, life, social security, and their place in society.

Tréanton is also studying the attitudes of managerial personnel over the age of 40, with special emphasis on the problems of aging and of social security. The first part of this study is being made on seventy managers in the chemical industry, to be followed by studies in other industries. The attitudes he is concerned with are hopes for stability of employment, attitudes toward the organization of managers, attitudes and provisions for retirement, attitudes toward work, and productivity in retirement work.

In the sociological field in France the study of aging suffered a great loss in the death of Jean Daric, who had made demographic studies of older people, more especially studies of age grading, and who had a number of projects under way. He had wide interests in all the social aspects of aging.

C. West Germany

Under the direction of Klaus Riegel, a large research project on the relation between the mental abilities and thinking processes of older persons and their interests, activities, attitudes, and adjustment was carried on at the University of Hamburg. For comparative purposes a control group of younger persons was used. In the pilot study in which the procedures were developed, 74 persons above 65 from old age homes were compared with 56 persons who had an average age 17 years. In the major study 450 persons above the age of 55 years from Middle and North Germany, stratified within groups of 150 cases from 55 to 64, 65 to 74, and 75 to 84 years, respectively, by sex, vocation, source of income, and residence were compared with 160 17-year-olds matched by sex, education, and vocation. The older subjects were secured in factories and clubs and by door-to-door contacts; the younger subjects, from various technical schools and high schools.

The Hamburg Wechsler Intelligence Scale was given to all subjects in order to study the effects of intelligence as well as to control it and to extend the norms of the test to age groups above 60. An item-by-item comparison between the younger and older subjects is being made. Six new verbal tests (synonym, antonym, selection, classification, analogy, and ordering) were also developed and applied in the pilot study, which showed no difference between the older and younger groups for the synonym test and increasing differences in the other tests in the order listed. The results of the tests have also been factor-analyzed. It is hoped that these new tests will give insight into intellectual changes in old age and yield an index of intellectual deterioration. A word-association test is also being used (made up of the same stimulus words of which the tests of verbal functioning are composed) in order to isolate changes in associative verbal behavior.

Attitude inventories of the Likert type are used to measure rigidity, dogmatism, and the attitude toward life. In the pilot study other measures of rigidity were tried out. A measure covering the intensity and span of interests is also being used. A general questionnaire covering personal data, life-history, social interactions, and social relations consisting of 125 questions, broken down into ten different subscales covering adjustment and activity within the family, social life, leisure, work, and other areas, was developed and is in use.

A very extensive statistical analysis of the data is now under way. This involves developmental and age comparisons as well as the interrelations between the variables. In addition, small samples are to be drawn out of the main sample for future studies of the verbal behavior and perceptual abilities of older persons. In drawing such samples, various controls can be exercised in terms of the data available on the subjects. This is a special advantage of the design.

While the present study represents a cross-sectional design, the records will be kept in the hope that some 5 or 10 years hence the study may be repeated on the same subjects. This investigation is aided by a grant from the foundation's Fund for Research in Psychiatry.

Another study is going forward under Hans Thomae at Erlangen. This is concerned primarily with personality changes in men between 30 and 50 years. Although it is a longitudinal study in which the men are interviewed every half-year, it also yields cross-sectional age comparisons. Questionnaires and semistructured inter-views are used which were developed on the basis of a preliminary pilot study. The final group to be followed consists of one hundred men. At present the project is financed for 3 years, with some hope that it will be continued longer. A preliminary report is in process of publication.

Although both the Riegel and the Thomae studies have implications for social behavior, there seems, in general, to be a lack of designed sociological studies. Nevertheless, at the international congress at Merano several theoretical and philosophical papers on aging were presented by professors from West Germany, who thus evinced interest in the implications of aging.

A major study of the characteristics of social security recipients is going forward under the Co-ordinating Committee of the Social Sciences Institutes, on which information can be obtained from the executive secretary, Professor Specht at Cologne-Lindenthal.[3] Within the framework of this larger project the Social Science Institute at the University of Frankfurt, under the direction of Professor Th. W. Adorno, is making a study of the old age expectations of workers and white-collar employees while they are still productively employed.

D. Scandinavian Countries

In the Scandinavian countries the care of older persons is generally at a very high level. One cannot but be impressed with the housing, the institutions, the philosophy, and the general organization of the programs. But a person who has grown up in scientific research wonders how this has all come about without an extensive series of studies, each rather specifically designed, which have been integrated into a sound body of practice. But the care of the old in society cannot wait for the results of the most recent investigations; it is with society as a practical problem always. Hence societies meet their problems as best they can in the light of their own present knowl-

[3] See Case Study No. 14, pp. 457–59.

edge and their own level of development. Involved also is a kind of social trial and error, like the trial and error in the learning of the individual, except that it may be much extended in time and involve many individuals and organizations. Some practices are eliminated in time, and some are retained and developed. But sometimes wrong directions are taken and rigidities develop. Because these may actually encumber the society and adversely affect many people, they need re-examination with modern techniques of research.

Since the advent of modern science, society increasingly substitutes a systematic and orderly method of solving its problems. At first it uses research techniques haltingly and with suspicion; later it uses them freely and with almost too ready acceptance. In the more advanced stages of its use of research techniques society subjects many of its current practices to critical examination, seeks to understand why one procedure rather than another is used, compares methods under controlled conditions, and refines and elaborates a process which already has been going on slowly and unsystematically within the social structure. Hence practice is in some respects and in some places ahead of science; in other respects and in other places, behind it. Sometimes the scientist conceptualizes and rationalizes what is already known; sometimes he moves out boldly from the present and changes wide ranges of practice.

Sweden.—In Sweden, despite the very high level of care and the interest in older people, pointed out by Havighurst in his chapter, there seem to be very few research projects. Nor does there seem to be much interest on the part of psychologists. However, sociologists, through the Swedish Institute for Public Opinion Research, made an interview study or poll in June, 1956, of a national sample of people over 56. The questions covered a wide range of interest, activities, and attitudes. (For some of the material from this poll consult chapters viii and ix.)

One interesting project is under way. Gunnar Boalt, at the Social Institute of Stockholm, is carrying forward a project in which he is studying a sample of people 60 years old who are leaving their jobs for pensions. They are first tested with a mental test designed by Carl Ramfalk and by simple physical fitness tests and then matched in pairs. One in each pair goes on pension, and the other is retained on his job. Both are tested each year for 3 years in order to determine whether the pension lowers their physical or mental fitness. The city of Stockholm is co-operating by letting a sample of pensioners remain at work while their paired mates go on pension. But Boalt has found difficulty in maintaining the non-working pension group because its members leave and then take other jobs with private employers. An attempt is being made to interest private companies in a project of this sort.

Denmark.—In Denmark, under the Ministry of Labor and Social Affairs, a health study of older persons is now being carried on in which a stratified sample of persons is being interviewed. While the questions center about health and its immediate problems, some have reference to adjustment. In the immediate future a study of the effects of isolation upon the adjustment and health of aged persons is contemplated.

The Danish Statistical Department is making a study on the living conditions of old age pensioners in different parts of the country, with particular reference to income and expenditures, the consumption of goods, and housing.

Another project contemplated by the Ministry of Social Affairs seeks to answer questions about the effects of the National Pensions Act of 1956 and will compare old age pensioners from the period before the new legislation with the pensioners after the new legislation and seek to find out why some apply and some do not apply for pensions. The study will also include a study of the attitudes of old people toward the pension scheme.

But the most significant feature on the

Danish scene is the Danish National Institute of Social Research, established by Parliament in 1958, which integrates work in the social sciences in government departments and universities. In the past the conduct of research projects by separate governmental departments has proved cumbersome, particularly in recruiting staffs that changed from study to study. This independent institute is financed by an annual grant from the government and is directed by a board composed of university professors in related fields and of representatives of government departments. The director of the Institute (who is Henning Friis) is appointed by the Minister of Social Affairs at the recommendation of the board. There is an Advisory Council composed of representatives of muncipalities, employers, labor, social welfare institutes, and individual experts, which may make suggestions for research. The Institute may receive grants from sources other than the government for special projects. The Institute is conducting substantial projects in collaboration with various governmental agencies and university departments and gives grants to scientists working on special projects.

The field of social gerontology has a high priority in the research program of the Institute. It is planned to make a sample survey of the elderly, with particular attention to the problems of retirement work and the need for social service.

Norway.—In Norway, so far as I could determine, there is at present little or no research on the psychological and social aspects of aging. There has been some discussion of a possible program in this area under the auspices of the National Association for General Health, which has requested Mrs. Eva Beverfelt to report on the possibilities.

Finland.—In Finland there is an active gerontological society which publishes a yearbook, *Geron,* that contains a variety of articles on older persons. While these are in the main of the statistical and survey type or are reports of agencies, there is an occasional research study. The journal reveals a broader interest in psychological and social problems than is true of many other European gerontological societies. Anitra L. C. Karsten, in particular, has been interested in the personality characteristics of older people and has recently concerned herself with the adjustment of older people in industry.

E. The Netherlands

In the Netherlands research on aging has been actively undertaken under the auspices of the National Health Research Council T.N.O. of the Netherlands Foundation of Applied Scientific Research. The latter organization covers industry, warfare, nutrition, agriculture, and health and promotes research in areas related to governmental activities. The term "health" is very broadly interpreted and includes the psychological and social aspects of welfare and of mental health. This organization sets up its own intramural projects and also gives extramural grants to scientists who apply. The Netherlands Foundation secures the co-operation of public officials, of universities and their staffs, and of interested community officials and agencies in co-ordinated efforts toward the solution of problems.

A particular area of concern to the National Health Research Council is aging. In approaching the problem of the aged person, it was felt that it was important to establish priorities by locating the central problems of aged persons. Later specific projects could be developed. The first step was to work out a questionnaire which covered the physical health and the psychological and social aspects of adjustment. Special attention was to be paid to the need for assistance and dependency or, conversely, to independence and self-help. In an early pilot study this questionnaire for an interview was distributed to some twenty physicians who interviewed patients above the age of 65. After criticizing results and analyzing the questions in terms of practicability, a new form of the interview is in use with the co-operation of general practitioners all over the Netherlands. Included is a section on psychological and social adjustment and a memory test similar to that in the Groningen survey mentioned later. The interview takes 3 hours per person.

In order to secure adequate sampling of the population, the lists of patients in the smaller towns are checked against the registrar's list and in the large cities against lists of sick-fund registrants and then plotted on a map for location, and a letter is written back to the doctor to get whatever number of persons of such-and-such qualifications as are needed to make up an appropriate sample. If there is no return from a particular area, a special attempt is made to secure data from that area. Lists are made up from the various sources, and, if a patient or person refuses, the next number is taken. Appropriate proportions of senile, deaf, and institutional cases are included. These questionnaires are returned to the central office and are checked. If part of the examination is incomplete or inadequate, the blank is returned to the doctor with a letter of explanation or request to supply the missing data.

The final sample is then a stratified sample of the whole population of Holland over the age of 65. The data are being machine-processed. From the data it is hoped to get a comprehensive picture of the situation of aged persons from the standpoint of their physical and psychological characteristics, together with their needs, their amount of dependency and/or invalidism, and their capacity for self-help. In addition to this large survey now being analyzed, more intensive surveys have been made in particular communities, of which the best known is the Groningen survey, in which three thousand persons over 65, randomly selected from four times that number, or all the aged persons in the city, were interviewed in their homes. This sample was divided into four age groups, 56–70, 70–75, 75–80, and 80 and over, and into two sex groups. The analysis of this data is now virtually completed and was of value in the development of the interviews being given over the whole of the Netherlands.

I have gone into some detail with respect to these surveys because I was impressed with the care taken in sampling as well as with the pilot studies and methods of checking the interviews. For more details the paper presented by van Zonneveld (1958) in the "Symposium on European Gerontology" at the Cleveland meeting of the Gerontological Society should be consulted. This presents the results and gives references to a number of health and medical surveys concerned with the aged which have been made in various countries in Europe. Often these surveys contain questions which are of much interest to the social scientist.

In addition to the surveys, there are other studies going forward under the auspices of the National Health Research Council. It has, for instance, subsidized research on aging in rats and mice, is making some studies of the housing of aged persons, and, in co-operation with various agencies, is studying social care. Still large in the planning stage is a project on how to develop and encourage independence and self-help in older persons. This particular study involves the co-operation of the Ministry of Social Welfare and will use five or six regions selected at random.

Other projects of special interest are now supported. One is a project in the Rotterdam Municipal Home for the Aged, which consists of a longitudinal study of the four hundred persons who are in that home from the present time until their death. The study involves periodic physical examinations, many types of laboratory tests, tests of sensory acuity, portraits at various ages, studies of psychological and social adjustment, and a final autopsy at death against which the cumulative records can be checked. It is hoped to view the subjects from every angle and to secure data which can be generalized to similar institutions in other parts of the country.

A second special project of general interest is being carried on at the Psychological Institute at the University of Groningen by F. Verhage, who is working in cooperation with a team composed of a psychologist, a statistician, and a clinical psychologist. They are developing an intelligence test, or tests, at the adult level that can be applied to older and younger people. At Groningen the Wechsler Intelligence Scale for Children has already been revised for use with Dutch children. The new project seeks to develop a test comparable to the Wechsler-Bellevue at the adult level. It is to be an individual rather than a group test, with scoring adapted to various kinds of persons and with a substantial number of subtests so that the tests which are not applicable may be left out in any individual case. Material must be adapted to Dutch standards and culture. Criteria relating to the level of difficulty as well as to the range and nature of the problems are to be used. While this test will be useful for all types of adults, a particular phase of the project involves a study of the applicability of tests to older people, including a search for items or subtests that will be interesting to older people and adapted to their background. At present pilot studies are under way with adults of various ages in order to make some preliminary selection of the test content. Later more intensive analysis will be made for the final selection and standardization. It is anticipated that 5 years is necessary to develop an adequate instrument.

There are some other special projects in the Netherlands under independent auspices. A study in Sittard in the south of Holland, under the auspices of J. M. A. Munnichs, of the Psychological Institute at Nijmegen, uses questionnaires and interviews in order to get together material that will reveal the thinking and needs of older people and the relations within the family of the older person with the members of the family. Frequency of visits between family members, where and how the older persons live, who their friends are and how often they are seen, the time schedule of their daily activities, their hobbies, and particularly their needs in terms of loneliness and social relations are being studied. Plans are being made for a similar study in rural areas.

F. Switzerland

In Switzerland there has always been much interest in the biological and medical aspects of aging and some emphasis upon methods of social care, but there has been little emphasis upon the psychological and sociological aspects of aging and not much interest on the part of university men in the behavioral and social sciences—all this in spite of the fact that good social statistics are available. A current project that may have implications for the future is the study by F. Verzar, at the University of Basel, which involves a longitudinal study of two hundred young employees of the Ciba Company by means of biannual physical and medical examinations. There is some discussion of the possibility of including psychological measures. At Basel there is also a rat colony of aging animals on which Jean Verzar-McDougall has carried on an interesting study on the relation of old age in white rats to learning and relearning.

G. Italy

In Italy there is very high interest in the medical and biological problems of aging and much less work on the psychological and social side. To a large degree the studies developed depend upon individual investigators and the resources available in the particular hospital or agency in which he is located. Most studies seem to be largely clinical in nature and to represent an accumulation of cases rather than a specific design attacking a research problem in terms of a particular hypothesis. Discussions with university men in psychology and sociology revealed only a mild interest in the problems of aging persons. Many of the generalizations with reference to psychological and social problems are left to medical men and social workers. There are a number of active journals in the field of geriatrics.

Some significant work has been done by individual investigators such as the recent study by Gemelli and Cesa-Bianchi of motor tests on persons from 20 to 80 years of age, and the Cesa-Bianchi study of an Italian version of the Wechsler-Bellevue Intelligence Scale and of the Rorschach on persons from 70 to 88 years. There also seems to be considerable interest in the use of psychometric and projective tests as diagnostic devices with older persons who become patients in clinics or residents of institutions.

H. Russia

While no visit was made to Russia, I did have an opportunity to talk with several Russian psychologists at the International Congress of Psychology at Brussels. They reported that there was virtually no interest in the problems of aging among Russian psychologists of their acquaintance. They said that Russia was a young country with much scientific concern with the psychological and social problems of children, adolescents, and young adults. There was some interest among physicians in the problems of the medical care of older people and some programs of social care. It was my distinct impression that there was no opposition to work on aging persons but rather that, because aging had not yet become a significant social problem, scientists had not yet been stimulated to work on it. Interviews with several psychologists from the satellite countries mirrored this impression.

III. Areas of Interest in Gerontology

Following are my impressions of the status of various areas of interest within psychological and social gerontology. While my activities were directed toward designed projects, I have occasionally included other types of studies. Even though one might expect interests within gerontology to reflect the dominating interests within the major scientific fields of a country at a particular time, this does not seem to be the case. Interest in aging is specialized and cuts across disciplines. Moreover, as one reads the scientific literature, there are many instances of investigators who work on a particular scientific problem and come up with data on older people, not so much because of interest in aging, but because older subjects were available or data were automatically collected on a large population which then was analyzed for age relations. Much of our earlier knowledge about aging came about as a by-product rather than a planned outcome.

1. *Polling and interview techniques.*—There is almost universal use of polling and interview techniques with various methods of sampling the general population. Public opinion polls with a limited number of questions are made across populations. Good examples are found in Sweden. A more restricted type of polling is that in which a community or region is polled—sometimes because it can be shown to be typical of the entire population. Another type of poll is a more detailed interview of persons, either taken at random or selected on some scheme of stratification, of which a good example is found in the Netherlands. Such polls, which contain a variety of questions concerning the life of older people and their attitudes toward their treatment and experiences, have both psychological and social significance. Van Zonneveld (1958) describes many types of surveys, chiefly of the interview type, that have been made in the various countries of Europe and comments on some of the problems involved.

2. *Age changes in perceptual, motor, and other psychological processes.*—In many countries studies of age changes in psychological processes are under way. In vision and audition these are often made

by persons interested in those areas rather than by persons concerned with aging. The most comprehensive studies of a series of psychological processes on the same individuals are those by Pacaud in France.

3. *Intelligence.*—An interest that runs across the cultural pattern concerns tests of intelligence. Intelligence tests for children have been either translated, adapted, or restandardized for use in almost every country, although interest in adult tests has lagged. Now, for a variety of reasons, such as clinical, industrial, and military use, work goes forward in many countries. Obviously, such measures, developed within the framework of a particular country and language, have many scientific and practical uses. For many years England has been advanced in this area. Recently tests have been developed in Italy and applied to older people. Holland and West Germany have major projects going.

4. *Personality tests.*—A somewhat similar statement could be made about the Rorschach Personality Test, in which there is wide interest because of its use for assessment and diagnosis in clinics. Studies made on persons of all age levels in various countries are scattered through the psychological literature. But other personality tests are in clinical use and are under study in various countries. Unfortunately, analyses of such results in relation to age are not always made.

5. *Learning and education.*—Except for the research done at Cambridge University, little work seems to be in progress on the acquisition of skills and the learning of simple and complex patterns, despite the obvious need of such information in working out educational programs for older people. When we turn to direct studies on educational methods for use with older people, the situation is even more striking. The analysis of the bibliographies and of the programs of international congresses revealed surprisingly little concern with this area, as did the conversations with psychologists and sociologists in various coun-

tries. While some data are available from the polls on the participation of older people in various activities, there is little concern with developing new activities or with exploring ways in which participation may be broadened by various kinds of educational programs geared to the older person.

6. *Retirement.*—In almost every country studies are concerned with the effects of retirement upon the health, behavior, interests, attitudes, and adjustment of older people. Since the number and the proportion of retired persons are increasing everywhere, problems arise. One would wish for more designed studies that are concerned, not so much with a descriptive analysis of the characteristics of retired persons, as with the exploration of methods that might be used to increase the participation of retired persons in community activities, to utilize their skills and knowledge, and to discover how to develop the feeling of being worthwhile that comes with participation.

7. *Self-help.*—Closely related to the problem of retirement as well as to the problem of care is that of building more autonomy in older persons with respect to their own care, that is, the problem of self-help. This is also related to the problem of rehabilitation. While workers in many countries are aware of the problem and, in fact, see it as of great importance because of the increasing burden placed upon the state by the care of the old, the amount of research designed to explore the underlying principles and give us the basis for a practical program is negligible.

8. *Social behavior.*—In the various polls and surveys some data on the extent and types of social participation of older persons and on their attitudes toward such activities are available. But there is little or no designed research on the organization of social groups, on how most effectively to secure participation, on the ways of reaching "lonely" old people and enriching their lives, etc. Nor are there experiments in which the group atmosphere, the

group size, and the group activities are varied systematically in order to compare different techniques and procedures.

9. *Housing.*—In many European countries there are fine housing developments for older people yet their practice seems to grow out of practical experience rather than systematic experiment. Much of the material seems to be on an ideological rather than an empirical level. Observations could well be made on the effects of various types of housing and equipment on the adjustment and attitudes of older people.

10. *Institutional organization and management.*—In all countries there are institutions of various sizes and types for older people, operated under a variety of auspices with various patterns of organization and staff arrangements. It occurred to me as I visited some of them that there was an opportunity for ecological and observational studies that would give us understanding of the various principles that underlie good institution organization and management in terms of the effects produced in the behavior and attitudes of older people.

11. *Working studies within departments and agencies.*—In all countries studies are made for administrative and departmental purposes within government units and agencies. Some of these concern old people. These studies concern needs, employment, housing, medical care, social services, income, retirement—almost any practical problem about which decisions have to be made. Much of this research is not conceived in terms of its significance for others, nor is it generalized in the scientific sense. Usually, such working studies are mimeographed or duplicated and given limited circulation. But among them are some using good techniques that seem to be of more general value and that could well be made more widely available.

12. *National and cross-cultural surveys.* —As one observes the work under way in various countries, he cannot help but be impressed with the desirability of making studies within them with similar techniques of sampling and similar methods in order to secure data that will permit cross-comparison. That there is interest in such a survey is indicated by a conference organized by the European Section of the Social Science Research Committee of the International Association of Gerontology and held at Copenhagen, October 19–23, 1956, and which has recently published a report entitled *The Need for Cross-National Surveys of Old Age.*

An introduction by Professor Titmuss of the London School of Economics, which makes a case for social research as a guide to the formulation of public policy, is followed by reports of working groups which formulated suggestions for cross-national research in three areas: (*a*) pensions, assistance, and levels of living; (*b*) work and retirement; and (*c*) family and institutional care. These reports are followed by papers prepared by research workers from various countries, giving examples of surveys undertaken or needed.

While this report is limited largely to surveys and collections of data which are related to the practical problems of the community and the state, there is no necessity to limit co-operation across national and cultural lines to the survey type of research. The techniques could be extended to designed studies, especially those concerned with the changes that take place with age and the factors which underlie change as well as to many other problems of psychological and social significance. In any event, it is likely in this field, as in other scientific fields looking to the future, that there will be an increase in the co-operation of scholars and scientists across national and cultural lines along with increased facilities for the interchange of information.

IV. FINANCE AND THE ORGANIZATION OF RESEARCH

That the conduct of research is affected by the financial aid made available from governmental and private sources and by the interrelations between governmental agencies and universities is clear from my impressions of the European scene. In some countries research is largely a matter of interest on the part of a particular investigator who uses whatever facilities he has himself or are available within his university without outside financial aid. In Great Britain there is a large foundation which promotes research by direct grants to investigators and to centers both within and outside universities that are interested in aging research. In the Netherlands there is a comprehensive governmental plan which brings governmental agencies and university investigators together. This agency also carries forward its own projects. In other countries there is some direct financing of research by particular government departments, but, even where foundation or governmental aid is available, some research is still carried on by individual investigators.

What seems to be clear is that the field of aging presents particular difficulties which operate to increase the cost of research. At younger ages, when children and youth are in school or university, numbers of persons are readily available. But the student of aging has to go out and secure his subjects either through the co-operation of industries and social agencies or by house-to-house canvass. Perhaps this also explains why university social scientists are not quite so interested in the problems of aging as some feel they might well be. Generally speaking, the projects now going on involve extensive co-operation over a period of time with many people. Usually, there are several investigators or an investigator who has the assistance of a staff or students. If research is to be developed on a substantial scale, financial support seems to be necessary.

Next, it is evident that, in spite of the fact that many European universities are financed by the state, just as are the departments of government, the strong tradition of intellectual independence which operates within universities, even though there are individual exceptions, creates difficulties for research projects which involve the co-operation of university departments and departments of government. Within universities, too, this strong tradition of independence limits the collaboration of departments on research projects. Although American universities and governmental divisions also vary greatly in this respect, nevertheless the rigorous separations of our earlier history seem to be breaking down in the face of the complex problems that are presented to the scientists of today. In many instances and in various sciences this leads to scientific teams rather than single individuals. Teams may be within a discipline or across disciplinary lines.

There is evidence in the formation of such bodies as the Netherlands Foundation for Applied Scientific Research and the Danish National Institute of Social Research that European countries are moving in the same direction as has the United States with its National Science Foundation and its National Institutes of Health. Since the National Institutes of Health carry on both an intramural program of research as a division of the Public Health Service and an extramural program by making grants to universities and research organizations, the Institutes probably afford the better model of what is likely to come. In any event it is clear that a type of organization can be developed with the modern state that will facilitate research both by groups and by individuals, both across and within disciplines. In talking about research organization with various people in different countries, there appears much similarity in the actual problems of conducting research. As far as the facilitation of research, either by financial support or by a form of organization that will free scientists within governments and within universities to work together, we are still in a process of social experimentation.

V. Conclusion

As we move across the various countries in Europe we see, first, that scientists are much more concerned with the medical and biological aspects of the aging problem than with the psychological and social aspects. The problems of the chronically ill as well as the problems of preserving life have been more pressing than the problems of psychological and social adjustment. Moreover, biologists who see the life-cycle in its completeness in lower organisms become interested in the process of aging as a significant area for research.

Second, it is clear that the problems of the practical care of aging persons and of economic assistance and government support arise in every country and that, with industrialization, problems of retirement arise. No one who has visited the various countries can fail to note the cumulation of much practical knowledge through social experience with reference to the care and handling of older people. With the development of social security and of pension plans, and the increasing longevity that results from modern medicine, the financial burden of caring for older people is increasing. As a result there is more awareness of the necessity of increasing the possibilities of self-help and of self-care through the design of living arrangements, household equipment, the provision of occasional nursing and domestic care at moments of great need, etc., in order that the person may care for himself the remainder of the time. What is sought from research workers is more accurate knowledge of means of assessing older persons, of their status in the community, of their resources and potentialities, and, in particular, some knowledge of the techniques by means of which they can become more effective during a longer portion of their life-span. This involves a study not only of age changes but of the factors that underlie dependence and independence and learning and adjustment.

Third, the scientific approach to the psychological and social aspects of aging is in most countries, as in the United States, in its infancy. Not many psychologists or sociologists, either in government or in universities, are directly concerned with the problem of aging. There is, of course, definite interest on the part of some, and, as has been shown, an appreciable amount of research is going forward. But it is quite evident that substantial research is necessary in order to build the basic methodology upon which practical applications can be made. We are concerned with substitution of valid or empirically supported generalizations for the half-formulated practical principles followed in the present development of programs. We are also concerned with understanding the basic processes of aging and the environment which facilitates or retards the process.

Fourth, each country attacks its problems in its own characteristic fashion in terms of its own traditions of scientific work. There are, however, common approaches and a substantial amount of interchange of scientific information.

Fifth, a beginning has been made in an attempt to secure comparable statistical and scientific information across national and cultural lines by means of standardized survey techniques. A similar cross-national or cross-cultural approach could well be extended to experimental and ecological studies of age changes and other psychological and social problems.

Sixth, there is great need of more financial support for research in the psychological and social aspects of aging. Support is now provided in a variety of ways, with substantial government support emerging as a typical pattern.

Seventh, almost everywhere it seems to be difficult to secure the interest of university social scientists in the practical problems presented to society by aging and aged persons and in the theoretical problems of aging. This problem is not unknown in the United States. It is being met both in the United States and in Europe by establishing institutes and making funds available for co-ordinating research efforts.

Eighth, there is also concern about the recruitment of advanced students and younger scientists for the field. Adequate financial support of research, the development of research teams, and the organization of institutes afford a partial answer to this problem. As the scientific literature in gerontology increases and more problems emerge, younger scientists in their formative years are more likely to be recruited.

REFERENCES

AMERICAN PSYCHOLOGICAL ASSOCIATION. 1927–54. Psychological abstracts, Vols. 1–28. Washington, D.C.

ANDERSON, J. E. 1956a. Child development: an historical perspective. Child Development, 27, 181–96.

——— (ed.). 1956b. Psychological aspects of aging. Washington, D.C.: American Psychological Association.

ANDREWS, P. W. S., and BRUNNER, E. 1955. The life of Lord Nuffield: a study in enterprise and benevolence. Oxford: Basil Blackwell.

BIRREN, J. E. (ed.). 1959. Handbook of aging and the individual: psychological and biological aspects. Chicago: University of Chicago Press.

———. 1960. Psychological aspects of aging. Ann. Rev. of Psychol., 11, 161–98.

HAVIGHURST, R. J. 1958. A world view of gerontology. J. Gerontol., 13 (Suppl. No. 1),2–5.

HERON, A. 1957. Psychological changes with age; the present status of research. In W. B. YAPP and G. H. BOURNE (eds.), The biology of ageing, pp. 91–100. New York: Hafner Publishing Co.

INTERNATIONAL ASSOCIATION OF GERONTOLOGY. 1955. Old age in the modern world. Report of the Third Congress held at London, 1954. London: E. & S. Livingstone.

———. 1957. Programme. Fourth Congress held at Merano, Italy, July, 1957.

———. 1958. The need for cross-national surveys of old age: report of a conference at Copenhagen, October 19–23, 1956. Ann Arbor: Division of Gerontology, University of Michigan.

SHOCK, N. W. 1951. A classified bibliography of gerontology and geriatrics. 1900–1948. Stanford, Calif.: Stanford University Press.

———. 1957a. A classified bibliography of gerontology and geriatrics, Supplement One: 1949–1955. Stanford, Calif.: Stanford University Press.

———. 1957b. Trends in gerontology. 2d ed. Stanford, Calif.: Stanford University Press.

TIBBITTS, C. (ed.). 1960. Handbook of social gerontology: societal aspects of aging. Chicago: University of Chicago Press.

VAN ZONNEVELD, R. J. 1958. Public health and the aged in Europe: research and programs. J. Gerontol., 13 (Suppl. No. 1), 68–91.

WELFORD, A. T. 1951. Skill and age: an experimental approach. London: Oxford University Press.

———. 1958a. Ageing and human skill. London: Oxford University Press.

———. 1958b. Psychological and social gerontology in Europe. J. Gerontol., 13 (Suppl. No. 1), 51–67.

XI

Résumé and Implications

ERNEST W. BURGESS

Five main questions challenge our attention in concluding our survey of aging in European countries of Western culture:

1. What general conclusions can be drawn from European experience in dealing with older persons and their problems?

2. What issues emerge in the comparison of developments from country to country in social action to cope with the problems of aging?

3. What values and meaning have the implications of the survey of European experience for our thinking and action in the United States?

4. What are the contributions from cross-national comparisons at present and to be expected in the future to the science of social gerontology?

5. What is the relation of social action in behalf of the aging upon their independence, initiative, and autonomy?

I. GENERAL CONCLUSIONS

The first conclusion from the survey of six European countries selected to be representative of Western culture is that the conditions which produced personal, societal, and governmental concern for the aging were similar in all these countries.

A. Similarities

The basic social change in each of these countries was the transition from agriculture to industry. Industrialization brought with it a series of consequences which impinge upon older persons: the growth of cities and urbanization, the shift of employment from the home to the factory, the accelerated breakdown of the extended family, and the emergence of the small unit of husband, wife, and children.

1. *Change in the economic structure.*— The basic change in the economic structure common to all six countries was the result of the industrial revolution. The old economic system of the family as the unit of production on the farm and in the shop was increasingly supplanted by the factory. Women as well as men gave up home production to work as employees in ever larger industrial organizations. The proportion of self-employed and entrepreneurs steadily declined.

Retirement of older workers at a fixed age at the initiative of the employer replaced the custom of gradual reduction of working time by the self-employed.

Even in farming, beginning before the industrial revolution, the nuclear family was replacing the three-generation family as the economic unit. The reason was that the iron plow, which needed only one man with two horses, was supplanting the old plowing system, which required two or three pairs of oxen operated by four or five men.

2. *Change in the social structure.*—The change in the social structure lagged behind that of the economic structure. The extended family dominated by the aging parents, deprived of its economic role, was

377

gradually reduced to a network of changing social relations. A transition stage of extended family relationship has been observed by Peter Townsend and others in certain working-class industrial urban districts in London. Here, after marriage, grown-up children tend to live near, but not often with, their aging parents. This type might be called the "maternal extended family" revolving around the grandmother and largely sustained by her daughters. City life in general, with its increasing residential and social mobility, still further disrupts the extended family and favors the emancipation of the conjugal or companionship unit of the husband, wife, and children from the control of the extended family. A decrease in the necessity and obligation of children to support needy parents has followed the general enactment of laws for old age insurance or pensions.

3. *The trend to the dependence of the aging upon organization.*—In the six countries of Western culture the tendency is for older persons to depend for the satisfaction of their needs less upon their children and other relatives and more upon organizations. The main reliance of the aging for economic support is now upon programs of old age and survivors' insurance, pensions, and old age assistance administered by the government. For meeting other needs, older people turn to an increasing variety of large organizations. Outstanding among these organizations are (*a*) the government, (*b*) business and industry, (*c*) labor unions, (*d*) the educational system, (*e*) the church, (*f*) welfare agencies, and (*g*) other voluntary associations. Fewer older people are now living with their children and more of them in dwellings specially designed for them and often subsidized by the government. In the field of health there is a network of clinics, hospitals, convalescent centers, visiting nurses, etc.

4. *Social action for the aging.*—All six European countries have shown concern for the problems of older persons. They all have taken much the same action for the welfare of the aging. The priority of measures has been similar in all these countries (Havighurst, 1958).

Legislation to insure a minimum of income for older persons tended to come first. Programs of old age and survivors' insurance were first introduced in Germany in 1889, in France in 1910, in Sweden and the Netherlands in 1913, in Italy in 1919, and in Great Britain in 1925.

Second, public concern and action were next in the area of housing and physical and mental health. In large measure this was a part of the larger interest in public health. In all Western countries concern and organization first were focused on child and maternal health, then upon the communicable diseases of middle age, and, finally, upon the health of older persons.

More recently interest has developed in the personal problems of aging people, such as those of family relations, loss of occupational role by retirement, lowered status, isolation, and loneliness.

B. Differences

The similarities among countries appear to be much more striking than the differences. Yet differences exist and deserve recognition.

1. *Industrialization.*—The degree of industrialization is greater in certain countries than in others. The United Kingdom and West Germany are the most highly industrialized. Sweden and the Netherlands are less industrialized. France and Italy are semiagricultural. The relative numbers of self-employed in the labor force vary in much the same way. The United Kingdom, being highly industrialized, has the smallest proportion; France and Italy, being semiagricultural, the highest percentage; and Sweden and West Germany are intermediate. The differences in urban and rural population show much the same distribution. The percentage of urban population is highest in the United Kingdom and West Germany, lowest in Italy, and intermediate in the other countries.

Differences in the stage of industrial growth appear to be more important for the status of the aging than variations of these countries in cultural heritage or historical background. At any rate, other differences significant for the welfare of older people among the countries seem to be largely the result of the degree of industrialization.

2. *Changes in economic structure.*—The degree of industrialization brings with it shifts of the aging in the economic structure. Consequently, in less industrialized countries a greater proportion of older as well as younger workers are self-employed, are engaged in work at home rather than in the factory, and thus determine the time and character of their retirement.

3. *Changes in social structure.*—The family structure has changed at a greater rate in the highly industrialized countries than in those which are still largely agricultural, such as Italy and France. The extended family as a social network survives with diminished functions in certain situations even in industrial districts, as in Great Britain. It flourishes with much of its earlier vitality and significance in certain rural districts in every country where farming is still largely a family operation.

4. *Differences in organizational structure.*—The movement in the development of large organizations has proceeded more rapidly in countries like the United Kingdom and West Germany than in less industrialized nations, such as France and Italy. But in all countries there has been a tremendous growth in governmental and other organizations. No attempt has been made in this survey to compare the development of the organizational structure country by country. Our assumption, however, is that it would correspond closely with the degree of industrialization.

5. *Differences in social action on behalf of the aging.*—While the general pattern for meeting the needs of the aging has much in common in European countries, there are considerable and often important differences in details. This is to be clearly seen in the legislation for social security.

All six European countries have laws for old age and survivors' insurance, yet the minimum age of eligibility in these six countries varies quite widely. For men it ranges from 60 to 67 and for women from 55 to 67.

Marked differences are observable in the sources of funds for insurance or pensions. In the Netherlands the cost of the system is borne entirely by the insured persons, except that the government contributes on behalf of low-income persons and bears any eventual deficit. In France and Italy the insured person and employer are the sources of insurance funds. In Sweden the contributions come from insured persons and the government. In Great Britain and in West Germany the cost of insurance is shared by the insured person, the employer, and the government.

The Netherlands is the only country that has an automatic adjustment of the benefit, calculated at 6-month intervals, and related to a 3 per cent increase in wages. West Germany has adopted the principle of adjusting outstanding pensions by special legislation to future changes in average taxable earnings on the basis of the status of pension finances and of the national economy. In Sweden old age benefits include, besides the basic amounts, a fixed supplement, a cost-of-living supplement, and a housing supplement.

The coverage by old age and survivors' insurance varies. The Netherlands includes all permanent residents aged 15–64. Sweden takes in all citizens 18–66. In Italy the program covers all employed persons, males from 14 to 59 and females from 14 to 54. In Great Britain the program embraces residents (men 15–65 and women 15–60) but is not compulsory for self-employed or persons with the lowest income or married women. West Germany has one system for wage-earners, another for salaried employees earning not more than DM. 15,000 annually, and special systems for miners, self-employed craftsmen, and civil servants. France has separate systems for non-agricultural employees, agricultural employees, miners, railroad employees, seamen, public employees, and self-employed persons.

Retirement from employment does not appear to be a requirement for receiving benefits except in Great Britain for 5 years beyond pensionable age and in West Germany if pensions are paid before reaching the normal eligibility age of 65.

Great Britain has flat rates of contributions and of benefits. In other countries contributions and benefits are graduated.

Other differences in social action on behalf of older persons may be briefly mentioned. Great Britain and Sweden lead in health services specially directed to the aging. France and Italy include older people in their general health programs. Similarly, Great Britain and Sweden are in the forefront with pioneering community services to enable older persons to remain in their own homes rather than to be cared for in institutions. Sweden has first place in housing specially designed for the aging. The Netherlands, closely followed by the United Kingdom, has pioneered in provision of social clubs and groups for older people which are conspicuous by their absence in other countries.

The patterns of societal change and action affecting the aging have been the same or similar in these countries considered as representative of Western culture. The details vary, owing more to the degree of industrialization than to differences in historical or cultural background, important though the latter may be, especially in Latin countries, such as France and Italy.

II. Emerging Issues

The countries of Europe may be thought of as an unintended laboratory in social experimentation for inventions to insure the welfare of the aging. Of course no conclusive findings can be presented on the relative value of policies, programs, and projects. But different ways of meeting the same problem permit comparisons and raise issues on policies and programs.

A statement of these emerging issues may be helpful at the present time. In preparation for the White House Conference on Aging we are now reviewing our philosophy and programs and projects in providing for the welfare of the aging and aged.

A. Employment of the Aging

A higher proportion of men 65 and over are employed in the United States than in any of the six European countries covered in our survey of Western culture. Yet in all these nations the present percentage is less than that of past decades and is slated to decline further in the future. What issues are suggested by our survey of European experience?

1. *Prolongation or shortening of the work life* as a policy for social action.
2. *Compulsory, flexible*, or *gradual* retirement.
3. *Optional retirement* as a modification of compulsory retirement.
4. *Objective criteria* of aging versus *chronological age* as the determinant of retirement.
5. *Employment by employer* or *self-employment* after retirement.
6. *Full-time* versus *part-time employment* after retirement.
7. *Employment of older or younger workers* in periods of unemployment.
8. *Special provisions* to encourage employment of older workers, such as reservation jobs, work modifications, training centers, and inducements to employers.
9. **Legislation against** *discrimination* in employment by age.

B. Income Maintenance

The widely different solutions to the problem of income maintenance of older persons by European countries disclose several important issues:

1. *Public versus private action* to insure basic minimum income maintenance has finally been decided in practically all countries of the world in favor of governmental control and administration. The issue, however, is still open on the question of the responsibility for further increments of in-

come beyond the basic minimum. Should these be obtained by action of the government, of the employer, of the union, or of the individual?

2. *Pensions and assistance grants versus insurance* as the pattern of old age benefits continue to be debated. Should the system of payments to older persons be paid out of general revenues or by contributions from insured persons and their employers? Some countries combine both patterns in their system of old age payments.

3. *Source of funds* from insured persons, employers, and government varies widely. Some countries rely on only one of these sources, others on all three, and still others on two.

4. *Flat-rate versus variable* contributions and benefits characterize different countries. Flat-rate contributions are typically associated with flat-rate benefits. But variable contributions may be tied to flat-rate benefits. Should the flat-rate benefit be adopted as an exemplification of the principle of equity, all beneficiaries would share alike in the basic minimum support in old age.

5. *The issue of adequacy of the benefit* covers a wide range of considerations. Perhaps in no country does the basic benefit meet a minimum of budget requirements without supplementation from other sources such as savings, homeownership, aid from relatives and friends, private pensions, etc. Different countries supply different forms of additional payments, generally under a means test either within the insurance or pension system or as assistance from other public funds. Adequacy is also related to rising standards of living and to changes in the cost of living. The issue here is whether adjustments should come through special legislation or should be changed automatically to meet changes in wage level or in the cost of living such as occur with rising production or with inflation. Then, too, adequacy is concerned with provision for disability before eligibility to retirement and to the meeting of medical expenses, including those of prolonged illness.

6. *The age of eligibility for benefits* varies widely in different countries, although the median age is 65 for men and 60 for women. Some countries have flexibility with reduced benefits with retirement at an earlier than normal age and increased benefits if the insured person retires later.

7. *The retirement test of eligibility* for benefits is required only in some countries but not in others.

C. Housing and Community Services

In providing special housing and community services for the aging, many European countries began earlier and have progressed further than the United States. Their experience compared with ours is valuable in stating the issues:

1. Remain in *home of middle years* or move to one suitable to the *later years*.
2. *General* versus *special* housing for the aging.
3. *Type of structure* as detached dwelling, row houses, apartments, etc.
4. *Towns for older people* versus dispersal in conventional community.
5. *Communal* housing for *able-bodied* or for *chronically ill*.
6. *Rehabilitation* versus *custodial care* of the chronically ill.
7. *Regulations and regimentation* versus *self-government and planning* of activities by residents.
8. *Institutional* versus *homelike climate* in communal housing.
9. Care of older persons in *institutions* or in their *own homes* through community services.
10. Medical services in the *home* versus in the *hospital*.
11. Comparative *costs of independent* versus *communal and institutional housing*.
12. Siting of institutions, communities, and smaller dwelling units in *urban* or *rural* areas.
13. *General* versus *specialized and professional personnel* for care of the aging.
14. *Financing of housing* by individuals and private agencies or by national and local governments.

D. Physical Health

The physical health of its citizens is of concern to each country in our survey of Western culture. Certain issues arise of concern to all medical workers.

1. The place of *the person and the family* in health care and prevention.
2. Proportions of older people needing *permanent hospitalization* and other institutional or communal care.
3. *Optimum number* of patients or residents in communal and institutional provision for the aging.
4. *Custodial care* or *physical rehabilitation* of the handicapped.
5. Equal emphasis upon *preventive* as upon *therapeutic* programs.
6. Adoption of *good nutrition* for different stages in the life-cycle.
7. *Public education* in the health problems and needs of the aging.
8. *Medical treatment at home* made possible by community services ("meals-on-wheels," homemakers, nurses, and visiting physicians) or all medical service in hospital.
9. Hospitalization for the aging: *curative, custodial,* or *pathological.*
10. *Special geriatric unit* in general hospital versus *geriatric hospital.*
11. Extension of the use of *day hospitals and consultative health centers.*
12. *General practitioner* versus *geriatric specialist.*

E. Mental Health

The mental health of its population is a subject of increasing concern to all countries of Western culture. The responsibility of care of mental patients is being transferred from the family to the government. In comparing countries, certain issues arise of interest to all workers in the field of mental hygiene in the United States.

1. *Special provision* versus *general care of older mental patients* is still a debated issue.
2. *Ratio of beds in mental hospital* varies from 2 per 100,000 population in Denmark to 4 per 100,000 population in Switzerland and Sweden. To what extent will the newer therapeutic methods, on the one hand, and the apparent trend to increasing extramural care, on the other, affect the number to be treated in hospitals?
3. *Size of the mental hospital* tends to be much smaller in European countries than in the United States.
4. *Voluntary admission as against legal commitment* seems to be the present trend in European countries, much more so than in the United States.
5. *Alternative* or *supplements to hospital treatment* by outpatient and day-center therapy.
6. *Classification of patients for treatment* in the community (short stay or long stay in the hospital).
7. *The optimum organization* of mental health services is already in the experimental and demonstration stage in some European countries.

F. Family Relationships

Before the industrial revolution a person's work and social life were usually carried on within the extended family and with its members. This pattern of living still survives, as we have seen, in certain rural areas of France, Italy, the Netherlands, and West Germany. Even when the extended family ceased to function as an economic unit, it still maintained a certain range of activities and responsibilities as a social unit. How much and what these should be are issues in every country of Western culture.

1. Restoration of *three-generation family relations* versus acceptance of priority of the *nuclear family.*
2. Reinforcement of *obligations of adult children* to support needy parents and to care for them in sickness versus development of *community services.*
3. Relative desirability of grandparents living *with, near,* or *at a distance from* children and grandchildren.
4. Promotion of conditions making for *mutual aid between generations* by governmental or private action.
5. Social life of the aging *independent of* or *completely with* adult children.
6. Grandparents as *disciplinarians* or *benevolent figures* to grandchildren.

G. Life beyond Family and Work

Compulsory retirement at either a fixed or a flexible age presented older persons and couples with an abundance of free time. Only recently have gerontologists in Europe and the United States become concerned with the issues involved in spending free time.

1. Continuing *work at career or other occupation* versus *volunteer activity* with some or similar meanings as work had.
2. *Passive* versus *active* use of free time.
3. *Informal social contacts* versus *membership in organized groups* for friendships, sociability, and meaningful activity.
4. Social participation in *mixed* or *own age* groups.
5. Segregation by locating in *retired* community versus integration by remaining in *normal* community.
6. Leisure-time objectives for *enjoyment and entertainment* or for *sociability, health, education, and culture.*
7. *Programs of preparation for retirement* to cover entire field or be limited to *financial aspects.*
8. Leisure-time activities and organizations to be planned *for* or *by* older persons.
9. Sponsorship of activities and organizations by *older persons* or by *churches, companies, unions, or welfare agencies.*
10. Activities and organizations supported by *subsidies* or financed entirely or in part by *fees and dues.*
11. *Governmental* or *private support* of activities and organizations.

The above issues emerging in seven areas of aging are real to persons confronted with decision-making upon a particular policy, project, or practice. But they fail to be impressive when viewed from the broad standpoint of social gerontology. The reason is that they appear to be an aggregate of individual issues.

Yet each one of these concrete issues derives its significance from underlying basic issues which pose challenges to our thinking, imagination, and creativeness. Seven of these basic issues are:

1. Ways of establishing the autonomy and independence of older people in place of dependency so as to release their energy, initiative, and creativity.
2. How to redefine roles and activities of older persons to have meaning in the modern world.
3. How to reconcile the conflict of interests of the aging with those of childhood, youth, and middle age.
4. Ways best to safeguard home living for older people and to make necessary institutional living more homelike.
5. Methods of the development of measures of prevention and rehabilitation.
6. How to enable the community to take advantage of the continuing contributions older people can make.
7. How government can best advance the welfare of the aging without becoming a welfare state.

III. Values and Meanings of European Experience

The implications of European experience for the United States should be stated with considerable caution. It is true of course that our country is part of Western culture. Therefore whatever happens in Europe in the field of aging has meaning for us. But the value to us of European experience must be viewed in terms not only of our likenesses but also of our differences.

The first difference is in the *vast extent* of continental United States as compared with countries of western Europe. The United States occupies nearly three million square miles as compared with less than half this area for western Europe excluding Communist-governed countries. France, with the largest area of the non-Communistic countries, has a little over two hundred thousand square miles, or about one-fourteenth of the area of the United States.

A second difference is that of *density of population.* The average population per square mile is a little over 200 for western Europe compared with less than 60 for the United States.

A third difference is the *higher mobility*

of the residents of the United States. This refers not only to the greater frequency of residential change but also to the higher fluidity of the population facilitated by rapid transportation, particularly in travel by airplane and automobile. Occupational and social mobility also proceeds at a more rapid rate.

Fourth, the United States comprises fifty states, with the problem of the allocation of responsibility for the welfare of the aging to be assumed by the federal or the state government, whereas most European programs are operated by the federal or central government.

Fifth, there is the greater *cultural diversity* of the United States which results from the more varied national and racial origins of the population and from regional differences.

Sixth, the *historical and traditional backgrounds* are more deeply impressed upon thought and action in the older European countries than in the young United States.

Seventh, the *level of personal and national income* is lower in European countries than in the United States (see Table 10, p. 473, in Part III).

Eighth, *private initiative* has been a traditional American characteristic, with reliance upon individual families and voluntary associations to take responsibility in dealing with problems.

These and other differences should be taken into account in judging the meanings and values of European experience for the United States.

These real differences between United States and European countries should not lead us to minimize the outstanding likenesses which have resulted directly or indirectly from industrialization. One of these, which has not been mentioned until now, is present in all countries of Western culture, namely, a *mass mood* in the population to act for the welfare of the aging.

In each of the countries of Western culture there exists a social movement to promote the welfare of the aging. This social movement is a response to a powerful mass mood which impels people to respond as individuals, uncritically and without deliberation, to proposals and programs in behalf of the aged and the aging.

A brief analysis of the behavior of the individual in the mass will enable us to understand the mechanism of action of people as aggregates of individuals rather than as members of social groups, social classes, and institutions. Individuals in the mass act on the basis of what is common to them, such as appetites, cravings, and vague and loosely organized feelings and sentiment. These feelings and sentiments toward older people which are common to people of Western cultures are:

1. *Filial sentiment* of adults to their parents.
2. *Guilt feelings* because of the difficulty or inability in the urban environment of discharging the full traditional responsibility of the son or daughter toward aging parents. This feeling includes social as well as financial obligation.
3. *Humanitarian sentiment* and welfare ideology. This generalized sentiment, which is stronger in some countries than in others, motivates action for the welfare of all disadvantaged groups including the aging.
4. *Identification* of adults 20–64 with the aging. This identification is a perception that sooner or later the young will also become old. Action for the benefit of the older generation is therefore also an act of self-interest of persons of all ages.

Action on the basis of mass mood is uncritical and impulsive. It therefore becomes necessary to attempt to find ways and means of providing direction to the expression of the mass mood for the welfare of the aging. Fortunately, the survey of European experience provides leads to guide the thinking and leadership of gerontologists in different countries of Western culture.

A. Objectivity

The need for objectivity is imperative for gerontologists if the hazards of the blind leading the blind are to be avoided. This survey of the experience of Western culture should markedly contribute to this end.

1. *Perspective* is gained by comparing the movement of social gerontology from country to country. It is thereby possible to perceive American problems, conditions, and programs in relation to the general progress of social gerontology in Western culture.

2. *Projects and programs perceived in the context* of a culture provides another aspect of objectivity. A given project can seldom be effectively transplanted unchanged from one country to another. It will need to be adapted to the conditions of living of the new environment.

3. *Clarification of issues* results from a comparison between countries of the thinking involved in establishing policies and programs for the welfare of the aging.

B. Critical Evaluation

The need for evaluation of policies, programs, and projects in the field of the aging is a further development in the expression of objectivity. The survey of European experience indicates that evaluation is in its infancy in Europe, as in the United States. Yet evaluation of policies, programs, and projects is essential if applied social gerontology is to arrive at maturity.

In all countries of Western culture, including the United States, many, if not most, pioneering projects are known to the public through favorable accounts by their sponsors. Such reports are far from being a valid basis for others to introduce such projects, however worthy their objectives and however pressing the problems which they are designed to solve. The cost of an evaluation of a promising pioneering project may be only a fraction of the funds likely to be wasted by attempts to copy an ill-conceived or inadequately reported project.

There are four types or levels of evaluation: (1) self-evaluation; (2) opinions of experts on a project; (3) factual appraisal; and (4) experiment and control.

1. *Self-evaluation* ranges all the way from news releases designed to obtain favorable publicity to serious self-study for the purpose of improving the operations of the project. The latter, if well done, is often of real value to the sponsoring agency. It may also be helpful to other agencies considering the introduction of the project. But, since it is geared to the needs of the sponsoring agency, it is likely to be less valuable to other organizations.

2. *Opinions of experts* represent the evaluation most generally relied on at present for a judgment on the value of a project. But experts differ. They are influenced by differences in previous background and training and by the weight they give to certain policies and practices. Then, too, the weight of expert opinion is likely to be inclined to favor existing standards, policies, and practices and to look askance at innovations which do not conform. Therefore expert opinion may be an unreliable guide in assessing pioneering ventures.

3. *Factual appraisal* is a survey of a project designed to gather and analyze the facts that are pertinent to an understanding and appraisal of the working of a project. It utilizes the various available techniques, such as schedules, scales, inventories, and interviews adapted for the purposes of the project. Its findings are helpful alike to the sponsoring organization and to other agencies. Its chief limitation is that it does not involve comparison with the operation of projects with the same or like purposes.

4. *Experimental and control projects* are the optimum type of evaluation. The District Mental Health Service at Worthing described in Part II (Case Study No. 6, pp. 432–35) is an excellent example. Here, two areas are compared with each other. One of these, the experimental area, is the locus of the health service experiment. The control area has been sending patients to the same two hospitals but does not have the new service. The object of the health service is to reduce hospital admissions by care in the home and in other facilities.

The result was a reduction of 59 per cent admissions to the two mental hospitals in the experimental district compared with an increase of 4 per cent in the control area.

The purpose of the control is to secure a project as identical or similar in its personnel and operations as is possible with the exception of the new variable introduced by the experimental project. The measurable changes which take place in the experimental as compared with the control project are then a convincing proof of the values of the pioneering project.

Experimental projects in the field of aging are conspicuous by their absence. This successful demonstration in Worthing should stimulate further studies of this type in Europe, the United States, and other countries of Western culture. The development of inquiries utilizing controls is likely to be a prominent characteristic of the forward movement of research in social gerontology.

C. Social Science Research

Evaluation studies are action research which focus on policies, programs, projects, and practices. They are not designed to yield basic knowledge about the aging process. Yet on occasion they may make a limited contribution.

What is imperatively needed to advance the new science of gerontology is a co-ordinated program of basic research. The closest approach to this objective is the continuing program of studies on aging and the care of the aging carried on by grants made by the Nuffield Foundation of England. This statesman-like program is described in detail in a document in Part II (Case Study No. 13, pp. 448–56). It discloses a remarkable record of achievement and suggests the possibilities in a program of social science research as over against an aggregate of individual projects.

IV. Cross-cultural Comparisons

Social gerontology is a youthful science. Research in the social aspects of aging is just beginning to get established. The progress already made in western Europe and United States in the last 15 years provides a sound foundation for the future.

Up to now studies have been confined to separate countries. The bulk of research will continue to be carried on country by country. But what are the conditions and the prospects for cross-cultural research? Such comparative studies will provide the essential body of theory and empirical findings to enable us to arrive at generalizations both (1) those that are universal in all societies and (2) those that are relative to economic, social, and cultural differences among countries.

The conditions favorable for cross-national studies are in the process of coming into existence. These are: (1) comparable statistical data; (2) national opinion polls; and (3) co-operative cross-cultural projects.

A. Comparable Statistical Data

The United Nations now provides roughly comparable statistical data gathered from practically all the countries in the world. It publishes annually a demographic yearbook and a statistical yearbook and a monthly report from its Statistical Office which presents a wealth of data on a wide range of topics.

The World Health Organization and the International Labour Organization also publish yearbooks with statistical data, respectively, in the fields of health and labor. Several other organizations issue annual or occasional volumes containing data of direct or indirect interest to social gerontology.

Selected tables derived from these sources are presented in Part III of this volume for nearly all European countries and a few other non-European countries. It is hoped that these data will be helpful to students interested in cross-cultural studies of aging.

The big difficulty in comparing statistics of different countries is the degree of comparability of the data on different items. There are, naturally, differences in reporting data and in the year for which data are available. The multitude of variations is in part indicated by the number of footnotes for each table describing them. It is to be expected that the reporting of data by countries and their comparability will continue to improve.

Statistical yearbooks of different countries are also available which may provide other data or more detailed data than are obtained in the international yearbooks.

B. *National Opinion Polls*

Certain data that are not available through statistical yearbooks may be obtained by cross-cultural sample surveys. The existing national opinion polls in various countries provide the mechanism. Two questions on retirement were recently asked by the International Research Associates, an association of national research institutes. One was on the preferred age of retirement and the other on opinions about the adequacy of governmental old age pensions and assistance.

This organization may be willing from time to time to canvass its national polling samples on items of interest to social gerontology. This co-operation will be helpful. But a great advance would be made if inquiries were organized to exploit the full potentialities of this new research facility. The cost would be much less expensive than would be required to set up research projects *de novo*.

C. *Co-operative Cross-cultural Projects*

Even more significant for research in social gerontology than the use of national opinion polls is the development of cross-cultural projects. These can take place in two ways. One method is to have a pioneering study in one country repeated in other countries. The other and generally more effective way is the formal organization of a cross-cultural project by representatives from different countries.

The Social Science Research Committee

of the International Gerontological Association is now promoting such an undertaking. As John E. Anderson has pointed out in the preceding chapter, the Copenhagen Conference in 1956 of the European Division of this committee outlined a program which was later published as *The Need for Cross-national Surveys of Old Age.*

In August, 1959, it held a second meeting in Italy to implement further planning and to draw up a research proposal. It also inspired an investigation by Peter Townsend and Brian Rees, carried out in England in 1959, to pilot a future cross national survey of aging. It has been published under the title, *The Personal, Family and Social Circumstances of Old People* (Townsend and Rees, 1959).

The European and American divisions of this committee sponsored a Seminar on Social Health of the Aging in Merano in July, 1957, where plans were discussed for co-operative projects on employment, budgets, family relations, and psychology of the aging.

A second seminar is planned at the time of the Fifth International Congress of Gerontology in San Francisco in August, 1960, to continue discussions of cross-cultural research and, if possible, to provide for planning of the research. Appraisal of present research and the possibilities of cross-cultural investigations are to be discussed in the areas of budgets and income, psychology, physical and mental rehabilitation, and retirement roles.

D. *Research Personnel and Methods of Research*

In the different countries of Western culture the basic conditions for valuable research in social gerontology exist. Cross-cultural studies are being planned. Pilot studies have been made or are in prospect.

Trained research personnel, who have had experience in research projects on the economic, psychological, and social aspects of aging, are available. They are familiar with the research of their colleagues in other countries and are personally acquainted through participation in seminars and conferences.

Methods of research especially adopted to the study of aging are being developed. A number of instruments and scales have been devised for the study of attitudes, roles, and personal and social adjustment in aging and retirement.

V. Welfare Policy and the Autonomy of the Aging

Finally, this survey of social gerontology in countries of Western culture poses a basic and puzzling question of welfare policy. Does provision by the government and by other organizations for the welfare of the aging mean regimentation, resulting in a breakdown of the independence, initiative, and autonomy of older people?

There is, as we have seen, in all European countries a growing tendency of older people to rely upon the government and on other economic and social organizations rather than upon themselves and upon their families and friends. This shift is natural and perhaps inevitable in the new society in which we live. Older individuals particularly are tending to demand more and more that society and the government do something for them, and the general public is more and more disposed to acquiesce.

The humanitarian mood of the public toward older persons and other disadvantaged groups, if misdirected, could radically change the American way of life. This disposition of the public to do something for the old and their tendency to accept it could undermine the initiative, the autonomy, and the independency of older persons.

The American way of life, if it is to be preserved for both older persons and all of us, is not merely to help older persons but to help them to help themselves. Every program and project designed to promote the welfare of older people, particularly those originating in other countries, needs to be thoroughly scrutinized to determine if it will result in the dependency of the aging or in strengthening their independence and freedom of action.

Up to the present time nearly all programs in behalf of the aging in the United States as well as in Europe are the products of the welfare mood, of expert opinion, and of uncritical adoption of untested projects. The time has come for critical evaluation of policies, programs, and projects and for reliance on basic research for the scientific knowledge of the capacities, needs, and potentialities of aging people.

REFERENCES AND BIBLIOGRAPHY

GREAT BRITAIN. GENERAL REGISTER OFFICE. 1952. Census 1951. One per cent sample tables. London: H.M. Stationery Office.

HAVIGHURST, R. J. 1958. A world view of gerontology. J. Gerontol., 13 (Suppl. No. 1), 2–5.

INTERNATIONAL ASSOCIATION OF GERONTOLOGY, EUROPEAN SECTION. 1958. The need for cross-national surveys of old age: report of a conference at Copenhagen, October 19–23, 1956. Ann Arbor: Division of Gerontology, University of Michigan.

MYRDAL, F. ALVA. 1945. Nation and family: the Swedish experiment in democratic family and population policy. London: Routledge & Kegan Paul.

SHENFIELD, BARBARA E. 1957. Social policies for old age: a review of social provision for old age in Great Britain. London: Routledge & Kegan Paul.

TIBBITTS, C. (ed.) 1959. Aging and social health in the United States and Europe. Ann Arbor: Division of Gerontology, University of Michigan.

TITMUSS, R. M. 1959. Essays on the welfare state. New Haven, Conn.: Yale University Press.

TOWNSEND, P., and REES, B. 1959. The personal, family and social circumstances of old people. London: International Association of Gerontology, Department of Social Science, London University.

U.S. SOCIAL SECURITY ADMINISTRATION. 1958. Social security programs throughout the world, 1958. Washington, D.C.: Government Printing Office.

PART TWO

Selected Case Studies

Introduction

Fourteen case studies are presented in Part II. The purpose of their inclusion is to supplement the survey and statistical data which were utilized in the comparisons of different countries in Part I.

The case studies cannot be considered as representative. They were rather selected to afford American readers a more intimate appreciation of significant aspects of aging in western European countries. Some cases give a glimpse into the cultural context of the process of aging. The majority of the cases, however, were selected as outstanding examples of European developments that merit special attention and consideration in this period when the American public is reviewing the present situation of the aging population and making plans for the future in preparation for the White House Conference on Aging to be held in January, 1961.

The first two case studies present the chief provisions of the laws on old age and survivors' insurance and on medical-care insurance in selected European countries. They show the common pattern as well as wide variations in provisions for income maintenance of older people.

The third case study is a pictorial representation of the outstanding features of housing design which embody the advanced thinking of Swedish gerontologists and architects. It should stimulate the creativity and resourcefulness of planners in the United States and other countries to raise their sights on combining the functional and aesthetic aims in special housing for older people.

The fourth case study gives an all-round description of the organization and administration of a home-help service to promote the health and happiness of old people.

The fifth case study presents the design and findings of a Swedish study of the mental health of a large Swedish rural population.

The sixth case study describes the evaluation of the pioneering demonstration of meeting the problem of mental-hospital overcrowding by the use of an intensive outpatient service.

The seventh and eighth case studies give an insight into the family relations of older persons in two Latin European countries where familial ties are still very strong. The first is an intimate view of extended family relations of an upper-middle-class French family. The second is a description of three-generation family living in an Italian low-income, rural district which is culturally backward.

The ninth case study is a report of a social worker on the attitudes toward their adult children of residents of an old people's home.

The tenth case study is a summary of the laws of six European countries on the duty of adult children to support needy parents.

The eleventh and twelfth case studies describe the workings of social clubs for older persons in the two European countries—Great Britain and the Netherlands—where these have had their greatest developments.

The thirteenth case study is that of the organized and continuous activity of the

Nuffield Foundation on aging and the care of the aged. It is a signal example of a program of research, evaluation, and demonstration. The studies and projects under its auspices have exemplified high standards of research design and competence and a lively interest both in basic research and in practical applications of knowledge for the welfare of aging persons.

The last case study describes and evaluates the objectives and results of a study of old age pensioners carried on under the joint auspices of four university research institutes in West Germany.

These fourteen case studies, considered individually, will give the reader some appreciation of significant aspects of European experience. Taken together, they mirror high points of achievement by and for older people in the cultures of the Old World—cultures not widely different from our own.

1

Old Age and Invalidity Insurance

Dates of Basic Laws

First law: 1924. Old age and survivors'
benefits: currently governed by laws of
1955 (wage-earners), 1956 (independent
workers), and 1957 (salaried employees),
as amended. Invalidity benefits: currently
governed by law of 1944, as amended.

Coverage

Gainfully occupied persons generally,
with separate systems for wage-earners,
salaried employees (provisions very similar
to those for wage-earners), and independent
workers (provisions different). Special systems for miners, seamen, railway employees, and permanent public employees.

Source of Funds

Insured person: Wage-earners, 4.25 per
cent of wages (rising in 1960 and each 5
years by 0.25 per cent, to ultimate 5.75
per cent). Salaried employees, 4.25 per cent
of salaries, with ceiling of 8000 francs[1] a
month (10,000 francs from 1960). Independent workers, 12,000 francs a year.

Employer: For wage-earners, 4.25 per
cent of wages paid (rising to ultimate 5.75
per cent). For salaried employees, 6 per
cent of salaries paid, with ceiling of 8000
francs a month (10,000 francs from 1960).

Government: For wage-earners, annual
subsidies, rising 40 million francs each year
to maximum of 2 billion francs (1957 subsidy, 1320 million francs). For salaried

[1] 1 franc = 2.0 U.S. cents.

employees and independent workers, subsidies of about 300 and 750 million francs
a year, respectively. All subsidies vary with
cost-of-living index.

Above contributions finance old age and
survivors' benefits only; invalidity benefits
financed through health and maternity
insurance.

Old Age Benefits

Amount: Pension of 60 per cent (single
person) or 75 per cent (married person) of
average earnings during lifetime (earnings
for each year revalued by coefficient reflecting cost-of-living changes). Minimum pension: single person, 18,700 francs a year;
married person, 28,000 francs. For salaried
employees, 36,000 and 45,000 francs, respectively. Independent workers: single
person, 12,000 francs a year; married person, 18,000 francs. Automatic adjustment
of pensions awarded to cost-of-living
changes.

Qualifying conditions: Age 65 (men) or
60 (women); payable up to 5 years earlier,
subject to reduction of 5 per cent per year
(ages for unhealthy occupations, 60 and
55). Qualifying period: 12 years of actual
or credited employment in last 15 years
(until 1960), 15 years in last 15 years
(1960–69), all years since 1955 (1970–99),
or 45 years for men and 40 for women
(thereafter); periods of incapacity, involuntary unemployment, etc., credited (pension reduced proportionately, if qualifying
period not satisfied). Retirement from gainful work, other than occasional work. Pensions for aliens reduced 20 per cent, unless

reciprocal agreement. Pensions not payable abroad, unless reciprocal agreement.

Invalidity Benefits

Amount: Pension of 60 per cent of earnings (continuation of sickness benefit under health insurance); reduced to 40 per cent after 6 months for pensioners without dependent, unless constant attendance required. Maximum: 100 francs a day for family heads and pensioners needing constant attendance; 68 francs for others. Automatic adjustment of pensions awarded to cost-of-living changes.

Qualifying conditions: Under age 65 (men) or 60 (women). Loss of 67 per cent of earning capacity in usual occupation. Six months of coverage, including 120 days of actual work (if under 25, 3 months and 60 days), and coverage during last quarter preceding onset of incapacity.

Survivors' Benefits

Amount: Widow's pension of 30 per cent of highest average earnings of deceased (earnings for each year revalued by coefficient reflecting cost-of-living changes); minimum pension: 14,000 francs a year. Widow of independent worker: 9000 francs a year. Automatic adjustment of pensions awarded to cost-of-living changes. Lump sum (if ineligible for pension): 1 year's pension.

Qualifying conditions: Widow, age 45, caring for child, or 67 per cent incapacitated. Husband insured or pensioner during last 12 months before death (if not, reduced pension payable proportionate to years of employment between age 20, or 1926 if later, and death). Married 1 year, and not remarried (lump sum of 2 years' pension on remarriage). Not payable if gainfully employed, unless occasionally only. Pensions for aliens reduced 20 per cent, unless reciprocal agreement. Pension not payable abroad, unless reciprocal agreement.

Administration

The Ministry of Labor and Social Welfare has general supervision. National Social Security Office, in Ministry, collects contributions and distributes to national agencies administering benefits. National Retirement and Survivors Pension Fund administers benefits; managed by administrator representing Ministry, assisted by joint employee-employer council. National Sickness and Invalidity Insurance Fund administers invalidity pensions (together with sickness benefits). Solidarity and Guarantee Fund administers pensions for independent workers, under supervision of Ministry of Middle Classes.

DENMARK

Dates of Basic Laws

First law: 1891. Currently governed by Social Insurance Act as amended on October 2, 1956.

Coverage

All Danish citizens not otherwise entitled to pensions from public funds. May be modified by reciprocal treaty.

Source of Funds

Insured persons: Old age national pension tax of 1 per cent of income subject to income tax. No contribution payable if national pension tax for person with dependents less than 40 crowns (kroner)[2] a year, or for a single person less than 25 crowns. Invalidity, 21.60 crowns a year.

Employer: Old age, none. Invalidity, 14.25 crowns a year.

Government: Balance of cost, from general revenues (estimated government share of national pension costs about 85 per cent).

Old Age Benefits

Amount: Minimum pension equal for single persons to 6 per cent and for a mar-

[2] 1 crown = 14.48 U.S. cents.

ried couple to 9 per cent of the average gross income of all breadwinners is payable irrespective of income or means; adjusted each year for cost-of-living changes; 1957 annual pensions, 680 crowns for single person and 1020 crowns for couple. National pensions and supplements also payable subject to income test and half-yearly cost-of-living adjustments, as shown in Table 1 (1957 rates, in crowns a year).

Reduction for other income follows a sliding scale starting at 60 crowns for each 100 crowns of income over specified exempted amounts (in Copenhagen, exemptions of 2600 and 1800 crowns from capital allowed couple and single person respective-

ly; other income exemptions, one-third higher).

Qualifying conditions: For minimum pension, age 67; no contribution or income test. For national pension and supplements, age 65 for men, 60 for women (to be increased to 66 and 61, respectively in April, 1959, and to 67 and 62 in April, 1961). National pension and supplements subject to income test.

Invalidity Benefits

Amount: Invalidity pension and supplements, subject to income test and half-yearly cost-of-living adjustments, are as shown in Table 2 (1957 rates, in crowns a year).

TABLE 1

DENMARK: NATIONAL PENSION AND SUPPLEMENTS ACCORDING TO PLACE OF RESIDENCE

(1957 Rates in Crowns per Year)

	COPENHAGEN		PROVINCIAL TOWNS		RURAL DISTRICTS	
	Couple	Single	Couple	Single	Couple	Single
Basic pension	5064	3360	4800	3228	4404	2952
Marriage supplement (if only one spouse entitled to pension)	....	564	....	504	....	444
Postponement supplement:						
To age 70 (single woman 65)	504	336	480	324	432	288
To age 72 (single woman 67)	756	492	708	480	648	432
Old age supplement (at age 80)	276	180	264	180	240	168
Supplement for surviving spouse	....	432	....	408	....	372
Supplement for each child under 15	924	924	804	804	684	684

TABLE 2

DENMARK: INVALIDITY PENSION AND SUPPLEMENTS ACCORDING TO PLACE OF RESIDENCE

(1957 Rates in Crowns per Year)

	COPENHAGEN		PROVISIONAL TOWNS		RURAL DISTRICTS	
	Couple	Single	Couple	Single	Couple	Single
Basic pension	5064	3360	4800	3228	4404	2952
Marriage supplement (if only one spouse entitled to pension)	....	564	....	504	....	444
Invalidity supplement	960	480	960	480	960	480
Supplement for each child under 15	924	924	804	804	684	684
Assistance supplement (in need of constant attendance, or blind)	1296	864	1224	816	1116	744
Helplessness supplement (in need of constant nursing)	2160	1440	2034	1356	1854	1236

Qualifying conditions: Inability to earn one-third of earnings of person with similar training and skill in locality. Income deductions and exemptions same as for old age membership in sick club and of good character.

Survivors' Benefits

None.

Administration

The Ministry for Social Affairs has general supervision. Old age pension claims adjudicated by social affairs committees of communes, and pensions disbursed by commune of residence. Administration of invalidity insurance interlocked with health insurance administration as to eligibility, income, etc. Invalidity Insurance Court, national body of five members appointed by the Minister, determines right to invalidity benefit.

FINLAND

Dates of Basic Laws

First law: 1937 (old age and invalidity insurance); assistance introduced 1952. Current insurance and assistance governed by law of June 8, 1956, effective January 1957.

Coverage

All residents age 16–64. (Subject to modification by reciprocal treaty.)

Source of Funds

Insured persons: $1\frac{1}{2}$ per cent of income starting in 1958 (no contribution ceiling).

Employer: $1\frac{1}{2}$ per cent of total payroll starting in 1958.

Government: National and local governments pay cost of assistance. Local share varies from 10 per cent to 30 per cent of assistance costs according to capacity to pay; resurvey of local share each 3 years.

Average national share of assistance costs approximately 77 per cent. National government also pays cost of basic pensions not financed by contributions and interest.

Old Age Benefits

Amount: Basic benefit of 24,000 marks (markka)[3] a year payable regardless of other income or employment. In addition, assistance payments of 72,000, 63,000, or 54,000 marks a year, according to cost-of-living zone; assistance payments reduced by 50 per cent of amount by which other income exceeds 34,000, 24,000, or 17,000 marks a year (according to cost-of-living zone). For aged couples, benefits are 160 per cent of above, and amounts of outside income permitted for assistance are correspondingly increased. Assistance pensions increased 10 per cent for each child under 16.

Persons deferring receipt of pension receive additional 12.5 per cent of basic pension for each year of postponement (maximum 5 years).

Benefits and income limits automatically changed with changes in cost-of-living index.

Qualifying conditions: Age 65. No requirement of insurance coverage or retirement. Single woman aged 63 and over may receive old age assistance. Residence and citizenship required for assistance (subject to modification by reciprocal treaty).

Property in excess of 2 million marks (single person) or 3 million marks (couple) taken into account for assumed income purposes in granting assistance.

Invalidity Benefits

Amount: Basic pension and assistance amounts same as for old age, with same income test.

Qualifying conditions: Age 16 and 64 years of age. Permanently incapable of maintaining self by work suited to strength and qualifications.

[3] 1 mark = 0.434 U.S. cent.

Survivors' Benefits

No pension. Funeral benefit equal to 1 year's basic pension, 24,000 marks, payable in following order: spouse, children under age 16, other heirs, parents, or person providing funeral.

Administration

The National Pension Institute is major administrative agency, with district offices throughout country ordinarily coinciding with commune borders; representative appointed by Institute in charge of each district office. Governing body of Institute named by the President. Local pension committees (instead of Institute's district offices) determine income of persons claiming old age assistance, with local representative of Institute acting as chairman of committee. Payments made monthly.

FRANCE

Dates of Basic Laws

First law: 1910. Non-agricultural system currently governed by law of 1945, as amended; agricultural system by law of 1935, as amended. National Solidarity Fund created by law of 1956. Assistance legislation dates from 1941.

Coverage

Non-agricultural system: All industrial, commercial, domestic, and other non-agricultural employees.

Agricultural system: Employees over 14 in agriculture and forestry. Special systems for miners, railway employees, seamen, public employees, and self-employed persons.

Source of Funds

Insured person: 6 per cent of wages up to 528,000 francs[4] a year; partly for health and maternity insurance (agriculture, 5 per cent of wages).

Employer: 10 per cent of payroll, ex-

[4] 1 franc = 0.24 U.S. cent.

cluding wages over 528,000 francs a year; partly for health and maternity insurance (agriculture, 5 per cent of payroll).

Government: None for insurance. Various 1956 increases in general taxes on income, alcohol, automobiles, inheritances, etc., earmarked to finance National Solidarity Fund. Government pays entire cost of ordinary assistance.

Old Age Benefits

Amount: Standard benefit, 20 per cent of average wages in last 10 years (wage ceiling, 528,000 francs a year; wages in earlier years revalued). Increment of 4 per cent of wages for each year benefit deferred after 60; e.g., at 65 (or 60 if unfit for work or with 20 years of "arduous" employment), 40 per cent of average wages; at 70, 60 per cent. Reduced benefit, 1/30 of standard benefit times years of insurance. Special benefit, 50 per cent of joint contributions paid in. Lump sum, 1 year's special benefit. Minimum annual benefit, 65,800 francs. Supplement of 50 per cent for dependent spouse, and 10 per cent if 3 children reared. Supplement from National Solidarity Fund of 31,200 francs a year also payable to all qualified low-income beneficiaries. Formerly employed workers not entitled to old age benefit and having limited income receive allowance of 68,640–72,380 francs a year according to residence, plus 50 per cent for spouse over 65 and 10 per cent if 3 children reared. (Assistance with income test available to destitute aged persons not entitled to other benefit or allowance.)

Qualifying conditions: Standard benefit, age 60 and 30 years of insurance. Reduced benefit, age 60 and 15 years of insurance. Special benefit, age 65 and 5 years of insurance. Lump sum, age 65 and less than 5 years of insurance. National Solidarity Fund supplement, age 65, or 60 if unfit for work; and annual income below 201,000 francs for single person or 258,000 if couple. Allowance for formerly employed worker, age 65, or 60 if unfit for work; French citizenship; 15 years of employment after age 50; and annual income including allowance below 201,000 francs for single person or 258,000 if couple. Retirement not required.

Invalidity Benefits

Amount: Partial invalid, 30 per cent of average wages in last 10 years (wage ceiling 528,000 francs a year; wages in earlier years revalued); total invalid, 40 per cent of average wages; total invalid needing constant attendance, 54 per cent of wages; 10 per cent supplement if 3 children reared. Minimum benefit, 72,380 francs a year.

Qualifying conditions: Under age 60 (replaced by old age benefit at 60). Partial invalid, loss of two-thirds of earning capacity of normal worker of same category in region; total invalid, loss of all capacity to carry on any occupation. Entry into insurance 12 months before invalidity, and 480 hours of employment in last 12 months or 120 hours in last 3 months. Benefit suspended if earning capacity rises above 50 per cent and reduced if benefit plus earnings exceed normal wages.

Survivors' Benefits

Amount: Widow or widower, 50 per cent of benefit of deceased spouse, plus 10 per cent supplement if 3 children reared; minimum benefit, 36,190 francs a year. No periodical benefit for other survivors. Lump-sum benefit, 90 times average daily wages of insured; maximum, 132,000 francs (lump-sum benefit under agricultural system, 25 times average monthly contribution).

Qualifying conditions: Widow or widower, age 65, or age 60 and unfit for work; dependent on deceased; married before deceased attained 60 or, if survivor's benefit payable before 65, 2 years of marriage. Deceased must have satisfied insurance requirements for invalidity or old age benefit or been recipient of allowance for formerly employed worker. Lump-sum benefit, 60 hours of insured employment or certified unemployment in quarter preceding

death; payable to dependent spouse, descendants, or ascendants.

Administration

The Ministry of Labor and Social Security has general supervision, with Superior Social Security Council as advisory body; General Social Security Directorate within Ministry prepares regulations, decrees, circulars, etc., for applying law. National, regional, and primary (district) social security funds, under elected tripartite or bipartite governing bodies, administer program; regional old age and regional invalidity funds are main administrative organizations, with primary funds collecting contributions and National Fund handling financing. (Agricultural system: Ministry of Agriculture, general supervision. Mutual Agricultural Social Insurance Fund in each department [province], with elected bipartite governing body, administers program including coverage, contributions, and benefits; co-ordinated by two central agricultural funds for invalidity or old age benefits.)

WEST GERMANY

Dates of Basic Laws

First law: 1889. Currently governed by National Insurance Code of 1911, as extensively amended by Wage-Earners' and Salaried Employees' Pension Laws of February 23, 1957.

Coverage

All wage-earners and all salaried employees earning not more than DM. 15,000[5] a year (separate system for each). Voluntary coverage for persons with 60 months of insurance in 10 years. Special systems for miners, self-employed craftsmen, and civil servants.

Source of Funds

Insured person: 7 per cent of wages, excluding those above twice average taxable

[5] 1 Deutsche mark = 23.81 U.S. cents.

earnings in last 3 years (1957 ceiling, DM. 750 a month). No contribution if wages 10 per cent or less of ceiling.

Employer: 7 per cent of payroll, excluding wages above twice average taxable earnings in last 3 years; 14 per cent of payroll for employees whose wages are 10 per cent or less of ceiling.

Government: Substantial lump-sum subsidy, fixed each year and varied with changes in average taxable wages. In 1957 equaled about one-third of cost of wage-earners' system and one-fifth of that of salaried employees' system.

Old Age Benefits

Amount: 1.5 per cent of individual's "assessed wages" times years of insurance. ("Assessed wages" computed by applying to average taxable earnings of all workers in last 3 years the percentage that individual's wages were of average wages of all insured persons throughout his contribution period; national average taxable earnings in 1954–56, DM. 357 a month. "Years of insurance" include credited periods of incapacity, unemployment, or schooling after 15.) Supplement for each child, 10 per cent of average taxable earnings of all workers in last 3 years (DM. 36 a month in 1957). Outstanding pensions to be adjusted by special legislation to future changes in average taxable earnings, on basis of status of pension finance and national economy.

Qualifying conditions: Age 65 (women at 60 if worked 10 of last 20 years and have retired; also, man or woman at 60 if unemployed 1 full year and remaining unemployed); 180 months of contribution (including credited periods of military service or internment). Retirement not required except for pensions before age 65. Not payable to non-Germans living abroad.

Invalidity Benefits

Amount: General disability benefit, 1.5 per cent, and occupational invalidity benefit, 1.0 per cent, of individual's assessed wages times years of insurance (see "Old Age Benefits" for explanation of "assessed wages" and "years of insurance"). If invalid under 55, and had 36 months of contributions in last 5 years or contributions in one-half of months since entry into insurance, benefit computed as if contributions paid until 1955. Supplement for each child, 10 per cent of average taxable earnings of all workers. Medical care and rehabilitation services provided.

Qualifying conditions: General invalidity benefit, inability to exercise any regular gainful activity; occupational invalidity benefit, reduction of earning capacity below 50 per cent of that of normal person with similar training and ability; 60 months of contribution (including credited periods of military service or internment). Not payable to non-Germans living abroad.

Survivors' Benefits

Amount: Widow or dependent widower, 100 per cent of deceased's actual or potential benefit for first 3 months after death; thereafter, if over 45, invalid or caring for child, 60 per cent of deceased's general invalidity benefit; otherwise, 60 per cent of occupational invalidity benefit. Each half-orphan, 10 per cent, and each full orphan, 20 per cent, of deceased's actual or potential benefit, plus regular children's supplements (10 per cent of average taxable earnings). Maximum for all survivors' benefits, 100 per cent of deceased's pension.

Qualifying conditions: Widow, not remarried (final lump sum of 5 years' benefit paid on remarriage). Widower, dependent on deceased and not remarried. Orphan, under 18 (under 25 if student and unmarried), or invalid; 60 months of contribution. Not payable to non-Germans living abroad, except to orphans when person responsible for care lives abroad.

Administration

Federal Ministry of Labor has general supervision. State insurance offices, one in each state, administer wage-earners' system. Federal Salaried Employees Insurance

Office administers salaried workers' system. Contributions collected by sickness insurance agencies.

GREAT BRITAIN

Dates of Basic Laws

Old age and survivors' insurance, first law: 1925. Invalidity insurance, first law: 1911. Currently governed by National Insurance Act, 1946, as amended.

The National Insurance Act, 1959, does not change the amount or payment of the standard flat old age pension. The major change is the provision for the payment of wage-related additional benefits based on the payment of graduated contributions. The new provisions do not apply to the one-third of the total working population now covered by pension plans, but employers may apply to bring their employees under its terms.

Coverage

Residents age 15–65 (men) or 15–60 (women). Insurance not compulsory for self-employed and non-employed persons with incomes below £156 a year, nor for married women.

Source of Funds

Insured person: Flat rate weekly contribution as follows: male employee, 7s. 5d.; male self-employed, 9s. 3d.; and male non-employed, 7s. 4d.; female employee, 6s.; female self-employed, 7s. 10d.; and female non-employed, 5s. 10d. (Lower rates if under age 18.)

Employer: Flat-rate weekly contributions as follows: each male employee, 6s. 2d.; each female employee, 5s. 1d. (Lower rates for employees under 18.)

Government: Flat-rate weekly contributions as follows: each male employee and non-employed, 1s. 10d.; male self-employed 2s. 6d.; female employees and non-employed, 1s. 10d.; female self-employed, 2s. 2d. (Lower rates for persons under 18.)

Also, if required, £325,000,000 between 1955 and 1960.

NOTE.—Above contributions also finance other national insurance benefits (e.g., sickness, maternity, unemployment); old age invalidity and survivor benefits represent about two-thirds of national insurance costs.

Old Age Benefits

Amount: Single person, 40s. a week; couple if both insured, 80s.; couple if wife not insured, 65s. Allowance for first child under 16, 11s. 6d. a week, and for each subsequent child, 3s. 6d. Pension increased 1s. 6d. a week for each twenty-five weekly contributions paid during first 5 years after pensionable age. Reduced for men under 70 and women under 65 by 6d. a week for each 1s. of earnings between 50s. and 70s. and by 1s. for earnings over 70s.

Qualifying conditions: Age 65 for men, 60 for women; 156 weekly contributions paid and for full pension, average of 50 paid or credited each year; proportionately reduced benefit if fewer than 50 contributions annually, with minimum of 13 contributions annually (contributions are credited in case of unemployment or sickness). Retirement required unless claimant 5 years past pensionable age. Residence in country not required, but pension amount not increased after leaving country unless reciprocal agreement provides otherwise.

Invalidity Benefits

Amount: Single person, 40s. a week; 25s. weekly supplement for adult dependent; 11s. 6d. for first child and 3s. 6d. for each other child (these are sickness benefits which are paid without limit on duration if qualifying conditions are met; there is no invalidity benefit as such). (Lower rates for married women and youths under 18.)

Qualifying conditions: 156 weekly employee or self-employed contributions paid and, for full benefit, 50 weekly contributions paid or credited in previous contribution year. Incapacity for work by reason of specific disease or bodily or mental disablement. Must reside in country or in another with which there is a reciprocal agreement.

Survivors' Benefits

Amount: Widow's allowance for first 13 weeks: 55s. a week, plus 16s. 6d. for first child and 8s. 6d. for each other child. Thereafter, widowed mother's allowance of 56s. 6d. a week plus 8s. 6d. for each child after the first; or, if no child, a widow's pension of 40s. a week. Allowance of 18s. a week paid to guardian of full orphan. Funeral benefit of from £6 to £20.

Qualifying conditions: For widows' benefits, 156 weekly contributions paid and, for full benefit, average of 50 paid or credited each year. Widow's allowance paid for 13 weeks regardless of age. Widowed mother's allowance payable if child of school age, but reduced 6d. a week for each shilling of earnings of 60–80s.; and shilling for shilling if earnings exceed 80s. Widow's pension normally payable only if marriage of 3 years' duration and widow was age 50 at husband's death. If mother over 40 when children attain school-leaving age, widowed mother's allowance becomes a permanent widow's pension. For guardian's allowances, one parent must have been insured, but no contribution is required.

Administration

The Ministry of Pensions and National Insurance administers program through regional and local offices. National Insurance Advisory Council appointed by Minister after consultation with the organization of employers and workers, friendly societies, and the Northern Irish Authority. Appeals lie to tripartite local tribunals and a commissioner appointed by the Crown.

ITALY

Dates of Basic Laws

First law: 1919. Currently governed by Act of April 4, 1952.

Coverage

Employed persons aged 14–59 (women, 14–54). Includes agricultural workers. Separate systems for seamen and public employees.

Source of Funds

Insured person: 2.4 per cent of earnings.

Employer: 6.6 per cent of payroll, plus small wage-class contributions equal to approximately 0.2 per cent of payroll. Flat-rate contributions for agriculture and domestic service.

Government: None currently; law states that government will eventually pay 25 per cent of cost.

Old Age Benefits

Amount: Men, 45 times 45 per cent of first 1500 lire[6] of contributions paid, 33 per cent of next 1500 lire, and 20 per cent of other contributions; increased by 6–40 per cent for postponement of pension from 1 to 5 years. Women, 45 times 35 per cent of first 1500 lire of contributions paid, 26 per cent of next 1500 lire, and 20 per cent of other contributions; increased by 3–62 per cent for postponement of pension from 1 to 10 years. 10 per cent supplement for each dependent child. Thirteenth monthly benefit paid each December. Minimum annual benefit, 45,000 lire if under 65 or 65,000 lire if over 65; maximum benefit, 80 per cent of average wages in last 5 years.

Qualifying conditions: Age 60 for men and 55 for women; 15 years since first entry into insurance, plus specified minimum total contributions (different for wage-earners and salaried employees and varying in agriculture by sex and occupational category; increased value is assigned contributions paid before 1948; periods of military service, sickness, and pregnancy credited). From 1962, 15 years of contributions will be required, with reduced benefit after 10 years (requirement increases 1 year at time from 1952 to 15 years in 1962).

[6] 1 lira = 0.16 U.S. cent.

Invalidity Benefits

Amount: Same as for old age, with minimum of 65,000 lire a year. Hospital or other care provided for prevention or cure of invalidity.

Qualifying conditions: Permanent reduction of earning capacity in suitable occupation by two-thirds for wage-earner and one-half for salaried employee; 5 years since first entry into insurance, plus specified minimum total contributions (different for wage-earners and salaried employees and varying in agriculture by sex and occupational category); 1 year of contribution in last 5 years. From 1962, 5 years of contributions will be required (gradual increase from 1 year of contributions in 1952). Benefit may be withheld if medical treatment refused.

Survivors' Benefits

Amount: Widow or incapacitated widower, 50 per cent of old age pension of deceased; each half-orphan, 20 per cent of pension; each full orphan, 30 per cent of pension; one parent or grandparent, 15 per cent of pension; two or more parents or grandparents, 30 per cent of pension divided equally. Minimum, 45,000 lire a year.

Qualifying conditions: Contribution requirements as for invalidity pension. Children under 18 or invalid and not gainfully occupied. Parents and grandparents entitled only if no spouse or orphan's benefit payable, age 65, and receiving no other pension.

Administration

The Ministry of Labor and Social Welfare has general supervision. National Social Insurance Institute, with branches throughout the country, administers program; managed by tripartite governing body.

NETHERLANDS

Dates of Basic Laws

First law: 1913. Currently governed by Act of May 31, 1956.

Coverage

All permanent residents age 15–64.

Source of Funds

Insured persons: 6.75 per cent of net income up to 6900 guilders[7] a year. No contribution payable if annual income below 1500 for single person or 2100 guilders for married person. Income ceiling varies with changes in wage index.

Employer: None.

Government: Contributions on behalf of low-income person and any eventual deficit.

Old Age Benefits

Amount: Full pension, 846 guilders for single person and 1404 guilders for aged couple, with automatic half-year adjustment for each 3 per cent change in wage index. Decrements of 1–2 per cent for each year of non-contribution.

Qualifying conditions: Age 65, though amount for couple paid irrespective of age of wife. Regular contribution each year until age 65 required for full pension. No retirement requirement. Persons over age 15 when act enacted must have 6 years of residence after attaining age 59 to qualify. Pensions payable to persons age 65 or over at start of Act if residents at least 6 years since age 59.

Invalidity Benefits

[Information not yet available on present status of older invalidity provisions.]

Survivors' Benefits

Widow over 65 receives old age benefit. Widow of deceased pensioner under 65 continues to receive benefit for 6 months only.

Administration

The Ministry of Social Affairs and Public Health has general supervision. Direct administration by Social Insurance Bank,

[7] 1 guilder = 26.32 U.S. cents.

which decides and pays claims; industrial associations may be assigned certain administrative functions. Contributions collected by Government Revenue Office.

NORWAY

Dates of Basic Laws

First law: 1936 (in force, as amended until end of 1958; provisions not charted below). Law of 1957 in effect from January 1, 1959.

Coverage

All resident citizens aged 18–69. Special systems for seamen, forestry workers, and government workers.

Source of Funds

Contribution amounts based on estimated annual expenditure under program. Initial amounts, based on estimated 1959 expenditure of 570 million crowns, are as follows:

Insured person: If income exceeds 6000 crowns (kroner)[8] a year, full premium (initially, 250 crowns a year); if income is 4000–6000 crowns a year, two-thirds of full premium (167 crowns); if income is 2000–4000 crowns a year, one-third of full premium (83 crowns). No contribution if income not in excess of 2000 crowns a year.

Employer: 60 per cent of employees' contributions.

Government: National government: amount equal to 15 per cent of contributions paid by insured persons. Communes: amount equal to 20 per cent of contributions paid by insured persons.

Old Age Benefits

Amount: Single person, 2208 crowns a year; couple, 3312 crowns a year, increased by 600 crowns for each child under 18. Pension supplement may be granted by commune, subject to income test; formula for reducing supplement because of outside income is to add 150 per cent of basic

[8] 1 crown = 14 U.S. cents.

pension to any other income and to reduce amount of supplement by half the sum of the two factors.

Qualifying conditions: Age 70, and either (1) citizenship with continuous residence during 5 years preceding claim, or (2), if not a citizen, residence for 15 years after age 20 with 5 years' continuous residence immediately prior to claim. Work on Norwegian ship deemed equivalent to residence. Wife eligible at age 60 if husband meets above qualifications. Invalid husband, formerly dependent on wife, also eligible at age 60 if wife meets above qualifications.

Invalidity Benefits

None.

Survivors' Benefits

Amount: Widow (or disabled widower) of pensioner entitled to same amount as deceased pensioner. Additional pension subject to income test may also be provided by commune.

Qualifying condition: Age 60.

Administration

The Department of Social Affairs has general supervision. Pension Board in Department administers national aspects of program and supervises operations. Claims handled at local level by communal pension committee, composed of chairman and vice-chairman named by governor of province on recommendation of communal council and of five members appointed by communal council.

SWEDEN

Dates of Basic Laws

First law: 1913. Currently governed by law of 1946, as amended.

The three new laws of May 14, 1959, establish a system of supplementary pensions in addition to the present universal flat "national pension." The system of supplementary benefits will be financed exclusively by employers. Their contributions are effective as of 1960, and benefits are payable 3 years later. Ultimately, the supplementary pension will equal 2 per cent of taxable earnings times years of coverage up to 30 years.

Coverage

All Swedish citizens aged 18–66.

Source of Funds

Insured persons: 2.5 per cent of income subject to income tax; maximum annual contribution, 250 crowns (kronor).[9] No tax if income is under 1200 crowns annually. (Contributions cover about 30 per cent of cost.)

Employer: None.

Government: National government pays approximately 55 per cent of cost of program from general revenue, and communes pay approximately 15 per cent of cost.

Old Age Benefits

Amount: Basic amounts and supplements in 1956 were as shown in Table 3 (in crowns per year).

TABLE 3

SWEDEN: NATIONAL PENSION AND SUPPLE-
MENTS ACCORDING TO MARITAL STATUS
(1956 Rates in Crowns per Year)

	Single Person	Aged Couple
Basic amount	1700	2720
Fixed supplement	200	320
Cost-of-living supplement	300	480
Total	2200	3520

About half the pensioners also receive a housing supplement varying with commune of residence and income. A housewife's benefit is also payable, subject to income test, if pensioner's wife is age 60–66 and if the marriage is of at least 5 years' duration; maximum, 1760 crowns a year.

[9] 1 crown = 19.33 U.S. cents.

Two additional allowances are payable if the pensioner has children—the regular family allowance of 290 crowns a year per child and the special children's allowance for persons with low incomes of 600 crowns a year per child.

Qualifying conditions: Age 67; Swedish citizen, or national of country having reciprocal treaty with Sweden and specified minimum residence in Sweden. (No relationship between contributions and benefit eligibility, and no income test for basic benefits.)

Housing supplement and housewife's benefits paid in full if outside income does not exceed 1000 crowns for single person and 1500 crowns for couple; reduced by one-third for income of 1001–1400 crowns; by two-thirds for income over 1400 crowns.

Invalidity Benefits

Amount: Flat amount of 200 crowns a year, plus invalidity supplements subject to income test, bringing the total maximum rates to the same total as for the old age pension (including cost-of-living and other supplements). Housing supplements and housewife's benefits are also payable as for old age.

Blind persons receive an extra allowance of 1000 crowns, plus the basic 200 crowns, without income test.

A sickness allowance of the same amount as the permanent disability benefit is payable in case of temporary but long-continued disability.

Qualifying conditions: Age 16–66. Permanently incapable of self-support in work corresponding to experience and training. Housing and housewife's benefits are subject to income tests the same as for old age pensioners. Blindness supplement is paid without income test to persons who have become blind before reaching age 60.

For the sickness allowance, disablement must exist as for invalidity, lasting 6 months, but not deemed permanent. This benefit is granted for specific periods in advance.

Survivors' Benefits

Amount: Widow's benefit is maximum of 1760 crowns a year, subject to income test. No provision under national pension legislation for other survivors. Both general children's allowances of 290 crowns a year and special children's allowances of 600 crowns a year are payable to full orphans and half-orphans; full orphans receive a special allowance, subject to reduction for outside income.

Qualifying conditions: Widow, age 55 at time of husband's death or caring for child under 12; marriage must have been of at least 5 years' duration. The income test is the same as for the housing supplement for a single person (above). Children's benefits are the same as for old age (above).

Administration

The Ministry of Social Affairs has general supervision. The National Pension Board administers program nationally. Local pension committees receive and process claims. Contributions collected with national income taxes.

UNION OF SOVIET SOCIALIST REPUBLICS

Dates of Basic Laws

First law: 1922. Currently governed by law of July 14, 1956.

Coverage

Wage and salary workers and students in higher specialized schools. Important exclusions: members of collective farms and producers' co-operatives. Special systems for scientists, writers, composers, architects, and other groups.

Source of Funds

Proportionate share of following combined social security contribution, which also covers cash benefits under health and maternity insurance and family allowances:

Insured person: None.

Employer: Percentage of anticipated payroll, budgeted at different rate for each industry, and varying from about 3.7 to 10.7 per cent of payroll.

Government: Usually pays employer contribution, though not directly, because industry and other business is nationalized. Act provides that "the State will pay pensions through funds provided in the U.S.S.R. State budget, including funds under the budget for State social insurance. . . ."

Old Age Benefits

Amount: Benefits (in rubles)[10] vary by wage class and work category, as shown in Table 4. Increased by 10 per cent of pen-

TABLE 4

U.S.S.R.: OLD AGE PENSION AS PERCENTAGE OF MONTHLY WAGES BY WAGE AND TYPE OF EMPLOYMENT

AVERAGE MONTHLY WAGE (RUBLES)	PENSION AS PERCENTAGE OF WAGES	
	Normal Employment	Unhealthy and Underground Employment
To 350 (inclusive)	100	100
350–500	85	90
500–600	75	80
600–800	65	70
800–1000	55	60
1001 and over	50	55

sion for 15 years' uninterrupted work and, if not employed, by 10 per cent for 1 dependent unable to work and by 15 per cent for two or more. Average wages computed over last 12 months or, at option of claimant, over any 5 consecutive years during last 10 years. Minimum pension, 300 rubles a month; maximum, 1200 rubles. Pension reduced to 150 rubles or to 50 per cent of pension in case of employees in unhealthy

10 1 ruble = 2.6 U.S. cents free-world rate, or about 10 U.S. cents official rate.

or underground work, if pensioner continues to work.

Qualifying conditions: Normal employment: for men, age 60 with 25 years' work; for women, age 55 with 20 years' work. Employment under "difficult" conditions: for men, age 55 with 25 years' work; for women, age 50 with 20 years' work. Unhealthy or underground work: for men, age 50 with 20 years' work; for women, age 45 with 16 years' work. At least half of time must have been in special employment to qualify for special conditions. Proportionately reduced pensions paid to persons reaching pensionable age while actively employed, with at least 5 years' work but not enough for a full pension; minimum reduced pension, one-fourth of full pension.

Invalidity Benefits

Amount: Complete invalidism: if needing constant attendance, 85 per cent of average monthly wages up to 500 rubles, plus 10 per cent of higher wages, with 300-ruble minimum and 900-ruble maximum; otherwise, 65 per cent of wages up to 450 rubles, plus 10 per cent of higher wages, with 230-ruble minimum and 600-ruble maximum; 10 per cent supplement for one dependent or 15 per cent for two or more dependents, 10 per cent supplement for 10–14 years of continuous employment or 15 per cent for 15 years, and 15 per cent supplement for needed attendance, with maximum supplement of 30 per cent.

Partial invalidism: 45 per cent of average monthly wages up to 400 rubles, plus 10 per cent of additional wages, with 160-ruble minimum and 400-ruble maximum.

Workers employed under "difficult" conditions receive above basic percentages but applicable up to 500 rubles, with 15 per cent of higher wages; for those in unhealthy or underground work, percentages apply to wages of up to 600 rubles, with 20 per cent of higher wages.

Qualifying conditions: Complete invalidism, incapacity for any work; partial invalidism, incapacity for usual work. Sliding scale of required years of employment, rising from 2 years for men and 1 year for women aged 20–23 to 20 years for men and 15 years for women over age 61; fewer years, rising from 1 to 14 years, for those in unhealthy or underground employment; no minimum employment period for invalids under age 20. Proportionally reduced pension payable to complete invalids with insufficient years of employment, with minimum of 25 per cent of full pension. Wages plus pension of employed partial invalids may not exceed previous earnings, except that at least 50 per cent of pension always payable.

Survivors' Benefits

Amount: One surviving dependent, 45 per cent of average monthly wages up to 400 rubles, plus 10 per cent of higher wages, with 160-ruble minimum and 400-ruble maximum; two dependents, 65 per cent of wages up to 450 rubles, plus 10 per cent of higher wages, with 230-ruble minimum and 600-ruble maximum; three or more dependents, 85 per cent of wages up to 500 rubles, plus 10 per cent of higher wages, with 300-ruble minimum and 900-ruble maximum. If survivors are full orphans, basic percentages above changed to 65, 90, and 100 for one, two, or three or more survivors.

If deceased employed under "difficult" conditions, basic percentages apply up to 500 rubles, with 15 per cent of higher wages; if employed in unhealthy or underground work, percentages apply to wages of up to 600 rubles, with 20 per cent of higher wages.

Ten per cent supplement if deceased had 10–14 years of continuous employment, or 15 per cent for 15 years.

Qualifying conditions: Eligible survivors include widow age 55, invalid or caring for child under 8; widower age 60 or invalid; children, brothers, sisters, or grandchildren under 16 (under 18 if student), or invalids; and parents age 60, invalid, or caring for child under 8. Must have been dependent on deceased. Sliding scale of required years of employment of deceased, rising from 2 years for men and 1 year for women aged 20–23 to 20 years for men and 15 years for women over age 61; fewer years, rising from 1 to 14 years for workers in unhealthy or underground employment. Proportionally reduced pensions if insufficient years of employment, with 25 per cent minimum.

Administration

All-Union Central Council of Trade Unions has general supervision. Regional and district trade-union committees have direct administration and decision of claims. Factory, shop, and local committees do preparatory work on claims. Department of Social Assistance has supervision over non-working pensioners.

2

Pensioners and Medical-Care Insurance in Eleven European Countries

INTRODUCTION

Patterns of medical care for persons receiving old age benefits of one type or another in eleven different countries reveal considerable variation. The following brief summary attempts to show whether or not such pensioners are covered for medical benefits, what they contribute, and what medical benefits they receive. The countries considered are Belgium, Denmark, Finland, France, West Germany, Great Britain, Italy, the Netherlands, Norway, Sweden, and the Union of Soviet Socialist Republics. Their systems include old age insurance programs, universal pensions, and old age assistance.

BELGIUM

Employed persons must join a mutual benefit society or the regional office of an official auxiliary fund. Pensioners are covered for medical benefits. Contributions from insured persons and employer are supplemented by a subsidy equal to 16 per cent of the above contributions.

Sickness benefits for insured persons provide 75 per cent of the cost of specialist care, surgery, hospitalization, laboratory services, and appliances and part of the cost of general medical care, medicines, dental care, and nursing.

DENMARK

Denmark's major benefit for aged persons is a pension based on the individual's income and resources.

Like other members of the population who have modest incomes, the Danish old age pensioner may choose between active and passive membership in a sick club. Active members receive free medical care from physicians, free hospital services, and three-fourths of the cost of medicines designated as necessary. They may, if the rules of their sick club permit, obtain specialist treatment, dental care, baths and massage, and certain other services.

The pensioner who is an active member pays, like other such members, about 4 crowns a month for medical care only. The fees vary somewhat among the clubs. At this contribution level there is a cash benefit of 40 öre a day.[1] The pensioner may choose to become insured for a somewhat higher cash benefit than the minimum, but not for more than 1 crown a day. Duration of cash benefit for pensioners is 13 weeks, or half the usual maximum duration of such payment. However, the provision of any cash sickness benefit is unusual, since most health insurance programs that make provision for pensioners under health insurance concern themselves only with services.

FINLAND

Finland has a pension payment composed partly of universal benefit and partly of a flat rate based on inquiry into the resources of the claimant. The latter may be three times as large as the former.

[1] 100 öre = 1 crown (14.88 U.S. cents).

408

Finland has no health insurance except non-subsidized programs, which are conducted in some cases by mutual societies and in others by insurance companies.

Old age pensioners, it appears, have no special position in relation to any medical-service benefits.

FRANCE

In France benefits for aged persons are provided through the social insurance system. The regular insurance benefit is supplemented—if the pensioner's income is small—by a substantial flat rate payment from the National Solidarity Fund, which is financed from various earmarked taxes.

Employer-worker contributions totaling 16 per cent of earnings finance both health and pensions insurance. The agencies of administration—local, regional, and national—are all part of the general system of social insurance for persons in non-agricultural occupations. Local agencies (*caisses primaires*) administer short-term benefits; regional agencies (*caisses regionales*), the long-term payments.

Old age pensioners and their wives and dependent children continue to be covered for medical benefits under the health insurance provisions after the individual's coverage as an active worker has ceased. The pensioner pays no contribution.

The benefits consist of an 80 per cent refund, according to fee schedule, of medical costs and of medicines and the provision of the full cost of hospital care either in a public hospital or at a rate not to exceed that of a public hospital.

WEST GERMANY

In the German Federal Republic old age benefits are payable under an insurance system.

Pensioners are insured for medical care, including those under the systems for wage-earners, salaried employees, and miners.

The contributions are paid by the insuring institution at rates fixed by the Federal Minister of Labor. Neither the health insurance funds nor the pension establishments have a direct influence in determining the level of contributions for pensioners.

The benefits consist of medical care, including services of a physician, medicines, and hospitalization.

GREAT BRITAIN

British retirement benefits are paid under the National Insurance System.

Medical care, which is free at the time the service is provided, is available separately under the National Health Service to all persons, whatever their age, whether insured or not.

ITALY

Italian benefits for the aged are paid under an insurance system.

Pensioners and their dependents—including wife, children, young brothers and sisters, and aged parents—are eligible for medical care under health insurance. This is a fairly recent development, the program of pensioners' benefits having started in November, 1955, under legislation of August 4, 1955.

The cost is not paid by the pensioner but is met from the joint employer-worker contribution to the Equalization Fund for Pensions and Sickness Benefit for Pensioners, which is the principal OASDI contribution. Since January 1, 1958, the rate of contribution has been 11.60 per cent of earnings, payable two-thirds by the employer and one-third by the insured wage-earner or salary worker.

Medical care for Italian pensioners consists of general and specialized services (the latter including obstetrical treatment), medicines, and hospitalization. Moreover, a decree of December, 1956, listed various special diseases of old age, which are treated without time limit.

NETHERLANDS

Dutch old age benefits are quasi-universal but are subject to a decrement for years of non-contribution.

The situation respecting health insurance services for pensioners has changed more than once in the past few years. Currently, as from January 1, 1957, there is a similarity to the Danish program in that pensioners are not subject to compulsory health insurance but may join a sickness fund voluntarily if not receiving income in excess of 3530 guilders a year.

Financial support for the benefits to pensioners is derived from the insured, the government, and the sick funds. The pensioner pays either 0.55 guilder a week, or 1.10 guilders, according to whether his income is less or greater than 2520 guilders annually. This meets from a quarter to one-half the cost, the remainder being financed half by government grant and half by the fund operating the compulsory health insurance program.

The medical benefits are general and specialist services, medicines, hospitalization, and dental treatment.

NORWAY

Norway has changed from pensions based on the means test to universal pensions; the change occurred on January 1, 1959.

The amendments to health insurance introduced by the Sickness Insurance Act of March, 1956, provided that "every person who is resident in Norway shall be insured under this act." There is no reference to pensioners by way either of emphasizing their compulsory affiliation or of making an exception. When pensions were based on the income test, the local government where the pensioner lived paid the health insurance contribution for coverage.

For pensions paid irrespective of income or insurance status, the normal position for the pensioner would appear to be that of any other old person. The medical-care premium, payable quarterly at the rate of 0.90 crown a week, is compulsory. There is also, for most non-employed persons, an optional added premium for obtaining cash

benefit (not considered further, since cash benefits are not under review). It would seem that under the new Norwegian pension act the pensioner himself would pay the premium, but no information has been received on this point.

The medical benefits include doctor's care, often through reimbursement by the sick club according to fee schedule, with the insurance program paying from two-thirds to three-fourths of the cost and the patient the difference. Also among the benefits are the full cost of hospitalization (surgery being a hospital service) in a public hospital, without time limit; essential medicines; physiotherapy; and limited dental care such as extractions and other work necessary for the individual's health.

SWEDEN

In Sweden benefits for aged persons are provided by a program of universal pensions.

Insurance for medical care is compulsory for all Swedish citizens over 16 and living in Sweden.

No health insurance contribution is paid by persons over age 67, or by national pensioners.

The medical service benefits are a 75 per cent refund of costs of physician's treatment and a refund of hospital costs at the rate for treatment in a public ward. There is partial payment of the cost of medicines, but some life-saving medicines are free.

UNION OF SOVIET SOCIALIST REPUBLICS

Benefits to aged persons are paid on an insurance basis.

Since medical services are provided outside the insurance system to all persons without cost except in the case of medicines or appliances, pensioners appear to have no special position in the U.S.S.R. As members of the community they are entitled to medical care.

3

Swedish Housing Design[1]

SWEDISH OLD PEOPLE'S HOMES

Swedish homes for the aged are in principle reserved for persons needing constant assistance but not requiring hospitalization. The buildings reflect the modern movement in architecture and are built on a friendly and sympathetic scale. They are designed for home-type living and to reduce institutionalism to a minimum. In consequence, sitting and dining rooms are kept small and repeated in various parts of the building. Halls are broken and related to living space through the use of functional walls, or are themselves furnished. Color is much used in rich warm tones, and designs reflect the traditional Swedish motifs. Simplicity without institutional sterility is achieved through the use of good textiles in rugs, draperies, and upholstery and of well-designed furniture. The open fireplaces, bright pieces of copper, and flowering plants add the warm touches of home.

The lovely homes shown here were designed by one of Sweden's most talented architects, Bo Boustedt of Kungälv, Sweden.

[1] This account was prepared by Wilma Donahue, Chairman, Division of Gerontology, Institute for Human Adjustment, University of Michigan, Ann Arbor.

Exterior of Starrkärr home for aged people fits the landscape

A RESTRAINED TOUCH OF ART

Entrance of Starrkärr

Entrance façade of Ryssby Home for thirty-six aged persons

Sculpture in pool in the yard of Ränneslöv Home for thirty aged persons

Modern motif, by sculptor R. Denman, Gothenburg, at Munkedal Home for forty aged persons

Cross-lighted,
broken corridors
at Vetlanda Home
for thirty-three aged
persons

HALLS DESIGNED TO OFFSET INSTITUTIONAL EFFECTS

Halls open to
daylight provide
comfortable
sitting rooms at
Sandared Home f
thirty aged persor

Corridors interrupted to include small living room at Vifolka Home for forty-two aged persons

LIVING ROOMS SMALL AND INTIMATE

Open fireplace in the living room of Vara Home for twenty-six old persons

The two rooms composing a little assembly hall at Vetlanda Home for thirty-three old persons

Living room adjacent to small dining room at Eksjö Home for fifty old people

One of the two dining rooms at Vetlanda Home for thirty-three old persons

Using her own furniture at Eksjö—one of fifty resident rooms

Furniture specially designed for the elderly at Vetlanda—single room

THE ENJOYMENT OF HOME

Enjoying the warmth of the open fire at Gislaved Home for thirty aged persons

Following his native skill at Munkedal Home for forty aged persons

Coffee kitchen, center of resident life at Eksjö Home for fifty aged people

A morning conversation at Frändefors Home for thirty-six aged persons

4

Older Peoples' Housework Scheme
Exeter, England.

It was four years ago that the Exeter Council of Social Service received a grant to set up a home-help scheme for elderly people, and a very modest start was made with the appointment of one helper and the preparation of a supply of forms for completion by old people requiring help.

The first results were not promising, and for 8 weeks I put off the painful experience of reviewing the progress of the scheme. Our first applications were received and the forms sent out; of these forms, however, the first two were never returned, and several others came back incomplete.

In spite of these setbacks the helper did actually visit a few homes, and I was satisfied that a satisfactory standard of cleanliness was being achieved. I was disappointed on my first two visits to the old people when they did not express appreciation of their cleaner and tidier homes, but I did not feel the full import of the situation until an old man told me in no uncertain terms what he thought. His sugar had been in the same place for 20 years, and he was not going to move it from the mantelpiece for anybody!

When the next application was received, I decided to make a visit myself instead of mailing a form. I found the old man in a sadly neglected state, but, in spite of the filth and the fleas, he was very happy. He agreed that the floor "could do with a sweep." He was 84, independent and intelligent, and it was apparent that, if any

improvements were to be made, they could be accomplished only with the old man taking an active part. I visited him several times, and we became friends and discussed the possibility of someone helping him. I arranged for a carefully selected helper to call to see him. They seemed to like each other, and soon she was visiting regularly, and many improvements were made. This helper remained with the old man until she retired 2 years later. During this time they had many rows, but the friendship remained firm. I was staggered to find that in the rehabilitation of this old man it had been necessary to contact no less than sixteen different departments and individuals.

From this experience it was clear that housework alone was not sufficient to insure the maximum well-being of our old people. Henceforward the forms were scrapped, and the term "health (physical and mental) and happiness" took priority over the word "cleanliness."

HOW THE SCHEME WORKS

Applications for help are received from local hospitals when an old person is ready to be discharged: from doctors; health visitors and old people themselves; relatives and friends of old people; the National Assistance Board; the Welfare Department; and sanitary inspectors.

We obtain as much information as possible when the application is made, including the name of the doctor, relationship with neighbors, church, etc., and we arrange to visit the old person to discuss the

[1] This study, written by Helen L. Slater, appeared in *Social Service*, **28** (Winter, 1954), 128–31. Minor changes have been made in the text.

type of help needed and the number of visits necessary. After talking the matter over with the old person and agreeing on the number of hours of help each week, we ask the selected helper to call so that the actual days and times of the visits can be fixed. We find this initial friendly visit very much worthwhile. Before the helper goes, we discuss the case and point out likely difficulties. This preliminary visit was arranged after an old lady told me that she had not slept all night because she had been wondering what "the helper would be like." It avoids a great deal of anxiety and often lays the foundation for a good relationship. When the inquiry comes from a hospital, the helper visits the old person there whenever possible and sometimes goes to get them when they are leaving. Similarly, when an old person is receiving help under this scheme and has to go to the hospital, we nearly always find that the helper is left with the key of the house or room (a very great privilege) and that she makes regular visits to the hospital. These visits are voluntary.

On the first day that the helper starts her duties we make a visit later in the day to check that all is well. This is essential, since it is at this stage that arrangements tend to go wrong. For instance, the old person may have changed her mind about having the help, or has decided she cannot afford to pay for help, etc.—then we have to start explaining all over again. Because having help in their homes—perhaps for the first time in their lives—is a big step for old people (it is a reminder of the process of aging), we accept it that installing a helper and establishing a good relationship is a delicate business and will not be achieved without some difficulties. Once the helper has visited two or three times, we experience little difficulty; but, if a satisfactory relationship is not established, we replace the helper. Sometimes the request comes from the helper herself.

We visit 91 old people every week; of these, 52 live alone and range in age from 60 to 92. The majority are in the 75-and-over group, and 9 are over 85. Last year, according to their time sheets, our helpers worked 9640 hours. In actual fact many more hours were worked, but these were done voluntarily.

The homes vary a good deal and range from dark, smelly rooms in condemned property to spic-and-span, well-preserved homes. Some of our most likable old people are to be found in the former group.

Frequently when we are first called in, we have to put in as many as 4 hours' help daily, particularly in cases of sickness, but we reduce this as quickly as possible. We encourage the old people to take as active an interest as possible because we believe that this is good for them, and for economic reasons we arrange the minimum number of hours' help. Many old people can manage with one visit of 2 or 3 hours of help weekly. Others need daily visits.

THE ACTUAL WORK

The helpers undertake anything that is necessary, such as cleaning, shopping, cooking, washing clothes, washing the old person, cutting toenails. These are the jobs they do when actually employed, and the list is considerably increased if those things they do voluntarily are included: shopping expeditions, visits to the sea, hot dinners on Sundays, the new cakes they take, the pensions they collect, and occasionally the gin or cider they call for—these and many other kindnesses could be enumerated.

We employ 38 part-time helpers; their ages range from 30 to 70, and 17 of these are over 60. They vary in social background from a tough old Irish lady whose language is formidable to smartly dressed young wives who are interested in social work. They vary as much as the old people they help. Many have children, and the work has a special appeal as the times of visiting can be arranged when the children are at school and can, when necessary, be altered by agreement with the old people. Sometimes the helpers with their children make friendly visits to their old people, and the whole relationship assumes a distinct family atmosphere. One helper has married the old man she visited.

There appear to be a few advantages, particularly in cases of sickness, in employing helpers of 60 years of age or more; they have a closer knowledge of the process of aging and usually have a good deal of spare time and can put in extra hours at short notice or can stay longer than the agreed-upon period in order to chat.

We have used several forms of newspaper advertisement to obtain helpers. When the applicants call, we listen to their reasons for applying; in the majority of cases it is because they like old people or like caring for someone and have perhaps lost their own parents. Economic reasons are seldom of primary importance. At the office we all agree that we cannot judge the applicant at this interview. Several times we have reluctantly engaged a helper simply because we had no alternative at the time and have found her to be excellent with old people. Only in a few cases is it apparent at the initial interview that an applicant would be unsuitable for the work.

In some cases it is obvious that the applicant would not fit in happily with a rough or dirty old person, and others would enjoy trying to improve the lot of "some poor old soul." Points like this are noted at the interview.

We go through our cards to try to find a suitable helper for each old person. Great care is taken in selection, and the value of the scheme is enhanced if the old person and the helper live near each other.

FINANCIAL MATTERS

We pay our helpers 1s. 9d. per hour plus bus fare. The old people pay 2s. 6d. per hour, and some of them receive the total cost from the National Assistance Board. Many battles are waged on this point. It frequently occurs that, when the old person receives the extra money from the National Assistance Board, he decides to do without the help or to have 2 hours instead of 4, etc. The skill and tenacity of old people on matters of finance are constant tests of our own intelligence.

In some cases sons or daughters pay the cost—one old lady pays the helper 2s. for her 4 hours' help, and the son and the daughter-in-law pay the balance direct to the office. The old lady does not know this, since she thinks 6d. an hour good money. A number of old people pay the full amount themselves and are very grateful for the service.

We receive a grant from the Dispensary Committee (a local charity), which covers insurance stamps, additional hours worked in emergencies, cases where payment is not recovered, and bonus of 10s. where a particularly dirty job is undertaken.

TRAINING

Training is done on an individual basis. There is such variety among our helpers that I would hesitate to try group talks, nor do I think that such talks would be appealing.

Each helper calls at the office at least once every week to pay in the money she has collected from her old people and to collect her own wages. On these occasions we discuss the old people she visits. If additional services, such as chiropody treatment or mobile meals, seem to be desirable, we ask the helper to discuss the matter with the old people. Other problems (like the reluctance of an old man to change his shirt or to get up in cold weather, or the old lady who spends 9s. a week on her two cats out of her National Assistance and then cannot pay the helper) are also talked over. By regularly discussing the problems, the helpers develop great skill in dealing with old people. Their techniques vary from threats to cease visiting to constant praise and flattery, and at the bottom of it all is a genuine affection.

5

An Important Swedish Epidemiological Study[1]

In 1954 Larsson and Sjögren published an exceedingly thorough and valuable study of the mental health of a large Swedish rural population.[2] Not only is their investigation important for the factual information it yields about indigenous mental health conditions but it is, in addition, an important methodological contribution.

The region studied consists of thirteen parishes located on two large islands and a number of adjacent smaller ones off the west coast of Sweden. These islands are situated near the mainland and for the purposes of the study are referred to as "AB:bo." In spite of its relative isolation, this population is considered as representative of the Swedish rural population as a whole. The very fact of isolation makes the area ideal for long-term study because it has been relatively free of large-scale migrations. During the present century it has tended to diminish some in population through emigration, but, in spite of this, it has remained reasonably stable and relatively uncontaminated by the influx of any appreciable numbers from parishes outside the region.

POPULATION STUDY

The investigators carefully searched the parish records for all instances of mental

[1] This account was prepared by Robert W. Kleemeier, professor of psychology, Washington University, St. Louis, Mo.

[2] T. Larsson and T. Sjögren, *A Methodological, Psychiatric, and Statistical Study of a Large Swedish Rural Population* ("Acta psychiatrica et neurologica Scandinavica," Suppl. 89 [Copenhagen, 1954]).

disorder or deficiency (see discussion of this registration in chap. vii above) for the period January 1, 1900, to December 31, 1944, and supplemented this effort by combing the records of mental hospitals and institutions normally serving the inhabitants of this area for additional cases. Finally, a thorough field investigation of the region was made to insure that the highest possible percentages of cases of mental disorder could be discovered and correctly diagnosed. In this way 1312 cases of psychosis, severe psychopathy, low-grade oligophrenia (marked mental deficiency), and suicide were identified for the 45-year period covered by the study. Among these were 763 psychotics, 65 psychopaths, and 320 oligophrenics.

Of methodological interest is the fact that only 83.6 per cent of the instances of psychosis and psychopathy were discovered through hospital records. While this is the great majority of cases, a not inconsiderable proportion of the study population would have been missed were these records the only source of information. That Sweden's unique parish records were of substantial value is indicated by the fact that 13.6 per cent of the cases were uncovered from this source alone, while an additional 2 per cent came from the records of the welfare organization. These percentages refer to the identification of the 745 psychotic and psychopathic probands or index cases upon which the genetic aspects of the study were based. Field investigation and interviews aided substantially in locating secondary cases related to the probands but who did not appear in any of the records mentioned above.

NON-HOSPITALIZATION

This careful work illustrates well the inadequacy of estimates of prevalence of mental illness based solely upon hospital records. While study of hospitalization rates are valuable and necessary in and of themselves, generalizations concerning the mental health of regional and national groups derived entirely from this source may be misleading. The reason for this cautious approach is made apparent in Table 1. Here we see that, of 1148 cases of mental disorder occurring in "AB:bo" during the 45-year investigation period, less than two-thirds were hospitalized or placed in an institution. Almost one-fifth of the psychotics did not enter a mental hospital, and only one-quarter of the mentally deficient were admitted to an institution for their disorder.

Of the 148 psychotics who were not hospitalized, 107, or 72 per cent, were registered as "undiagnosed psychosis." This is not surprising, since such persons are less likely to be observed by a competent diagnostician than are hospitalized patients. Larsson and Sjögren assume, however, that they would be distributed according to diagnosis in frequencies similar to those found in the hospitalized cases.

AGE AT ONSET OF PSYCHOSIS AND AGE AT HOSPITALIZATION

Estimates of the amount of "non-hospitalization" when based upon data gathered within a sharply defined period of time will contain some error, because cases developing near the end of the period and hospitalized after the termination date are wrongly classified. In other words, the late-occurring case is placed in the "non-hospitalized" category even though hospitalization may in fact occur after the end of the study period.

This technical point brings up the problem of the relationship between time of

onset of psychosis and time of hospitalization, which has important bearing upon the estimation of prevalence of psychosis by age. Heretofore (in chap. vii above) we have had to rely completely on age at hospitalization or upon age-frequency distributions of hospital populations in order to form a picture of the mental health of the aged. For Sweden, however, the thorough methods of the present study give us a clue concerning the age of onset of mental disorder of an entire regional population.

TABLE 1*

"NON HOSPITALIZATION" OF THE MENTALLY ILL AND MENTALLY DEFICIENT IN A SWEDISH RURAL AREA ("AB:BO"), 1900–1944

DIAGNOSIS	CASES NOT HOSPITALIZED		TOTAL NO. OF CASES
	No.	Per Cent	
Men..........	239	41.0	583
Psychosis......	69	19.9	346
Psychopathy...	23	60.5	38
Oligophrenia...	147	73.9	199
Women.........	187	33.1	565
Psychosis......	79	18.9	417
Psychopathy...	14	51.3	27
Oligophrenia...	94	77.7	121
Both sexes.......	426	37.1	1148
Psychosis......	148	19.4	763
Psychopathy..	37	57.0	65
Oligophrenia...	241	75.0	320

* Source: T. Larsson and T. Sjögren, *A Methodological, Psychiatric, and Statistical Study of a Large Swedish Rural Population* ("Acta psychiatrica et neurologica Scandinavica," Suppl. 89 [Copenhagen, 1954]), p. 101, Table 22.

In 628 of the psychotic cases discovered in "AB:bo" the date of onset of the disease was definitely known. The distribution of these by age is given in Table 2 and is represented graphically in Figure 1, along with the age distribution of first admissions to hospital of the hospitalized group. The composition of the groups is obviously not identical, but the great majority are represented in both distributions. Figure 1 shows clearly the extent of the tendency for hospitalization to occur at a later age than the onset of the psychosis; note that the modal age of onset is between 20 and 24 years, while the mode for hospitalization falls in the age interval 35–39.

The records reveal that in only about one-third (37 per cent) of the cases did hospitalization take place during the same calendar year as the onset of the disease. In 3 years about two-thirds of the hospitalized cases were admitted, and in 6

TABLE 2*

DISTRIBUTION OF PSYCHOTIC CASES IN A RURAL SWEDISH AREA BY AGE AT ONSET OF PSYCHOSIS AND AT FIRST HOSPITALIZATION†

AGE	ONSET OF PSYCHOSIS		FIRST HOSPITAL- IZATION
	All Cases‡	Verified Cases Only§	
Under 14	13	13	3
15–19	54	49	21
20–24	102	82	54
25–29	71	68	61
30–34	88	79	74
35–39	78	70	80
40–44	63	47	56
45–49	68	55	56
50–54	66	47	53
55–59	58	43	50
60–64	43	30	39
65–69	27	20	31
70–74	19	13	19
75 and over	13	12	18
Total	763	628	615

* Source: T. Larsson and T. Sjögren, *A Methodological, Psychiatric, and Statistical Study of a Large Swedish Rural Population* ("Acta psychiatrica et neurologica Scandinavica," Suppl. 89 Copenhagen, 1954)), pp. 125–26, Tables 30 and 31.

† Does not include psychopathy.

‡ Includes all cases, including those in which age of onset was estimated.

§ Includes only those cases in which age at onset was verified.

per cent of the cases the interval was 20 years or more. The delay in hospitalization for the senile mental disorders tends to be somewhat less than the average because of the high age of onset and the rapid progress of the disease; that is, unless hospitalization is fairly early, the patient may die before being admitted.

The mean age at onset for the various diagnostic categories of this population were as follows:

	Age at Onset (Years)
Schizophrenia:	
Male	28.0
Female	31.8
Hebephrenia	23
Catatonic schizophrenia	35
Paranoid schizophrenia	46
Manic-depressive psychosis:	
Male	42.4
Female	40.4
Senile psychosis	70.5
Presenile psychosis	54.4

DIAGNOSIS

Of the 763 cases of psychosis identified over the 45-year period of the "AB:bo" study, 34.2 per cent were diagnosed as schizophrenia and 18.1 per cent as manic-depressive psychosis. Senile and presenile psychosis accounted for 14.9 per cent of the total. Other specified diagnoses were given in 18.1 per cent of the cases, and the remaining 14.7 per cent could not be diagnosed. These data emphasize the tremendous burden imposed by the single cluster of diseases known as schizophrenia. In 1951 it was estimated that, of all Swedish hospital beds for both somatic and mental illnesses, some 22 per cent were occupied by schizophrenic patients.

EXCESS MORTALITY

Various mental diseases affect future life-expectancy to markedly different extents but always unfavorably. In Table 3 the "AB:bo" data provide a basis for the estimates of these influences in Sweden; undoubtedly, these figures have considerably wider application. Here the relatively poor prognosis for senile psychosis is emphasized. Hospitalized or previously hospitalized male patients with this disease can expect on the average only 35 per cent of the number of years of life remaining to their age group. In general, psychosis appears to have a more severe effect for women than for men, and hospitalization as a consequence of psychosis seems to be an additional indication of further reduction in life-expectancy.

MORBIDITY RISK

The morbidity risk for a particular disease at any age may be defined as the percentage of the total population at this age affected by the disease. Thus the morbidity risk for disease *x* at age 30 in Sweden would be the percentage of all the 30-year-olds in the entire population of Sweden who had this particular disease. The *aggregate* morbidity risk for this disease would be the sum total of the morbidity risks of the disease for all ages. Note particularly that aggregate morbidity risk is *not* the percentage of people in a population affected by a disease but rather is the sum of the percentages of persons affected at each age.

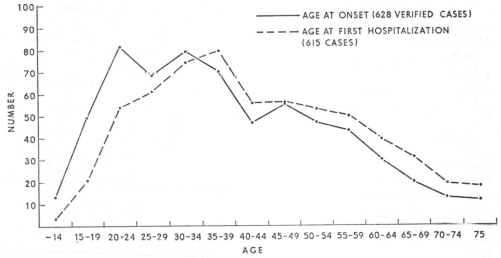

AGE AT ONSET (628 VERIFIED CASES)

AGE AT FIRST HOSPITALIZATION (615 CASES)

Fig. 1.—Distribution of psychotic cases in a rural Swedish area by age at onset of psychosis and at first hospitalization. (After T. Larsson and T. Sjögren, *A Methodological, Psychiatric, and Statistical Study of a Large Swedish Rural Population* ["Acta psychiatrica et neurologica scandinavica," Suppl. 89 (Copenhagen, 1954)], pp. 125–26, 160, Tables 30 and 31.)

TABLE 3*

LIFE-EXPECTANCY FOR PSYCHOSIS AND OLIGOPHRENIA, SWEDEN

	REMAINING MEAN EXPECTATION OF LIFE AS A PERCENTAGE OF THAT FOR THE GENERAL POPULATION, 1900-1944			
MAIN DIAGNOSIS	All Affected and Previously Affected Cases		All Hospitalized and Previously Hospitalized Cases	
	Male	Female	Male	Female
Schizophrenia	72	63	68	54
Manic-depressive psychosis	95	91	88	75
Senile psychosis	50	60	35	45
Presenile psychosis	60	67	52	63
Psychosis: all forms	71	67	66	57
Low-grade oligophrenia	70	70	60	60

* Source: T. Larsson and T. Sjögren, *A Methodological, Psychiatric, and Statistical Study of a Large Swedish Rural Population* ("Acta psychiatrica et neurologica Scandinavica," Suppl. 89 [Copenhagen, 1954]), p. 179, Table 44.

In the "AB:bo" study aggregate morbidity risks were calculated for various mental disorders. For the purposes of the study the calculations were based only upon data up to and including age 80, and various corrections were applied to minimize the effects of incompleteness of data and lateness in registration. The results of these calculations are as follows:

	Per Cent
Schizophrenia	1.6
Manic-depressive psychosis:	
Male	0.9
Female	1.2
Presenile psychosis:	
Male	0.7
Female	1.0
Senile psychosis:	
Male	0.6
Female	0.8

Since the aggregate morbidity risks are not based upon ages over 80, the estimates for senile psychosis are necessarily less stable than are the others. The aggregate morbidity risks for all forms of psychosis are estimated to be 4.7 per cent for men and 5.7 per cent for women. Larsson and Sjögren believe that, because of the difficulty in securing absolutely complete data, these estimates are, if anything, too low. They feel that the risk is more likely to be 5 per cent for males and 6 per cent for women than any lesser figure.

ASSESSMENT OF PREVALENCE OF
PSYCHOSES IN SWEDEN

With the knowledge gained in the "AB:bo" study about morbidity risk and excess mortality in relation to psychoses, it was possible to make estimates about the prevalence of mental disease in Sweden. Since population projections were available, future predictions as well as estimates for the past could be made. These figures for the years 1945 and 1965 are given in Table 4.

This table reveals the almost staggering problem mental illness presents, and there is no reason to believe that it is unique to Sweden. We see that the estimate of the number of persons affected or previously affected by psychosis at the end of 1945 was 90,000 and that by 1965 this number is expected to increase to 108,000. When one takes into account the fact that this is for a population of between 7 and 8 million people, one can imagine the extent of the problem in the United States with a population well over twenty times that of Sweden.

TABLE 4*

ESTIMATED NUMBER OF PERSONS WITH PSYCHOSIS OR PREVIOUSLY AFFECTED
WITH PSYCHOSIS IN SWEDEN, 1945 AND 1965
(In Thousands)

MAIN DIAGNOSIS	CALCULATED NO. OF AFFECTED AND PREVIOUSLY AFFECTED PERSONS IN TOTAL SWEDISH POPULATION AT END OF YEAR					
	1945			1965		
	Men	Women	Both Sexes	Men	Women	Both Sexes
Schizophrenia	21	18	39	24	20	44
Manic-depressive psychosis	8	14	22	10	17	27
Senile and presenile psychosis	3	6	9	5	8	13
Other psychoses	10	10	20	12	12	24
All psychoses	42	48	90	51	57	108

* Source: T. Larsson and T. Sjögren, *A Methodological, Psychiatric, and Statistical Study of a Large Swedish Rural Population* ("Acta psychiatrica et neurologica Scandinavica," Suppl. 89 [Copenhagen, 1954]), p. 210.

MENTAL HEALTH NEEDS IN SWEDEN

Larsson and Sjögren are quick to point out the implications of their findings for Sweden. They admit that their calculations are in many respects uncertain and that their predictions may be influenced by as yet unknown trends and factors (e.g., increased inland migration, urbanization, industrialization, etc.). Nevertheless, they believe that their findings "clearly show the extensive problems in this field that will confront the public health authorities, and the great demands that must be made for a rapid extension of accommodation for the mentally diseased and the mentally deficient."[3]

No specific mention is made of the increasing pressure exerted by the mounting numbers of the aged in this aggregate of the mentally ill, but Hagnell documents well the increasing importance of this aspect of the problem.[4]

[3] *Ibid.*, p. 211.

[4] O. Hagnell, "Psykoser hos äldre människor, ett växande psykiatriskt problem" ("Psychosis in the Aged, an Increasing Psychiatric Problem"), *Nord. med.*, 51 (1954), 737–42.

6

A District Mental Health Service[1]

Now being carried out in a town on the Sussex coast is an experimental attempt at demonstrating a superior way of meeting the problem of hospital overcrowding by use of an intensive outpatient service which has special implications for the aged mentally ill. Carse, Panton, and Watt, the authors of the first report on this study, point out that for more than a century therapeutic emphasis has been upon treatment of the mental patient in hospital. Until 1930 in Great Britain there were few outpatient clinics, and little encouragement existed for early treatment. "Even today [1958]," they say, "for the great majority of mentally ill patients, treatment still means admission to mental hospital."[2]

Recognizing the full importance of the problem of overcrowding, they dismiss the possibility of its solution by the building of new hospitals not only because of tremendous construction and operating costs but also because the difficulties in staffing new institutions would be too great. Their solution calls for great expansion of outpatient treatment facilities, and the apparently successful experiment at Worthing supports the validity of their claims. This experiment, designed as a 2-year pilot study, began on January 1, 1957. The following report is based upon the experience of the first 10 months.

Worthing is a Sussex coastal resort town of about 70,000 population, located some 60 miles south of London. The experimental catchment district extended over a semicircular area radiating between 8 and 9 miles from the clinic center and including in its boundaries approximately 160,000 people. This district is served by Graylingwell Hospital, and the Worthing unit was set up as an experimental outpatient and domiciliary treatment facility of that hospital. Worthing is located 22 miles from the parent institution—a deliberately chosen factor in the experimental situation in order to test the practicability of providing "psychiatric treatment for large numbers of patients without the immediate availability of the resources of a modern mental hospital."

All patients of the unit were referred by the family physician excepting a few patients who were directed by the courts to attend. All admissions to Graylingwell from the Worthing catchment area were screened by the unit. The population of this region is varied and contains one of the highest percentages of aged people in England and Wales.

STAFF

The twenty-bed unit served as an active treatment center and day hospital. There were no resident patients. On the staff were three psychiatrists (two full time and one part time), a trained psychiatric nurse, two staff nurses, two ward orderlies, an occupational therapist, a medical secretary, and a clerical helper, plus some additional per-

[1] This account was prepared by Robert W. Kleemeier, professor of psychology, Washington University, St. Louis, Mo.

[2] J. Carse, N. E. Panton, and A. Watt, "A District Mental Health Service: The Worthing Experiment," *Lancet,* January 4, 1958, pp. 39–41.

sonnel from Graylingwell. Social work was done by a psychiatric social worker and a hospital almoner.

PATIENTS

During the first 10 months, 1192 patients (376 male and 816 female) were seen; of these, 318 were 65 years or older. The psychiatric outpatient clinic of the general hospital was included in the service, thereby strengthening the relationship with local general practitioners—a relationship necessary for the success of the scheme.

1957 the admissions from the catchment area served by the Worthing unit decreased by 324, a drop of 59 per cent, while admissions from a control area, similar in size and composition of population, increased by 4 per cent.

As might be expected, the Worthing service appears to have a greater effect upon admissions to the short-stay unit at Summersdale than to the main hospital, Graylingwell. This was anticipated because it had been thought that many of the recoverable patients being sent to Summers-

TADLE 1*

ADMISSIONS TO GRAYLINGWELL HOSPITAL AND SUMMERSDALE HOSPITAL

ADMISSIONS	YEAR		DIFFERENCE
	1956	1957	
From catchment area served by Worthing service......	548	224	−324 (−59%)
From catchment area *not* served by Worthing service...	603	626	+ 23 (+4%)
Total..	1151	850	−301 (−26%)

* Source: J. Carse, N. E. Panton, and A. Watt, "A District Mental Health Service: The Worthing Experiment," *Lancet*, January 4, 1958, pp. 39–41, Table I.

TREATMENT

Over a thousand domiciliary visits were made by the unit's psychiatrists to 432 patients during the period of report. The social workers assisted here to sort out the problems presented by these patients. Each patient received a thorough physical examination. Psychiatric treatment included extensive use of electroconvulsant therapy and some modified insulin therapy, while, for many, psychotherapy was the main treatment. The latter was given individually or in a weekly group psychotherapy session. No patient fees were charged.

EFFECT ON HOSPITAL ADMISSION

In Table 1 the effect of this experimental effort at Worthing on admissions to Graylingwell and Summersdale hospitals is shown. Summersdale is a short-stay subsidiary hospital for Graylingwell. During

dale could indeed forego hospitalization, provided other help were available. What was surprising to the investigators, however, was the 40 per cent drop in admissions to Graylingwell, because cases admitted there were usually intractable. As is indicated in Table 2, a greater percentage reduction was experienced for women than for men.

The reduction in admissions from the Worthing area was somewhat less for aged patients than for the total for all age groups, although here, too, it was substantial, as may be seen in Table 3. With advanced age, beyond 75, the reduction seems least; but, nevertheless, even for this age group, the 1957 admissions were less than two-thirds of those in the corresponding 1956 period. Elderly patients (those between ages 65 and 75) are quite reluctant to enter the mental hospital, and for these the Worthing service was particularly well suited. The authors take a cautious attitude, however, concerning the results with older patients; for, although the reduction in admissions was maintained for the full 10 months covered in the report, marked fluctuations in the admission of senile patients may be expected.

OBSERVATIONS

The investigators believe that hospitalization is unnecessary for a large proportion of patients now being admitted to mental hospitals and that these persons may be treated successfully as outpatients. While

to it. It is seen "as a hospital for selected patients, mostly with good prognosis, but needing special treatment and conditions which cannot be provided by an outpatient service."

Good public relations are viewed as a basic requirement for the successful outpatient service; in Worthing the public had been prepared through various educational and publicity media for a number of years before the establishment of the service. This groundwork had also in large measure dissipated the fear of Graylingwell, for, in 1956, 85 per cent of new admissions to this

TABLE 2*

ANALYSIS OF ADMISSIONS FROM WORTHING AREA

YEAR	GRAYLINGWELL HOSPITAL			SUMMERSDALE HOSPITAL			TOTAL		
	Male	Female	Total	Male	Female	Total	Male	Female	Total
1956.............	108	152	260	69	219	288	177	371	548
1957.............	69	88	157	22	45	67	91	133	224
Reduction......	39	64	103	47	174	221	86	238	324
Per cent reduction........	36	42	40	68	79	77	49	64	59

* Source: J. Carse, N. E. Panton, and A. Watt, "A District Mental Health Service: The Worthing Experiment," *Lancet*, January 4, 1958, pp. 39–41, Table II.

TABLE 3*

ADMISSIONS AMONG ELDERLY PATIENTS

AGE	YEAR		DIFFERENCE
	1956	1957	
65–69.......	57	20	$-37\brace-18$ −55 (−51.4%)
70–74.......	50	32	
75–79.......	31	18	$-13\brace-11$ −24 (−38.7%)
80 and over.	31	20	
Total.....	169	90	−79 (−46.9%)

* Source: J. Carse, N. E. Panton, and A. Watt, "A District Mental Health Service: The Worthing Experiment," *Lancet*, January 4, 1958, pp. 39–41, Table III.

the mental hospital is not considered as being outmoded, it is believed to have a more limited function than is now assigned

hospital were either non-statutory or voluntary, a figure above the national average.

IMPLICATIONS

The implications of the Worthing experiment are not being disregarded by either the politicians or the public. British attitudes toward mental health are in flux, and traditional methods in dealing with the problem of mental illness are subject to criticism and widespread change is inevitable. Dr. Donald McI. Johnson, Member of Parliament for Carlisle, says that the improper admission of patients is one of the greatest problems confronting mental hospitals today.[3] Though always legally

[3] Donald McI. Johnson, "New Deal Lies Ahead for Mentally Sick," *Bristol Evening Post*, February 5, 1958, p. 2.

correct, he charges that in too many cases the basis for hospitalization is medically and psychiatrically unsound. He supports his argument by referring to the Amsterdam system and the Worthing experiment. General adoption of similar services throughout Britain, he believes, would save upward of $28 million (£10 million) annually and would produce vastly superior therapeutic results than are at present obtained. Unquestionably, much can be learned by observing the steps taken in Great Britain during this period of critical self-examination and change.

7

A Case Study of Family Relations

The following case is typical of the well-to-do bourgeoisie, professional, Catholic family in which familial ties are very strong. The same type of relations would be found in the upper middle class. They are, however, more extensive in the upper-upper-class family. The frequency and solidarity of these relations are conditioned by residential proximity. But in France, where geographical mobility is not nearly so extensive as in the United States, neighborhood proximity is less rare. Children intermarry and live in the same city as the parents. With important economic aid of the grandparents, vacations are very often taken together by three generations. For example, the grandparents own or rent a villa on the seashore or in the mountains.

Residence of the family is in a French city of 100,000 inhabitants 150 miles from Paris. It has machine and textile industry and is quite prosperous.

THE GRANDFATHER

The grandfather is 61 years of age.

Occupation. He is a non-specialist physician in general medical practice, with the responsibility for hospital service, to which he devotes his mornings. He receives patients at his home 5 days a week from 2:00 to 5:00 P.M. and afterward makes home visits to 8:00 P.M.

Economic level. His professional income is about $10,000 a year, to which is added a certain income (about $4000) derived

[1] This account was prepared by Dr. Jean-René Tréanton, Centre National de la Recherche Scientifique, Paris.

from his investments. These are constituted in large part of the estate which he inherited from his father.

Of this $14,000, he expends about $6000 and invests the remainder in stocks.

Social status. He belongs to the first rank of the "professionals" of his city, who confer on him numerous honorific duties and consider him as the moral leader of doctors not only of the city but of the country.

His type of life and the esteem which he enjoys are characteristic of the upper middle class. The upper-upper class in the city is constituted of about fifty industrial families who have very considerable income and form a quite closed circle.

Hobbies. He buys books (especially literary ones); follows daily the transactions of the stock exchange; listens to the radio a little; sees a movie once a year; purchases some "long-playing" records; participates in several learned societies (medical and literary); and travels to the French provinces one month each year but never in foreign countries.

THE GRANDMOTHER

The grandmother is 54 years of age. Her social origin is in a Parisian social milieu of an older and more refined bourgeoisie than her husband's. She is interested in fashions, in beautiful furniture, in the latest novel, and in the current plays in Parisian theaters. She has little use for social life. She spends her days at home, where she manages her household (having one servant). She goes to Paris once every week, where she sees her mother (82 years old), her sister, and the members of the family who live in Paris.

RELATIONS WITH CHILDREN

There are four children: a daughter Madeleine, 28 (married); a son Jacques, 26 (married); a daughter Helene, 24 (married); and a son Henri, 21 (unmarried).

THE CHILDREN

The two daughters attended high school before their marriage but do not have an occupation apart from marriage. The son Jacques pursues his highly specialized medical studies; the son Henri, the science of agriculture. During their childhood they spent one month each year during the summer at the seashore. The grandparents have offered them several trips outside France. Each of them equally had the opportunity of spending 15 days nearly every year in the mountains during the winter in order to ski.

The youngest child, Henri, is still entirely supported by his parents, who take care of his expenses at the technical college. They offer him a trip during the summer vacation and 15 days in the mountains in winter. They give him about $30 a month for his personal expenses. For the last 3 years he has made his internship on a large farm, where he is learning practical agriculture. He has saved about $100. His great ambition is to own an automobile, provided his father helps him out. He hopes to get it now that he has completed his 2 years of military service, which expired at the beginning of 1960.

The three married children are no longer supported by their parents. There is an exchange of presents at Christmas and certain holidays and anniversaries. The presents given by the parents are generally a little more valuable than those which they receive from the children.

There is one exception to this general picture. The son Jacques, who pursues his medical studies and who has been recently married, is lodged free by his parents in a small apartment which they own in Paris.

RELATIONS WITH THE GRANDCHILDREN

Only the older daughter, Madeleine, has children: one boy of 8 years, Remy; a daughter of 5 years, Martine; and a son of 2 years, Gerard. They live a short distance from the grandparents in the same city two blocks away. Also the relations between the grandparents and the grandchildren are very frequent. Some of the examples are:

1. Mutual visits are exchanged at least once every day. Generally, the grandchildren come to see the grandparents at the close of the elementary school. Very often one of the two older children remains to take lunch with the grandparents.

2. When one of the children is ill, the two others live with the grandparents to avoid contagion.

3. The grandchildren are entirely taken in charge by the grandparents if the parents go on a trip or out for the evening.

4. Almost every Sunday there is the family meal, which brings the three generations together at the home of the grandparents. After lunch the grandparents generally take the grandchildren and their mother out for a walk. The father takes advantage of this to play golf or to remain at home to read or work.

5. During the summer vacation the grandparents take the grandchildren several times to the seashore or the mountains, thus giving their children their freedom. At other times they rent a villa in common, and the three generations spend the vacation together.

The ties of affection between the grandparents and the grandchildren are very strong. The grandparents play an essential role in the socialization of the grandchildren (e.g., reading out loud or explaining the "comics" or telling them stories). The grandchildren have the tendency to consider the house of their grandparents as their real dwelling and their preferred home.

THE GREAT-GRANDMOTHER

The great-grandmother (82 years), mother of the grandmother, lives in Paris but visits her daughter every 2 months. She remains almost 3 weeks (so much that in the course of a year she lives with her daughter about 15–18 weeks). She spends with them equally the greater part of the summer vacation. During the remainder of the year her daughter will visit her at least once a week and often takes one or two of the great-grandchildren with her. The great-grandmother gives them numerous presents. The ties of affection between them are very strong, although the great-grandchildren have a tendency to consider her as "terribly old."

OTHER RELATIVES

The great-grandmother has two other children, a daughter, Anne (57 years), married, without children, and a son, Pierre (47 years), who has six children between 6 and 18 years of age.

Relations with Anne. Anne lives in Paris, some 500 feet from the great-grandmother. Anne would like to move to the outskirts of the city, but she has decided not to do so as long as her mother is alive. They meet every day, Anne having her mother over for dinner or for lunch at least once a week. As Anne has a car, she is often ordered by her mother to bring her to the center of the city to do some shopping, which is the favorite diversion of this old lady. Anne generally tries to escape it, and this is one of the subjects of complaint by her mother.

Relations with Pierre. The great-grandmother spends practically all Sundays at Pierre's house when she is in Paris. The daughter-in-law complains a little that the responsibility of carrying on the conversation with the great-grandmother is entirely hers and is not shared by Pierre, who is accustomed to escape. The grandchildren slip away too. The great-grandmother greatly enjoys giving them lessons in education or in speaking of their "beaus" with the two elder granddaughters.

Another very important person in the great-grandmother's life is her brother (76 years). They meet at least twice during the week (one being a lunch at his home). A wealthy retired executive, he helps her financially with some small gifts. His health is not very good, and, certainly, his death would deeply affect her.

The great-grandmother was completely ruined financially in 1930 by a dishonest broker. Since that time, she has lived on a small pension given her by her three children.

Except for her health (bad legs and high arterial tension), she is well adjusted: very talkative, always busy with problems of hats and dresses, not at all religious but very fearful of leaving this good world. Her daughters consider her "childish"; they joke about her taste for reading love stories. She reads a great deal or listens to the radio when alone, but she is rarely alone.

8

The Three-Generation Rural Family in Italy[1]

In the twelve rural villages in Abruzzia the three-generation family is the rule. The old people never live alone in the house. Usually the oldest son, his wife, and his children live with them. Sometimes the old parents prefer to live with a daughter and her husband.

The living-together of the generations is economical. The old women in one of the twelve villages make the ancient *ricamo* and *merletto,* which is very fine embroidery work. In wintertime this work of the grandmother is almost the only economic resource of the family. This fact is very important, since it gives the grandmother a significant economic role in the family.

When the young couple is working in the fields, the grandmother keeps house. The grandparents take care of the children. They are more strict with them than the parents. Obedience and reverence for the grandparents are general. One of their rules is that of educators of the grandchildren. The grandmother is accustomed to help the grandchildren with their homework.

It is natural to have the old people at home. They do not constitute a problem. Sometimes we find only old people and their grandchildren in the household. The mother and father will be elsewhere in Italy or in other countries.

At times the old father-in-law lives alone because it is hard for him to keep in accord with the daughter-in-law. In this case the daughters-in-law take turns in caring for

him. Such a situation often is a subject for discussion in the community. The people are divided between those who say that it is wrong and those who say that it is right.

In case of sickness the old people are well attended. The community is likely to criticize a daughter-in-law who does not take good care of her father-in-law and mother-in-law.

When old people are sick, the relatives do not call the doctor, because they are convinced that the doctor can do nothing for old people. The old people are always kept in the home of one of the children— sometimes one of the daughters if they feel that they are better looked after by daughters than by daughters-in-law.

The old women are counselors in matters of maternity, cooking, medicine, and clothes. People are often afraid of the power of their chatter. For many hours of the day they sit in front of the houses on the village square commenting on and controlling every event.

The old people are very influential even if they are poor and propertyless. People go to them to find a mediator in case of fights. Old people are deeply respected.

There are fifteen residents in the home for old people in this area. They are all without families. There is no one living there who has family or relatives to care for him. In nearly every case this situation is a result of emigration of the adult children.

One village woman took an old blind woman into her home when she became too

[1] This account was prepared by Miss Angela Zuccino, dean, School of Social Work, Rome, Italy.

frail to work or to care for herself. The latter had no one left of her family. She has been there now for over a year. She is bedbound. The daughters in the family keep her bed clean. They gave her their own room when she came. It would never occur to them to resent in any way her being taken into their home. They treat her with great respect.

Today changes are taking place in the villages. Old people are much more connected with the church than are their children. Young people go to church more indifferently. The young generation does not buy books. The books in the home belong to the old generation. Social security is changing the role of old people and their relationship with their children.

Relations with Their Children of Parents in an Old People's Home[1]

Miss Margrit Kessl, of the School of Social Work in Zurich, has made a study of the relations with their children of parents living in an old people's home in Switzerland. Interviews revealed that with nearly all of them some kind of relation was maintained, especially through mutual visits. Less often were letters exchanged, common trips undertaken, or any kind of services provided. Most parents received presents now and then from their children, while it was seldom possible for them to give their children presents, since as a rule they had only limited pocket money.

Family relationships were differently assessed by those questioned. Barely a half described them as "good." The remainder characterized them as "average" or "bad." The answers of the old and the young did not always agree. It appeared that external factors (such as social class, dwelling accommodations, the distance from the residence to the old people's home, or the state of health on both sides) were not primary for good, indifferent, and bad relations. The attitudes to one another of parents, children, and grandchildren counted far more.

In particular, the attitudes of the parents to their entrance into the old people's home influence the mutual relations. The old people report the relation to their children as good only if they have reconciled themselves to living in the old people's

home. Others are embittered not to be able to live with a son or daughter. Even if this were attempted, it might lead to unfortunate results on both sides. It strikes many parents as unnatural not to live with the child. For this most of them blame the in-law child. The old generation grew up in the period when the three-generation family was the norm. The loss of the functions of the family through industrialization and individualization resulted in the family's becoming smaller. In the small family there was seldom any room for relatives of the married pair. Or, if so, living together led to constant irritations. Numerous old men could not keep step with this change and therefore suffer under the present conditions, which they can recognize only as a personal fate and not as social change.

Where the children do not report the relation as good, the cause is overwhelmingly to be discovered that in childhood or youth they experienced too little parental love. This clearly was expressed in several cases. Nevertheless, they worry about their progenitors because of feelings of their duty. Yet very few of these would take the father or mother to live with them.

It is questionable how one can help the old people who are unhappy in the old people's home because they feel rejected by their children. A realistic influencing of their attitudes can scarcely be possible. Yet a regular hearing of their grief by a volunteer helper can somewhat mitigate the bitterness of the feeling.

[1] This account has been translated from *Pro senectute*, **36** (June, 1958), 52–54.

10

Duty of Children To Support Parents[1]

FRANCE

According to Article 205 of the Civil Code of 1804, as amended by the law of March 9, 1891, "the children owe support to their father and mother as well as to other ascendants who are in need of support."

Under Section 206 of the Code, as amended by the law of August 9, 1919, a duty of support is also incumbent upon a son-in-law and a daughter-in-law as against a father-in-law or a mother-in-law.

WEST GERMANY

Under Sections 1601 *et seq.* of the Civil Code of 1896, mutual duties of support exist between relatives in the ascending and descending line. A person is therefore under a duty to furnish support to his father, his mother, his grandfather, his grandmother, and also to more remote ascendants if they are in need of such support.

GREAT BRITAIN

Under the common law of England children are under no duty to provide support for their parents. A limited duty was established, however, under the poor laws, the latest version of which was contained in the Poor Law Act, 1930 (c. 17), Section 14. This law was repealed by the National Assistance Act, 1948, Sixth Schedule, paragraph 19(1). By Section 42 of the National Assistance Act, 1948, duties of support are incumbent only upon a husband as against his wife, upon a wife as against her husband, and upon both a man and a woman as against their children.

ITALY

Under the Civil Code of 1942, Section 433, a person in need has the right to be supported by his legitimate or legitimated children or, if they are dead, by his more remote descendants. Under the same section mutual rights and duties of support also exist between son-in-law and daughter-in-law, on the one side, and father-in-law and mother-in-law, on the other side.

NETHERLANDS

Under the Civil Code of 1836, Article 376, "the children are under the duty to provide support to their parents and their ascendants in more remote degrees whenever such persons are in need of support." Article 377 provides a duty to support a person's father-in-law and mother-in-law.[2]

SWEDEN

Under the Law on Family Relations (*Föraldrabalken*), Chapter 7, Article 3, children are under a duty to provide support for their parents. Under Chapter 3 of the Law on Public Assistance, children are also under a duty to reimburse the assistance authorities for support furnished their parents.

---

[1] This account was prepared by Dr. Max Rheinstein, Max Pam Professor of Law, University of Chicago.

[2] [The duty of grandchildren to support grandparents is in process of being repealed.—EDITOR.]

11

Clubs for Older People in an English Community

Throughout the ages people of like tastes have met together to enjoy discussion of subjects of mutual interest and to exchange ideas, for example, in monasteries, medieval guilds, coffeehouses, political clubs and, in this century, townswomen's clubs, women's institutes, and the like. Since the second World War, sponsored mainly by such voluntary bodies as old people's welfare committees, women's voluntary services, the British Red Cross Society, and many churches, there has been a rapid and nation-wide development of clubs for the elderly. Some of these clubs meet once weekly, some meet twice a week, and some are open every day. Some meet in church halls, some in village halls, some in buildings specially designed to suit their special needs—with a kitchen, toilet facilities, a stage, and a hall—and some in a room in a private home. The clubs usually meet from 2:00 to 4:30 P.M.

MEMBERS

Members of these clubs join sometimes at 60 years of age, but more often at 65.

[1] This is a description of the clubs for older people sponsored by the Old People's Welfare Committee of Chislehurst and Sidcup in Kent, on the outskirts of Greater London. There are twelve clubs, with the following names: Sunshine Club, Cosy Club, Good Companions, Jolly Rogers, Albany Park Over 60 Club, Home from Home Club, Merry and Bright Club, Gay Venture Club, Happy Wanderers, Friendly Club, Rodney Club, and Rest Awhile Club.

This account was prepared by Miss Bertha James, chairman of the Northwest Kent Old People's Welfare Committee and of the Homes, Housing and Home Services Committee of the National Old People's Welfare Council.

There are many members well over 80 years of age and a few over 90. Most of the members come from the lower-income group, with a few retired clerical workers. To the best of my knowledge, no retired member of any of the professions is a member of any of our clubs. Women members greatly outnumber the men in all clubs.

LEADERS

The majority of club leaders are middle-aged married women whose children have left school and who find themselves with more leisure time. A few of the helpers are younger married women with children in school. A few retired single women are glad to interest themselves in this work.

FINANCE

The clubs are self-supporting. Rents vary very much indeed. Some clubs pay only 2s. a week; some, 7s. 6d.; and one club, a guinea a week. The club funds are raised by (1) a weekly subscription—mostly 4d., or 3d., including tea and a cake or bread and butter; (2) raffles; and (3) a "Bring-and-Buy Sale" once or twice a year, when members sew and knit, bake cakes, and make jam for the stalls at the sale (sometimes these sales are opened by some well-known man or woman in the district).

Once a year each club receives a proportion (about £4) of a grant made to the Old People's Welfare Committee by the Borough Council from the Sunday Cinema Fund. Some clubs receive a few annual donations or gifts in kind from individuals, local organizations, or tradesmen.

ACTIVITIES

All clubs arrange a number of outings during the year—to the sea, to churches, to cathedrals, to beauty spots, to historic houses, to factories, etc. All clubs have a Christmas party, a carol service, an Easter service, and a harvest festival. Most clubs have a minister of religion who interests himself in their activities. Many clubs have a charity in which they interest themselves —such as the blind or deprived children. Some clubs have a concert party which goes round to hospitals and homes and entertains the patients. Many clubs have film shows provided by British railways or coach companies or private individuals. All clubs greatly enjoy entertaining visitors from overseas. Most clubs play dominoes, checkers, darts, and whist and other card games. One club issues, and sells for 2*d.*, a quarterly newssheet which gives items of interest about members and helpers and club activities generally. This is particularly appreciated by club members when they are too frail to attend regular weekly meetings. Some club members regularly visit sick members in hospitals. Some clubs enjoy learning to make baskets. The club leaders, week by week, listen to many stories of difficulties, often connected with housing and health, and their practical help and advice in these matters are greatly appreciated. Many clubs receive gifts of clothes, dishes, and furniture. These are usually sold, for very small sums, to members for the benefit of the club. Some clubs have members represented on a committee. Many club members belong to two or even more clubs. Three members from one club served as models for the girls' grammar school, and one modeled for the art school. Of course the tea provided by the helpers is greatly enjoyed at every club meeting, and teatime is the highlight of the afternoon.

INTERCLUB EVENTS

A number of interclub events—bulb shows, luncheons, holiday trips, etc.—are held each year.

Bulb show.—The clubs plant daffodils, hyacinths, crocuses, tulips, scillas, etc., every autumn, and an interclub bulb competition is held each February. Five challenge cups have been given for this event, and about thirty prizes are awarded annually in a number of different classes.

Luncheons.—Six members of each club are invited to a luncheon in the Civil Defense Hall in Sidcup about four times a year. The meal is prepared by helpers, and members pay 2*s.* each. There is always a speaker, and slides are often shown. This is one of the more recent activities and is rapidly growing in popularity.

Holidays.—Holiday schemes have been operating for some 9 years now. Members are received in hotels in May and October at reduced prices, and transport by coach is provided. Last year a most successful holiday was arranged at Pitlochy in the Highlands of Scotland. At least one club helper accompanies each party.

Adult education.—Through the co-operation of the Kent Education Committee, for the last 3 years about forty club members (drawn from all clubs) have attended a course of four afternoon lectures in the warm and comfortable library of the Adult Education Centre at Lamorbey Park. The subjects have been local history, national history, historic homes, and the appreciation of music. A coach picks up members at various points in the district and drives them to and from Lamorbey. The members pay 6*d.* each, and the committee meets the balance of the cost. Last year—and again this year—three prizes were awarded for the three best essays on the course. After the course, a visit was made to Canterbury Cathedral the first year, to Haslemere Museum the second year, and to Ightham Mote and Penshurst Place last year.

Handicrafts.—An interclub handicraft competition, including classes for sewing, knitting, crocheting, embroidering, painting, basketry, woodworking, etc., is held every autumn. Two challenge trophies have now been presented for this event.

Church service.—Last year a service was

held in Canterbury Cathedral which was attended by some two hundred of our club members.

THE FUTURE

During the last years certain trends have been noticeable. Wider and newer interests have been aroused—a greater willingness to travel and to try new activities. A greater wish to play a part in the life of the community has been observed. A loyalty to their clubs is most noticeable in members.

One wonders what people of 50 and 55 years of age today will expect in their clubs in 10 years' time. What part will club leaders play then? Is there need for further development in these clubs for the elderly, which are now a part of the national life? Should or could members participate more themselves? Should we provide more opportunities for them to do so? Should we be content with, very often, our drab premises? Is there room for a greater variety of clubs to cater for different tastes and interests so that members could use their gifts and talents? What part could further education committees play in providing courses for some club members?

12

Clubs for Older People in the Netherlands[1]

Old people's clubs may be originated both by church organizations and by non-church societies. There is no standardized club organization or program, though there are similarities among the various clubs. The larger church denominations in the Netherlands each has an old people's organization which organizes clubs as well as other programs for older church members.

The Catholics have the Union of Diocesan Associations of Old People, with a membership of 40,000. Fees are 25 Dutch cents a month for a single person and 40 cents for a married couple. Besides clubs, the associations organize retreats, stimulate mutual visits by older people to support each other spiritually, and give advice on pensions and financial problems.

Thus the club is only one of the activities of an association, but it also is the focal point of many of the other activities. The Catholic clubs number about 350, with an average attendance at a club meeting of 50. The members are mostly from lower-middle and working classes. They are now attempting to reach upper-middle-class people. Membership is generally accepted at age 60. While the local branches of the diocesan associations are run by the older people themselves, leadership in the clubs is generally exercised by members of the Catholic women's organizations.

[1] This account was prepared by Dr. Robert J. van Zonneveld, of the National Health Research Council in The Hague, Netherlands. Dr. van Zonneveld has made medicosocial studies of older people and is a leader in the field of gerontology in the Netherlands. Since the majority of old people's clubs in the Netherlands are sponsored by churches, these have been described by him.

The clubs are financed by dues from the members and by a subsidy from the local municipal government and occasionally from the church organization or from trade and industrial organizations.

A LOCAL CATHOLIC PROGRAM

At The Hague, with 610,000 inhabitants, about a third of whom are Catholic, the Catholic Union of Diocesan Associations of Old People has 23 clubs, with about 1400 members. Women may join at age 60; men, at 65. The members are mainly working-class people.

In one particular club the leader is a woman of about 60, assisted by six young married women who are childless. She prefers such women, since they have more spare time and are less tied down than women with children.

This club meets two afternoons a week. Many members arrive at noon, while officially the club meeting starts at two o'clock or even later, because they can save coal then by not using their stoves. The meeting place is in a building of the Catholic church. Other clubs meet in a youth clubhouse or in a parish house. Attendance of this specific club is about 100 at a time. They pay 10 Dutch cents each time they come, for which they get three cups of coffee, tea, or chocolate and a biscuit or a sweet. (The minimum income, the state pension, to which, with some minor exceptions, every aged citizen is entitled, is 1584 Dutch florin a year for a couple and 972 florin for a single person.) The costs for rent of the clubroom, light, heating, and other expenses are partly met by a subsidy from the local welfare department, which contributes 10 cents for each attendant. Therefore, all who attend have to sign an attendance list. Sometimes the pastor of the parish makes some money available when there is a deficit. The work of the men and women who are doing handicrafts at home (though the material is given by the club) is on display at a show from time to time, and, if the aged want these to be sold, the profits go to the Association of Old People in case it provided the material.

In this club (as well as in the other 33) the activities are mostly restricted to chatting; playing cards, chess, dominoes, checkers, or shuffleboard; knitting or embroidering by women; preparation for the annual one-day trip; some festivities; a show; occasional visits to sick colleagues; etc. The leaders have tried several times to introduce more cultural activities, but mostly the members are not much interested. They like to say, "We are here for our pleasure, not to learn anything or to be really active." At carnival time the people dress themselves up a little. Sometimes there is a motion picture or popular music by an accordionist.

Classical music and cultural films, however, are in general not much liked. Many old people want to talk with the leader about personal difficulties. The old people do not assist much in serving tea, collecting fees, etc. Nor do they lead the club, as this would often cause jealousy or misunderstandings. There are some magazines on display; generally, the members look a little at the pictures, but, if they want to read the articles, they take them to their own homes.

An attempt was made to organize a meals-on-wheels service, but there was strong opposition to this idea. A beginning has been made to visit occasionally an ill colleague or leader, and also occasionally one old woman goes once a week to another old woman to help her with the housekeeping. The leaders also visit the sick old people.

The oldest Catholic club has existed for 12 years, and the organization of clubs started about 1950.

OTHER CLUB PROGRAMS

In the Protestant sector there are now at least 550 clubs, with an average membership of 30. The local clubs are more the result of local initiative by churches and less the result of a co-ordinated movement. Meeting places for the clubs are clubrooms, village centers, vestries, or, occasionally, schoolrooms. The club members are mainly working-class people. The leaders are mostly women (occasionally men) of middle age or younger. Exceptionally, the leader is an older person.

The finances come from the sponsoring churches and from the members (who each pays 10–25 cents a time) and often again from subsidies by the local welfare authorities on a fifty-fifty basis. In general, the club activities are of a simple character, consisting mostly of recreational activities. At some places—as a rule, in the larger cities, though sometimes also in rural areas—more cultural activities are incorporated into the program. This depends on the availability of expert assistance and experience. Thus there are some programs going on in which old people meet in a well-equipped educational center and co-operate actively in setting up well-defined club programs. The latter activities are financed both by member contributions and by subsidies. The tendency is to develop such programs.

So again one can say that, though the general lines along which the clubs of old people in the Netherlands are developing are more or less the same and that at the moment these are still rather simple, there may exist considerable difference among the programs of geographically or denominationally closely allied clubs.

13

The Nuffield Foundation and the Study of Aging[1]

The Nuffield Foundation has taken a continuous and intensive interest in the problems of the old since its inception in 1943. Indeed, "the care and the comfort of the aged poor" is specifically prescribed by its trust deed. This phrase has the ring of orthodox Victorian philanthropy, but in practice the Foundation has gone far beyond the prescription.

The origin of its policies on aging is an appreciation of the national as well as the individual human problem. In Britain the proportion of old people to the rest of the population is between two and three times greater than it was a century ago and is increasing as still more people are living into old age. This does not necessarily mean that the rest of the community will have to support an increasing burden. The frontiers of real old age are being slowly pushed back, and the theoretical retirement age could possibly be later than it is—60 for women, 65 for men. But there are difficulties. Industry is highly organized, machinery is complex and is constantly developing new forms, and industrial processes are continuous and set the pace for the worker. The person who is slowing up mentally and physically and is irregular in attendance is the least desirable employee. The social situation is also worsening for those old people who are not well or strong enough to work or to look after themselves, for the tendency in a modern industrial society is for the extended family to scatter, leaving more old people unable to live with

relatives and in need therefore of social help.

In this situation the Foundation's policy has been: (1) in general, to find out the facts about old people; (2) to discover what public and voluntary effort can do to deal with their problems and to help the voluntary bodies to do their share; (3) to encourage experimental psychologists to find out the capabilities of the aging, how they can be taught to adapt to work, and how work can be adapted to their capacities; (4) to discover how particular industries actually deal with their aging workers and how they could do better; (5) to have the special medical problems of the old investigated and to encourage the establishment of special hospital departments; and (6) to have the biological problems of aging investigated by the best scientists who can be attracted to the task.

SOCIAL SURVEYS

On projects arising out of this policy the Foundation has spent something like $6 million in the last 12 years. It is possible in this review to mention only the most interesting of them.

The first major creative act of the Foundation in the field of aging was to set up a committee under an eminent social investigator, the late B. Seebohm Rowntree, to inquire into the problems of old age, into the work being done, and into the resources available for the care of the old and to recommend what action should be taken by public and private bodies (the latter to include the Foundation).

[1] This account was prepared by John C. Beavan, assistant director of the Nuffield Foundation.

Appearing in 1947, when the foundations of the British welfare state were being laid, the Rowntree Committee's report had almost the status of that of a Royal Commission, and some of its recommendations were speedily made the object of legislation or of administrative action.

The committee found that the vast majority of old people present no problem at all to society—though more of them ought to seek a social solution of their problems. The committee urged the building of small houses of special design for the old. It called for a review of charities for the old, some of which were ancient. It found that state pensions were sufficient to abolish acute poverty at current prices. It suggested that large poor-law institutions be abolished and that local authorities create several thousands of small homes. Voluntary communal homes should be officially inspected. Better provision was needed for the chronic sick. More recreational facilities and clubs should be provided. There should be financial inducements for fit people to stay at work if they wanted to, beyond the age at which they were entitled to draw a pension. The recommendation to the Foundation was that it should set up a strongly endowed central body to study the changing needs and conditions, make experiments, give advice, and stimulate and support voluntary effort.

One of the studies arising out of the Rowntree Committee's report was an intensive inquiry into the personal health and circumstances of the old people of Wolverhampton, done by Dr. J. H. Sheldon, then director of medicine at the Royal Hospital in that town. The report, *The Social Medicine of Old Age,* was regarded as a minor classic.

Sheldon found that only 3 per cent of the old people were undernourished, and this was generally due to domestic circumstances. Over 70 per cent of the men and women between the ages of 60 and 74 were able to enjoy unlimited movement outside their homes, and, even between 75 and 84, over half continued to do so.

The small number of bedridden people at home (2.5 per cent) was probably due to the fact that most of them had been removed to institutions. The factors causing limitation of movement were shortage of breath, weakness, arthritis, vertigo, painful feet, and fear of traffic. Steep stairs lacking hand rails caused many accidents and impeded domestic work.

About 60 per cent wore dentures, and 38 per cent who were without adequate teeth had no symptoms of indigestion. About 40 per cent suffered from bronchitis and 55 per cent from pain in the feet; deafness was very prevalent, and liability to fall, often due to vertigo, seemed to be connected with defective hearing. A third of the poorer old people had unsatisfactory spectacles. Over 80 per cent were normal mentally, and a further 11 per cent were only slightly impaired. About 3 per cent were eccentric, and nearly 4 per cent showed signs of mental breakdown.

One of the most important conclusions was that old people living in their homes were more intelligent and cheerful than old people in institutions. The feeling of being necessary to the world gave them a sense of having something to do and was essential for the mental health of old people.

About one-fifth of the old people suffered from loneliness, sometimes amounting to a desolation of spirit that was heart-rending to meet. Widowers were lonelier than widows. Of those living alone, nearly one-third had relatives within half a mile, and in 40 per cent of cases happiness and domestic efficiency depended upon the nearness of children and relations. Women up to the age of 75 and occasionally older were found to be helping with domestic tasks, including the rearing of grandchildren, and gave more than they took in domestic responsibility.

A survey of the health of the elderly at home was made in Sheffield by William Hobson, professor of social and industrial medicine at the University of Sheffield; John Pemberton, senior lecturer in the same subject; and a team of collaborators. It was found that, of those who were living on a state pension or on a pension supplemented by National Assistance benefit, 16 per cent of the married couples and 10 per cent of those living alone were below the standards of subsistence defined by the Beveridge Report, though the average incomes were up to this standard.

The group whose position was most unsatisfactory was those who had only a state pension and had not applied for supplementary National Assistance, perhaps through ignorance or prejudice. Dental conditions were unsatisfactory, but, since the provision of the National Health Act, more people had adequate spectacles. About 20 per cent of the men were still in whole-time work, and it seemed that it was easier for the professional or managerial worker or the unskilled worker to stay at work than it was for the skilled workers to do so. These researchers found that 29 per cent of those aged 65–74 who had retired were fit. It seemed fairly certain that at least one-third of retired men between the ages of 65 and 74 could continue in whole-time employment if they wished and if suitable employment were available.

Another important investigation was made some years later in the late fifties by Peter Townsend and published in his book, *The Family Life of Old People*. Townsend based his observation on old people selected at random in Bethnal Green, an old working-class area of London. In an area like this— which is probably not typical— Townsend found that comparatively few old people were seriously isolated. Each old person had on average thirteen members of an extended family living within a mile and kept in touch with most of them. Elderly women got a good deal of help from their relatives, but they did what they could to help in return by looking after grandchildren and providing midday meals. About two-fifths of them were infirm or living with an infirm spouse, and one in three had been in hospital within the last 5 years. One in eight had caused a relative

to give up paid work in order to look after them.

Townsend suggested that, to help the family in its task of supporting the old, there should be a comprehensive family-help service to experiment with alternatives to institutional care—boarding out the isolated and converting old houses into one-room flats with housekeepers in charge. The existing home-help arrangements should be extended to relieve relations in the evening and for holidays. A health visitor with nursing qualifications could do much to prevent the gradual deterioration in old people, and interest in life could be preserved by old people's clubs and unofficial friendly visiting by volunteers. Physiotherapy in the home might have a useful future.

Townsend is now making a study of the institutional care of the aged and is attached to the London School of Economics.

Although so much has been done to get at the medical and social facts of old age, little is known about the income and expenditure of elderly people. The Department of Applied Economics at Cambridge made a pilot survey in 1957 to look at this problem in a selected area and to find out what old people were earning from part-time work or receiving by way of private pensions, encashment of savings, and help in money or kind from relatives. They also found out something about the spending and saving behavior of the elderly. The pilot study was encouraging, and the Foundation made a grant to extend the investigation to other areas.

In Britain, unlike the United States, the organization of classes and groups for "senior citizens" is not a recognized part of education, although, in fact, some people do prepare for retirement by using educational facilities to learn domestic craft or arts or to equip themselves for social or political activities. The Foundation made a grant to the National Institute of Adult Education to collect information about the existing facilities, the use made of them, and the general role played by adult education in helping people to adjust themselves to retirement and to continue leading an active life. The report is to be completed soon.

THE NATIONAL CORPORATION FOR THE CARE OF OLD PEOPLE

The Foundation followed the advice of the Rowntree Committee and set up in the same year (1957) the National Corporation for the Care of Old People. The Foundation put in $1.5 million to equip it for the next 5 years, and the Lord Mayor of London's National Air Raid Distress Fund, which had been financing old peoples' homes in bombed areas, gave the corporation an equal sum. It also attracted a grant of $500,000 from the gift which the peoples of South Africa made to Britain and took over the administration of other trusts with total resources of $1 million.

In the beginning most of its money went into the provision of voluntary homes for relatively able-bodied people needing care and attention. But as the local authorities implemented the National Assistance Act, which enjoined them to provide such homes, the corporation began to look for other ways in which voluntary bodies could help old people. It helped to establish 1200 non-residential clubs for old people, a cheap laundry service in the city of Bristol, a chiropody service (to keep old people literally on their feet), a system to bring cooked meals to old people living alone, and a system of night sitters-in. There was public accommodation for the elderly sick and for the elderly able-bodied, but there was no provision for those who were neither well nor sick. The corporation helped to provide six rest homes to show how the gap could be filled and insisted they should have a proper link with hospitals with geriatric units. For its new work the Foundation provided a further $750,000, and recently it has renewed the grant at the same rate.

The next phase in the corporation's work was concerned with the care of old people at home and finding out how they could best be helped to remain there. Many old people were unaware of the services available to them to help to keep their independence. The corporation tried to discover how many applicants for places in communal homes would really have need to move if they made full use of the domiciliary services. It appointed, in three areas, social workers to visit the old people who had asked advice about moving out of their own homes. In another town an intensive study was made of the use old people were making of social services and of what additional ones were needed. It also ran a night attendance service for those who were acutely ill and in need of institutional care which was not immediately available.

Although the corporation felt that it was generally desirable to keep old people in their own homes, it did however make preliminary investigations into comparative costs and found that occasionally it cost a good deal more to provide services enabling them to stay at home than to take them into hospital. The corporation is still stressing the need to keep as many old people as possible within the community to which they have been accustomed and is urging public bodies to provide more housing for old people. It is busy at present trying to close the gap between those doing research into the problems of aging and those engaged on practical work with the old so that they benefit from each other's experience.

SOME PRACTICAL EXPERIMENTS

The Nuffield Foundation has always worked in close collaboration with the Nuffield Provincial Hospitals Trust. Indeed, the chairman of the Foundation, Sir Geoffrey Gibbs, is chairman of the Trust and also of the National Corporation for the Care of Old People. The director of the Foundation, Leslie Farrer-Brown, is a governing trustee of the Trust and is honorary secretary to the ordinary trustees. He is also a governor of the National Corporation. The Trust's main concern in recent years has been to investigate the working of the National Health Service and to undertake experiments which might point the way to its improvement. The Trust too has been concerned with the care of the aged. It has provided an occupational day center for the elderly at Nottingham in the hope of preventing by simple measures mental and physical breakdown. The principle is to arrange, for elderly people who are showing signs of instability, daily or frequent attendance at the center where in the atmosphere of a social club they can feel that they are wanted. There are facilities for modest creative work, indoor and outdoor, and a good meal is provided. The center is run by the Health Committee of the City Council.

At Belfast the Trust and the City Hospital experimented with the home care of the elderly. It was believed that there were elderly invalids, well cared for at home, whose recovery was delayed or who even risked being disabled or becoming bedfast through lack of facilities which are usually available only in hospital.

Patients were selected for treatment in consultation with their family doctors, and often physiotherapy was given. About two-thirds of them made satisfactory progress and usually at a lower cost than if they had gone to the hospital.

The Trust has also sponsored a sociological and medical sample survey of old people in northeastern Scotland which is being carried out by the Department of Social Medicine at Aberdeen. The department hopes to examine some aspects of old age which have not been sufficiently explored. It is likely that attitudes and behavior in later life are largely the outcome of experience in earlier years. So an attempt will be made to relate family, occupational, and other past influences to the problems of the present.

At Cowley Road Hospital, Oxford, there has been a combined operation by the Foundation, the Trust, and the National Corporation to help the Oxford Geriatric Unit, under Dr. L. Z. Cosin. A combination rest home and day hospital has been pro-

vided and has been designed by the Division for Architectural Studies, another unit which is housed with the Foundation and the Trust at Nuffield Lodge, London, and is supported from Nuffield funds.

The rest home, Hurdis House, is a forty-bed annex of the unit where convalescent patients waiting to go home or into local authority homes can be rehabilitated. This often cuts down their stay in the acute wards of the hospital and the costs of care. The idea is to replace the antiquated concept of custodial care of old people by that of continuing care, which implies that a program of medical care does not begin when a patient enters hospital or end when he is discharged.

Many Oxford family doctors have found that day-hospital care for elderly patients is the answer to their environmental problems. There is useful co-operation between family doctors and the hospital's medical and auxiliary staff, and there are joint discussions on treatment. Arrangements have also been made with the public health authority for bringing in the mental health visitors, and it is hoped that one result will be that cases of mental disability will be received earlier.

A Nuffield mental health research team has operated from this unit for 3 years and has assessed the improvement of social behavior in a group of deteriorating old men in a local authority home. This has led to permanent programs of occupation being provided for them. An evaluation has been made of the relative load of mental-health work done for the elderly by the local mental hospital and the Geriatric Unit (the unit was found to be dealing with 75 per cent of the mental-health problems). A close study was done of fifty permanently confused old people and their social background, and an evaluation was made of the function of occupational therapists.

ELDERLY PEOPLE AT WORK

While the social aspects of aging have been the concern of the National Corporation, the Foundation itself has concentrated on research. As long ago as 1946 the Foundation set up a Nuffield Research Unit in problems of aging in the Psychological Laboratory of the University of Cambridge, under Professor Sir Frederic C. Bartlett, F.R.S., and, after his retirement, under A. T. Welford. Its main job has been to study changes of human performance in middle and old age likely to have a bearing on capacity for work in industry.

Most of the work consisted of laboratory experiments to compare the performances of people at different ages from the twenties to the seventies at tasks which may be termed "skilled." The laboratory work was supplemented by the study of industrial and agricultural employment and production and accident records.

The work was described by Welford in a book published last year, *Ageing and Human Skill* (Oxford University Press). The team found that the well-known slowing of performance with age is not due to old people's being physically incapable of moving faster but to their taking longer to perceive what has to be done, to their brains requiring more time to control their muscles, and to their tending to exercise more care and caution than younger people. The changes of perception with age appear to be far greater than can be explained by age deterioration of sight, though factors such as good lighting are still very important.

It is in jobs which call for fast, light, manipulative work that one sees most clearly the increased time that older people take in perceiving and relating what is perceived to what is done. This kind of job often becomes difficult some 5 or 10 years before heavy muscular work does. Again, older people may find that, although the mechanization of their job may reduce the physical burden, it replaces one kind of difficulty by another, because it substitutes arbitrary, complex control actions for the simple direct eye-hand co-ordination of manual work.

One of the most important ways to make work more suitable for older people is to organize it so that it is straightforward and free from complications as well as reducing the muscular effort required. Examples are given in the book which open up the possibilities of greatly improved methods for training or retraining people in middle or old age.

The studies done by this unit are the most extensive series undertaken anywhere in the world on age changes in performance. On the whole, old people show up rather well. Although age takes its toll in many ways, its effect is shown often to be of little importance, and, even when it does make a substantial difference, older people are seen again and again to change their manner of work to make the best use of their abilities.

It was appreciated that the results of research on the employment of older people must be tested on the shop floor, and a grant was made to K. F. H. Murrell, joint honorary secretary of the Ergonomics Research Society, to do such field experiments from the Department of Psychology at the University of Bristol. The first activities were mostly concerned with confirming that aging affects performance on the shop floor, and a study was made of the age structure of engineering jobs throughout the country. The broad conclusion was that the hierarchy of jobs is determined by their difficulty, with the older worker doing the simpler tasks.

A study of accidents was also made, and it was found that older men working on the jobs usually given to younger men suffered more personal accidents. The unit then tried to discover by means of job analysis what the typical job functions were that militated against the older worker. In general, it appeared that the complexity of a job was to be related to such things as the proportion of the available controls people had to operate, the amount of stooping, and the amount of vision that was required.

For the last 18 months the unit had people doing simulated tasks in the laboratory in order to find out more clearly how people perform at work as they grow older. A study is being made of training in relation to age.

An effort was made to discover what had happened to a number of men who in middle life had left highly complex jobs. Although some had elected to change to less skilled jobs, the main trend was to find the same kind of job but in a smaller firm.

Meanwhile Dr. J. Szafran, lecturer in psychology at the University of Exeter, who was Mr. Welford's assistant director at Cambridge, is studying the effects of aging on the performance of tasks of varying complexity. Much recent work implies that in the analysis of human performance the amount of both "information" or "organization" being delivered to the human operator should be considered rather than the "load" he is supposed to deal with. What Dr. Szafran is aiming at is a closer analysis of the effects of aging on two components of complexity—the information content and the discrimination difficulty. One of the surprising conclusions suggested by the results so far available is that the older adult may be as efficient as the younger in making rather elaborate decisions, although lagging behind in the simpler discriminations and choices. These findings may provide some justification that with age there is an increasing level of random activity in the central nervous system.

FACTORY PROBLEMS

Over a number of years F. Le Gros Clark has been doing for the Foundation an investigation of the social aspects of the continued employment of elderly workers. He has published a series of short studies on the extent to which various kinds of modern industry can absorb the labor of aging persons and the social and traditional influences that really determine the attitude of management, including foremen and welfare and personnel managers.

Le Gros Clark began with a study, *Older Men in the Building Industry,* which dealt with 320 men, all apparently fit at the be-

ginning of the study, from the age of 60 to the end of their working lives. Clark found that, of every 100 men fit at 60, about 70 were still fit as building workers 5 years later. At 70 about 30 of the original 100 were still working.

In the later sixties many men had to quit as a result of degenerative complaints such as rheumatism or bronchitis. At least 17 per cent of them went back to work too soon after a serious illness and retired a few months later. Measures of rehabilitation might have given them a few more years at work. About three-quarters of the men over 60 did not want to, or would not, work at heights. More than 40 per cent refused jobs calling for speed, and 20 per cent were reluctant to work in bad weather.

But about a third of the whole labor force is engaged on repair and maintenance work with a slower tempo, and foremen say that they can employ twice as high a proportion of older men as they can have on new-building sites. Clark suggested that older men should change over to such work in time to adjust themselves to it. This industry is fairly well adapted to give older men a chance of employment, provided that they are carefully distributed.

In *New Jobs for Older Workers,* Clark found that about 20 per cent of the men who reach their early sixties in reasonable health will need lighter jobs before they pass beyond their mid-sixties.

With Agnes C. Dunne, Clark did a more comprehensive study called *Aging in Industry,* covering 32 jobs. This showed that 70 per cent of carpenters, bricklayers, and foresters carry on well into the late sixties, since they are able to adjust pace to age, and that 60 per cent of dockers, plasterers, bargemen, warehouse men, and welders can also carry on to this age but that only 40 per cent of foundrymen, bus conductors, bus-drivers, truck-drivers, and paperworkers can do so.

Such industries as bricks, glass, boots and shoes, cabinet-making, and paper show a greater tendency than they used to show to lose operatives around their mid-sixties.

Most old-time craftsmen, such as watch-makers and makers of musical instruments, remain on their jobs until a late age.

Each year probably 40,000 elderly men who are still reasonably fit will need alternative work, and it is doubtful whether sufficient suitable jobs are available. Clark thinks that appeals to industry are not sufficient, because most industries are not flexible enough to absorb more than a small proportion of their own aging workers. He suggests that various social agencies should be established for the purpose and reminds us that only under conditions of high employment will the matter be taken seriously.

In a trade recession the older men are the first to go (we had experience of this in the recession of December, 1958). In 1957 Clark published a further study, *Ageing on the Factory Floor,* an inquiry into the prospects of aging men with a mechanized industry, the production of domestic furniture. The report concludes that some working adjustments or concessions had to be made to one man in ten in their late fifties, three in ten in their early sixties, and six in ten in their late sixties.

Le Gros Clark's most recent study, *Age and the Working Lives of Men,* states that one of the problems of industry and of the nation is that of the aging man whose job is getting beyond him. In most cases he is by no means finished; but, if he is to go on in paid employment, he has either to take his job more easily or find a new one. This investigator has tried to calculate how many men are in this difficult transitional stage. The evidence is incomplete, but he estimates that, by the age of 65, about 10 per cent of manual workers have become chronic invalids and have retired; about 20 per cent are no longer holding down their normal jobs but have either moved to a lighter job or need to do so at once; almost three out of four of those who need to change their jobs retire around 65 after an unsuccessful attempt, not always a very pertinacious one, to find a more suitable job; and 12 per cent or more retire at 65 by custom or inclination, though in theory they might have gone on working.

On the whole, Le Gros Clark concludes that able-bodied men in their sixties need not be a problem for industry. The real difficulty arises with those who are compelled by their age to work less strenuously, for often the system of production leaves few jobs suitable for elderly workers.

THE BIOLOGICAL APPROACH

The Foundation has for many years made biology its foremost interest in the sciences, and a good deal of the fundamental research in this field is indirectly linked with the process of aging. Some, however, of these studies have been directly linked with the process. With the co-operation of the Royal Society, the Foundation established gerontological research fellowships of professorial status. The first two Fellows appointed under the scheme were Dr. P. L. Krohn, of Birmingham, designated Nuffield Professorial Research Fellow, and Dr. D. A. Hall at Leeds. Dr. Hall has been making experiments to substantiate his somewhat controversial belief that an elastin-like substance is prepared by the fission of collagen molecules. At Birmingham, Professor Krohn has been concerned with changes that take place in the aging ovary and has been grafting tissues between old and young mice which were all closely related members of one inbred strain. He discovered that oestrous cycles may be restored in anoestrous old mice by grafting young ovaries. It appears, therefore, that changes in the ovary itself are primarily responsible for the failure of the reproductive processes. The aging process in the ovary is manifest as a progressive loss of oöcytes, that is, of the egg cells before they have reached maturation. Professor Krohn has shown that this process can be retarded by removing the pituitary. Animals have been treated in this way, and their ovaries have been removed at an age when they would ordinarily have lost their reproductive capacity. When such ovaries are transplanted in suitable young hosts, they can still give rise to pregnancies.

In the Department of Physiology at St. Bartholomew's Hospital, Professor K. J. Franklin, F.R.S., made a plan of research along broad lines, dividing human life into four phases: conception, evolution, maturation, and involution. This provided for an exploration of the physiology of aging from conception to death, with sample experiments along the line rather than over a small portion of the life-span. Studies have been made of the mechanism of parturition and renal physiology at various ages and of the reactivity of the gingival epithelium on short-lived animals. The department has also investigated thyroid activities in rats of different ages, renal function following hypotension, and the aging effects of ionizing radiations on rats and mice. This last has become the most important activity and has significance for cancer research. It looks as though the effects of radiation persist in subsequent generations.

The Geriatric Unit at Sunderland General Hospital has for some years been studying physiological and pathological changes in the aged and aging. A phenomenon found in almost all aging tissues is shrinkage, and in this process changes in content of water and electrolytes take place insidiously. The unit has been studying the reversible and irreversible effects of these changes on kidneys, the heart, and the brain.

Its recent work has concerned a group of young subjects suffering from degenerative diseases of the central nervous system, and it has been found that a chronically ill person of 40–50 years has the body-water distribution of a normal person of 70–80 years. An attempt has also been made to investigate protein absorption in the aged. To extend knowledge of the metabolism of normal pathological aging, the unit has studied serum lipids and lipoproteins in normal young people, schizophrenics, arteriosclerotics, and sufferers from coronary artery disease. Some of the findings were reported at the first meeting of the European Clinical Section of the International Association of Gerontology, which took place in Sunderland last year.

In the Department of Zoölogy at University College, London, Dr. Alex Comfort, Nuffield Research Fellow in Gerontology, has been engaged for some years on an expanding program of research into the biological problems of aging. He is seeking information about the pattern of aging in vertebrates other than man and laboratory rodents. The work he has now in hand includes a long-term study of the actuarial aging of fish under various conditions of growth in order to see whether their behavior differs from that of mammals and whether retardation of growth also produces prolongation of life.

In the same department Dr. J. Maynard Smith has studied the process of aging in the *Drosophila* fly, finding that the life-span of the insect is roughly halved for each degree rise in temperature, over a range from 20° C. (3 months) to 35° C. (25 minutes). This relationship between temperature and life-span suggested that causes of senescence at normal temperatures and the causes of death at high temperatures might have something in common.

THE FUTURE

The technique of the program—looking at a large and complex problem from a variety of angles, personal, social, industrial, medical, and biological—is one which a foundation is peculiarly well placed to use. It is a fruitful technique, for it may indicate from time to time not only what the solution of a recognized problem may be but also what the new problems are and what their degree of urgency is.

The study of aging is one of the Nuffield Foundation's original interests. It is, of course, an enduring one. The more we learn about aging, the more we see we have yet to learn.

14

The Condition of the West German Pensioner before the Social Reform[1]

In Germany in the last decade, as in other countries of Western industrial society, the life-span of persons of advanced age has become a problem which has evoked a lively scientific and a still more animated public discussion. The topic of this discussion was, in particular, the system of the financial care of the aged workers and the compulsory insured employees whose state-fixed pension, in view of the mounting living standards of the gainfully employed, became ever more unsuitable and turned people on social security into an underprivileged and needy group.

In connection with the plans of the federal government for social reform, H. Achinger, J. Höffner, H. Muthesius, and L. Neundörfer submitted an expertise (*A New Ordering of the Social Services* [Cologne: Greven Verlag]) which tried to proceed from social facts as well as these could be ascertained. At the same time the authors complained of the scarcity of knowledge of the social reality of the older workers and employees and asserted that a successful reorganization of the social security system seemed hardly possible without such knowledge.

Thanks to the efforts of Neundörfer and Achinger, in conjunction with G. Mackenroth, the Association of Research Social Science Institutes, with the financial support of the German National Science Foundation, began a common research project in 1954 which was supposed to furnish the material facts on the condition of the pensioners, on the conception of old age, and on the provision for older workers and employees.

According to the research proposal of Neundörfer, it was not the amount of the pensions (which were imperatively in need of being increased) or the procedure of their calculation and payment (complicated, hard to understand, and time-consuming) which was to be the subject matter of the study. Rather it was to be an investigation of the significance of other sources of the maintenance of the pensioners, such as ownership of houses, real estate, and garden, income-producing activities, additional pensions, and public assistance, as well as support by younger members of the family in the joint household. The working hypothesis was that the old age pension of public social insurance had lost its dominant role as a source of support in the last 50 years. Furthermore, the investigation aimed at eliciting the differences between the condition of the pensioners in urban and in rural communities. According to a second hypothesis, the opportunity for a full and secure life in old age should be greater in the country than in the city.

In order that the substantive and methodological experiences and interests of the separate institutes be better utilized, the study group decided not to conduct a unified regionally subdivided investigation by

[1] This account of a research project of the Association of Research Social Science Institutes was prepared by Ludwig von Friedeburg, Institut für Sozialforschung an der Johann Wolfgang Goethe-Universität, Frankfurt am Main.

which all institutes used the same methods but rather to divide the research project into a series of single co-ordinated studies. The co-operation between the institutes should be limited to an occasional exchange of experiences, and the findings of the separate studies would be later co-ordinated into a complete report.

Of the suggested single themes, the following were worked on principally in the year 1955. I. Berghaus and I. F. Poser, Institute for Economics and Sociology in the Federal Research Institution for Home Economics, Bad Godesberg, carried through a "Comparative Investigation of 510 Households of Pensioners in City and Country with and without Home Production," in which they studied both the meaning of family ties for economic subsistence and the personal satisfaction of the pensioner. W. Brepohl, Social Research Institute of Dortmund, investigated the "style of life of pensioners" with like pensions and like family conditions, in which 200 couples of pensioners were investigated, stratified as to rural and urban communities and region of the Federal Republic. H. J. Seraphim and F. J. Hessing, Institute of Homesteading and Home Economics, Münster University, investigated in metropolitan areas "the significance of the small garden from the standpoint of social security" by way of a statistical analysis of 40,000 small gardeners and by personally interviewing 260 of these.

O. Neuloh, Social Research Institute, Dortmund, was concerned with the economic and social situations of aged miners and their pension system and interviewed 300 pensioners in the Ruhr district. Neundörfer, K. G. Specht, and S. Groth, Sociographical Institute, Frankfurt, used monographs to compare "men in retirement from railway, mailpost, and industry," the condition of the pensioned small civil servants, with that of the pensioners of the general public old age insurance in urban and rural communities.

In contrast with the forementioned studies, which were concerned with pensioners,

L. von Friedeburg and F. Weltz, Institute of Social Research, Frankfurt, attempted in their study of the conceptions of aging and the provisions for old age of workers and employees to investigate the economically active who were expecting to receive a pension in their old age. Their findings are based on questionnaires of a representative sample for the Federal Republic of 1000 cases of male employed persons of non-agricultural occupations between the ages of 20 to 65 years who are members of the disability or employee insurance and upon 348 interviews with wives of the interviewed workers.

During the course of the investigation the representatives of the institutes met twice for a discussion of the entire research project. At the end of the investigations each institute submitted a research report (usually mimeographed) of its part of the study. The first published report on the study of the Institute for Social Research, by Friedeburg and Weltz, was *The Conception of Aging and Provisions for Old Age* (Frankfurt: Europäische Verlagsanstalt, 1958). This was followed by the findings of the study of the Institute of Homesteading and Home Economics, by F. J. Hessing, on *The Economic and Social Significance of the Small Garden* (Münster: Verlag Joseph Kiekenbeck, 1958). The plans of a projected publication of a complete report integrating the individual studies have not been realized as yet, in view of the changed conditions in the social pension system through the reform legislation in 1957.

Owing to the division of the general project into loosely connected individual studies, the rich and varied material and the results of the different investigations on the condition of pensioners before pension reform are difficult to compare and to integrate into a representative picture. If one, nevertheless, attempts a summarization of the findings with respect to the research objectives of the total project, it appears that the two working hypotheses have been disproved. The old age pensions of social insurance, grossly insufficient as they may have been before the reform, had nevertheless their importance as the main source of subsistence even for the minority of those pensioners who had a significant source of additional income. It was the amount of the pensions (apart from the state of health) that was the major source of concern of the old retired worker and employee, as well as of the young and still gainfully employed worker so far as the latter was at all concerned with the problems of old age. Material need and a poor state of health made all the other problems of old age look insignificant—problems arising from the loss of function of the no longer employed old member of the developing industrial society: loneliness, boredom, and loss of prestige.

These questions, which are the major concern of the gerontologist, can only now, after the pension reform of 1957, which decisively bettered the economic situation of the pensioner, become really significant and adequately investigated. In view of the acquiescing helplessness of the aged and the ignorance of the young, it can be shown that up to now every provision is missing to prepare a person for the role of pensioner assigned to him by society, namely, to lead his life for himself alone.

The second working hypothesis also could not be substantiated in its general application, namely, that the pensioners in the country have more opportunities for a full and secure life. Certainly, pensioners who own houses and lands are better off (and they are found more often in small communities than in the large cities), but pensioners who live in the country without such property are, as a rule, worse off than comparable groups in the city.

The second working hypothesis was mainly oriented to the advantages of the living-together of the generations under one roof of a single household. Yet the conception that the family is responsible for the old and offers them social security makes the assumption of the persistence of the intact large family functioning as a solidified community, a survival which has more and more vanished in the course of industrial evolution.

The findings of the investigations show that the dwelling-together of at least two adult generations only seldom occurs and that it is not basically desired and included in the self-planning by the vast majority of workers and employees. Therefore the recommendation for a dwelling and economic policy of the restoration of the large family can hardly lead to a practical social political initiative. In addition, the expansion of public provision by the increase in state pensions will not mechanically curtail the efforts of individuals to make their own preparations for old age or, on the other hand, to be stimulated automatically by the restriction of the governmental policy of assistance and the support of primary insurance societies.

It is much more apparent that the initiative for the care of the individual and of the family depends decisively upon the assumption of basic risks by the state and on the assurance of being able to plan ahead for a longer time without risk. A social policy which plans and secures its standards from the state will therefore promote self-care more strongly than a direct appeal to the initiative of the individual and his support by private acquisition of property. As soon as, to be sure, the governmental planning shall make, from its duty of guardianship, an equal responsibility for all citizens, irrespective of their personal financial preparation, it would have to surmount the opposition of traditional conceptions of the individual's participation which has to be honored according to performance. These findings explain even at the time of the investigation the clear vote of the workers and employees for the system of German social insurance, although their inadequate pensions were sharply criticized.

PART THREE

Selected Statistical Tables

Comparative Data on Socioeconomic Conditions
and the Aging in Different Countries

A wealth of statistical data is available for comparing the countries of the world on the aging population and on the social economic conditions affecting their status and welfare. The most important sources to be consulted by students on the comparative study of aging are the following: the *International Labour Organization Yearbook*, the *United Nations Demographic Yearbook*, the *United Nations Statistical Yearbook*, and the *World Health Organisation Yearbook*.

The selected tables in Part III are presented for gerontologists who may wish ready reference to data on other countries besides those given in the chapters of this volume. The tables do not cover all the countries of the world. They do include all the European countries—Communist and non-Communist—except the smallest coun-

tries, such as Albania, Luxembourg, and Monaco. In addition, data are presented for four non-European countries of Western culture—Australia, Canada, New Zealand, and the United States—and four relatively underdeveloped countries—Brazil and Mexico in the Western Hemisphere and Egypt and India in the Eastern Hemisphere.

The inclusion of countries outside Western culture gives evidence of the wide differences among the nations of the world in their social and economic characteristics which affect the aging of their populations.

Comparisons between countries need to be made with great caution, owing to national differences in methods of census-taking and in definitions of terms. Many of these discrepancies are described in detail in the original sources of these tables.

TABLE 1*

Area, Density, Population, and Latest Population Estimate

Country	Date of Census	Total Population	Estimate Midyear 1957 Population (in Thousands)	Area (Km.²)	Density (1957)
Austria..................	1951	6,933,905	6,997	83,849	83
Belgium..................	1947	8,512,195	8,989	30,507	295
Bulgaria..................	1956	7,600,525	7,667	111,493	69
Czechoslovakia.............	1950	12,338,450	13,353	127,859	104
Denmark.................	1955	4,448,401	4,500	43,042	105
Finland..................	1950	4,029,803	4,336	337,009	13
France...................	1954	42,843,520	44,091	551,208	80
East Germany.............	1950	17,199,098	16,401	107,431	153
West Germany.............	1956	50,974,500	51,469	247,960	208
Greece...................	1951	7,632,801	8,096	132,562	61
Hungary.................	1949	9,204,799	9,815	93,030	106
Ireland..................	1956	2,898,264	2,885	70,283	41
Italy.....................	1951	47,158,738	48,483	301,226	161
Netherlands..............	1947	9,625,499	11,021	32,450	340
Norway..................	1950	3,278,546	3,494	323,917	11
Poland...................	1950	25,008,179	28,300	311,730	91
Portugal.................	1950	8,441,312	8,909	92,200	97
Rumania.................	1956	17,489,450	17,829	237,500	75
Spain....................	1950	27,976,755	29,431	503,486	58
Sweden..................	1950	7,041,829	7,367	449,682	16
Switzerland...............	1950	4,714,992	5,117	41,288	124
United Kingdom:........	1951	50,225,224	51,657	244,016	212
England and Wales.......	1951	43,757,888	45,043	151,113	298
Northern Ireland........	1951	1,370,921	1,399	14,139	99
Scotland...............	1951	5,096,415	5,211	78,764	66
Yugoslavia...............	1953	16,990,617	18,005	255,804	70
U.S.S.R.................	1939	170,467,186	200,200	22,403,000	9
Australia.................	1954	8,986,530	9,643	7,704,159	1
Canada..................	1956	16,080,791	16,589	9,974,375	2
New Zealand.............	1956	2,174,062	2,229	267,995	8
United States.............	1950	150,697,361	171,196	7,827,976	22
Brazil...................	1950	51,976,357	61,268	8,513,844	7
Mexico..................	1950	25,791,017	31,426	1,969,269	16
Egypt...................	1957	22,992,150	24,026	1,000,000	24
India....................	1951	356,741,669	392,440	3,281,769	120

* Source: *United Nations Demographic Yearbook, 1958*, Table 1.

TABLE 2*

PERCENTAGE OF PERSONS AGED 65 AND OVER OF ALL PERSONS OF THE SAME SEX
IN OR AROUND 1850, 1900, AND 1950

COUNTRY	MALE			FEMALE		
	1850	1900	1950	1850	1900	1950
Austria.	. . . .	4.7	9.5	. . . .	5.3	11.5
Belgium.	5.5	5.7	9.8	6.3	6.6	11.6
Bulgaria.	. . . .	. . . .	. . . .	. . . .	. . . .	. . . .
Czechoslovakia.	. . . .	. . . .	. . . .	. . . .	. . . .	. . . .
Denmark.	4.9	6.1	8.7†	6.0	7.1	9.5†
Finland.	. . . .	. . . .	. . . .	. . . .	. . . .	. . . .
France.	6.1	7.6‡	9.7	6.9	8.7‡	13.8
East Germany.	. . . . .	. . . .	. . . .	. . . .	. . . .	. . . .
West Germany.	. . . .	4.4	8.9§	. . . .	5.3	9.6§
Greece.	. . . .	. . . .	. . . .	. . . .	. . . .	. . . .
Hungary.	. . . .	. . . .	. . . .	. . . .	. . . .	. . . .
Ireland.	. . . .	. . . .	. . . .	. . . .	. . . .	. . . .
Italy.	4.2‖	6.2#	7.7	4.1‖	6.2#	8.8
Netherlands.	4.3	5.6	7.4	5.2	6.4	8.0
Norway.	5.1**	7.6	8.7	6.4**	8.3	10.6
Poland.	. . . .	. . . .	. . . .	. . . .	. . . .	. . . .
Portugal.	4.4‖	5.2	5.7	4.9‖	6.2	8.1
Rumania.	. . . .	. . . .	. . . .	. . . .	. . . .	. . . .
Spain.	. . . .	. . . .	. . . .	. . . .	. . . .	. . . .
Sweden.	3.9	7.6	9.7	5.6	9.1	10.9
Switzerland.	5.1‖	5.4	8.5	5.1‖	6.2	10.6
United Kingdom:††	4.3	4.2	9.3‡‡	5.0	5.2	12.3‡‡
England and Wales.	. . . .	. . . .	. . . .	. . . .	. . . .	. . . .
Northern Ireland.	. . . .	. . . .	. . . .	. . . .	. . . .	. . . .
Scotland.	. . . .	. . . .	. . . .	. . . .	. . . .	. . . .
Yugoslavia.	. . . .	. . . .	. . . .	. . . .	. . . .	. . . .
U.S.S.R.	. . . .	. . . .	. . . .	. . . .	. . . .	. . . .
Australia.	. . . .	4.4§§	7.4	. . . .	4.2§§	8.6
Canada.	. . . .	5.1	7.8	. . . .	5.0	7.7
New Zealand.	. . . .	4.7	9.1	. . . .	3.3	10.1
United States.	. . . .	4.0	7.8	. . . .	4.1	8.5
Brazil.	. . . .	2.1‖‖	2.3	. . . .	2.1‖‖	2.7
Mexico.	. . . .	. . . .	. . . .	. . . .	. . . .	. . . .
Egypt.	. . . .	. . . .	. . . .	. . . .	. . . .	. . . .
India.	. . . .	2.3§§	3.4##	. . . .	2.5§§	3.8##

* Source: United Nations, Department of Economic and Social Affairs, *The Aging Population and Its Economic and Social Implications* (New York, 1956), Table 7.

† From *United Nations Demographic Yearbook, 1956*.

‡ Excluding non-declared and those 95 and over.

§ Data for Federal Republic.

‖ 1860.

Comparability after 1901 affected by territorial changes.

** 1855.

†† Great Britain.

‡‡ Based on 1 per cent sample.

§§ 1910.

‖‖ Excluding Federal District and Indian population.

Based on 10 per cent sample.

TABLE 3*

EXPECTATION OF LIFE AT SPECIFIED AGES FOR EACH SEX
(In Years)

COUNTRY	PERIOD	MALE				FEMALE			
		0	60	65	70	0	60	65	70
Austria.............	1949–51	61.9	15.1	12.0	9.3	67.0	17.3	13.6	10.4
Belgium.............	1946–49	62.0	15.4	12.3	9.5	67.3	17.4	13.9	10.7
Bulgaria.............	1925–28	45.9	16.4	13.5	10.9	46.6	17.2	13.9	11.0
Czechoslovakia........	1929–32	51.9	14.4	11.3	8.7	55.2	15.4	12.1	9.2
Denmark.............	1951–55	69.9	17.5	13.9	10.7	72.6	18.4	14.6	11.2
Finland.............	1951–55	63.4	14.1	11.2	8.7	69.8	16.9	13.2	10.0
France..............	1952–56	65.0	15.2	12.1	9.3	71.2	18.5	14.8	11.3
East Germany........	1954–55	66.2	16.3	13.0	10.0	70.2	18.2	14.3	10.8
West Germany........	1949–51	64.6	16.2	12.8	9.8	68.5	17.5	13.7	10.4
Greece.............	1926–30	49.1	16.0	13.1	10.6	50.9	17.5	14.1	11.0
Hungary.............	1955	64.7	15.9	12.6	9.6	68.7	17.5	13.8	10.6
Ireland.............	1950–52	64.5	15.4	12.1	9.2	67.1	16.8	13.3	10.2
Italy...............	1950–53	63.8	16.0	12.6	9.6	67.2	17.5	13.7	10.4
Netherlands..........	1953–55	71.0	17.8	14.1	10.8	73.9	18.9	15.0	11.5
Norway.............	1951–55	71.1	18.5	14.9	11.6	74.7	19.9	16.0	12.3
Poland.............	1952–53	58.6	14.7	11.7	9.1	64.2	17.3	13.7	10.6
Portugal............	1955–56	58.8	14.8	11.6	8.7	63.8	17.6	13.8	10.3
Rumania............									
Spain..............	1950	58.8	15.2	12.0	9.1	63.5	17.7	14.0	10.6
Sweden.............	1951–55	70.5	17.4	13.8	10.6	73.4	18.6	14.8	11.3
Switzerland..........	1948–53	66.4	15.7	12.4	9.5	70.8	17.8	14.0	10.7
United Kingdom:									
England and Wales...	1956	67.8	15.0	11.8	9.2	73.3	18.7	14.9	11.4
Northern Ireland.....	1954–56	67.4	15.5	12.3	9.5	71.0	17.6	14.0	10.7
Scotland...........	1955–57	65.9	14.5	11.6	9.0	71.1	17.5	13.8	10.6
Yugoslavia§..........	1952–54	59.2	14.9	11.8	9.0	63.5	17.0	13.4	10.3
U.S.S.R.............	1955–56	63.0	......	......	......	69.0	......	......	......
Australia.............	1953–55	67.1	15.5	12.3	9.6	72.8	18.8	15.0	11.6
Canada.............	1950–52	66.3	16.5	13.3	10.4	70.8	18.6	15.0	11.6
New Zealand†........	1950–52	68.3	16.2	12.9	10.0	72.4	18.5	14.8	11.5
United States‡........	1956	67.3	15.9	12.9	10.3	73.7	19.3	15.5	12.2
Brazil‖.............	1890–1920	39.2	13.0	10.6	8.5	......	......	......	......
Mexico.............	1940	37.9	13.4	10.9	8.7	39.8	13.5	10.9	8.5
Egypt..............	1936–38	35.6	13.3	10.5	7.9	41.5	16.3	12.8	9.6
India..............	1941–50	32.4	10.1	8.2	6.5	31.7	11.3	9.3	7.5

* Source: *United Nations Demographic Yearbook, 1958*, Table 31.
  † European population only.
  ‡ White population only.
  § Croatia.
  ‖ Data for both sexes.

TABLE 4*

Specific Death Rates by Age for Males

Country	Year of Data	All Ages	50–54	55–59	60–64	65–69	70–74	75–79	80–84	85 and Over
Austria	1953	13.1	11.2	17.3	26.9	43.3	62.5	102.2	161.6	264.0
Belgium	1953	13.1	11.1	17.8	26.2	38.9	59.9	98.4	156.7	248.6
Bulgaria	1945	16.7				38.4				
Czechoslovakia										
Denmark	1954	9.4	7.6	11.8	19.6	29.8	50.0	82.0	137.7	243.1
Finland	1953	10.3	13.7	22.8	32.7	51.9	77.1	120.6	178.9	283.8
France	1953	13.6	12.4	18.5	26.7	41.0	64.1	106.4	169.8	302.1
East Germany										
West Germany	1953	12.0	9.9	15.8	24.3	38.3	63.2	105.7	169.9	277.7
Greece										
Hungary†	1953	11.7	11.3		29.3			105.5		
Ireland	1951	14.9	11.7	17.7	28.0	43.1	71.3	118.6	196.1	294.5
Italy	1951	11.0	10.6	15.5	22.8	35.1	58.5	99.4	159.2	301.8
Netherlands	1953	8.0	6.9	11.3	17.5	27.9	47.9	80.9	131.9	233.5
Norway	1953	8.7	6.6	10.3	16.4	26.3	43.9	67.9	114.4	218.3
Poland										
Portugal	1954	11.5	11.1	16.3	25.5	38.9	66.2	111.9	203.7	
Rumania										
Spain	1950	11.6	9.8	21.5				74.3		
Sweden	1953	9.9	6.7	11.9	18.6	30.0	48.8	82.1	136.1	245.7
Switzerland	1953	10.8	9.7	15.2	24.4	38.3	60.2	96.6	162.0	264.5
United Kingdom:										
England and Wales	1953	12.2	10.3	17.2	28.1	43.9	66.7	105.1	162.4	258.1
Northern Ireland	1954	11.5	10.3	16.3	25.5	41.0	68.4	89.2	145.2	280.0
Scotland	1954	12.9	12.6	21.1	32.0	46.5	69.3	110.3	169.7	274.5
Yugoslavia	1953	12.8	11.8	18.6	29.2	46.1	70.1	113.4	185.7	332.4
U.S.S.R.										
Australia	1953	10.0	10.5	17.2	27.4	40.7	63.3	98.7	144.7	279.2
Canada	1953	9.8	10.4	15.7	24.2	35.3	53.6	82.4	129.3	231.9
New Zealand	1954	10.0	8.4	14.1	25.8	37.5	56.1	88.0	138.1	229.4
United States	1953	11.1	12.9	19.4	29.2	42.6	58.2	89.8	132.5	195.8
Brazil	1950	14.5	26.4		51.8		100.6		196.8	
Mexico	1950	17.3	17.6	23.8	31.7	44.5	66.0	89.8	119.4	229.2
Egypt	1947	23.5	20.3	22.1	30.3	50.2	70.7	134.2	183.6	664.8
India										

* Source: *United Nations Demographic Yearbook, 1955,* Table 27.
† Data are given for both sexes, together with specific death rates by age for males.

467

TABLE 5*

SPECIFIC DEATH RATES BY AGE FOR FEMALES

COUNTRY	YEAR OF DATA	All Ages	50–54	55–59	60–64	65–69	70–74	75–79	80–84	85 and Over
Austria	1953	11.0	6.3	9.4	15.5	26.6	48.5	83.8	137.8	238.4
Belgium	1953	11.1	5.8	9.2	15.3	26.6	45.5	79.0	127.4	215.8
Bulgaria	1945	13.0				32.0				
Czechoslovakia										
Denmark	1954	8.7	5.4	8.7	13.8	24.6	43.7	76.7	130.1	233.4
Finland	1953	9.0	6.6	10.7	17.6	31.4	54.6	96.6	151.5	285.9
France	1953	12.4	6.8	9.7	14.7	23.9	42.0	74.0	126.5	232.4
East Germany										
West Germany	1953	10.1	6.0	9.5	15.6	28.4	51.8	92.8	152.8	252.9
Greece										
Hungary†	1953	11.7								
Ireland	1951	13.7	9.5	13.7	22.3	36.1	60.3	104.6	171.7	257.3
Italy	1951	9.7	6.2	9.7	15.8	27.7	48.5	88.8	137.8	271.2
Netherlands	1953	7.3	5.4	8.2	13.4	23.5	41.8	74.8	122.5	218.0
Norway	1953	8.2	4.4	7.2	10.8	19.5	34.6	60.5	105.4	211.9
Poland										
Portugal	1954	10.4	6.1	9.1	15.0	24.9	44.4	81.8	185.8	
Rumania										
Spain	1950	10.2	5.9	12.9			62.4			
Sweden	1953	9.5	5.5	8.6	13.9	24.2	43.7	74.4	129.0	230.0
Switzerland	1953	9.6	6.0	8.9	14.4	25.8	44.7	80.7	133.9	244.1
United Kingdom:										
England and Wales	1953	10.7	5.8	9.0	14.6	24.4	41.7	74.1	122.8	218.8
Northern Ireland	1954	10.4	7.3	10.6	18.0	27.3	52.4	72.0	141.1	244.2
Scotland	1954	11.2	7.5	10.6	18.7	28.9	48.7	82.8	143.6	233.9
Yugoslavia	1953	12.1	8.5	13.3	22.2	36.5	61.1	101.4	173.7	310.0
U.S.S.R.										
Australia	1953	8.1	6.6	9.6	15.3	23.9	40.2	71.8	115.5	249.9
Canada	1953	7.4	6.4	9.5	15.4	24.3	39.9	67.6	111.0	208.8
New Zealand	1954	8.0	5.7	9.5	14.1	22.5	39.6	68.0	106.5	211.2
United States	1953	8.1	7.3	10.5	16.2	26.3	39.7	67.8	110.7	179.9
Brazil	1950	11.6	15.1		29.5		65.2		163.2	
Mexico	1950	15.2	13.1	18.1	26.5	41.1	60.1	88.5	121.8	260.6
Egypt	1947	19.6	12.7	11.0	18.0	31.5	45.7	100.2	141.7	723.0
India										

* Source: *United Nations Demographic Yearbook, 1955*, Table 27.
† Data for both sexes.

TABLE 6*

DEATH RATES BY MARITAL STATUS FOR MALES 65 AND OVER

COUNTRY	YEAR OF DATA	SINGLE		MARRIED		WIDOWED		DIVORCED	
		No.	Per Cent	No.	Per Cent	No.	Per Cent	No.	Per Cent
Austria................									
Belgium..............	1950	3,154	......	15,951	......	12,279	......	286	......
Bulgaria..............									
Czechoslovakia..........									
Denmark..............	1955	958	......	6,674	......	4,867	......	268	......
Finland..............	1950	1,070	11.6	4,569	7.2	2,978	11.3	101	11.2
France...............	1954	11,293	8.8	82,547	6.0	54,499	11.5	1,514	6.8
East Germany.........	1956	1,537	......	38,403	......	23,367	......	901	......
West Germany.........	1950	7,177	6.9	74,084	5.5	49,793	9.6	1,412	8.9
Greece...............									
Hungary.............									
Ireland..............	1955	3,853	......	5,129	......	4,056			
Italy................									
Netherlands...........									
Norway..............	1950	1,035	6.4	4,344	5.0	3,679†	9.6†		
Poland..............									
Portugal.............	1950	1,638	8.9	9,351	6.1	6,274	10.8	76	6.9
Rumania.............									
Spain...............									
Sweden..............	1950	3,174	7.3	10,113	5.2	9,410†	9.8†		
Switzerland...........									
United Kingdom:									
England and Wales....	1951	14,299	8.8	90,551	6.9	63,087†	12.6†		
Northern Ireland......	1956	979	......	2,175	......	1,607			
Scotland.............	1951	2,557	9.5	9,048	7.3	7,479	12.1	28	9.2
Yugoslavia............									
U.S.S.R..............									
Australia..............	1954	3,463	9.1	13,657	6.1	7,617	10.8	192	6.6
Canada...............									
New Zealand‡..........	1956	785	......	3,523	......	2,022	......	72	......
United States...........	1950	40,771	8.5	214,981	5.7	135,189	9.8	10,240	9.6
Brazil................									
Mexico...............									
Egypt................									
India................									

* Source: *United Nations Demographic Yearbook, 1958*, Tables 13 and 6.

† Includes divorced.

‡ European population only.

TABLE 7*

Death Rates by Marital Status for Females 65 and Over

Country	Year of Data	Single		Married		Widowed		Divorced	
		No.	Per Cent	No.	Per Cent	No.	Per Cent	No.	Per Cent
Austria.................									
Belgium................	1950	4,186	......	9,003	......	19,720	......	264	......
Bulgaria..............									
Czechoslovakia.........									
Denmark...............	1955	1,904	......	3,407	......	7,038	......	302	......
Finland................	1950	1,657	6.4	2,038	5.0	7,702	7.9	138	6.8
France.................	1954	18,487	5.5	31,696	3.4	125,409	6.8	2,357	4.2
East Germany..........	1956	5,205	......	17,259	......	49,659	......	1,479	......
West Germany..........	1950	14,103	5.5	36,954	4.5	93,941	7.1	1,515	6.7
Greece.................									
Hungary...............									
Ireland................	1955	3,007	......	2,184	......	6,707	......		
Italy..................									
Netherlands...........									
Norway................	1950	1,956	5.4	2,462	4.0	6,140†	7.9†		
Poland................									
Portugal...............	1950	3,740	7.2	4,402	3.9	14,157	7.4	100	6.3
Rumania..............									
Spain.................									
Sweden................	1950	5,059	6.3	5,996	4.5	13,716†	8.0†		
Switzerland...........									
United Kingdom:									
England and Wales.....	1951	29,831	6.6	45,499	4.5	116,479†	8.3†		
Northern Ireland.......	1956	1,303	......	947	......	2,821	......	2	......
Scotland..............	1951	4,682	7.4	4,673	5.3	12,537	9.1	44	9.3
Yugoslavia............									
U.S.S.R...............									
Australia..............	1954	3,339	6.0	5,761	3.9	13,999	7.0	114	4.2
Canada...............									
New Zealand‡..........	1956	759	......	1,512	......	3,369	......	34	......
United States..........	1950	32,887	5.7	85,596	3.7	233,501	6.6	4,180	5.7
Brazil.................									
Mexico................									
Egypt.................									
India.................									

* Source: *United Nations Demographic Yearbook, 1958,* Tables 13 and 6.

† Includes divorced.

‡ European population only.

TABLE 8*

ECONOMICALLY ACTIVE POPULATION 65 AND OVER FOR BOTH SEXES

COUNTRY	YEAR OF DATA	MALES 65 AND OVER			FEMALES 65 AND OVER		
		Total Population	Economically Active		Total Population	Economically Active	
			No.	Per Cent		No.	Per Cent
Austria...............	1951	305,881	95,836	31.3	427,156	57,169	13.4
Belgium..............	1947	409,522	101,179	24.7	500,367	26,841	5.4
Bulgaria..............							
Czechoslovakia.........							
Denmark..............	1950	184,332	66,211	35.9	205,853	17,187	8.3
Finland...............	1950	99,675	56,489	56.7	166,851	34,331	20.6
France................	1946	1,763,856	959,296	54.4	2,591,594	578,747	22.3
East Germany.........	1946	760,035	273,181	35.9	967,445	110,058	11.4
West Germany........	1950	1,992,479	533,393	26.8	2,431,394	235,803	9.7
Greece...............	1951	225,349	138,743	61.6	284,809	14,080	4.9
Hungary..............	1949	305,705	189,364	61.9	387,152	75,560	19.5
Ireland...............	1951	155,038	90,517	58.4	161,353	27,356	17.0
Italy.................							
Netherlands...........	1947	325,844	115,675	35.5	357,295	22,648	6.3
Norway..............	1946	130,352	62,968	48.3	163,827	17,403	10.6
Poland................							
Portugal..............	1950	231,747	155,815	67.2	357,768	43,592	12.2
Rumania..............							
Spain.................							
Sweden...............	1950	335,224	121,110	36.1	385,869	29,926	7.8
Switzerland...........	1950	194,058	98,414	50.7	259,168	30,726	11.9
United Kingdom:......	1951	2,174,800	695,300	32.0	3,125,200	166,000	5.3
England and Wales....							
Northern Ireland......	1951	60,748	23,918	39.4	74,245	5,554	7.5
Scotland............	1951	214,704	74,601	34.7	292,191	13,508	4.6
Yugoslavia............	1953	423,000	255,000	60.3	587,000	69,000	11.8
U.S.S.R..............							
Australia.............	1947	279,809	94,775	33.9	325,088	15,968	4.9
Canada...............	1951	550,709	212,399	38.6	534,667	27,188	5.1
New Zealand..........	1951	84,613	22,461	26.5	92,846	3,074	3.3
United States.........	1950	5,734,250	2,379,545	41.5	6,522,600	507,345	7.8
Brazil................	1950	329,187†	186,463	56.6	424,686†	19,462	4.6
Mexico...............	1950	412,603			453,011		
Egypt................	1947	267,121	234,217	87.7	319,072	211,332	66.2
India.................							

* Source: *United Nations Demographic Yearbook, 1956*, Table 11.
† Age 70 and over.

TABLE 9*

Economically Active Males Engaged in Agriculture†

Country	Year of Data	Economically Active Male Population		
		Total	Engaged in Agriculture	
			No.	Per Cent
Austria...................	1951	2,055,630	510,971	24.9
Belgium...................	1947	2,660,111	361,647	13.6
Bulgaria.................				
Czechoslovakia.............	1947	3,793,420	1,123,235	29.6
Denmark..................	1950	1,368,975	396,941	29.0
Finland..................	1950	1,176,053	542,724	46.1
France..................	1954	12,855,000	3,371,000	26.2
East Germany..............	1946	4,464,149	1,046,107	23.4
West Germany.............	1950	14,125,000	2,316,000	16.4
Greece..................	1951	2,328,901	1,152,292	49.5
Hungary.................	1949	2,950,228	1,544,656	52.4
Ireland..................	1951	947,190	436,172	46.0
Italy....................	1951	14,663,427	6,227,713	42.5
Netherlands..............	1947	2,892,392	578,500	20.0
Norway..................	1950	1,059,894	332,696	31.4
Poland..................				
Portugal.................	1950	2,551,389	1,329,641	52.1
Rumania.................				
Spain...................	1950	9,084,227	4,853,160	53.4
Sweden..................	1950	2,285,686	578,708	25.3
Switzerland..............	1950	1,515,232	325,321	21.5
United Kingdom:...........	1951	15,662,200	997,500	6.4
England and Wales........				
Northern Ireland.........	1951	420,790	92,897	22.1
Scotland................	1951	1,585,335	150,435	9.5
Yugoslavia...............	1953	5,145,000	3,079,000	59.8
U.S.S.R.................				
Australia.................	1947	2,479,269	473,581	19.1
Canada..................	1951	4,130,802	969,593	23.5
New Zealand..............	1951	568,963	126,220	22.2
United States.............	1950	43,542,293	6,719,975	15.4
Brazil...................	1950	14,609,798	9,154,034	62.7
Mexico‡.................	1950	8,345,240	4,823,901	57.8
Egypt...................	1947	7,058,302	3,685,532	52.2
India...................	1951	85,460,898	59,313,352	69.4

* Source: *United Nations Demographic Yearbook, 1956*, Table 12.

† Includes forestry, hunting, and fishing.

‡ Data for both sexes.

TABLE 10*

NATIONAL AND PER CAPITA INCOME, 1949, IN NATIONAL CURRENCIES AND UNITED STATES DOLLARS

COUNTRY	QUALITY OF INCOME ESTIMATE	1949 NATIONAL INCOME		1949 INCOME PER CAPITA (U.S. DOLLARS)
		Unit	Amount	
Austria.....................	O†	Million schillings	29,198	216
Belgium....................	O	Million francs	250,775	582
Bulgaria...................				
Czechoslovakia..............	E‡	Thousand million koruny	244	371
Denmark...................	O	Million kroner	16,480	689
Finland....................	O	Thousand million markkaa	323.2	348
France.....................	O	Thousand million francs	6,930	482
East Germany...............				
West Germany..............	O	Thousand million Deutsche marks	64.5	320
Greece.....................	O	Thousand million drachmae	19,200	128
Hungary...................	E	Million forints	24,875§	269
Ireland....................	E	Million pounds	342	420
Italy......................	O	Thousand million lire	6,192	235
Netherlands................	O	Million guldens	14,135	502
Norway....................	O	Million kroner	9,640	587
Poland.....................	O		#	300
Portugal....................	C‖		#	250
Rumania...................				
Spain......................				
Sweden....................	O	Million kronor	22,500	780
Switzerland.................	O	Million francs	16,940	849
United Kingdom:...........	O	Million pounds	10,420	773
England and Wales........				
Northern Ireland..........				
Scotland.................				
Yugoslavia.................	E	Thousand million dinars	191	146
U.S.S.R....................	E		#	308
Australia**.................	O	Million pounds	1,896	679
Canada....................	O	Million dollars	12,977	870
New Zealand††.............	O	Million pounds	473	856
United States..............	O	Million dollars	216,831	1,453
Brazil.....................	E	Thousand million cruzeiros	170	112
Mexico....................	O	Million pesos	25,600	121
Egypt.....................	E	Million pounds	650	100
India**....................	O	Million rupees	93,200	57

* Source: United Nations, Department of Economic and Social Affairs, *National and Per Capita Incomes of Seventy Countries in 1949 Expressed in United States Dollars* (New York, 1950), Table 1.

† Official or semiofficial estimate.

‡ Estimate or extrapolation by the Statistical Office of the United Nations.

§ Figure for 1949 not available; based on older estimate or on an assumed per capita income.

‖ Crude estimate by the Statistical Office based on assumed per capita figure.

In prices of January, 1947.

** For 1948–49.

†† For 1949–50.

TABLE 11*

CHANGES IN THE COST-OF-LIVING INDEX, 1948–58
(1953 = 100)

COUNTRY	YEAR 1948	YEAR 1958	PER CENT INCREASE
Austria............	50	114	128.0
Belgium...........	95	108	13.7
Bulgaria..........			
Czechoslovakia......			
Denmark..........	81	117	44.4
Finland...........	64	128	100.0
France............	60	121	101.7
East Germany.......			
West Germany......	93	110	18.3
Greece............	63	131	107.9
Hungary..........			
Ireland...........	79	117	48.1
Italy.............	86	113	31.4
Netherlands........	77	117	51.9
Norway...........	74	117	58.1
Poland...........			
Portugal..........	96	105	9.4
Rumania..........			
Spain............	79	140	77.2
Sweden...........	77	119	54.5
Switzerland........	96	107	11.5
United Kingdom:.....	77	119	54.5
England and Wales..			
Northern Ireland....			
Scotland..........			
Yugoslavia.........		125	
U.S.S.R...........			
Australia..........	56	115	105.4
Canada..........	84	108	28.6
New Zealand........	75	119	58.7
United States.......	90	108	20.0
Brazil............	62	238	283.9
Mexico...........	71	150	111.3
Egypt............	95	102	7.4
India.............	92	109	18.5

*Source: *International Financial Statistics*, Vol. **10**, No. 10, and Vol. **12**, No. 10.

TABLE 12*

CIRCULATION OF DAILY NEWSPAPERS AND PER CAPITA NEWSPRINT CONSUMPTION

COUNTRY	CIRCULATION OF DAILY NEWSPAPERS Year	CIRCULATION OF DAILY NEWSPAPERS Per 1000 Population	NEWSPRINT CONSUMPTION PER CAPITA, 1957 (IN KILOGRAMS)
Austria...........	1956	187	6.5
Belgium...........	1952	383	9.5†
Bulgaria..........	1956	170	2.4
Czechoslovakia.....	1956	170	....
Denmark..........	1955	376	15.5
Finland...........	1956	420	18.1
France...........	1956	244	10.7
East Germany......	1954	118 }	8.0‡
West Germany.....	1956	277 }	
Greece............	1952	71	1.8
Hungary..........	1956	122	....
Ireland...........	1955	269	10.3
Italy.............	1952	107	4.4
Netherlands.......	1956	264	11.3
Norway...........	1956	374	11.0
Poland...........	1956	150	1.7
Portugal..........	1954	61	3.1
Rumania..........	1957	149	1.7
Spain............	1956	68	1.9
Sweden...........	1956	462	24.8
Switzerland.......	1956	296	12.7
United Kingdom:...	1954	573	20.0
England and Wales			
Northern Ireland..			
Scotland.........			
Yugoslavia........	1956	48	1.5
U.S.S.R..........	1956	107	1.6
Australia..........	1957	381	27.2
Canada...........	1956	244	25.1
New Zealand......	1956	390	28.4
United States......	1956	337	36.3
Brazil............	1955	50	....
Mexico...........	1952	48	....
Egypt............	1952	25	0.8
India.............	1953	7	0.2

*Source: *United Nations Statistical Yearbook, 1958*, Tables 180 and 181.

† Belgium and Luxembourg.

‡ Figure combined for West Germany and East Germany.

TABLE 13*	TABLE 14*
NUMBER OF RADIO RECEIVERS AND RECEIVERS PER 1000 POPULATION	ANNUAL PER CAPITA ATTENDANCE AT CINEMAS

TABLE 13*

NUMBER OF RADIO RECEIVERS AND RECEIVERS PER 1000 POPULATION

Country	Year of Data	No. of Receivers (in Thousands)	No. of Receivers per 1000 Population
Austria............	1957	1,838	263
Belgium...........	1957	2,307	257
Bulgaria...........	1956	400	53
Czechoslovakia.....	1957	3,323	249
Denmark.........	1957	1,551	345
Finland...........	1957	1,121	259
France...	1957	10,881	247
East Germany......	1957	5,397	329
West Germany.....	1957	14,634	284
Greece............	1957	545	67
Hungary...........	1956	1,774	180
Ireland............	1957	477	165
Italy.............	1957	6,759	139
Netherlands........	1957	3,128	284
Norway...........	1957	985	282
Poland............	1957	4,028	142
Portugal...........	1957	596	67
Rumania..........	1957	1,499	84
Spain..............	1957	2,105	72
Sweden............	1957	2,695	368
Switzerland.......	1957	1,308	256
United Kingdom:...	1957	14,654	284
England and Wales	......	......	......
Northern Ireland..	......	......	......
Scotland.........	......	......	......
Yugoslavia........	1957	890	49
U.S.S.R............	1956	29,571	148
Australia..........	1956	2,089	222
Canada...........	1956	9,050	563
New Zealand.......	1957	531	238
United States......	1956	150,000	892
Brazil.............	1954	3,500	61
Mexico............	1955	2,500	84
Egypt.............	1956	850	36
India.............	1956	1,076	3

* Source: *United Nations Statistical Yearbook, 1958,* Tables 1 and 185; *United Nations Statistical Yearbook, 1957,* Table 1; *United Nations Statistical Yearbook, 1956,* Table 1; and *United Nations Statistical Yearbook, 1955,* Table 1.

TABLE 14*

ANNUAL PER CAPITA ATTENDANCE AT CINEMAS

Country	Year of Data	Per Capita Attendance
Austria................	1955	15.8
Belgium................	1957	11.5
Bulgaria...............	1957	10.1
Czechoslovakia..........	1957	13.9
Denmark...............	1956	11.7
Finland.................	1957	7.4
France.................	1957	9.7
East Germany...........	1955	17.2
West Germany..........	1956	15.4
Greece.................	......	......
Hungary...............	1956	11.5
Ireland................	1957	18.0
Italy...................	1954	16.8
Netherlands............	1957	5.9
Norway................	1957	10.0
Poland.................	1957	8.2
Portugal................	1957	3.1
Rumania...............	1957	4.9
Spain..................	1954	10.4
Sweden................	1958	9.4
Switzerland.............	1957	7.2
United Kingdom:........	1957	17.8
England and Wales.....	......	......
Northern Ireland.......	......	......
Scotland...............	......	......
Yugoslavia.............	1957	6.0
U.S.S.R................	1957	15.1
Australia	1956	14.5
Canada................	1957	10.6
New Zealand...........	1957	16.9
United States...........	1957	14.0
Brazil..................	1955	5.3
Mexico.................	1957	8.5
Egypt..................	1955	2.7
India..................	1953	2.0

* Source: *United Nations Statistical Yearbook, 1958,* Table 183B.

TABLE 15*

ESTIMATED PER CAPITA CONSUMPTION OF
COMMERCIAL SOURCES OF ENERGY
1937 AND 1956

(Expressed in Coal Equivalents in Metric Tons)

Country	1937	1956
Austria.................	1.04	2.43
Belgium-Luxembourg.....	4.02	4.34
Bulgaria................	0.14	0.60
Czechoslovakia..........	1.78	3.98
Denmark...............	1.71	2.62
Finland.................	1.03	1.89
France.................	2.12	2.68
East Germany..........	....	3.66
West Germany..........	....	3.60
Greece.................	0.18	0.36
Hungary...............	0.72	1.52
Ireland................	1.10	1.38
Italy..................	0.66	1.12
Netherlands............	1.79	2.45
Norway................	3.44	5.66
Poland.................	0.75	2.74
Portugal...............	0.24	0.42
Rumania...............	0.37	1.28
Spain..................	0.40	0.88
Sweden................	2.50	4.59
Switzerland............	1.81	3.18
United Kingdom:	4.24	5.03
England and Wales.....	....	....
Northern Ireland.......	....	....
Scotland...............	....	....
Yugoslavia.............	0.18	0.58
U.S.S.R................	0.87	2.45
Australia...............	2.27	3.85
Canada†................	4.91	8.25
New Zealand............	1.94	2.81
United States...........	5.89	8.58
Brazil..................	0.13	0.39
Mexico.................	0.44	0.75
India..................	0.09‡	0.12
Egypt..................	0.13	0.24

* Source: *United Nations Statistical Yearbook, 1957*, Table 128.

† Including Newfoundland.

‡ Including area now Pakistan.

Contributors

JOHN E. ANDERSON, PH.D.
Professor, Institute of Child Welfare, University of Minnesota, Minneapolis, Minnesota

JOHN C. BEAVAN
Assistant Director, Nuffield Foundation, London, England

ERNEST W. BURGESS, PH.D.
Professor Emeritus of Sociology, University of Chicago, Chicago, Illinois

WILBUR J. COHEN
Professor of Public Welfare Administration, School of Social Work, University of Michigan, Ann Arbor, Michigan

WILMA DONAHUE, PH.D.
Chairman, Division of Gerontology, Institute for Human Adjustment, University of Michigan, Ann Arbor, Michigan

LUDWIG VON FRIEDEBURG
Institut für Sozialforschung an der Johann Wolfgang Goethe-Universität, Frankfurt am Main, Germany

PHILIP M. HAUSER, PH.D.
Professor of Sociology, University of Chicago, Chicago, Illinois

ROBERT J. HAVIGHURST, PH.D.
Professor of Education, University of Chicago, Chicago, Illinois

BERTHA JAMES
Chairman, Northwest Kent Old People's Welfare Committee, and Chairman, Homes, Housing and Home Services Committee of the National Old People's Welfare Council, England

MARGRIT KESSI
School of Social Work, Zurich, Switzerland

ROBERT W. KLEEMEIER, PH.D.
Research Professor, Department of Psychology, Washington University, St. Louis, Missouri

JEROME S. PETERSON, M.D.
Director, Division of Organization of Public Health Services, World Health Organization, Geneva, Switzerland

VERA J. PETERSON, M.D.
Honorary Secretary, Medical Women's International Association, Geneva, Switzerland

MAX RHEINSTEIN, J.U.D.
Max Pam Professor of Law, University of Chicago, Chicago, Illinois

HELEN L. SLATER
Secretary, Exeter Council of Social Service, Exeter, England

JEAN-RENÉ TRÉANTON, PH.D.
Centre d'Études Sociologiques, Centre National de la Recherche Scientifique, Paris, France

ROBERT J. VAN ZONNEVELD, M.D.
National Health Research Council, TNO, The Hague, Netherlands

RAUL VARGAS, M.P.H.
Statistician, World Health Organization, Buenos Aires, Brazil

SEYMOUR L. WOLFBEIN, PH.D.
Deputy Assistant Secretary of Labor, Department of Labor, Washington, D.C.

ANGELA ZUCCINO
Dean, School of Social Work, Rome, Italy

Indexes

Index of Names

Index of Subjects

[Page numbers followed by (c), (f), or (t) indicate that the reference is to a chart, figure, or table.]

Adult education: participation of the aged in, Sweden, 309–11, United Kingdom, 334–35; preparation for retirement programs, United States, 348–49; school and library programs for the aged, United States, 348

Age changes, biological research regarding, 455–56

Aged: characteristics of, related to housing, 114; as a heterogeneous group, 163–64, 186; increase in numbers of, and social policy, 55; roleless role of, 20–21; scientific study of, 356 ff.; social policy for 303–4; welfare policy and the autonomy of the, 388

Ageing and Human Skill, 453

Ageing in Industry, 454

Aging: attitudes toward, 19; criterion of, 4; effects of, on capacity for and performance of work, 453–54; effects of social trends on, 5 ff., 14 ff.; increase in scientific interest in, 359 ff.; as a social problem, 299–300

Aging, societal aspects of: aging of nations, 32 ff.; population changes, 29–33; *see also* Population age structure; Population aging

Aging process, study of, 356

Automation, and leisure time, 12

Belgium: health insurance law for the aged in, 408; medical care for the aged, 189–90; old age and invalidity insurance law in, 393–94

Beveridge report, and old age pensions, 101

Biology of aging, 156–57

Birth rate: and population age structure, 43–44; for selected European countries, United States, and Canada, 1905–54, 43(t); for seventy-two countries, around 1950, 31–32(t)

Bouwcentrum (Housing Center), Rotterdam, 109

Cancer, changes in importance as cause of mortality in Western cultures, 171, 172(t)

Cardiovascular-renal disease, as leading cause of mortality in old age among Western cultures, 171, 172(t)

Chronically ill, types of shelter for, 108

Clubs for old people: description of a program in an English community, 443–45; in Denmark, 311–12; in Netherlands, 323–25, 446–47; in Switzerland, 315; in United Kingdom, 328–30; in United States, 342–43

Community services for the aged, 23–24, 143–50; as adjuncts to medical care programs, 182, 184–86; costs of home services versus cost of institutionalization, 143–44; eligibility criteria for,

149–50; living at home, England, 451; in the Netherlands, 188; recruitment of personnel, 151–53; relation to housing needs, 115; sponsorship and financing of, 150–51; types of, 144–49; *see also* Clubs for old people

Cost of living, changes in, 1948–56, for selected countries, 17(t)

Day centers for the aged, 452; in United States, 344

Day hospitals, and mental health services, 260–62

De Gamles By, Copenhagen, 108, 116

Death rate: for selected European countries, United States, and Canada, 1905–54, 41(t); for seventy-two countries, around 1950, 31–32(t); world changes in, 29–33; *see also* Mortality

Democracy, growth of, in Western cultures, 3

Denmark: community services for the aged in, 144 ff.; expenditure of public funds for pensioners in various types of accommodations, 144(t); gerontological research in, 367–68; health insurance law for the aged in, 408; independent housing for the aged in, 116 ff.; mental health services in, location of, 234(f), plans for, 231–32; mental illness in, 225–37; national pension, invalidity pension, and supplements by place of residence, 1957, 395(t); provisions of old age and invalidity insurance in, 394–96; social roles of the aged in, 311–14

Dependency ratio: and persons 65 years and over as percentage of younger age groups in selected European countries, United States, and Canada, 1900–1950, 36(t); in selected European countries, United States, and Canada, 1850–1950, 37(f); social, political, and economic implications of, 37–38

Disability insurance: adoption of, in United States, 93; provisions in European countries, 93; and vocational rehabilitation, 99; *see also* Social security

Diseases and disorders of the aged: common restrictive, 165–70; diagnoses among older patients in selected western European countries, 169–70

Divorce: and the aged, 291 ff.; percentage of population 65 and over, by sex, five western European countries, 292

Domestic aid; *see* Home-help services

Economic factors, changes in cost of living, 1948–56, for selected countries, 17(t)

Economic status of the aged: and its effects on housing, 111; in West Germany, 316–17, 457–59

485